Probate Practitioner's Handbook

SIXTH EDITION

PROBATE PRACTITIONER'S HANDBOOK

SIXTH EDITION

General Editor: Lesley King

The Law Society

ISBN-13: 978-1-85328-814-2

First published in 1991
2nd edition 1995
3rd edition 1999
4th edition 2003
5th edition 2006

This sixth edition published in 2011 by the Law Society
113 Chancery Lane, London WC2A 1PL

Typeset by Columns Design XML Ltd, Reading
Printed by TJ International Ltd, Padstow, Cornwall

The paper used for the text pages of this book is FSC certified. FSC (the Forest Stewardship Council) is an international network to promote responsible management of the world's forests.

FSC
www.fsc.org
MIX
Paper from responsible sources
FSC® C013056

Contents

PART III: PRACTICAL PROBATE

Preface to the sixth edition

This is the sixth edition of the Handbook. I hope that it will be as useful to the profession as the previous ones. Practice in general is changing with frightening speed and probate practice particularly so. Practice development will be much more challenging in the next few years with the introduction of alternative business structures in 2011 – as Heather Stewart says in **Chapter 3**, 'the marketplace will change forever'.

While coping with all this change, private client practitioners still need to be aware of recent developments in law, tax, practice and client care. It is a daunting task, and I hope that this Handbook will assist by gathering together the different areas into one book.

This edition has been updated to take into account the introduction of the transferable nil rate band, differential rates of capital gains tax, the change in approach to the making of statutory wills resulting from the Mental Capacity Act 2005, the 2009 changes to the intestacy rules and the new rules on perpetuities and accumulations. It also includes references to recent cases, where appropriate.

I am very grateful for all the help I have received from the Law Society, and from the contributors who have been so generous with their time.

Professor Lesley King
November 2010

Notes on contributors

Meg Andrews is a partner at Hartley & Worstenholme Solicitors, West Yorkshire and former chair of the Law Society's Wills and Equity Committee.

Peter Camp runs his own training consultancy, Educational and Professional Services, and is a visiting professor of ethics at the College of Law.

Charles Christian is an ex-barrister who has been writing about IT for 30 years. He is the editor of the Legal Technology Insider newsletter and The Orange Rag.com blog.

Helen Clarke is a solicitor, member of the Law Society council and Private Client Section and former chair of the Wills and Equity Committee.

Gillian E. Cockburn is a partner at RHW Solicitors LLP, Guildford, where she heads the tax, trusts and estates department.

Henry Frydenson is the principal at Frydenson & Co., London, and the chair of ACTAPS.

Beatrice Gosford is a solicitor at Withers LLP, London.

David Hodson is a specialist family law solicitor, mediator and arbitrator and an Australian qualified solicitor and arbitrator, and is a consultant with The International Family Law Group in London, and a deputy district judge at the Principal Registry of the Family Division, London.

Professor Lesley King is a solicitor and principal lecturer at the College of Law, and a member of the Law Society's Wills and Equity Committee.

Alexander Learmonth is a barrister at New Square Chambers, Lincoln's Inn, where he specialises in traditional chancery work, in particular the law of succession. He is an editor of *Theobald on Wills* (Sweet & Maxwell) and a former chair of the Young Barristers' Committee.

Sue Medder is a partner at Withers LLP, London.

Adrian O'Loughlin is principal of the private client department at TWM Solicitors LLP, Guildford, and specialises in inheritance tax planning and trusts. He is a notary public and a member of the Law Society's Private Client Section.

Gill Steel is a solicitor and director of LawSkills Ltd, consultants and trainers, and a member of the Law Society's Wills and Equity Committee.

Heather Stewart worked as a solicitor in private practice before completing a doctorate on research into client evaluation of legal services and is currently a management consultant with Otterburn Legal Consulting.

Kim Tasso is a strategic marketing consultant and freelance journalist specialising in management in the professions.

Table of cases

Table of statutes

Table of statutory instruments

Table of international instruments

Abbreviations

ABS	alternative business structure
ACTAPS	Association of Contentious Trust and Probate Specialists
BMA	British Medical Association
CA 1989	Children Act 1989
CDD	customer due diligence
CGT	capital gains tax
CIT	Chartered Institute of Taxation
COB Rules	Solicitors' Financial Services (Conduct of Business) Rules 2001
CPR	Civil Procedure Rules 1998, SI 1998/3132
CRM	client relationship management
DPA 1998	Data Protection Act 1998
DPB	designated professional body
ECA 2000	Electronic Communication Act 2000
EPA	enduring power of attorney
FSA	Financial Services Authority
FSMA 2000	Financial Services and Markets Act 2000
GLO	Group Litigation Order
HMRC	HM Revenue & Customs
HTA 2004	Human Tissue Act 2004
ICO	Information Commissioner'sOffice
IFA	independent financial adviser
IHT	inheritance tax
IHTA 1984	Inheritance Tax Act 1984
IPFDA 1975	Inheritance (Provision for Family and Dependants) Act 1975
IT	information technology
ITT	invitation to tender
IVA	Individual Voluntary Arrangement
LCS	Legal Complaints Service
LDP	legal disciplinary practice
LeO	Legal Ombudsman
LLP	limited liability partnership
LPA	lasting power of attorney

LSA 2007	Legal Services Act 2007
LSC	Legal Services Commission
MCA 2005	Mental Capacity Act 2005
MPAIS	Multi-Party Action Information Service
NCPR 1987	Non-Contentious Probate Rules 1987, SI 1987/2024
OLC	Office for Legal Complaints
OPG	Office of the Public Guardian
PESTE	polititcal – economic – sociological – technological – environmental
PET	potentially exempt transfer
POCA 2002	Proceeds of Crime Act 2002
PPC	pay per click
PR	personal representative
RAO 2001	Financial Services and Markets Act 2000 (Regulated Activities) Order 2001, SI 2001/544
ROI	return on investment
RSC	Rules of the Supreme Court 1965, SI 1965/1776
SAR	Solicitors' Accounts Rules 1998
Scope Rules	Solicitors' Financial Services (Scope) Rules 2001
SIF	Solicitors Indemnity Fund
SMART	specific – measurable – achievable – realistic – timed
SOCA	Serious and Organised Crime Agency
SRA	Solicitors Regulation Authority
STEP	Society of Trust and Estate Practitioners
SWOT	strengths – weaknesses – opportunities – threats
TCGA 1992	Taxation of Chargeable Gains Act 1992
TLATA 1996	Trusts of Land and Appointment of Trustees Act 1996
TMA 1970	Taxes Management Act 1970

PART I

Probate and the professional rules

CHAPTER 1

Solicitors and instructions

Adrian O'Loughlin

1.1 WHO IS THE CLIENT?

1.1.1 Personal representatives

In probate and estate administration, the solicitor's clients are the personal representatives (PRs) and not the beneficiaries or friends and family of the PR. Problems can arise if a PR is elderly and a son or daughter offers to help him or her, because here, as in other legal work, a solicitor's instructions should come directly from the client. A person appointed as PR who does not feel able to act should consider renunciation, allowing those next entitled to apply for the grant, or the appointment of an attorney (a relative or perhaps you, as solicitor, to act on their behalf). There are circumstances in which it may well be preferable for an executor to renounce. In a useful article in [1995] *Solicitors Journal*, 13 January, Philip Rossdale identified five situations in which an executor or executrix should consider renouncing.

1. Where there is a danger that the executor or executrix would infringe the rule against self-dealing, typically where the named executor or executrix was the deceased's business partner or a trustee of a trust under which the deceased was a beneficiary.
2. Where the executor or executrix is a debtor of the deceased whose debt is statute barred.
3. Where the deceased was an executor or executrix (because of the possibility of the chain of representation applying).
4. Where the deceased was a sole trader.
5. Where there are substantial overseas assets and modest UK ones (because the executor or executrix may find himself or herself facing a UK tax liability with insufficient UK assets to discharge it).

A PR may be replaced under Administration of Justice Act 1985, s.50 or passed over under Senior Courts Act 1981, s.116.

As an alternative to renunciation, one of two or more executors may choose to have power reserved to him or her, which gives that person the option to get involved later (the power reserved process is simpler than that for renunciation). Renunciation or the reservation of power might also be considered by prospective PRs who plan to be away for long periods of time, or who do not wish to be involved in the administration. If this is suggested, the pros and cons should be clearly pointed out to those concerned.

Problems can arise where the two PRs cannot agree on a solicitor to represent them. If it is not practicable for the solicitors to represent both PRs it makes no sense for both solicitors to fully replicate the work required to obtain a grant and administer the estate. Instead, the solicitors acting should seek to come to some kind of agreement which will allow one solicitor to deal with the administration of the estate, while the other will review what has been done on behalf of his or her client.

1.1.2 Beneficiaries

Some recent cases may point the way to an extension of the liability of professionals to third parties. (Aspects of liability for a client's fraud are considered in **Chapter 13**.) However, in general, beneficiaries' rights in estate administration are limited. They have the right to have the estate properly administered, but are not entitled, unless they are also PRs, to make decisions about the conduct of the administration, nor to be involved in the day-to-day business of administering the estate. (Residuary beneficiaries can have rights as entitled persons under the Solicitors' (Non-Contentious Business) Remuneration Order 2009, SI 2009/1931.)

Beneficiaries who are not PRs are not clients of the solicitor acting for the PRs, so it is not up to them to instruct those solicitors. It is for the PRs. Where appropriate, of course, beneficiaries' wishes, and particularly those of residuary beneficiaries, can be taken into account. This may be of particular relevance if the beneficiary is a charity and can, for example, reclaim income tax paid or avoid capital gains tax where assets are appropriated to the charity prior to sale so that they may then be sold on behalf of the charity as bare trustee. (Charitable beneficiaries are considered further at **17.9.7** and **17.8** below.)

Bear in mind that most beneficiaries will have no idea of what needs to be done to complete the winding up of an estate and how long it can take to do it. They may expect payment of their legacies or to be able to take possession of their gifts within an unrealistically short time frame. This, together with their lack of involvement in the administration, can mean worry and uncertainty for them and may possibly result in expression of unjustified dissatisfaction with the firm involved. Accordingly, obtaining the PRs' consent to informing the beneficiaries briefly of the expected timescale for completing the administration, or how long an unexpected hold-up may take to resolve, is likely to be beneficial to all concerned. It is a good idea, when establishing the terms of the retainer with the PRs, for solicitors to agree the extent of any communication with beneficiaries and the specific information which may be divulged.

It is the usual practice of many firms to notify all beneficiaries of their entitlements or legacies at an early stage. Legatees may simply be informed or sent a copy of the relevant part of the will, and residuary beneficiaries may be sent a copy of the whole will. Taking this action, and including an indication of the realistic likely date of payment, may put the beneficiaries' minds at rest and avoid unrealistic expectations, as well as saving time and costs in unnecessary correspondence. However, you will need to provide updates to those concerned if the anticipated timetable changes.

Solicitors approached for information by beneficiaries during the administration may wish to agree with the PRs as to the information to be given, and to advise the PRs on what is appropriate. This will depend on factors such as the beneficiaries' status and relationship to the PRs (and the deceased), the nature of the questions, and the costs which would be involved in dealing with them. Although beneficiaries are not clients, the Legal Complaints Service (LCS) and from 6 October 2010, the Legal Ombudsman (LeO) expect replies to letters of enquiry to be as courteous and as informative as they can be in the circumstances, and for these to be sent reasonably promptly.

More information about trustees and beneficiaries, and the information which beneficiaries are entitled to have, is available in works such as *Underhill and Hayton: Law Relating to Trustees*, 18th edn (LexisNexis, 2010).

What is most important in any administration is to establish good communication with the executors and residuary beneficiaries. The vast majority of complaints against solicitors arise out of inadequate communication. It makes sense, therefore, for solicitors to try and agree with the executors and any residuary beneficiaries how often the solicitor will communicate with them so that their expectations can be met.

Solicitors should be aware of the dangers of committing a money laundering offence when administering an estate. See the Law Society's Anti-Money Laundering Practice Note (Law Society, 29 October 2009) and the discussion in **Chapter 4**.

See also the remainder of this chapter and **Chapter 2**, and Mike Frith's article 'Who is the probate client?' [2000] *Gazette*, 10 February, 38.

1.2 INSTRUCTIONS

1.2.1 General reminders

Solicitors need to be as sure as they can be that the person purporting to instruct them has authority to do so. Remember that if the next of kin are to be administrators under an intestacy, there might be an as yet untraced will appointing others as executors. Next, the solicitor needs to establish exactly what the client wants him or her to do, and it is important to agree with the client precisely what is possible and what the firm can do. Making a summary of the client's instructions for the front of the file can be a useful reminder of the extent of the original retainer, particularly if more than one person is likely to be working on the file or if there are unusual instructions which might get buried in a thick file. Extensions or alterations to the retainer can be dealt with in the same way, together with the date. As a matter of routine, instructions and alterations should, of course, be confirmed in writing as soon as possible.

The case of *Cancer Research Campaign* v. *Ernest Brown & Co* [1997] STC 1425 illustrates the importance of identifying the scope of the retainer.

At this stage, it is also appropriate for solicitors to consider what information the client needs from them. This Handbook contains some specimen materials which solicitors in private practice may adapt or adopt. They are intended to cover certain basic points relating to succession and estate administration work.

Other materials for clients can be obtained from the Law Society (see **www.lawsociety.org.uk/choosingandusing/commonlegalproblems.law**).

1.2.2 Difficulty with instructions

If difficulty is experienced, it may be possible to shed some light by going back to the beginning and finding exact answers to the following questions:

- Who is my client? (usually, but not always, this will be the same as the answer to the question 'Who will pay my bill?')
- What have I been instructed to do?
- What is my role – professional, legal, practical?

The answer to the first question will help disentangle conflicts in areas where these might arise; contradictory or unacceptable instructions can be revealed by the answer to question two; and the answer to the third question can often pinpoint where the difficulty lies.

Some of the problems which can arise in the course of estate administration are dealt with in **Chapter 16**.

1.3 CONFLICTS AND DISPUTES

Clients sometimes find that conflicts arise between their roles as beneficiary and PR. It may be preferable for a PR to renounce before taking the grant if there are reasons to suspect that a conflict is likely to arise which cannot be addressed in any other way. A renunciation can only take place before the executor or executrix has acted in the administration. If the conflict arises at a later stage an alternative way to address the conflict will need to be found. Another problem, particularly where an intestacy or a step-relationship is involved, is that one PR may feel left out or that the other is being favoured, especially if the firm acting is the other PR's usual solicitor. Both PRs should be involved in the decision taking and it may be helpful, in these sensitive situations, to ensure that the content of conversations and correspondence with one PR is fully and promptly reported to the other.

Disputes can, of course, arise on any number of grounds, for example because a will is challenged, through disappointment on the part of the family about the disposition of the estate, or regarding the identity of the PRs. It may be appropriate to advise the client what steps the other side may take, whether seeking an opinion from counsel or a specialist solicitor or even commencing litigation, and about the costs and time implications. Clear preliminary instructions need to be obtained and confirmed in writing. Family companies, in particular, can be a fertile source of difficulty. Firms who have acted for the founder and members of his or her family personally and on behalf of the business may find that the various parties are at logger-heads after the death. This may result in the firm having to cease to act for some or all of those involved.

Rule 3 of the Solicitors' Code of Conduct 2007 sets out the formal obligations in this area. Solicitors must not put their duty of confidentiality to a client or former client at risk by accepting instructions to act for another client with an adverse interest (see rule 3.03).

Problems of conflict and confidentiality may arise where a solicitor has drafted wills for a husband and wife, and one party later asks for a new will to be drafted without disclosing this fact to the other. See Duncan Bailey, 'Serving two masters' (2006) 73 *Trusts and Estates Law & Tax Journal.*

1.3.1 Independent advice

From time to time, beneficiaries or PRs may seek independent advice about their position, perhaps because they think a lay or co-PR is mishandling an administration, or because they consider a solicitors' firm is working too slowly. Such a move creates some practical difficulties, the main issue usually relating to costs. The opinion set out at **16.10** below, although it relates to PRs seeking independent advice only, may be of interest in this connection. In any event, solicitors may wish to discuss the costs issue with those involved early on. It may also be appropriate to discuss the implications for the administration of what has happened.

Another difficulty may relate to access to papers, particularly if the disagreement centres on dissatisfaction with the firm of solicitors handling the administration. Finding a solution to these problems is difficult, but dealing with the following questions may shed some light on the matter:

- Who is the original client of the firm?
- Has the retainer been terminated? By whom?
- To whom will duties, such as the duty of confidentiality, be owed?
- To whom should reports be made?
- If a conflict appears to have arisen, is there a conflict for the firm, or is it in fact a conflict for the PR?

For a useful discussion on termination of retainers, see Roger Billins, *Solicitors' Duties and Liabilities*, 2nd edn (Law Society, 2009), p. 21. A solicitor may have to advise a client to seek independent advice if he or she has made a mistake or there is concern that a mistake may have been made by the solicitor (see **16.18** below). Solicitors should remember that they must comply with the terms of their insurance contract in informing insurers of possible claims against them.

1.3.2 Solicitors giving evidence as to circumstances in which will was made

Solicitors may be drawn into disputes about a will after a death, for example if it is questioned whether the testator or testatrix had capacity.

Some years ago the Council of the Law Society obtained the opinion of leading counsel as a result of *Larke* v. *Nugus* [2000] WTLR 1033 on the duty of a solicitor who had acted for a testator in drawing up his will which, after the death, had been the subject of a dispute.

It was decided that a solicitor should make available a statement of his or her evidence regarding the execution of the will and circumstances surrounding it, to a person who is either a party to probate proceedings or whom the solicitor believes to have a reasonable claim under the will but who is not yet a party to any proceedings, whether or not the solicitor acted for those propounding the will. See the Law Society's Practice Note: Disputed Wills (Law Society, 16 April 2009) and **Chapter 12**. While the facts of each matter will differ, the principle that the available information should be made accessible impartially to both sides is likely to be of value.

Solicitors may seek advice from the Solicitors Regulation Authority on all such points (see **Appendix F** for address).

1.4 EXECUTORS IN THE OFFICE

1.4.1 Retired and non-practising solicitors

Many solicitors take up executorships during retirement or during a period in which they are consultants to their previous firms. As far as charging clauses are concerned, these will need to be interpreted to see whether they are wide enough to cover charging by a person not involved in any business. A person may not act as a solicitor, of course, unless he or she holds a current practising certificate. Solicitors merely on the Roll, i.e. non-practising and retired solicitors not holding practising certificates, may not describe themselves as solicitors or act as such, by, for example, making an application for the grant of representation as a solicitor. See the decision in *Glenister* v. *Moody* [2005] WTLR 1205 for a discussion of when an accountant who was winding down his practice could be said to have retired.

1.4.2 Fee earners about to retire or move firms

When a fee earner leaves the firm, it may be necessary to resolve the question of his or her appointment as executor or executrix. What is to happen? Was the appointment of the individual personally (so that the testator or testatrix will probably wish the fee earner to continue to act after going to the new firm) or was it, in effect, appointment of the firm (so that someone else in the original firm should now be appointed)? Ideally, the client's instructions should be obtained. Making contact in this way can also usefully remind the client that other aspects of the will may need review and revision. From a marketing point of view, it might be useful to include an invitation to make an appointment for this; and why not send a copy of the firm's brochure too? (For more on marketing, see **Chapter 21**.)

1.4.3 Supervision of employee personal representatives

For supervision generally see Supervision Practice Note (Law Society, 10 March 2010).

Firms may wish to consider whether it would be appropriate to prohibit unqualified staff from being appointed executor or executrix for clients of the firm by inserting appropriate clauses into the contracts of employment of those staff. However, the solicitor's duty to act in the best interests of the client may mean that such a blanket prohibition would be inappropriate, for example where the client was a close friend or relative of the member of staff. Therefore, consideration should be given to clauses restricting unqualified staff from being named as executor or executrix unless prior approval of a partner is obtained. Any such restrictions must not prejudice the interests of the firm's client. The contract could also provide that where an unqualified member of staff becomes executor or executrix on the death of a client, all estate monies should be paid into the firm's client account. In practice, a client who is not a close friend or relative of a staff member is unlikely to be prejudiced by such a restriction.

Similar points should be borne in mind where an unqualified member of staff is asked to be appointed attorney or enduring attorney for a client. It is better for a solicitor to be appointed, even if the day-to-day work is delegated to the member of staff.

It is worth noting that the Solicitors' Accounts Rules 1998 impose some record-keeping requirements where money is held outside a firm's client bank account (e.g. where a client's own bank account is operated). See **Chapter 5** for a fuller discussion.

CHAPTER 2

Costs and charging

Adrian O'Loughlin

2.1 SOURCES OF INFORMATION

- Disability Discrimination Acts 1995 and 2005;
- Solicitors' (Non-Contentious Business) Remuneration Order 2009, SI 2009/1931;
- Equality Act 2010;
- Solicitors' Code of Conduct 2007, rule 2.03;
- Law Society Practice Advice Service, *Non-Contentious Costs* (Law Society, 2010) at **www.lawsociety.org.uk**;
- Law Society Practice Advice Service, *Contentious Costs* (Law Society, 2010) at **www.lawsociety.org.uk**;
- P. Camp, *Companion to the Solicitors' Code of Conduct 2007*, 2nd edn (Law Society, 2009).
- R. Billins, *Solicitors' Duties and Liabilities*, 2nd edn (Law Society, 2009).

See also **Chapter 3** on Client care.

2.2 COSTS AND THE CLIENT

The Law Society wants openness about costs. The final charge for the administration of an estate may be difficult to predict at the outset, but most clients will not understand the reasons why, and are likely to interpret vagueness and uncertainty about costs as a signal that the costs will be enormous, or that the firm is not being frank. Either way, openness is in the firm's interests (as well as in accordance with the obligations imposed by the Solicitors Regulation Authority). See in particular the Solicitors' Code of Conduct 2007, rule 2.03(1) and (5):

> (1) You must give your client the best information possible about the likely overall cost of a matter both at the outset and, when appropriate, as the matter progresses. In particular you must:
>
> (a) advise the client of the basis and terms of your charges;
> (b) advise the client if charging rates are to be increased;

...

(5) Any information about the cost must be clear and confirmed in writing.

If an indication of the cost for the whole administration cannot be given, the solicitor can tell the client why, as well as what work will have to be done before the total costs can be estimated and how much it will cost the client to reach that point. If nothing else, clients can be told the hourly charging rate of the person handling their work, and given an idea of the number of hours involved, plus details of any known disbursements or a range within which their costs are likely to fall.

Such evidence as is available indicates that most clients feel they get good value from solicitors. Do not shrink from discussing fees and do include everything the client is likely to have to pay for, including disbursements. Plain speaking about costs is in everyone's interests. (See **2.6** below and also **Chapter 3**.)

Solicitors should always remember Solicitors' Code of Conduct 2007, rules 1 and 10.01 when it comes to billing, and they should never put their own interests before those of the client. This is particularly important in a contentious probate where the legal costs may quickly become disproportionate to the amount in issue. See, for example, *Perrins* v. *Holland* [2009] EWHC 2558 (Ch), where legal costs in excess of £183,000 were incurred in relation to an estate of only £160,000.

2.3 CHARGING FOR WILLS

Although this Handbook is primarily about estate administration, will drafting is, of course, closely related. A number of general points about wills are included in **Chapter 14**. As with estate administration, there is a need to be open with clients and potential clients about the cost involved. However, it is often feasible to quote a definite fee for drafting a will.

Some firms offer will preparation at a price similar to the unregulated will selling services; while making this known may encourage clients to consult solicitors, it is important that solicitors do not compromise the quality of their advice. If your firm's charges are higher, be open about the cost and explain why the service offered is good value. What solicitors have, which is of great value to most clients, is the ability to advise in the broader area of what happens when someone dies and also any tax issues, and it may be helpful to explain to a potential client all the reasons why seeing a solicitor is worth the extra amount. Where the solicitor has a Legal Help contract with the Legal Services Commission, some clients can still get help with will drafting under the Legal Help scheme (see **14.1.7**).

2.4 REMUNERATION ORDER 2009

The Solicitors' (Non-Contentious Business) Remuneration Order 2009, SI 2009/1931 (the 2009 Order) is set out in **Appendix B**.

2.4.1 Article 2: interpretation

Note the definition of 'entitled third party'. This is:

> a residuary beneficiary absolutely and immediately (and not contingently) entitled to an inheritance, where a solicitor has charged the estate for his professional costs for acting in the administration of the estate and the only personal representatives are:
>
> (a) solicitors whether or not acting in a professional capacity;
> (b) solicitors acting jointly with partners, managers or employees in a professional capacity;
> (c) employees of a solicitor sole practitioner acting in that capacity; or
> (d) managers or employees of a recognised body acting in that capacity.

'Residuary beneficiary' includes a person entitled to all or part of the residue of an intestate estate.

2.4.2 Article 3: matters taken into account 'in particular'

Amongst the matters which are relevant to the question of whether a solicitor's costs are fair and reasonable is the express or implied approval of the entitled person or the express approval of the testator to the solicitor undertaking the work giving rise to the costs and to the amount of the costs (art.3(i)).

It is therefore important when taking instructions for a will to provide the client with sufficient information to enable them to make an informed decision regarding the appointment and the costs of such an appointment.

At the time of writing, the Law Society was preparing a Practice Note recommending that solicitors should:

- inform clients that it is not a requirement that a professional is appointed as an executor;
- explain that a professional will charge;
- give a clear explanation of the current basis of charging to enable clients to form a view of the likely impact of charges on the estate.

It will be good practice when preparing wills in which the firm or a partner is appointed as executor to include, in the letter of engagement for taking instructions for the will, a section which sets out your firm's charging structure for acting as executor. Once the client has signed this letter of engagement, a copy can be put with the will, and this express approval will come squarely within art.3 of the Remuneration Order.

A related question which was attracting interest at the time of writing is whether a solicitor should renounce probate if requested to do so by the family. The Law Society's Practice Note referred to above also deals with this issue. The advice is that a solicitor should always consider such a request from the beneficiaries. However, there may be good reasons for continuing to act. A solicitor will need to consider:

- the client's reason for appointing a professional executor;
- the client's understanding of the cost implications;
- whether circumstances have changed from the time the will was made and the best interests of the estate.

2.5 ASSESSMENT OF COSTS

Under rule 2.05 of the Solicitors' Code of Conduct 2007 a solicitor must inform the client in writing that there may be a right to object to the bill by making a complaint to the Legal Complaints Service or the Office for Legal Complaints (OLC) and/or by applying to the court for an assessment of the bill under Part III of the Solicitors Act 1974.

2.6 NON-CONTENTIOUS COSTS GUIDANCE

2.6.1 Guidance from the Law Society's Practice Advice Service

The following extract from the Law Society's Practice Advice Service booklet *Non-Contentious Costs* (last updated March 2010) may be helpful:

> **VALUE ELEMENT**
>
> In certain areas of work, such as probate, mortgages, commercial leases and domestic conveyancing amongst others, it may be appropriate to include a value element in the method of charging. Information on these specific areas is discussed in the subject areas below.
>
> However, the question of whether a value element is used is a matter for agreement between the solicitor and the client; it is not mandatory. Where a value element is used, practitioners may wish to use the guidance that follows, which has been distilled from the decisions made by assessors in dealing with applications for remuneration certificates.
>
> . . .
>
> **CHARGING IN PROBATE AND IN THE ADMINISTRATION OF ESTATES**
>
> *Fair and reasonable*
>
> In all cases the overall consideration must be that the charges are fair and reasonable, having regard to all the circumstances of the matter. The figures below should not be regarded as scale charges in any way and must always be exercised with discretion. In *Jemma Trust* v. *Liptrott* [2003] EWCA Civ 1476, the Court of Appeal stated that it would be best practice to agree the charging regime in advance with not only the executors but also, where appropriate, with any residuary beneficiary who is an entitled third party under the Solicitors' (Non-Contentious Business) Remuneration Order 1994 (now replaced by the Solicitors' (Non-Contentious Business) Remuneration Order 2009). The Court of Appeal held that a value charge can either be made in addition to an hourly rate, or

it can be included in the hourly rate, but the value element must not be reflected in both charges. The comments of the court are reproduced in Appendix 4 below but it is recommended that practitioners read the Jemma Trust judgment in its entirety.

Where appropriate, charges may consist of two elements:

(a) *Hourly rate*

This should be an inclusive figure incorporating the fee earner's expense rate and any appropriate care and conduct uplift.

(b) *Value element*

Account may be taken of the value of the assets in the estate. In calculating the value element of the charge, the following approach may be helpful:

- **Consider the value nature and number of assets.** It is usual to divide the estate (i.e. total value of the assets left after death) into two parts:
  - (i) The deceased's residence. (The value of the deceased's home, or as much of it as he or she owned, if it was shared with another person. For example, where the property is jointly owned, the value is reduced by half.)
  - (ii) Value of rest of the estate.
- **Apply an appropriate percentage.** An appropriate percentage should be considered in the light of the circumstances of the case but the following may be helpful.

Solicitor not acting as an executor

Value of gross estate less residence: 1%
Value of residence: 0.5%

Worked Example 1 – Solicitor not acting as executor

So, for example, if the residence was valued at £200,000 and was owned by the deceased alone this would be calculated as follows: £200,000 × 0.5% = £1,000.

Then consider the value of the rest of the estate, which is say, £50,000 ignoring the value of the residence then apply 1%. The remaining calculation therefore is:

Rest of estate is £50,000 then apply 1% = £500
Therefore total value element = £1,000 + £500 = £1,500.

Solicitor acting as sole executor or joint executor with another person

Value of gross estate less residence: 1.5%
Value of residence: 0.75%

Worked Example 2 – Solicitor acting as executor

So, for example, if the residence was valued at £200,000 and was owned by the deceased as a joint tenant this would be calculated as follows:

Value of residence (£200,000 ÷ 2) = £100,000 × 0.75% = £750.

Note the value of the residence is reduced by half as the deceased owned it jointly with another person.

Then consider the value of rest of the estate which is say £50,000 ignoring the value of the residence then apply 1.5%.

The remaining calculation is therefore:

Rest of the estate is £50,000 then apply 1.5% = £750
Therefore total value element = £750 + £750 = £1,500

High value estates

When dealing with high value estates, consideration should be given to reducing the value element percentage charged in order to ensure that the overall level of charge is fair and reasonable. For general guidance on this point, see the case of *Jemma Trust* v. *Liptrott* [2003] EWCA Civ 1476. In that case the Court of Appeal held that an appropriate charging regime was as set out in Appendix 3 of this booklet.

In the case of *Jemma Trust*, the Court also noted that in the appropriate circumstances a regressive scale may also need to be applied to the value element related to the principal residence.

It is for individual practitioners to exercise their own professional judgment as to whether or not to apply the value element when charging for the administration of an estate.

...

APPENDIX 2: HIGH VALUE PROBATE CASES

In *Jemma Trust* v. *Liptrott* [2003] EWCA Civ 1476, the Court of Appeal held that there should be a regressive charging regime in respect of high value non-contentious cases and that the following bands would be applicable to cases such as this in 1993 (see paragraph 31):

(1)	Up to £750,000
(2)	£750,000 – £3 million
(3)	£3 million – £6 million
(4)	above £6 million.

That would suggest that the appropriate figures for bills rendered for work done in 2003 would be:

(1)	Up to £1 million	1.5 %
(2)	£1 million – £4 million	0.5 %
(3)	£4 million – £8 million	0.1666%
(4)	£8 million – £12 million	0.0833%
(5)	Over £12 million	0.0416%

The appropriate percentages should be 1½%, ½%, 1/6%, 1/12% and 1/24% (1.5%; 0.5%; 0.1666%; 0.0833% and 0.0416%).

Thus for an estate worth £11,500,000 in 2003, the appropriate value element would be:

£1 million × 1.5% =	£15,000
£3 million × 0.5% =	£15,000
£4 million × 0.1666% =	£6,664
£3.5 million × 0.08333% =	£2,915.50
Thus total value element =	£30,579.50

Solicitors calculating all or part of their bill on a value basis should, therefore, ensure that they calculate the amount using appropriate bandings for the year in which the work was done.

2.6.2 Guidance from *Jemma Trust* v. *Liptrott*

Nowadays, many firms have high charge-out rates, as a necessity to cover high bills for salaries and premises. Many of these practices will, in practice, be recording a profit mark-up at or below 25 per cent, on top of the expense-of-time rate. In this situation, a value element will invariably be appropriate. Each firm will need to do expense-of-time calculations to know where it is. If the percentage profit of the firm is significantly higher than, say, 25 per cent, it may be that the firm is already recovering a profit percentage through higher charge-out rates, and all or part of that value may already be being indirectly charged for through those higher hourly rates.

Clearly, the model under which both time and value are both charged is a genuine attempt to have a basic model which can work for small and larger estates to produce a fair result. In a survey carried out for the Law Society for the Probate Section (now Private Client Section) in 2002, 70 per cent of the practitioners charged in this way. This area had a major review in the case of *Jemma Trust* v. *Liptrott*, and this method (value + time) of calculating costs was accepted as a fair basis for charging. The Court of Appeal had the following advice to solicitors for the future (para.33):

THE FUTURE

We have been asked to give the profession such guidance as we can for the future in the light of the issues to which the appeal has given rise. This is difficult and, for our part, we cannot do better than to suggest that it would be appropriate for solicitors to adhere to the following principles:

1. Much the best practice is for a solicitor to obtain prior agreement as to the basis of his charges not only from the executors but also, where appropriate, from any residuary beneficiary who is an entitled third party under the 1994 Order. This is encouraged in the 1994 booklet [An Approach to Non-Contentious Costs] and letter 8 of Appendix 2 to the 1999 booklet [Practice Advice Service booklet called Non-Contentious Costs] provides a good working draft of such agreement. We support that encouragement;
2. in any complicated administration, it will be prudent for solicitors to provide in their terms of retainer for interim bills to be rendered for payment on account; this is, of course, subject to the solicitor's obligation to review the matter as a whole at the end of the business so as to ensure that he has claimed no more than is fair and

reasonable, taking into account the factors set out in the 1994 Order [Solicitors' (Non-Contentious Business) Remuneration Order 1994];

3. there should be no hard and fast rule that charges cannot be made separately by reference to the value of the estate; value can, by contrast, be taken into account as part of the hourly rate; value can also be taken into account partly in one way and partly in the other. What is important is that

   (a) it should be transparent on the face of the bill how value is being taken into account; and
   (b) in no case, should it be taken into account more than once;

4. in many cases, if a charge is separately made by reference to the value of the estate, it should usually be on a regressive scale. The bands and percentages will be for the costs judge in each case; the suggestions to the costs judge set out in paragraph 30 may be thought by him to be appropriate for this case but different bands and percentages will be appropriate for other cases and the figures set out in paragraph 30 cannot be any more than a guideline;
5. it may be helpful at the end of the business for the solicitor or, if there is an assessment, for the costs judge, when a separate element of the bill is based on the value of the estate, to calculate the number of hours that would notionally be taken to achieve the amount of the separate charge. That may help to determine whether overall the remuneration claimed or assessed is fair and reasonable within the terms of the 1994 Order.
6. it may also be helpful to consider the Law Society's Guidance in cases where there is no relevant and ascertainable value factor which is given in the 1995 booklet at paragraph 13.4. If the time spent on the matter is costed out at the solicitors' expense rate (which should be readily ascertainable from the Solicitors' Expense of Time calculations) the difference between that sum (the cost to the solicitor of the time spent on the matter) and the final figure claimed will represent the mark-up. The mark-up (which should take into account the factors specified in the 1994 Order including value) when added to the cost of the time spent must then be judged by reference to the requirement that this total figure must represent 'such sum as may be fair and reasonable to both solicitor and entitled person'.

It is for individual practitioners to exercise their own professional judgment as to whether or not to apply the value element when charging for the administration of an estate. Whatever method is adopted, it is vital that it should be transparent on the face of the bill how it is being treated and in no case, should value be taken into account more than once.

2.6.3 Estimates, quotations or other indications of cost

The word 'indication' is used where appropriate to include quotations and estimates. It is advisable that indications are given by an authorised responsible member of a firm and that a standard procedure for giving indications is adopted within the firm. All such indications should be readily visible on the file.

All indications should be confirmed in writing to the client. The final amount payable should not vary substantially from the relevant indication unless the client was informed in writing at the time that there was a change of circumstances.

A solicitor may wish to give a qualified indication, for example by stating that it may be reviewed if the matter develops in an unforeseen manner or turns out to be more complex or difficult than originally envisaged. However, even if such complications arise, the original indication will still be binding on the solicitor unless the solicitor informs the client immediately and in writing of the change in circumstances. The solicitor should point out that the original indication no longer stands and/or the client's instructions to proceed should be sought.

In cases where the solicitor's fee is to be paid by a third party, it may be that the indication has only been given to the third party and not to the client. In such cases (depending on the overall circumstances) the same principles as set out above in relation to solicitor and own client indications will generally apply.

2.6.4 Consumer Protection from Unfair Trading Regulations 2008

Inaccurate indications can amount to an offence under the Consumer Protection from Unfair Trading Regulations 2008, SI 2008/1277, reg.9. Regulation 5 sets out the circumstances in which a misleading indication could give rise to a criminal offence.

2.6.5 Change of circumstance

A solicitor is required to notify the client immediately, and in writing, if a change of circumstances has occurred so that the original qualified indication no longer applies. It is appreciated that some special circumstances, e.g. a contract race, may make it impractical for the solicitor to revise the indication in the way contemplated by the statement.

Solicitors should take extra care in these circumstances to ensure that the client does not rely on the indication if it has become misleading.

2.6.6 Split transactions

Where a transaction has a number of parts (e.g. the purchase of a property, the creation or discharge of a mortgage or the registration of title) the indication, unless it states otherwise, will be deemed to include all of these matters. The view that an indication only covers the basic transaction and that a charge can be raised in addition for ancillary matters such as registration of title is not acceptable and this may well be (depending on the circumstances) a misleading indication.

2.6.7 Petty disbursements

The practice of adding petty disbursements such as postage, telephone calls and faxes to the final bill is generally unacceptable. Petty disbursements are considered to be part of the overheads of the firm. They are expenses of the firm and should be included in the calculation of the fee even if there is an indication that petty disbursements will not normally be allowed, unless there is a specific agreement to the contrary.

Where a transaction is likely to involve substantial telephone work, faxing or photocopying, it should be made clear to the client if such items are to be charged in addition to any indication of costs.

2.6.8 Abortive matters

In general, where an indication has been given for a completed transaction and it does not proceed to completion, the charge for the abortive work should be made on a pro rata basis. In the context of conveyancing, an indication given for a sale will normally be held to include all abortive sales unless the solicitor has revised the indication at the appropriate time.

In a purchase transaction, it is in both the solicitor's and the client's interests that the extent of the indication is revised in writing as soon as abortive matters make it clear that the original indication is no longer appropriate.

See **16.9** in connection with estates which turn out to be insolvent.

2.6.9 Approximations

Where an indication is expressed in forms such as 'about £500', or 'approximately £500', it would normally be expected that the final fee charged would be within 10 per cent of the indicated figure. Any fee outside that tolerance may (depending on the circumstances) be viewed as a substantial variation resulting in the original approximation restricting the solicitor's fee.

2.6.10 Time limits

When confirming an indication, it is advisable to make clear the time period within which the indication will remain valid. Failure to do so may well (depending on the circumstances of the case) result in solicitors being held to what they consider to be an out-of-date figure, particularly where it is clear that the client still viewed the indication as an incentive to instruct the solicitor and relied upon it.

CHAPTER 3

Client care

Heather Stewart

3.1 INTRODUCTION

Legal practices are the same as any other business – you have services you want to sell to make a desired level of return on your investment. In the case of a probate department, these services will include wills and powers of attorney, estate administration, trusts and tax planning. Clients will only buy these services and the department will only make that return if its products are what clients want and they consider the price charged to be fair.

Clients' expectations of, and attitudes towards, legal services have changed significantly in the last 25 years. Many legal services are regarded as commodities by clients, which impacts on the price sensitivity of the service. Solicitors already operate in mature markets for most of their services – numerous other legal practices offer the same technical skills. Successful firms have differentiated themselves on their service package, the way in which they deliver advice, and on their culture, in order to attract and retain clients who feel comfortable dealing with like-minded people.

The various elements of the Legal Services Act (LSA) 2007 will have an even greater impact on the marketplace and the way in which legal practices are regulated. The ethos of LSA 2007 is to open up the legal marketplace for the benefit of consumers. When legal practices can attract external investment and be owned by non-lawyers, the marketplace will change forever.

LSA 2007:

1. Establishes the Legal Services Board to oversee the regulation of legal services by all approved regulators such as the Solicitors Regulation Authority, the Bar Standards Board and the Council for Licensed Conveyancers.
2. Enables new forms of legal practice to develop and will allow lawyers to form multidisciplinary practices offering legal services in conjunction with non-legal services. It will also allow non-lawyers, including commercial organisations to own firms that provide legal services. Legal disciplinary practices (LDPs) came into being in March 2009 and the market will be open to external service providers in the form of alternative business structures (ABSs) in 2011.

3. Creates the Office for Legal Complaints, the Board which set up the new independent Legal Ombudsman (LeO) to deal with all consumer complaints about legal services from 6 October 2010, taking over from the Legal Complaints Service (LCS) and bringing with it a new consumer-focused regime for reporting and handling complaints. The Legal Ombudsman will cover the work of all lawyers and will deal with redress – not with regulation.

The changes to the way in which the Solicitors Regulation Authority (SRA) exercises the regulation of solicitors and legal practices from 2011 will also be significant. The proposed outcomes-focused regulation will concentrate on high-level principles governing practice and the quality of outcomes for clients, rather than tick-box compliance with the rules of the Solicitors' Code of Conduct 2007.

It is no longer a question of *whether* external suppliers will enter the market, but *when*. Probate services were opened up in 2004 when s.55 of the Courts and Legal Services Act 1990 was implemented, allowing bodies to apply to become 'approved' for the purposes of applying for grants of representation. Although potential entrants may not have experience of delivering legal services, they do understand the needs of their customers. Although some legal firms have excellent senior management, the external competition is likely to have superior management skills throughout their organisation. Even if such organisations are not in direct competition, the impact of those skills will gradually be felt across all firms. New entrants are likely to have a more commercial approach and deeper pockets, and the way in which they provide services may be quite different from the way solicitors have provided legal services in the past. Clients' expectations of all legal services providers are likely to rise even further.

We think we look after our clients well and give them a good level of service, but do our clients think so? Research has shown that, increasingly, our services are seen as expensive and that the level of service received does not match the expectations of clients. Put yourself in your client's position – who would you instruct in the future?

There are great opportunities in the marketplace but not necessarily by continuing to work as we have done in the past, and not by delivering a substandard level of service or one which is seen as not offering value for money. To compete, firms will constantly have to ensure their service actually meets clients' needs, continuously consider how profitability can be maintained or enhanced while meeting those needs, and be willing to adopt new ways of working.

Understanding customer needs and delivering a service to meet them will be crucial for success. Focus on the specific services you offer and understand what clients in the market you are targeting really want.

- How important is price?
- Where do clients think you can improve?
- Are your processes and procedures really aligned to give clients the type of service they want?
- How can you rethink service delivery?

- Do your processes and procedures just operate solely for the benefit of internal efficiency without considering your clients at all?
- What impression do your letters, e-mails and other means of communication make on clients? Are they user friendly and approachable, easy to understand or stiff and formal – and off-putting?

Talk to your clients and understand what they want from you before it is too late.

3.2 CULTURE AND LEADERSHIP

The critical difference between successful and less successful firms, irrespective of size is often culture. Culture is something a firm 'is' rather than 'has', but it does not just happen. Although partly derived from a firm's history, culture is in fact managed on a daily basis by the attitudes, behaviours and leadership demonstrated by a firm's partners, the organisational structures and processes by which it is managed and success measured, and the decisions taken in running the firm. Culture provides the guidelines for the behaviour of everyone in the firm, for their attitudes towards work and the way in which it is handled, for relationships within the firm and with clients. Firms that have a distinctive culture have a real advantage because this is what differentiates them from other firms. Aspects of service that create confidence and value for clients relate back to a firm's ethos and the way its people consistently treat clients and build relationships with them. Solicitors might profess to care for their clients but, unless their attitude and behaviour actually back that up, they will fail as far as their clients are concerned.

In legal services, more than in any other profession or business, reputation is essential in attracting and retaining clients. Clients who need help in the private client area often lack familiarity with the provision of legal services. This means they take a leap of faith when instructing a legal practice. This leap is much easier when they have experienced or heard positive things about a firm. The client has to know that you will protect their interests and look after them to achieve the best possible outcome. It is for this reason that no modern legal practice can afford to overlook the importance of client care, yet few solicitors appreciate that importance. Spending more time and resource on understanding and improving the service given to existing clients rather than using the majority of a marketing budget on trying to attract new work will invariably be more cost effective and provide a better return. For firms that get service levels right as far as clients are concerned, repeat business, recommendation and referral are still the principal ways of attracting new work and will become increasingly so albeit by different means such as social interactive websites.

Quality accreditation schemes such as the Law Society's practice management standard, currently Lexcel v4, can act as a catalyst for a change of behaviours and consequently the culture of a firm, in addition to promoting better management and greater effectiveness in the way in which work is handled. However, beware of hiding behind accreditations to avoid dealing with the internal cultural issues which are the real barrier to delivering excellent client service. Many firms only treat client care as part of risk and compliance. Senior managers often do not realise that their client care performance is not up to standard and are unaware that the level of complaints their firm generates is above the 'norm'. The technical expertise offered may be of a high standard but the level of service over and above that is increasingly important. A recent client care initiative undertaken by the Law Society has shown that processes and procedures are not the primary requirement for delivering excellent client care. A significant proportion of firms with quality accreditations were among those with a higher than average number of complaints referred to the LCS. Good client care comes down to attitude backed up by compliance, not compliance alone.

Consider:

- How important is client care in your firm?
- How clear and strong is your message about it?
- Is client care taken into account at appraisals, performance review?
- What emphasis is put on client service compared to fee income targets?

3.3 PROFESSIONAL CONDUCT

The legal profession is currently regulated by the Solicitors Regulation Authority (SRA) under the Solicitors' Code of Conduct 2007 (the Code) and other regulations which have already been updated several times to take account of the introduction of elements of LSA 2007. On 31 March 2009 the Code was amended as part of a general updating of the rules to introduce firm-based regulation and LDPs with the effect that the SRA received new powers to apply the rules to non-solicitor managers and employees (see the Law Society Practice Note on firm-based regulation). There have been several further updates to the rules and practitioners should always check on the SRA website (**www.sra.org.uk**) that they have the most up-to-date version.

Rule 1 of the Code sets out six core duties, the principles of professional conduct, and rules 2–25 address in more detail the minimum standards required to achieve compliance with those. The professional standards in respect of client care are principally set out in rule 2 (Client relations) although rules 2–11 focus on delivering a high standard of service to clients. Each of the 25 rules is accompanied by guidance which assists with the interpretation of the rules in different situations and shows practical ways of complying with them. The guidance and explanatory introductions issued with the rules are not mandatory and do not form part of the Code. However, if you do not follow the guidance you may be required to demonstrate how you have nevertheless complied with the rule.

Rule 2 (Client relations) and rule 5 (Business management) have the greatest impact on client care and its management within a legal practice.

The Law Society, in its representative capacity, issues Practice Notes on a variety of issues for the use and benefit of its members. They represent the Law Society's view of good practice in a particular area but are not intended to be the only standard of good practice that solicitors can follow. You are not *required* to follow them, but doing so will make it easier to account to the SRA for your actions. Practice Notes are not legal advice, nor do they necessarily provide a defence to complaints of misconduct or of inadequate professional service. While care has been taken to ensure that they are accurate, up to date and useful, the Law Society will not accept any legal liability in relation to them. Always ensure that you have the most up-to-date version of a Practice Note: they can be downloaded from **www.lawsociety.org.uk**.

3.3.1 Rule 1 (Core duties)

These regulatory principles, definitions of which are given in rule 1 and its guidance, are enforceable in their own right and applicable in all circumstances, are as follows:

1.01 Justice and the rule of law.
1.02 Integrity.
1.03 Independence.
1.04 Best interests of clients.
1.05 Standard of service.
1.06 Public confidence.

Breaches of the core duties may amount to inadequate professional service (a level of service falling below that which a client could reasonably expect) or even misconduct. Breaches of the other rules may also amount to a breach of one or more of the core duties. For example, not complying with aspects of rule 2 (Client relations) may mean that you are not acting in the best interests of your client (1.04) and some breaches of rule 5 may amount to a breach both 1.04 and of 1.05 (Standard of service).

3.4 RULE 5 (BUSINESS MANAGEMENT)

The aim of rule 5 is that firms should be able to give a continuing standard of service to clients. It sets out the minimum standards applying to the supervision of their matters and the minimum requirements in relation to business arrangements considered essential to good practice and integral to compliance with supervision and other duties to clients.

Under rule 5.01(1) firms and managers of recognised bodies must make arrangements for the systematic and effective management of the firm. Firms must have systems, procedures, processes and methods of organisation in place to achieve the required outcome. These will depend on the size and structure of the firm, types of work it undertakes and the experience and qualifications of staff. What is important is that the arrangements must be seen not only to exist but to actually be used in operation and, to be seen to be effective, they must also be reviewed periodically. The following requirements of rule 5 have particular relevance to client care.

3.4.1 Supervision of staff and direction of clients' matters (rule 5.01(1)(a))

Managers have a duty to supervise the work of all employees, including independent consultants or locums, wherever the work is carried out, whether in the office, or away from the office such as visiting clients or working from home. You can delegate supervision provided that it is delegated within a framework of reporting and accountability. There is a separate duty under rule 5.03 to have procedures for supervising work for clients. To comply, there must be appropriate and effective systems in place to check:

- the quality of work;
- with reasonable regularity;
- by suitably experienced and competent people.

If you receive a complaint you will have to show that work checking procedures exist and are in operation to avoid a breach of rule 5.

The Law Society's Supervision Practice Note gives further guidance. Probate departments have traditionally been staffed with a range of fee earners, many of whom are experienced and therefore may not be supervised to any great extent. In some instances this can lead to fee earners carrying far too heavy a workload to be able to handle files effectively and efficiently, which may lead to poor client service, complaints and potential negligence claims.

3.4.2 Conflict of interest (rule 5.01(1)(d))

You must also have effective procedures to identify and avoid conflicts of interest, dealing with conflicts between the duties of confidentiality and disclosure, and maintaining client confidentiality. Rule 3 (Conflict of interests) and rule 4 (Confidentiality and disclosure) and the respective guidance to both rules should always be read together. The Law Society Practice Note on File Retention: records management – retention and wills, deeds and documents together with supporting data, contains useful guidance for probate practitioners. It includes information in relation to confidentiality and legal professional privilege after a death and in connection with trusts and beneficiaries.

Conflict searches should be comprehensive and meaningful. Be particularly mindful when you merge with another firm or take on new fee earners from other firms that conflict or confidentiality situations do not arise with regard to the former clients of the old or other firm. The Law Society Practice Note on Initial Interviews (2008) gives guidance on conflict checks to be made in situations in which initial interviews are given without subsequent work being undertaken.

Pay particular attention to rule 3.04 (Accepting gifts from clients). If anything more than a token amount is accepted without the client having separate advice (other than where you are acting for a family member as permitted by 3.04), you may be exposed to allegations of misconduct. You can prepare a will for a family member under which you receive a significant gift without requiring the client to seek independent advice on that gift. However, extreme caution should always be exercised. The guidance to the rule states that the risk of conflict is high. See *Franks v. Sinclair* [2006] EWHC 3365 (Ch) where a will prepared by a solicitor for his mother which left the estate equally between himself and his sister was held to be invalid for lack of knowledge and approval. The will differed substantially from the deceased's previous will which had left the bulk of the estate to a grandchild.

Take particular care when acting for more than one member of a family in a conflict situation under the 'common interest' exception set out in rule 3 and its guidance. It is essential that you take an objective view of your position.

You must make the implications of 3.04 clear to all members of your firm who take instructions from clients, whether solicitors or not. Back this up by training and supervision. Staff training should cover reminders about confidentiality. Use your induction process to emphasise the importance of confidentiality to all support staff, particularly those who have not worked in the legal profession before. Take a critical look at confidentiality in your reception area. Do not discuss matters with clients there, even just signing documents. Can other clients overhear your receptionist talking about confidential matters with another client on the phone? Be careful when using laptops on trains and in public places. Remind everyone about the use of mobile phones in public places, particularly on trains.

3.4.3 Compliance with client relations rule (rule 5.01(1)(e))

Firms must have systems and procedures to ensure compliance with rule 2.02 (Client care), 2.03 (Costs information) and 2.05 (Complaints handling). You will need to be able to demonstrate with evidence from files that these aspects of rule 2 have been complied with. These issues are covered in the section in this chapter on client care. Do your supervision and file review systems cover these aspects of rule 2?

3.4.4 Safekeeping of documents and assets (rule 5.01(1)(g))

Documents and assets include client money, wills, deeds, investments and other property entrusted to the firm by its clients and others. It is up to you to design the systems but, as a minimum, you must be able to identify to whom documents and assets belong and in connection with which matter. Always ensure that you:

- maintain an accurate record of all wills retained for clients. If records are computerised, ensure regular back up, including items stored off site;

- if a will is released, obtain a receipt and ensure that the recipient and his or her address are noted on the register/computer record;
- if the original will is sent to the client, make a file note and ensure that a completed copy is retained;
- ensure that clients are aware where their papers are located, particularly if the firm moves office, merges or changes name.

The Law Society's File Retention Practice Note gives additional guidance.

3.4.5 Maintaining competence (rule 5.01(1)(i))

Training for everyone is particularly important to maintain a level of competence appropriate to their work and level of responsibility. Firms must have systematic procedures to ensure both that training needs are recognised and that training actually happens. Ensure that employees are trained on the requirements of the rules to the extent necessary for the roles they undertake in the firm.

3.4.6 Risk management (rule 5.01(1)(l))

Firms must also have a systematic approach to the management of risk, including client-related risk. Lexcel v4 has requirements for supervision and file audit within its supervision and risk management sections which require that firms have procedures to cover:

- inactivity checks;
- file reviews;
- how work is accepted;
- conflict of interest;
- risk assessments;
- risks by work type;
- key dates;
- key information on retained on file.

3.5 TAKING ON CLIENTS

Both rule 2 and rule 5 emphasise risk management in relation to clients and their matters. Risk should be analysed before new clients are taken on, when new matters are opened and during matters as well. There is no point in saying six months down the line, 'I wish we had not taken on this work' or 'I wish we had not taken on this client'. Clients and the nature of their work vary. Many will be existing clients but, nevertheless, a risk assessment should be carried out at the start of anything other than routine work. Greater knowledge allows for the better assessment of the level of risk in potential work and for planning the appropriate level of fee earner to undertake it with appropriate supervision. The fact that partners and many fee earners 'know their clients' is often taken for granted in firms but the information is rarely shared. It is important to both store and share key information about clients and decisions made about what information to keep and how to make that information accessible to others:

- What information do you need to hold about existing clients?
- Do you have systems in place to gather, collate, store and update that information?
- Do you have guidelines about which types of work you will/will not undertake and a clear decision making process?
- Have you established and communicated clear criteria, in relation to value, complexity for example, for taking on new clients?
- Do you ensure that you complete your money laundering procedures before you accept money on account?
- Do you complete your conflict of interest searches before you send your terms of engagement letter?

Remember that if you do not want to act for a client, you must decline before you send out your terms of engagement letter and/or your terms and conditions of business.

The guidance to rule 2.01 provides that, before taking on a new matter, you must consider whether your firm has the resources – including knowledge, qualifications, expertise, time, sufficient support staff and, where appropriate, access to external expertise such as agents and counsel – to provide the support required to represent the client properly. The obligation continues throughout the matter and you must ensure that an appropriate or agreed level of service can be delivered even if circumstances change, for example if an experienced member of your team leaves and you cannot find an immediate replacement.

3.6 UNDERSTANDING YOUR CLIENTS' PERSPECTIVE

For some clients, making a will or dealing with a relative's estate may be their first contact with a lawyer, while other clients may be sophisticated users of legal services. However, for all clients, the matters that a solicitor will be dealing with on their behalf are likely to be of immense personal importance to them. They want to feel confident they are receiving the best advice and that your charges are fair and reasonable. Unfortunately, they cannot assess either of those issues beforehand and so may approach a solicitor's service with feelings of uncertainty and trepidation. Their lack of knowledge manifests itself in a need for information, particularly in a long-running probate matter. Unfamiliarity with what could or should happen, or the time that each stage should take, often makes clients feel that things are out of their control. Nor can they anticipate the likely level of costs, which increases their feeling of vulnerability.

Clients cannot judge the accuracy your advice and therefore focus on what they understand: how it is delivered. Complaints rarely arise from poor advice. Client expectations may be quite unrealistic but unless solicitors explain what they can and cannot do, the likely timescale involved in each stage of the matter, and give an explanation of the cost estimate, their expectations will continue to be unrealistic. Managing a matter should be a two-way process: you need the client's instructions, and, although you have the professional knowledge and skill, you have to manage the relationship to your client's satisfaction. First meetings are all important – they are your opportunity to understand what your client wants and to manage their expectations. Clarity at the beginning gives less cause for complaint later. Discuss four issues with your client:

- What they want to happen: their objective.
- What should or could happen.
- The type of service you can offer.
- How much it is going to cost.

The purpose of rule 2 (Client relations) is to help you to establish and manage the relationship with your client. The requirements of the rule should be viewed positively and not merely as box ticking necessary for compliance.

3.7 RULE 2.02 (CLIENT CARE)

Good communication is essential in establishing a good relationship but it is two way: it not only involves giving advice, it also involves listening. Clients complain that lawyers are not good listeners and often assume that they know what the client wants. It is essential to listen to clients to understand, or to help them to formulate, their wishes and to ensure that you understand their concerns. Some clients may be unclear themselves of what they want, what they would like to happen or what it may be possible to achieve. By going through all the issues you will help them to clarify their own thoughts. What are they hoping to achieve? What is really important to them? If you do not clarify issues, you may pursue a course of action your client does not want to follow, resulting in an unhappy client.

Rule 2.02 requires that you agree your client's objectives and the way to achieve them at the outset and periodically as a matter progresses if there is any significant change. Complaints can arise because solicitors fail to check the client's instructions when there has been a change in circumstances.

Clients may not be totally clear about what they want at the outset. When talking about a complicated issue, feedback to your client what they have told you and explain the implications of a course of action to allow your client to consider whether it is really what they intended. Summarise discussions periodically to ensure that you both fully understand each other and always write to confirm instructions where there may be any cause for doubt. Ensure that you have given clear advice on all the issues raised by your client or where your client could reasonably expect that you would give advice. Explain fully any reason why you cannot follow a client's instructions. Bear in mind that clients who are going through emotional or stressful times find it particularly difficult to absorb information.

Clients will rarely be familiar with the technical language often used in wills and trusts or the intricacies of an inheritance tax calculation. It is essential that the terms are explained to all clients in clear and simple language without legal jargon. Wherever possible, straightforward language should be used in documents, as clients will want to be able to understand them when they revisit them in several years' time. If the provisions are complicated, provide a separate written note giving an explanation in simple terms together with the reason for their inclusion. See *Franks* v. *Sinclair* [2006] EWHC 3365 (Ch), where David Richards J described a residuary gift containing substitutional gifts for the issue of deceased children as being expressed in 'the customary technical language of wills, which most lay people will find impenetrable and many may consider to be gobbledegook'. He said it required explanation in simple language to enable the testator to understand its effect.

Remember that your client is unlikely to be familiar with the legal process. First meetings are your chance to tell your client what is likely to happen and when, and to explain the usual process in matters of that type. Run through any potential complications and their impact. It can help to have a leaflet explaining these issues for your client to take away afterwards. Think about the different types of work; probate for instance will inevitably have gaps where nothing appears to be happening. Explain that to your client at the start along with the various steps involved in obtaining a grant and administering an estate with likely timescales. Case planning at each stage of a matter in which you identify with your client the steps involved and agree how the issues are to be dealt with serves to give the client a sense of involvement and an awareness of progress. Whether information should be given to beneficiaries is discussed later in this chapter, but providing information at least on timescales is likely to promote better understanding on their part and gives a better impression of your firm.

At the end of the meeting, your client should understand:

- the steps that you will take up to the next stage of the matter;
- that their own responsibility is to provide you with information to allow you to achieve their objective;
- when things are likely to happen;
- when to expect to hear from you next;
- when you will need to hear from your client.

Rule 2.02 also requires that you agree a level of service with your client. This is not about the level of fee earner who will do the work but the method and timing of communication between you and the level of service the client can expect. Listen to your client: what do they think you will be able to do for them? You should agree when and how you will communicate at the outset and be proactive with information. Does your client want regular letters from you, or regular reports or do they want to wait until you have reached an agreed point before you get back to them?

However, bear in mind that the matter is likely to be uppermost in your client's mind a lot of the time but you should explain to your client at the outset that calling five times a day will be expensive. Although they may say that they do not want to hear from you until a certain point, it will be worthwhile to get back to them in the interim just to confirm that everything is going according to plan. Clients are not mind readers and you cannot assume that a client is aware that that you are working on their file; they need information about progress in a timely way. A client should not have to chase you for an update of their file.

At the end of the meeting, your client should always know:

- how often you will be in touch;
- the agreed form of regular communication.

It is up to you to establish your client's confidence and build their trust in you:

- Listen to the client; ensure that all relevant information is obtained to enable draft documentation to be prepared which gives effect to the client's wishes.
- Communicate with the client clearly, simply and in a timely way.
- Agree when and how the client will be updated with progress.
- Give an indication of timescales for each stage of the matter.
- Be proactive in explaining any delay.
- Return phone calls, voice mails and e-mails promptly.
- Always keep the client informed of the process and involved in the decision making of the matter.
- Ensure that the client feels that he or she can easily contact either the solicitor or a member of the team.
- Follow the client's instructions and deliver the service when and how agreed.
- Keep promises and be reliable and efficient, including in relation to billing.
- Reassure clients on the safety of their documents.
- Treat clients with respect and show genuine interest in them and their concerns.
- Demonstrate the effort put in on the client's behalf.

On a practical note:

- Establish your client's objectives at the outset and at significant stages in a long-running matter. Case planning with the client is a discipline and an opportunity to ensure that this is addressed.
- Where appropriate, consider whether the likely outcome justifies the expense or risk involved.
- Clearly note all instructions on file for any other person who may have to take over or supervise the matter.
- Agree how frequently you will be in touch and the most convenient method.

- Discuss the likely timescales involved. For example, agree a timescale with the client for drafting, engrossing and executing a will. Operate a reminder system and ensure the will is executed, or the file is closed and the client notified.
- Explain when a client can expect a distribution of assets, if appropriate.
- Use diary systems and file review systems to maintain regular contact with clients.
- Ask clients whether the matter has been completed to their satisfaction and whether the service provided might have been improved in any way.
- Do not delay in acting on instructions, for example the sale of assets, as their value may go down.
- Ensure beneficiaries are correctly identified and that correspondence is sent to the correct address.
- Write to confirm as soon as a matter is completed.
- Bill promptly, while a client still remembers the value of your efforts.
- Account promptly for all client-related funds held (together with interest if appropriate).
- Hand over all papers and property to which the client is entitled (subject to any lien for unpaid bills).
- Handle all post-completion matters speedily.

3.8 WHO IS YOUR CLIENT?

Information required by 2.02 (Client care), 2.03 (Information about the cost) and 2.05 (Complaints handling) must be given to your client and it is important that it is given to the correct person or persons:

- Who is your client for the purposes of rule 2?
  - Identify the right client and client name.
  - Who gives you instructions/whom do you report to?
- Ensure instructions are from all clients or that you have the authority of all to accept from one.

Identifying the client may be not be straightforward if you are a solicitor-executor or trustee. What relationship should the solicitor have with the beneficiaries? How much information should be given in respect of costs or the conduct of the matter in general?

In *Jemma Trust* v. *Liptrott* [2003] EWCA Civ 1476 the Court of Appeal stated that it would be best practice to agree the charging regime in advance not only with the executors but also, where appropriate, with any residuary beneficiary who is an entitled third party under the Solicitors' (Non-Contentious Business) Remuneration Order 1994, SI 1994/2616 (now replaced by the Solicitors' (Non-Contentious Business) Remuneration Order 2009, SI 2009/1931). The clear message was the need for transparency between solicitor, executor and residuary beneficiary.

Note 26 of the guidance to rule 2 recognises that 'beneficiaries', not just residuary beneficiaries, are 'interested parties'. It states:

> Where you are, in effect, your firm's client – for example, as an executor administering a deceased's estate or a trustee of a trust – you should consider what information, if any, should be given to interested parties. There is no requirement, for example, that beneficiaries under a will or trust should be treated as though they were clients. It may, however, be good practice to provide some information – for example, about the type of work to be carried out and approximate timescales.

The test applied by the LCS when dealing with complaints is one of reasonableness in each particular case. In an application by a beneficiary for a remuneration certificate, an adjudicator stated:

> Whilst it is not necessary to send a client care letter to residuary beneficiaries, it is regarded as good practice to do so, just as it is regarded good practice to have on file a client care letter addressed to the solicitor executor.

Where a solicitor is an executor with a lay co-executor, both are in effect the firm's clients but all too frequently the lay executor is not consulted on matters connected with the estate or kept informed on progress or costs and a complaint to the LCS results. You should be able to provide evidence either that the person with conduct of the file had communicated with both executors or that there was an agreement (preferably in writing) confirming that the lay executor had agreed that all general instructions could be taken from one executor only. If not, there is a potential breach of rule 2.02(2)(a), (b) and (c) in that the person handling the file had not explained either his or the client's responsibilities in relation to the administration of the estate and/or had not agreed a level of service with the lay executor, all of which might lead to a finding of inadequate professional service, i.e. a level of service falling below what the client might reasonably expect.

When complaints are dealt with by the Legal Ombudsman (LeO) from 2010, it is proposed that the LeO will have power to investigate complaints made by a beneficiary of the estate or trust in question about a solicitor (referred to as 'the respondent') where the services complained of were provided by the respondent:

- in the respondent's capacity as a personal representative or trustee; or
- to a person acting as a personal representative or trustee.

If you receive instructions from someone other than your client, you must still give the information required under rule 2 to your actual client. There are, however, exceptions to this. For example, where your client has an attorney appointed by an enduring power of attorney which has been registered with the Court of Protection, or a donee of a lasting power of attorney which has similarly been registered, or a deputy for financial affairs, the information required by 2.02 should be given to the attorney, donee or deputy. However, because the question of capacity relates to the particular decision that needs to be made (that is, just because a person lacks capacity as defined in the Mental Capacity Act 2005 to make certain decisions they do not necessarily lack the capacity to instruct a solicitor in other matters), you need to have regard to the provisions of that Act and its accompanying Code of Practice and must not assume that a person subject to the provisions of that Act lacks the capacity to instruct you in an area not covered by the power of attorney or the scope of the deputy's appointment.

These may appear basic issues but you need to give relevant training to staff and to check compliance on file review to comply with rule 5.

3.9 CLIENT CARE/TERMS OF ENGAGEMENT LETTERS

These letters are a vital tool in helping your client to focus on the exact parameters of the retainer with them particularly at a time when they are primarily concerned with achieving the successful resolution of their problem. Clarity at the outset on what you will do for them, the level of service they can expect to receive and price that they will pay will prevent problems and possible complaints at a later date.

The Law Society's Client Care Letters Practice Note gives guidance on the content, style and length of the letter and gives sample terms and conditions of business. The Law Society's Provision of Services Regulations 2009 Practice Note includes details of the information to be given to clients required by those regulations.

In effect, your letter should be a contemporaneous record of what you have agreed with your client at the first meeting. It should identify the work that you have agreed to do and equally what you have not agreed to do for the price which you have agreed with your client. Sending out a letter in vague terms may well cause confusion and problems with your client at a later date. Always ensure that the letter is addressed to the actual client.

Although the majority of information required under 2.02 does not need to be included in your client care/terms of engagement letter, including the key issues will be helpful. It can also provide evidence of compliance for supervision purposes. The following information must be given in writing to your client at the outset:

- the name and status of the person dealing with the matter;
- the name of the person responsible for its overall supervision.

Costs information must be given in writing at the outset under rule 2.03. Information on whom your client should contact in the event of a problem with your service or bill must also be included under rule 2.05.

3.10 MANAGING COSTS

The relationship on costs is different from the solicitor–client relationship based on building trust and confidence. Getting the costs relationship right obviously adds to your client's confidence in you and equally, getting it wrong breaks that confidence. But the relationship on costs is with the firm, not the individual fee earner, and the firm has to have as much information as possible to allow fee earners to give accurate forecasts of costs or fixed prices wherever possible. Good credit control starts at the beginning of a matter. Setting up the agreement with clients and then sticking to it and always keeping clients informed about current costs levels is far more likely to mean that your bills will be paid promptly.

It is important that someone with knowledge of the implications for the firm of different costs arrangements sees the client at the first meeting. In *Reynolds* v. *Stone Rowe Brewer (A Firm)* [2008] EWHC 497 (QB) a firm was bound by an original estimate plus 15 per cent because a client had been given an estimate on which the client could rely. The estimate had been given by a trainee solicitor.

Obviously, the firm has needs when it comes to costs and billing and these must be taken into account when discussing costs with a client. However, agreements can often be mutually beneficial, for example, agreeing on interim billing. For clients, it means they never have a huge weight of costs on their shoulders and they are far more likely to feel in control of the costs situation – little and often. Be reliable in respect of the agreement. If you agree to bill monthly, do so, even if there is only a small amount to bill, or notify the client why you have not done so. Otherwise your client thinks that you are not very good at housekeeping and wonders whether your internal inefficiency will be reflected in the way you handle their matter.

Agree to bill periodically rather than when the matter has reached a specific stage as by then the costs may be quite a large sum. By billing frequently, the client will also remember the value of what you have done and you are less likely to write off time before submitting the bill.

Costs are an area of major concern for all clients. Rule 2.03 supports client needs in respect of costs and it is vital that you follow it and the guidance to the rule. The guidance states that you are not acting for your client in costs negotiations so you *must* give the best information possible to enable your client to make an informed decision.

Rule 2.03(1) provides that:

> You must give your client the best information possible about the likely overall cost of a matter both at the outset and, when appropriate, as the matter progresses.

The guidance to that rule states (note 36):

> It is often impossible to tell at the outset what the overall cost will be. Rule 2.03 allows for this and requires that you provide the client with as much information as possible at the start and that you keep the client updated. If a precise figure cannot be given at the outset, you should explain the reason to the client and agree a ceiling figure or review dates.

3.10.1 Managing costs at the outset

The Law Society Client Care Letters Practice Note suggests that giving the 'best information possible' may include:

- agreeing a fixed fee; or
- giving a realistic estimate; or
- giving a forecast within a possible range of costs; or
- explaining why it is not possible to give the above, and instead giving the best information possible about the costs of the next stage of the matter.

Probate clients may be extremely distressed and it may be difficult to discuss costs at an initial meeting, but it should not be avoided. It may not be possible to give an estimate of the likely overall cost or of the timescale involved in a complicated matter until what is involved has been fully investigated, but an estimate can be given for the first investigatory stage and the client informed that you will be in a better position to discuss costs fully after that. You must tell clients in clear, simple, non-jargon language what they will get for their money. Always be totally transparent about costs information. Make sure that all correspondence relating to costs is clearly set out and unambiguous.

Agree the basis of your charges with your client and how your client will pay at the outset. Give the hourly rates of everyone to be involved in the matter and a realistic estimate of the time to be charged. Merely setting out the hourly rate in your terms of business or retainer letter, even if supported by information leaflets, does not comply with the requirement to give your client 'the best information possible about the likely overall cost'. Give your client the opportunity to set an upper limit on costs.

All possible options should be considered, discussed and then confirmed in a client care/retainer letter that accompanies your terms and conditions of business. It is important that you do cost/benefit analyses with your client not only at the outset but if a matter changes as it progresses. Your client will then have to decide whether the potential outcome will justify the risks involved, including that of having to pay a third party's costs.

Clients regard an estimate as a fixed price for the work which you state that you will do for that figure. It is essential that you set out both price and work to be done for that price precisely in your client care/terms of engagement letter, including the assumptions as to the progress of the matter on which you have based your estimate. Your client will not understand if the original estimate has been exceeded because more work has been involved than originally anticipated unless you establish at the outset what your price or estimate is to cover.

The Law Society's Practice Advice Service booklet, *Non-Contentious Costs* (see **Appendix A7**) sets out the basis for charging in non-contentious business and refers to the Solicitors' (Non-Contentious Business) Remuneration Order 2009 dated 16 July 2009 and in particular to art.3, which states that: 'A solicitor's costs must be fair and reasonable having regard to all the circumstances of the case.' The guidance is based on the decisions of assessors dealing with applications for remuneration certificates and covers charging in probate and the administration of estates, including what is deemed 'fair and reasonable'.

Clients may find it difficult to accept the concept of a 'value' element in addition to what they may consider to be a high hourly rate. The *Non-Contentious Costs* guidance states that it may be appropriate to include a value element but whether a value element is used is a matter for agreement between the solicitor and the client: it is not mandatory. In the *Jemma Trust* case the Court of Appeal held that a value charge can either be made in addition to an hourly rate, or it can be included in the hourly rate, but the value element must not be reflected in both charges. The guidance recommends that practitioners read the full *Jemma Trust* judgment, an extract of which is set out in Appendix 3 to the booklet.

Your client should be clear about the following:

- How much it will cost.
- The work to be included for the price given.
- What will happen if additional work has to be carried out, beyond what you have anticipated and quoted for.
- That the work quoted is up to a certain stage in a matter and that further costs will be payable for future stages.
- What will happen on costs if the matter is not completed.
- The basis of your charges and that VAT is payable in addition. When and how the work is to be billed.
- How much money is required on account and when are initial and subsequent payments to be made. Whether you charge for reading letters, for photocopying etc., and if so, how much.
- Who will be involved in the matter and their respective charge-out rates.
- If the first interview is free, how long can it last?
- What disbursements or payments to third parties will have to be paid, the likely amount and when the client will have to pay them.

3.10.2 Managing costs as a matter progresses

Many fee earners give clients information on costs at the outset but often fail to give clear, up-to-date costs information as a matter progresses. Remember the guidance to rule 2.03 states that if a precise figure cannot be given at the outset, you should explain the reason to the client and agree a ceiling figure or review dates. Agree these at the outset. However, even where costs estimates are given or ceilings on costs agreed, they are frequently exceeded without obtaining the client's agreement. It is essential that communication about costs takes place throughout; clients will not necessarily ask you for the information, you must proffer it. Lexcel v4 provides that this is done at least every six months, but costs updates should happen far more frequently if costs are accumulating quickly. Where you can only bill on the conclusion of a lengthy matter, send clients regular statements of accrued costs either electronically or in hard form. Discuss the regularity of these statements with the client at the outset. Do not assume that a client will realise that costs are mounting, even if they are aware of the work you are doing for them.

You must get back to your client to revise an estimate and secure the client's acceptance to the new figure before it is exceeded. However, the decision in *Reynolds* v. *Stone Rowe Brewer* [2008] EWHC 497 (QB) was based on the estimate having been a significant underestimate and even though the firm had complied with rule 2 by giving updates on costs and getting back to the client to discuss costs, the firm was unable to recover a substantial balance from its former client. It is not enough to revise an estimate where nothing material has changed in the retainer since the original estimate was given.

In the case of *Barrett* v. *Father Benjamin Rutt-Field* [2006] WTLR 1505, Costs Judge Rogers made it clear that the breach of the requirement to tell the client in advance if a final bill is going to exceed an estimate applies just as much in non-contentious as in contentious work.

Because all costs information has to be in writing, an informal chat about costs will not do. Write to confirm all information given orally as soon as possible. There must be no ambiguity; if you send a series of letters about costs, ensure that they are consistent and present a short summary of previous information.

- Ensure that your terms of engagement letter allows you to renegotiate costs if the matter does not follow the anticipated path.
- Setting the flag available on your computer systems at 75–80 per cent of an estimate warns fee earners to get back to their client.
- Remember to notify your client of any changes in hourly rates before incurring any costs at a new rate.
- Take courage and speak to the client in advance before sending a bill if you think there will be any problem.
- Avoid purge billing at the year end. These bills rarely accord with the costs agreement and it upsets clients.
- Set and enforce firm-wide protocols for managing costs and billing.

Some organisational issues:

- Who sees clients initially? There are a lot of issues that an inexperienced person will not be able to handle.
- Do your fee earners have the knowledge to discuss costs issues with clients and to give estimates?
- How is the first meeting to be recorded? Some aspects will have to be included in your client care/terms of engagement letter but how will you maintain file notes on other client care issues that may not be set out in the letter?

3.11 COMPLAINTS

Many practitioners perceive a complaint to be the same as a negligence claim, but few complaints arise from bad advice. Complaints are a business risk that must be managed positively; by handling client dissatisfaction well you can learn and recover from mistakes and build client loyalty. They not only offer the opportunity to correct immediate problems but also provide constructive ideas for improving services and service levels. Research into complaint behaviour indicates that only a fraction of dissatisfied clients actually complain. Clients are unwilling to do so either because they are sceptical of the reception their complaint will receive or because they do not have the courage to complain. You may be unaware of a client's dissatisfaction but they will tell colleagues, family and friends thus damaging your reputation and the prospect of recommendation and referrals. Therefore, it is important to have a complaints management system that is visible and easily accessible. Informing clients about the way you handle complaints is not inviting a complaint; well-run organisations now publicise the way in which a consumer can register any dissatisfaction.

Managing complaints well minimises their negative impact such as loss of fees, potential loss of reputation, and loss of future work in addition to the hassle and time that it takes to resolve them. Guidance on good complaints management is available in the Law Society's Practice Note: Complaints Management and from its Lawyer-line service (0870 606 2588) and from both LCS publications and its website (**www.legalcomplaints.org.uk**).

Under rule 2.05(1)(b), you must inform your client in writing at the outset or existing clients at the next appropriate opportunity:

(i) that, in the event of a problem, the client is entitled to complain; and
(ii) how and to whom the client should complain;
(iii) that this could include a complaint about the firm's bill;
(iv) that the firm has a complaints procedure, a copy of which is available on request;
(v) of their right to complain to the Legal Ombudsman at the conclusion of your complaint process, the timeframe for doing so and full details of how to contact the Legal Ombudsman;
(vi) that there may also be a right to object to the bill by applying to the court for an assessment of the bill under Part III of the Solicitors Act 1974; and
(vii) that if all or part of a bill remains unpaid the firm may be entitled to charge interest;

The Practice Note on complaints management suggests that a paragraph such as the following should be included in client care letters about complaints:

> [Practice Name] is committed to high quality legal advice and client care. If you are unhappy about any aspect of the service you have received or about the bill, please contact [name] on [phone number and e-mail] or by post to our [place] office. We have a procedure in place which details how we handle complaints which is available at [details of how to obtain it].
>
> If you are not satisfied with our handling of your complaint you can ask the [Legal Complaints Service or the Legal Ombudsman after 6 October 2010] at [contact details] to

> consider the complaint. Normally, you will need to bring a complaint to the Legal Ombudsman within six months of receiving a final written response from us about your complaint.

The guidance to rule 2.05 (note 52) states:

> **52.** Where your client is unhappy with your bill you should treat this like any other complaint about your service. In such circumstances it may be helpful, when responding to the complaint, to provide a detailed narrative of your bill so that your client can clearly understand how the costs were incurred. You may be required to provide the Legal Ombudsman with such a narrative where a complaint about your bill is referred to them. You should inform clients that the Legal Ombudsman may not deal with a complaint about a bill if the client has applied to the court for assessment of that bill.

It also states at note 53 that:

> **49B.** In some circumstances it will be appropriate to remind the client at a later stage whom they should approach under the firm's complaints procedure if they want to complain (or for the firm to inform the client of this at a later stage if the client has not been told at the outset). This will be appropriate if:
>
> (a) the client is particularly vulnerable;
> (b) the client is a private client and you are delivering a bill more than two years after the original information was given;
> (c) you are taking your costs from money held on client account and have not previously supplied the information; or
> (d) you are suing on a bill, and have not previously supplied the information.

3.11.1 Complaints handling

If a client makes a complaint, rule 2.05(1)(d) provides that they must be told in writing:

(i) how the complaint will be handled; and
(ii) timescales within which they will be given an initial and/or substantive response.

Under the rule complaints must be handled promptly, fairly and effectively.

You must have a written complaints management policy, a clear and concise outline of general processes the firm will follow when a complaint is made, to be given to clients on request. The Practice Note on complaints management provides a link to a sample policy.

Firms must also have internal procedures for handling complaints. The content of these is up to each firm but they must be in writing, clear and unambiguous. Everyone in the firm must ensure that clients know whom to contact if they have a problem and be aware of the information to give to the client if a complaint is made.

It is anticipated that the LeO, which took over the handling of new complaints from October 2010, will have an even greater consumer focus. Complaints must be dealt with in-house under a firm's complaints procedures but if not resolved within eight weeks, the client may use the ombudsman service. All parties will be entitled to make representations and its determinations and awards will be 'fair and reasonable' with a limit of £30,000. Further information is available on the LeO website (**www.legalombudsman.org.uk**).

3.11.2 Dealing with complaints

Most lawyers are articulate and have an assertive air of certainty when arguing a point which can give an impression of confidence and sometimes arrogance. This does not necessarily mean they are also thick skinned and able to take feedback easily. Many solicitors find it hard to acknowledge that they may be at fault and too often become defensive when criticised, even constructively. They do not feel comfortable reflecting on feedback to see if it contains any element of truth. However, an aggressive stance does nothing to assist client relations; a more constructive response is to be conciliatory. Few clients make complaints lightly and, even if you do not think a complaint is justified, you should at least acknowledge that the client is upset and apologise for this.

Treat clients with fairness and respect and do not:

- reject the complaint immediately without a good reason;
- forget clients are your livelihood;
- give the impression that only you know all the answers;
- be patronising;
- be critical that your client expects money as a remedy.

3.11.3 Learning from complaints

Consider how to collate and analyse the information that complaints contain, whether within a department or centrally, and then review and use the information:

- What does it tell you?
- Is there an underlying cause of the complaint?
- Are there any trends?
- What must be done to ensure that the complaint is not repeated?

There may be a raft of reasons for a complaint arising: for example, too much work, poor supervision, poor delegation, lack of competence, or a breakdown of internal communication. When analysed, many problems are caused by inadequate management or lack of skills training, such as interviewing or listening skills, too much focus on compliance and processes rather than a culture of openness and a real desire to give clients an excellent service, or the inadequate setting and enforcement of standards. No one is infallible, nor is any firm immune from receiving complaints, irrespective of size.

It is far better to resolve a complaint in-house rather than to allow it to escalate and result in a complaint being made to the LCS or the LeO.

3.12 MANAGEMENT ISSUES

Although the relationship develops between fee earner and client it cannot be seen in isolation. That individual fee earner must be backed up by the following:

- Good leadership that promotes a culture in which client care is recognised as being of prime importance and which manages the resources of the practice to an optimum level.
- Good training not only in technical skills but also in the soft skills needed to manage the relationship with the client, in financial matters to enable fee earners to understand costs issues and in the practice's IT systems so that the maximum benefit is derived from them.
- An appropriate organisational structure within the team or department offering the service so that a person with knowledge discusses costs with clients and supervises the fee earner at an appropriate level, where a fee earner has the optimum amount of work and where delegation works effectively.
- The right level of support and resources to enable a fee earner to give excellent client care – a client is not interested in the fact that the letter to them is at the bottom of a pile of dictation.
- Good office systems and procedures that work to enable the fee earner to deliver the service and that produce meaningful information for the practice's leaders to manage well.
- Good financial management that enables fee earners to understand financial information and managers to assess the profitability of work and clients.
- The best use of practice management systems to provide management information to manage the practice effectively and of case management systems to maximise their benefit to provide an excellent service to clients.

CHAPTER 4

Estate administration and statutory regulation

Peter Camp

4.1 FINANCIAL SERVICES AND MARKETS ACT 2000

4.1.1 Terminology

The Financial Services and Markets Act (FSMA) 2000 which came into force on 1 December 2001 enables the Financial Services Authority (FSA) to regulate providers of investment business. Under FSMA 2000, s.19(1), no person can carry out a 'regulated activity' unless he is 'authorised' by the FSA or 'exempt'. Although the exemptions and exclusions in FSMA 2000 mean that few solicitors need to be authorised by the FSA, it is important for firms to identify the exact nature of these exemptions and exclusions. Undertaking regulated activities without authorisation and outside the statutory exemptions or exclusions is a criminal offence.

The main statutory exemption for certain professionals, including solicitors, is contained in FSMA 2000, Part XX. It permits professional firms to carry out a regulated activity if regulated by a designated professional body (DPB) and if such activity is 'incidental' to the professional services offered by the firm. As the Law Society is a DPB, solicitors regulated by the Solicitors Regulation Authority (SRA) may carry on a regulated activity in the course of their other work, such as probate and trusts.

The SRA makes rules to govern the solicitors' firms which carry out regulated activity under the Part XX exemption. These rules are:

- the Solicitors' Financial Services (Scope) Rules 2001 (the Scope Rules); and
- the Solicitors' Financial Services (Conduct of Business) Rules 2001 (the COB Rules).

Both sets of Rules have been amended in the light of the extension of financial services regulation to regulated mortgages and insurance work.

Solicitors conducting regulated activities (whether mainstream activities or exempt activities) must also comply with the Money Laundering Regulations 2007, SI 2007/2157 (see below, at **4.2**).

4.1.2 Sources of further advice

Probate work is, generally speaking, the area where most solicitors come into contact with regulated activities, FSMA 2000, the Scope Rules and the COB Rules. It is, therefore, important that solicitors are aware of the compliance requirements and also the investment business opportunities involved.

The SRA offers confidential guidance on the Solicitors' Code of Conduct 2007, the Scope Rules and the COB Rules, including whether or not authorisation is required.

4.1.3 Do you need to be authorised?

Solicitors carrying out probate and trust work are likely to be potentially undertaking regulated activities. However, the exclusions and exemptions contained in the legislation mean that most solicitors will not need to be authorised by the FSA.

4.1.4 What are 'investments' and what is a 'regulated activity'?

'Investments' are defined in the Financial Services and Markets Act 2000 (Regulated Activities) Order 2001, SI 2001/544 (RAO 2001) (as amended). Examples include stocks and shares, unit trusts and life and other insurance policies. Further, regulated mortgage contracts will also be 'investments' for these purposes. (National Savings products are outside the scope of FSMA 2000.) The activities constituting 'regulated activities' are also defined in RAO 2001: examples include dealing and arranging deals in investments, giving investment advice and the discretionary management of investments. The activities of 'sending dematerialised instructions' and 'custody of investments' are also potentially regulated activities. 'Custody of investments' involves safeguarding *and* administering investments and this is likely to be relevant to firms conducting probate/trust work. Further guidance is available from the SRA.

4.1.5 What exclusions apply?

Under the terms of RAO 2001 there are exclusions for dealing and arranging deals where the activities are carried out using an authorised person. However, of greater relevance to trust and probate practitioners are the exclusions contained in RAO 2001, art.66 which apply to arranging deals, discretionary management, investment advice, sending dematerialised instructions and custody of investments where the activity is being carried out by a trustee or personal representative (PR). Note that these exclusions are not available where a firm is simply acting for outside trustees or PRs. However, where a member of the firm is a trustee or PR (whether alone, with another member of the firm or with an external trustee or PR) these exclusions are valuable. Practitioners must check carefully the conditions contained in art.66. Where they apply the firm will not be carrying on regulated activities and will be subject to no compliance requirements other than those applicable to solicitors generally. There is, however, a very important restriction on the use of the exclusions. The 'authorised person' exclusion and the 'trustee' exclusion do not, generally, apply where the investment is an insurance policy. Solicitors who advise on or make arrangements for a PR client to obtain, for example, a missing beneficiary insurance policy will not be able to benefit from any of these exclusions.

4.1.6 What exemptions apply?

As discussed above, whilst RAO 2001, art.66 is invaluable for those matters where a member of the firm is a trustee or PR, it will offer no assistance in those circumstances where the firm is simply acting for outside trustees or PRs or where an insurance policy is involved. Here, an alternative solution must be found to avoid the need for authorisation. Under Part XX of FSMA 2000 certain professionals can undertake 'exempt regulated activities' without the need for authorisation. The exempt regime is available where the member of the profession is regulated by a DPB, and the Law Society is such a body. Certain conditions must apply before regulated activities can be treated as exempt. These include the requirement that the activities must be incidental to the provision of other professional services, and that the activities are of a type not prohibited by the rules of the DPB. The SRA's Scope Rules contain a number of prohibitions. Most of these prohibitions will not be relevant to probate practitioners but one is worthy of note. The Scope Rules prohibit solicitors entering into a regulated mortgage contract (where credit is provided to an individual or trustees secured by a first legal charge over residential property) as lender unless it is done in the firm's capacity as a trustee or PR and the borrower is a beneficiary under the trust, will or intestacy.

Where the Part XX regime is relied upon, care must be taken to ensure that the specific prohibitions relating to 'packaged products', 'securities' and other 'relevant investments' are identified. In most cases these prohibitions apply to recommendations and arrangements to *buy* such investments. Investment activities undertaken by probate practitioners usually relate to the disposal of investments. However, trust practitioners may need to take care in relying upon the Part XX regime as a result of these Scope Rules restrictions. Where policies other than life insurance policies are involved (e.g. advice on or arrangements made in respect of missing beneficiary policies) solicitors should be able to use the Part XX regime. However, any advice or arrangement relating to an insurance policy (life or general insurance) will amount to 'insurance mediation'. Where a firm undertakes insurance mediation, the Scope Rules require the firm to appoint a compliance officer and to ensure that the firm's name is registered in the FSA register.

4.1.7 The 'incidental' nature of probate

If a solicitor is involved only in winding up estates on behalf of outside PRs, then the investment business work is likely to be 'incidental' to the main activity, which is the administration. The effect of this is that the work will be capable of falling within Part XX of FSMA 2000 and the requirements for compliance relating to non-insurance products are very few: see below.

4.1.8 Compliance requirements

Where the statutory exclusions apply, as noted above, no special compliance requirements will apply. Where a solicitor relies upon the Part XX regime, the COB Rules will apply. These rules are designed to be simple and generally will not impose a major burden upon practitioners. However, it is necessary for probate practitioners who rely upon Part XX to familiarise themselves with the COB Rules. They cover obligations relating to status disclosure, record keeping, systems for safe custody and confirmation of execution only business. Where insurance mediation is undertaken, the status disclosure requirements include an obligation to provide the client with a statutory statement (see COB rule 3) before undertaking any insurance mediation. Further, if the insurance mediation includes the recommendation of a policy to a client, the requirements of COB rule 8A will apply. This rule requires firms to indicate whether or not a full market analysis of insurance products was undertaken before making any recommendation; to ensure that whether or not a full market analysis was undertaken, the recommendation was suitable to the client's demands and needs; and to provide the client with a demands and needs statement.

4.1.9 Relevance of the Solicitors' Code of Conduct 2007

Solicitors who are involved in investment business activities (whether benefiting from a statutory exclusion or from the 'exempt' regime under Part XX of FSMA 2000) are bound by the Solicitors' Code of Conduct 2007. As with any aspect of a solicitor's practice, the Solicitors' Code of Conduct 2007 will apply, but of particular relevance to probate work and investment business services are rules 1, 2, 7, 9, and 19.

4.1.10 Solicitors' Accounts Rules 1998

Solicitors are also subject to the Solicitors' Accounts Rules 1998. Brief guidance on these can be found at **Chapter 5**.

4.1.11 Investment business opportunities

If a firm decides to offer investment services to its clients, either by seeking authorisation or by using an exclusion or exemption, then there are a number of investment business opportunities deriving from probate work. Examples include offering investment advice to beneficiaries and tax planning for beneficiaries.

4.2 ANTI-MONEY LAUNDERING

Anti-money laundering is too large a subject to address adequately in this book. Practitioners should refer to the Law Society's Anti-Money Laundering Practice Note, which has been approved by the Treasury (see also **13.5**). The SRA and the courts will have regard to the Practice Note when considering whether a solicitor's conduct was reasonable in relation to allegations of:

- money laundering;
- failing to report suspected money laundering; and
- failure to comply with the requirements of the Money Laundering Regulations 2007.

This Practice Note confirms that solicitors could be at risk of money laundering where their work involves assisting with the management or distribution of assets.

4.2.1 Offences under the Proceeds of Crime Act 2002

If the assets are (or include) 'criminal property' (defined as the benefit or representation of the benefit, from criminal conduct), the solicitor could be involved in one or more of the money laundering offences contained in Proceeds of Crime Act 2002 (POCA 2002), ss.327–329. Under these provisions it is an offence:

(a) to conceal, disguise, convert, transfer or remove from the United Kingdom the proceeds of criminal conduct (s.327);
(b) to be concerned in an arrangement which facilitates the acquisition, retention, use or control of another person's proceeds of criminal conduct, where there is knowledge or suspicion that this is the case (s.328); or
(c) to acquire, use or possess the proceeds of criminal conduct (s.329).

Further, even if solicitors are not themselves involved in the management or distribution of assets, they may be subject to an obligation under POCA 2002, s.330 to report to the authorities, information which gives rise to knowledge or suspicion of money laundering where such knowledge or suspicion came into their possession as a result of business in the 'regulated sector'.

The 'regulated sector' applies to:

- the provision by way of business of advice about the tax affairs of another person;
- the provision by way of business of legal services which involves participation in a financial or real property transaction concerning:
  - the buying and selling of real property or business entities;
  - the managing of client money, securities or other assets;
  - opening or management of bank, savings or securities accounts;

- the organisation of contributions necessary for the creation, operation or management of companies; or
- the creation, operation or management of trusts, companies or similar structures.

The administration of estates is in the regulated sector.

Probate practitioners will be subject to the Money Laundering Regulations 2007, SI 2007/2157. These apply to 'relevant persons', which, in the context of legal advisers is defined in the same way as the 'regulated sector' (see above). Where the regulations apply, solicitors must establish procedures relating to:

(a) customer due diligence (which includes the verification of clients' and beneficial owners' identities);
(b) record keeping;
(c) reporting procedures;
(d) training.

4.2.2 Summary

1. Solicitors can be at risk of an offence if their work involves assisting with the distribution of assets which include suspected 'criminal property'.
2. A defence may be available if a report is made to the Serious Organised Crime Agency (SOCA), and if relevant, 'appropriate consent' is obtained or can be deemed through lapse of time (see Chapter 8 of the Anti-Money Laundering Practice Note).
3. However, because of the judgment in *Bowman* v. *Fels* [2005] EWCA Civ 226, before a solicitor reports to SOCA a key consideration will be whether the solicitor's knowledge or suspicion of money laundering is based on information received in legally professionally privileged circumstances.
4. Customer due diligence (CDD) is required by the Money Laundering Regulations 2007, SI 2007/ 2157. Regulation 7(3) provides that you must:

   (a) determine the required extent of customer due diligence measures on a risk-sensitive basis depending on the type of client, business relationship, product or transaction; and
   (b) be able to demonstrate to your supervisory authority that you took appropriate measures in view of the risks of money laundering and terrorist financing.

   Solicitors can use a risk-based approach to determine the extent and quality of information required and the steps to be taken to meet the requirements. Chapter 4 of the Practice Note deals with CDD and in particular with the requirements in relation to trusts.
5. Although will writing is not a regulated activity, ancillary services provided

by solicitors when drafting wills may be. For example, tax advice and the creation, operation or management of trusts, companies or similar structures are included.

4.2.3 Warning signs

The following warning signs relevant to probate practitioners are identified in Chapter 11 of the Law Society's Anti-Money Laundering Practice Note:

11.3 PRIVATE CLIENT WORK

11.3.1 Administration of estates

The administration of estates is a regulated activity. A deceased person's estate is very unlikely to be actively utilised by criminals as a means for laundering their funds; however, there is still a low risk of money laundering for those working in this area.

Source of funds

When you are acting either as an executor, or for executors, there is no blanket requirement that you should be satisfied about the history of all of the funds which make up the estate under administration; however you should be aware of the factors which can increase money laundering risks.

Consider the following when administering an estate:

- where estate assets have been earned in a foreign jurisdiction, be aware of the wide definition of criminal conduct in POCA and the provisions relating to overseas criminal conduct
- where estate assets have been earned or are located in a suspect territory, you may need to make further checks about the source of those funds

The wide nature of the offences of 'acquisition, use and possession' in section 329 of POCA may lead to a money laundering offence being committed at an early point in the administration. The section 328 offence may also be relevant.

Be alert from the outset and monitor throughout so that any disclosure can be considered as soon as knowledge or suspicion is formed and problems of delayed consent are avoided. A key benefit of the *Bowman* v. *Fels* judgment is that a solicitor who makes a disclosure is now able to continue work on the matter, so long as they do not transfer funds or take any other irrevocable step.

How the estate may include criminal property

An extreme example would be where you know or suspect that the deceased person was accused or convicted of acquisitive criminal conduct during their lifetime.

If you know or suspect that the deceased person improperly claimed welfare benefits or had evaded the due payment of tax during their lifetime, criminal property will be included in the estate and so a money laundering disclosure may be required. Information on the financial thresholds for benefits can be obtained from **www.dwp.gov.uk** or **www.hmrc.gov.uk**.

While administering an estate, you may discover or suspect that beneficiaries are not intending to pay the correct amount of tax or are avoiding some other financial charge (for example, by failing to disclose gifts received from the deceased less than seven years before death). Although these matters may not actually constitute money laundering (because no criminal conduct has yet occurred so there is no 'criminal property'), you should carefully consider their position in conduct terms with respect to Rule 1.01 of the Solicitors' Code of Conduct.

Grant of probate

A UK grant of probate may be required before UK assets can be released, while for overseas assets the relevant local laws will apply. Remain alert to warning signs, for example if the deceased or their business interests are based in a suspect territory.

If the deceased person is from another jurisdiction and a lawyer is dealing with the matter in the home country, it may be helpful to ask that person for information about the deceased to gain some assurances that there are no suspicious circumstances surrounding the estate. The issue of the tax payable on the estate may depend on the jurisdiction concerned.

11.3.2 Trusts

Trust work is a regulated activity.

Trusts can be used as a money laundering vehicle. The key risk period for trusts is when the trust is set up, as if the funds going into the trust are clean, it is only by the trustees using them for criminal purposes that they may form the proceeds of crime.

When setting up a trust, be aware of general money laundering warning signs and consider whether the purpose of the trust could be to launder criminal property. Information about the purpose of the trust, including why any unusual structure or jurisdiction has been used, can help allay concerns. Similarly, information about the provider of the funds and those who have control of the funds, as required by the Money Laundering Regulations 2007, will assist.

Whether you act as a trustee yourself, or for trustees, the nature of the work may already require information which will help in assessing money laundering risks, such as the location of assets and the identity of trustees. Again, any involvement of a suspect jurisdiction, especially those with strict bank secrecy and confidentiality rules, or without similar money laundering procedures, may increase the risk profile of the retainer.

If you think a money laundering offence has, or may have, been committed that relates to money or property which already forms part of the trust property, or is intended to do so, consider whether your instructions involve you in a section 328 arrangement offence. If they do, consider the options for making a disclosure.

11.3.3 Charities

In common with trusts, while the majority of charities are used for legitimate reasons, they can be used as money laundering/terrorist financing vehicles.

If you are acting for a charity, consider its purpose and the organisations it is aligned with. If you are receiving money on the charity's behalf from an individual or a company donor, or a bequest from an estate, be alert to unusual circumstances including large sums of money.

There is growing concern about the use of charities for terrorist funding. HM Treasury maintains a consolidated list of individuals and entities to whom you may not provide funds, economic resources, and in relation to terrorism, financial services. See also **7.10** of this practice note.

11.3.4 Powers of attorney/deputyship

Whether acting as, or on behalf of, an attorney or deputy, you should remain alert to money laundering risks.

If you are acting as an attorney you may learn financial information about the donor relating, for example, to non-payment of tax or wrongful receipt of benefits. You will need to consider whether to make a disclosure to SOCA.

Where the public guardian has an interest – because of a deputyship or registered enduring power of attorney – consider whether the Office of the Public Guardian (OPG) needs to be informed. Informing the OPG is unlikely to be tipping off because it is unlikely to prejudice an investigation.

If you discover or suspect that a donee has already completed an improper financial transaction that may amount to a money laundering suspicion, a disclosure to SOCA may be required (depending on whether legal professional privilege applies). However, it may be difficult to decide whether you have a suspicion if the background to the information is a family dispute. You can get legal advice on this through the Law Society's AML directory.

CHAPTER 5

Solicitors' Accounts Rules 1998

Lesley King

5.1 INTRODUCTION

The Solicitors' Accounts Rules 1998 (the SAR) were made by the Council of the Law Society with the approval of the Master of the Rolls on 22 July 1998. The SAR include notes which form part of the rules and are mandatory.

The SAR are published online (**www.sra.org.uk**) and in the *Solicitors' Accounts Manual*, 11th edn (Law Society, 2009).

5.2 AN OUTLINE OF THE RULES

5.2.1 Who is governed by the SAR?

The SAR apply to solicitors, registered European lawyers, registered foreign lawyers and recognised bodies. They also apply to non-solicitor lawyer managers and non-lawyer managers (a manager being a partner in a partnership, a member of a limited liability partnership (LLP) or a director of a company), and to employees of firms. They do not apply to solicitors who are employed by, for example, a local authority or to a solicitor when carrying out the function of a coroner or other judicial office or a sheriff or under-sheriff (rules 4 and 5).

All of the partners in a practice are required to ensure compliance with the SAR by fellow partners and everyone else in the practice, and to remedy breaches (rules 6 and 7). (This duty extends to directors of recognised bodies which are companies, and to members of recognised bodies which are limited liability partnerships.) The case of *Weston* v. *The Law Society* (1998) *The Times*, 15 July is a reminder that solicitors are under a heavy obligation in securing compliance with the SAR. The Court of Appeal confirmed that it was appropriate to strike off a solicitor where no dishonesty was alleged but the partner in question was guilty of breaches through his partners' activities of which he was unaware. Lord Bingham referred to 'the duty of anyone holding anyone else's money to exercise a proper stewardship in relation to it'.

The SRA guidelines – accounting procedures and systems (Appendix 3 to the SAR) state that compliance with the SAR is the equal responsibility of all partners.

Responsibility for day-to-day supervision may be delegated to individual partner(s) but it is not acceptable to delegate total responsibility to a cashier or book-keeper.

Liquidators, trustees in bankruptcy, Court of Protection deputies and trustees of occupational pension schemes are subject to some of the record-keeping requirements of the SAR (rule 9 and see **5.4** below). The reason for this extension of the Rules is to protect the vulnerable against defalcations and to protect the profession from claims on the Compensation Fund, but with a lighter regulatory touch because of the existence of other statutory regulatory frameworks.

Similarly, solicitors who operate joint accounts with clients, another solicitors' practice or another third party, or operate the accounts of clients, are subject to certain record-keeping requirements (rules 10 and 11 and see **5.4** below).

The obligations on reporting accountants are set out in Part F of the SAR.

5.2.2 Classification of money (rule 13)

All money held or received in the course of practice falls into one of the following two categories.

Client money

Client money is money held or received for a client or as trustee, and all other money which is not office money (rule 13).

A 'client' is defined by rule 2 as a person for whom the solicitor acts. However, client money includes money held as a bailee, agent, or donee of a power of attorney. It also extends to money held as stakeholder, liquidator, trustee in bankruptcy or Court of Protection deputy.

Client money also includes money received:

- for unpaid professional disbursements;
- for other unpaid disbursements where the solicitor has not incurred a liability to pay them (for example, stamp duty land tax, Land Registry registration fees, telegraphic transfer fees and court fees);
- on account of costs;
- as commission paid in respect of a client unless the solicitor is entitled to retain it (see rule 2.06 of the Solicitors' Code of Conduct 2007).

Professional disbursements include the fees of counsel, other lawyers, and other professionals, agents or experts instructed by the solicitor – this will include interpreters, translators, process servers, surveyors and estate agents instructed by the solicitor. It does not include travel agents' charges.

Office money

Office money is money which belongs to the solicitor or practice. It includes:

- money held or received in connection with running the practice, for example PAYE or VAT on the firm's fees;
- interest on general client accounts;
- money received for profit costs where a bill or written notification of costs has been sent;
- money received to repay the solicitor for disbursements already paid;
- money received for disbursements which are unpaid but for which the solicitor has incurred a liability to pay (e.g. items settled by a credit account such as Land Registry search fees, taxi fares or courier charges); however, unpaid professional disbursements are expressly excluded and money received for them is client money (see above under 'Client money' for the definition of a professional disbursement);
- money received for an agreed fee (see rule 19(5)); and
- money held in the client account but earmarked for costs and awaiting transfer (see rule 19(3)).

5.3 USE OF CLIENT ACCOUNT

A solicitor who holds or receives client money must keep one or more client accounts (see rule 14(1)).

5.3.1 What is a client account? (rule 14)

A client account is an account of the practice kept at a bank or building society in England and Wales. It must include the word 'client' in the title. There are two types of client account:

- a separate designated client account which is a deposit or share account for money relating to a single client, other person or trust; or
- a general client account which is any other client account.

5.3.2 What money goes into the client bank account? (rule 15)

Rule 15(1) states that all client money must be paid without delay into a client account.

There are some exceptions, for example when a client instructs the solicitor not to pay in money (rule 16(1)) or where a trustee operating in accordance with his or her powers pays money into a non-client account or retains it as cash (rule 17(ca)).

Rule 15(2) states that no other money may be paid into the client account. Again, there are exceptions so, for example, a solicitor can use his or her own money to open or maintain the client account and can advance money to the client where the solicitor is holding too little client money for a client or trust to fund a payment.

5.3.3 When can money come out of the client account?

This is governed by rule 22. The situations in which solicitors can withdraw client money include:

- making payments on behalf of the client or trust;
- paying disbursements on behalf of the client or trust;
- reimbursing themselves for money spent on behalf of the client or trust;
- transferring to another client account.

The money taken out of a general client account must not exceed the total held for that client or trust in all the general client accounts.

There is one exception to this, which is where a solicitor holds money in a separate designated client account for a client or trust. A solicitor can withdraw from a general client account a sum in excess of the amount held there for the client or trust provided that a transfer is immediately made from the separate designated client account.

A solicitor can withdraw money from the client account to meet the cost of disbursements that have already been paid from the office bank account without sending a bill. Solicitors can only withdraw money for their professional charges once they have sent the bill or other written notification of costs, or agreed a fee under rule 19(5). Once the bill has been sent the money due for professional charges becomes office money and it must be transferred within 14 days. See **5.3.6** below.

5.3.4 Mixed receipts (rule 20)

Where office money is received mixed with client money, either the cheque must be split or the whole amount paid into the client account.

If it is all paid into the client account, all office money must be transferred out of the client account within 14 days. (But see also rule 19 (at **5.3.5** below) in the case of costs payments.)

5.3.5 Special rules for dealing with money received for bills (or other notifications of costs) (rules 19 and 21)

There are four possibilities:

1. Identify the type of money received and deal with it appropriately:

    - if the money is all office money, put it all in the office account;
    - if the money is all client money, put it all in the client account;
    - if the money is a mixture, deal with it under rule 20 – either splitting it or paying it all into the client account and then transferring out the office element within 14 days of receipt.

2. Where the money is all office money and/or client money in the form of unpaid professional disbursements for which the solicitor has incurred a

liability to pay, in this one circumstance client money can be paid into the office bank account for a limited period (rule 19(1)(b)). To fall within rule 19(1)(b) the receipt must consist only of office money and client money for unpaid professional disbursements (see rule 2(2)(s) for definition). The solicitor must have already incurred liability for the disbursement. If the disbursement is not paid by the end of the second working day following receipt, the client money must be transferred to the client bank account. The advantage of this option is that it simplifies dealing with receipts of costs, allowing more money to be paid straight into the office bank account and resulting in fewer transfers between client and office bank accounts.

3. Irrespective of the type of money, pay it all into the client bank account and transfer out any office money within 14 days of receipt. This may be done where the person dealing with the money is uncertain as to its correct classification. This option allows the money to be banked promptly pending a decision as to how it should be treated. It is also a useful option where a client wishes to make direct payments into a bank account. The client can be given the number of the client bank account and all payments can be made into that account.
4. Follow rule 21 in relation to payments from the Legal Services Commission (LSC):

   - A special dispensation for costs payments in relation to certificated work means that a payment for costs may be paid into the office bank account, even when mixed with client money for unpaid disbursements, provided the disbursements are paid or money representing them is transferred to the client bank account within 14 days of receipt (see rule 21(1)(b) and note (iii) to rule 21).
   - Standard monthly payments from the LSC in respect of civil and criminal contracts are dealt with in rule 21(2). These regular payments are office money and must be paid into an office account at a bank or building society in England and Wales (rule 21(2)(a)–(b) and note (vii) to rule 21). Professional disbursements relating to a matter (see rule 2(2)(s)) must be paid, or an amount for their settlement transferred to a client account, within 28 days of the solicitor reporting to the LSC on the completion of that matter (see rule 21(2)(c) and notes (viii)–(ix) to rule 21).

There is a special rule for payments from a third party (see rule 21(3)). Where the LSC has already paid any costs to a solicitor (or has paid professional disbursements direct) and costs are subsequently settled by a third party, the entire third party payment must be paid into the client bank account.

Any balance belonging to the solicitor must be transferred to the office bank account within 14 days of the solicitor sending a report to the LSC containing details of the third party payment. The amount retained in the client bank account must be recorded as held for the LSC (either on the individual client's ledger account or on a separate ledger in the LSC's name).

It must be kept there until the LSC informs the solicitor that it has recouped an equivalent sum from subsequent legal aid payments due to the solicitor. The retained sum must be transferred to an office bank account within 14 days of notification of recoupment.

5.3.6 Time limit on transfers (rules 19–21)

The SAR impose a standard 14-day time limit on all transfers needing to be made to or from the client bank account (apart from the two-day period for unpaid professional disbursements under rule 19(1)(b), and the 28-day time limit for the payment of professional disbursements (or transfer to a client account of an equivalent sum) under rule 21(2)(c)). The time limit on transfers is imposed in order to prevent unclaimed costs concealing a shortfall on the client account.

5.3.7 Transfers between clients (rule 30(2))

Solicitors are required to obtain the written authority of both clients in the case of private loans between clients. This does not apply to loans made by an institutional lender.

5.3.8 Authority for withdrawals from client account (rule 23)

A withdrawal of funds from client account may be made without the bank which actually makes the transfer having to hold a written authority, for example, it can be done by telephone. However, before the transfer is made there must be in existence a specific authority in respect of the particular withdrawal, signed by one of the persons specified in rule 23(1). It is also of paramount importance that there are appropriate safeguards, such as passwords. Note that in the case of a withdrawal by cheque, the signature on the cheque is usually the specific authority. Signing a blank cheque is not a specific authority.

5.3.9 Who may authorise withdrawals from client account? (rule 23)

Withdrawals from client account may be authorised by:

(a) a solicitor who holds a current practising certificate or a registered European lawyer;

(b) a Fellow of the Institute of Legal Executives or licensed conveyancer who is a manager of the practice, where the practice is a recognised body;

(c) a Fellow of the Institute of Legal Executives or licensed conveyancer who is an employee of the practice, where the practice is a recognised body or recognised sole practitioner;

(d) a registered foreign lawyer who is a manager of the practice, where the practice is a recognised body; or
(e) any other individual who is a manager of the practice.

See note (v) to rule 23 for the position when solicitor-trustees instruct an outside manager to run the trust or estate on a day-to-day basis.

5.3.10 Minimising the risk of money laundering (rule 15)

A client account should not be used to provide banking facilities to a client or third party (see rule 15, note (ix)).

5.4 RECORD-KEEPING REQUIREMENTS (RULE 32)

Solicitors must keep records to show all dealings with client money and office money relating to any client or trust matter. The dealings must be recorded on a cash account (or record of inter-client transfers) and on a client ledger account for each client or trust. The current balance for each client must be shown or be readily ascertainable.

The records must show all dealings with client money. It is, therefore, important to record any change in the person(s) for whom money is held.

For example, during or at the end of an administration beneficiaries will become entitled to funds. Normally, there will be a cash payment to the beneficiaries which will be recorded as a cash payment from the client account on behalf of the personal representatives. However, the beneficiaries may ask the solicitor to retain funds for them in the client account for a specific reason (but banking facilities must not be provided through the client account – see rule 15, note (ix)). In such a case the solicitor must record – on the client ledger accounts and also on the transfer record – that money is no longer held for the PRs but is now held for the beneficiary. Separate client ledger accounts are necessary.

5.4.1 Relaxation of requirements when acting for both institutional lender and borrower (rule 32(6))

To regularise the practice of a solicitor opening one ledger account where he or she is acting for both lender and borrower in a conveyancing matter, rule 32(6) permits the opening of only one ledger account, provided that the funds belonging to each client are clearly identifiable on the ledger. The permission does not extend to private loans.

Rule 32(6) is expressed to apply to mortgage *advances*. There is no mention of mortgage *redemptions*. The normal rules will, therefore apply. If the solicitor holds money for the lender, it will be necessary to show this in the accounts by opening a separate ledger account for the lender. The proceeds of sale can then be shown as held partly for the seller and partly for the lender. Frequently, however, the solicitor acting for the seller will not hold any money after completion for the lender so there will be no need for a separate ledger.

5.4.2 Record keeping when acting for a trust

Solicitors must keep full records of all dealings with client money arising from a trust unless an outside manager is used to run the trust on a day-to-day basis. In such a case the manager must keep and retain appropriate accounting records which must be available for inspection by the SRA. See rule 32, note (ii)(d).

5.4.3 Record-keeping requirements for liquidators, etc. (rule 9)

Provided liquidators, trustees in bankruptcy, Court of Protection deputies and trustees of occupational pension schemes comply with their own statutory rules and regulations, they will be deemed to have complied sufficiently with the SAR so long as they also comply with the limited record-keeping requirements of rule 9. They must:

- keep a central record or file of bills;
- retain for at least six years any records kept under the statutory rules;
- keep such records centrally, or maintain a central register of appointments;
- make such records available for monitoring and inspection by the Law Society; and
- produce such records to the reporting accountants to enable them to check compliance.

5.4.4 Record-keeping requirements for joint accounts (rule 10)

The SAR in general do not apply to solicitors operating joint accounts but various record-keeping requirements do apply (to protect against fraud). Solicitors must:

- keep a central record or file of bills;
- retain statements and passbooks (or duplicates and copy entries) for at least six years;
- keep such statements and passbooks (or duplicates and copy entries as permitted by the Rules) centrally;
- make such records available for monitoring and inspection by the SRA; and
- produce such records to the reporting accountants to enable them to check compliance.

5.4.5 Record-keeping requirements for client's own account (rule 11)

The SAR in general do not apply to solicitors operating a client's own account (for example, under a power of attorney) but various record-keeping requirements do (to protect against fraud). Solicitors must:

- receive and keep statements and passbooks (or duplicates and copy entries) for at least six years;
- keep such statements and passbooks (or duplicates and copy entries as permitted by the SAR) centrally;
- make such records available for monitoring and inspection by the SRA; and
- produce such records to the reporting accountants to enable them to check compliance.

5.4.6 Regular bank reconciliations (rule 32(7))

Solicitors are required to prepare bank reconciliations for all general client accounts and separate designated client accounts containing client money at least once every five weeks (in effect monthly).

However, where money held by solicitor-trustees is kept in a passbook-operated separate designated client account, solicitors need only prepare a reconciliation for that money every 14 weeks. There is no requirement to check that interest has been credited since the last statement or entry in the passbook.

5.4.7 Retention of paid cheques and bank statements, etc. (rule 32(9) and (10))

Paid cheques must be retained for at least two years (see note (xiv) to rule 32 as to the extent of this requirement). It is not necessary for the bank to return paid cheques, if it is arranged in writing that the bank will keep paid cheques (either the originals or digital images of the front and back of each cheque) for at least two years. Other authorities for withdrawals from the client account must also be kept for at least two years (rule 32(10)).

Bank statements and all other records must be kept for at least six years (rule 32(9)). These requirements extend not just to client accounts but to any other account where client money is held.

Notes (xv)–(xvii) to rule 32 deal more specifically with the retention of digital images of paid cheques in place of the originals.

5.5 RULES ON INTEREST (RULES 24–28)

Solicitors must account to clients for all interest earned on separate designated client accounts (rule 24(1)). Rule 25(1) requires solicitors to aim for a reasonable rate of interest on such money.

Where money is not held in a separate designated client account, the general rule is that solicitors must account to the client for a sum in lieu of interest (rule 24(2)). However, there are exceptions (see rule 24(3)) where there is no need to account. These are as follows:

(a) if the amount calculated is £20 or less;
(b) (i) if the amount held does not exceed the amount, and the time for which it is held does not exceed the period, set out in the table below:

Amount £	**Time (weeks)**
1,000	8
2,000	4
10,000	2
20,000	1

(ii) if the amount held exceeds £20,000 but is held for one week or less, unless it is fair and reasonable to account having regard to all the circumstances;

(c) on money held for the payment of counsel's fees, once counsel has requested a delay in settlement;
(d) on money held for the LSC;
(e) on money held in the client account as a result of an advance from the solicitor to the client to cover a payment for which the client had insufficient funds;
(f) if there is an agreement to contract out of the interest provisions of the SAR.

Solicitors are still allowed to retain any interest earned on client money held in a general client account over and above the amount they are required to pay out. It is expressly provided in rule 13, note (xi)(b) that interest earned in this way is office money.

A client may fail to present a cheque for payment promptly. Note (vii) to rule 24 states that whether or not it is reasonable to recalculate the amount due will depend on all the circumstances of the case. Solicitors can make a reasonable charge for any extra work carried out but only if they are legally entitled to make a charge for such work.

When calculating the amount due to a client in lieu of interest, rule 25(1) requires solicitors to account for a 'fair' sum. It need not necessarily reflect the highest rate of interest available but it is not acceptable to look only at the lowest rate of interest available. Rule 25(2) provides that the sum must be calculated:

- on the balance(s) held over the whole period for which cleared funds are held
- at a rate not less than whichever is the higher of:
  - the rate payable on a separate designated client account for the amount(s) held; or

- the rate payable on the relevant amount(s) if placed on deposit on similar terms by a member of the business community

at the bank or building society where the money is held.

5.6 ACCOUNTANTS' REPORTS

Accountants' reports are dealt with in the SAR at Part F (rules 35–49).

Reporting accountants must have registered auditor status together with membership of one of the accountancy bodies listed in the Rules (see rule 37). To enable the SRA to maintain accurate records solicitors must inform the SRA of any change of reporting accountant (rule 39).

Solicitors must produce a letter of engagement for accountants incorporating the terms set out in rule 38(1). The letter (and a copy) must be signed by the solicitor (or a partner, director or member) and by the accountant. The letter must be kept for at least three years after the termination of the retainer and produced to the SRA on request (rule 38(2)).

Accountants are also required to report on any substantial departure from the SRA Guidelines for Accounting Procedures and Systems (see rules 29, 43 and 44(e), and Appendix 3 to the SAR).

In addition to the requirements for testing already contained in the Rules, reporting accountants have to complete and sign an SRA checklist which the solicitor must keep for at least three years from the date of signature and produce to the SRA on request. The checklist is intended to be an assurance to the solicitor and to the SRA that the work required to be done has indeed been done. It does not impose any additional obligations on accountants. See Appendix 4 to the SAR.

A solicitor who has operated a client's own account as signatory must deliver an accountant's report for the accounting period within six months of the end of the period (rule 35). The reporting accountant will check compliance with rule 11.

The reporting accountant will have to check that records, statements and passbooks are being kept as required by the SAR for solicitors acting as liquidators, Court of Protection deputies, trustees in bankruptcy and trustees of certain occupational pension schemes (rule 9). The reporting accountant will also check the requirements for joint accounts (rule 10).

The reporting accountant is required to check that the solicitor has a certificate(s) of qualifying insurance for the period covered by the report (rule 42(1)(p)). The reporting accountant should check that the insurance is issued by a qualifying insurer, a list of whom can be found on the SRA's website (see **www.sra.org.uk/solicitors/code-of-conduct/indemnity**); and that the end date of the certificate(s) is 30 September. The accountant also needs to check the level of cover (£3 million for recognised bodies and £2 million for other firms (see the Solicitors' Indemnity Insurance Rules 2010).)

5.7 HOW DO THE SAR AFFECT PROBATE WORK?

When solicitors are doing trust and/or probate work they will handle client money. They will have to pay money into the appropriate bank accounts and follow the rules as to withdrawals. In particular, solicitors will have to classify money correctly as client or office.

5.7.1 Which bank account?

Client money can go into the general client account or a separate designated client account. It can also be retained in cash or paid into a 'non-client account' if the client so instructs (rule 16).

Client money arising from a trust can also be paid into a 'non-client account' if the trustees' powers permit it, or be retained in cash in the performance of the trustees' duties (rule 17(ca)).

5.7.2 Reconciliation

Where money is paid into a general client account it will be subject to the requirement for reconciliations at least once every five weeks (rule 32(7)).

This requirement will apply to money held by solicitor-trustees in separate designated client accounts unless the account is passbook-operated in which case the requirement is at least once every 14 weeks. Reconciliations are necessary even where the client money is held in a 'non-client account' under rules 16 or 17(ca) (see rule 32(7)(a)).

5.7.3 Records

Where solicitor-trustees instruct an outside manager to run the business or property portfolio of an estate or trust, the manager must maintain, and then produce, appropriate records for inspection by the SRA (rule 32, note (ii)(d)).

Remember that if acting as a Court of Protection deputy, operating a joint account or operating the client's own account, solicitors will be required to keep limited records and have them checked by the reporting accountant.

5.7.4 Interest

There may be problems for solicitors in calculating how much interest is due to clients. For example, the administration may have been completed and cheques sent to beneficiaries. If the beneficiaries fail to cash those cheques, the solicitor may be under an obligation to pay the beneficiary interest unless the amount falls into one of the exceptions set out in rule 24(3). The notes to rule 24 say that whether or not a solicitor has to recalculate interest will depend on the circumstances of the case.

PART II

Probate, wills and the law

CHAPTER 6

The law on wills and succession: a review

Lesley King

There are many excellent works covering the law relating to wills and succession (see **Appendix E**). A brief summary of the principal legal issues is included here on the basis that this may be helpful generally, and also may act as a pointer to some of the grounds on which the validity of a will, or parts of it, may be challenged.

6.1 IS THE WILL VALID?

Check the following matters.

6.1.1 Age

Was the testator or testatrix over 18 (or, if a minor, a soldier on actual military service or a mariner or seaman at sea) at the time the will was made?

6.1.2 Formalities

Wills Act 1837, s.9 states:

> No will shall be valid unless –
>
> (a) it is in writing, and signed by the testator, or by some other person in his presence and by his direction; and
> (b) it appears that the testator intended by his signature to give effect to the will; and
> (c) the signature is made or acknowledged by the testator in the presence of two or more witnesses present at the same time; and
> (d) each witness either:
>
> (i) attests and signs the will; or
> (ii) acknowledges his signature, in the presence of the testator (but not necessarily in the presence of any other witness),
>
> but no form of attestation shall be necessary.

Whereas originally the signature had to be at the foot or end of the will, the rule is now as set out in (b) above. The emphasis is on giving effect to the will as far as possible whilst not opening the door to fraud.

'Signature' is given a wide meaning: a mark, an initial, and even a thumb print have all been held to suffice, but not a seal. Even an incomplete signature will do: *Re Chalcraft* [1948] P 222; *In the Estate of Cook* [1960] 1 All ER 689. See also *Weatherhill* v. *Pearce* [1995] 1 WLR 592. 'Presence' is also given a wide meaning: see *Couser* v. *Couser* [1996] 1 WLR 1301.

Attestation clause

Whilst an attestation clause is not required by Wills Act 1837, s.9, if such a clause is included and recites that the formalities of s.9 were observed, it will raise the presumption of due execution. Further, the inclusion of such a clause will normally avoid the necessity of providing the registrar with an affidavit of due execution.

The presence of an attestation clause reciting that the formalities have been complied has been held to create a powerful presumption which requires the strongest evidence to rebut. See the Court of Appeal decision in *Sherrington* v. *Sherrington* [2005] EWCA Civ 326 and the discussion of recent cases in **Chapter 12**.

6.1.3 Mental capacity

Requirements

For the classic statement of the test of testamentary capacity, see *Banks* v. *Goodfellow* (1869–70) LR 5 QB 549. The testator or testatrix must understand:

- the nature of the act;
- the claims he or she ought to consider;
- the extent of the property he or she has to dispose.

In addition, the testator or testatrix must not be subject to any disorder of the mind as shall 'poison his affections, pervert his sense of right or prevent the exercise of his natural faculties', i.e. he or she must not be suffering from an insane delusion.

The test was to some extent extended by Briggs J in *Key* v. *Key* [2010] EWHC 408 (Ch) who found that an 89-year-old man who was left devastated by the sudden death of his wife of 69 years lacked capacity. He said that this was not a case in which it was possible to point to a conspicuous inability of the deceased to satisfy one of the distinct limbs of the *Banks* v. *Goodfellow* test. Rather, taking the evidence as a whole, it was clear that Mr Key was simply unable during the week following his wife's death to exercise the decision-making powers required of a testator – or, at least, the daughters had not proved that he was:

> To the extent that such a conclusion involves a slight development of the *Banks* v. *Goodfellow* test, taking into account decision-making powers rather than just comprehension, I consider that it is necessitated by the greater understanding of the mind now available from modern psychiatric medicine, in particular in relation to affective disorder.

Proof of capacity

Those putting forward a will have to prove that it is valid. Therefore, they have to prove that the testator had the appropriate mental capacity when the will was made. They are assisted by the presumption of capacity where the will is rational and there is nothing to cast doubt on capacity; so those opposing the will must produce evidence to suggest lack of capacity. It will then be for those putting forward the will to establish capacity. A will fails if the person putting it forward cannot discharge the burden of proof (see *Vaughan* v. *Vaughan* [2002] EWHC 699). If the testator or testatrix generally lacked mental capacity (e.g. he or she was mentally ill), lack of capacity is presumed; this can be rebutted. A person alleging that a will was made in a lucid interval will have to prove this (see *Brown* v. *Deacy* [2002] WTLR 781).

Has the Mental Capacity Act 2005 affected the position?

Section 1(2) provides that 'for the purposes of this Act' a person must be assumed to have capacity unless it is established that he lacks it.

Section 2 provides that for the purposes of the Act, a person lacks capacity in relation to a matter if at the material time he is unable to make a decision for himself in relation to the matter because of an impairment of, or a disturbance in the functioning of, the mind or the brain.

Section 3(1) provides that a person is unable to make a decision for himself if he is unable:

(a) to understand the information relevant to the decision;
(b) to retain that information;
(c) to use or weigh that information as part of the process of making the decision; or
(d) to communicate his decision (whether by talking, using sign language or any other means).

The fact that a person is able to retain the information relevant to a decision for a short period only does not prevent him from being regarded as able to make the decision

Section 1(2) of the Act throws the onus of proof of incapacity on the person who alleges lack of capacity. This would obviously change the common law position. However, the Act may not be relevant in relation to testamentary capacity. Section 1(1) says that the principles set out in s.1 apply 'for the purposes of this Act'. The making of a will does not appear to be within the purposes of the 2005 Act. The only provisions relating to wills are in ss.16–18 and concern the power of the court to make or authorise the making of wills on behalf of persons who lack capacity, not the ascertainment of whether a particular testator had capacity when a will was made.

The Mental Capacity Act Code of Practice at para.4.33 states expressly that there are existing common law tests of capacity for certain tasks, including making a will. It says that the Act's new definition of capacity does not replace them although, when cases come before the court on such issues, judges can adopt the new definition if they think it is appropriate:

> The Act's new definition of capacity is in line with the existing common law tests, and the Act does not replace them. When cases come before the court on the above issues, judges can adopt the new definition if they think it is appropriate.

In *Scammell* v. *Farmer* [2008] EWHC 1100 (Ch) one of the few cases which at the time of writing have actually considered the implications of the Act, the judge held that the 2005 Act did not apply for two reasons:

- first, the death occurred and the litigation was commenced before the Act came into force; and
- second, he accepted that the making of a will was not a case within the purposes of the 2005 Act, as required by s.1(1).

At the time of writing, therefore, it seems likely that the Act has not affected the test of testamentary capacity or the burden of proof directly although it is likely to influence the way in which courts approach capacity issues.

The time for testing capacity is normally when the will is executed. However, if the testator or testatrix was competent when giving instructions, but not at actual execution, the will is nonetheless valid if he or she recalls giving the instructions and believes the will to accord with them: *Parker* v. *Felgate* (1883) 8 PD 171. For recent examples of the principle being applied to save a will see *Clancy* v. *Clancy* [2003] EWHC 1885 and *Perrins* v. *Holland* [2010] EWCA Civ 840 where the interval between giving instructions and making the will was more than 12 months.

6.1.4 Statutory wills

Where, of course, the Mental Capacity Act 2005 is of direct relevance is in relation to statutory wills made on behalf of those who lack testamentary capacity.

In *Re P* [2009] EWHC 163 (Ch) Mr Justice Lewison said that before the Act the court's job was to make the will that the patient himself (if not mentally disordered) would have made. This approach has sometimes been called the 'substituted judgment' approach. The patient was assumed to have had a brief lucid interval at the time when the will is made and the court attempted to make the will which the actual patient would have made taking into account the patient's antipathies and affections – unless beyond reason.

The Mental Capacity Act, s.1(5), however, provides that a decision made under the Act for or on behalf of a person who lacks capacity must be done, or made, in his 'best interests'. Section 4 sets out the matters that the person making the determination must consider when taking a decision in a person's 'best interests'. Just one of the matters included in s.4 is the person's past and present wishes and feelings. Having followed a structured decision-making process, the court must form a value judgment of its own, giving effect to the paramount statutory instruction that any decision must be made in the protected person's best interests.

Munby J took the same approach in *Re M*; *sub nom. ITW* v. *Z* [2009] EWHC 2525 (Fam).

There is a difficulty in determining what is in the best interests of a person in relation to a will. Both Lewison J and Munby J agreed that it was in a person's best interests to be remembered 'as having done the "right thing", either in life or, post mortem, by will'. In *Re D*; *sub nom. VAC* v. *JAD* [2010] EWHC 2159 (Ch) the court accepted that in a case where there were serious doubts as to the validity of previous wills, 'best interests' could require the execution of a statutory will, rather than leaving the estate to be eroded by the costs of litigation after death, and the testator's memory to be tainted by the bitterness of a contested probate dispute between her children.

For a fuller discussion of the principles governing statutory wills, see the *Elderly Client Handbook*, 4th edn (Law Society, 2010).

6.1.5 Intention

Requirements

The testator or testatrix must intend:

- to make a will; and
- to make the particular will executed. He or she must, therefore, know and approve its contents: *Guardhouse* v. *Blackburn* (1865–69) LR 1 P&D 109.

Where a capable testator or testatrix has signed the will, there will normally be a presumption of knowledge and approval. There may be suspicious circumstances which rebut the presumption so that the burden falls on the beneficiary to dispel suspicion that the will was not the product of the testator's or testatrix's free will: *Barry* v. *Butlin* (1838) 2 Moo. PC 480.

Proof of intention

Knowledge and approval of the particular will are presumed from the fact that the testator or testatrix had capacity and executed the will, unless one of the following applies:

- He or she was blind or illiterate or the will has been signed by someone else on his or her behalf (e.g. in the case of someone totally paralysed). Here the registrar must be satisfied that the testator or testatrix had knowledge of the will's contents and execution.

- Suspicious circumstances are present (e.g. the will substantially benefits the person who prepared it). Here, the greater the degree of suspicion, the stronger must be the affirmative proof to remove it: *Fulton* v. *Andrew* (1874–75) LR 7 HL 448; *Wintle* v. *Nye* [1959] 1 WLR 284. If there is a question of suspicious circumstances, is there a careful and full record of events? In some cases the burden of proof may be so heavy as to be impossible to discharge, as in *Wintle* v. *Nye* itself.

Cases such as *Fuller* v. *Strum* [2002] 1 WLR 1097 and *Hart* v. *Dabbs* [2001] WTLR 527 suggest that where a will is simple and straightforward and the testator or testatrix had an opportunity to read it, the court may well accept that he or she knew and approved the contents even where a beneficiary was concerned in the preparation of the will. See also *Shuck* v. *Loveridge* [2005] EWHC 72 (Ch).

Rebutting the presumption of knowledge and approval

If knowledge and approval are presumed, those opposing the will must prove that such knowledge and approval were absent by establishing that:

- the testator or testatrix was induced to make the will by force, fear or fraud; or
- he or she was subjected to undue influence and so did not make the will voluntarily. In the case of a will, undue influence must be tantamount to coercion, i.e. the testator or testatrix being driven to make the will against his or her wishes, e.g. by physical threats or actual violence, or incessant nagging may suffice: *Wingrove* v. *Wingrove* (1886) LR 11 PD 81. However, persuasion (appeals to sentiment, ties of kindred, etc.) is permissible.

For a recent example of a will being set aside on the basis of undue influence, see the first instance decision in *Gill* v. *Woodall* [2009] EWHC B34 (Ch). At the time of writing, the Court of Appeal was considering an appeal.

Motives are irrelevant.

6.1.6 Mistake

Mistake will invalidate a will, or that part of it included by mistake, but only if the relevant words are present without the testator's or testatrix's knowledge: it will not save a disposition where the testator or testatrix was mistaken as to the effect or meaning of the words used. Thus, he or she is deemed to know and approve the technical language used by the person drafting the will: even though that person was mistaken as to its legal effects, such language must be admitted to probate: *Re Horrocks (Deceased)* [1939] P 168.

Conversely, a mere clerical slip or error (such as a typing mistake) will generally be omitted from probate unless it has been brought to the testator's or testatrix's notice: *Re Morris* [1971] P 62.

In *Parkinson* v. *Fawdon* [2009] EWHC 1953 (Ch) the court was willing to amend a will which got the name of the beneficiary wrong when there was strong evidence to identify the intended beneficiary.

6.2 HAS A DOCUMENT BEEN INCORPORATED?

To be incorporated as part of a will an unexecuted document must be:

- in existence at the date of execution of the will;
- referred to in the will as already existing; and
- clearly identified in or identifiable from the will.

Care should be taken to avoid reference in a will to an existing document if incorporation is not intended. The registrar may require production of any such document, with evidence of possible incorporation.

The consequence of incorporation is that the document incorporated will be open to public scrutiny, as it will be admitted to probate with the will.

6.3 ARE TWO WILLS MUTUAL?

See **14.1.5** for a discussion of the requirements for mutual wills.

Be aware that once one testator or testatrix dies with a will in the agreed terms, the property of the survivor becomes subject to a trust. The property will pass to the agreed beneficiary even if the surviving testator or testatrix makes a new will purporting to leave the property elsewhere.

Re Hobley Deceased (1997) *The Times*, 16 July (reported at [2006] WTLR 467) shows that there can be difficulties in deciding whether or not the first testator has died with a will in the agreed terms where there has been any kind of alteration to the agreed will.

Olins v. *Walters* [2008] EWCA Civ 782 is an interesting case as the surviving husband denied that he and his deceased wife had intended to make mutual wills. The Court of Appeal agreed with the trial judge that there was sufficient evidence to establish the existence of an agreement to make the mutual wills with the result that the survivor was subject to an immediate constructive trust.

It is clearly good practice to set out the terms of any agreement within the wills. See the comments of the judge to this effect in *Charles* v. *Fraser* [2010] EWHC Civ (Ch) 2154.

6.4 TYPES OF LEGACY

Legacies may be categorised as follows.

6.4.1 Specific

This is a gift of property forming part of the testator's or testatrix's estate at death and distinguished in the will from other property of the same kind, e.g. 'my race horse Red Rum', 'my dwelling-house Blackacre, or such other dwelling-house in which I shall reside at the date of my death'.

Even a gift of money may be a specific legacy (*Re Wedmore* [1907] 2 Ch 277) although this is relatively rare.

6.4.2 General

This is a gift of property not distinguished in the will from other property of the same kind, e.g. 'to X the sum of £5,000; to Y £5,000 shares in ICI'. Whilst most general legacies are of money, it is not essential that they be so – although clearly an attempt to give a general legacy of some types of property would create problems and might well be void for uncertainty (e.g. 'to X a horse' – how does one define a horse, what value, etc.?).

6.4.3 Demonstrative

This is a general legacy payable out of a specific designated fund, e.g. '£1,000 payable out of my paid-up share account with X Building Society'. Here, in so far as the fund is still in existence at the testator's or testatrix's death, it will be treated as a specific legacy. In so far as it is not, it will be treated as a general legacy and abate accordingly should there be insufficient in the estate to discharge debts without recourse to the other general legacies.

The distinction between specific, demonstrative and general legacies is particularly important because:

- a specific legacy is subject to ademption; a general one is not, e.g. if Red Rum (see above) has been sold, given away, or has died during the testator's or testatrix's lifetime, the legatee will get nothing unless there is a substitutional provision (as in the case of the gift of Blackacre (again, see above));
- a general legacy must be applied for payment of debts before a specific one;
- a demonstrative legacy is only treated as a specific legacy in so far as the designated fund remains at the testator's or testatrix's death.

6.4.4 Pecuniary

This is a gift of money which may be specific, general or demonstrative. Administration of Estates Act 1925, s.55(1)(ix) defines a pecuniary legacy as including:

> an annuity, a general legacy, a demonstrative legacy, so far as … not discharged out of the designated property, and any other general direction by a testator for the payment of money, including all death duties free from which any devise, bequest or payment is made to take effect.

Thus, a legacy specified to be free of tax or free of expenses will be treated as a legacy conferring an extra benefit, the amount of which would be equivalent to the tax or expenses being paid out of the estate.

6.4.5 Residuary

The residue is what is left after all debts, liabilities, legacies and other expenses have been paid.

Where residue is left to be divided between an exempt and a non-exempt beneficiary (e.g. a charity and a member of the deceased's family) problems arise as to how the burden of tax should fall. See the discussion of *Re Benham* at **17.9**.

With regard to legacies to institutions (including charities), the solicitor will need to know whether or not the institution is charitable, as the cy-près doctrine only applies to charities, and charities are not bound by the rule against perpetuities. This means that a charity can generally take an interest under a will, no matter how distantly in the future it vests.

The Charity Commission (see **Appendix F** for address) may be able to advise if problems arise. More information on charitable beneficiaries is included at **17.8** onwards.

6.5 IS INTEREST PAYABLE?

Legacies should be paid with due diligence and usually within the executors' year. Even where the will directs earlier payment, this cannot be compelled (though interest will become payable from the earlier date – see below).

Interest (payable from residue) is payable to pecuniary legatees to compensate them for late payment. It is, therefore, normally payable from the end of the executor's year unless the will directs earlier payment. The will may, of course direct that interest is to be paid from the date of death. Exceptionally, interest runs from death where the legacy is:

- charged on realty;
- in satisfaction of a debt.

A contingent pecuniary legacy does not normally carry a right to receive income or interest until the contingency is fulfilled unless the will expressly gives such a right. Exceptionally interest will be payable (from death) where the legacy is:

- directed to be set aside as a separate fund;
- to the testator's or testatrix's minor child(ren); or
- to any other minor if the will shows an intention that the income is to be used for maintenance or education.

Where interest is not payable to the pecuniary legatee, the personal representatives (PRs) will have to invest a sum sufficient to produce the required amount and pay any income produced to the residuary beneficiary. The residuary beneficiary will be liable to income tax on the income and will have an immediate post-death interest for inheritance tax purposes. When the contingency is fulfilled the immediate post-death interest will terminate and the residuary beneficiary will be deemed to make a potentially exempt transfer to the pecuniary legatee. Most testators would not want this result so in the case of anything other than very small amounts it will normally be preferable to direct that the legacy fund is to be held on trust for the legatees and to make express provision for the treatment of income.

6.5.1 At what rate is interest paid?

Unless the will provides otherwise, interest is paid at the same rate that it would be payable if the court ordered an account of legacies. The Civil Procedure Rules 1998, SI 1998/3132 (CPR), Practice Direction 40 provides that this is normally at the basic rate payable for the time being on funds in court. At the time of writing the rate is derisorily low. There is a useful leaflet on the Court Funds Office website which gives interest rates going back to October 1965.

6.6 PROVISION ON INTESTACY

As from 1 February 2009 the levels of the statutory legacy for spouses and civil partners increased. Lower rates are payable for deaths before that date.

On 29 October 2009 the Law Commission issued a consultation paper (Intestacy and Family Provision Claims on Death No.191) asking for responses on possible reforms to the law in this area. This chapter deals only with law as it is at the time of writing.

6.6.1 Deceased married or in a civil partnership at death

1. If the intestate leaves issue (e.g. children and/or grandchildren) the spouse or civil partner takes:

(a) personal chattels absolutely (as defined by Administration of Estates Act 1925, s.55(1)(x)); and
(b) £250,000 plus interest at the rate of 6 per cent from death until payment (free of tax, with costs and interest coming from the residue); and
(c) a life interest in half the residue, the remainder and the other half going to the children on the statutory trusts.

2. If the intestate leaves no issue, but does leave a parent or brother or sister of the whole blood or their issue, the spouse or civil partner takes:

   (a) the personal chattels absolutely; and
   (b) £450,000 plus interest as above; and
   (c) half the residue absolutely.

3. If the intestate leaves no issue, no parents, no brothers or sisters of the whole blood or their issue, the spouse or civil partner takes the whole estate absolutely.

Spouses and civil partners must survive 28 days in order to benefit on intestacy (Administration of Estates Act 1925, s.46(2A) but only in relation to deaths occurring on or after 1 January 1996).

A person will only be treated as a spouse or civil partner under the intestacy rules if the marriage or civil partnership was continuing at the time of the death. Therefore, if a decree absolute of divorce, or a final dissolution order in relation to a civil partnership, has been made, the ex-spouse does not qualify under the intestacy rules. A decree nisi has no such effect.

If a decree of judicial separation, or a separation order, has been made, the intestacy rules operate as though the ex-spouse/civil partner had already died (Matrimonial Causes Act 1973, s.18(2) and Civil Partnership Act 2004, s.57).

There are no cases on intestacy and polygamous marriages in England and Wales but by analogy with family provision and matrimonial relief, it appears that there can be more than one spouse for this purpose. See *Re Sehota* [1978] 1 WLR 1506, *Chaudhry* v. *Chaudhry* [1976] Fam 148. The statutory legacy would be divided amongst the various widows. See, for example, *Cheang Thye Phin* v. *Tan Ah Loy* [1920] AC 369.

6.6.2 Deceased dies without a spouse or civil partner

The estate goes to:

1. the intestate's issue on the statutory trusts; if none
2. the intestate's parents; if none
3. the intestate's brothers and sisters of the whole blood on the statutory trusts, failing whom to remoter relations; if none
4. to the Crown or the Duchy of Cornwall or the Duchy of Lancaster.

The Crown and Duchies have discretion to make grants from the estate for dependants of the deceased and 'other persons for whom the intestate might reasonably have been expected to make provision' (Administration of Estates Act 1925, s.46(1)). These might include, for example, unmarried partners, friends or neighbours, or relatives by marriage or civil partnership. The Treasury Solicitor's Department publishes guidelines as to the way in which this discretion will be exercised on behalf of the Crown as do the solicitors for the two Duchies.

'Personal chattels' excludes any which are used for business purposes. It also excludes money or securities for money, but has been held to include, for example, valuable collections.

Under the statutory trusts (Administration of Estates Act 1925, s.47), a child of the intestate has a contingent interest in the estate. This is satisfied if the child reaches 18 or marries or forms a civil partnership before that. A child dying under 18, unmarried and without having formed a civil partnership, is treated as never having existed.

If a child of the intestate does not survive the intestate, but he or she leaves a child or children, then that child or those children will take his, her or their deceased parent's share (in equal shares if more than one), again contingently on attaining 18 or marrying or forming a civil partnership before that.

6.6.3 Spouses and civil partners: special rights

A surviving spouse or civil partner may elect (generally within 12 months of the grant) to do the following:

- Redeem any life interest in the estate in return for a lump sum (Administration of Estates Act 1925, s.47). If the spouse or civil partner so elects, this does not count as a transfer of value for inheritance tax (IHT) purposes. He or she is treated as if, instead of being entitled to the life interest, he or she had been entitled to the lump sum from the outset.
- Take any dwelling house included in the undisposed-of property in which the survivor was resident at the date of death, or the deceased's share in it, in or towards satisfaction of any absolute or capitalised interest in the estate (Intestates' Estates Act 1952, Sched.2). The value of the house is taken at the date of appropriation, not of death: *Re Collins* [1975] 1 WLR 309. To qualify, the surviving spouse or civil partner must be living in the house concerned at the intestate's death.

Exceptions to the right of the surviving spouse or civil partner to take the dwelling house include cases where the intestate's interest in the property was a tenancy determinable (by notice or otherwise) within two years of death and where the house forms part of a commercial unit, such as a farmhouse on a working farm or a flat in a family hotel.

If the value of the dwelling house is more than the statutory legacy, the spouse or civil partner may make up the shortfall.

Under this provision the surviving spouse or civil partner is able to require PRs to make this appropriation. This is in direct contrast to the position under Administration of Estates Act 1925, s.41, under which PRs have the power (whether the deceased died testate or intestate) to appropriate his or her property in (or towards) satisfaction of interests in the estate. Such an appropriation will require the consent of the beneficiary unless the will has removed the need for consent.

The right cannot be exercised while the surviving spouse or civil partner is a sole PR. An additional personal representative has to be appointed.

6.6.4 Hotchpot

The Law Reform (Succession) Act 1995 abolished the rules as to hotchpot in their entirety for deaths occurring on or after 1 January 1996.

6.7 JOINT PROPERTY

Joint property can cause a number of problems for solicitors.

In *Carr-Glynn* v. *Frearsons* [1998] 4 All ER 225 the testatrix wished to leave her interest in a house to her niece. She was uncertain whether her interest was held as joint tenant or as tenant in common with her nephew. The solicitor explained to her that the will would be ineffective if the house was held as joint tenants and that it would be necessary to sever the joint tenancy. The solicitor offered to obtain the title deeds to check. The client said that she would do it herself but did not do so. When she died, it was discovered that the house had been held as joint tenants so the will was ineffective.

The Court of Appeal found the solicitor negligent: the service of a notice of severance was part of the will-making process. The niece was as much an intended beneficiary of the severance as she was of the new will. The solicitor should have explained that it was possible to serve the notice of severance as a precaution without any need to check the title deeds:

> She did not tell the testatrix that the doubt, identified in her letter of 6 February 1989, could and should be laid to rest by the service of a notice of severance before or at the same time as the will was executed; that there was no need to obtain the deeds before serving the notice; and that there was nothing to be gained, and potentially much to be lost, by delay.

It is important to check the basis of ownership and, if there is any doubt, advise service of a notice of severance.

Although many people think only of a notice of severance in relation to severing a joint tenancy, this is not the case. The Law of Property Act 1925, s.36(2) expressly preserved the pre-1925 methods of severance. *Williams* v. *Hensman* (1861) 1 John & H 546 lists three methods:

1. an act of any one of the persons interested operating upon his or her own share may create a severance as to that share;
2. mutual agreement; and
3. any course of dealing sufficient to intimate that the interests of all were mutually treated as constituting a tenancy in common.

This means that although a client may appear to be the sole beneficial owner of property as a result of survivorship, there may have been an earlier severance by conduct. This is what happened in *Re Woolnough (Deceased)* [2002] WTLR 595.

In *Re Woolnough* a brother and sister had made wills leaving their interest in a house owned as joint tenants to the other for life with a gift over to a third party. After the sister's death the brother left the house to charity. If the joint tenancy had already been severed, only half of the value of the house was in his estate. If it had not, the whole value of the house was his.

The fact that the two had made wills giving each other a mere life interest in the property was sufficient to amount to an agreement to sever:

> It is not a case of one of them acting behind the back of the other. The reference in the will to a half share makes it clear that they were treating their share as disposed of by their wills.

It would not, of course, have amounted to severance had one joint tenant alone made a will dealing with the half share.

When administering an estate there may be cases where it is necessary to investigate whether or not there was an earlier severance by consent. Although an estate may appear to have acquired the entire interest in a property by survivorship, there may have been severance by consent at an earlier stage.

It is also important to be aware of the implications of the case when taking instructions for a will. As in *Re Woolnough*, a solicitor may be consulted by two clients who are beneficial joint tenants but who indicate by the instructions they give for their wills that they are treating the joint tenancy as at an end. Probably merely giving the instructions (as opposed to executing the will) is sufficient to amount to severance. However, it will be helpful if the solicitor ensures that there is clarity as to when the severance takes place – consider preparing a signed statement or notice of severance on the spot.

6.8 RELEVANT STATUTES

6.8.1 Law of Property (Miscellaneous Provisions) Act 1994

The Law of Property (Miscellaneous Provisions) Act 1994 came into effect on 1 July 1995. Helpful articles on this, by Philip Rossdale and Robin Towns, appeared in [1995] *Solicitors Journal*, 28 July ('Administration of estates') and [1995] *New Law Journal*, Probate Supplement, 29 September ('Trustees' lot not a happy one').

The 1994 Act affects sales of land by PRs and also vests intestates' property pre-grant in the Public Trustee (instead of the President of the Family Division).

6.8.2 Trusts of Land and Appointment of Trustees Act 1996

The Trusts of Land and Appointment of Trustees Act 1996 (TLATA 1996) came into force on 1 January 1997. It prevents the creation of new trusts for sale and strict settlements in respect of land and introduces the 'trust of land'. Trustees of land have all the powers of an absolute beneficial owner including the power of sale. Property of an intestate is no longer held on a trust for sale.

Where a will creates a continuing trust, s.11 imposes an obligation on trustees of land to consult beneficiaries of full age with an interest in possession when exercising any function in respect of land.

Section 12(1) gives a beneficiary with an interest in possession a right to occupy land if:

(a) the purposes of the trust include making the land available for his occupation (or for the occupation of beneficiaries of a class of which he is a member or of beneficiaries in general), or
(b) the land is held by the trustees so as to be so available.

There had been fears of adverse capital gains tax consequences where a spouse leaves his/her interest in the matrimonial home to a discretionary trust and the surviving spouse continues in occupation by virtue of the right to occupy. The survivor's interest will pass to his or her personal representatives at market value at the date of death without a disposal (Taxation of Chargeable Gains Act 1992, s.62(1)). But the trustees would be liable to tax on any increase in value since the death of the first spouse, unless the principal private dwelling house exemption is available under Taxation of Chargeable Gains Act 1992, s.225. *Sansom* v. *Peay* [1976] 3 All ER 375 decided that the exemption is available where the trust is discretionary and the beneficiary occupies as a result of the exercise of the trustees' discretion. But have the trustees permitted the surviving spouse or civil partner to occupy if they are already entitled to occupy as a person with an interest in possession? Many people thought that there might be a charge to tax. However, an article by Gill Steel and Richard Dew 'Can TLTA 1996 be interpreted as a fiscal bill' in (2009) 106 *Trust and Estates Law & Tax Journal*, 11 reported that the Revenue accepts that the principal private dwelling house exemption is available under Taxation of Chargeable Gains Act 1992, s.225 in such circumstances

Section 13 allows trustees to regulate the respective rights of beneficiaries where more than one has an interest in possession.

Section 19 allows beneficiaries of full age and capacity entitled to the whole beneficial interest to compel the existing trustees to retire in favour of new trustees of their choice. See **6.9.3** below.

All of these provisions can be varied by the will.

Helpful articles appear in [1996] *Solicitors Journal*, 1154 ('Trusts of land: will-drafting implications' by Lesley King and Sheila Bramley); in [1996] *Family Law*, December, 736 on the provisions of the Act relating to joint ownership ('Trusts of land and family practice' by Simon Baughan); and in [1997] *Conveyancing*, July/August, 263 on drafting to restrict trustees' powers ('Escaping s.8(1) provisions').

6.8.3 Trustee Delegation Act 1999

The Trustee Delegation Act 1999 came into force on 1 March 2000. It prescribed a new short form of power of attorney, amended Trustee Act 1925, s.25 and repealed Enduring Powers of Attorney Act 1985, s.3(3), which it was felt had gone too far in removing the safeguards of the Trustee Act 1925.

Trustee Act 1925, s.25, as amended, allows trustees to delegate all powers and discretions but subject to various restrictions. The appointment cannot exceed 12 months (although the appointment can be renewed); cannot be to a sole trustee; the donor remains liable for the acts of the attorney; and notice of the delegation must be given to all co-trustees.

The main effects of the Trustee Delegation Act 1999 are as follows:

- Section 7 confirms and strengthens the rules that capital money must be paid to, and a valid receipt for capital money must be given by, at least two trustees, and that a conveyance or deed must be made by at least two trustees to overreach any interests affecting a legal interest. In effect two individuals must always act. So, for this purpose a trustee acting on his or her own behalf and as attorney for all the other trustees only counts as one person. The provisions relating to delegation must be read subject to this.
- Prior to the 1999 Act co-owners could not delegate by using a general power of attorney. They had to use a Trustee Act 1925, s.25 trustee power of appointment or an enduring power. Section 1 of the 1999 Act allows trustees with a beneficial interest in the trust property (e.g. co-owners) after 1 January 2000 to use a general power of attorney to delegate their trustee functions in relation to land, the proceeds of sale of land and income arising from it. The effect is that they are freed from the restrictions of s.25 so there is no limit on the length of time the delegation can last, it can be to a sole co-trustee and notice need not be given to co-trustees. In a typical husband and wife co-ownership, one could delegate to the other. However, under s.7 of the 1999 Act there will still need to be two individuals to give a good receipt for capital money. If the attorney wanted to sell, there would have to be another trustee appointed.
- Section 8 amends Trustee Act 1925, s.36 to provide, for an attorney who cannot sell because there is no other trustee, a limited power to appoint a further trustee. The amended s.36 applies only where there is a registered enduring power or lasting power under which the attorney is authorised to exercise the donor's trustee functions.

Helpful summaries of the Trustee Delegation Act 1999 appear in [2000] *Solicitors Journal*, 3 March ('Trustee powers of attorney' by Trevor Aldridge), (2000) 64 *Conveyancer* and [2000] *Gazette*, 2 March ('Trustee Delegation Act' by Denzil Lush). An interesting letter published in (2002) 33 *Trusts and Estates Law Journal*, 13 suggests including in wills and trusts a wider power for specified persons to remove trustees who are becoming mentally incapable and, in appropriate cases, to appoint a replacement.

6.8.4 Mental Capacity Act 2005

The Mental Capacity Act came into force on 1 October 2007. The Act has had profound effects on dealings on behalf of those who lack capacity. For the possible effects of the Act on the test of testamentary capacity, see **6.1.3** above.

The Act makes it clear that a person's capacity is to be assessed in relation to a specific decision and at the material time that decision is to be made.

Section 1 sets out the principles to be applied. In particular, a person must be presumed to have capacity and where it is established that they do not have capacity to make a decision, a person who acts on their behalf must act in their best interests. Section 3 sets out the test to be applied when determining whether or not a person has capacity to make a particular decision and s.4 sets out the procedure to be followed when deciding how to act in a person's best interests.

One of the most important changes made by the Act was the introduction of lasting powers of attorney (LPAs) to replace enduring powers of attorney.

Lasting powers of attorney are dealt with in ss.9–14. A lasting power has to be registered before it can be used. The donor must get an appropriate person to certify that the donor understood the purpose of the power and the scope of the authority that it confers and also that the donor was not subject to any fraud or undue pressure.

Regulation 5, and Parts 1 and 2 of Sched.1 to the Lasting Powers of Attorney, Enduring Powers of Attorney and Public Guardian Regulations 2007, SI 2007/1253 provide two prescribed forms of lasting power: one for property and affairs, and one for health and welfare. A donor cannot confer on her attorneys the authority to make health and welfare decisions in the form prescribed for property and affairs. If a donor includes provisions dealing with welfare in a property and affairs power (or vice versa) the offending provisions will be severed.

From 1 October 2007 it is not possible to create new enduring powers of attorney although existing powers continue to be effective. The provisions relating to enduring powers of attorney are contained in Sched.4 to the Mental Capacity Act 2005.

It is fair to say that the introduction of lasting powers was not entirely trouble free. A number of forms were returned because of technical errors such as a failure by the certificate provider to tick the necessary boxes. The forms were amended as a result of the initial teething problems.

At the time of writing the most common errors relate to replacement attorneys.

There are a number of restrictions on what attorneys can do. For example, Sched.1, para.2(3) to the Mental Capacity Act 2005 says that 'the persons who may be named persons do not include a person who is appointed as donee under the instrument'. A 'named person' in this context is a person identified by the donor in a statement listing the people whom the donor wishes to be notified of the registration of his LPA. Initially, there was uncertainty as to whether a person who was merely a replacement attorney could be a named person. In the case of *Howarth* July 2008 (see Court of Protection website at **www.publicguardian.gov.uk/information-professionals.htm**), it was held that this was not possible. A person appointed as a replacement attorney is subject to the same restrictions as someone appointed an immediate attorney. Hence, a replacement attorney cannot:

- be a named person;
- witness the donor's signature in Part A;
- provide the certificate in Part B;
- be under the age of 18.

6.8.5 Trustee Act 2000

The Trustee Act 2000 came into force on 1 February 2001. It implies a set of default powers into trusts unless the trust document specifies differently by exclusion, modification or widening and applies irrespective of whether the trust was created before or after 1 February 2001. The powers implied include a general investment power, power to use agents, nominees and custodians and a general power to insure. These are dealt with at **16.10.1** below.

The Trustee Act 2000 makes various changes to the law on charging clauses. Under s.28:

- a trustee of a non-charitable trust who acts in a professional capacity (defined as one providing services in connection with the management and administration of trusts) can charge for work that a lay person could do without express authorisation in the charging clause;
- a charging clause is no longer treated as a legacy so:
  - a partner in a firm with the benefit of a charging clause can witness the will without losing the benefit of the clause;
  - the charges will not abate with other pecuniary legacies where there are insufficient funds (so it is no longer necessary to provide for this expressly in the clause).

Under s.29 a trustee of a non-charitable trust who is acting in a professional capacity can charge reasonable remuneration for his or her services without a charging clause, provided a majority of co-trustees authorises it. This does not apply to a sole trustee (other than trust corporations).

The Act also imposes a general duty of care. Whenever the duty applies, the trustee must exercise such care and skill as is reasonable in the circumstances, having regard in particular:

- to any special knowledge or experience that the trustee has or holds himself out as having; and
- in the case of a professional trustee, to any special knowledge or experience it is reasonable to expect that person to have.

6.8.6 Perpetuities and Accumulations Act 2009

This is a very brief summary of the effect of the Perpetuities and Accumulations Act 2009 in relation to non-charitable trusts. The rules relating to charitable trusts are different.

The Act came into force on 6 April 2010. It provides a new perpetuity period of 125 years to replace the two current alternatives of:

(i) a life or lives in being plus 21 years (at common law); or
(ii) a specified number of years, not exceeding 80 years (under Perpetuities and Accumulations Act 1964).

It removes the statutory rules limiting accumulation of income.

Which wills and trusts are affected?

The Act applies only to trusts taking effect and wills executed after the Act comes into force. Trusts already in existence are not affected.

There is one exception to the rule that existing trusts continue to be governed by the old law. Section 12 allows trustees of settlements where the perpetuity period is defined by reference to a life or lives in being and it is difficult, or not reasonably practicable, to ascertain whether the lives have ended, to opt for a fixed period of 100 years. Trustees who want to opt for the 100-year period must execute a deed stating that they believe there is such a difficulty and that the instrument is to be treated as if it specified a period of 100 years (no other period is possible).

It is unclear whether the Act applies where a will executed before commencement is republished after commencement by a codicil. It must apply to the contents of the codicil document itself, but does it apply to the contents of the original will document if these are not expressly restated in the codicil? *Re Heath's Will Trusts* [1949] Ch 170, which concerns a statute using similar language, suggests that it may not.

Testators who want to be sure that the Act will apply to apply to any trusts in wills executed before 6 April 2010 should do one of the following:

- execute a new will after commencement;
- execute, after commencement, a codicil that restates in full the trusts contained in a will executed before commencement.

Drafting implications

Trusts to which the Perpetuities and Accumulations Act 2009 applies will have the new 125-year period whatever the trust instrument may say. It is not necessary to state a perpetuity period but it will be helpful to do so. Future practitioners will not necessarily remember the exact date that the Act came into force. A suitable clause would be:

> The 'Trust Period' shall mean the period ending on the last day of the period of 125 years from the date of my death which period (and no other) shall be the applicable perpetuity period.

It is important to amend the trust period as well as the perpetuity period. The trust period is the period within which trustees can exercise their powers.

The rule against excessive accumulations is abolished. However, the Act does not override provisions in trust documents so the unrestricted power to accumulate will be subject to any express provisions in the trust instrument. A possible clause would be:

> The accumulation period shall be the Trust Period.

Alternatively, if the instrument is silent, there will be no limitations on the trustee's powers to accumulate.

Trusts created by the exercise of powers of appointment

Section 6(2) provides that the perpetuity period for an instrument created in the exercise of a special power of appointment will begin on the date on which the instrument creating the power took effect.

Example

A trust created on 1 July 1980 with an 80-year perpetuity period from that date includes a special power of appointment. The perpetuity period for any trust created by the power, whether before or after 6 April 2010, will be 80 years starting on 1 July 1980.

Similarly, new trust interests created by the exercise of a special power of appointment will be governed by the original accumulation period, even if the power is exercised after 6 April 2010.

The rules are different for trusts created under a general power of appointment taking effect after commencement of the Act. A person with a general power is treated as, in effect, the absolute owner of the property subject to the power. If the trust is created on or after 6 April 2010, the perpetuity period will be 125 years, beginning on the date on which the power is exercised, not the date on which it was created and there will be an unrestricted power to accumulate.

Post-death variations

What is the position if a beneficiary of a will executed before 6 April 2010 uses a post-death variation to create a settlement on or after that date?

The rules here are logical. Reading back takes effect only for inheritance tax and capital gains tax purposes. For other purposes the person making the variation is making a lifetime disposition. So if a beneficiary with an absolute entitlement, varies the will today to leave property on trust, that beneficiary is creating a new trust today and the new provisions will apply.

If the will itself had created a trust and a beneficiary of the will trust had varied his beneficial entitlement, there would be an assignment of an interest in a pre-Act trust and the new provisions would not apply.

Perpetuities and pension schemes

At the time of writing, there is concern and some uncertainty as to the position where trustees of a pension scheme are asked to exercise their discretion to appoint death benefits to a trust established in the member's lifetime to receive the benefits (a pilot trust).

The generally accepted view is that:

- As each member joins a pension scheme, there is a new settlement. irrespective of when the scheme itself began. See the Privy Council in *Air Jamaica Ltd* v. *Charlton* [1999] 1 WLR 1399, 1409:

  > Every time an employee joins the scheme, a new settlement is created. The settlement comprises the contributions made in respect of the employee whether by him or by the company. The rule against perpetuities must be applied separately to each individual settlement, and each employee must be treated as a life in being in relation to his own settlement.

- Hence, where a member joined the scheme pre-6 April 2010 the trust is governed by the old rules (which probably give a perpetuity period of member's life + 21 years). If he joins after that date the trust will be covered by the new rules (perpetuity period of 125 years).
- If the trust created by the member to receive the benefits is created on or after 6 April 2010, it will automatically have a perpetuity period of 125 years. This cannot be varied. (However, it is possible to limit the trust period and, as we will see in a moment, this can be useful.)
- If trustees of a pre-6 April 2010 pension scheme appoint benefits to a trust created after that date using a special power of appointment, the appointment will be subject to the old rules and the property must vest within the old perpetuity period, even though the new trust has the new 125-year perpetuity period. This does not mean that the appointment is immediately void. It will be possible to wait and see.

- However, it will make for easier administration if the trustees of the new trust are given power to limit the trust period so that the new trust can be made to coincide with the funds transferred.

Where a member himself creates a trust of the death benefit, the perpetuity period starts with the date on which the trust is created; so, for a trust created today, the 125-year period is available. For a discussion of perpetuities and pension schemes, see John Woolley's article on spousal by-pass trusts in (2010) 165 *Taxation* 16.

6.8.7 Civil Partnership Act 2004

The Civil Partnership Act 2004 came into force on 5 December 2005. It deals separately with changes to the law in England and Wales, Scotland and Northern Ireland. The aim is to put civil partners on the same statutory footing as spouses within each of the three jurisdictions. The relevant property provisions in relation to succession to property are found in ss.71–72 and Sched.4. Enactments relating to wills, administration of estates, claims under the Inheritance (Provision for Family and Dependants) (IPFDA) Act 1975 and the provisions of Married Women's Property Act 1882, s.11 are amended to apply in relation to civil partnerships as they do to marriages.

The Act does not contain any general statement that the word 'spouse' is to be construed as including civil partners in private documents. In wills and trusts if the intention is to include a civil partner in a class of beneficiaries it is necessary to say so.

The Act has some implications when it comes to the wording of oaths. If a deceased dies intestate without ever marrying or forming a civil partnership, he or she will be described as a spinster or bachelor. If there is a surviving civil partner, the civil partner must be described as the:

> lawful [male] [female] civil partner and [the only person now entitled to] [one of the persons entitled to share in] the estate of the said intestate.

If the intestate had a civil partner who predeceased, it will be necessary to declare that the intestate died:

> without a surviving lawful [male] [female] civil partner.

6.8.8 Gender Recognition Act 2004

The Gender Recognition Act 2004 came into force on 4 April 2005. Its purpose is to provide transsexuals with legal recognition in their acquired gender. Legal recognition will follow from the issue of a full gender recognition certificate by a Gender Recognition Panel.

Before issuing a certificate, the Panel must be satisfied that the applicant:

- has, or has had, gender dysphoria;
- has lived in the acquired gender throughout the preceding two years; and
- intends to continue to live in the acquired gender until death.

Where applicants have been recognised under the law of another country or territory as having changed gender, the Panel need only be satisfied that the country or territory in question has been approved by the Secretary of State.

The effect of legal recognition is that, for example, a male-to-female transsexual person will be legally recognised as a woman in English law for all purposes (s.9(1)). The transsexual will receive a new birth certificate in the new gender. There will be no link between the original certificate and the new one, which will presumably make life difficult for genealogists.

Section 15 provides that a change of gender does not affect the distribution of property under a will or other instrument made before the day on which the Act comes into force. For wills or other instruments made after that day, the general principle stated in s.9(1) will apply. For example, if a will refers to the 'eldest daughter', and a person who was previously a son becomes the 'eldest daughter' following recognition in the acquired gender, that person (subject to s.18) will inherit as the 'eldest daughter'.

There is protection for PRs under s.17. They are relieved from any fiduciary duty to inquire whether a gender recognition certificate has been issued to any person or revoked, even if that fact could affect entitlement to property which the PR is responsible for distributing.

The beneficiary will nevertheless retain his or her claim to the property and may enforce this claim, for example, by following the property into the hands of another person who has received it instead.

Under s.18, the court has power to make orders to deal with the situation where the devolution of property under a will or other instrument is different from what it would be but for the change of gender. If, for example, a will left property to 'eldest daughter' of X, and there is an older brother whose gender becomes female under the Act, then the person who was previously the 'eldest daughter' will cease to enjoy that position. A person who is adversely affected by the different disposition can apply to the court and the court, if it is satisfied that it is just to do so, may make such order as it considers appropriate in relation to the person benefiting from the different disposition of the property. There is no guidance as to how the court should exercise its powers.

Neither the Act nor the explanatory notes deal with the situation of a legacy leaving property to 'my son, John' and by the date of death there is no son, John but instead a daughter, Joanna. If there is no one who fulfils the description, will the use of the name be sufficient to identify the person intended?

Obviously, testators who know of the change can review their wills. From a general drafting point of view, it is probably advisable to refer to the desired beneficiaries by name or by a non-gender related description rather than to use a description such as 'the son/daughter of X'. An alternative approach is to include a clause stating that the will is to be construed as if the Act had not been enacted and that gifts are to pass to those who fulfil the relevant description at the date the will was made.

6.9 APPOINTMENT AND REMOVAL OF TRUSTEES AND PERSONAL REPRESENTATIVES

6.9.1 Retirement

There is no power for a PR who has taken a grant simply to retire from the office of executor in favour of another person. However, where a will appoints a person to act as executor and trustee, it will be possible for that person to retire from the office of trustee.

When does a personal representative become a trustee?

This can be a difficult question. Once the PR has ascertained the amount of residue available to the residuary beneficiary and, if appropriate, obtained approval of the estate accounts it is likely that the PR then holds the remaining assets as trustee. If, however, other assets or liabilities were discovered, the PR would have to deal with these assets or liabilities as PR since that office is never lost.

In what circumstances can a trustee retire and/or appoint new trustees?

The circumstances may be covered by the will. If not, the provisions of Trustee Act 1925, ss.36 and 39 will apply. These sections allow a trustee to retire or be removed provided this does not result in there being a sole remaining trustee and provided the continuing trustees consent. Continuing trustees can appoint replacement or additional trustees. The PRs of a sole trustee who has died can appoint replacements.

A trustee who is incapable of acting can be replaced under s.36(1). However, be careful of s.36(9), which requires the Court of Protection to authorise the replacement if the trustee is entitled in possession to a beneficial interest in the trust property.

6.9.2 Removal of personal representatives by the court

Administration of Justice Act 1985, s.50

Under Administration of Justice Act 1985, s.50 the court has a discretion to appoint a new PR or PRs in the place of existing PRs or any of them, or to terminate the appointment of one but not all of the PRs (unless appointing at least one substituted PR).

The court's jurisdiction under s.50 is not limited to cases of conflict between PRs. It can be used where a PR wishes to retire.

There have been a number of recent cases on the principles governing the court's exercise of its s.50 powers.

In *Letterstedt* v. *Broers* (1883–84) LR 9 App Cas 371 the court was at pains to point out that there are no hard and fast rules and that the main guide in these cases must be the welfare of the beneficiaries. In *Loftus Deceased* [2005] EWHC 406 (Ch) the court held that removal under s.50 is a matter for the discretion of the court, and it is reasonable for the court to take a pragmatic approach, to consider the views of the beneficiaries and the interests of the estate as a whole. It will often be appropriate for the court to appoint an independent expert in place of the original PR.

In *Thomas and Agnes Carvel Foundation* v. *Carvel* [2007] EWHC 1314 (Ch) Lewison J said that the court's power to remove and replace a personal representative is in no way limited to cases of misconduct. If the administration has come to a standstill because relations between the personal representatives have broken down, or relations between the representatives and the beneficiaries have broken down, the court will ordinarily remove the personal representatives and appoint new ones to enable the administration to be completed. This approach was endorsed in *Angus* v. *Emmott* [2010] EWHC 154 (Ch) where, although there was no misconduct, a situation had been reached in which there was such a degree of animosity and distrust between the executors that the due administration of the estate was unlikely to be achieved expeditiously. The safest and most appropriate course to ensure the proper administration of the estate in the interests of all beneficiaries was to remove all the current executors and to replace them with a suitably qualified professional.

Friction or hostility between trustees and the beneficiaries is not of itself a reason for the removal of the trustees. But where the hostility is grounded on the mode in which the trust has been administered, it is certainly not to be disregarded. For an example of the court refusing to remove executors, see *Kershaw* v. *Micklethwaite* [2010] EWHC 506 (Ch), where there was friction and hostility between one of the beneficiaries and the executors and some errors had been made. The court declined to remove the executors, saying that poor relationships need not and should not interfere with the administration of the estate and not every mistake will induce a court to remove an executor.

In *Alkin* v. *Raymond* [2010] All ER (D) 48 (May), the following useful comments on s.50 were made by George Bompas QC sitting as a deputy judge:

(1) If the friction or hostility is generated by the behaviour of the beneficiary, the court will need more than the mere fact of friction and hostility. It will need to be satisfied that the friction or hostility was impeding the proper execution of the trusts and the welfare of the beneficiaries.

(2) Where the friction or hostility is with someone who is merely a discretionary beneficiary, this is of less significance than when the beneficiary is the 'possessor of the trust estate' although it will be relevant to form a judgment as to the ability of the trustees to give proper consideration to the claims of that beneficiary, as well as the other beneficiaries.

(3) The testator's selection of executor should not lightly be set aside. It should not be disregarded except for serious reason.

Court administering estate

Where the court has ordered the administration of the estate under its supervision (a comparatively rare event) it has power to appoint PR(s).

Trustee Act 1925, s.41

The court has power to remove PRs and appoint new ones under Trustee Act 1925, s.41 where, without an order, it is 'inexpedient, difficult or impracticable' to appoint a new trustee or new trustees (including PRs). Such appointees may be 'in substitution for or in addition to any existing trustee or trustees'. The wording of s.41 is sufficiently wide to enable the court to remove PRs and trustees from office for other than the common causes – residing permanently abroad, becoming mentally disordered, becoming bankrupt or being convicted of serious crime.

Judicial Trustees Act 1896, s.1

There is power under Judicial Trustees Act 1896, s.1 for the court to appoint a judicial trustee. See **Chapter 12** at **12.5.4** for an example of the use of the section in connection with a trust arising from a mutual will agreement.

6.9.3 Trusts of Land and Appointment of Trustees Act 1996, s.19

It is worth noting that under TLATA 1996, s.19, beneficiaries who are of full age and capacity and between them entitled to the whole beneficial interest can compel the retirement of the existing trustees and the appointment of trustees of their choice.

In the past, beneficiaries who were at odds with their trustees could not simply change the trustees (*Re Brockbank* [1948] Ch 206). In such circumstances they had to bring the trust to an end and then resettle the property with trustees of their choice, but this would frequently have had adverse capital gains tax (CGT) consequences. Section 19 is subject to contrary intention in the will or trust instrument. However, for most people the CGT advantage will outweigh the concern over arbitrary replacement of trustees, so only rarely will it be appropriate to exclude the s.19 power.

It is important to note that because of the requirement for full age and capacity and absolute entitlement to the whole beneficial interest there will be comparatively few occasions where s.19 will be relevant.

6.10 POWERS AND DUTIES OF EXECUTORS AND TRUSTEES

6.10.1 Powers

Unless the powers of executors and trustees are extended or varied by the will, the powers are limited to those given by statute. The main statutory powers are set out below.

Trustee Act 2000, s.3 gives a general power to invest in anything other than land as if the trustees were absolute owners. The power is in addition to any express power but subject to any restrictions contained in the trust instrument. However, nothing in a trust instrument made before 3 August 1961 will be treated as restricting or excluding the general power of investment (s.7(2)). While this power will make little difference to modern, professionally drafted trusts, it makes an enormous difference to trusts arising on intestacy and to older or home-made trusts.

The Act does have important implications for all trustees even those acting under express investment clauses as it imposes additional duties.

Section 4(1) provides that when exercising any power of investment trustees must take into account the statutory investment criteria which are:

- the suitability to the trust of investments of the type proposed and of that particular investment as an investment of that type; and
- the need for diversification of investments of the trust, in so far as is appropriate to the circumstances of the trust.

Section 4(2) provides that trustees must review investments from time to time and consider whether they should change investments.

Unless the trustees reasonably conclude that it is unnecessary or inappropriate in all the circumstances to do so, they must obtain and consider proper advice before investing and when reviewing (s.5).

Gregson v. *HAE Trustees Ltd and Others* [2009] 1 All ER (Comm) 457 is one of the few cases to discuss the implications of s.4 for trustees. The court held that the duty to review is a separate and independent duty which applies both to property originally settled and to subsequent investments. The court accepted that when considering the need for diversification, trustees could properly take into account matters such as the nature and purposes of the settlement, directions in the settlement, letters of wishes and the effects of sales on shareholdings of family members.

Trustee Act 2000, s.8 gives power to acquire freehold or leasehold land in the United Kingdom. This can be for investment or residence by a beneficiary. It does not provide power to buy land abroad or an interest in land.

Trustee Act 2000, ss.11–27 authorise the appointment of agents, nominees and custodians subject to certain safeguards. Trustees will not be liable for the acts of their appointees unless they fail to exercise reasonable care and skill in the appointment or in keeping the arrangements for employment under review.

Section 14 provides that where trustees wish to delegate their asset management function, they must do so in writing and must prepare a policy statement giving guidance as to how the agent is to carry out its functions. The statement should deal with such matters as:

- attitude to risk;
- the balance to be maintained between income and capital;
- level of liquidity;
- attitude to capital gains (undesirable if the life tenant is very elderly and there is a possibility of tax-free uplift on death in the relatively near future);
- willingness to be exposed to foreign currency.

There is a helpful article on the relationship between trustees and investment managers by Robert Smeath in [2001] *Private Client Business*, Nov/Dec, 371 and one by Toby Harris outlining the main provisions in [2002] *New Law Journal*, Wills and Probate Supplement, 21 June, 945.

Administration of Estates Act 1925, s.19, as substituted by Trustee Act 2000, s.30, gives trustees a general power to insure any trust property against all risks and to pay the premiums out of income or capital.

Administration of Estates Act 1925, s.39 gives PRs all the powers of trustees of land (generally the powers of an absolute owner).

Administration of Estates Act 1925, s.41 gives power to appropriate assets.

Administration of Estates Act 1925, s.42 enables payment of a minor's gift to be made to a trust corporation or at least two trustees, if the minor is absolutely entitled. The section is less important since the Children Act 1989, which provides that all parents with parental responsibility have the same rights, powers and duties as guardians appointed under the Children Act. These rights are set out in s.3 and include the right to receive property in their own name for the benefit of the child.

Trustee Act 1925, s.31 gives power of maintenance in relation to income. Trustee Act 1925, s.32 gives power of advancement in relation to capital.

6.10.2 Exercise of powers

These powers are fiduciary. A sole, or sole surviving, executor or executrix may act alone in all cases. Where there is more than one executor or executrix, authority is joint for land (i.e. all must execute any deed) and joint and several for some personalty (i.e. just one may deliver an asset (e.g. jewellery) to a beneficiary and get a good receipt and discharge).

The Law of Property (Miscellaneous Provisions) Act 1994 covers aspects of sales of land by PRs, including the contract for sale: see **6.8.1** above.

6.10.3 Duties

The executors must safeguard the estate and, with due diligence:

- collect and realise the assets;

- pay the debts and legacies; and
- distribute the residue of the estate among the beneficiaries.

6.11 FOREIGN ASSETS AND DOMICILES

6.11.1 Foreign assets

Some clients may own property abroad because of a family connection; others because they have bought second homes or businesses. Potentially disastrous consequences can ensue if those clients are not fully advised about local laws regulating the inheritance of land and other property. In certain civil law jurisdictions, for example, children are automatically entitled to a fixed share of the estate regardless of any will to the contrary.

Solicitors need to be aware of the possibility both when preparing wills and when dealing with estates, and solicitors may need to refer clients to a solicitor in the United Kingdom with the necessary knowledge and experience or a local lawyer in the jurisdiction. The Law Society can help with the names of appropriately qualified lawyers (contact the International division, see **Appendix F** for address).

See discussion of negligence in relation to international clients at **14.3.10**.

6.11.2 Wills for clients with foreign assets

Sometimes an English will dealing with foreign property can put the testator's or testatrix's wishes into effect, but it is often helpful for the client to make a will in accordance with the requirements of the other jurisdiction to deal separately with those assets. Once a client has a foreign will, it is important to ensure that any new English or foreign will does not start with a standard revocation clause revoking all other wills.

It may be helpful to provide clients with a list of questions for lawyers in a foreign jurisdiction. For example, whether there are any fixed inheritance laws and whether the basis of ownership alters the way in which property passes.

6.11.3 Dealing with the estates of clients with foreign assets

If the deceased died domiciled in England and Wales, but with assets in another country, a foreign will may have been made. A lawyer of that country may have to be instructed. Usually it is necessary to extract the grant in England and Wales first and then send it accompanied by a sealed and certified copy of the will to a local practitioner. This does not apply in a country where the Colonial Probates Act 1892 applies, or in Scotland or Northern Ireland. There are many publications dealing with buying property abroad which often contain helpful sections on wills and probate.

6.11.4 Foreign domiciles

If the deceased died domiciled outside England and Wales, but left assets in England and Wales (unless the Colonial Probates Act 1892 applies, or the deceased was domiciled in Scotland or Northern Ireland) it will be necessary to obtain a grant in England and Wales: see the Non-Contentious Probate Rules (NCPR) 1987, SI 1987/2024, rule 30.

Questions of domicile arise with increasing frequency. Probate practitioners may be involved with the question of domicile either in relation to IPFDA 1975 (claims can be brought only if the deceased died domiciled in England and Wales) or in relation to liability to IHT. The following cases are useful: *Morgan* v. *Cilento* [2004] EWHC 188 (Ch); *Allen* v. *HMRC* [2005] WTLR 937; *Agulian and Another* v. *Cyganik* [2006] EWCA Civ 129; *Holliday* v. *Musa* [2010] EWCA Civ 335; *Mark* v. *Mark* [2005] UKHL 42.

6.12 LIFETIME GIFTS AND UNDUE INFLUENCE

Probate practitioners may find that after death, there are allegations that lifetime gifts made by the deceased are void on the basis of undue influence. There have been cases where virtually no assets remain to pass under the terms of the will. See, for example, *Special Trustees for Great Ormond Street Hospital for Children* v. *Rushin* [2001] WTLR 1137. Such allegations can be very distressing for all concerned and will inevitably prolong and complicate the administration of the estate. However, the law is relatively well established.

The decision of the House of Lords in *Royal Bank of Scotland* v. *Etridge* [2002] AC 773 made the following points:

1. There are two forms of unacceptable conduct which will cause the courts to find a transaction void for undue influence.
2. The first consists of overt acts of improper pressure or coercion such as unlawful threats.
3. The second arises from a relationship where one person has acquired a measure of influence or ascendancy over another a person of which the ascendant person takes advantage. There is an irrebuttable presumption that one person has influence over another in the case of certain relationships (parent/child, lawyer/client, doctor/patient). In other cases the complainant must prove that there was a relationship of trust and confidence.

Once such a relationship is proved, it is sufficient for the complainant to show that there was a transaction requiring an explanation. There is no need to prove that the transaction was the result of undue influence.

A presumption of undue influence arises and the court will infer that the transaction was the result of undue influence unless sufficient evidence is produced to show that this was not the case.

In *Hammond* v. *Osborn* [2002] EWCA Civ 885 the Court of Appeal emphasised that in cases of presumed undue influence the court intervenes not on the ground that any wrongful act has actually been committed by the donee but on grounds of public policy to prevent any abuse of the relationship of trust and confidence.

In *Niersmans* v. *Pesticcio* [2004] EWCA Civ 372 the Court of Appeal emphasised that the submission that the donee had 'done nothing wrong' was an instance of the 'continuing misconceptions' as to the law of presumed undue influence mentioned by Sir Martin Nourse in *Hammond* (above). The basis of the court's intervention is not the commission of a dishonest or wrongful act by the defendant, but that, as a matter of public policy, the presumed influence arising from the relationship of trust and confidence should not operate to the disadvantage of the victim, if the transaction is not satisfactorily explained by ordinary motives.

In *Aldridge* v. *Turner* [2004] EWHC 2768 (Ch) the court accepted the proposition that gifts of individually modest amounts could give rise to the presumption of undue influence when added together.

There were 62 transactions which depleted the deceased's resources by £25,000 at a time when his regular monthly income was less than £2,000. On the facts, some of the transactions were legitimate but others were wholly unauthorised or the result of undue influence. The defendant, the deceased's son, had to account to the estate for the unauthorised withdrawals and also for some loans made in the 1990s which he had never repaid.

See also: *Randall* v. *Randall* [2004] All ER (D) 570; *Macklin* v. *Dowsett* [2004] EWCA Civ 904; *Vale* v. *Armstrong* [2004] EWHC 1160 Ch; *Stevens* v. *Newey* [2005] EWCA Civ 50; *Watson* v. *Huber* [2005] All ER (D) 156; *Wright* v. *Hodgkinson* [2004] EWHC 3091; *Turkey* v. *Awadh and Another* [2005] EWCA Civ 382 and *Hughes* v. *Hughes* [2005] EWHC 469; *Gill* v. *Woodall* [2009] EWHC B34 (Ch).

6.13 ARTIST'S RESALE RIGHT REGULATIONS 2006

The Artist's Resale Right Regulations 2006, SI 2006/346, were made under European Communities Act 1972, s.2(2) and implement Directive 2001/84/EC of the European Parliament and Council. They came into force on 14 February 2006. Initially, the rights were not to apply to the estates of deceased artists until 1 January 2010. The Directive allowed Member States this option to enable the operators in that Member State to adapt gradually to the resale right system while maintaining their economic viability. Commencement was deferred in October 2009 by a further two years until 1 January 2012 by virtue of the Artist's Resale Right (Amendment) Regulations 2009, SI 2009/2792.

The regulations provide for a royalty to be paid to an artist:

- on any sale of 'any work of graphic or plastic art such as a picture, a collage, a painting, a drawing, an engraving, a print, a lithograph, a sculpture, a tapestry, a ceramic, an item of glassware or a photograph';

- during the copyright period (usually 70 years) that is subsequent to the artist's first disposal;
- where the price exceeds €1,000 (but this does not apply to any sale made less than three years after acquisition from the author where the price is less than €10,000);
- but only where the buyer or the seller, or (where the sale takes place through an agent) the agent of the buyer or the seller, is acting in the course of a business of dealing in works of art.

These regulations apply to all types of resale, both public and private sales, auctions and private treaty.

The seller is jointly and severally liable for the royalty with his agent, or if there is no seller's agent, the buyer's agent, or if there no buyer's agent then the buyer.

Schedule 1 sets out the percentage of the sale price payable as a royalty on each sale (the price used is net of any sales tax, but not commission and the euro conversion rate will be at a reference rate set by the European Central Bank). There is a maximum on any single sale of €12,500.

Sale price	Royalty on each sale
€0–50,000	4%
€50,001–€200,000	3%
€200,001–€350,000	1%
€350,001–€500,000	0.5%
over €500,000	0.25%

This right is capable of passing on death as personal or moveable property to a natural person or charity (reg.9).

Where an author died before the introduction of the regulations and would have been a qualifying person, the regulations provide for the author's royalty under these regulations to be inherited by:

1. the person inheriting the copyright from the author if he or she owned it;
2. the person inheriting the work if the author owned the work but not the copyright to it;
3. otherwise, the person(s) inheriting the personal estate.

Management and collection of the royalty will be through a mutual collecting society. There are two ways in which PRs may be affected by the regulations:

1. An outstanding liability for the royalty is a debt which will reduce the IHT value of a seller's estate.
2 An artist's right to royalties under these regulations will be an asset of his or her estate and will need to be investigated and valued.

6.14 STATUTORY ORDER FOR PAYMENT OF DEBTS

6.14.1 Solvent estates

Where an estate is solvent, all the creditors will be paid but some beneficiaries will have their share of the assets reduced. Administration of Estates Act 1925, s.34 and Sched.1, Part II set out the order in which legacies are reduced to provide assets to pay debts (residue, retained pecuniary legacy fund, specific gifts). Where there are insufficient funds to pay all the pecuniary legacies in full, they abate proportionally unless the will provides otherwise.

Personal representatives who choose to distribute assets before paying all the debts should follow the statutory order. Paying pecuniary legacies too early may mean that there are insufficient assets to meet the debts without recourse to items specifically given. Personal representatives would then be personally liable to the disappointed beneficiaries. (See *Mitchell and Others* v. *Halliwell and Others* [2005] EWHC 937 (Ch).) See a helpful article by Hugh Jones and Lauren Killilea ('Insolvent estates: safety first') in *Trusts and Estates Law & Tax Journal* (2006) March.

6.14.2 Insolvent estates

An estate is insolvent if, when realised, it will be insufficient to meet in full all its debts and other liabilities. No beneficiaries will receive anything and some creditors will not be paid in full.

The relevant statutory instrument is the Administration of Insolvent Estates of Deceased Persons Order 1986, SI 1986/1999, as amended by Administration of Insolvent Estates of Deceased Persons (Amendment) Order 2002, SI 2002/1309.

An insolvent estate can be administered under the directions of the court (CPR Part 50) but this is rare. It will normally be done by the deceased's PRs out of court following the relevant regulations or in bankruptcy following an insolvency administration order made by the bankruptcy court. Whichever option is adopted, the priority for payment of debts is the same: funeral and testamentary expenses first, followed by the bankruptcy order. Personal representatives will be personally liable if they pay an inferior debt before a superior one and there are insufficient funds for the superior one.

If the PRs or creditors decide that a trustee in bankruptcy is required, perhaps to set aside voidable lifetime transactions, they can apply at any stage for an administration order to be made. The form of the petition is set out in Sched.3 to the Administration of Insolvent Estates of Deceased Persons Order 1986, SI 1986/1999.

An insolvency administration order can be made at any time during the administration of the estate. If such an order is made, any disposition made by the personal representatives in the period between death and the vesting of the estate in the trustee in bankruptcy is void, unless made with the consent of the court or subsequently ratified by the court. This means that a solicitor who has charged for acting may have to repay sums received. The court will only ratify payments made for the benefit of the estate at a time when there was no reason to suppose that the estate was insolvent. See *Dick* v. *Kendall Freeman* [2005] WTLR 1619.

CHAPTER 7

Revocation and revival of wills

Alexander Learmonth

7.1 INTRODUCTION

A will may appear duly executed on its face, and indeed be duly executed. The testator may have had the necessary mental capacity to make a will, have known and approved its contents, and have done so free from any undue influence or mistake. (See **12.3** below.) Yet the will may not be eligible for a grant of probate, because it has been revoked since its execution. Conversely, a will that has been revoked may be revived and 'revalidated', so that it may again be eligible to be admitted to probate.

There are four ways to revoke a will. Three of them can only be done deliberately, with the necessary intention to revoke the will, but one can, and often does, happen without the testator realising that his will has been revoked. They are as follows:

- revocation by deed or subsequent will;
- revocation by destruction;
- revocation by obliteration or alteration (usually only partial);
- revocation by marriage or civil partnership.

In addition, certain dispositions in a will are partially revoked by divorce or annulment, or the dissolution of a civil partnership.

7.2 REVOCATION BY DEED OR SUBSEQUENT WILL

7.2.1 No automatic revocation by subsequent consistent will

By far the most common form of revocation is the execution of a subsequent will. But it is important to remember that this is not automatic. One testator may have several wills. In the absence of a revocation clause, a will only revokes a previous will in so far as it is inconsistent with it. Provisions of more than one will that can be read consistently with each other will all take effect. Thus, if the first will leaves £10,000 to A and the residue to B, and a later will leaves £10,000 to C and the residue to D, it is possible that both A and C will receive £10,000, even if that leaves nothing for D. In cases such as this, however, extrinsic evidence of the testator's intention will usually be admissible to resolve any ambiguity as to whether he intended the earlier will to be completely revoked.

7.2.2 Standard revocation clauses

That is why it is usual practice to insert a revocation clause at the beginning of every will. However, this ought not to be done automatically or unthinkingly, and its presence and effect should expressly be brought to the testator's attention during the reading over. A testator may have other wills dealing with particular assets (such as assets related to his or her business) or property in a particular location (such as a holiday home abroad), which he may not wish revoked. It is important to check that a testator understands that a general revocation clause will affect wills made abroad.

Where a revocation clause has been introduced by mistake, without the testator's knowledge and approval, 'it has over and over again been laid down that probate of a paper may be granted of a date prior to a will with a revocatory clause, provided the court is satisfied that it was not the deceased's intention to revoke that particular legacy or benefit' (*Gladstone* v. *Tempest and Others* (1840) ER 989). This happened in *Re Wayland* [1951] 2 All ER 1041, where a testator made a Belgian will dealing with his Belgian property and later that day an English will dealing with his English property, even though the latter contained a general revocation clause.

7.2.3 Revocation by written instrument

A will may also be revoked by deed. However, the formalities for the deed are the same as for a will, so it must be executed in the presence of two witnesses, who must both sign the will (save in the case of a privileged testator).

7.3 REVOCATION BY DESTRUCTION

Section 20 of the Wills Act 1837 provides that a will may be revoked by the testator burning, tearing, or otherwise destroying his will, or by someone else doing it at the testator's direction and in his presence, with the intention of revoking it. Thus a solicitor cannot revoke a testator's will for him by destroying the original on instructions over the telephone; the testator must be present. Crossing out the will does not amount to destruction, but it is likely that erasing the writing (e.g. if in pencil) will.

7.3.1 Intention to revoke – *animus revocandi*

The testator must intend the revocation, so that accidental destruction will not revoke the will. Nonetheless, it would be sensible to re-execute an accidentally destroyed or damaged will. The intention to revoke can be proved by what the testator says at the time, by inference from what he actually does to the will, or by inference from the circumstances (*Clarke* v. *Scripps* (1852) 163 ER 1414; 2 Rob Ecc 563). If a will that has been in the testator's possession is found torn up, it is rebuttably presumed that it was so torn by the testator with the intention of revoking it.

7.3.2 Partial destruction

The will does not need to be completely destroyed. Partial destruction may also effect a revocation. Any act of tearing, burning or other destruction, such as tearing the will partly in half, will revoke the will if the testator intends by so doing to revoke the will. But a mere symbolic gesture of tearing is not enough – some damage must actually be caused – nor will an interrupted act of destruction, if the testator intended to do more to complete the revocation. Thus, if a partially destroyed will is found after the testator's death, the burden of proof is on the person contending that the will has been revoked to show that revocation was intended.

7.3.3 Mental capacity

It follows that a testator must have testamentary capacity in order to revoke a will; the test is the same as that required to make a will in the first place: *Re Sabatini* (1969) 114 SJ 35. But under the Mental Capacity Act 2005, the court will always assume mental capacity unless grounds for doubting it is shown, and so the burden of proof is on the person who contends that the testator was of unsound mind at the time of the destruction. Someone who is so drunk as not to be responsible for his actions cannot revoke his will by destroying it. For testamentary capacity and the effect of the Mental Capacity Act 2005, see **6.1.3** above.

7.3.4 Copies of wills

Destruction of a copy of a will does not suffice to revoke the original. But destruction of one of two original duplicate wills, both properly executed, can suffice to revoke the will if done with the requisite intention. It is also possible to revoke only certain provisions of a will by carefully destroying that part.

7.3.5 Missing wills and the presumption of destruction

A will that can be traced into the testator's possession, which then cannot be found after searching following the testator's death, is presumed to have been destroyed by the testator with the intention of revoking it. This presumption therefore does not apply where a will is lost that was never in the testator's keeping. Nor will this presumption operate where the first search of the testator's safe or other repository was carried out by those who stand to gain from its destruction. Some recent cases on this are *Rowe* v. *Clarke* [2006] WTLR 347; *Nicholls* v. *Hudson* [2007] WTLR 341 and *Wren* v. *Wren* [2007] WTLR 531.

Evidence is admissible to rebut the presumption that a missing will has been revoked, including things said by the testator close to the time of his death. But a court should be sceptical about the declarations of a testator: 'Few declarations deserve less credit than those of men as to what they have done by their wills' (*Pemberton* v. *Pemberton* (1807) 13 Ves 290). Indeed, in each of the three recent cases mentioned above, the presumption was rebutted on the facts. In cases where the court is not able to conclude that a missing will was destroyed by the testator with the requisite *animus revocandi*, a copy of the missing will may be admitted to probate.

As these cases show, the problem with revocation by destruction is that it leaves no written record of it having taken place, and can create uncertainty as to whether the destruction was effective to revoke the will. For that reason, testators who wish to revoke a will without executing a new one should be advised to do so by a duly executed instrument. Practitioners supervising a destruction should of course make a careful attendance note.

7.4 REVOCATION BY OBLITERATION OR ALTERATION

Another mode of revocation or partial revocation that is not recommended for general use is obliteration.

7.4.1 Later additions and amendments invalid

Attempting to amend a will after its execution by inserting words, crossing them out or a combination of both will not be effective. Similarly, additional unexecuted sheets that are inserted between the pages of an executed will or attached to it will not be admitted to probate (although the court will normally presume that all the sheets of a will which is executed on its last page were together at the time of execution, in the absence of evidence to the contrary). Such amendments must themselves be executed in the margin of the page near the relevant amendment.

The other way of giving effect to subsequent amendments of this type is to execute a codicil confirming the will; it is then confirmed in the state it was at the date of the codicil.

The exception to these rules is where an obliteration of the original words of the will is so complete that the original words are no longer 'apparent', in the sense that they cannot be read. If so, then those words will be treated as having been revoked even though the obliteration has not been subsequently executed. In determining whether the original words are 'apparent', the test is whether they can be read using a magnifying glass by, if need be, an expert. But the use of special techniques such as chemicals or infra-red photography is not permitted.

7.4.2 Additions made before execution

Amendments, additions, obliterations, etc. to a will that are made before its execution are in principle valid, regardless of whether they are separately executed. But it is nonetheless important to avoid making such amendments wherever possible. This is because a court will presume, in the absence of evidence to the contrary, that amendments to a will that have not been separately executed were added *after* the original execution of the will. and are therefore invalid. They will not be admitted to probate unless there is evidence (such as an attendance note or the evidence of an attesting witness) to establish that they were added before execution. It is therefore far preferable to use a clean copy of the will for execution, rather than making manuscript amendments to save time, except in cases of great urgency.

7.5 REVOCATION BY MARRIAGE OR CIVIL PARTNERSHIP

A will is completely revoked by the subsequent marriage or civil partnership of the testator (Wills Act 1837, s.18(1)). This is so even if the will in question made express provision for the intended spouse or civil partner. Many testators do not realise this, and so it is all too easy for a testator inadvertently to put his or her new spouse or civil partner in a worse position than they were before, particularly now that it is common for couples to live together and have children before marrying or becoming civil partners.

7.5.1 Wills made in expectation of marriage or civil partnership

There are only two exceptions to this rule. Both arise where the will itself states that it is made in contemplation of marriage or civil partnership. The first is where it appears from the will both that the testator is expecting to be married to, or to enter a civil partnership with, a specific person, and that the testator intends that the will should not be revoked by that subsequent marriage or civil partnership (Wills Act 1837, s.18(3)). The second is a modified version of this rule relating to particular dispositions: the will must show that testator expects to marry or enter a civil partnership with a particular person, and that he intends a particular disposition to survive the marriage or civil partnership (s.18(4)). If that is the case, that disposition will not be revoked by the subsequent marriage or civil partnership, nor will any other dispositions unless the will shows that the testator intended them to be revoked by it.

The recent case of *Re Ikin; Court* v. *Despallieres* [2009] EWHC 3340 (Ch) emphasised that the provisions require there to be a specific marriage or civil partnership in mind. It is not enough simply to direct that a subsequent civil partnership or marriage should not revoke the will.

The best course is therefore to ensure that a will made prior to marriage or civil partnership is subsequently confirmed by codicil, so as to revive it (see below).

7.5.2 Marriage or civil partnership does not revoke the execution of powers of appointment

It is also to be noted that the revocation of a will by marriage only affects dispositions of property owned by the deceased. The exercise in a will of any power of appointment over settled property is not revoked by marriage, and the will therefore survives to that extent (Wills Act 1837, s.18(2)).

7.6 PARTIAL REVOCATION BY DIVORCE, DISSOLUTION OR ANNULMENT

Since 1982, certain rules apply where a testator's marriage or civil partnership was dissolved or annulled after the execution of a will. In that case, any provision in that will relating to the former spouse or civil partner (whether as to the appointment of the spouse or civil partner as executor, or as a beneficiary) will take effect as if the spouse or civil partner had died on the day of the divorce, annulment or dissolution. Deeming the former spouse or civil partner to have predeceased the testator in this way has the advantage over simply invalidating the disposition in that an interest in remainder or gift over on death can take effect immediately, rather than the property in question being undisposed of during the life of the spouse or civil partner (as where a testator leaves property to his wife during her life and thereafter to his children).

7.7 CONDITIONAL REVOCATION

A revocation by any of the three deliberate means mentioned above may be conditional. Whether it is conditional or not will depend upon the testator's intention: 'was his intention absolute or qualified, so as to be contingent or conditional? If it was absolute, that is the end of the investigation, for the act take effect as a revocation. If however it was qualified, the further question that arises is, what was the nature of the qualification?' (*Re Jones* [1976] Ch 200).

A qualification of this sort may arise out of a misapprehension by the testator as to the effect of the revocation. One common case is where the testator erroneously believes that by revoking his last will, his previous will is revived. Other examples are where the testator proceeds in a false assumption as to the effect of intestacy, or destroys a will he wrongly believes to be invalid. As set out below, that is not the case. If the revocation was, on a true interpretation, based on such a belief, then it will not take effect.

Another case of conditional revocation is where a testator destroys his last will in preparation for making a new one, which for some reason is then not validly executed. If the revocation can be shown to have been conditional upon the new will taking effect, the earlier will survives the purported revocation.

In all these cases, the court must be satisfied that the testator would want the earlier will to continue in those circumstances. However, the court will generally approach such cases with the presumption that a testator does not intend to be intestate.

7.8 REVIVAL OF WILLS

A will that has been revoked may be 'revived' by re-executing it, or by executing a codicil that confirms the revoked will (Wills Act 1837, s.22). But simply revoking the instrument that itself revoked an earlier will does not restore the earlier will.

7.8.1 Intention to revive

The intention to revive the will must be stated with sufficient certainty. But it is not necessary to identify the will to be revived by date, provided the court can be clear which will is intended. As with other questions of construction, where it is ambiguous whether a codicil confirms an earlier will, extrinsic evidence of the testator's intention is admissible.

It would, of course, be unusual for a codicil to a later will to be intended to revive an earlier will that has been revoked. The court is therefore cautious about reading a mere reference to a will be date (which may be given in error) as indicating an intention to revive.

7.8.2 Effect of revival

Reviving a will has the same effect as if the will were executed afresh on that date. Problems may arise however when the will being revived had codicils to it. Do the codicils revive even though they are not expressly referred to by the reviving instrument? It is in every case a question of the testator's intention, and in general merely referring to the original revoked will does not suffice to revive a revoked codicil to that will.

Where a will or codicil has first been partly revoked (for example by obliteration), but then wholly revoked (for example by written instrument), a subsequent revival will not re-establish the whole will, but only the parts of the will that remained unrevoked after the first, partial revocation (Wills Act 1837, s.22).

7.8.3 A note on 'republication'

One sometimes hears of the 'republication' of wills, particularly in early cases. This term was used prior to the Wills Act 1837, when a will would only dispose of real property owned by the testator at the date of execution. Republication was therefore a means of including after-acquired property. Now that wills are treated as disposing of all property owned at the date of death, this term is no longer appropriate: *Berkeley* v. *Berkeley* [1946] AC 555.

7.9 FURTHER READING

The reader is referred to Bridge, Martyn and Oldham, *Theobold on Wills*, 17th edn (Sweet & Maxwell 2010), Chapter 8 and Caddick and Martyn, *Williams, Mortimer and Sunnocks*, 19th edn (Sweet & Maxwell, 2007), Chapter 14 for a more detailed treatment of this subject (see **Appendix E**).

CHAPTER 8

Time for probate

Gillian E. Cockburn

Time limits are of crucial importance in probate and estate planning. This chapter considers, in brief, some of the more important time limits that practitioners should bear in mind during the administration of an estate.

8.1 OBTAINING THE GRANT

In general, a grant of probate will not issue from the probate registry within seven days of the date of death and a grant of letters of administration will not issue within 14 days of the date of death. In exceptional cases, a district judge or probate registrar may give leave for the grant to issue earlier but the applicant will first have to explain the need for expedition by way of a letter accompanying the application (Non-Contentious Probate Rules (NCPR) 1987, SI 1987/2024, rule 6(2)).

8.1.1 Caveats

If a caveat is entered to prevent a grant of representation being issued in an estate it should be remembered that the caveat will only remain in force for a period of six months from the date of entry (NCPR 1987, rule 44(3)(a)–(c)). It may be extended for further periods of six months but each application for extension must be made in the last month prior to the expiry of the caveat.

8.2 RECTIFICATION OF THE WILL

It is possible to correct errors in wills of testators dying on or after 1 January 1983 provided that the court is satisfied that the will fails to express the testator's intentions as a result of either a clerical error or a failure by the drafter to understand the testator's intentions (Administration of Justice Act 1982, s.20). An application for rectification of a will must be made within six months of the date that representation to the estate is first taken out.

The court does have power to consider applications outside the six-month period but the applicant has to show that there was a good reason why the application was not made within the time limit. See, for example, *Chittock* v. *Stevens* [2000] All ER

(D) 239. If there is a possibility of rectification the PRs should not distribute the estate within the six-month period referred to above. See Administration of Justice Act 1982 regarding distributions once the six-month period has expired.

8.3 FAMILY PROVISION CLAIMS

Certain individuals have the right to apply for financial provision from the estate of a person who dies domiciled in England and Wales (Inheritance (Provision for Family and Dependants) Act (IPFDA) 1975, s.1). See also **Chapter 11**.

A claim must be made within six months of the date that representation to the estate is first taken out (IPFDA 1975, s.4). If there is a possibility of a claim the PRs should not distribute the estate within this period (see IPFDA 1975, s.20 on distributions). The court has power to allow a claim to be made outside the six-month period. The basis for the court exercising its discretion was set out by Megarry V-C in *Re Salmon (Deceased)* [1981] Ch 167, where he identified six guidelines. Examples of cases in which the court has exercised its discretion are *Re Hancock (Deceased)* [1998] 2 FLR 346 and *McNulty* v. *McNulty* [2002] WTLR 737 in which assets of the estate had increased substantially in value. Note that the court can only use its power under s.9 to make an order against the deceased's share of property held as beneficial joint tenants if the application is made within the six-month period. There is no power to extend the time limit.

Civil partners also have the right to apply for financial provision under the Civil Partnership Act 2004.

8.4 INTEREST AND LEGACIES

Personal representatives must administer the estate properly and should not unduly delay the payment of legacies (see also **Chapter 17**). Personal representatives who delay payment without good reason may find themselves personally liable to pay interest to aggrieved beneficiaries. In certain cases, legatees have the right to interest at the basic rate payable for funds in court, at present 0.3 per cent per annum (CPR Practice Direction 40, para.15) on their legacies, if they are paid late, as follows:

- General pecuniary legacies should be paid within one year ('the executors' year') from the date of death. Where they are paid outside that period they must carry interest calculated from the first anniversary of the death (when the right to receive the legacy arose). Any interest paid will come from the residue of the estate (from monies which might otherwise have passed to the residuary beneficiaries).
- Specific legacies do not carry the right to interest but they do carry any income arising from the gift, subject to the wording of the will.

- Immediate legacies will carry interest from the date of death if it is clear from the will that the testator or testatrix intended that the payment should be made immediately on death. Legacies (whether immediate or contingent) providing for the maintenance of the testator's or the testatrix's children will also carry interest from the date of death.
- Future or contingent legacies will in general carry interest from the date the future event or contingency occurs.
- Residuary gifts do not carry interest in accordance with these provisions. However, residuary beneficiaries are entitled to a share in any income the estate generates after payment of estate liabilities and legacies.

8.5 ADVERTISING FOR CREDITORS

Personal representatives should consider advertising for creditors and potential beneficiaries before starting to distribute the estate (Trustee Act 1925, s.27). The point during the administration at which the advertisement is inserted will depend on a number of factors, varying with each estate. The advertisement gives notice of the PRs' intention to distribute to those who may have claims against the estate. A suitably worded advertisement should be inserted in the *London Gazette* and in a newspaper circulating in any area where the deceased owned land. In addition, the PRs should also consider advertising elsewhere if there are any special factors affecting the estate. The advertisements must give claimants at least two months to notify the PRs of their claim. After the advertisements have been inserted, and assuming that no claimants have come forward in the two-month period, the PRs may distribute the estate with reference only to claims known to them at the time of distribution.

8.6 INTESTACY

Under s.1 of the Law Reform (Succession) Act 1995 and with effect from 1 January 1996, a spouse must survive for 28 days before becoming entitled under the intestacy laws.

The surviving spouse also has the following rights, both of which should be exercised within 12 months of the date that representation to the estate is first taken out:

- to redeem the life interest and instead receive a capital sum (Administration of Estates Act 1925, s.47A, as amended by Administration of Justice Act 1977); and/or
- to have the deceased's interest in the matrimonial home appropriated as part of the surviving spouse's interest in the estate (Intestates' Estates Act 1952, Sched.2).

A partner in a civil partnership has the same rights as a surviving spouse under an intestacy (Civil Partnership Act 2004, Sched.4, paras.7–12, which amend the Administration of Estates Act 1925).

It should be noted that statutory legacy payable to spouses and civil partners payable under the intestacy rules increased for deaths on or after 1 February 2009.

8.7 INHERITANCE TAX

8.7.1 Payment of tax

The due date for payment of inheritance tax (IHT) on death is six months after the end of the month in which the death occurs (Inheritance Tax Act (IHTA) 1984, s.226). Late payment will result in interest charges under ss.233 and 234. However, when the application for the grant of representation is made, any IHT payable on the non-instalment option assets (e.g. money, chattels, quoted shares, etc.), must be paid at that time even if prior to the due date.

IHT on instalment option assets (as set out in IHTA 1984, s.227, i.e. land including agricultural property or shares or other property qualifying for business property relief) may be paid by 10 equal yearly instalments if the personal representatives so elect. If this election is made, the first instalment is due six months after the end of the month in which the death took place and the remaining nine instalments on successive anniversaries of that six-month date. The election is usually made within the account sent to HM Revenue and Customs (HMRC) but it may also be made separately at a later date. In practice there does not appear to be any specific time limit within which this election should be made.

8.7.2 Delivery of accounts

An account must be delivered to HMRC within 12 months of the end of the month in which the death occurs or, if later, three months from the date the personal representatives first act (IHTA 1984, s.216). Regulations may be made under s.256 dispensing with this requirement in certain cases (e.g. excepted estates). Failure to deliver an account within the time limit may render the PRs liable to financial penalties (IHTA 1984, ss.245 and 245A, as amended by Finance Act 1999, s.108).

Although not yet in force in relation to the payment of IHT, Finance Act 2009, Sched.56 imposes new penalties for paying IHT late. The schedule has at the time of writing only been brought into force in relation to income tax.

8.7.3 Reliefs and exemptions

If an estate includes a holding of qualifying investments (usually quoted shares) which are sold within 12 months of the date of death for less than the probate value, the PRs, or other person liable for the tax, may apply to have the lower sale price substituted for the probate value (IHTA 1984, ss.178 and 179). In addition if land or an interest in land is sold within four years of the date of death for less than the probate value, the PRs, or other person liable for the tax, may be able to substitute the lower sale price for the probate value (IHTA 1984, ss.190 and 191). Note in both cases the claims have to be brought within four years from the dates referred to in IHTA 1984, ss.179(1)(a) and 191(1)(a) (Finance Act 2009, Sched.51, para.9). The moral is: if you wish to make a claim do so as soon as possible.

From October 2007 the transferable nil rate band was introduced allowing the use of any unused portion of a late spouse's or civil partner's nil rate band. It is important to note that the relief must be claimed within 24 months of the end of the month in which the second spouse or civil partner dies.

8.7.4 Variations and disclaimers

It is possible to vary the terms of a will or the provisions applicable to an estate under the intestacy laws so that the varied provisions take effect (for IHT and/or capital gains tax (CGT) purposes) as if those provisions had been included in the deceased's last will (IHTA 1984, s.142 and Taxation of Chargeable Gains Act (TCGA) 1992, s.62(6)–(7), as amended by Finance Act 2002). A variation must be made in writing by the people who would otherwise benefit from the varied assets within a period of two years from the date of the death. For instruments made on or after 1 August 2002, formal elections to the Board of the Inland Revenue are no longer necessary. Instead of elections, a statement must be contained within the instrument made by all the relevant parties that they intend IHTA 1984, s.142(1), and TCGA 1992, s.62(6) to apply to the variation. If more tax is payable as a result of the variation then a copy of the deed must be delivered to HMRC within six months of the date of the deed informing them of the additional tax to be paid and the personal representatives must join in the deed.

A disclaimer of an interest under a will or under the intestacy laws must also be made in writing and within two years of the date of death. No elections are necessary for the disclaimer to be treated as though made by the deceased for IHT or CGT purposes.

8.7.5 Property settled by will

Capital distributions or appointments from a discretionary will trust (i.e. from a settlement and before any interest in possession arises) within two years of the date of death (or any shorter period stated in the will) will be treated as having been made under the deceased's will and taking place at the date of death (IHTA 1984, s.144). This provision only applies if the capital distribution or appointment is an event which would otherwise have been chargeable to IHT. Thus a capital distribution or appointment from the property to a beneficiary absolutely within the first three months after death will not qualify for reading back (IHTA 1984, s.65(4)).This can mean that the estate fails to benefit from the expected spouse exemption as in

Frankland v. *IRC* [1997] STC 1450, where trustees appointed property to the surviving spouse five days before the end of the three-month period and giving rise to an unwanted IHT bill of £2 million.

The section was amended by Finance Act 2006 to allow reading back where appointments create immediate post-death interests, trusts for bereaved minors or trusts for bereaved young people. In these cases because of the wording of the section there is reading back where the appointment is made within the first three months after death.

8.7.6 Quick succession relief

If the deceased's estate was increased by a chargeable transfer within five years of the date of death then quick succession relief will be available to reduce the IHT payable on the death (IHTA 1984, s.141). The reduction is a percentage of part of the IHT paid on the earlier transfer. The percentage applicable will depend upon the period between the transfer and the date of death.

8.7.7 Overpayments of tax

Claims for repayment of overpaid IHT (including interest) must be made within six years of the payment of the tax (IHTA 1984, s.241). However, if too much tax was paid as a result of a mistake by HMRC then a repayment can be claimed within 20 years.

8.7.8 Underpaid tax

HMRC will not bring any proceedings for underpaid tax once a period of four years has expired from the later of:

- the date when the payment of tax or the last instalment was made and accepted; and
- the due date for payment of the tax or last instalment (IHTA 1984, s.240, as amended by Finance Act 2009, Sched.51, para.11).

The period is extended to six years where the loss of tax is brought about carelessly by a person responsible for the tax. Careless behaviour is defined in IHTA 1984, s.240A.

In cases of deliberate behaviour the HMRC can go back 20 years from the end of the relevant period.

8.7.9 Events prior to death

There are a number of important time limits for probate practitioners in relation to pre-death events. For instance, chargeable transfers and potentially exempt transfers made within a period of up to seven years before death must be taken into account by the PRs in the calculation of the IHT due on the transferor's estate at death (IHTA 1984, ss.7 and 3A).

Gifts with reservation may also have to be taken into account when calculating the IHT due on death if the gifts are either still subject to the reserved interest at the date of death or alternatively the reservation was released within seven years before the date of death (Finance Act 1986, s.102 and Sched.20).

There may also be a liability to IHT payable by the transferees of these different types of lifetime transfers following the death of the transferor within the seven-year period. Any additional IHT payable by a transferee as a result of the death will be due for payment six months from the end of the month in which the death occurs, but payment by instalments may be available in certain cases (IHTA 1984, s.226).

However, if the transferee does not pay within 12 months of the end of the month in which the death occurs HMRC may look to the PRs for payment of the tax (IHTA 1984, ss.200, 204; see also **Chapter 16** on PRs and IHT). It is important, therefore, for the PRs to make full enquiries to discover any lifetime transfers. If any are discovered, the estate should not be fully distributed until the tax due on these transfers has been settled and an appropriate certificate of clearance issued by the Capital Taxes Office.

8.8 CAPITAL GAINS TAX

Personal representatives are entitled to the individual's annual CGT exemption for the tax year of death and the following two tax years (TCGA 1992, s.3(7)). After that time an annual CGT allowance will not be available unless the PRs qualify in another capacity, e.g. as trustees. It should be noted that under the self-assessment regime the due date for payment of CGT is 31 January following the end of the tax year in which the gain was made.

8.9 INCOME TAX

8.9.1 Appeals

An appeal against an income tax (or CGT) assessment or an appeal against an amendment to a self-assessment must be made in writing and lodged within 30 days of the issue of the assessment or notice of amendment (Taxes Management Act (TMA) 1970, s.31A). *Inland Revenue* v. *Wilkinson* [1992] STC 454 demonstrates the importance of making a formal appeal against tax assessments. An application for postponement of payment of some or all of the tax assessed may be made at that time. HMRC may allow appeals to be made outside the 30-day period but it is under no obligation to do so.

8.9.2 Returns

During the course of the administration it may be necessary to submit income tax returns. In order to avoid the possibility of automatic penalties and surcharges (see **8.9.3** below) always make enquiries of HMRC about the deceased's income tax affairs and do so as soon after the death as possible. To avoid interest and penalties under the self-assessment regime completed returns must be submitted to HMRC by 30 September following the end of the tax year (if the taxpayer wishes HMRC to calculate the tax due). If taxpayers calculate the tax themselves then the return should be submitted to HMRC by 31 January following the end of the tax year (or if the return is issued after the end of October, then within three months of the date of service of the return). Taxpayers who do not submit self-assessment returns by the due date will be subject to an automatic penalty of £100 (TMA 1970, s.93, as amended by later Finance Acts). A further penalty of £100 will be charged if the return is still outstanding after a further six months. In cases of more serious delay other penalties will be charged. It should be noted that, in general, a self-assessment return is not considered to have been submitted unless it is complete. Thus 'to be advised' figures are not acceptable (although best estimates may be).

8.9.3 Payment of tax

Under the self-assessment regime, tax must be paid in full by 31 January following the end of the tax year. In addition, payments on account in two equal instalments for the current tax year may be required to be paid by 31 January in the tax year and the following 31 July. A balancing payment may then be required on the following 31 January. Interest will be charged on overdue tax plus a 5 per cent surcharge if the balancing payment is outstanding more than 28 days after the due date (TMA 1970, s.59C, as amended by later Finance Acts). A further 5 per cent surcharge may be payable if the tax is still unpaid more than six months after the due date.

8.9.4 Changes to time limits for assessments and claims

With effect from 1 April 2010 there has been introduced a normal four-year time limit for assessments and claims (Finance Act 2009, Sched.39). This affects claims for repayment under self-assessment as well capital gains tax and other elections. This would include important elections such as for capital gains tax hold over relief. So beware and make all claims and elections promptly!

8.10 PREVENTING PROBLEMS

Missing just one time limit could prove to be an expensive error involving an application for extension of the normal time limit, interest charges, and even a claim for damages. It may also spoil a good solicitor–client relationship.

How can a practice guard against missing an important time limit? It is clear that there are too many time limits for it to be safe to rely on memory alone. The use of a central diary (whether handwritten or on computer) operated by a responsible member of the practice may be of considerable benefit. Most practices will now have computerised systems and so notices of time limits are likely to be automatically generated with appropriate warnings as the time limits approach. Fee earners would need to provide the diary keeper with a list of their important dates, perhaps by completing a pro forma list or enter the dates direct on the computer system. If a fee earner was unexpectedly absent, important dates would not be missed as the computer system or diary keeper would be able to bring the date to the attention of another member of the practice. Used in this (or a similar) way, a central diary system could prove to be invaluable in the running of an efficient and trouble-free probate practice.

CHAPTER 9

Appointing guardians of children

Gillian E. Cockburn and David Hodson

9.1 INTRODUCTION

A guardian of a child is someone who is appointed to take over responsibility for a child in the event of the death of the child's parent or other carer. The appointment is necessary not only if a child has property or money but also to provide day-to-day care for the child, as the guardian will have the right to decide on the child's upbringing, healthcare, religion and education. It is very important to ensure that the right person or persons are appointed as guardians in accordance with the law. It is unrelated to the appointment of guardians who look after children in public law care proceedings.

The law on the appointment of guardians changed radically as a result of the Children Act 1989 (CA 1989) which came into effect from 14 October 1991. It is essential for the will drafter and probate practitioner to understand the main elements of CA 1989 and in particular the concepts of parental responsibility and residence orders. In some cases it may also be important to liaise with a family law practitioner to find out what court orders have been made concerning a child which may in turn affect the appointment of guardians under the will.

9.2 WHO MAY APPOINT A GUARDIAN?

This is governed by CA 1989, s.5, which provides that guardians may be appointed by:

1. a parent with parental responsibility for the child (CA 1989, s.5(3)); or
2. an existing guardian of the child (CA 1989, s.5(4)); or
3. a court order in family proceedings (CA 1989, s.5(1) and (2)).

Except as set out below, the appointments in (1) and (2) become effective when the person who makes the appointment dies. At that time, the guardian will acquire parental responsibility for the child.

9.2.1 Parental responsibility

The Children Act 1989 defines parental responsibility for a child as all the rights, duties, powers, responsibilities and authority which by law a parent of a child has in relation to that child and the child's property (CA 1989, s.3(1)).

9.2.2 Who has parental responsibility?

If the child's parents are married at the time of birth (or the child has been legitimated or is adopted), the parents (or adopting parents) will each have parental responsibility (CA 1989, s.2(1) and (3)) and both may appoint guardians for the child in the event of their respective deaths (CA 1989, s.5(3)).

If:

- the parents of a child were not married to each other at the time of the birth; and
- the child has not been legitimated by the parents' later marriage or adopted; and
- the father's name is not registered on the birth certificate,

the mother alone has parental responsibility for that child (CA 1989, s.2(2) and (3)). The father does not have automatic parental responsibility and so will not be able to appoint a guardian of the child on his death. However, the father may *acquire* parental responsibility (and therefore be able to appoint a guardian) in the following ways:

- through a court order granting him parental responsibility (CA 1989, s.4(1)(c)); or
- by entering into a parental responsibility agreement with the child's mother (CA 1989, s.4(1)(b)); or
- by being appointed, either by the mother or by the court, to assume parental responsibility after the mother's death; or
- by becoming registered as the child's father primarily on the birth certificate (CA 1989, s.4(1)(a)), provided that the child was born after 1 December 2003 (if the child was born before that date, the father will not acquire parental responsibility through this method unless the birth was re-registered after that date with the father's name then appearing).

The parental responsibility agreement must be in accordance with the Parental Responsibility Agreement Regulations 1991, SI 1991/1478, reg.2, as amended. The agreement must contain the names of the child's parents and of the child to whom the agreement is to relate, and must contain the signature of both parents and be witnessed. It must provide for only one child, not more than one. Both parents must have their signature witnessed at court by a JP or court official and provide evidence of their identity (including a photograph and signature). The mother must also provide the child's full birth certificate.

The agreement will only take effect once it has been received and recorded in Section A at the Principal Registry of the Family Division (see **Appendix F** for address). A stamped copy is then given to each parent.

The agreement may be brought to an end only by a court order (CA 1989, s.4(3)) or upon the child reaching 18. It should be noted that a parental responsibility agreement can only be made with an unmarried father and not with any other family member.

The Adoption and Children Act 2002 introduced a concept of 'special guardians'. They are only appointed by the court; only a limited category of persons connected with the child can apply; they cannot be a natural parent and have to give three months' prior notice of the application to the relevant local authority. They must be vetted by the local authority which then prepares a report, dealing with the suitability of the applicant, for the use of the court. It is a stage short of a full adoption and is a semi-permanent order, lasting until the child attains 18. A special guardian has parental responsibility and is entitled to exercise parental responsibility to the exclusion of any other person with parental responsibility apart from other special guardians. They are therefore in a more powerful position than a natural parent with parental responsibility, in that they can override their wishes. In addition, a parent with parental responsibility has to apply for the court's leave to discharge a special guardianship order, and the court may not make that order unless there has been a 'significant change in circumstances' (CA 1989, s.14D(5)). A special guardian may appoint another individual to be the child's guardian in the event of his or her death. In many ways, the position of the special guardian is the same as the orthodox guardian. Both are substitutes for the parent rather than a substitute parent. Special guardianship is intended to meet the special needs of children who will benefit from a secure placement rather than adoption, e.g. due to cultural or other issues with adoption itself. On parental death, an appointment of an orthodox guardian will invariably be more appropriate than appointment of a special guardian.

A parent with parental responsibility can give parental responsibility to their partner if they are married to them (CA 1989, s.4A, as inserted by Adoption and Children Act 2002, s.112) or by court order. All other persons with parental responsibility must agree. This took effect from 5 December 2005. A step-parent who is the civil partner of a parent with parental responsibility may also be able to obtain parental responsibility by agreement with the parents of the child or by court order. In addition, the Human Fertilisation and Embryology Act 2008 inserted new s.4ZA into the Children Act 1989, enabling a birth mother's female partner (regardless of whether the mother and partner are in a civil relationship or not) to be registered as the child's second parent along with the birth mother. This applies to couples that received fertility treatment on or after 6 April 2009.

9.2.3 Who can be a guardian?

Subject to **9.2.4** below, a parent with parental responsibility for a child, or a properly appointed guardian, may appoint another individual to act as guardian for the child on his or her death (CA 1989, s.5(3) and (4)). Although CA 1989 refers to an individual in the singular, more than one individual may be appointed in accordance with Interpretation Act 1978, s.6(c). In addition, CA 1989, s.6(1) also contemplates the subsequent appointment of further guardians. However, the term 'individual' would not include a trust corporation, local authority or other non-individual.

9.2.4 Residence orders

A residence order is a court order settling the arrangements to be made about the person with whom a child is to live (CA 1989, s.8(1)). It also affects the testamentary appointment of guardians and so needs to be considered by the will drafter.

Shared (or joint) residence orders are sometimes (and increasingly) made in favour of both parents, or a parent and another carer of the child (CA 1989, s.11(4)). It may not even be the case that the parents and/or carers have the child living with them for approximately equal periods of time.

A residence order may be made in the context of divorce, judicial separation or nullity proceedings. It can be made in freestanding applications under the Act, for example to unmarried parents, grandparents or others who are given leave of the court to apply (CA 1989, s.10). It is not an automatic replacement of the care and control orders made under the pre-Children Act law; in many respects it is wider and more flexible. Also, unlike parental responsibility which is bestowed by law on all parents except as set out in **9.2.2** above, residence orders can only be granted by a court.

However, residence orders are not automatically granted on or post divorce to, say, the parent who has the child primarily living with him or her. The court shall not make any order in respect of the arrangements for a child unless it considers that doing so would be better for the child than making no order at all (CA 1989, s.1(5)). In practice, most family courts do not make residence orders and other child orders on divorce if the arrangements between the parents for the child are working satisfactorily. Will drafters should therefore enquire of clients whether there is an existing residence order and not presume that there is one simply because a child is living with a particular parent following a divorce or other family law proceedings. It should also be drawn to the parents' attention that if, in the future, circumstances change and a residence order is made in either parent's favour, they should then review their wills and testamentary dispositions.

9.3 APPOINTMENT OF A GUARDIAN

If, on the death of the appointor of a guardian (even if the parents are separated or divorced):

- there is a surviving parent with parental responsibility; and
- the deceased did not have a residence order in his or her favour,

the appointment of the guardian *does not take effect until the death of the surviving parent with parental responsibility* (CA 1989, s.5(8)). Then effective appointments by both parents will take effect simultaneously: this can lead to conflicts between the two separately appointed guardians which the court may have to resolve.

A parent of a child can only appoint a guardian to act jointly with the surviving parent if the deceased parent with parental responsibility had a residence order in his or her favour and in force at the date of his or her death and it was not a joint or shared residence order with the surviving parent (CA 1989, s.5(7)) or he or she was the child's only (or last surviving) special guardian. This situation of an appointed guardian acting jointly with a surviving parent can lead to some bitter and contested children proceedings as the surviving parent often resents the interference and involvement of the guardian appointed by the deceased parent, from whom the surviving parent may have been divorced, etc. Great care and sensitivity is needed and the matter is invariably better dealt with by specialist family lawyers. The outcome is determined by the paramountcy of the child's welfare.

If:

- on the death of the appointor the child has no surviving parent with parental responsibility; or
- immediately before the death of the appointor, a court residence order was in existence in the appointor's favour regarding the child; or
- he or she was the child's only (or last surviving) special guardian,

then the appointment of the guardian takes immediate effect on the death of the appointor (CA 1989, s. 5(7)).

A properly appointed guardian of a child may also appoint another individual to take his or her place as the child's guardian on his or her death (CA 1989, s.5(4)). However, if there is a surviving parent with parental responsibility and the guardian does not have a residence order in his or her favour (or was not the last surviving special guardian) then the appointment by the guardian will only take effect on the death of the surviving parent (CA 1989, s.5(8)).

9.3.1 How is a guardian appointed?

Under CA 1989, the appointment by a parent or guardian will not be effective unless it is made in a written document and dated. It must also be signed by the person appointing the guardian, except in the case of a document signed at the appointor's direction, in his presence and in the presence of two witnesses who each then attest the signature (CA 1989, s.5(5)). An appointment made by will (or other testamentary document) signed at the appointor's direction must be properly witnessed as required under the provisions of Wills Act 1837, s.9.

The court can also appoint a guardian (on specific application or in general family proceedings) if either:

- a child has no parent with parental responsibility; or
- a residence order has been made in favour of a parent or guardian who has died whilst the order was still in force (CA 1989, s.5(1)).

The former applies to orphans or to children of unmarried fathers without parental responsibility. The latter applies even though the child may have a surviving parent, albeit without a residence order. In practice, the court is only likely to appoint a non-parent as sole guardian when the deceased, having a residence order in his or her favour, did not make a lifetime appointment and a third party is likely to be better able to care for the child than the surviving parent. (An account of the full circumstances in which courts appoint guardians is beyond the scope of this book.)

9.3.2 Can the appointment be revoked or refused?

During the lifetime of the person who has made the appointment, he or she may revoke the appointment in the following ways:

- by a further appointment of a guardian unless clearly consistent with the appointment of an additional guardian rather than revoking the first appointment (CA 1989, s.6(1));
- by specifically revoking the appointment in writing, subject to the same conditions for the appointment of guardians as set out in **9.3.1** above (CA 1989, s.6(2));
- if the appointment is made other than in a will or codicil, by destroying the original written document which provided for the appointment of the guardian, with the intention of revoking the appointment (CA 1989, s.6(3));
- by revoking the will or codicil which contains the appointment (CA 1989, s.6(4)); or
- if the person appointed is the spouse of the appointor and their marriage is dissolved or annulled in England or Wales, or abroad and recognised here, unless a contrary intention appears by the appointment (CA 1989, s.6(3A)); or if the person appointed is the civil partner of the appointor and the civil partnership is dissolved or annulled as before.

The court has power to revoke the appointment at any time under CA 1989, s.6(7). In addition, the person who is appointed guardian may refuse the appointment by any document in writing signed by him or her made within a reasonable time of his or her first knowledge that the appointment has taken effect (CA 1989, s.6(5)).

The provision concerning spouses came into effect from 1 January 1996 (and civil partners from 5 December 2005). If such a spouse or civil partner has parental responsibility, his or her right over any children would be unaffected. The result is that, unless there is anything in the will to the contrary, the appointment of a step-parent as guardian in such circumstances would be revoked unless the step-parent had parental responsibility.

9.3.3 Effect of the 1989 Act on appointment of guardians by will or codicil

An appointment of a guardian may still be made in a will or codicil as these documents are written instruments under CA 1989, s.5(5). Although an appointment may be made in any written document, there is an advantage in appointing in a testamentary document as such documents are likely, by their nature, to be preserved, easily identifiable and be considered by those dealing with the estate of the appointor on death. However, as substitute or additional guardians may also be appointed in other written documents, the probate practitioner cannot assume that the guardians appointed in the will are the only guardians and enquiries should be made as to any other appointments which might take effect either instead of, or in addition to, the appointment in the testamentary document.

Even if a guardian is appointed in the will or codicil, the appointment may be revoked in any written document in accordance with CA 1989, ss.5 and 6 or may be revoked by a dissolution or annulment of the marriage or civil partnership. This latter may be excluded in the will or other appointment so that notwithstanding the dissolution or annulment the appointment of guardians will remain valid. Thus a will may be valid, apart from the appointment of guardians which may have been revoked in a later non-testamentary document or by dissolution or annulment of the marriage or civil partnership. The converse situation could never arise, i.e. a revoked will but a valid appointment of guardians due to the provisions of CA 1989, s.6(4), so that if a will or codicil is revoked, the appointment of a guardian contained in the testamentary document will also be revoked.

It is advisable, when dealing with an estate involving minors, to check whether there are any other written documents which may have revoked an appointment of guardians in a will or codicil. Also check to see whether the marriage or civil partnership was dissolved or annulled after the appointment. However, a contrary intention in a will or other testamentary document would mean that the appointment of the ex-spouse or ex-civil partner as guardian would remain valid.

It is, of course, possible to have an invalid will (e.g. if the formalities for signing and witnessing the will have not been complied with) which contains a valid appointment of guardians. The appointment will be valid provided that the invalid will qualifies under CA 1989, ss.5 and 6 as a document in writing, is signed by the appointor, and is dated.

It has been common in the past for both parents to appoint a guardian or guardians, the appointment to take effect on the death of the second parent. In general, it is no longer necessary that such a specific condition should be included within a will because under the terms of CA 1989, where both parents have parental responsibility (and there is no residence order in force), the appointment will not take effect until the second death. Some parents may, however, feel happier knowing that the provision is in place were they to be the first to die.

At any one time, more than one person may have the right to appoint a guardian for a child but the appointment of guardians on death will not, in general, take effect until the child's last surviving guardian or parent with parental responsibility dies. The situation may then arise of two or more separately appointed guardians acting. This should be taken into account by the probate practitioner.

As noted from **9.3** above, the position will be further complicated if there are any residence orders in force with respect to the child. Will drafters and probate practitioners should also take this into account. If clients are at all unclear as to the existence of residence orders, the prudent will drafter should make enquiries of a specialist family law practitioner to ascertain the correct position.

If the will drafter is acting for the mother of a non-marital minor child, enquiries should be made as to whether the father is registered on the birth certificate (and if so, the date) or the existence of any parental responsibility agreement, as the father of the child may then be able to appoint testamentary guardians. As the significance of parental responsibility is of such importance for the appointment of guardians, and the requirements for parental responsibility agreements are strict, it may be prudent for the will drafter or probate practitioner, in appropriate cases, to check the existence of a valid agreement at the Principal Registry. Enquiries should be directed to the Searches Department, and a fee (currently £40) is payable to include a copy of any agreement found.

There is no provision in CA 1989 for successive appointments by the original appointor (i.e. 'I appoint Jane Smith as guardian of my minor children and when she dies then I appoint her husband William Smith as guardian'). However, there seems to be no prohibition on substitutional appointments taking effect if the first choice as guardian does not survive the appointor (i.e. 'I appoint Jane Smith as guardian of my minor children but if she has pre-deceased me then I appoint her husband William Smith as guardian').

There are often a number of clauses included in wills giving executors, trustees and appointed guardians certain rights and powers in relation to financial provision for minor beneficiaries under the will. If the will refers to provision for the child being made to the child's guardian, care should be taken by executors and trustees as well as those administering estates to ensure that the named guardian is properly and effectively appointed.

CHAPTER 10

Probate and benefits

Meg Andrews

10.1 INTRODUCTION

Some clients may not be concerned about potential inheritance tax liability or how best to invest their legacy but, more practically, how they are going to cope financially without the person who has died.

10.2 FUNERAL COSTS

The first problem is often: how is the funeral to be paid for? One does come across the enterprising client who has withdrawn the money for the funeral refreshments and flowers using the deceased's cashpoint card, or paid for the funeral using a power of attorney before the bank is aware of the death, but clearly this should not be encouraged.

More and more funeral directors are asking for disbursements like doctors' or cremation fees to be paid in advance. If the client is in touch early enough, it may be possible to direct them to a funeral director who submits the bill a few weeks after the funeral and will include newspaper notices and funeral refreshments on the account. For a family used to paying cash on the nail, the prospect of a bill of £2,500 or more hanging over them can be distressing. The suggestion that they take the funeral account to the deceased's bank or building society as soon as it is received may be all that is required. If they are fortunate, the deceased banked with one of the institutions who will reimburse the cost of disbursements on sight of a receipted account. Banks will not pay separate florist's or caterer's bills as a matter of course.

Where someone has a collection of small accounts, closing them all by cheques payable to the funeral director can be cheaper than a collection of statutory declarations in lieu of a grant, particularly if the deceased died intestate leaving a number of people equally entitled to benefit.

Unfortunately, some financial organisations make a habit of referring the bereaved customer to a solicitor as soon as they find out a will is involved, when the bank's own small estates procedure would be perfectly appropriate. The fairest thing to do in those circumstances (unless there is a pending flotation, when other considerations may apply) is to refer the client back to the institution involved, perhaps having telephoned the branch manager first. On the other hand, where a bank has actual knowledge of the state of the personal representative's own financial situation, it may insist on a grant for a very modest estate, in order to protect its own position and that of the beneficiaries.

If the deceased was a member of a trade union or hospital fund, it is worth contacting the organisation before the funeral arrangements are made. Some will only pay funeral benefits if the claim is made before the funeral, while others, especially if a funeral bond is involved, may wish to specify a particular funeral director. Many make their cheque payable to the funeral director, rather than the family, which can present problems if the family have already clubbed together to pay the bill. The funeral director should be prepared to refund money, but negotiating cheques can cause delays.

The Social Fund will pay the costs of a basic funeral, if the person responsible for paying for it is on income support, in receipt of pension credit, income based job-seeker's allowance, council tax benefit, housing benefit, disabled person's tax credit or working families' tax credit. The funeral payment will cover the costs of a burial plot and interment or cremation costs, including the doctors' certificates, the cost of a hearse and up to £700 for any other funeral expenses. The claimant's savings are ignored.

The cheque is normally payable to the funeral director and the application can be made immediately or up to three months after the funeral. The application form asks for some detailed information about the relationships between the claimant and the deceased and between the deceased and other members of his or her family, to confirm that the applicant is the appropriate person to have responsibility for paying for the funeral. The Social Fund will be able to recover its costs from the estate, if it turns out that there are liquid assets after all. Although some funeral directors keep a stock, the application form (SF200) can be obtained from the local social security office or downloaded from the website of Direct Gov (**www.direct.gov.uk**).

A relative on income support, pension credit, income related employment and support allowance or certain other benefits can apply for a Community Care Grant to help with the cost of attending the funeral. The grant is not repayable and can be of real benefit at a difficult time, when the option of cheap advance fares may not be available.

10.3 BEREAVEMENT

10.3.1 Bereavement payment

Since April 2001, a surviving spouse has been able to claim a tax-free lump sum bereavement payment of £2,000. This is not means tested, but is conditional on the deceased having paid appropriate national insurance contributions and either not being entitled to state retirement pension when he or she died or the surviving spouse being under retirement age at the date of death. As from December 2005, the surviving partner in a registered civil partnership can also claim on the same basis.

The claim can be made at the local Jobcentre Plus office or online (**www.jobcentreplus.gov.uk**).

10.3.2 Bereavement allowance

If the surviving spouse or registered civil partner is over 45 years old at the time of death, they may be entitled to bereavement allowance, a taxable weekly benefit, for 52 weeks from the date of death. Again, this can be conditional on the deceased having paid appropriate national insurance contributions, but will also be paid if death was caused by their employment. The amount payable (rates correct at April 2010) depends on the age of the surviving spouse or partner, with those aged over 55 getting the full rate of £97.65 per week and those aged between 45 and 54 getting only part of this (£29.30 per week if the surviving spouse or partner was 45 at the time of bereavement). Unfortunately the rate is fixed and does not go up if the claimant crosses an age threshold during the year in question. Current rates and claim forms can be found on the Jobcentre Plus website (**www.jobcentreplus.gov.uk**) or **www.direct.gov.uk**.

10.4 ORPHANS

If the surviving spouse or registered civil partner is under state pension age and has children entitling them to child benefit, or was expecting the deceased's child, then widowed parent's allowance will be paid instead of bereavement allowance. This is taxable and continues for as long as the claimant meets the conditions, generally until the youngest child leaves school. The widowed parent's allowance is paid at the rate of £84.25 per week (as at April 2010).

A lone parent who was not married to the deceased or in a registered civil partnership may, like a widow or widower, be entitled to income support, help with rent in the form of housing benefit or council tax benefit. Those receiving income support are also eligible for budgeting loans to buy things for the home or Social Fund crisis loans if immediate help is needed in an emergency. If the child is under five, income support also entitles the claimant to cold weather payments. Other triggers for this last benefit are the claimant being disabled or over 60.

Child benefit is not means tested or taxable and is payable to any person bringing up children, while the child is under 16, or under 19 and studying full-time either A level, NVQ level 3 or an equivalent qualification, or under 18 and actively looking for work or a training place while registered for work or training with the Careers Service or Connexion Service. It is paid in respect of each child, at the rate of £20.30 a week for the first child and £13.40 a week for others.

If the carer is not the child's parent and both parents are dead, or one has died and the other is in prison or cannot be found, or the parents were divorced, the carer may also be entitled to guardian's allowance. Guardian's allowance is not taxable and is paid at the rate of £14.30 for each child, on top of child benefit.

10.5 INCAPACITATED DEPENDANTS

Sadly it is often the ostensibly fitter half of a couple who dies first, and it may only then be apparent how much care the surviving partner has been receiving. If he or she was under pension age and became disabled before 27 October 2008, then there may be an entitlement to incapacity benefit, if the right to statutory sick pay has expired. This benefit is dependent on national insurance contributions, unless the claimant became unable to work between 16 and 20 years of age, or the claimant is under 25 and was in education or training when under 20. Rates (at April 2010) vary between £68.95 and £91.40 per week, depending on the age of the claimant, the length of time that they have been incapacitated and the level of incapacity.

New claimants on or after 27 October 2008 will need to apply for employment and support allowance. This follows the principle that, in general, work is good for you. For the first 13 weeks, the claimant's capability for work is assessed and an allowance is paid at a maximum of £65.45 per week. After that, if it is agreed that illness or disability affects the ability to work, the claimant will receive either a work-related activity allowance of up to £91.40 per week if they are able to work, or a support grant of up to £96.85 per week if they are unable to do so.

Attendance allowance is available to those over 65 who have needed help looking after themselves for at least six months or who have received a terminal diagnosis. The claim forms can be completed on behalf of a claimant, so that the fact of a terminal diagnosis need not be disclosed to them.

The need may be for daytime care, help at night, or both, with the rate payable depending on the need (£71.40 per week for day and night attendance or if there is a terminal diagnosis, or £47.80 per week if day or night care is required as at April 2010). Attendance allowance is not means tested or taxed and does not count as income for income support assessment purposes. It does, however, open the door to additional severe disability benefits which are paid with pension credit, council tax benefit or housing benefit.

It may also entitle a claimant in England to obtain a grant from the Warm Front Scheme towards the cost of home insulation or heating improvements, including changing an open coal fire to a modern glass fronted one.

10.6 OTHER SOURCES OF HELP

The right to means-tested benefits may have been lost by cohabitation as man and wife or in a same sex relationship, even if there is no registered civil partnership. The death of one of a couple may mean the survivor can resume claiming in their own right.

Apart from state help, it is worth looking at what pension rights the deceased had or what pensions the deceased was receiving. Most pension schemes make provision for widows or widowers and dependent children of any age and more will now pay pensions to cohabitants. The old-fashioned schemes where a widower was only entitled to a pension from his late wife's pension if he was disabled are no longer found. A spouse should now be interpreted as covering a registered civil partner. If the deceased had not reached retirement age, an employer's pension scheme will generally provide that a lump sum or pension is payable at the discretion of trustees, who will be guided by any letter of wishes signed by the deceased. In the absence of any such expression, trustees generally follow the intestacy rules, but it may be possible to persuade them to pay money into a purpose-built discretionary trust, if this would avoid the beneficiary losing means-tested benefits.

It is always worth checking the death certificate to see what the person died of, or what illnesses they suffered from at the time of death. The number of industrial diseases for which compensation can be claimed is growing all the time. If the deceased was a miner's widow or child, it is wise to ask if the late miner suffered from emphysema or chronic obstructive airways disease, as his claim for compensation did not necessarily die with him and may not have been recognised at the time of his death.

Many types of employment have their own charities attached, from the Royal Agricultural Benevolent Association to the Solicitors Benevolent Association. The Civil Service has its own charity, which offers emotional as well as financial support, as do each of the services. The Armed Forces Compensation Scheme pays compensation for death due to service, even if the person concerned had retired from the services by the time of their death, and pensions for dependants. Counsel and Care is a charity which specialises in pointing people, including legal advisers, in the direction of appropriate charities who may be able to assist elderly people in financial need or requiring help or advice (see **Appendix F** for address).

Benefit advice can be given under the Legal Help scheme or, of course, *pro bono*.

CHAPTER 11

Claims under the Inheritance (Provision for Family and Dependants) Act 1975

Sue Medder and Beatrice Goford

11.1 SUMMARY OF COURT'S APPROACH TO CLAIMS

The court approaches the Inheritance (Provision for Family and Dependants) (IPFDA) Act 1975 claims in stages:

1. Was the deceased domiciled in England and Wales on death? If not, IPFDA 1975 does not apply.
2. Does the claimant have standing – do they fall into one of the classes set out at IPFDA 1975, s.1(1): spouse or civil partner, former spouse or civil partner who has not entered into a subsequent marriage or civil partnership (IPFDA 1975, s.1(l)(a) has been amended to include civil partners on an equal footing with spouses), cohabitants of at least two years' standing, children (including adopted and non-marital children and those treated as children of the family) or persons maintained by the deceased immediately before death? If not, they cannot bring a claim under IPFDA 1975.
3. There is then a two-stage assessment:
   (a) Whether reasonable financial provision has been made for the applicant by the deceased under the will or through the intestacy rules; and
   (b) If it has not, and only if it has not, what, if any, provision should be made?
4. In the case of claimant spouses and civil partners, the test is what is reasonable in the circumstances, but for all other categories of claimant the test is what is reasonable for their maintenance.

11.2 HOW TO PREVENT A CLAIM WHEN DRAFTING WILLS

It is not possible to exclude the possibility of a claim under IPFDA 1975 but there are some simple steps that can be taken when drafting wills which may reduce the likelihood of a claim or, if one is made, reduce its chances of either succeeding or diminishing the estate by court proceedings.

11.2.1 Check background facts

Establish the extent of all the client's family and dependants. Sensitivities should not prevent you from asking about any unknown relationships and non-marital children. It is only by being aware of potential claimants that you may try to protect against any specific threat they may hold.

11.2.2 Ask questions

A client may have dependants who are not immediately obvious to them as such. For example, they may be making gratuitous payments to a niece or nephew, or providing accommodation for a mother-in-law, or companion.

11.2.3 Options

The clients may have been providing for people who could claim against the estate as dependants, but who do not otherwise fall within any of the other categories of claimant under IPFDA 1975, s.1(1). If the client has been providing for people he or she should be advised that the chance of a claim could be reduced by:

- making some provision by will or otherwise for them; or
- ceasing to maintain them.

If the first option is taken, the provision should be 'reasonable', although what is reasonable will depend very much on the circumstances of the testator and the prospective beneficiary and the relationship between them. The solicitor will need to consider carefully the factors set out at IPFDA 1975, s.3, such as the resources and needs of the beneficiaries and any claimants (charitable beneficiaries are unlikely to be able to show the same needs as individuals), and the size and nature of the client's estate.

One example of the nature of the estate being taken into consideration was an award to a claimant surviving spouse tailored to avoid disturbing a business which the adult children continued to run following their deceased father's death (*Baker* v. *Baker and Others* [2008] EWHC 977 (Ch)).

If the second option is taken, the solicitor should also advise the client to make it clear to any dependants that he or she no longer assumes responsibility for their maintenance. A memorandum can be left with the client's will explaining that maintenance has ceased. It is preferable for the client to send a letter (keeping a copy) to each dependant explaining that maintenance (or the assumption of responsibility) is ceased. The assumption of responsibility is a necessary element of a successful claim under this head. In *Baynes* v. *Hedger* [2009] EWCA Civ 374 the Court of Appeal held that once it was demonstrated that the deceased had not assumed responsibility, the applicant's claim failed.

11.2.4 Leaving a memorandum

If the client considers there is a possible claimant under IPFDA 1975 but does not wish to make provision for the potential claimant, the client should be encouraged to leave a memorandum with the will explaining why no provision was made, unless the reasons for making no provision are unreasonable, in which case the memorandum could do more harm than good. As with a will, a memorandum should be updated as and when the potential claimant's financial circumstances alter from those in place at the date of the memorandum. A memorandum based on outdated financial facts may assist a claimant in securing provision if the reasoning behind the limited provision by the deceased spouse/civil partner no longer reflects the reality of the claimant's financial circumstances.

In addition to leaving a memorandum with the will, it may be helpful if the client makes it clear to the potential applicants that they will not be provided for on the deceased's death. In *H* v. *Mitson* [2009] EWHC 3114 Fam a significant factor in the court's decision to award nothing to the deceased's only daughter was that the estranged daughter had lived all her married life in the belief that she had no expectations and had expressed regret that her mother was not going to leave anything to her grandchildren. It was not a case of disappointed expectations.

There appears to be a trend in IPFDA 1975 actions towards the introduction by claimants of parallel claims (such as proprietary estoppel, declarations as to beneficial interests, mutual will obligations, and claims based on a contractual relationship with the deceased). Such claims are based on a combination of fact and the deceased's intentions. The claim will only be made after the deceased's death. Unless the deceased documented his intentions or discussed them with independent persons who are subsequently willing to come forward as witnesses, the claimant is free to give their version of the deceased's intentions, unchallenged by contemporaneous evidence.

With this in mind, it may well be appropriate for a detailed attendance note of the initial instructions to be copied to the client with the draft will. The client should be asked to confirm the attendance note details are correct when confirming instructions to engross the will. The attendance note should be kept, as with any memorandum, with the will.

Property falling outside the estate may be considered in the context of an IPFDA 1975 claim. The court has considered the position where a deceased owned a house with his first spouse on a joint tenancy, but lived in it with a second spouse. The court included his notional half share of that house in his estate when considering the second spouse's IPFDA 1975 claim. As a result, the second spouse received half the value of the property, calculated as at the date of the award, rather than immediately before death (*Dingmar* v. *Dingmar* [2006] EWCA Civ 942). When making a claim against an estate containing property passing by survivorship, it is vital to remember that the time limit of six months from the date of the grant cannot be extended in relation to joint property (see IPFDA 1975, s.9(1)).

11.2.5 Consider prospective claimants

Surviving spouses or civil partners

Some clients will say they are making no or little provision for their wife, husband or civil partner because their spouse or civil partner has his or her own personal assets which are sufficient for his or her needs. This may reflect a misunderstanding on the client's part about what would be regarded for these purposes as adequate assets, so make further enquiries and ensure that the client understands the real financial position of his or her spouse or civil partner.

It may be prudent to remind the client that one of the criteria the court will use for assessing what is reasonable provision is what the spouse or civil partner would have received if the marriage had been terminated by divorce rather than death.

As a result of the ancillary relief decision in *White* v. *White* [2001] 1 AC 596 the 'yardstick of equality' may be referred to as a starting point when considering the quantum of a surviving spouse's or civil partner's claims in long marriages/relationships. This analogy has shaped the level of provision that the court views as appropriate in IPFDA 1975 claims brought by spouses and civil partners. See the favourable decisions for spouses in *Fielden* v. *Cunliffe* [2005] EWCA Civ 1508 and *P* v. *G, P&P* [2006] 1 FLR 431.

Bear in mind, however, that where a marriage has ended by death, there is only one party who needs provision as opposed to two on divorce. This is likely to have the result of increasing the provision a spouse or civil partner would expect to receive on an IPFDA 1975 claim because their marriage has been ended by death as opposed to divorce.

Former spouses or civil partners

A former spouse or former civil partner (who has not remarried or entered into another civil partnership) may make a claim if he or she is receiving maintenance at the time of the ex-spouse or civil partner's death. It is sensible to check whether the client is bound by the terms of any ancillary relief orders for transfer of matrimonial assets, ongoing maintenance payments, or obligations to provide by will or life assurance: if the latter, check whether the policy is still valid.

People with special needs

If a client has dependants with mental or physical disabilities, and is assuming that the state will support them, the client should be warned that the local social services department can make an application on behalf of the dependants for provision from the estate. Solicitors may wish to consider with such a client the advantage of making provision for such a dependant in the form of a discretionary trust with the possibility (not guaranteed) that this will protect the fund from a claim from public services and/or alternatively will not be taken into account when assessing the capital resources of the dependant.

Cohabitants

A client who is living with someone as a cohabitant should be advised that the cohabitant has no entitlement under the intestacy rules.

The Law Commission is reviewing the intestacy rules and is considering giving cohabitants entitlement comparable to that of spouses and civil partners, perhaps depending on the length of the cohabitation and whether there are children of the relationship – see the consultation paper at **www.lawcom.gov.uk/docs/cp191.pdf**.

The cohabitant will not be able to make a claim under IPFDA 1975, if:

- he or she was not living together with the deceased for two years prior to the death (note: the Law Commission proposes that this minimum requirement be removed where the deceased and cohabitant have children); or
- he or she was not maintained by the deceased.

If a cohabitant can bring a claim under IPFDA 1975, this will be assessed on the basis of reasonable provision for maintenance, rather than the higher level of reasonable provision in all the circumstances. Cohabitants can therefore be severely disadvantaged by the death of a partner because the provision that they will expect to recover will not be assessed as that of a spouse or civil partner. The Law Commission proposes to remove this qualification so that cohabitants can claim the same level of provision as surviving spouses or civil partners.

IPFDA 1975, s.3(2A) sets out guidelines the court should consider when an application is made by a cohabitant. These are:

- the age of the applicant and the length of the period during which the applicant lived as the husband or wife of the deceased and in the same household as the deceased; and
- the contribution made by the applicant to the welfare of the family of the deceased, including any contribution made by looking after the home or caring for the family.

Examples of factors the court will take into consideration in cohabitation cases include whether:

- the claimant and deceased lived together as spouses or civil partners (*Re Watson (Deceased)* [1999] 1 FLR 878);
- any separations were transitory and did not affect the continuity of the relationship (*Gully* v. *Dix* [2004] 1 WLR 1399);
- the relationship was publicly acknowledged (*Baynes* v. *Hedger and Others* [2008] EWHC 1587 (Ch)); and

- the deceased and claimant shared a joint domestic economy, although this is possible even where there were separate properties (*Churchill* v. *Roach* [2003] All ER (D) 348).

Generous provision may be made, particularly in cases of lengthy cohabitation. The court has a wide discretion to make value judgments. The Court of Appeal on 28 February 2008 refused an application for permission to appeal against a first instance decision where the court had awarded maintenance based on the lavish lifestyle she had enjoyed with the deceased rather than the more modest lifestyle the claimant cohabitant had enjoyed before she met him (*Negus* v. *Bahouse* [2007] EWHC 2628 (Ch)). The court took the same approach in *Webster* v. *Webster* [2008] EWHC 31 (Ch).

Children

As children are a separate class of claimant, there is no requirement for a claimant who is a child of the deceased to have been maintained by the deceased, although arguably a child who has been maintained would bring a stronger claim to provision than one who has not. The level of provision deemed reasonable will be considered on a maintenance basis.

There has been an increase in the volume of claims by adult children, and in the level of those that succeed. Traditionally the court's view was that persons who could maintain themselves should not expect others to provide for them (*Re Dennis* [1981] 2 All ER 140).

Arguably a child is more likely to be able to show legitimate expectation of provision, which may form a solid basis for their claim, and may give rise to a tandem claim under another head, such as proprietary estoppel. There is no special requirement to show that the deceased had any moral obligation to make provision for the claimant. An adult child needs to prove their case in the same manner as any other claimant (*Espinosa* v. *Bourke* [1999] 1 FLR 747).

Contact between the deceased and the adult child will be taken into consideration. A 15-year estrangement has resulted in an adult child being considered to have no claim to their deceased parent's bounty so that it was held to be reasonable that no provision was made by the deceased parent (*Garland* v. *Morris* [2007] EWHC 2 (Ch)). However, the nature of the relationship between the deceased and the claimant child has been taken into consideration. Adult children who had been estranged from their deceased parents or had difficult relationships with them prior to their death have been awarded provision from their estates (*Gold* v. *Curtis* [2005] WTLR 673). However, in *H* v. *Mitson* [2009] EWHC 3114 Fam the very lengthy estrangement between mother and daughter was a significant factor in the court's refusal to make an award.

11.3 WHAT TO DO IN THE EVENT OF A CLAIM

If a claim has been issued, personal representatives in the estate (PRs) should be cautious about how they administer the estate. Broadly speaking, PRs faced with a claim should pay debts and funeral expenses and collect in the assets of the estate; but they should not distribute until the claim has been disposed of.

11.3.1 Small legacies or cases of hardship

If there are small legacies which are unlikely to be affected by the claim, or beneficiaries are experiencing hardship, PRs can seek the agreement of parties affected, including the claimant, to payment of legacies or a distribution to relieve hardship (*Re Ralphs; sub nom Ralphs* v. *District Bank* [1968] 1 WLR 1522). If consent is not forthcoming, an application can be made to the court for directions (CPR, rule 64.2(a)).

If the converse applies and the claimant is suffering hardship, PRs can, again, make an interim payment to them with the agreement of the beneficiaries. If the beneficiaries will not agree to a distribution, the claimant can apply under IPFDA 1975, s.5 for an interim payment.

11.3.2 Time limit

Claimants have six months from the issue of the grant to put in a claim, so PRs will not be liable if they distribute the estate more than six months after obtaining the grant if no IPFDA 1975 application has been issued. However, claimants can apply for leave to apply out of time. *McNulty* v. *McNulty* [2002] WTLR 737 is an example of a successful application. Remember though that the court has no power to allow out of time applications in relation to property passing by survivorship (see IPFDA 1975, s.9(1)).

When considering whether to grant leave to apply out of time, the court will take into account the effect on any party affected, including any hardship caused to the beneficiaries by allowing the claim. The court will consider whether distribution has taken place, so a PR may reduce the prospects of success of an application to bring a claim out of time – and consequently the claim itself – by distributing as soon as practicable once six months have passed from the issuing of the grant.

Claimants who might otherwise seek to reach negotiated settlement may be driven to issue by the impending expiry of the six-month deadline. Parties may be able to avoid a claim being issued by agreeing not to oppose an application to bring the claim out of time. There may be considerable merit in reaching such an agreement and avoiding the pressure of a court timetable and the additional costs.

A Trustee Act 1925, s.27 advertisement does not protect PRs who distribute after two months has expired from the date of advertisement but within six months from the grant of probate.

11.3.3 Acting for personal representatives as claimants

Obviously, as a solicitor for the PRs, you cannot act both for potential claimant and potential defendant(s) in an IPFDA 1975 claim.

The PRs as a body should adopt a neutral role and not attempt to defeat the claim. The proper parties to defend the claim are the residuary beneficiaries whose share will be reduced by a successful claim. PRs taking steps to actively defend an IPFDA 1975 claim could be at risk on recovery of their costs, as would any other actively participating defendant. If the PRs are not seen to be adopting a neutral approach, the administration of the estate is likely to grind to a halt while the claim is pending.

A claimant who is one of the proposed PRs may choose to have power reserved. It is not necessary to renounce if he or she is going to make a claim. A PR who has taken out a grant and proposes to claim need not be removed from office.

11.3.4 Sole personal representatives

If the intending claimant is the sole PR, he or she might prefer not to take out the grant (although power might be reserved). In such a case, the grant may have to be taken out by the person next entitled, or by a nominee of the intending claimant pursuant to s.166 of the Senior Courts Act 1981.

11.3.5 Personal representatives as beneficiaries

The PRs are also often beneficiaries who are resisting a claim. Although PRs in their capacity as PRs should adopt a neutral stance, leaving it to the claimant and the beneficiaries to fight the matter out, beneficiary PRs are not obliged to be neutral *in their capacity as beneficiaries*. They must not pay the costs of defending the claim out of the estate: such costs are their personal liability.

Difficulties arise where one or more PRs are professionals and another is a beneficiary who wishes to contest the claim. If all PRs are content to accept your advice, or that of counsel, on how to respond to the claim, and are not causing costs to be incurred unnecessarily, you should not have a conflict of interest in acting for all the PRs.

Nevertheless, it is much better to ensure that the PR with the beneficial interest is separately represented in his or her capacity as beneficiary.

11.4 HANDLING A CLAIM

Once the claim is issued, the PRs should promptly provide the information required by CPR, rule 57.16(5) and Practice Direction 57, para.16 unless all parties agree not to enforce the obligation to respond by witness statement in order to save costs.

PRs must comply with their obligations to bring to court matters within their knowledge which may be relevant to the court's exercise of its discretion. Equally, they should maintain a neutral position with regard to the merits of any claim and not usurp the function of the beneficiary defendants.

Although PRs have extensive common law and statutory powers (see Trustee Act 1925, s.15, as substituted by Trustee Act 2000) to compromise claims against the estate, provided that they act in good faith, these powers do not extend to compromising an IPFDA 1975 claim because the claim, instead of being against the estate is a claim against the beneficiaries of the estate and they are the proper parties to defend and compromise a claim. The PRs ought to leave the claimant and the beneficiaries to negotiate a settlement but should indicate:

- their readiness to assist by providing up-to-date information on the composition and administration of the estate;
- their desire to be involved at the final stage of negotiations to ensure that the agreement reached between the parties is workable from the administrative point of view and that the PRs' own position on costs is protected.

Solicitor PRs should be concerned to ensure the part that they play is as limited as possible. The estate should not be put to unnecessary additional expense. It may be appropriate for PRs to seek directions from the court that the beneficiaries' advocate represent them during proceedings.

It is likely that the parties will seek to engage in alternative dispute resolution. The PRs' knowledge of the estate is likely to assist and PRs should be prepared to attend with the agreement of all parties, or to be available by telephone to assist with information. If the PRs are trustees of trusts created under the deceased's will, their increased involvement may be required as they will need to indicate which agreements they would be prepared to carry into effect.

11.5 OTHER CONSIDERATIONS

11.5.1 Charity beneficiaries and IPFDA 1975

(For more on charity beneficiaries see **Chapter 17**.) A charity can agree to a compromise of proceedings through its duly authorised officer. The charity may need separate advice on whether to agree a compromise and if in doubt can seek an order from the Charity Commissioners or a letter of opinion or advice under ss.26 and 29 of the Charities Act 1993, although this is not normally necessary.

In some cases, charities may feel a moral obligation to renounce part of their entitlement and under s.27 of the Charities Act 1993 the Charity Commissioners have powers to authorise charity trustees to give effect to a perceived moral obligation. Charities cannot give effect to a moral obligation without such authority. The Charity Commission has produced a very useful leaflet CC7, *Ex Gratia Payments by Charities* (available from **www.charity-commission.gov.uk**).

11.5.2 Costs

Unless the PRs have acted unreasonably (such as by adopting too proactive a stance) or for their own benefit rather than that of the estate, they should receive their costs out of the estate on the indemnity basis (CPR, rule 48.4). PRs and trustees should be aware of the provisions in CPR Practice Direction 48, para.50A.1–3, which list the criteria that the court will use in assessing whether the costs were properly incurred. . Where a personal representative wishes to remain neutral in relation to the claim, and agrees to abide by any decision which the court may make, he should state this in Section A of the acknowledgement of service form. He will then be protected from personal liability for costs.

The PRs will also be expected to act in accordance with the overriding objective of CPR, rule 1.1(2) in dealing with the claim and will be expected to do so in a way which is proportionate to the amount of money involved, the importance of the case, the financial position of each party, and the complexity of the issues. In making costs orders the court will give consideration to whether the parties have complied with the overriding objective.

A successful claimant's costs are usually paid from the estate, commonly on the standard basis; conversely, an unsuccessful claimant's costs are not always borne by him or her. Frequently, an unsuccessful claimant is not ordered to pay the costs of the PRs or other defendants. PRs should be aware of the effect on the estate of costs orders in favour of a number of parties and it may be appropriate to bring this to the attention of the claimant and beneficiaries.

11.5.3 Wasted costs

Solicitors for the PRs should be aware that, if they have acted improperly and unreasonably or have been negligent, and in consequence any party to the proceedings has incurred additional costs, they can be disallowed their costs or asked to meet all or any wasted costs of another party (Senior Courts Act 1981, s.51(6), as amended; CPR, rules 44.14 and 48.7). An example of causing wasted costs would be the negligent provision of incorrect information about the size and nature of the estate when preparing the PR's witness statement under CPR, rule 57.16(5).

The case of *Ridehalgh* v. *Horsefield and Another (No.2)* [1994] 3 WLR 462 provides an analysis of when it would be appropriate to bring an application for a wasted costs order and reference was made to this analysis in *Morris* v. *Roberts (Inspector of Taxes)* [2005] PNLR 41.

CHAPTER 12

Contentious probate

Henry Frydenson

12.1 INTRODUCTION

The proportion of contentious work in private client departments is growing rapidly. The growth is partly the result of an increasingly litigious society and partly the result of the fact that there is more wealth around for people to argue over.

12.1.1 ACTAPS

Practitioners who find that more work of this type is coming their way may be interested in joining the Association of Contentious Trust and Probate Specialists. (More information and application forms are available online from their website **www.actaps.com**.)

The purposes of the Association include raising the standard of contentious work and developing a common approach. Members agree to endeavour to act in accordance with a voluntary Code of Conduct. Under this Code members agree where appropriate to try to use the full range of solutions, in particular alternative dispute resolution.

12.1.2 Alternative dispute resolution

Alternative dispute resolution is an informal alternative to formal litigation and an attempt to overcome and avoid the acrimony, expense and frustration of litigation, as a way of settling disputes. Increasingly its main method is mediation. In mediation, the parties select an independent third party who will assist the parties in reaching their solution to the problem. The mediator will have experience in this method of problem solving. He will air the problem with both sides initially together and then privately with each party. The private sessions will be blunt and open and the mediator will do his best to get both sides to look at their real interests and priorities. Mediation produces non-binding solutions until the parties reach agreement and then the parties are able to agree between themselves that the new agreement is to be binding. The mediation process is a without prejudice one.

A refusal to mediate can have unfortunate results. See the case of *Dunnett* v. *Railtrack* [2002] EWCA 303, where the court penalised a party in costs for failing to mediate; *Halsey* v. *Milton Keynes General NHS Trust* [2004] EWCA Civ 576, where the court highlighted the importance of mediation before court proceedings were issued, and stated that an unreasonable refusal to mediate would attract cost sanctions; and *Burchell* v. *Bullard and Others* [2005] EWCA Civ 358, where the Court of Appeal added weight to the *Halsey* decision. Lord Justice Ward said:

> *Halsey* has made plain not only the high rate of a successful outcome being achieved by mediation, but also its established importance as a track to a just result running parallel with that of the court system.

He continued:

> The profession can no longer with impunity shrug aside reasonable requests to mediate. The parties cannot ignore a proper request to mediate simply because it was made before the claim was issued. With Court fees escalating, it may be folly to do so.

12.2 IDENTIFICATION OF ISSUES

When advising a client it is important to identify the points which are likely to be in issue.

If there is a will there will be two possible questions relating to the will:

- Is the will valid? This may require considering any of the following questions:
  - Have the formal requirements for making a will been complied with? (See Wills Act 1837, s.9.)
  - Did the testator have the capacity to make a will?
  - Do claims of undue influence or lack of knowledge and approval arise?
- How is a particular provision in a will to be construed?

12.3 METHODS OF ATTACK

Where a person is unhappy with the terms of a deceased's will or the provisions which would arise on intestacy, there are various grounds of possible attack. Before considering these grounds in detail, thought should always be given as to what the outcome of a successful attack will be. For example, the overthrow of a will may result in intestacy or in the provisions of an earlier will remaining in effect. There is absolutely no point in overthrowing the later will if your client will have no rights on intestacy or under the earlier will.

Consideration must also be given to the all-important question of costs (see **12.6.5** below).

12.3.1 Lack of due execution of the will

The burden of proving that the will was executed in accordance with Wills Act 1837, s.9 (as substituted by Administration of Justice Act 1982, s.17) is on the party seeking to establish the validity of the will.

It may be possible to challenge the will on the following grounds:

- the signature was not made by the testator or testatrix in the presence of two witnesses present at the same time, but see *Couser* v. *Couser* [1996] 1 WLR 1301;
- the two witnesses did not subscribe or acknowledge their signatures to the will in the presence of the testator or testatrix;
- the signature of the testator or testatrix was not intended to give effect to the will; or
- the signature which appears on the will was not in fact made by the testator or testatrix himself or herself, or for him or her, or in his or her presence, or by his or her direction.

12.3.2 Attestation clause

To be effective, the attestation clause must state that the witnesses signed or acknowledged their signatures to the will in the presence of the testator. Where a will contains an attestation clause showing that the will was signed by the testator in the presence of two witnesses, and each witness signed it in the presence of the testator, no other evidence as to execution is required.

The court will require 'the strongest possible evidence' before accepting that a will which contains a correct attestation clause was not duly executed, otherwise the greatest uncertainty would prevail in the proving of wills' (*Wright* v. *Rogers* (1865–69) LR 1 P&D 678 at 682). A number of more recent decisions have taken the same approach. See for example: *Sherrington* v. *Sherrington* [2005] EWCA Civ 326, where Peter Gibson LJ said at para.42: 'In general, if a witness has the capacity to understand, he should be taken to have done what the attestation clause and the signatures of the testator and the witness indicated.'

In *Fuller* v. *Strum* [2002] 1 WLR 1097, the will was challenged on the ground that the testator did not know or approve the whole contents of the will. It was held that while the court could accept that the testator knew of and approved one part, but not another, such cases were unusual. The Court of Appeal held that if the party putting forward the will, had prepared the will, that would be an instance which made the court want to examine the evidence in support of the will so that it could satisfy itself that the testator knew and approved of the contents when he executed, and that they set out the real intentions of the deceased.

And see also the decision of the Court of Appeal in *Channon* v. *Perkins* [2006] WTLR 425. The Court of Appeal reversed the decision at first instance and held that where witnesses accept that a will carries their signatures, but neither attesting witness has any recollection of attesting the will, their inability to remember the event was not sufficient to displace the presumption of due execution. Much stronger evidence is required, for example proof that the witness was elsewhere at the relevant time.

12.3.3 Lack of testamentary capacity

The test of testamentary capacity is still that established in 1870 in *Banks* v. *Goodfellow* (1869–70) LR 5 QB 549. For a more recent example of the *Banks* v. *Goodfellow* test, see *Brown* v. *Deacy and Others* [2002] WTLR 781. A person may suffer from a mental disorder and yet still be able to fulfil that test.

Capacity is issue specific, though mental states are presumed to continue, so if a person is normally mentally capable it will be presumed, provided the will appears rational, that he or she had capacity when the will was made. For examples of the importance of this presumption, see *Vaughan* v. *Vaughan* [2002] EWHC 699 and *Sharp* v. *Adam* [2005] EWHC 1806. However, this presumption is rebuttable by evidence. Where a person lacks general mental capacity, the person putting forward the will has to prove testamentary capacity.

In *Key* v. *Key* [2010] EWHC 408 (Ch) a testator in his 80s made a will a few days after the sudden death of his wife of 65 years, an event which left him 'devastated'. He changed the main beneficiaries from being his two sons to his two daughters. The solicitor who drew up the will took no steps to investigate the testator's capacity. The court found that the testator did not have testamentary capacity and, in addition, that if he had possessed capacity, the daughters had not discharged the burden of showing he knew and approved of the contents of his will. Two important points emerged:

1. Testamentary capacity requires volition as well as cognition. Volition is impaired by affective disorders, i.e. disorders of mood, and includes depressive illness, bipolar disorders and bereavement reactions. Mr Justice Briggs found that the testator was simply unable during the week following his wife's death to exercise the decision-making powers required by a testator. He said that if this involved a slight development of the *Banks* v. *Goodfellow* test taking into account decision-making powers rather than just comprehension, he considered that to be necessary because of the greater understanding of the mind now available from modern psychiatric medicine.
2. Substantial weight was attached to the opinion of medical experts.

In addition, the judge criticised the solicitor for not following the 'golden rule' set out in *Kenwood* v. *Adams* (1975) *The Times*, 29 November.

Finally, the judge stressed the importance of attendance notes, without which the solicitor who drew up the will was unable to refresh his memory.

Impact of Mental Capacity Act

Scammell v. *Farmer* [2008] EWHC 1100 (Ch) was the first case involving testamentary capacity to be considered after the Mental Capacity Act (MCA) 2005 came into force. Although the judge decided that, because of the date of death, it was appropriate to base his decision on the old law, it contains helpful comments on the differences between MCA 2005 and the common law.

He said that while MCA 2005, s.3 (which sets out the test for determining whether a person lacks capacity to make a particular decision) can be regarded as largely restating the *Banks* v. *Goodfellow* test, there is an obvious difference between the position at common law and the position under MCA 2005, in that under s.1(2) a 'person must be assumed to have capacity unless it is established that he lacks capacity'. However, s.1(1) states that the principles set out in s.1 apply 'for the purposes of this Act'. The making of a will is not within the purposes of MCA 2005. The only provisions relating to wills are in ss.16–18 and concern the power of the court to make or authorise the making of wills on behalf of persons who lack capacity, not 'the ascertainment of whether a particular testator had capacity when a will was made'.

The Mental Capacity Act 2005 Code of Practice at para.4.33 states expressly that there are existing common law tests of capacity for certain tasks, including making a will. It says that the Act's new definition of capacity does not replace them although, when cases come before the court on such issues, judges can adopt the new definition if they think it is appropriate.

It will be interesting to see the approach of the courts in later cases but at the moment it looks as if MCA 2005 may not have affected the existing position.

12.3.4 Lack of knowledge and approval

The burden of proving that a testator or testatrix knew and approved the contents of his or her will rests with the person seeking to prove that will. However, where testators read through a will (or have had the contents read to them) there is normally a presumption that they knew and approved the contents of the will.

There is no presumption if the testator or testatrix was deaf and dumb or blind or if there were suspicious circumstances (such as where a major beneficiary prepares the will or is active in arranging its execution). See *Richards* v. *Allan* [2001] WTLR 1031. The burden of proof is then upon the person attempting to set up the will to remove any such suspicions and to prove positively that the testator or testatrix knew and approved of the contents of the will.

It is usually preferable to plead lack of knowledge and approval rather than to allege undue influence. Once you can show suspicious circumstances the burden of proving knowledge and approval falls on the person putting forward the will. In a case of undue influence, the person alleging it must prove it. There can be adverse costs consequences where an allegation of undue influence fails.

12.3.5 Undue influence

Undue influence is one of the most difficult allegations to sustain, since the primary witness – the deceased – is by definition unavailable to give evidence and not able to assist the court. There is no presumption of undue influence in relation to wills, unlike the position in relation to lifetime gifts (see below).

Where a solicitor makes an allegation of fraud or undue influence and loses, the solicitor will be particularly at risk of a costs order being made against his or her client.

It should be clearly understood that there is nothing inherently wrong with influence by itself; people who make wills are influenced by various factors when deciding on what they will include in their will. What the law will not allow is *undue* influence.

As mentioned above, proving undue influence in relation to a will is extremely difficult whereas sustaining an allegation of lack of knowledge and approval is somewhat easier. However, you are not allowed to disguise what is in reality a plea of fraud or undue influence as a lesser plea of lack of knowledge (*Re Stott (Deceased)* [1980] 1 WLR 246).

It is, however, important to be alert to the possibility of covert undue influence as was found to be the case in *Gill* v. *Woodall* [2009] EWHC B34 (Ch).

There have been an increasing number of cases involving allegations of undue influence in relation to lifetime gifts.

There is a presumption of undue influence where the donee is in a position of trust and confidence in relation to the donor and the transaction is one that requires an explanation – see the House of Lords decision in *Royal Bank of Scotland* v. *Etridge* [2002] AC 773. Recent cases, such as *Watson* v. *Huber* [2005] All ER (D) 156, and *Turkey* v. *Adwadh and Another* [2005] EWCA Civ 382, have applied the principles set out in *Etridge*.

Daniel v. *Drew* [2005] EWCA Civ 507 has clarified the differences between actual and presumptive undue influence, while the other cases have focused on the significance of the relationships, the nature of the transaction, and the rebuttable characteristic of the presumption.

12.3.6 Beneficial interest under resulting or constructive trust

It may be possible to claim a beneficial interest under a resulting or constructive trust.

12.3.7 Claim under Inheritance (Provision for Family and Dependants) Act 1975

If the client falls within one of the categories set out in s.1 of the Inheritance (Provision for Family and Dependants) (IPFDA) Act 1975, it may be possible to make a claim under the Act.

12.4 PRACTITIONER'S TOOLS

12.4.1 Law Society guidance and *Larke* v. *Nugus*

There is often a need for information about the circumstances in which a will was made. Solicitors are under an obligation to provide information about wills which they have prepared.

On 16 April 2009, the Law Society re-formulated in its Disputed Wills Practice Note the guidance previously given in 1959 and dealing with the issue of where a practitioner has prepared a will which is subsequently disputed, and the practitioner is asked to disclose information about the circumstances surrounding its preparation and execution (see **Appendix A3**). The guidance deals with the circumstances in which a practitioner should disclose the contents of a will. The guidance was affirmed by the Court of Appeal in *Larke* v. *Nugus* SW Vol 123 (1979) CAP 337, and later reported in [2000] WTLR 1033. The Law Society's Disputed Wills Practice Note deals with good practice on receipt of a request for information, the risks of acting in disputes, the risk of incurring cost, conducting litigation on behalf of the beneficiary and protecting the estate pending resolution of the dispute.

12.4.2 Caveats, warnings and appearances

Caveats

Where a person wishes, for example, to bring a probate claim or issue a citation or even to look into the question of whether there are sufficient circumstances for him to oppose the grant of probate, it is necessary to issue a caveat. Rule 44 of the Non-Contentious Probate Rules (NCPR) 1987, SI 1987/2024 sets out the provision for the entry of a caveat – a notice in writing that no grant be sealed in the estate of the deceased without notice to the caveator.

It is important that an application is made for a caveat only where it is appropriate to do so. The purpose of a caveat is to prevent the issue of a grant. It should not be applied for where someone is making an application for financial provision under IPFDA 1975. The appropriate procedure there is for the applicant to make a standing search. The Probate Registry will then inform the applicant when a grant is issued so that the applicant will know when the six-month time limit for applications commences. A caveat remains in force for six months from the date it is entered, though the caveator can extend the caveat for a further period of six months by paying a further fee.

The application for extension must be received by the Probate Registry within the last month of the current six-month period.

12.4.3 Citations

Where a probate dispute can be seen on the horizon, those named as executors may well feel a natural reticence towards doing anything. In addition, very often if the validity of a last will is called into question, the executors may be unhappy to release earlier wills.

In all these cases it is necessary to seek the assistance of the Principal Probate Registry by way of a citation (NCPR 1987, rules 46 and 47). A citation is a document issued out of the Principal Probate Registry or a district registry and can be issued for any one of the following reasons.

Citation to accept or refuse a grant

Where there is a delay in obtaining the grant and the person entitled does not renounce his or her entitlement to do so, a citation may be issued.

Citation to take probate

Where the executor has intermeddled in the estate and thereby accepted office but has not applied for a grant within six months of death, the citation is to take the grant. The citor may be any person with an interest in the estate. A grant to the citor is allowed as an alternative to an order directing the executor to take a grant within a specific time (NCPR 1987, rule 47).

Citation to propound a will

Where the validity of a will is doubted, a person entitled on intestacy or under an earlier testamentary document may cite the executors and persons interested under the alleged will to propound it. It should be noted that a citation is not appropriate for executors appointed by a will doubting the validity of a codicil.

The procedure with a citation is to lodge it in draft form with the district judge/district probate registrar so that he can settle it.

There are alternatives to the citation procedure which may be more effective such as the subpoena procedure or an application under s.116 of the Senior Courts Act 1981 to pass over the person entitled to a grant. Citations are often used to try to force someone who is being dilatory to do something. However, even if the citation is successful in the short term, future progress may still be slow.

12.4.4 Subpoena procedure

If the original will/codicil is in the possession of a person who will not release it and is thus preventing an application for a grant by the person entitled, an application may be made under Senior Courts Act 1981, s.123 for the issue of a subpoena by the district judge/registrar. The application must be supported by an appropriate affidavit (NCPR 1987, rule 50(2)). The effect of the subpoena is to require the person in possession of the will to file it in the registry. The subpoena must be served personally and endorsed with the penal notice. Committal is not normally the result of disobedience, and more usually the person is ordered to attend for examination as to possession of the testamentary document.

If a person is not in possession of the will but has knowledge of it, s.122 of the Senior Courts Act 1981 allows the court to require the attendance of such a person for examination and it is a contempt of court not to comply. This could apply to the witnesses to a will who have declined to swear an affidavit of due execution.

12.4.5 Senior Courts Act 1981, s.116

Where there are appropriate circumstances the court can pass over the persons entitled to a grant and appoint such person or persons as the court feels expedient. This form of application is particularly useful where those entitled to a grant cannot be traced or where it is desired to appoint some person who is not interested in the estate as beneficiary or creditor.

The application is made *ex parte* under NCPR 1987, rule 52 to a district judge or probate registrar, supported by an affidavit. It is possible to pay a fee of £5 to have the affidavit approved by the registrar.

12.5 TYPES OF PROBATE ACTION

12.5.1 Probate action re validity of a testamentary document

The action is commenced by the executor or someone else with an interest under the document or someone opposing a grant. Persons entitled on intestacy may put executors to proof of the will. The attesting witnesses may be called for examination or to swear an affidavit of due execution.

12.5.2 Action regarding interests

An interest action is one in which a person's interest in opposing a will or claiming the right to letters of administration is disputed. Such an action may involve proof of a person's entitlement, for example by production of a birth certificate. Such actions are often about validity of a marriage or legitimacy. The applicant in an interest action will ask the court for a declaration against the person who is claiming entitlement to a grant and instead to make an order in his favour. If the court can be persuaded to make an order, the person who was not entitled to the grant will have their right 'cleared off' and the grant will issue to the person who is properly entitled to administer the estate.

12.5.3 Action regarding revocation of a grant

Such an action is appropriate where a grant has been improperly obtained by a person not entitled or where the will is invalid. On an intestacy the action may force a person who has obtained letters of administration to prove his entitlement. If a will is subsequently found the action will be to revoke the earlier grant and pronounce the will's validity. The court will be asked to pronounce against any earlier will and in favour of the later document, which will in turn enable a correct application for a grant to then be made.

Where a grant has been obtained by mistake, e.g. a filing department has produced the wrong will which has then been proved, an application should be made by the person who obtained the grant with an affidavit specifying the error. The district judge/registrar will then make an order revoking the grant and a further correct application may then be made (see NCPR 1987, rule 41).

In a revocation action the original grant should be filed within seven days of the claim form or within 14 days of service on the defendant of the original grant.

12.5.4 Action for the removal of personal representative

This form of action was introduced by s.50 of the Administration of Justice Act 1985. It allows a personal representative or a person who is beneficially interested in an estate under the will of the deceased or under intestacy rules to apply for the removal of a personal representative.

If the application by summons does not request the appointment of a substituted PR, the court will not allow the estate to be unrepresented. The applicant will swear an affidavit giving reasons for the removal and as to the suitability of the replacement PR who must consent to act. An example of this would be where a partner in a firm is an executor and then leaves the firm. It would be appropriate for him to be removed and replaced with another partner. Part 57 of the Civil Procedure Rules 1998 (CPR) requires every PR to be joined as a party and for the grant to be lodged in court.

Under s.116 of the Senior Courts Act 1981, as stated above, the court has discretion to appoint as administrator any person it considers expedient even if the person entitled, for example on intestacy, would thereby be passed over.

A district registrar or district judge may be willing to contemplate revoking a grant where a PR refuses or neglects to participate properly in the administration of an estate. (See **Chapter 16**.)

It should be noted that a beneficiary of a mutual will is not a beneficiary of an estate and so cannot apply under s.50 of the Administration of Justice Act 1985. See *Thomas & Agnes Carvel Foundation* v. *Carvel* [2007] EWHC 1314 (Ch) where Lewison J held that a person claiming under the doctrine of mutual wills is a beneficiary of a trust which comes into effect not under the will of the surviving testator but on the death of the predeceased testator. Therefore, the beneficiary is not beneficially interested in the estate 'under the will of the deceased' and cannot make an application under s.50. However, such a person is a beneficiary of a trust for the purposes of s.1 of the Judicial Trustees Act 1896 and can apply for the removal of a trustee.

There have been several recent decisions on s.50 applications which are helpful in indicating the court's approach. See, for example, *Angus* v. *Emmott* [2010] EWHC 154 (Ch) and *Alkin* v. *Raymond* [2010] All ER (D) 48 (May) and **6.9.2** above.

12.5.5 Appointment of a judicial trustee

Applications are governed by the Judicial Trustees Act 1896 and the Judicial Trustee Rules 1983, SI 1983/370.

This can be a more expensive exercise than the appointment of a new PR under s.50 of the Administration of Justice Act 1985, but may be the more practical solution where, for example, the sole PR has a beneficial interest in the estate and there has been a substantial breakdown in confidence and/or communications between the PR and the other beneficiaries.

Where an application is made in relation to an estate, s.1(7) of the Judicial Trustees Act 1896 provides that the court may, if it sees fit, proceed as if the application were made under s.50 of the Administration of Justice Act 1985.

The judicial trustee has all the powers and discretions of a properly appointed PR but the court has wide powers to give directions as to the custody of the funds in the estate. Following the appointment of the judicial trustee the trustee or any beneficiary interested can apply to the court for further directions by letter.

12.5.6 Breach of trust or breach of fiduciary duty

Executors who, through negligence and default, have caused loss to an estate will clearly be open to an action by a beneficiary of the estate. Such neglect or default might consist of failures to carry out the provisions of the will; making distributions to persons not named in the will; a failure to maintain neutrality between the beneficiaries on the one hand and the claimants on the other; executors who derive a personal benefit from the estate; or failure to obtain sufficient information regarding the estate.

12.5.7 Claims relating to the administration of estates and trusts

It is possible to apply to court under CPR, Part 64 for:

- the court to determine any question arising in the administration of an estate or in the execution of a trust;
- an order for the administration of an estate or the execution of an estate to be carried out under the direction of the court (an 'administration order').

It is unusual for the court to take over the administration of an estate or trust. It will only do so if it considers that the issues between the parties cannot properly be resolved in any other way. It is more likely to give directions on specific points.

Practice Direction 64A which accompanies Part 64 gives the following examples of the types of claims which may be made for specific directions under Part 64:

- the determination of any question as to who is included in any class of persons having:
  - a claim against an estate;
  - a beneficial interest in an estate;
  - a beneficial interest in any property subject to a trust;
- the determination of the rights or interests of any person claiming:
  - to be a creditor of an estate;
  - to be entitled under a will or intestacy;
  - to be beneficially entitled under a trust;
- a claim for an order requiring a trustee to:
  - provide and, if necessary, verify accounts;
  - pay into court money which he holds in that capacity;
  - do or not to do any particular act;
- a claim for an order approving any sale, purchase, compromise or other transaction by a trustee;
- a claim for an order directing any act to be done which the court could order to be done if the estate or trust in question were being administered under the administration of the court.

Claims under Part 64 can be made by beneficiaries, trustees, PRs or other interested parties. They must use a Part 8 claim form.

12.5.8 Summons to deliver an inventory and account

This is an extremely useful procedure. It is available in the probate registry and is therefore relatively cheap. Every deponent to an oath leading to a grant of administration swears 'to exhibit on oath ... a full inventory of the estate and when so required render an account of the administration'. (See s.25 of the Administration of Estates Act 1925, as amended by s.9 of the Administration of Estates Act 1971.)

This means that anyone with a beneficial interest in the estate can apply by summons at any time for an inventory and account. The summons issues out of the registry from which the grant issued and should be supported by affidavit.

When an inventory is requested, it is a good idea to ask for an order for costs. If an outline of the costs incurred is available when attending the summons, the registrar can assess costs there and then, which avoids the 7.5 per cent taxing fee which would otherwise be payable.

The probate registry's jurisdiction is limited to ordering an inventory and account. For an administration order it will be necessary to go to the Chancery Division under CPR, Part 64.

12.5.9 *Beddoes* summons

A problem often faced by PRs is whether in the administration of an estate they should defend a claim brought against them, initiate an action on behalf of the estate, or compromise a claim on behalf of the estate. A PR who brings or defends a claim without obtaining leave of the court may find himself exposed to the costs that arise. A PR can obtain protection by applying to the court for directions. This is often referred to as a *Beddoes* order, from the case of *Re Beddoes* [1893] 1 Ch 547. The decision as to the granting of a *Beddoes* order is a matter which the court will decide in its absolute discretion in each case, and a *Beddoes* order is not given as of right by the court.

The case of *Singh* v. *Bhasin and Another* [2000] WTLR 275 is a salutary illustration of the risks of not seeking an order.

In some cases it will also be prudent for executors to seek directions from the court under CPR, Part 64.

12.5.10 Rectification under Administration of Justice Act 1982, s.20

Under s.20 of the Administration of Justice Act 1982 the court may order that a will be rectified so as to give effect to the testator's intention. There are two grounds for such rectification:

- in consequence of a clerical error; or
- in consequence of a failure to understand the testator's or testatrix's instructions.

It is important to appreciate that s.20(1)(b) of the Administration of Justice Act 1982 applies where the testator's or testatrix's instructions are not understood, which is not the same as a failure to carry out those instructions. Thus, rectification will not be available where the testator or testatrix, or his or her solicitor, does not understand the meaning and effect of words used, unless it is unclear what his or her instructions were or he or she had failed to inform the solicitor.

If the person seeking rectification has obtained the grant and has the will in his or her possession, these must be lodged with the court when the claim form is issued. If a defendant has the probate or letters of administration in his or her possession, or under his or her control, the defendant must lodge them in the relevant office within 14 days after the service of the claim form on the defendant.

12.5.11 Claims against solicitors

If rectification is not available because of an error by the solicitor who prepared the will, the disappointed beneficiary may have a claim against the solicitor.

12.6 CPR, PART 57

With effect from 15 October 2001, CPR, Part 57 and the accompanying Practice Direction deal with probate claims, claims for the rectification of wills and claims to replace or remove a PR. For this purpose a 'probate claim' is:

- a claim for the grant of probate or letters of administration;
- a claim for the revocation of such grant; or
- a claim for a decree pronouncing for or against the validity of an alleged will not being a claim which is non-contentious (or common form) probate business (such matters being dealt with by Senior Courts Act 1981, s.128).

Non-contentious probate business remains outside the scope of the CPR and is still governed by the Rules of the Supreme Court (RSC).

Note: Transitional provisions – contentious probate proceedings for the rectification of wills started before 15 October 2001 continue to be dealt with by the Practice Direction which supplements CPR, Part 49. Applications for the removal or substitution of PRs made before that date continue to be dealt with under CPR, Sched.1, Ord.93, rule 2.

12.6.1 Commencing a probate claim under CPR, Part 57

Probate claims issue from:

- Chancery Chambers at the Royal Courts of Justice; or
- a Chancery District Registry; or
- a county court which has a Chancery District Registry (at present this means Birmingham, Bristol, Cardiff, Leeds, Liverpool, Manchester, Newcastle-upon-Tyne or Preston) if:
  - an application for grant has been made in the Principal Registry of a district probate registry; and
  - the value of the net estate after payment of expenses and debts does not exceed the county court limit (currently £30,000).

The CPR, Part 57 procedure must be used for probate claims, and CPR, Part 57 Practice Direction, para.2.1 sets out the requirements for the probate claim form (form N2). It is a standard claim form save that it is headed 'In the estate of X deceased (Probate)'. The notes for the claimant (form N2A) are helpful and set out most of the special requirements.

12.6.2 Response to probate claim

The defendant must file an acknowledgement of service on the new form N3. Moreover, if the particulars of claim are served with the claim form, the defendant must file the acknowledgement of service form within 28 days of service of the claim form.

12.6.3 Lodging testamentary documents and filing of evidence of them

Any testamentary documents (previously known as testamentary scripts) in the possession or control of any party must be lodged with the court. Unless the court directs otherwise, these documents must be lodged by the claimant when the claim form is issued and by a defendant when the defendant files his or her acknowledgement of service.

In addition, the claimant and every defendant who acknowledges service must in written evidence describe any testamentary document of which he or she has knowledge or if he or she does not know of any such document, state that fact. Also, if the claimant/defendant has knowledge of any testamentary document which is not in his or her possession or control, the claimant/defendant must give the name and address of the person in whose possession or under whose control it is. If the claimant/defendant does not know the name and address of such persons, he or she must state that fact. There is a prescribed form for written evidence set out in the CPR Part 57 Practice Direction.

In cases of urgent need, the court may permit the claimant to issue the claim form against an undertaking to the court to lodge the documents and file the evidence within such time as the court may specify.

12.6.4 Contents of claim form

The claim form must contain a statement of the nature of the interest of the claimant and each defendant in the estate.

A plea of want of knowledge and approval must be particularised as must a claim that a will was not duly executed, that the testator or testatrix was not of sound mind, memory and understanding or that the execution of the will was obtained by undue influence or fraud.

CPR, Part 57 also deals with revocation actions, judgments in default, summary judgment, discontinuance and settlement, rectification of wills, substitution and removal of PRs.

It is important to appreciate that CPR, Part 57 and its Practice Direction are not a comprehensive reformulation of procedure and accordingly practitioners must bear in mind the other relevant provisions of the CPR.

12.6.5 Costs

Section 51 of the Senior Courts Act 1981 provides that in contentious probate actions all parties' costs are at the discretion of the court.

It is, however, true to say that a 'wind of change' has been blowing for some time in relation to the old 'rule of thumb' that, if the proceedings were reasonable, costs would usually come out of the estate. The issue of costs is now looked at very carefully, and the parties who lose can often find themselves saddled with *inter partes* standard costs (and on occasion with indemnity costs) particularly if it is found that they have instituted untenable or unreasonable proceedings. A prudent practitioner will therefore always keep the question of costs under review and where appropriate make a 'without prejudice save as to costs' offer or a Part 36 offer. Also as stated at the beginning of this chapter, reasonable requests for mediation must be carefully considered, since failure to do so can attract meaningful costs consequences.

Practitioners are also referred to the summary of the rules on costs in *Kostic* v. *Chaplin* [2008] Costs LR 271. The normal rule is that costs come out of the estate and the court will only order otherwise if one of the two exceptions applies, namely:

1. the testator's conduct has caused the litigation;
2. it was reasonable to investigate the position.

See *Perrins* v. *Holland* [2010] EWHC 2558 (Ch), where the court would have let costs lie where they fell had it not been for the son's unreasonable rejection of a settlement offer.

CHAPTER 13

Liability for a client's fraud

Alexander Learmonth

13.1 INTRODUCTION

A solicitor may, in good faith, assist a client in a financial transaction which appears at the time to be perfectly proper, but which turns out to involve a fraud on a third party. In the context of a probate practice, this could consist of helping a client obtain probate of a will the client knows to be forged or otherwise invalid, falsely completing an inheritance tax return, or in distributing an estate on the basis of false information provided by a client. The solicitor will then want answers to three questions:

- Can I be held liable in any way to the injured third party?
- Can I disclose details of the client's transaction to the third party once I discover (or more likely suspect) the client's wrongdoing?
- Have I committed a criminal offence under POCA 2002?

This chapter gives basic guidance on these issues. It does not consider a solicitor's liability for his or her own fraud *per se*, or for actions taken in his or her capacity as an executor under a will, which are considered elsewhere in this book. The next section deals with the extent of liability for a client's fraud in the light of the leading cases. Section **13.3** deals with the solicitor's duty of confidentiality. Section **13.4** suggests what action solicitors should take when they know or suspect that a client has involved them in a fraudulent transaction. The final section considers POCA 2002.

13.2 HOW LIABILITY CAN ARISE

A number of recent cases illustrate the way in which a solicitor (or other professional adviser) can become drawn into a client's improper scheme, and face a claim. In one case, the defendant solicitor acted for several members of the same family in relation to a complex network of family trusts, which included his appointment as trustee. The assets had been acquired by the father of the principal beneficiaries, who was also a trustee and beneficiary under certain of the trusts. The solicitor was asked to exercise his powers as trustee to support the business run by the father, which involved a substantial risk to the assets of the trust. The solicitor was one of the defendants sued by the other members of the family after the business collapsed and the father was declared bankrupt (*Walker* v. *Stones* [2001] QB 902). The court had to decide whether the solicitor was guilty of a breach of his own fiduciary duties, or guilty of assisting others to contravene their own obligations. Though this was not a probate case, such a situation could equally arise under a will trust.

Another illustration involved a firm of accountants acting for an oil company, which was being defrauded by its in-house accountant. The firm took instructions from a French lawyer, and did not discover the nature of the transactions in which they had assisted until the oil company sued them. They thought that they had been involved in a scheme to circumvent exchange controls. Again, the court had to decide whether they were liable for the losses suffered by the company (*Agip (Africa) Ltd* v. *Jackson* [1991] Ch 547).

In both cases, the professional advisers were found to be liable for the losses suffered, although in neither case had they been personally enriched beyond the payment of fees. It is at least conceivable that solicitors could become unwittingly caught up in similar situations in the probate context.

13.2.1 Liability for receipt and liability for assistance

There are two main ways in which liability can arise:

- for receiving the proceeds of fraud through:
  - unjust enrichment and the common law of restitution;
  - the tort of conversion;
  - a proprietary constructive trust in equity;
  - knowing receipt;
- for assisting in the fraud through:
  - dishonest assistance in a breach of trust or fiduciary duty;
  - breach of contract;
  - the tort of negligence.

Each of these will be briefly examined in turn. It goes without saying, of course, that any practitioner in doubt as to whether a particular transaction is lawful, or faced with a claim under one of these heads, should consult specialist textbooks or seek other advice before proceeding.

13.2.2 Liability for receiving the proceeds of fraud

Liability for unjust enrichment

In *Lipkin Gorman* v. *Karpnale Ltd* [1991] 2 AC 548 the House of Lords set out the conditions under which a claim for unjust enrichment can succeed:

- the defendant must be enriched;

- the enrichment must be at the claimant's expense;
- the enrichment must be unjust, which means that there must be a factor, such as mistake or duress, which renders the enrichment reversible, not simply that the enrichment is 'unfair'; and
- there must be no defence (such as bona fide purchase or change of position).

Liability does not depend on fault by the defendant: the fact of enrichment, combined with the lack of a defence, will justify the court giving judgment for the claimant.

The application of these tests means that, in practice, solicitors and other professional advisers are unlikely to incur liability to make restitution. There will normally be no enrichment beyond the receipt of fees: while substantial sums may pass through a client account, the professional is not enriched by this, and so no liability will arise.

Liability for conversion

It is easier to incur liability as a result of handling chattels (including cheques and bankers' drafts) on behalf of a client. Liability can arise under the tort of conversion, which applies to any dealings with a chattel inconsistent with the rights of the person entitled to immediate possession. A person who deals with a stolen cheque or bankers' draft will be strictly liable for its face value if there is anyone entitled to immediate possession (*Morison* v. *London County and Westminster Bank* [1914] 3 KB 356; *International Factors Ltd* v. *Rodriguez* [1979] QB 315; *Lipkin Gorman* v. *Karpnale Ltd* (above)). There is no defence of change of position, although the Bills of Exchange Act 1882 provides limited defences based on acting in good faith and for value.

Liability under a proprietary constructive trust

A proprietary constructive trust is a trust attaching to property, or its proceeds, which can be followed or traced from the claimant to the defendant under the equitable rules of tracing. Liability arises here because the defendant is in possession of property which belongs, in equity, to the claimant. Equity will not trace property into the hands of a bona fide purchaser for value without notice of the equitable claim.

The greatest risk for a professional in relation to this form of liability is to be faced with competing claims on clients' monies; for example, a third party claiming that funds held in a client account are in fact the traceable proceeds of a fraud which the client has received. In such a situation, a professional faced with a claim which is not obviously hopeless should consider making an application to court for directions: paying the money to the client with notice of the claim attaching to it might lead to liability for knowing assistance in a breach of trust, as described below.

13.2.3 Personal liability to account 'as a constructive trustee'

Personal and proprietary claims distinguished

The use of the term 'constructive trust' to describe two entirely different situations has caused confusion for a long time. In deciding a claim based on a proprietary constructive trust, the court has to ask whether a person takes property subject to or free from an equitable claim. The court looks at whether the defendant had notice of the equity, whether the defendant gave value, and whether he or she still has the property or its traceable proceeds.

The phrase 'liable to account as a constructive trustee' is also sometimes also used to describe the situation where the defendant is to have imposed upon him or her the personal burdens and obligations similar to those of a trustee. This usage has been criticised, and is 'no more than a formula for equitable relief' (*Paragon Finance* v. *D. B. Thakerar & Co* [1999] 1 All ER 400, 409). Such liability will arise where the defendant has either received and subsequently disposed of trust property, or become involved in a breach of trust in circumstances in which it is equitable for the defendant to be treated as a trustee. The court therefore looks at the defendant's knowledge, rather than the more technical rules of actual and constructive notice. Liability may extend to the total amount knowingly received by the defendant, or the total foreseeable loss suffered by the claimant as a result of the breach of trust in which the defendant assisted (*Target Holdings Ltd* v. *Redferns* [1995] 3 All ER 785).

Liability for knowing receipt and dealing

To be liable for knowing receipt and dealing, defendants must receive property, beneficially belonging to the claimant, for their own benefit. Consequently, a professional who legitimately receives trust property on behalf of a client (holding it in a client account), and passes it on, cannot be held liable under this head, because there is no beneficial receipt (*Agip (Africa) Ltd* v. *Jackson* (above)).

Again, the difficulty for professionals arises where their fees have been paid out of the property claimed by the claimant. In the earliest case to address this issue, *Carl Zeiss Stiftung* v. *Herbert Smith and Co (No.2)* [1969] 2 Ch 276 the question was whether the solicitors involved could retain the fees which had been paid to them for defending a claim that their client held all of its assets on trust for the claimant. The court held that as the firm acted honestly and provided full consideration, it could not be liable for knowing receipt.

The other, and most difficult, ingredient is what the defendants' state of mind must be. *BCCI* v. *Akindele* [2000] 4 All ER 221 made it clear that dishonesty is not an essential element of a claim for knowing receipt. It is enough that the defendant should receive property in circumstances in which the defendant's state of knowledge makes it unconscionable to retain it. In particular, there is now a possibility that professionals may be required to repay fees which were received honestly, but where they had sufficient notice of the claimant's interest to make the receipt 'unconscionable'. In cases of doubt, professionals are likely to be best advised to insist upon payment from another source, or where they already hold the funds when the claim is notified to them, it could well be appropriate to make an application to the court for directions (*Finers* v. *Miro* [1991] 1 All ER 182, and see below as to duties of confidence.)

Liability for dishonest assistance

While dishonesty is not an essential element in a claim for receipt of trust property, it remains the most important element in liability for assistance (*Royal Brunei Airlines* v. *Tan* [1995] 3 WLR 64). A person who helps another to misapply trust property will be liable to the beneficiaries if he or she does so dishonestly; no liability arises if the assistance is provided honestly, even if the defendant acted negligently. It is therefore unlikely to be a claim that will concern most professionals.

If the defendant acts dishonestly, he or she will be liable even if the breach of trust itself is not dishonest. Lord Nicholls in *Royal Brunei Airlines* v. *Tan* (above) gives the example of trustees who wish to deal with the trust funds in their care in such a way as to amount to a breach of trust, without realising. If a solicitor acts for them in the knowledge that a breach of trust is being committed, he or she will be liable to the beneficiaries.

The test for dishonesty is now definitively stated in *Twinsectra* v. *Yardley* [2002] 2 AC 164, a case of particular relevance to solicitors. Money was paid to Yardley's solicitor on the undertaking that it would be used to buy a particular property. But the solicitor paid it to a second solicitor acting for Yardley, on oral assurances that the money would be so applied, but without any undertakings as such. The second solicitor paid it to Yardley himself, who dissipated some of the money without investing it. T sued (*inter alia*) the second solicitor for dishonest assistance. The majority of the House of Lords adopted a test that combined both objective and subjective elements:

> before there can be a finding of dishonesty, it must be established that the defendant's conduct was dishonest by the ordinary standards of reasonable and honest people and that he himself realised that by those standards his conduct was dishonest.

Since the second solicitor – owing to a mistake as to the law – had not appreciated that his conduct was dishonest by ordinary standards, he was not liable. This is reassuring for solicitors.

However, the Privy Council has added a gloss to this test in *Barlow Clowes International (In Liquidation)* v. *Eurotrust International Ltd* [2005] UKPC 37, which has subsequently been applied. The *Twinsectra* test was explained as requiring not an understanding of what the generally accepted standards of honesty were, but knowledge of those elements of the transaction that made it dishonest by those standards.

It is not necessary to know the precise details of the fraud being carried out provided the defendant knows that something illegal or improper is being planned. In *Agip (Africa) Ltd* v. *Jackson* (above): the defendant accountants thought that they were assisting in a scheme to contravene Tunisian exchange controls, rather than a fraud on the claimant, but were nevertheless held to have acted dishonestly.

Negligence

Solicitors engaged in financial transactions will clearly owe a duty to safeguard the client's interests. But solicitors may also owe a duty of care in tort to third parties. In the area of probate, it is now clear that solicitors may be liable to a testator's intended beneficiaries if a will is inexpertly drafted (at least to the extent of the costs incurred in having it rectified), if its execution is inordinately delayed or inadequately supervised by the solicitor, or if the necessary steps to give effect to the will are not taken (e.g. the severance of a joint tenancy). Solicitors also need to give thought to the tax consequences of transactions, and although the question of liability to a deceased's estate for avoidable inheritance tax is fraught with difficulty, there seems little doubt in principle that such a claim can succeed.

13.3 FRAUD, PRIVILEGE AND CONFIDENTIALITY

13.3.1 Nature of the problem

Solicitors who fear that they may inadvertently have become involved in a fraudulent transaction are placed in a difficult position with regard to client confidentiality. If the solicitor has acted properly, there should be no liability in relation to past actions. However, the solicitor may incur liability by continuing to act after his or her suspicions have been aroused, and assistance previously provided to the client may allow that client to continue to defraud innocent persons in the future.

Further, the position under the general law as set out below is subject to the radical changes effected by POCA 2002, considered below.

13.3.2 Decision of the Court of Appeal in *Finers* v. *Miro*

The leading case on the options available to an inadvertent participant in a fraud at common law remains the decision of the Court of Appeal in *Finers* v. *Miro* [1991] 1 WLR 35. The solicitors in that case helped their client to set up a complex series of trusts which made his ownership of his assets difficult to detect, and did so in such a way that they found themselves holding the assets as bare trustee for the client. They then discovered that the client was accused of defrauding an insurance company, and feared that the assets in the trusts were the proceeds of the fraud. They applied to the court for directions, and asked whether the liquidator of the insurance company should be notified of the application. The Court of Appeal held that the liquidator should be notified because, on the evidence available, there was proof on the balance of probabilities that the alleged fraud had been committed. Communications between a solicitor and client for the purpose of furthering a client's fraud are not confidential, because committing a fraud is no part of the solicitor–client relationship. Professional obligations are regarded as never having arisen if solicitors discover in the course of acting that clients have been using them to commit a fraud, and so disclosure can be made without the client's consent. For these purposes, 'fraud' covers all forms of dishonesty, as long as the conduct in question amounts to real dishonesty, and not merely disreputable conduct or a failure to maintain good ethical standards (*Gamlen Chemical Co (UK) Ltd* v. *Rochem* (1980) 124 SJ 276 (per Goff LJ), followed in *Finers* v. *Miro* (above)).

A solicitor can disclose information if he or she is consulted by a client who wants help to plan, execute or conceal a fraud. However, if the fraud is already complete, and the client is seeking advice which would not further it or conceal it, the solicitor cannot disclose the fraud to the injured party. The solicitor would be in breach of both the legal duty of confidentiality and the rules of professional conduct if any disclosure were to be made without a court order. But that position is now subject to POCA 2002, discussed below.

13.3.3 Privilege and confidentiality

The position of solicitors is complicated by the fact that information may be privileged as well as confidential. The two concepts are distinct: privilege is much narrower than confidentiality, as it relates only to the inadmissibility of solicitor–client correspondence in litigation. *O'Rourke* v. *Darbishire* [1920] AC 581 is authority that as fraud is outside the solicitor–client relationship, information relating to the solicitor's furtherance of a fraud is not privileged.

13.4 ACTION BY SOLICITORS INVOLVED IN DISHONEST TRANSACTIONS

Having outlined the basic legal position in relation to fraud and confidentiality, we now turn to the appropriate course of action for any solicitors who fear that a client has been using their services to defraud an innocent third party.

13.4.1 Professional rules

Rule 4 of the Solicitors' Code of Conduct 2007 deals with confidentiality and disclosure. Of particular significance is note 8(a) of the guidance to the rule, which provides that the contents of a will cannot be disclosed to anyone other than the executors without their consent until the will is admitted to probate. The guidance also acknowledges the existence of exceptions to the rule of confidentiality in cases of proceeds of crime and money laundering, and sensibly suggests that practitioners refer to the SRA's Professional Ethics Team.

However, it is submitted that the guidance in the relevant parts of the old rules ('The duty to keep a client's confidences can be overridden in certain circumstances' – guidance to rule 16.02 of the Solicitors Practice Rules 1990) remains an accurate summary of the general law:

> The duty of confidentiality does not apply to information acquired by a solicitor where he or she is being used by the client to facilitate the commission of a crime or fraud, because that is not within the scope of a professional retainer. If the solicitor becomes suspicious about a client's activities the solicitor should normally assess the situation in the light of the client's explanations and the solicitor's professional judgment.

The greatest problem arises when a firm cannot simply refuse to act because it is still holding some of the proceeds of the suspected fraud. When the client has failed to satisfy the solicitor of the honesty of the transaction, the solution is to apply to the court for directions on how to apply the funds held on trust, as in *Finers* v. *Miro*, where the court held that it has jurisdiction to give directions for the administration of a bare trust, even where the apparent beneficiary opposes the application and asks for the funds to be paid direct to him or her.

13.5 PROCEEDS OF CRIME ACT 2002

The Act, the relevant parts of which came into force on 24 February 2003, contains a number of parts, of which the most important to solicitors are those dealing with anti-money laundering provisions in Part 7. This chapter provides only a summary of the relevant law. Solicitors should refer to the Law Society's Anti-Money Laundering Practice Note (**www.lawsociety.org.uk**).

13.5.1 Money laundering

Probate practitioners are perhaps particularly likely to encounter danger in this field, because their work will frequently involve their clients disclosing their affairs in great detail, and then require them to manage or distribute their client's property. Solicitors must carefully consider their position as soon as they know or suspect, or have reasonable grounds for suspicion, that the client's property may be 'criminal property' within the meaning of POCA 2002; that is to say, any property which the defendant knows or suspects to represent a benefit from criminal conduct, either directly or indirectly, in whole or in part. From a probate practitioner's perspective, it is important to note that it appears that criminal property will continue to be criminal property even after the death of the person guilty of the original criminal conduct.

There are a number of offences to consider:

- concealing, disguising, converting or transferring criminal property, or removing it from the jurisdiction (s.327);

- making arrangements to facilitate the acquisition, retention, use or control of criminal property by or on behalf of another (s.328);
- acquiring, using or having possession of criminal property without having given adequate consideration (s.329).

It is a defence to each of these offences if a person makes an authorised disclosure and has obtained the appropriate consent, or where the defendant intended to make such a disclosure but had a reasonable excuse for not so doing. Authorised disclosures must be made to a constable or customs officer, or to the nominated officer of the disclosing party's employer, who will then pass on the disclosure to the Serious Organised Crime Agency (SOCA). Where an authorised disclosure is made prior to a transaction which would otherwise be an offence, the disclosing party must wait for consent before proceeding with the transaction in question.

The most important offence for solicitors in general is that of making arrangements under s.328. The Court of Appeal in *Bowman* v. *Fels* [2005] EWCA Civ 226, [2005] 1 WLR 3083 has provided some welcome guidance on the scope of that offence. It was held that s.328 was not intended to cover the ordinary conduct of litigation, which included any step taken from the issue of proceedings to final judgment, and it is thought that litigation also extends to pre-action steps and the disposal of property in accordance with any judgment or settlement. However, 'sham proceedings' would still be caught, and would probably involve misleading the court in any event.

Section 328 is therefore of more importance in transactional work. Almost all transactions involving criminal property, including its distribution under the terms of a will, might be said to facilitate the retention, use or control thereof. Distribution of property under the terms of a will might also constitute an offence of transferring or removing criminal property from the jurisdiction under s.327. However, accepting suspected criminal property as fees will not be an offence under s.329, provided they are reasonable fees and provided the fees are not paid for services which are known or suspected to help another carry out criminal conduct.

The only safe course is to make an authorised disclosure, and refrain from taking further steps until consent is given, or the time for considering whether to give such consent has expired. However, solicitors may be in breach of their duty of confidentiality and the client's legal professional privilege if they do so, unless they have prima facie evidence that they are being used in furtherance of a crime. The Law Society recommends that in such circumstances, solicitors should either obtain a waiver of privilege from the client (subject to tipping-off issues), or withdraw from the case altogether.

13.5.2 Disclosure obligations and tipping off

POCA 2002 created the following offences of particular relevance to solicitors who acquire detailed knowledge of their clients' affairs:

- failing to make an authorised disclosure of information received in the course of a business in the 'regulated sector' (for example managing investments) that another person is engaged in one of the above offences (s.330);
- tipping off: disclosing the fact that a suspicious activity has been made or that an investigation into money laundering is being carried out or is being contemplated, so that any investigation which might follow the disclosure would be prejudiced (s.333A).

There are a number of defences to tipping off. These include that the person who made the disclosure did not know or suspect that the disclosure would prejudice an investigation (s.333D(3) and (4)). Another defence is that the disclosure is made to the client for the purpose of dissuading the client from engaging in the alleged money laundering (s.333D(2)).

CHAPTER 14

Wills and best practice

Lesley King with Helen Clarke

14.1 DRAFTING POINTS

14.1.1 Appointment of solicitor-executor

Probate registries report frequent problems with the wording of clauses appointing solicitor-executors. An appointment of 'one of' or 'two of' the partners in a firm is void for uncertainty. The appointment should be of 'the partners' in the firm at the date of the deceased's death and express the wish that only two should prove.

The clause included in *Williams on Wills*, 9th edn (Sweet & Maxwell, 2007) (as B3.9), has the approval of the Principal Registry of the Family Division. The commentary usefully outlines the issues.

Incorporation and conversion into limited liability partnerships (LLPs) have caused problems where there is a will appointing 'partners in the firm of'. The probate registrars decided at their annual conference in 2003 that where a firm becomes an LLP an appointment as executors of 'partners in the firm' is void. The basis of their decision was that the members of the successor LLP were not 'partners' in a 'firm'.

In *Re Rogers (Deceased)* [2006] 2 All ER 792 Mr Justice Lightman considered the effect of a standard appointment of 'partners' in relation to a firm which had become an LLP. He said that the wishes of the testatrix should not be frustrated by the decision of the solicitors to alter the legal nature of the vehicle through which they carry on that practice. He therefore held that profit-sharing members of the LLP were to be treated as partners and could apply for probate.

The decision was welcome. It made no mention of incorporated practices but the spirit of the judgment would suggest that the owners of an incorporated practice ought to be treated as partners for this purpose.

Notice that the judgment drew a clear distinction between profit sharing partners/ members and others. The judge said:

> ... even as the 'partner in the partnership' means in the case of a partnership a profit sharing partner and not merely a salaried partner or a person merely held out (but not in fact) a partner, so when transposed to a limited liability partnership the member must mean a profit sharing member.

This distinction causes problems for partnerships where salaried partners have been in the habit of obtaining grants of representation as this will no longer be possible if the appointment is of 'partners'. Going forward, the will can be drafted to define 'partner' as including 'salaried partner'. Precedents B3.9–B3.12 in *Williams on Wills*, 9th edn (Sweet & Maxwell, 2007) have been redrawn to take account of the implications of a future change in the nature of the firm.

In the case of existing wills, it would be possible for all the profit sharing partners to grant a power of attorney to the salaried partner to allow the salaried partner to take a grant on their behalf.

Partners applying for a grant under standard appointment clauses should describe themselves as 'profit sharing partners'.

14.1.2 Sole practitioners

Sole practitioners should include in their own wills an appointment of a special executor to deal with the affairs of the practice. Suitable clauses were published in the *Probate Section Journal* (November, 2001). They are also available from the Solicitor Sole Practitioners Group (see **www.spg.uk.com**).

14.1.3 STEP: standard conditions for wills

On behalf of the Society of Trust and Estate Practitioners (STEP), barrister James Kessler has prepared a set of standard administrative clauses for wills and settlements (see **Appendix F** for address). STEP's aim in publishing the standard provisions was to enable wills and settlements to be shortened, and to provide the necessary standard powers in language which is lucid, contemporary and easily understood by non-lawyers.

A Practice Direction from the Principal Registry of the Probate Division dated 10 April 1995 allows wills incorporating the STEP provisions by reference to be proved in the normal way without providing the text of the provisions themselves.

At the time of writing the second edition of the standard provisions was being prepared.

If incorporating the STEP provisions it is helpful to place a copy of the edition current at the date the will is made with the will. Testators may not die until many years later, by which time the provisions may have been amended several times. Life will be much simpler for the person dealing with the administration if the relevant provisions are to hand.

14.1.4 Clauses excluding liability for negligence in respect of professional executors/trustees

Many people feel that it is inappropriate to include in wills and settlements clauses which seek to limit the liability of a solicitor or other professional trustee, when acting as an executor or trustee, to loss or damage through fraud or dishonesty and to exclude liability for negligence. Solicitors should in any event be fully insured against their own negligence. Of course, there are clearly special cases where it would be reasonable for the trust document to exclude or restrict liability more widely (for example, estates or trusts involving assets held overseas in countries with unreliable legal systems, long-running and serious family or other disputes, or continuing litigation).

In *Armitage* v. *Nurse* [1997] 3 WLR 1046, CA and *Bogg* v. *Raper* (1998) *The Times*, 22 April, [1998] CLY 4592, the Court of Appeal stated that clauses limiting liability for negligence were not contrary to public policy nor to the nature of a trust. Millett LJ stated that, although many people felt such clauses had gone too far, it would require legislation to change their validity.

Bogg v. *Raper* confirmed that a solicitor who prepares a will or settlement which appoints the solicitor or a partner as an executor or trustee and which then restricts or excludes liability for negligence, does not 'receive a benefit'. The clause merely limits liability.

On 19 July 2006 the Law Commission published a report (No.301) on trustee exemption clauses favouring a non-legislative solution. It recommended that professional and regulatory bodies should adopt rules or guidance to the effect that any paid trustee, who causes a settlor to include a trustee exemption clause in a trust instrument which has the effect of excluding or limiting liability for negligence, must before the creation of the trust take steps to ensure that the settlor is aware of the meaning and effect of the clause.

The Law Society was consulted by the Law Commission prior to publication of the report and supported this approach.

Rule 2.07 of the Solicitors' Code of Conduct 2007 states that solicitors must not exclude or attempt to exclude by contract all liability to clients. However, it is permissible to limit liability, provided that such limitation:

(a) is not below the minimum level of cover required by the Solicitors' Indemnity Insurance Rules for a policy of qualifying insurance;
(b) is brought to the client's attention; and
(c) is in writing.

There is further guidance in the notes to the rule. In particular, when preparing a trust instrument for a client which limits trustees' liability in negligence, a solicitor should take reasonable steps before the trust is created to ensure that the client is aware of the meaning and effect of the clause. Extra care is needed if the solicitor, or anyone in or associated with the firm is a paid trustee of the trust. The guidance makes the point that it is prudent to ensure that there is evidence that the appropriate steps were taken and that the evidence is retained for as long as the trust exists and for a suitable period afterwards.

On 14 September 2010 the Parliamentary Under-secretary of State for Justice (Mr Jonathan Djanogly) announced the government's acceptance of the Law Commission's recommendations in its 2006 report on Trustee Exemption Clauses (see *Hansard*). He said that they had already been adopted by the leading regulatory and professional bodies but that the Government would be promoting further uptake by writing directly to the relevant regulatory and professional bodies to urge them to adopt the approach recommended by the Law Commission.

14.1.5 Mutual wills

For wills to be mutual wills there must be evidence of an agreement between two people that:

- they will each leave their property in a particular way (not necessarily to each other, *Re Dale (Deceased)* [1994] Ch 31); and
- neither party will revoke unilaterally.

The mere fact that the wills are 'mirror-images' does not make them mutual.

In fact the agreement is impossible because wills cannot be made irrevocable. Each party is always free to revoke. Revocation may be out of the hands of the survivor as where a later marriage revokes an earlier will.

However, revocation does not assist the survivor as equity will intervene. If the first party to die has carried out his or her part of the agreement, the law imposes an obligation on the survivor to give effect to the agreement. In effect, assets of the survivor are held under a trust.

Apparently the trust is a floating one during the lifetime of the survivor and crystallises on the survivor's death (*Re Goodchild (Deceased)* [1996] 1 WLR 694 confirmed by the Court of Appeal [1997] 1 WLR 1216). There is some uncertainty as to how the trust works. What if the survivor spends or gives away everything before death? In *Birmingham* v. *Renfrew* (1937) 57 CLR 666 the court said:

> No doubt gifts and settlements, *inter vivos*, if calculated to defeat the intention of the compact, could not be made by the survivor and his right of disposition, *inter vivos* is, therefore not unqualified.

This means that the survivor is free to dispose of the assets unless such disposal is made with the object of defeating the interests of the agreed ultimate beneficiary. Mutual wills may provide little protection for the agreed beneficiary as there may be few assets left by the time the surviving testator or testatrix dies. At the same time they may prove troublesome for the survivor who may be uncertain as to the extent of his/her powers to deal with the combined assets.

Birch v. *Curtis* [2002] WTLR 965 illustrates the need for evidence of an agreement that the wills were to be irrevocable. In that case Rimer J accepted that there may well have been an agreement between the husband and wife as to how the husband was to leave his property after the wife's death. However, there was no evidence of an agreement that he would not revoke his will. Therefore, the wills were not mutual and the husband was free to leave his property as he wished. Always include an express statement if there is such an agreement.

Even more importantly, however, consider including a statement that there is no such agreement in other wills. This makes the true position clear to the clients. It will also help deter disgruntled family members from incurring the expense and ill-feeling of challenging the will of the survivor.

If the agreement relates to land it is necessary to comply with the requirements of the Law of Property (Miscellaneous Provisions) Act 1989 which provides that there must be a written agreement signed by both parties. In *Healey* v. *Brown* [2002] All ER (D) 249 a husband and wife had made mutual wills dealing with their respective beneficial interests in the matrimonial home. The wife died first and the husband transferred the house into joint names with his son from a previous marriage. On the husband's death the court held that the agreement was void as there was no writing signed by both parties. If making mutual wills relating to land, it is, therefore, important to have a separate written agreement which both parties sign. It is not sufficient that each party signs his or her own will. Both parties must sign one document. It is possible for a solicitor-appointed executor or executrix to employ and pay individual partners in the firm, provided there is an express agreement that the solicitor PR shall not participate in the profits nor derive any benefit from the charges (*Re Gates* [1933] Ch 913).

In *Walters* v. *Olins* [2008] EWCA Civ 782 the survivor of the alleged contract denied that there had ever been an agreement not to revoke. However, the Court of Appeal agreed with the trial judge that the terms of a codicil which included the following words:

> This codicil is made pursuant to an agreement made between my husband and me for the disposal of our property in a similar way by mutual testamentary dispositions.

together with a letter from the solicitor explaining the effect of the agreement amounted to sufficient evidence to establish a binding agreement. It is clearly much more satisfactory for the terms of the agreement to be set out in the will. In *Charles* v. *Fraser* [2010] EWHC 2154 (Ch) the judge described the failure to include such a statement in the will as 'remarkable' and said:

> I think it was the plain duty of any solicitor, then as now, faced with two sisters wishing to make reciprocal wills, to ascertain their intentions as to revocation, to advise as to the effect of making mutual wills and to ensure that the agreement the testatrices wished to make was clearly and accurately recorded.

At first instance in *Olins* ([2007] EWHC 3060 (Ch)) the issue of the effect of the Law of Property (Miscellaneous Provisions) Act 1989 had arisen, as the property which was subject to the agreement included land. Norris J held that the Act did not apply on the facts. *Healey* v. *Brown* had held that the contract to make a will had to comply with the formalities required to dispose of the property actually described in the will. In *Olins*, although the matrimonial home which was owned by the deceased wife passed as part of the residue, the will did not refer to it expressly. The deceased directed her executors to convert her estate, and after directing them to pay her testamentary and funeral expenses, debts and taxes, disposed of the residue so realised. Norris J held that no formalities are required for such a disposition. The result, therefore, appears to be that the requirements of the Act need only be complied with where the will expressly describes the property.

Mutual wills present a number of problems and will rarely present the best solution for a client. Problems include:

- There is uncertainty as to the extent of the trust binding the survivor.
- Does the trust bind the property inherited or does it extend to the property owned by the survivor at the death of the first to die or to the after-acquired property of the deceased? The answer probably depends on the terms of the agreement but the problems are clear.
- Do the parties really understand the implications?
- The first to die will have little certainty that the assets will pass as intended. The survivor may have spent the assets by the date of death; the terms of the agreement may not become apparent on the survivor's death so that no one realises the estate is bound by a trust.

See 'Mutual wills and future ills' by Peter Nellist in (2008) 98 *Trusts and Estates Law & Tax Journal*, 23 for more information on problems associated with mutual wills.

14.1.6 Making provision for animals

This is often a difficult problem for clients. In an interesting article in the July 2003 issue of the *Probate Section Journal*, Julia Abrey, a principal of the London firm Withers, gave three possible solutions to the problem of caring for animals after the owner's death:

1. The animal and a sum of cash are left to the executors with a note of wishes that a particular person should care for the animal using the money available.
2. The animal and a sum of cash are left to a named legatee with the proviso that the legatee only gets the money if they care for the animal. A substitute legatee can also be named.
3. The animal and the money are left to an animal charity, such as the RSPCA asking them to find a suitable home. This leaves the money free of IHT, but the gift cannot be made conditional.

The article made the point that first two solutions place a burden on the executor in terms of policing the arrangement and means that IHT will be payable on the funds left for the care of the animal. A spokesperson for the RSPCA confirmed that it comes across problems involving animals and legacies quite regularly:

> We are becoming a more and more litigious society and some people are not happy when they find they have been cut out of a will in favour of an animal. Sometimes they have a good case under the Inheritance Act, but some are try-ons by the family. We look at each case individually and we take legal advice. We will do what we can to avoid going to court. Unfortunately costs usually end up coming out of the estate in these cases. At the same time we will do what is necessary to protect our interests.

The charity confirmed that in every case where it has been left an animal to re-home, it has so far been successful: 'The welfare of the animal is our priority and even if an animal is elderly we have managed to find a home.'

Anyone wanting advice on drawing up specific clauses involving the RSPCA undertaking care of an animal can contact the RSPCA's Legacy Department for furthcr information.

14.1.7 Wills and public funding

The making of wills and matters of trusts law generally are amongst the services that cannot normally be publicly funded as part of the Community Legal Service scheme (Sched.2 to the Access to Justice Act 1999). However, s.6(8) gave the Lord Chancellor power to issue directions authorising the Legal Services Commission (LSC) to fund certain services which would normally be excluded. On 2 April 2001 he issued *Scope of the Community Legal Service Fund – Exceptions to the Exclusions* which authorises the LSC to fund Legal Help where the client is:

(a) aged 70 or over; or
(b) a disabled person within the meaning of the Disability Discrimination Act 1995; or
(c) the parent of a disabled person (as defined in (b) above) who wishes to provide for that person in a will; or
(d) the parent of a minor who is living with the client but not with the other parent, and where the client wishes to appoint a guardian for the minor in a will.

Applications for funding under this direction must still satisfy all relevant criteria in the Funding Code and regulations.

14.2 MENTAL CAPACITY

The classic test of testamentary capacity is set out in *Banks* v. *Goodfellow* (1869–70) LR 5 QB 549. See **6.1.3** for a fuller discussion.

14.2.1 The 'golden rule'

Questions of capacity frequently cause problems for solicitors taking instructions for a will.

In particular, when taking instructions from an elderly or mentally frail client, solicitors need to consider the 'golden rule'. This was first articulated by Templeman J (as he then was) in *Kenward* v. *Adams* [1975] CLY 3591 and followed in *Re Simpson (Deceased)* (1977) 121 SJ 224. The rule as stated in *Kenward* v. *Adams* is as follows:

> In the case of an aged testator or a testator who has suffered a serious illness, there is one golden rule which should always be observed, however straightforward matters may

> appear, and however difficult or tactless it may be to suggest that precautions be taken: the making of a will by such a testator ought to be witnessed or approved by a medical practitioner who satisfies himself of the capacity and understanding of the testator, and records and preserves his examination and findings.
>
> There are other precautions which should be taken.
>
> If the testator has made an earlier will this should be considered by the legal and medical advisers of the testator and, if appropriate, discussed with the testator. The instructions of the testator should be taken in the absence of anyone who may stand to benefit, or who may have influence over the testator.
>
> These are not counsels of perfection. If proper precautions are not taken injustice may result or be imagined, and great expense and misery may be unnecessarily caused.

The presence or absence of such precautions will not affect the validity of the will. Validity is a matter for the court to decide and depends on whether or not the testator actually had the appropriate capacity and knew and approved the contents of the will and whether or not there was any force, fraud or undue influence. In *Sharp* v. *Adam* [2006] EWCA Civ 449 May LJ said:

> The golden rule is a rule of solicitors' good practice, not a rule of law giving conclusive status to evidence obtained in compliance with the rule. Nevertheless, where a testator's apparent mental state is observed and recorded at the time when he actually executes the will in complete compliance with the rule and with the care with which it was in the present case; and where professional people concerned reached a properly informed and recorded conclusion that the testator does have testamentary capacity, it will require very persuasive evidence to enable the court to dislodge that conclusion.

In *Sharp* v. *Adam* the Court of Appeal did conclude despite a contemporaneous medical opinion and the 'meticulous' way in which the solicitor had taken instructions that the testator had lacked capacity.

The danger for solicitors who do not follow the golden rule is that a court may take the view that the failure has led to probate proceedings which might have been avoided had contemporaneous medical evidence been available. See, for example, *Corbett* v. *Bond Pearce* [2001] EWCA Civ 531, where Sir Christopher Slade said of *Worby* v. *Rosser* [1999] Lloyd's Rep PN 972:

> ... the significance of this case lies in the fact that the Court of Appeal accepted that in a case where a solicitor's negligence in regard to the preparation or execution of a will was the cause of expensive probate proceedings after the testator's death, this could give rise to a claim for damages against the solicitors at the suit of the testator's personal representatives for the benefit of the estate generally.

In *Key* v. *Key* [2010] EWHC 408 (Ch) Briggs J was extremely critical of a solicitor who made a will for a recently bereaved 89-year-old testator without obtaining any medical advice. He said that the failure to comply with the golden rule had 'greatly increased the difficulties to which this dispute has given rise and aggravated the depths of mistrust into which his client's children have subsequently fallen'.

However, much will depend on the facts of the case. In *Perrins* v. *Holland* [2009] EWHC 2558 (Ch) the unsuccessful challenger of a will claimed costs from the estate on the grounds that the litigation had been induced by uncertainty over the testamentary capacity of the testator, and that the real cause of these uncertainties was the failure of the legal executive who took instructions for the will to follow 'the golden rule'. Lewison J rejected the claim. He did not consider that the failure to follow the 'golden rule' caused the litigation. Even where the 'golden rule' has been obeyed, a will may still be successfully challenged on the ground of testamentary incapacity. He made the important point that the claimant's expert witness had been very sceptical of a GP's ability to assess the mental capacity of a person, like the testator, who was suffering from severe multiple sclerosis. The practical point for solicitors is that the opinion of an ordinary GP may not carry much weight in a case where the client suffers from a disease which is difficult to assess.

The problems are most acute where capacity is borderline but the will needs to be made urgently either because of approaching death or because it is clear that the testator's capacity will not improve. It is important that an individual is not denied an opportunity to have their wishes carried out.

In an interesting article in the 87th edition of the ACTAPS Newsletter Judge Alastair Norris QC considered the vexed question of what a solicitor should do if faced with a would-be testator who in the draftsman's opinion is competent but who according to a medical practitioner lacks capacity:

> My own view is that the position should be explained to the testator. And the will offered for signature. It is then for the testator to decide whether to sign it or not …
>
> The client is the testator. He has given instructions on which the will draftsman has felt able to act. He should be told there is a doubt about his legal capacity to sign a will that day. The options should then be explained. If there is a prospect of improvement in capacity (a change in a drug regime, a refreshing rest, the passing of a temporary infection) the possibility of postponement can be discussed, but the risk that the will might never be signed recognised.
>
> If there is no prospect of improvement in capacity, then the choice presented to the testator would simply be either to forego the will-making power or to sign a will that is likely to be the subject of challenge.
>
> In my view it is for the testator to choose whether to sign the will in the light of that advice. If he cannot understand the advice or make a choice then that might suggest that the will draftsman's assessment of testamentary capacity might require review. ('Might suggest' because there will be cases where capacity to sign a document which accords with instructions earlier given will constitute sufficient testamentary capacity, though capacity to give instructions is lacking.) If he can understand the advice, then it might suggest that the medical practitioner's assessment might require review. But if they remain at odds, and the client wants to sign I cannot see why he should not. His instructions are lawful and he (and those in whom any right of action will vest on his death) cannot complain that they were given without the benefit of advice: and the probate court will be able to decide whose assessment was right.

This is a difficult area. It may not always be practical in terms of cost and time to obtain a medical opinion. Even when one is obtained, it may not address the issues which are relevant to the question of testamentary capacity; the medical practitioner may not recognise the particular problems of the testator. See, for example, *Charles v. Fraser* [2010] EWHC 2154 (Ch) where the medical report said that the testator had testamentary capacity yet she had forgotten the existence of her family. The best solution will often be for the solicitor to ask questions to test the client's ability to fulfil the elements of the *Banks* v. *Goodfellow* test and to make a full attendance note. Unless it is possible to cross-check the information given, however, this will not help in a case where the client has forgotten the existence of family members.

14.2.2 Association of Contentious Trust and Probate Specialists checklist

The Association of Contentious Trust and Probate Specialists (ACTAPS) has published a checklist on capacity. We have reproduced it below with their kind permission.

RISK ASSESSMENT: Factors to be taken into account in the assessment of mental capacity/undue influence

By Christopher Allen, consultant with Lawrence Graham and Member of the Association of Contentious Trust and Probate Specialists Committee

A 'Golden Rule' was reemphasised by Mr Justice Templeman (as he then was) in *Re Simpson deceased* (*Solicitors Journal*, 1 April 1977). Templeman J there said that the events of this case, which involved the disputed will of an old and infirm testator 'constrained him to repeat the warning he had given in *Kenward* v. *Adams*, *The Times*, 29 November 1975, that the making of a will by such a testator ought to be witnessed and approved by a medical practitioner who satisfies himself as to the capacity and understanding of the testator and makes a record of his examination and findings'.

The points in issue were recently reinforced by *Re Morris, Trustees of Great Ormond Street* v. *Rushin and Others* (Lawtel, 15 May 2000). In referring to the rule, Rimer J stated that the rule must always be observed 'however straightforward matters appear and however difficult or tactless it may be to suggest that precautions be taken'. The desirability of review and discussion of earlier wills with testators and for instructions to be taken in the absence of a potentially influential beneficiary were also emphasised.

In the light of these cases and *Killick* v. *Pountney*, *The Times*, 30 April 1999, ACTAPS with assistance from Susan Midha of the [Private Client Section] has drawn up a suggested checklist which has now been adopted by the [Private Client Section].

Possibly there has been diffidence about producing a 'Code of Conduct' lest the already heavy duties placed on practitioners be further increased. It seems to me to make little difference what one calls the following; we have Lord Templeman's 'Golden Rule' and individually we have to decide how to apply it in the many and various situations with which we are faced.

Preliminary notes

1. The test of testamentary capacity remains that established in *Banks* v. *Goodfellow* (1870) LR5QB 549, namely:
   (a) the testator must not be affected by any disorder of mind or insane delusion. A disorder which operates only in respect of a particular individual may amount to lack of capacity although it must be sufficient to affect the testator's judgment – mere eccentricity or irrationality does not in itself invalidate the will;
   (b) he should appreciate the nature and consequences of making a will, e.g. understanding that the will operates only on death, that it can be changed or

revoked and beneficiaries might die before him. He should generally be aware of the purposes of appointing executors;

(c) he must understand the extent of his property (in general terms). He ought also to realise that his estate may reduce (or increase) over time and know if any assets are jointly owned;

(d) the testator should consider the moral claims of those persons for whom he ought to make provision.

2. Lack of capacity and vulnerability to undue influence may go hand in hand but equally one may exist without the other. It is felt helpful to separate them because the precautionary measures to be taken by the practitioner (e.g. the attendance of a doctor) are not necessarily the same in each case.
3. The following constitute important areas for practitioners to raise with their clients. It should, however, be noted that the list is not exhaustive, nor are all items compulsory (e.g. in the case of an elderly and very alert client whom the practitioner has known for many years) but there may well be additional points to be raised in particular cases.

Capacity

- Client's name and date of birth
- Have you any reason to doubt your client's testamentary capacity?
- Are you aware of any medical problems of your client? What are they?
- Is your client taking any medication and if so what?

If in the light of the above, you feel that your client's capacity may be questioned:

- Have you advised the client of the importance of having either a medical report or medical witness or both if he/she has any medical or other condition which could invalidate the will?
- Have you kept contemporaneous file notes?

Undue influence

- Do you consider there are any issues of vulnerability or suggestibility in the client or do you feel that the client might be subject to undue influence as defined by case law?
- Who contacted you to see the client or to draft the will?
- Who else was present when the instructions were given?
- Has your client made an earlier will or wills?
- What changes is your client making?
- Was the client able/prepared to tell you why the changes were being made?
- Attach a brief family tree.
- What relationship do the main beneficiaries have with your client?
- Has your firm acted for the client (or his or her family) before?

If there seems to be a problem:

- Did you discuss the existence of lifetime gifts with the client? If so, were they made to someone with whom your client had a 'special relationship' as defined in case law? Has that person subsequently benefited under the will?
- Who was present, apart from the witnesses, when the will was executed?

14.2.3 Mental Capacity Act 2005

The Mental Capacity Act 2005 came into force on 1 October 2007. The provisions of the Act which are most relevant to testamentary capacity are contained in ss.1–3.

For a discussion of the impact of the Act on the test of testamentary capacity see **6.1.3**.

14.2.4 Instructing medical practitioners

The Law Society and the British Medical Association have prepared guidelines in *Assessment of Mental Capacity: A Practical Guide for Doctors and Lawyers*, 3rd edn (Law Society, 2009) which provides answers to many awkward questions. It sets out the specific legal tests of capacity to make particular decisions or carry out legal transactions, and explains how these relate to the medical practicalities of assessing capacity. Appendix H of this book provides a sample letter to a GP requesting evidence of testamentary capacity, reproduced below:

Dear Dr [name]

RE: [CLIENT'S NAME] [DATE OF BIRTH] AND SOLICITOR'S REFERENCE [...]

I am instructed on behalf of [X] who wishes me to prepare a will on his/her behalf. As you may be aware, the courts have advised that wills that are drawn up for an elderly person or for someone who is seriously ill should be witnessed or approved by a medical practitioner. In accordance with good practice I am therefore writing to request that you assess [X]'s capacity to make a will and prepare a report which may be used in evidence in the event that there is any subsequent legal challenge.

I attach evidence of [X]'s consent for you to disclose medical information for the purpose of this report.

As you may know, under the Mental Capacity Act 2005, we are required to presume that [X] has capacity to make specific decisions unless there is proof that s/he does not and also to take steps to enable him/her to make decisions. In relation to making a will, I have seen [X] personally and have explained the legal consequences of the wishes s/he would like to be put into effect in the will. The fact that [X] has made choices that others may think are unwise does not, by itself, indicate that s/he lacks capacity.

You may wish to note that you need only show on the balance of probabilities whether [X] has or does not have testamentary capacity, in other words, that it is more likely than not. I also request that you pay particular attention to the following points, and indicate whether [X] understands them:

- The nature of the act of making a will. This involves understanding that s/he will die and that when s/he does the will comes into operation. Further, s/he can change or revoke the will before his/her death, but only for as long as s/he has the mental capacity to do so.
- The effect of making a will. This includes the appointment of executors, deciding who receives what, whether the gifts are outright or limited or conditional in some way, the

consequences of a depleted estate, that a beneficiary may pre-decease him/her, the effect on any previous will, and the reasonably foreseeable consequences of making or not making a will at this time.

- The extent of the estate. This includes the amount of property or money or investments s/he holds (although not necessarily the exact value) and the fact that some may be jointly owned, whether s/he has any debts, that some benefits may be payable only on his/her death irrespective of his/her will, and that the estate may change during his/her lifetime.
- The possible claims of others. This involves the ability to distinguish between individuals who may have some claim on the estate and to reach some kind of moral judgment in relation to them. Beneficiaries may be left out because they are otherwise well provided for, or because of personal reasons or preferences. [X] must be aware of these reasons and the possibility that these could be challenged.

I attach details of [X]'s estate for your reference along with a draft will which s/he has agreed to disclose.

As you may be aware, a diagnosis of mental disorder does not necessarily mean that [X] lacks capacity. It would be helpful therefore to include in your report details of any impairment of, or disturbance in the functioning of, [X's] mind or brain and whether that has any effect on his/her ability to make decisions concerning the will. I would be grateful if you would also include reference to [X]'s physical state in so far as it is relevant to this report.

I have requested you prepare this report because [X] informs me that you have been his/her family doctor for a number of years. If, however, in the course of taking a psychiatric history and conducting a mental state examination you consider a specialist report is required (for example from a psychiatrist or psychologist), please let me know.

If you are of the opinion that [X] has the capacity to make a valid will, I would be grateful if you would agree to act as one of the witnesses when the time comes for him/her to sign it.

I confirm that we have agreed the sum of [£ ...] for the purposes of the examination and preparation of this report. In the unlikely event that you are required to give evidence at court a further fee will be negotiated. Please mark your invoice with the reference stated at the top of this letter.

If you require any further information or clarification on any points please do not hesitate to contact me.

Yours sincerely

Mind has issued a booklet on wills and trusts to help people with mental health problems gain greater financial control of their lives. *Find Peace of Mind* is a step-by-step guide to wills. It can be ordered via its website (**www.mind.org.uk**).

14.3 NEGLIGENCE AND WILLS

Clients are much swifter to allege negligence than used to be the case. There are a number of problem areas in connection with taking instructions for a will.

14.3.1 Preparing a will for someone who lacks capacity without making adequate checks

Solicitors who do not take appropriate steps to satisfy themselves that a client has appropriate capacity may be liable to the estate for the costs of a successful challenge to the validity of the will. See *Worby* v. *Rosser* [1999] Lloyds Rep PN 972 and *Corbett* v. *Bond Pearce* [2001] EWCA Civ 531.

14.3.2 Failing to take steps necessary to make the will effective

A solicitor may be held liable to a disappointed beneficiary who cannot benefit under a will because the solicitor has not taken steps necessary to ensure that an asset is part of the estate (for example, failing to advise on the possibility of severing a beneficial joint tenancy). In *Carr-Glynn* v. *Frearsons* [1998] 4 All ER 225 the Court of Appeal held that the solicitor was negligent because she had allowed the testatrix to execute a will at a time when neither she nor the testatrix knew whether the testatrix was able to leave her interest in her house to the desired beneficiary. According to the Court of Appeal the solicitor should have advised the client that it was possible to serve a notice of severance as a precaution irrespective of whether the property was actually owned as beneficial joint tenants or tenants in common.

14.3.3 Failing to clarify the property owned

Clients do not always remember how they own property. In *Chittock* v. *Stevens* [2000] 1 WTLR 643 the matrimonial home was believed to be in joint names but eight months after the death of the husband (partially intestate) it was discovered that it had been in his sole name.

Property in joint names may be held on a resulting trust for the original purchaser. In *Carlton* v. *Goodman* [2002] 2 FLR 259 the Court of Appeal found that although a property had been conveyed into joint names, it was in fact in the sole beneficial ownership of the deceased.

Be careful in this context of the House of Lords decision in *Stack* v. *Dowden* [2007] UKHL 17. The House of Lords held (Lord Neuberger dissenting) that in a domestic consumer context (as opposed to a purchase for investment) the presumption is that beneficial title follows legal title. Hence, a person who claims that the beneficial ownership is different from the legal ownership must produce evidence to prove this. So in sole ownership cases the burden of proof falls upon the non-owner to show that he has any interest at all. In joint ownership cases, the burden falls upon the joint owner who claims to have other than a joint beneficial interest. In a number of cases since the House of Lords decision courts have found that the evidence to rebut the *Stack* v. *Dowden* presumption was inadequate. See, for example, *Jones* v. *Kernott* [2010] EWCA Civ 578.

What does 'In a domestic consumer context' mean? In *Adekunle* v. *Ritchie* [2007] WTLR 1505 the court held that it is not limited to cohabiting couples living together in a platonic or sexual relationship and applied the *Stack* v. *Dowden* approach in a case where a property had been purchased by a mother and son. However, the question is always one of fact. In *Laskar* v. *Laskar* [2008] All ER (D) 104 (Feb) the Court of Appeal held that where property was purchased jointly as an investment, albeit by a mother and daughter, it was not appropriate to apply the presumption of joint ownership. Despite the familial relationship between the parties, it was clear that the purchase was nothing more than a business venture.

Proprietary estoppel may mean that someone else can claim an interest in property 'owned' by the client. See *Gillett* v. *Holt* [1998] 3 All ER 917; *Campbell* v. *Griffin* [2001] WTLR 981; *Jennings* v. *Rice* [2002] WTLR 367; *Thorner* v. *Curtis* [2009] UKHL 18; *MacDonald* v. *Frost* [2009] EWHC 2276 (Ch).

The existence of such an interest ought to reduce the value of the property to the legal owner for IHT purposes. Valuation for IHT is at open market value at the date of death (IHTA 1984, s.160). Hence, where a promisee has been given a right to occupy, the value of the property in the promisor's estate ought to be reduced to reflect the fact that the promisor no longer enjoys the property unencumbered. However, HMRC is not keen to admit such a reduction: see 'What price a promise?' by Peter Nellist in (2009) 109 *Trusts and Estates Law & Tax Journal*, 17, in which he makes the point that, while HMRC's arguments may not be correct '... it can hardly ever be in a client's interests to become involved in litigation with the Revenue: so give and take in negotiations may be essential ... Some clients like a fight, most do not'. He does, however, give two examples of cases where he was able to negotiate a reduction in the value transferred on the basis that the property was subject to occupation rights which reduced its open market value.

Does the client have a power of appointment over trust property? If it is a general power of appointment, an ordinary residuary gift will be sufficient to exercise it without any express reference to the power. The client may not realise this and may believe that, because the power has not been expressly exercised, the trust property will pass to the person entitled in default. In *Gibbons* v. *Nelsons* [2000] PNLR 734 the court found that a solicitor was in breach of duty in not clarifying the client's wishes in such circumstances.

Solicitors should always try to resolve any ambiguities or uncertainties when taking instructions. In *Sillett* v. *Meek* [2007] EWHC 1169 (Ch) there was criticism of a legal adviser who had drafted a will and enduring power of attorney for a client who had recently put an account containing substantial funds into joint names with a friend, Mrs Meek. The judge expressed surprise that the adviser:

> ... should have neither known, nor, apparently, cared whether the account was to pass by survivorship to Mrs Meek beneficially, or whether it was to pass to Mrs Meek as sole legal owner, to be distributed under the will of which he and Mrs Meek were appointed executors.

Where there is any doubt, the solicitor should record that the will has been prepared on the basis of the information provided by the client.

Be aware that serving a notice of severance is not the only way of severing a joint tenancy (see **6.7**). Section 36(2) of the Law of Property Act 1925 expressly preserved the pre-1925 methods of severance.

This means that, although a client may appear to be the sole beneficial owner of property as a result of survivorship, there may have been an earlier severance by conduct. See *Re Woolnough (Deceased)* [2002] WTLR 595.

14.3.4 Failing to prepare a will sufficiently quickly

The speed required depends on circumstances. In *X (A Child)* v. *Woollcombe-Yonge* [2001] WTLR 301 a solicitor was alleged to have been negligent where a testatrix, known to be suffering from terminal cancer, died before he had prepared a will. He had intended to have the will ready for signature one week after taking instructions. Neuberger J held that on these facts the amount of time taken was not unreasonable. It was significant that although the testatrix was terminally ill, she was not expected to die in the near future. Neuberger J went on to say that:

> Where there is a plain and substantial risk of the client's imminent death, anything other than a handwritten rough codicil prepared on the spot for signature may be negligent. It is a question of the solicitor's judgment based on his assessment of the client's age and health.

Note the useful decision of *Atkins* v. *Dunn & Baker (A Firm)* [2004] All ER (D) 324 in which the Court of Appeal held that the retainer to prepare a will normally extends only to the preparation of a will which the client is free to execute or not. There will normally be no obligation to 'chase' a client who does not execute a will.

14.3.5 Failing to keep an appointment

A solicitor who cancelled an appointment to visit a client in hospital for execution of the client's will was held to be negligent in *Hooper* v. *Fynmores (A Firm)* [2001] WTLR 1019:

> there is a positive duty on the solicitor to satisfy himself that the additional delay caused by his (not the client's) request is not to the client's detriment.

14.3.6 Allowing a will to be executed conditionally

In *Corbett* v. *Newey* [1996] 3 WLR 279 solicitors allowed a testatrix to sign a will but not to date it. Her intention was that the will was not to come into effect until she had completed certain lifetime gifts. The will was held to be invalid because executed conditionally. The solicitors therefore were liable to compensate the disappointed beneficiaries.

14.3.7 Failing to offer an opportunity to execute the will under supervision

In *Esterhuizen* v. *Allied Dunbar* [1998] 2 FLR 668 Longmore J said:

> It is in my judgment not enough just to leave written instructions with the testator. In ordinary circumstances just to leave written instructions and to do no more will not only be contrary to good practice but also in my view negligent.

To protect themselves solicitors should have in writing an offer in the following terms:

- the client can visit the solicitor's office for execution;
- if the client prefers, the solicitor will visit the client's house with a member of staff; or
- if the client prefers, the client can make his or her own arrangements.

Although the safest course is clearly to follow *Esterhuizen*, it is worth noting that in the earlier case of *Gray and Others* v. *Richards Butler* [2000] WTLR 143 Lloyd J found that a solicitor who had not offered to oversee execution had not been negligent in the circumstances of the case. He referred to the 'very clear terms of the attestation provision of the will' and went on to say that:

> What steps are appropriate in discharge of these various duties in any given situation may depend on who the client is and the view that the solicitor has formed, or ought to have formed if acting with reasonable competence, as to the ability of the client to understand and follow advice as to the relevant procedures.

14.3.8 Failing to inspect a will returned after execution

In *Ross* v. *Caunters* [1979] 3 All ER 580 Megarry V-C accepted that the solicitors had breached their duty by *inter alia*:

- not checking the will after execution;
- not noticing that one of the witnesses was a spouse of a beneficiary; and
- not bringing that fact to the attention of the testator.

In *Gray and Others* v. *Richards Butler* [2000] WTLR 143 the court accepted that there was nothing about the particular will under consideration which should have aroused suspicion. However, the case proceeds on the basis that solicitors have a duty to inspect a will that has been returned.

In *Humblestone* v. *Martin Tolhurst Partnership* [2004] EWHC 151 (Ch) the court accepted that a solicitor has a duty to inspect a will returned for safekeeping whether or not asked to do so.

14.3.9 Failing to offer a client advice required for the transaction being carried out

In *Hurlingham Estates Ltd* v. *Wilde & Partners* [1997] STC 627, Lightman J had to consider whether or not a property lawyer had entered into an effective agreement with his client to exclude any obligation to advise on the tax aspects of a property transaction. He concluded that there was insufficient evidence of such an agreement. It ought to have been recorded in a letter to the client so that the client could have considered the implications and discussed them with others, but it had not been. He also held that to be effective such a limitation on liability would require fully informed consent on the part of the clients.

He went on to consider whether, in the absence of an effective retainer limiting liability, a solicitor carrying out a commercial conveyancing transaction for a client has an obligation to advise on tax implications. Obviously this is an issue for probate practitioners too.

Lightman J said that the test was whether, having regard to all the circumstances, the solicitor should reasonably have appreciated that the client 'needed his advice and guidance in respect of the tax liabilities to which entry into the transaction would expose it'.

A solicitor cannot gain protection from liability by claiming to rely on counsel's opinion. In *Estill* v. *Cowling* [2000] WTLR 417 an estate suffered unnecessary IHT because a discretionary trust was established in inappropriate circumstances.

Arden J said that he endorsed the approach taken in *Locke* v. *Camberwell Health Authority* [1991] 2 Med LR 249 that a solicitor does not abdicate his professional responsibility when he seeks the advice of counsel.

The principles to be derived from the relevant authorities were, he said, as follows:

1. In general, a solicitor is entitled to rely upon the advice of counsel properly instructed.
2. For a solicitor without specialist experience in a particular field to rely on counsel's advice is to make normal and proper use of the Bar.
3. However, he must not do so blindly but must exercise his own independent judgment. 'If he reasonably thinks counsel's advice is obviously or glaringly wrong, it is his duty to reject it ...' (per Taylor LJ, at 254, with whom Sir George Waller and Parker LJ agreed).

Arden J went on to consider what in his view a reasonably competent solicitor would do to give himself sufficient general knowledge of the subject:

> as respects the tax considerations, he would have read some general outline of the tax implications of setting up a trust, and (having discovered IHT applied to all transfers of value subject to exemption) looked to see what exemptions were available. The point was not some obscure point of tax law. It was a basic principle of IHT which had been discussed in the professional press at the time, particularly when the law was changed to make transfers to IIP trusts PETs. As it was, Mr Anderson did no research of his own ... His conclusion that a transfer of value to the settlement was a PET was negligent.

14.3.10 Failing to recognise an international element

A number of problems can arise here. There are the obvious ones of unfamiliarity with the client's local law or not recognising that the client may be subject to forced heirship rules or, if married, to community of property but there are many more. A number arise in relation to domicile and were listed by Sophie St John in a helpful article 'A wolf in sheep's clothing' on the dangers of hidden international aspects in (2009) 105 *Trusts and Estates Law & Tax Journal*, 24. They include the following:

- If a client has a non-domiciled spouse or civil partner, the spouse exemption for IHT will be limited to £55,000.
- A woman married before 1 January 1974 took her husband's domicile (called a domicile of dependency). After that date she would retain it as a domicile of choice unless and until she abandoned it and acquired a different domicile.
- A child is deemed to have a domicile of dependency but only until 16, at which point the child may establish a domicile of choice.
- Clients will obtain deemed domicile in this country if they have been resident in the United Kingdom for 17 years out of 20. Alarmingly, this can be triggered where a taxpayer is resident for 15 years and two days as residence for part of a tax year counts as residence for that tax year.

14.4 WILLS PROCEDURE CHECKLIST

Some practitioners like to use a checklist with their clients. Others prefer to have one available for their own use as an *aide-mémoire*. The following checklist was compiled by the Law Society after discussions with the various probate registries around the country. It is intended to be used while taking instructions, as an *aide-mémoire* of the topics to cover and record of those instructions.

The checklist draws attention to common mistakes which can lead to delay in obtaining the grant and other points, certain of which are mentioned in this Handbook, which can easily be overlooked. Probate registries report difficulties in relation to the drafting of clauses appointing solicitor-executors (see **6.3.1** above).

Wills procedure checklist

1. Did you obtain full, clear instructions from the client?
2. Was there any reason to suspect a later challenge to the client's testamentary capacity? If so, did you ask questions to satisfy yourself? And record them in a full written attendance note?
3. Did you check the client's eligibility for public funding: age; capacity; intention?
4. Did you check that any charity mentioned is really charitable? And the correct charity name, number and address? And that the estate is likely to be solvent and all the legacies can be paid?
5. Have you explained to the client (in no particular order):

- the pros and cons of appointing members of the family/solicitors/others as executors?
- the implications of the clauses extending or varying the executors' general law powers and duties?
- the impact of the general law on the will (e.g. effect of marriage, formation of civil partnership)?
- the implications of any charging clause?
- the need for parents to appoint guardians of minor children?
- the position of single parents under the Children Act 1989?
- the law relating to specific, general or demonstrative legacies, where appropriate, e.g. the need to review specific legacies if the property the subject of the gift alters or is sold or destroyed?
- the terms and effect of any residuary gifts made?
- whether there will be any secret or half-secret trusts?
- whether the will is to be mutual, i.e. not to be revoked unilaterally?
- the effect of mutual wills? (are they appropriate for the client?)
- whether the will incorporates any document – was that intended?
- the general law concerning the payment of tax, testamentary expenses or other liabilities (especially those items which will not be paid out of residue)?
- the tax planning considerations which affect the terms of the will, e.g. lifetime gifts within seven years of death?
- the likelihood of a claim under the Inheritance (Provision for Family and Dependants) Act 1975 and, if any, what should be done?
- about the position of a cohabitee (with and without an interest in the home)?
- the consequences for the beneficiaries if the residue is much larger (say because of an unexpected windfall) or smaller (say because a property has had to be sold to pay for care) than anticipated?
- the advisability of making an enduring power of attorney and discussed with the client a procedure for making the will available to the attorney (to avoid problems such as accidental ademption)?
- the need to sever a joint tenancy if the client wants to make a gift of property held as beneficial joint tenant?

6. Have you agreed the arrangements for valid execution of the will, and advised the client accordingly? Have you offered to inspect the will after execution?
7. What is to happen to any previous wills or codicils? It is advisable to destroy them so as to avoid any possible confusion; similarly letters of wishes relating to personal chattels.
8. Have you asked the client if there are any other practical or legal steps they want to consider in relation to their financial and other arrangements – writing a life insurance policy in trust, drawing up an enduring power of attorney making an advance directive or living will?
9. Was the will executed within a reasonable time? If not, did you:

   - explain to the client the implications of not executing the will, i.e. intestacy or non-revocation of existing will?
   - sought instructions about new provisions, if the client is unhappy about the terms or effect of the draft will?
   - ensured that existing provisions have not been overtaken by events in the intervening period?

10. After the will has been executed, have you:

    - checked it was executed and witnessed properly by people who are neither beneficiaries nor married to beneficiaries?

- kept a copy for your files?
- if you are holding the original, have you given a copy to the client?
- advised on the importance of placing the will where it will be found, and telling executors and family where it is?
- advised on the desirability of the client placing a Personal Assets Log [*available from the Law Society*] with their papers?
- explained to the client that it is necessary to review a will every two to five years and sooner if there is a major change of financial or personal circumstances?
- agreed the extent of your retainer? Is the client aware that you will/will not be reminding them of the need to review their will in five years' time or in any other situation, and will/will not be notifying them about tax changes affecting provisions made? [*The dramatic changes to the taxation of trusts introduced in the Finance Act 2006 were a good illustration of the importance of being clear as to whether or not the solicitor has an obligation to inform clients of changes in the tax rules.*]
- if partners of the firm have been appointed as executors have you a separate record of this so that the client can be approached if a partner leaves, retires or dies?

14.5 SOLICITOR'S DUTY AFTER WILL EXECUTED

This guidance was approved by the Law Society's Standards and Guidance Committee and Property and Commercial Services Committee in 1991:

1. It is for clients to ensure that their wills are kept up to date and solicitors may help clients to do this by retaining in a manual or computer database (note the requirements of the Data Protection Act 1984 [repealed by Data Protection Act 1998] and European legislation in relation to manual records and databases) the names of clients for whom they have drawn up wills in the past. Solicitors may write to these clients from time to time reminding them of the need to review a will regularly and of their firms' services.
2. The preparation of a will for a client is in the ordinary case an entire contract so that when the work is completed and the final bill is submitted, the relationship of solicitor and client may be assumed to have ended as far as will preparation is concerned. Of course, the relationship of solicitor and client may continue with that client on other matters. Where solicitors have a continuing relationship with clients, they may wish to consider agreeing with those clients whether or not the client wishes the firm to maintain a watching brief on legal changes or tax changes which might affect their will; the Society considers that it would be appropriate for a charge to be made for such a service in addition to charges for preparation of a will.
3. Without specific instructions from the client, a retainer for will preparation would not entail the solicitor in maintaining any such 'watching brief', but it is possible for a solicitor by his or her conduct to change a retainer so that a client comes to have a reasonable expectation that such a watching brief will be maintained. Solicitors would be well advised to ensure that these matters are clear between themselves and their clients.
4. Many firms store clients' wills as a free service and a courtesy to their clients. The storage of a will does not of itself create a retainer. Solicitor and client may agree otherwise.
5. In relation to wills stored by firms, should a solicitor or clerk named as executor or executrix in such a will retire, move to another practice, or die, or otherwise become unable or unwilling to act, the firm should consider writing to the testator

or testatrix at the client's last known address detailing the changed circumstances. Informing clients of such internal changes to a firm is not considered to be any indication that a watching brief on matters of law has been agreed upon, but is, rather, part of the necessary changes which follow retirement or resignation, etc., of a solicitor from a firm, such as changes to the notepaper.

6. Some firms may retain large numbers of wills for clients from whom they have not heard for many years. Solicitors wishing to clarify the position in relation to these wills may wish to consider writing to a testator or testatrix at the last known address. However, even if no reply is received, such wills should never be destroyed as they remain the clients' property or the property of the clients' PRs.

In February 2001 the Law Society's Probate Section obtained counsel's opinion (from Sian Warnock-Smith and Tracey Angus) on client retainers. The opinion deals with a variety of aspects of retainers and contains some useful clauses for inclusion in a client care letter.

It contains the following paragraphs:

> A solicitor who is instructed to prepare a Will would not, unless he has expressly agreed to do so, owe any duty to conduct a regular review of the client's Will which he holds (for example, an annual review in the light of the Budget). However, a solicitor who is instructed to prepare a codicil, would usually owe a duty to review the contents of the Will and any earlier codicils.
>
> Firms that provide Will drafting services should certainly review their standard precedents in the light of any important reported authority (such as *Re Benham*) or change in the law. However, once this task is performed, the firm does not, in our opinion, owe any duty to its past clients to review its old Will files and to contact clients for whom it has prepared Wills in the past in order to advise them of the implications of that decision or change in the law unless it had agreed with the clients in question that it would provide this service.

14.6 RETAINERS GENERALLY

Also note the cases of *Cancer Research Campaign* v. *Ernest Brown & Co* [1997] STC 1425; *Gibbons* v. *Nelsons* [2000] PNLR 734 and *Gray* v. *Buss Murton* [1999] PNLR 882, all of which emphasise the importance of clarity in the terms of a solicitor's retainer. In *Gibbons* v. *Nelsons* (above) Blackburne J stressed that a solicitor has a general duty to the client when preparing a will and the burden is on the solicitor to demonstrate any limitation on that retainer:

> Although the burden of proof rests with the claimant to establish what the scope was of the solicitor's retainer, once the claimant establishes that the solicitor was retained to prepare a will, the burden must, I think, shift to the solicitor to show, if he can, that his responsibility for the preparation of the will did not extend to advising the client on some aspect of the will relevant to the claim.

In *Gray* v. *Buss Murton* (above) Rougier J said that any ambiguity in the retainer would be determined in favour of the client. It is the solicitor's duty to clarify precisely the terms of any retainer.

Lightman J in *Hurlingham Estates Ltd* v. *Wilde & Partners* [1997] STC 627 emphasised the need for a client to give informed consent to any limitation in the retainer and to the importance of a clear written record of any agreement to limit the retainer.

In *Atkins* v. *Dunn & Baker (A Firm)* [2004] All ER (D) 324 Pill LJ held that the retainer for preparing a will did not normally extend to sending reminders to a client who failed to execute it.

The evidence was that the instructions were that a draft will should be prepared and submitted to the client. That was done promptly in accordance with instructions. The solicitor had completed the task which he had been asked to perform. It does not necessarily follow from the retainer rules, which cover a variety of situations, that in this situation there was inevitably a duty upon a solicitor to send a reminder.

The Probate Section opinion referred to above contains useful precedent clauses setting out the extent of the retainer. The following is included by way of illustration:

1975 Act Advice

The Inheritance (Provision for Family and Dependants) Act 1975 may enable certain persons to seek additional provision out of your estate after your death. If an application is made under this Act it is likely to involve your estate in expense and may result in a variation of the dispositions made in your will.

If the information which you provide to us for the purposes of preparing your will suggests that there is a real risk of such an application being made in respect of your estate, we will advise you that this is the case. However, we will not offer more detailed advice in relation to IPFDA 1975 unless you ask us to do so and, in those circumstances, an additional fee will be charged.

14.7 ADVANCE DECISIONS TO REFUSE MEDICAL TREATMENT

14.7.1 Introduction

'Advance decisions' are sometimes referred to as 'living wills' or as advance directives. They are documents intended to allow individuals to specify the extent and nature of the medical treatment they would or would not find acceptable should they lose capacity in the future. The term 'living will' is confusing since such documents have no connection with ordinary wills. The Mental Capacity Act (MCA) 2005 uses the term 'advance decision' and this is becoming more usual.

Competent patients can authorise or refuse consent to treatments, both contemporaneously and in advance. They cannot make legally enforceable demands about specific treatments they wish to receive. *R (on the application of Burke)* v. *General Medical Council* [2005] EWCA Civ 1003 confirmed that medical practitioners are under no obligation to provide a specific treatment requested by the patient if in their view it is clinically inappropriate.

The case of *Re B (Consent to Treatment: Capacity)* [2002] 2 All ER 449 reviewed the authorities and states very clearly that a mentally competent patient has an absolute right to refuse consent to medical treatment for any reason, rational or irrational, or for no reason at all.

The difficulty with advance decisions is that they are normally in issue in cases where patients are unable to speak to make their wishes known.

The British Medical Association (BMA) published a statement in 1992 on advance directives (as they were then called). It stated that the BMA 'strongly supports the principle of an advance directive' and points out that 'patients have a legal right to decline specific treatment, including life prolonging treatment'. It stressed 'the significant ethical and legal difference between the concept of an advance statement and the issue of euthanasia ... [which] is illegal' and emphasises that its conclusion on advance directives should not be seen as supporting euthanasia. See also the BMA's current guidance, *Advance Decisions and Proxy Decision-Making in Medical Treatment and Research* (BMA, June 2007).

A number of cases supporting advance directives followed: *Re T (Adult: Refusal of Treatment)* [1992] 3 WLR 782; *Airedale NHS Trust* v. *Bland* [1993] 2 WLR 316, HL; *Re C (Adult: Refusal of Medical Treatment)* [1994] 1 All ER 819 and *HE* v. *A Hospital NHS Trust and AE* [2003] EWHC 1017 (Fam). In *Re T* (above) the Court of Appeal said that an anticipatory choice will bind a medical practitioner if it is:

- clearly established; and
- applicable in the circumstances.

The position is now clarified by MCA 2005. Section 24 provides that a person who is 18 or over and who has capacity can make an advance decision to refuse specified treatment at a later date in specified circumstances. If in the future the person loses capacity their decision will remain valid provided it has not been withdrawn or altered.

The decision can be expressed in layman's terms. It does not need to be in writing unless (as, in fact, will usually the case) it relates to life-sustaining treatment. Where it does relate to life-sustaining treatment MCA 2005, s.25(5) provides that the decision must be made in writing and include a statement that it is to apply to that treatment even if life is at risk, and further:

- it must be signed by the person making it (P) or by someone else in P's presence and by P's direction;
- the signature must be made or acknowledged by P in the presence of a witness; and
- the witness must sign it, or acknowledge his signature, in P's presence (s.25(6)).

An advance decision can be withdrawn at any time when the person who made it has capacity to do so and a withdrawal need not be in writing. An alteration of an advance decision need not be in writing (unless MCA 2005, s.25(5) applies in relation to the decision resulting from the alteration).

An advance decision to refuse medical treatment will only be effective if it is applicable to the treatment in question. MCA 2005, s.25(4) provides that it is not applicable if:

> (a) that treatment is not the treatment specified in the advance decision,
> (b) any circumstances specified in the advance decision are absent, or
> (c) there are reasonable grounds for believing that circumstances exist which P did not anticipate at the time of the advance decision and which would have affected his decision had he anticipated them.

There will often be cases where the decision will not be applicable. See, for example, the pre-Act case of *Re B* (above). Ms B had executed a living will in 1999 after she had first become ill. It said that if she was unable to give instructions, she wished treatment to be withdrawn if she was suffering from 'a life-threatening condition, permanent mental impairment or permanent unconsciousness'. When she became paralysed from the neck down and needed ventilation, the doctors concluded that the terms of the directive were not specific enough to authorise withdrawal of ventilation. Although she was able to make her wishes known, the doctors argued that she had lost her mental capacity to make decisions as to her treatment. The Court of Appeal did not agree and Ms B was allowed to reject ventilation.

Section 26 of MCA 2005 allows application to the court to determine whether or not an advance decision is applicable.

The problems of drafting an advance decision to cover all future possibilities means that many people will choose the alternative of making a health and welfare lasting power of attorney. The donor of a lasting power can authorise the attorney to give or refuse consent to the carrying out or continuation of life-sustaining treatment.

There is a common misconception that the next of kin are normally responsible for making treatment decisions. This is not so. In *Re T*, Lord Donaldson pointed out that the responsibility lies with the doctor:

> There seems to be a view in the medical profession that in ... emergency circumstances the next of kin should be asked to consent on behalf of the patient and that, if possible, treatment should be postponed until that consent has been obtained. This is a misconception because the next of kin has no legal right either to consent or to refuse consent. This is not to say that it is an undesirable practice if the interests of the patient will not be adversely affected by any consequential delay. I say this ... because contact with a next of kin may reveal that the patient has made an anticipatory choice which, if clearly established and applicable to the circumstances ... would bind the practitioner.

Clients who are concerned about their future treatment need to consider either an advance decision or a properly drafted lasting power of attorney. Living wills or advance directives which predate MCA 2005 and which deal with the refusal of life-sustaining treatment should be reviewed as they may not comply with the requirements of MCA 2005, s.25(5).

Information on the assessment of capacity to consent to or refuse medical treatment is contained in Nicola Greaney, Fenella Morris and Beverley Taylor, *Mental Capacity Act 2005: A Guide to the New Law*, 2nd edn (Law Society, 2008) and BMA and Law Society, *Assessment of Mental Capacity: A Practice Guide for Doctors and Lawyers*, 3rd edn (Law Society, 2009).

14.7.2 Specimen advance decisions

There are numerous precedents for advance decisions available. For more information see: the NHS website (**www.nhs.uk**) on end of life care. See also: *Finance and Law for the Older Client* (LexisNexis, looseleaf).

14.8 ISLAMIC WILLS

There is a lot of interest in Islamic wills, and useful articles by Hajj Ahmad Thomson, head of chambers at Wynne Chambers, London, have been published in [2005] *Probate Section Journal*, April and in (2006) 156 *New Law Journal*, 24 March ('No usury').

Muslims are normally free to leave a portion of their estates to whomever they wish, but the balance must be divided amongst surviving relatives in prescribed shares. They can leave the whole estate to be divided amongst the surviving relatives but may not allocate an extra portion from the one-third to a relative who is already going to receive a fixed share out of the two-thirds. Such a gift will be void. Not all of the deceased's surviving relatives will necessarily be entitled to a fixed share. The closer relatives exclude the more distant relatives who will only be entitled to shares if the closer relatives have predeceased the testator.

At the time the will is prepared, it will be impossible to know which relatives will survive the testator so a discretionary trust and letter of wishes is likely to be the most appropriate solution. Some testators will be willing to consider a life interest to the surviving spouse with power for the trustees to appoint capital elsewhere.

A software package called IRTH: the Islamic Inheritance Program, which can calculate who would be entitled to what share if the client had just died – and who would not – is available on the internet free of charge (**www.IslamicSoftware.org/irth.html**). Bequests to those not entitled can then be included in the will. If when the testator dies such a relative is, in fact, entitled to a fixed share, the bequest is automatically nullified and the fixed share is given instead. Note that the Islamic Inheritance Program offers a choice of which Sunni school of jurisprudence to follow as there are variations between them as to the fixed shares. The program is not suitable for a Shi'a client.

14.9 HOW LONG SHOULD WILL FILES BE RETAINED?

The Law Society's File Retention Practice Note (11 September 2007) suggests that despite the problems of storage solicitors should err on the side of caution and makes the point that in the case of wills the limitation period does not start to run until the testator has died. The Practice Note is extremely helpful and all private client departments should download it.

14.10 INTERNET WILLS

14.10.1 Using the internet

The number of solicitors' firms who promote their legal services through their own websites continues to rise and so does the variety of legal services including will drafting offered via the internet. The delivery of legal services via the internet raises important issues in respect of the use of this modern technology when taking instructions and preparing wills, including the solicitor's duty of care in relation to e-commerce.

Some solicitors are keen to use the internet to its full potential and have readily embraced the e-commerce age, whilst others are more cautious and some are hostile to the idea of preparing wills via the internet. As the legal and technical difficulties surrounding electronic signatures are resolved it will become technically possible for wills and other documents to be completed and executed online. The possibility of wills executed electronically has serious implications, so it is worth reviewing the advantages and disadvantages of using the internet for the preparation of wills.

The type of legal services offered by legal firms via the internet varies, although e-mail communication with clients, companies and government departments is increasingly the norm. Many firms who do private client work use their websites to promote their services to existing and new clients and to provide legal knowledge. Other firms offer a more interactive site, enabling the client to download forms and to complete and return questionnaires and information to the firm. Some legal firms now offer different options to the client, including the option for a client to create their will online. The will is then checked by the firm and returned electronically to the client to print and sign. This option is likely to increase in popularity in the future.

14.10.2 Advantages of using the internet for wills

The internet provides easy access for computer literate clients possibly on a 24-hour basis and is heavily used by the younger generation who consider it to be an essential part of their life. Giving instructions via an interactive site is likely to appeal particularly to the under 35s who, overall, tend to resist making wills. Many firms now regard a sophisticated IT set-up as an essential and vital part of their practice, rather than just an alternative marketing option.

It *should* be possible to offer a less expensive service as overheads and reduction in staffing could cut costs in the long term; however, the start-up costs of setting up a truly interactive site are not insignificant and it can require a considerable amount of time and effort to develop an accurate and responsive system. Nevertheless, external competitors, such as banks and other institutions, already have sophisticated IT systems in place which consumers have readily embraced, so why should they expect anything less from the legal profession?

The internet knows no boundaries, therefore the drafting of wills can be carried out at a different location where the overheads may be cheaper. This may result in more flexible working practices for staff, as if the instructions are received via the internet there is no need for the staff to be located in a central office. Accessibility problems may be overcome for disabled clients or staff if they choose to use the internet instead of attending at the solicitor's office. A considerable amount of information can be presented to clients via the website, which they can access in the privacy of their home and at their own speed.

If regularly updated a firm's website can provide clients with useful information about recent legislative changes which affect the client, for example the introduction of the Mental Capacity Act 2005 and the latest tax changes.

If the appropriate prior consent has been obtained from clients, newsletters, mail alerts and marketing information can be distributed to clients via e-mail in a quick, cost-effective manner. Remember that overuse of the e-mail format in order to send newsletters and or other information can be very annoying and counter-productive – most private clients are unlikely to want a weekly or even a monthly newsletter from their solicitor.

However, face-to-face access should continue to be made available, as a significant proportion of clients for the foreseeable future are likely to choose to have a meeting in person at the solicitor's office when discussing complex issues.

14.10.3 Disadvantages of using the internet

A will is not a commercial contract; it is a unilateral document which may not become operative for many years. To create a valid will the statutory requirements of s.9 of the Wills Act 1837 and an adequate level of testamentary capacity must be satisfied. What sets a will apart from other forms of commercial transactions is the fact that by the time the will is challenged the testator or testatrix (and possibly the witnesses) will be dead and unable to verify the will.

Without a personal interview with the client it would be difficult to spot underlying problems or the 'hidden agenda'. There is a potential risk of fraud or coercion of clients, particularly if they are vulnerable or elderly.

A solicitor offering services via the internet remains subject to the Solicitors' Code of Conduct 2007, which in particular includes obligations to:

- act in the best interests of each client (rule 1.04);

- refuse to act or cease to act for a client where the solicitor knows or has reasonable grounds for believing the instructions are affected by duress or undue influence, and not acting on those instructions until the solicitor has satisfied himself they represent the client's wishes (rule 2.01(d));
- provide a good standard of service, regardless of the means of delivery (rule 1.05).

It can be time-consuming for the client to access the appropriate information on the taxation system, or information concerning claims under Inheritance (Provision for Family and Dependants) Act 1975 or complexities which can occur where second marriages are involved. There is a real risk that the clients may lack the ability to use the software properly or to understand key explanations and definitions in the computer software. For example, 'children' includes illegitimate and adopted children but not step-children, and clients may not appreciate this distinction.

Some firms to try 'filter' out potentially complex situations with a series of questions and advise clients with complex needs to contact the firm to arrange a meeting.

It is essential that any website is regularly maintained and upgraded. Regrettably some existing sites run by solicitors (both small and larger firms) are not maintained regularly, and so include out-of-date or ambiguous advice.

Issues of mental capacity cannot be easily resolved. If you have not had a meeting with your client when taking the instructions and discussing the same, how would you be able to confirm to any court in the event of a dispute that the client did actually have the necessary mental capacity to make a will?

Draft wills should be sent by encrypted e-mail and include a 'draft watermark' when they are printed. If the final will is downloaded and printed out by the client, it will be impossible for the solicitor to ensure that the pages have in fact been printed correctly on suitable quality paper. Some firms specifically suggest the will should be printed on durable (acid free) paper and bound with a secure form of binding.

Databases recorded in certain old computer formats are already obsolete and it is now impossible to retrieve the data. There is also evidence that floppy disks and CDs degrade after a relatively short period. An electronic will should be capable of being stored for at least 75–80 years and easily retrievable, but at present there is no technical standard or guarantee that data can be stored for any long-term period, i.e. 50 years or more.

14.10.4 Confidentiality

The client, understandably, will expect confidentiality but *this cannot and should not be guaranteed.* Many large global organisations have set up complex security systems, which have then been compromised by computer hackers. Nevertheless, solicitors will be keen to try and emphasise that efforts have been made to make the website as secure as possible. Possible means of doing this will be by using a guaranteed encrypted system, or software, which includes other security devices to protect the information from being intercepted.

Protecting personal information and privacy are likely to be key issues for most clients. In the past, fear of credit card abuse caused consumers to resist purchasing products online, but this has changed in recent years and online consumer purchases have significantly increased. Nevertheless, solicitors' firms wishing to encourage clients will need to consider confidentiality and security very seriously. Some firms have had their information systems independently audited and arranged for an attempted penetration to check the levels of security. An American security company challenged hackers to break into its security system which it described as the 'Fort Knox' of computer security. It took the hackers one day to access the main server and claim their prize of £35,000.

Verifying the authenticity of the message and the sender/recipient is important. Cameras linked into the computer are likely to become increasingly important in the future alongside electronic keys and electronic signatures as a means of confirming the identity of the client. The cost of creating and, in particular, maintaining the computer software to support security systems will have cost implications for solicitors.

14.11 E-COMMERCE: STATUTORY FRAMEWORK

14.11.1 Introduction

The UK Government, as a member of the European Union, is required to implement the Electronic Commerce Directive 2001/31/EC (the E-Commerce Directive), which requires all Member States to ensure that their legal systems permit contracts to be executed by electronic means. The Directive was adopted by the EU on 8 June 2000 but has not yet been fully implemented by the United Kingdom.

The Electronic Communications Act 2000 (ECA 2000), which partly came into force on 25 May 2000, seeks to create public confidence in e-commerce by:

- confirming the legal status of electronic signatures;
- creating a statutory framework for the approval of cryptography providers; and
- providing a system to facilitate the removal of any legal barriers against the use of electronic communications.

14.11.2 What is an electronic or digital signature?

An 'electronic signature' is defined by ECA 2000, s.7(2) as something which incorporates or is linked to electronic data or an electronic communication with the purpose of establishing the authenticity or the integrity of the communication or data.

ECA 2000 did not attempt to define the basis on which an electronic signature would be treated as valid. ECA 2000, s.7(1) states that an electronic signature and the certification by any person of the signature are deemed to be admissible in any legal proceedings, but it is left to the courts to decide what evidential weight to give to an electronic signature.

A paper signature can be treated as a record of the intention of the signatory to be committed to a course of action. An electronic 'signature' can be used to verify the identity of the person and to bind them in the same manner as a manual signature. An electronic signature is not a scanned image of the individual's normal signature.

The Electronic Signatures Regulations 2002, SI 2002/318 came into effect on 8 March 2002 with the purpose of implementing the provisions of the Electronic Signatures Directive 1999/93/EC. The regulations include a definition of an 'advanced electronic signature' by reference to certain specific requirements and are intended to encourage their legal recognition throughout the EU. The electronic signature is treated as an 'advanced electronic signature' if the signature:

1. is uniquely linked to the signatory;
2. is capable of identifying the signatory;
3. is created using means that the signatory can maintain under his or her sole control; and
4. is linked to the data to which it relates in such a manner that any subsequent change of the data is detectable.

The term 'digital signature' is somewhat misleading as the 'signature' consists of complex information which is encrypted. The system relies on the signature having been approved by way of a digital certificate issued by a certification authority. The system relies on 'keys' which are in fact complex mathematical algorithms; the complexity of the algorithms means that only the specific individual should be able to sign the e-mail or other electronic document. There are public and private keys, which when matched together enable encrypted information to be decrypted and read. So the keys enable information to be encrypted with a public key which can then be simply sent via the internet and only be decrypted with a private key.

The Government, financial institutions and commerce are all trying to create secure systems which will enable fully integrated electronic business to be conducted via the internet. The whole area of digital and electronic signatures is likely to continue to change dramatically in the next few years. At the moment there is no specific legislation which prohibits the use of an electronic signature to effect the creation of a will, although it still has to satisfy the requirements of the Wills Act 1837, as amended.

14.11.3 Privacy and Data Protection Act 1998

Solicitors when they collect and store personal information are required to comply with the obligations set out in the Data Protection Act 1998 (DPA 1998). These include the eight principles of good information handling, which are set out on the Information Commissioner's Office (ICO) website (**www.ico.gov.uk**).

The eight principles state that the data must be:

- fairly and lawfully processed;
- processed for limited purposes;
- adequate, relevant and not excessive;
- accurate and up to date;
- not kept longer than necessary;
- processed in accordance with the individual's rights;
- secure;
- not transferred to countries outside the European Economic area, unless there is adequate protection.

Personal data includes information such as lists of names and addresses. Most solicitors' firms are likely to handle personal data and will need to notify (register) under DPA 1998.

It is possible to check online whether a firm or company is registered by searching the Data Protection Public Register held by the ICO.

The Seventh Principle contained in DPA 1998, Sched.1, Part II requires appropriate technical and organisational measures to be taken against unauthorised or unlawful processing of personal data and against accidental loss or destruction of or damage to the personal data. This means that if solicitors are in receipt of personal information about a person they will have an obligation to ensure the reliability of all the employees that have access to that personal data to ensure that it is not misused. Non-compliance is an offence and directors/officers of a company can be held personally liable.

The Law Society's Information Security Practice Note (September 2008) contains useful information and guidance about data protection issues which may arise from personal information contained in e-mails whether sent or received.

If a firm fails to comply with the provisions of DPA 1998, it may be liable to claims for compensation from the party providing the data as well as to criminal proceedings (DPA 1998, s.13).

14.11.4 Consumer Protection (Distance Selling) Regulations 2000

Firms intending to develop a website which is more than an information portal will need to comply with the Consumer Protection (Distance Selling) Regulations 2000, SI 2000/2334 (as amended) which became operative from 31 October 2000. These regulations were primarily aimed at mail order catalogues, telephone sales and other types of 'distance selling', but the regulations also affect faxes, newspaper advertisements, the internet and contracts that are not made face to face. The regulations only apply to transactions involving consumers; they do not apply where the services are being offered to a business.

The regulations set out the minimum requirements concerning the information which must be supplied to the client/customer by the supplier. A solicitor or legal firm which is offering to sell legal services or legal knowledge to a consumer or lay client over the internet is deemed to be a supplier of legal services.

The regulations include an automatic seven-day cooling-off period (unless agreed between the parties that the contract will commence at an earlier point) and unless the time is specifically extended, all contracts must be completed within 30 days.

The right to return 'goods' to the supplier after they have been received by the consumer does not apply if the goods that are supplied are customised for that particular client (reg.13(1)(c)). Most wills should be capable of being treated as specific to the client and therefore should not be caught by the right of return.

A cooling-off period should, however, be incorporated into the firm's terms and conditions of business regardless of whether the transaction is over the internet or in written form.

In addition to the firm's business terms and conditions, the E-Commerce Directive requires solicitors who either provide services electronically or advertise electronically to inform their clients or customers that the service is provided by solicitors of England and Wales, that they are regulated by the Solicitors Regulation Authority (SRA) and information on how to access the SRA's rules (the easiest way to do this is to provide a link to **www.sra.org.uk**). The name, address, e-mail address and VAT number of the firm must also be provided. If there is electronic trading, such as the purchase of legal forms or the purchase of a will online for a specific fee, additional information about the steps required to enter into the contract have to be displayed on the website.

14.11.5 Contractual implications of wills via the internet

The internet may not recognise geographical boundaries but anyone providing services via the internet needs to define in which country or legal jurisdiction any contractual disputes are to be to be decided. It is also necessary to define the place of performance of the contract or the provision of services. Failure to define the terms clearly could result in the case being heard in another country and the legislation of that country being applied. Although this problem is less likely to apply to wills than to the purchase of other goods, such as books or videos, it is obviously preferable to avoid uncertainty wherever possible. An EU Council Regulation 44/2001 on jurisdiction and the recognition and enforcement of judgments in civil and commercial matters imposes additional restrictions if there is a consumer contract.

14.11.6 Duty of care limiting liability

Using e-mail, a website or other internet facilities to provide legal services does not negate the basic duty of care which a solicitor owes to a client. E-commerce is simply a different modern method of delivering solicitor's services.

E-mail and the internet may increase the pressure for an immediate response to the client, but it does not reduce the professional standard of care to which a solicitor is expected to adhere.

Different levels of information may be agreed or may be appropriate for different clients. Ideally, the client should normally be told in appropriate language at the *outset of a matter or as soon as possible thereafter* the issues in the case and how they will be dealt with. In particular, the immediate steps to be taken in a transaction must be clearly explained.

It may be helpful to provide linked specialist text for the client to access explaining particularly complex issues, i.e. parental responsibility if the parents are unmarried, or when and why including a life interest trust would normally be recommended.

Costs information

It is important that the client is able to understand the cost implications of the transaction, particularly if the decision may have future consequences, i.e. the appointment in the will of a legal firm or an individual solicitor as the executor. Clear information should be included in the online instructions to inform the client of the consequences of selecting such an option when giving will instructions via the internet.

If the proposed will appoints a solicitor or the firm as executors the solicitor must ensure that the client makes an informed decision. The client must be informed that they do not have to appoint professional executors, and that if they appointed lay executors, such as friends or family members they could choose a different solicitor to act and that those costs would be paid from the assets in the estate.

The client should also be informed of how the solicitor's firm charges for administering an estate and also that these rates and the method of charging may change by the time the estate is administered.

Drafting questionnaires

The emphasis therefore is on *informing* the client. So, if a client is asked to complete an online questionnaire the client needs to understand the legal language used. For example, it might contain a statement such as:

> This questionnaire is only appropriate if your assets and possessions do not exceed the inheritance tax threshold – £325,000 for tax year 2010/2011.

This statement assumes that the client understands what is meant by the term 'assets'. Many clients and members of the public might query what from a legal perspective appears to be a straightforward question. The client might want to ask the following questions:

- Does that include my half share in the house I own jointly with my wife – I thought that was tax-free and did not count?

- What about my life policies – I think they go to my children if I die – are they included?
- I also have a timeshare in Gran Canaria – I wonder if that is included?

The example given above demonstrates that even a simple statement concerning the client's assets may require a considerable amount of further knowledge and information to be available in order for the client to make a reasoned judgment. If such information is to be gathered electronically, detailed additional information and checks need to be included and this can make the process time-consuming and off-putting to the client.

Very few wills are straightforward, and in fact more and more wills are becoming complex. Second or third marriages, children from different partners and a variety of pension schemes and investments mean solicitors must take a detailed profile in order to prepare a suitable will.

It is unlikely that the internet is going to be the appropriate method for preparing complex wills which involve tax planning. This is already recognised by some of the unregulated will writer websites, which suggest the customer seeks 'independent advice' where the assets include business or farming interests, foreign domicile, or complex trusts.

14.11.7 Can you limit your liability?

Some solicitors using the internet to provide will services have tried to limit their liability to the information provided in the will questionnaire and stressed the importance of the client providing accurate information.

It is understandable that a solicitor does not want to be held liable if the client has provided inaccurate or inadequate information which the solicitor has then relied upon to draft the will. However, if the solicitor has failed to provide an adequate level of information to assist the client in completing the questionnaire, any clause attempting to limit liability is unlikely to be given effect by the courts. Furthermore if the questionnaire is completed electronically how does the solicitor know that *the client* actually completed it? Even if the completed questionnaire is handed to the solicitor, specific confirmation should be obtained that the client completed the form (see *Clancy* v. *Clancy* [2003] EWHC 1885).

Hurlingham Estates Ltd v. *Wilde & Partners* [1997] STC 627 suggests that the obligations of the solicitor to the client appear to be widening, and *Hurlingham* cannot be viewed as an isolated case as it has since been followed in *Estill* v. *Cowling* [2000] WTLR 417. It should be noted that both the cases of *Hurlingham* and *Estill* refer to express agreements with the client. This would seem to indicate that simply sending terms of engagement or a retainer letter, whether through the post or via e-mail, may not always be enough.

There are also certain implied duties, which a solicitor cannot exclude. The problem for the draftsperson is ascertaining which tasks should be included or excluded.

Some IT experts argue that if a basic 'no frills' service is offered it is unreasonable for the client to expect a high level of information or service. However, if the site offers a service by a person holding himself out as a solicitor, a standard of care of a competent solicitor will be expected irrespective of the standards offered by other internet sites which may be offering a will-making service. An interesting question will be whether the courts when dealing with other internet sites offering will-drafting services will be willing to follow the principles formulated in the case of *Esterhuizen* v. *Allied Dunbar* [1998] 2 FLR 668, where the court stated that a commercial company, Allied Dunbar, had to apply the same standards of care as a solicitor when carrying out a will-making service.

Where a retainer has been agreed, the status of the parties may be significant. An elderly client who does not have detailed knowledge of tax or trust law is unlikely to be expected to understand the significance of clauses which seek to limit the solicitor's areas of responsibility under a retainer unless it can clearly be shown that the client understood the consequences of the clauses, as was identified in the Jersey Court of Appeal decision *Pickersgill* v. *Riley* [2004] UKPC 14. In *Pickersgill* the court recognised that the duty of care was variable (at para.8):

> The scope of the duty may vary depending on the characteristics of the client, in so far as they are apparent to the solicitor. A youthful client, unversed in business affairs, might need explanation and advice from his solicitor before entering into a commercial transaction that it would be pointless, even sometimes an impertinence, for the solicitor to offer to an obviously experienced businessman.

It is arguable that in these circumstances the duty towards the client will widen and solicitors should take additional time and effort if necessary to explain the terms of the retainer to their client. If the only communication is by e-mail, how can solicitors assess the situation?

14.11.8 Accessibility

The Disability Discrimination Act 1995 made it a legal requirement for companies and businesses to ensure that as many people as possible can access services and information, including internet services (see **16.5**). This requirement will continue under the Equality Act 2010, which was given Royal Assent on 8 April 2010 and repeals the 1995 Act. The Equality Act 2010 brings together existing discrimination legislation in a single Act. The bulk of the Equality Act 2010 came into force on 1 October 2010 (see SI 2010/2317).

See also *Equality Act 2010: A Guide to the New Law* (Law Society, 2010); and the Law Society's Disability Discrimination Practice Note.

14.12 INTERNET SERVICES OFFERED BY FIRMS

14.12.1 Larger firms

Although private client work has been eschewed by many of the very large commercial firms in the city of London and elsewhere as not being cost effective, some commercial firms have focused only on established commercial clients and individuals with a high net worth and aim to offer a bespoke service. There are other large firms which have developed highly sophisticated IT case management systems (usually for property transactions), capable of carrying out a high volume of legal work via the internet. The expertise in providing volume legal services is now being expanded into other areas, such as will writing. The significant changes in the Legal Services Act 2007 have started to be implemented and large commercial organisations such as the Co-operative Trust Corporation Limited are offering an increasing range of legal services including will-writing services, and it is likely that many of the services will be delivered electronically.

Several large legal firms have developed will-drafting packages for their institutional clients, which the clients can then market through their individual high street shop or premises. Instructions will be taken in the commercial premises of the company or institution from the individual and then e-mailed back to the legal firm to implement. The legal firm does not actually deal with the individual client directly. The legal firms acting on behalf of the institutions are hopefully aware of the potential risks in drafting wills via the internet but they are likely to make a commercial judgment based on risk assessment. If the volume of business generated is sufficiently large, they will be prepared to take the commercial risk of having to deal with some potential problems/claims.

However, as the threats from computer viruses, computer hackers and criminals continues to increase the level of technical expertise and knowledge needed to maintain a fully interactive website will also rise. Certainly the levels of financial investment available to the largest firms enable sophisticated security systems and rigorous quality checks to be undertaken which would not be realistically cost effective for smaller firms to undertake.

14.12.2 Small firms' potential use of the internet

An increasing number of small firms have recognised that the internet offers a possible way of widening their client base without the need to purchase costly additional premises. The smaller firms face competition from unregulated will writers who actively market their services via the internet, so an increasing number of smaller firms have set up low cost websites to offer will packages via the internet.

Potential problems that may occur will be the failure to maintain and to upgrade the website at regular intervals; out-of-date or inaccurate information on which a client relied could result in a negligence claim. A general disclaimer from liability on the website may not be enforceable: the court is likely to consider that any firm of solicitors, regardless of size, should be able to provide up-to-date information on the basic UK tax regime. It is relatively easy to set up a simple website and to claim an expertise in will drafting; the question is whether or not some of the solicitors' firms have the necessary levels of competence actually to draft the documentation.

There is an expectation by courts when considering negligence claims against solicitors and by clients themselves (perhaps even more so because they are using the internet) that the work will be completed quickly and this may place considerable pressure on a small firm with limited resources.

There will be an ongoing need to update and upgrade security systems including contingency plans in case a security incident compromises data. The website will need to be protected by a firewall and intrusion detection software, which will have resource implications for small firms.

14.12.3 Areas to define and limit when using the internet

The terms of the retainer will need to reflect the type of will-drafting service that is being offered via the internet and might include the following.

Foreign assets

Foreign assets such as a holiday home in France or Spain require careful thought and specialist advice. In most circumstances, therefore, the retainer should explain that such specialist advice is not provided as part of the will-making service offered through this particular internet service. The internet has no geographical boundaries and the issues concerning domicile and residence may be relevant. A client's e-mail address will not necessarily give any indication of where the client is resident, and this could affect the legal advice that should be offered.

Solicitors may, if appropriate, suggest that they meet the client in person to discuss the matter further, but they should make it clear that an additional charge will be made.

Inheritance tax advice

In most circumstances solicitors will be expected to ascertain the extent and the nature of the estate. If the estate is well below the nil rate band for tax purposes is it reasonable to try and exclude tax advice?

Some solicitors' firms who are already offering legal services over the internet have sought to restrict their liability to give tax advice by excluding such advice in the terms of their retainer. If the *Hurlingham* and *Estill* decisions (above) are followed such a clause may not be enough as it is necessary to establish that the client had informed consent. So if a solicitor is seeking to try to limit liability for tax advice, at least a résumé of tax principles should still be provided and this information must be up to date.

It may be prudent to include a clause within the terms of the agreed retainer with the client defining clearly that the advice given and the prepared will are based on the law at a definite moment in time and that the firm does not accept responsibility to notify the client of any future changes in the law or any legal decisions which might affect the terms of the will.

Due execution of the will

Clients using the internet for will drafting are perhaps less likely to be willing to attend in person at the solicitor's office to execute the will. Provided the client is willing and able to understand instructions on how to execute the will and a clear set of written instructions has been provided, the solicitor in normal circumstances should have discharged his duty of care. The danger lies in the fact that having taken instructions via the internet, the solicitor may not have identified possible complications and if there are unusual circumstances any exclusion in the retainer is unlikely to be effective.

As problems concerning the correct execution of the will have been a fertile area of litigation in recent years with cases such as *Esterhuizen* v. *Allied Dunbar* [1998] 2 FLR 668, the risk of failing to provide adequate instructions should not be underestimated.

Printed documentation

Where the will-drafting service is via the internet an additional issue may arise concerning the printing of the will as well as the execution of the will and storage of the will.

In these circumstances any retainer should very clearly state the potential risks and seek to define whether or not the solicitor is responsible for checking the will if it is returned to the firm. However, there is still the risk that the courts would not accept the retainer as being reasonable in all circumstances: see *Humblestone* v. *Martin Tolhurst Partnership* [2004] EWHC 151 (Ch).

14.12.4 Is it worth the risk?

Solicitors are already carrying out a significant amount of their legal work via the internet and this is likely to increase further in the future. However, wills by their nature are very specialist documents, which require specific procedures, i.e. careful drafting and correct execution in order to be valid. There is real danger that firms that do not have specialist knowledge will simply set up websites offering services without considering the relevant dangers and risks and this in turn will lead to negligence claims at a later date.

Even for the experienced practitioner, the time required to provide the essential detailed information for the client should not be underestimated. Furthermore such information will still not negate the obligation to explain (in person, if necessary), complex issues to clients who are vulnerable or have special needs.

It is inevitable that the internet increasingly will be used to deliver a wide range of legal information, knowledge and services to the public. Although cost is undoubtedly a factor for some individuals, superstition and a reluctance to make decisions are also key inhibitors which cause people to delay making a will and these are likely to remain the same whether the will is created via the internet or made in person.

The speed with which consumers are embracing new opportunities to purchase goods and services online should not be underestimated – online banking services and electronic ticketing for train and airline tickets are now the norm for consumers. However, while electronic signatures may be appropriate for contracting to purchase the weekly shopping online, the creation of a will is quite different. In addition to satisfying the legal formalities of the Wills Act 1837 (as amended), ensuring that there are adequate safeguards against abuse or exploitation of the vulnerable will continue to provide a considerable challenge to those seeking to offer a fully automated will-writing service. An advantage offered by the use of IT is the ability to store and then easily retrieve specific information about the client, which enables the firm to provide a more client-focused service. For example, the client database can be programmed automatically to generate a reminder letter to clients of the need to review a will/enduring/lasting power of attorney after a given period of time. Such a system may, however, be counter-productive if there are insufficient staff available to respond to the work generated.

Whilst the use of the internet to prepare and send draft wills inevitably will increase, the creation and recognition of totally electronic wills using electronic signatures is a more complex matter and is unlikely to be widely implemented in the near future.

14.12.5 Further advice and information

At the time of writing, the Law Society's Wills and Equity Committee is planning to produce a Wills and Modern Technology Practice Note in late 2010. This will replace existing guidance in connection with the preparation of wills on the internet, which was published by the Law Society in May 2000.

The Law Society has also issued:

1. E-mail Guidelines for Solicitors, last revised in November 2005, available at **www.lawsociety.org.uk.**
2. Information Security Practice Note (September 2008).
3. Execution of Documents by Virtual Means Practice Note (February 2010).
4. Data Protection Practice Note (February 2009).

The Department for Business, Innovation and Skills website (**www.bis.gov.uk**) contains useful information concerning electronic signatures and other e-commerce issues.

Points and actions that solicitors should consider regarding wills prepared via the internet include the following:

- Consider your market carefully – do you prepare a lot of simple wills or are they complex?
- Litigation involving wills has increased dramatically in recent years – do you have the necessary expertise and the IT knowledge to provide the service?
- You could create a website of services offered by the firm, plus information for clients and a checklist that the client can download to use to collate information before a face-to-face meeting (this could be an effective marketing tool).
- You could create an interactive website enabling clients to complete a questionnaire to send to the firm, but then still post the will to the client.
- You could set up a totally electronic system, with payment by credit card and the will dispatched electronically.
- Any information on the website must be accurate and regularly updated.
- Insurance-loading may become an issue in the future.
- Be careful about relying on retainers and make sure you have a written agreement from clients and that they understand the terms of the agreement.
- Any website should be protected by a firewall and up-to-date intrusion detection software.

14.13 CONSUMER PROTECTION REGULATIONS

The Cancellation of Contracts made in a Consumer's Home or Place of Work etc. Regulations 2008, SI 2008/1816 came into force on 1 October 2008. A helpful Practice Note was published by the Law Society on 2 March 2010 and can be downloaded from the Law Society's website.

The regulations apply to contracts made between a 'consumer' (natural person acting outside his trade or profession, reg.2) and a 'trader' (person acting in a commercial or professional capacity, reg.5, so including solicitors) for the supply of services which are made:

(a) during a visit by the trader to the consumer's home or place of work, or to the home of another individual;
(b) during an excursion organised by the trader away from his business premises; or
(c) after an offer made by the consumer during such a visit or excursion.

The Practice Note states that, until it is clarified by case law, it is prudent to assume that limb (b) would apply to any situation where a solicitor arranged to meet a client away from his business premises. Therefore, if you arrange to meet a client in hospital you should assume that this falls within limb (b), even though the meeting would not be social in nature and the client and solicitor would not go anywhere or do anything together.

Regulation 7 gives a consumer the right to cancel a contract to which the regulations apply within the period of seven days starting with the date of receipt of the notice of the right to cancel. The trader must give the consumer a written notice of his right to cancel the contract:

- at the time the contract is made; or
- in the case of a contract made after an offer during a home visit or excursion organised by the trader, at the time the offer is made by the consumer.

Failure to give notice is a criminal offence carrying the maximum penalty for a summary offence (fine of £5,000 or six months' imprisonment).

Unless the client has provided a written request, a solicitor who starts work within the cooling-off period has no right to recover payment if the client cancels the contract.

A client who wants the work to start immediately must request the solicitor to start work immediately and must pay for the work done in accordance with the reasonable requirements of the cancelled contract (reg.9(2)).

The implications for solicitors are serious. If making a home visit, unless the contract has already been made before the visit:

- You should take with you a notice informing the client of their rights to a cooling-off period.
- If you intend to start work within the cooling-off period, you will also need a written request for the client to sign.

The regulations will not apply if a contract is completed before a visit is made but difficult questions may arise where discussions take place with a client in the office, either face to face or on the telephone, and then those discussions are continued during a visit. In general, where there is doubt, the Practice Note suggests that it is safer to assume that the regulations do apply, to avoid criminal penalties for any breach.

PART III

Practical probate

CHAPTER 15

Inheritance tax

Lesley King

15.1 CONTACTING HM REVENUE AND CUSTOMS (INHERITANCE TAX)

For details on contacting HM Revenue and Customs (Inheritance Tax), see **Appendix F**.

15.2 INHERITANCE TAX RATES 1999–2010

(For transfers to non-exempt beneficiaries.)

15.2.1 Transfers on deaths occurring on or after 6 April 1999 and lifetime transfers taking place within three years of death

The table gives the inheritance tax (IHT) threshold limits, beyond which the 40 per cent rate applies.

For deaths after 5 April	IHT threshold £
1999	231,000
2000	234,000
2001	242,000
2002	250,000
2003	255,000
2004	263,000
2005	275,000
2006	285,000
2007	300,000
2008	312,000
2009	325,000

In the Finance Act 2010 it was announced that the nil rate band would be frozen at £325,000 until 2014–15.

15.2.2 Lifetime transfers taking place between three and seven years of death

There is a tapering relief available on such gifts but it takes the form of a reduction in the tax which would otherwise be payable. Thus, it only becomes effective if the total of the lifetime transfers made between three and seven years of death exceeds the limit of the nil rate band.

Years before death in which transfer made	Percentage of death rate tax payable
3–4	80%
4–5	60%
5–6	40%
6–7	20%

Note: Lifetime chargeable transfers made between seven and 14 years before the death, although themselves not liable to tax, may affect the rate of IHT applicable to gifts within the seven-year period.

15.2.3 Annual exemption

£3,000 (plus £3,000 for the previous tax year if unused).

15.2.4 Reliefs

Business property relief/agricultural property relief

Each at 100 per cent or 50 per cent of the value of the property transferred, depending on the nature of the assets and subject to minimum ownership requirements. These reliefs are particularly valuable so good IHT planning should always aim to safeguard them.

Woodlands relief

The value of trees or underwood growing in non-agricultural woodlands can be left out of account by election and the tax deferred until disposal of the timber.

National heritage property

Exempt from IHT if so designated by HMRC and undertakings regarding the property are given and complied with. The notes to IHT400 explain in detail how to deal with heritage property.

HMRC guidance *Capital Taxation and the National Heritage* (also known as IR67) was last published in 1986. It contained information about conditional exemption from the capital taxes (inheritance tax, capital gains tax and estate duty). It also included guidance on maintenance funds for national heritage property and the 'acceptance in lieu scheme' – acceptance of works of art and other property in satisfaction of inheritance tax and estate duty.

At the time of writing HMRC was about to complete a revised text. Currently available are *Guidance Notes on Public Access*.

Quick succession relief

Available on a sliding scale when a transfer on death takes place within five years of an earlier transfer on which tax was paid, the point on the scale depending on date of the second death.

15.2.5 Transferable nil rate band

The introduction of the transferable nil rate band for deaths on or after 9 October 2007 has revolutionised estate planning for married couples and civil partners.

A spouse or civil partner who dies on or after 9 October 2007 can inherit an unused nil rate band from a predeceased spouse or civil partner. It is not the unused amount of the first spouse's or civil partner's nil rate band that is transferred. It is the unused percentage of the nil rate band.

Example

Harry dies at a time when the nil rate band is £180,000 and he used only half of his nil rate band. His wife, Wanda dies when the nil rate band has increased to £400,000. Her estate will have an additional 50 per cent of the current nil band available to it, i.e. an additional £200,000.

It does not matter when the first spouse or civil partner died, although if it was before 1975 the full nil rate band may not be available to transfer, as the amount of spouse exemption was limited before that date.

The additional nil rate band is claimed using form 402. In the case of deaths occurring after the introduction of the transferable nil rate band HMRC will require full documentation to prove that the nil rate band was unused (this will comprise the will, IHT400, any post-death variation or appointment under Inheritance Tax Act (IHTA) 1984, s.144). Where the first death occurred before that date, such documentation may well be unavailable. HMRC accepts that it may not be possible to produce documentary evidence in such cases.

There is helpful guidance available on the HMRC website under the heading 'Transferring an unused Inheritance Tax threshold'. It includes worked examples and a table of nil rate bands going back to 1914.

15.2.6 Killed or missing in action and the transferable nil rate band

The introduction of the transferable nil rate band has meant that on a surviving spouse's death, practitioners have had to look at the circumstances relating to the estate of the first to die to ascertain whether or not there is any nil rate band available for transfer. Where a spouse died in the days of estate duty leaving everything to the spouse, the lack of a spouse exemption before 1975 means that the nil rate band will often have been exhausted.

However, the death in service exemption may be applicable. The April 2009 IHT and Trusts Newsletter explains how the exemption works for deaths before 12 March 1952. Two separate schemes of relief from estate duty for those killed or missing in action were in force. One was a complete exemption and the other a conditional remission. The service rank of the person killed or missing determined which scheme applied.

For deaths on or after 12 March 1952 a single scheme of complete exemption from estate duty, replacing the two schemes described above, was introduced for anyone killed or missing on active service. It was very similar to the exemption that applies under inheritance tax.

Anyone requiring more information should telephone 0115 9742406 (the contact number for Estate Duty cases).

15.3 ACCOUNTING FOR INHERITANCE TAX

15.3.1 Is an account necessary? Excepted estates

As from 1 November 2004 an account of some sort is required for all estates.

If the estate fulfils the requirements for an excepted estate, the application for a grant of representation must be accompanied by a return of estate information on form IHT205 (or IHT207 for those domiciled abroad).

In other cases a full IHT400 (or 401 for those domiciled abroad) is required.

Which estates are excepted?

For deaths on or after 6 April 2004 the rules relating to excepted estates are set out in Inheritance Tax (Delivery of Accounts) (Excepted Estates) Regulations 2004, SI 2004/2543. There are three types of excepted estate. The first two apply where the deceased died domiciled in the United Kingdom at death (the Channel Islands and Isle of Man are not in the United Kingdom); the third applies where the deceased was never domiciled in the United Kingdom. The estate cannot be excepted if any of the anti-avoidance provisions dealing with alternatively secured pensions apply (IHTA 1984, s.151A–151C).

CATEGORY 1

An estate is excepted where:

- the estate consists only of property passing by will or intestacy, nomination, survivorship or under a single settlement in which the deceased had an interest in possession; and
- if the estate includes assets held in trust, their gross value does not exceed £150,000*; and
- if the estate includes foreign assets, their gross value does not exceed £100,000*; and
- if there are any 'specified transfers', their chargeable value does not exceed £150,000*; and
- the gross value of the estate and any 'specified transfers' or specified exempt transfers does not exceed the threshold for IHT.

CATEGORY 2

An estate is excepted where:

- the estate consists only of property passing by will or intestacy, nomination, survivorship or under a single settlement in which the deceased had an interest in possession; and
- if the estate includes assets held in trust, their gross value does not exceed £150,000*; and
- if the estate includes foreign assets, their gross value does not exceed £100,000*; and
- the deceased died without having made any chargeable transfers in the seven years before death other than specified transfers not exceeding £150,000*; and
- the gross value of the estate and any 'specified transfers' or specified exempt transfers does not exceed £1 million; and
- the net estate after deducting debts and the spouse and charity exemption does not exceed the threshold for IHT. (In cases where the deceased had the benefit of a transferred nil rate band, the estate must fall within the deceased's own nil rate band; the transferred nil rate band is ignored for this purpose.)

CATEGORY 3

An estate is excepted where:

- the deceased was never domiciled nor treated as domiciled in the United Kingdom at death; and

- the deceased's United Kingdom estate consists only of cash or quoted shares or securities passing under a will or intestacy or by survivorship in a beneficial joint tenancy and the gross value does not exceed £150,000*.

* Note that different figures apply for deaths occurring before 1 September 2006.

'Specified transfers' are chargeable transfers of cash; personal chattels or corporeal moveable property; quoted shares or securities; or an interest in or over land save to the extent that the property became settled on the transfer or was subject to a reservation of benefit.

Business and agricultural property relief must be ignored in calculating the value of any 'specified transfers'. This means that in respect of an estate where £500,000 of property attracting 100 per cent business property relief is left to issue and the remaining £200,000 to the spouse, the estate is not excepted even though no tax is payable.

At the time of writing, when determining whether an estate is within the IHT threshold for categories 1 and 2, the benefit of any transferred nil rate band is ignored. HMRC has announced proposals to increase the threshold to take account of any transferred nil rate band. This would increase the threshold criteria (at current rates) to £650,000 in those cases. This, however, will be subject to:

- the full nil rate band being available for transfer from the earlier death so that the deceased's nil rate band is increased by 100 per cent as a result of the transfer;
- there being only one pre-deceased spouse or civil partner; and
- a suitable claim being made to transfer the unused nil rate band.

HMRC proposes further amendments to the regulations. The first is to remove an unintended consequence to category 2 excepted estates to ensure that only estates where the transfers are exempt because they are transfers to a spouse, civil partner or charity fall within the category.

The second proposal is to extend the principle of including certain tax-free transfers within the value transferred by a chargeable transfer. The regulations currently provide that where the value of a transfer is deemed to be reduced by virtue of a business or agricultural property relief, the actual value transferred is taken into account. In future, transfers that are exempt as normal expenditure out of income will similarly be added in but only if such transfers exceed £3,000 in the tax year concerned.

When can HMRC insist on delivery of a full account?

If you have taken out an excepted estate grant, HMRC can still insist on delivery of a full IHT account. There will be automatic discharge after 35 days (60 in Scotland) unless HMRC has asked for a full account. It will do so on a random basis across the whole population but will also use information available to identify cases near the threshold where tax may be at risk. The regulations require that notice requiring an account is given to the legal personal representatives rather than any solicitor acting for them.

What if additional assets are discovered which mean that the estate is not excepted?

If an excepted estate grant has been taken out before you find out that the estate did not meet the conditions, you have six months from discovery to deliver a corrective account containing details of the changes. The same applies should the beneficiaries execute a variation which changes the devolution of assets so that the estate no longer qualifies.

Different rules apply to deaths before 6 April 2004. HMRC provides a helpline (see **Appendix F**).

15.4 WHERE AN ESTATE IS NOT EXCEPTED

Practitioners must complete IHT400 inheritance tax account together with the relevant schedules and the probate summary, It may be possible to complete the simple IHT calculation on the IHT400 which is appropriate where certain conditions are satisfied: there is no interest due, no tax is to be paid in instalments, lifetime transfers are below the IHT threshold and there is no relief for double tax or quick succession. Where these conditions are not fulfilled, the calculation has to be made on the form 'IHT400 Calculation'.

There is a useful checklist of what the personal representatives must send to HMRC on p.14 of the IHT400.

It is possible to deliver a reduced IHT account where:

- the deceased died domiciled in the United Kingdom; and
- most of the assets passing under will or intestacy pass to a spouse domiciled in the United Kingdom (either absolutely or through an interest in possession trust) or pass immediately to a charity or similar body; and
- the gross value (before liabilities, reliefs or exemptions) of other property chargeable on death plus chargeable gifts (after deducting liabilities, reliefs or exemptions) made in the seven years before death does not exceed the IHT threshold.

The IHT threshold for this purpose will be increased if the deceased had the benefit of any transferred nil rate band.

A reduced account can also be delivered if the deceased's estate qualifies for exemption from inheritance tax under the death in service exemption (IHTA 1984, s.154).

15.5 HMRC GUIDANCE

There is a substantial amount of guidance on the HMRC website.

The simplest guidance is contained in *A Guide to Understanding Tax when Someone Dies* (available online at **www.hmrc.gov.uk**).

This explains the tax liabilities that may arise when someone dies, gives basic information about income tax and capital gains tax and briefly mentions inheritance tax, and explains what you need to do if you are a:

- personal representative (PR);
- beneficiary;
- trustee.

This guidance was formerly named *What to Do About Tax When Someone Dies*.

The IHT Manuals give more technical advice and are particularly useful as they give insight into HMRC's approach to matters.

In addition there is detailed guidance on the following:

- Inheritance tax.
- Grossing up calculator.
- Grossing, interaction and abatement.
- Guaranteed annuity calculator.
- Discounted gift schemes.
- Inheritance tax clearance service for business owners.
- IHT press release – 'Wartime compensation payments'.
- How to calculate inheritance tax.

15.6 ADDITIONAL REMINDERS

15.6.1 Calculation of the tax and interest

Personal representatives have a duty to complete their IHT account properly and will become liable to a penalty if they do not (see **15.7** below). They have a legal responsibility to pay the full amount of tax for which they are liable, before they send the account to the probate registry with their application for a grant of representation. Practitioners acting as, or on behalf of, PRs are expected to calculate the correct amount of tax due themselves.

HMRC has introduced a common interest rate regime that will apply across all taxes and duties. The legislation came into effect on 12 August 2009 and is contained in Finance Act 2009, ss.100–103 and Scheds.53 and 54 and the Taxes and Duties (Interest Rate) (Amendment) Regulations, SI 2009/2032.

The effect of the regulations is that with effect from the September 2009 meeting of the Bank of England's Monetary Policy Committee, the old single rate of interest for inheritance tax, capital transfer tax and estate duty was replaced by one rate for charging interest on unpaid tax and another, lower, rate for the repayment interest supplement that is added to repayments.

The regulations stipulate that the rate for charging interest on unpaid tax is the Bank of England base rate plus 2.5 per cent. The rate of interest that will be paid on repayments of tax and interest will be the Bank of England base rate minus 1 per cent, although the rate for the repayment interest supplement is subject to a floor of 0.5 per cent.

There may be circumstances where it is necessary to apply for a grant quickly and there is not time to obtain final valuations, in which case solicitors should phone the Probate and Inheritance Tax Helpline and explain the problem.

The IHT and Trusts Newsletter for August 2009 included the following paragraph in an item on payment of IHT:

> If you have to use estimates and are encountering difficulties in obtaining the actual figures let HMRC Inheritance Tax know what the problems are. Having this information at an early stage helps to demonstrate that you are doing everything reasonable to produce the actual figures.

In *Robertson* v. *Inland Revenue Commissioners (No.1)* [2002] STC (SCD) 182 a solicitor who submitted an account containing estimated values which turned out to be substantially below the true values was ordered to pay a penalty by the Revenue. Eventually the Special Commissioner found that he had acted properly because he had disclosed that his values were estimates and had paid the extra tax required within six months from the end of the month of death. However, it is clearly preferable to avoid the possibility of any argument with HMRC by making arrangements in advance.

Practitioners should supply HMRC with as much information as possible with the account to enable more focused enquiries to be raised after the grant has been issued. Both HMRC and practitioners want to provide an efficient and speedy service to their respective customers. It will save time if the IHT400 contains a statement of the basis of an ownership claim rather than waiting for HMRC to raise enquiries.

Care should be taken when valuing household and personal goods. In the December 2004 Newsletter the Revenue stated that it was anxious to establish whether the value of such goods had been ascertained in accordance with correct statutory principles as set out in IHTA 1984, s.160, i.e. 'the price which the property might reasonably be expected to fetch if sold in the open market'. The Newsletter sets out circumstances which might lead the Revenue to make further enquiries as to the basis of valuation. In the April 2006 Newsletter, HMRC reported that there were still problems with the valuation of household and personal goods. Practitioners should be particularly careful of the following:

- if there are such goods but the PRs consider that they are valueless, it is still necessary to report that such goods exist;

- where items are valueless, complete form D10 to explain why they are considered to have no value;
- do not simply give a value without explanation; attach a valuer's report if one was obtained; if the valuation was a PRs' estimate, explain how the estimate was arrived at and what comparisons were made;
- a valuer's report must state that it was made on an open market basis;
- if there is a car, state its value separately on form D10 and give details of its make, model, year of registration and registration number;
- if the deceased owned a holiday home, separate details of the contents must be provided even if the PRs consider them to be valueless;
- when taking an inventory, be sure not to overlook items which are not in the house; check garden sheds and garages; ascertain whether there is a car parked in the street and whether any items have been placed with friends or relatives for safekeeping.

The value of property comprised in the estate is the price which the property might reasonably be expected to fetch if sold on the open market at that time, provided that such price is not assumed to be reduced on the ground that the whole property is to be placed on the market at the same time (IHTA 1984, s.160). In other words, the value will be the open market value of the property immediately before the death. Where an estate includes land or buildings, it is necessary to include any development or hope value. The IHT Newsletter for April 2006 states that, when valuing, PRs must take into account any feature that may make the property attractive to builders or developers such as a large garden or access to other property. The Newsletter concludes: 'where it is evident that reasonable and adequate steps have not been taken to ascertain the open market value, based on all information that was available, penalties may be sought'.

The IHT and Trusts Newsletter August 2009 addressed the question of when HMRC would seek a penalty if land was sold for substantially more than its valuation. It said that where instructions for valuation are given on the correct basis, i.e. as a hypothetical sale in the open market under normal market conditions and marketed properly with no discounts for a quick sale or the time of year, etc., then any uplift in value is unlikely to attract a penalty. The most important questions for HMRC are about the actual steps that were taken:

- Was professional advice sought?
- Were instructions given on the correct basis?
- Was the valuer's attention drawn to particular features of the property (such as development potential)?
- Was anything unusual about the valuation questioned?

HMRC has recently amended its guidance on how to value land and buildings (*IHT400 Notes: Guide to Completing Your Inheritance Tax Account*). The new guidance says:

> If, having obtained a valuation and before you apply for a grant, you find out about other information that casts doubts on the initial valuation, you must reconsider it. For example, if you have a valuation that shows the property was worth £250,000, but when you try to sell the property you market it at £270,000 and receive some offers at that figure or more, it suggests that the open market value for the property may be more like £270,000.

The August 2010 Newsletter for Estates and Trust Practitioners published the revised guidance with the following commentary:

> In these circumstances, HMRC recommends that the taxpayer should ask the valuer to reconsider it and, if appropriate, amend the date of death value, taking into account such things as the length of time since the death and movements in the property market.
>
> HMRC hopes that this will make it clearer to both practitioners and personal applicants that it is important to instruct a properly qualified person on the current basis and to reconsider the initial valuation if any offers received suggest the property may be worth more. Valuing the property in this way will help prevent the risk of substantial undervaluation and HMRC charging penalties as a result.

This advice from HMRC seems to require taxpayers to take a very proactive approach to valuations.

It is important to remember that if a taxpayer challenges the imposition of a penalty, the courts do not always support HMRC. For an example where the court supported the taxpayer, see *Cairns* v. *HMRC* [2009] UKFTT 67 (TC).

Where land is sold within three years of death for less than the probate value, loss relief under IHTA 1984, s.191 may be available. HMRC requires claims to be on form IHT38. Claims by letter or on a C4 corrective account are not acceptable. A similar relief applies under s.179 where quoted shares are sold for less than probate value within 12 months of death.

When valuing gilts or other fixed interest stocks with and without accrued interest, it is interest net of basic rate income tax which is added or subtracted (see IHT Manual, para.18098).

Note: HMRC Helpsheet 343 provides useful guidance on the accrued income scheme (see **www.hmrc.gov.uk**).

15.7 THE RULES ON PENALTIES

HMRC is developing one consistent penalty regime for inaccuracies in tax returns and other tax documents that will apply across almost all the taxes and duties HMRC administer. The new income tax and capital gains tax regime applies to trust and estate returns filed after 1 April 2009. This regime is extended to IHT for all chargeable events that occur on or after 1 April 2009 (Finance Act 2008, Sched.40, which amended Finance Act 2007, Sched.24). The provisions of IHTA 1984, s.247(1) and (2) continue to apply to events before that date imposing liability where a person 'fraudulently' or 'negligently' furnishes an incorrect account.

The Finance Act 2008 regime applies to events on or after that date both to persons submitting documents and to third parties providing information to those submitting documents (Finance Act 2007, Sched.24, para.1A).

There are three categories of error (see Finance Act 2007, Sched.24, para.3):

(a) 'careless' if the inaccuracy is due to failure by P to take reasonable care,
(b) 'deliberate but not concealed' if the inaccuracy is deliberate on P's part but P does not make arrangements to conceal it, and
(c) 'deliberate and concealed' if the inaccuracy is deliberate on P's part and P makes arrangements to conceal it (for example, by submitting false evidence in support of an inaccurate figure).

In addition, HMRC will have regard to the nature of disclosure of the inaccuracy – whether it was prompted or unprompted. The legislation sets out a minimum penalty for each combination of behaviours.

Behaviour	Disclosure	Min penalty	Max penalty
Careless	Unprompted	0%	30%
	Prompted	15%	30%
Deliberate	Unprompted	20%	70%
	Prompted	35%	70%
Deliberate & concealed	Unprompted	30%	100%
	Prompted	50%	100%

There is information about the new regime on HMRC website. The following is a summary of points relevant to IHT:

1. The test is now of 'reasonable care' rather than 'negligence'. HMRC considers the PRs will have taken reasonable care where they:
   - follow the guidance provided about filling in forms such as the IHT400 and IHT205/207/C5;
   - make suitable enquiries of asset holders and other people (as suggested in the guidance) to establish the extent of the deceased's estate;
   - ensure correct instructions are given to valuers when valuing assets;
   - seek advice about anything they are unsure of;
   - follow up inconsistencies in information they receive from asset holders, valuers and other people;
   - identify any estimated values included on the form.
2. Where the PRs leave all this in the hands of an agent, HMRC expects them to check through the form before signing it and to question anything that does not accord with what they know about the deceased. Simply signing an account completed by an agent is not taking reasonable care.
3. Where IHT is payable other than on death, HMRC expects the transferor (or

trustees) to deliver a full and complete return of the transaction concerned, and to have sought professional advice as necessary. Again, simply signing an account completed by an agent is not taking reasonable care.

4. A penalty can be charged where an inaccuracy in the liable person's document is attributable to another person. This is particularly relevant to IHT, where the PRs will inevitably be relying on other people to provide them with information about the deceased's estate.

Where it can be shown that the other person deliberately withheld information or supplied false information to the liable person, with the intention that the IHT account or return would contain an inaccuracy, a penalty may be charged on that other person.

But that will not necessarily mean that the PRs may not also be chargeable to a penalty. If the withheld or false information gave rise to inconsistencies in the information they had received about the estate and they did not question those inconsistencies, the liable person may still be charged a penalty for failing to take reasonable care as well.

Are professional advisers at risk of a penalty?

In response to a question from the Chartered Institute of Taxation (CIT), the Revenue indicated (as reported on 17 December 2009 in the CIT news archive at **www.tax.org.uk**):

> … a penalty cannot arise upon an agent under Paragraph 1 because the clear intention of the legislation is that the person becoming liable to a penalty under this penalty is the taxpayer. Indeed, as you have indicated, there would be no coherence to Paragraph 18 if this were not the case.
>
> Moreover, we would not usually expect agents to become liable to penalties under Paragraph 1A of Sched.24, since we would not normally expect an agent to cause an inaccuracy in a return by deliberately supplying false information to the person making the return. Ordinarily, a tax adviser receives information from a person and then gives advice based on that information.

However, there is clearly a risk of liability in negligence. Problems tend to arise in two areas:

- valuations;
- undiscovered assets.

As explained at **15.6** above, it is important to instruct valuers to provide an open market valuation as at the date of death including all development and hope value. In the case of unusual properties where accurate valuation is difficult, it may be sensible to use a chartered surveyor who will provide a reasoned valuation rather than to rely on a more speculative 'selling' valuation from an estate agent.

To limit the risk of overlooking assets it may be sensible to use a company such as Landmark Financial Assets Search, which will carry out a search against the deceased's name.

15.8 DEATH OF A LIFE TENANT: APPROVED STANDARD LETTER

A life tenant may be treated as the beneficial owner of the trust capital under IHTA 1984, s.49.

The Finance Act 2006 made changes to the taxation of trusts but many life interests will still qualify under IHTA 1984, s.49.

In the case of trusts created before 22 March 2006, a life tenant will continue to be treated as the owner of the underlying trust capital. In the case of trusts created after 22 March 2006 this will only be the case if the interest is an immediate post-death interest created on death or a transitional serial interest.

Where a beneficiary is treated as entitled to the underlying trust capital, the IHT payable as a result of the beneficiary's death will be apportioned between the beneficiary's own estate and the trust fund. It is necessary to inform HMRC of the beneficiary's death. HMRC approves the notification letter below, and adds that applications for clearance should not be made until all issues on both the free estate and settled property are finalised. There is no point in applying with, for example, the IHT100.

As a result of the changes to the excepted estates rules, some estates that include assets held in trust may still qualify as excepted estates (see **15.3**). HMRC Capital Taxes will return any accounts IHT100 in connection with trust assets the gross value of which does not exceed £100,000, if it is not clear whether the estate as a whole may qualify as an excepted estate.

The Director
HMRC Inheritance Tax
DX 701201
Nottingham 4

[Date]

Dear Sir

The Trust of Mr Fred Bloggs (Settlement 1953/Will dated 10/4/55)

Date of Death: 1/5/58
Your Reference: F/123456/53
Life Tenant: Mrs Freda Payne
Date of Death: 25/10/06

The Life Tenant of this Trust has died. She was entitled to a qualifying interest in possession. We enclose a copy of the Trust Instrument.

We also enclose a completed form IHT 100 with supporting schedules. Please acknowledge receipt.

The Life Tenant's Estate will be dealt with by: Morse & Co, Solicitors, Lewis House, 22 Burt St, Oxford OX1 2OX

*[We have not yet been able to ascertain the value of the Life Tenant's free estate.]

OR

*[We understand that the value of the deceased's free estate is about £X.]

We look forward to receiving an assessment or, in due course, confirmation that we may lodge form IHT 30.

Yours faithfully

(Jaguar & Co)

---

* Include as necessary: this will help HMRC Inheritance Tax decide whether to issue a provisional assessment immediately. It can only do this if it knows the value of the free estate.

15.9 PAYING IHT

Where IHT is payable on an estate, it is necessary to apply for an IHT reference number and payslip before you pay. The reference number is unique to the estate and you should use it on all IHT forms, payments and correspondence with HMRC.

HMRC frequently complains that taxpayers apply for an IHT reference number when no IHT is payable. This is unnecessary and a waste of time. When no IHT is payable, HMRC will allocate a reference number when it receives the forms and paperwork as part of the probate process.

Where a reference number is required, you can apply online or by post.

HMRC will send by post a note of the reference, a payslip and a payment envelope. Taxpayers can then arrange to pay any tax due using the Direct Payment Scheme, at a bank, using electronic bank transfers (BACS/CHAPS) or by cheque (using the payment envelope provided and payslip). The completed form IHT400 should include the reference number on the top of the front page. It is important to apply for the reference number in good time. The HMRC website suggests allowing at least three weeks.

15.9.1 How to apply online

1. Gather the following information about the deceased before filling in the form, as you cannot save the form and go back to it later:

- full name;
- date of death;
- date of birth;
- national insurance number.

2. Access the online form using the link provided on the HMRC website in the section 'Do it online – Get an Inheritance Tax reference number'.
3. Ensure all information included matches the information on form IHT400.
4. HMRC sends the reference number by post together with a pre-referenced payslip (unique to the estate).

You will not be able to use the online form if the deceased did not have a national insurance number (for example, because the deceased did not live in the United Kingdom or was a minor). In these cases you will need to apply by post.

15.9.2 How to apply by post

You need to download form IHT422 from the HMRC website and use it to request the reference number and payslip to go with form IHT400. For those based in England and Wales and Northern Ireland the address is:

HM Revenue & Customs
Ferrers House
PO Box 38
Castle Meadow Road
Nottingham
NG2 1BB

15.10 FUNDING IHT

Inheritance tax on property which does not attract the instalment option has to be paid with the IHT400 before obtaining the grant. The PRs are, therefore, unable to access the deceased's assets to produce funds. It is always worth asking the deceased's bank whether it is prepared to pay funds directly to HMRC to meet the pre-grant IHT. Many banks will do this and it is normally the quickest and cheapest method of dealing with the payment.

15.10.1 Interest on loans

The interest payable on qualifying loans taken out by the PRs to pay IHT pre-grant is deductible for income tax purposes from income in the PRs' hands in respect of a period of one year from the making of the loan.

15.10.2 Sources of funding

It is advisable to consider options other than borrowing from the deceased's bank first.

Many banks and building societies will make funds available direct to HMRC on an informal basis.

However, since 31 March 2003 there has also been a more formal scheme called the Direct Payment Scheme to which many banks and building societies belong. The procedure for using the Direct Payment Scheme is as follows:

1. Contact the banks or building societies that you would like to transfer the money from and ask them what they need to see in order to grant you power as a personal representative to arrange for the transfer – and how long the transfer will take once they have everything they need from you. To avoid delays later on, it is best to do this even before you apply for the grant of probate.
2. Apply to HMRC for an inheritance tax reference number (see **15.9** above). You will need to put the reference number on the Direct Payment Scheme application form, so you will need to do this in good time.
3. Fill in form IHT423 Direct Payment Scheme bank or building society account. You will need a separate form for each bank or building society that will be transferring funds.
4. Send form IHT423 to the banks and building societies and at the same time send form IHT400 inheritance tax account, form IHT421 probate summary and any supplementary pages or supporting documents to HMRC using the address details shown below.

The bank or building society will transfer the money to HMRC and should be able to give an indication of how long it would normally take them to make the transfer.

It is possible to pay IHT by encashing National Savings certificates or British Government Stock (no grant being needed for this); however, the process is not quick. After HMRC Inheritance Tax receives the request, it takes at least four weeks for the cash to be transferred and so this can slow down the obtaining of a grant quite substantially.

When encashing Government Stock, write to the registrars explaining that you want to transfer funds from the British Government Stock to pay IHT, and how much you would like to transfer. You will need to provide a copy of the death certificate.

Computershare Investor Services PLC
PO Box 2411
The Pavilions
Bridgwater Road
Bristol BS3 9WX
Tel: 0870 703 0143
E-mail: gilts@computershare.co.uk

Computershare may need the stock reference number to help them find a particular investment. They aim to deal with requests within five working days.

Once you have done this you need to send HMRC:

- a letter stating how much of the tax you want to be paid out of the British Government Stock (use the relevant address shown below);
- form IHT400 inheritance tax account;
- form IHT421 probate summary.

If encashing National Savings products, contact the relevant National Savings & Investment Office for the type of product and ask them to send you a withdrawal form and letter stating:

- the value of the deceased's National Savings investments at the date of death;
- the National Savings reference.

This is what you will send to HMRC with your IHT forms.

When you get your letter from National Savings, write to HMRC enclosing:

- a letter detailing the National Savings investments to be used;
- any official letters stating the value of those investments;
- form IHT400 inheritance tax account;
- form IHT421 probate summary (or C1 confirmation in Scotland).

At the same time as you write to HMRC, send the completed withdrawal form back to National Savings.

Other possible sources of funding are investments in nominee names or family members.

Below are two specimen letters: the first to a bank seeking a global loan facility; the second letter to a building society seeking the early release of funds.

15.10.3 'Global' loans facility – letter to bank

This is an edited version of a letter used by one practice to obtain special favourable facilities. If such an arrangement is established, consider in each case whether there are any issues which would make it advisable to suggest that clients seek separate independent advice on the arrangements for the loan on to them: for example, is this the cheapest arrangement currently available? Also, explain the details the bank will want, and obtain the client's consent to passing on the information shown in item 6 of the specimen letter.

Your Ref [...]
Our Ref [...]

The Manager [...] Bank [etc.]
Date [...]

Dear

GLOBAL PROBATE LOANS FACILITY

I should like to discuss a new facility to enable us to arrange short-term bridging loans for clients to meet inheritance tax and probate registry fees.

As you will be aware, personal representatives have to pay inheritance tax and probate registry fees when they apply for a grant of representation (whether of probate or letters of administration) to a deceased's estate. In a typical situation, no funds will be available from the estate until the grant has been issued, which means a loan has to be arranged, usually from the deceased's bank.

The personal representatives may well not be familiar with the deceased's bank, and may therefore instruct us to make the necessary arrangements. In such cases, it would save my firm time and paperwork if we were able to arrange the necessary loan through your bank on an agreed basis.

I would estimate that, on average, the loans would be repaid after approximately six to eight weeks, or nine to 11 weeks if quoted securities have to be sold, allowing for the settlement period and registration with the company registrars.

May I suggest that the basis on which your bank may agree the provision of this facility might be along the following lines:

1 **'In principle' agreement.** I accept that the bank will need to treat the provision of this facility as being an 'in principle' agreement because each loan, for reasons including taxation, branch monitoring and the liabilities of the borrowers, will be set up separately but taken within the 'umbrella' limit. I would hope that the advantage of having this agreement in place would be that the setting up of such accounts could be negotiated with you locally on an immediate basis, rather than suffering delays while negotiating and setting up relevant arrangements with the deceased's bank in each instance.

2 **Global limit.** Having regard to the normal volume of estate administration conducted by this firm, I would suggest that this should be £[100,000].

3 **Availability.** I anticipate that the bank would wish the facility to be expressed to be available for 12 months and that it will be described by you as being technically 'repayable on demand'. If this be the case, I should appreciate your confirmation that the only likely circumstances under which such a demand might be made would be if for some reason the lending had become 'unsatisfactory'.

4 **To whom available.** The facility would be available to the personal representatives of deceased persons where this firm is acting for them.

5 **Purpose.** To enable the personal representatives to deal with the estate's liability to inheritance tax and probate registry fees.

6 **Account arrangements.** I anticipate that you will wish the firm to complete the bank's form of application to open an account on each occasion and it would be helpful if we could be supplied with a stock of these. If you wish, having obtained the agreement of the personal representatives, the firm can provide the bank with the application form, the appropriate HMRC forms (IHT 400, IHT 401, IHT 402) confirming the amount due by way of inheritance tax and the details of the estate assets.

7 **Drawdown.** Each facility will be drawn as a separate loan, although partial drawings against that loan would need to be permitted.

8 **Interest.** I suggest that the rate of interest payable on the amount of each facility outstanding from time to time might be [2 per cent] per annum above the bank's base

rate from time to time in force. Presumably interest will be calculated on a daily basis and charged at quarterly intervals to each separate loan facility.

Please confirm that it will be possible, on request, for the bank to apportion the interest between the amount of loan drawn for payment of inheritance tax (on which tax relief can be claimed) and any part of the loan taken up for other outgoings such as the Probate Registry fees – which do not attract income tax relief.

9 **Arrangement fee.** I would hope that in view of this firm's connection with your bank no arrangement fee will be charged in respect either of the setting up of this facility or the taking up of each individual loan within it.

10 **Repayment and security.** Repayment would normally be made either from liquid assets, e.g. cash accounts, building society accounts, stocks and shares, etc., or from the sale proceeds of assets of the estate. As regards security, if each account is opened in the name of the firm and designated with the name of the estate, the firm will be responsible to the bank for the payment of each loan facility. We will, of course, secure our own position with the personal representatives in the context of this liability.

11 **Discretionary arrangements.** There will be occasions when the size of the estate is such that the amount required by way of loan would be too large to take under the global 'umbrella' facility. In such circumstances I would expect that we would approach you on behalf of the personal representatives to negotiate terms for a similar facility for the estate and which might involve a discounted rate of interest. I appreciate that you would not necessarily be able to provide as quick a response in this case.

If this facility is provided, my firm will be able to offer an improved service to its clients and the bank will derive benefit as well. I hope that I have covered everything which is relevant in this letter but please let me know if there is any further information you require.

Yours sincerely [etc.]

15.10.4 Release of funds – specimen letter to building society

Your Ref [...]
Our Ref [...]

The Manager [...] Bank [etc.]

Date [...]

Dear

THE LATE MRS VICTORIA JONES

Mrs Jones' personal representatives would like to arrange for a withdrawal from her account[s] no[s] [...] [to pay] [the funeral expenses] [the inheritance tax] [Probate Court fees] [so the grant of representation can be obtained].

The payments needed are:

[Funeral expenses: £[...], payable to [...]]

[Inheritance tax: £[...], payable to HMRC.]
[Probate Court fee: £[...], payable to HM Paymaster-General.]

We hope that you will be able to agree the personal representatives' requests. If so please send the forms they must sign. We will register the grant with you when we have it.

Yours faithfully [etc.]

15.11 HMRC NEWSLETTER

HMRC produces a quarterly publication, *HMRC Newsletter for Trusts & Estates Practitioners*, available to download from the HMRC website which deals with inheritance tax and trusts issues (**www.hmrc.gov.uk/cto/newsletter.htm**). It is extremely useful.

15.12 FOREIGN ASSETS

The IHT Newsletter for August 2006 stated:

> For the remainder of 2006 we will be paying particularly close attention to foreign assets. In appropriate cases we will open an enquiry and ask you for further information to satisfy ourselves that all of the foreign assets have been valued on the statutory basis. We will tell you if the estate is one that has been selected for enquiry in this way. Where it appears that the accountable people have been negligent we will consider whether a penalty is appropriate.

15.13 HMRC INHERITANCE TAX TOOLKIT

On 29 September 2010 HMRC published a helpful toolkit which provides guidance on the errors that commonly occur in relation to form IHT400 and the steps that can be taken to reduce the risk of those errors.

The toolkit has three key elements:

- a checklist – to help you address the areas of possible error that it identifies as key risks when completing the form IHT400;
- explanatory notes – which identify the underlying risks of error, how to mitigate those risks and a brief outline of the tax treatment;
- cross references – linking to the more detailed guidance available online if required.

It does not purport to be comprehensive, being focused on the most common errors. In particular, risks arising in connection with claims to business and agricultural property relief, and relief associated with works of art and other national heritage assets are not dealt with.

CHAPTER 16

Probate problems

Lesley King

16.1 MISSING BENEFICIARIES

Personal representatives (PRs) have an obligation to distribute to those entitled and will incur personal liability if they omit someone. Section 27 of the Trustee Act 1925 offers protection to PRs who comply with the requirements to make searches but only in their capacity as PR. A claimant retains rights to claim from beneficiaries including beneficiaries who were PRs. In any event s.27 only protects against unknown claimants; it offers no protection where the existence of claimants is known but their whereabouts are unknown. See *MCP Pension Trustees Ltd* v. *Aon Pension Trustees Ltd* [2010] EWCA Civ 377 for an illustration of the limited protection afforded by the section where trustees had notice of the existence of beneficiaries. It is, therefore, very important for PRs to try to trace beneficiaries.

The following can be tried:

- Make advertisements and searches under Trustee Act 1925, s.27 as early as possible in case they reveal helpful information.
- Instruct genealogists to trace the beneficiaries. Firms divide into those that charge on a time-costing basis and those that charge the beneficiaries a share of their inheritance. Improvements in research technologies and techniques make establishing the existence of entitled kin much more straightforward now than it was even a few years ago. See below for reasons why it may be more appropriate to use a firm which charges on a time basis rather than charging a contingency fee.

In the case of a gift to a wide class of relatives, for example 'my nieces and nephews', PRs should be very cautious about accepting an assurance from one part of a family that 'X died without any children'. It is necessary to check or risk distributing assets wrongly.

The question of where the cost of tracing a beneficiary should fall often concerns practitioners. Is it a general administration expense or should it fall on the share of the missing beneficiary? The position is not clear but the following points are relevant:

- There is nineteenth-century authority that the estate should bear expenses 'incidental to the proper performance of duties of personal representatives as personal representatives': *Sharp* v. *Lush* (1878–79) 10 Ch D 468. In *Evans* v. *Westcombe* [1999] 2 All ER 777 the court approved the cost of insurance falling on the general estate.

- RSC, Ord.65, rule 14B provided that the costs of inquiries to ascertain the person entitled to a share of the estate should fall on that share unless the court directed otherwise. Order 65 was repealed but a modern court would not necessarily find that the position has reverted to *Sharp*. The just result may be that the costs of ascertaining the beneficiaries entitled to a distinct asset or share of the estate should fall on that asset or share. There is probably a difference between ascertaining how many distinct shares there are (cost to fall on the general estate) and then locating the claimants to a share (cost may properly fall on that share). See an interesting article 'Personal representatives and commissions to agents tracing beneficiaries' (2005) 5 *Private Client Business*, 293.
- The safest course is, however, to ask the court for directions. The court may make one of two types of order:
  - The best known order in cases of uncertainty is one permitting the estate to be administered on the basis that a beneficiary who cannot be traced has died (*Re Benjamin* [1902] 1 Ch 723).
  - Alternatively, the court may order that known beneficiaries are entitled to their share of the estate immediately. The practical effect is that the cost of further investigations falls on those who have yet to be traced. (See CPR Practice Direction 40A, para.7.)

If there is no success in locating a beneficiary, the following options should be considered:

- Take personal indemnities from the other beneficiaries (but from a risk management point of view, these are of doubtful value).
- Take out missing beneficiary insurance; but as the case of *Evans* v. *Westcombe* [1999] 2 All ER 777 shows, it is necessary to insure for an amount large enough to cover the capital entitlement *and* the payment of interest should the missing beneficiary appear. Only a limited number of firms now offer this insurance and, before providing it, they will normally require that genealogists attempt to trace the beneficiaries.
- The entitlements may be paid into court under Trustee Act 1925, s.63 if appropriate (see *Underhill and Hayton: Law Relating to Trustees*, 17th edn (LexisNexis, 2006)).

Another concern for professional advisers is the basis on which the remuneration of heir locators is calculated. The possibilities are normally time costing or a contingency fee. There are reasons for solicitors and PRs to be cautious about the use of employing heir locaters on the contingency fee basis:

1. It is the duty of the PRs to distribute the estate to the correct beneficiaries. If a PR agrees that an heir locator can take a 30 per cent contingency fee which is

in excess of a proper time-based fee, the PR is likely to have breached the duty to distribute the estate to those entitled. Many firms of genealogists will offer a fee structure based on their recorded time and the necessary disbursements (certificates of birth, marriage and death, etc.), which represents significantly better value to the estate.

2. The effect of an agreement to allow an excessive contingency fee will be to reduce the value of a part of the estate (analogous to allowing an asset to fall into disrepair). The PR could be held to have committed a *devestavit*.
3. If the PR is also a residuary beneficiary, there is a clear conflict of interest in that the PR will benefit from the use of the contingency fee. The PR's share of the residue will be bigger because it will be untouched by the cost of tracing the missing beneficiary.
4. If the heir locator exploits the beneficiary in any way (for example, by charging an excessive fee or inducing the beneficiary to enter into an agreement by misrepresentation) the PR may be held complicit in such an arrangement.
5. A PR could not make a valid agreement with a beneficiary to take 30 per cent of his entitlement in return for giving him details of his entitlement. It follows, therefore, that they cannot authorise an employee or agent to do the same.
6. A PR cannot give confidential information about the estate to a third party.

Solicitors may be consulted by a beneficiary who has been approached by an heir locator who is offering to inform them of an entitlement in return for a substantial part of the inheritance. In such cases, it is worth looking at the list of recent *bona vacantia* estates published by the Treasury Solicitor to see if the client can recognise a name.

It is also worth pointing out to the beneficiary that the agreement may not be enforceable on any of the following grounds.

- The information provided to the beneficiary by the heir locator may be misleading, in which case the agreement can be rescinded by the beneficiary.
- It may be possible to have the agreement set aside as an unconscionable bargain.
- The particular agreement entered into may be champertous. There are a number of cases where agreements have been set aside on this basis. An agreement to provide information, in itself, is not champertous. However any agreement to provide information and evidence to support legal proceedings will be void for champerty.

In *Rees* v. *De Bernardy* [1896] 2 Ch 437 Romer J set aside a contingency fee agreement on the basis that it was champertous and an improvident bargain on the part of the beneficiaries, obtained as a result of the defendant taking an unfair advantage of the beneficiaries. There are two Irish cases, *McElroy* v. *Flynn* [1991] ILRM 294 and *Fraser* v. *Buckle* [1996] 2 ILRM 34, in which arrangements were set aside. See, however, an interesting article by David Capper 'The heir locator's lost inheritance' in [1997] *Modern Law Review*, 286 in which he regrets the failure of the Irish Supreme Court to examine whether public policy requires heir locator agreements to be void for public policy in the present day and considers the arguments for and against.

16.2 DECEASED WITH NO KNOWN RELATIVES

Is there a will appointing the solicitor as executor? If so, he or she can take the steps set out at **16.1** above to trace claimants.

Where the deceased is intestate, the usual action is to refer the matter to the Treasury Solicitor's Bona Vacantia Division (see **Appendix F** for address) (or in the Duchies of Cornwall and Lancaster to the corresponding Crown Agent, Farrer & Co). However, this is likely to mean that the solicitor will lose the opportunity to deal with the administration.

If the solicitor wishes to investigate the existence of entitled kin who could instruct the solicitor in the administration of an apparently *bona vacantia* estate, he or she should beware of incurring unrecoverable costs, unless prepared to write them off if the exercise is fruitless. However, the breadth of our intestacy provisions and the national demographic mean that the overwhelming majority of estates which appear to be *bona vacantia* do, in fact, yield heirs in priority to the Crown. In this situation, a solicitor might consider asking a firm of professional genealogists if it is willing to establish the position, without committing the solicitor to fees. Some firms will do this by deferring their fee (which should be agreed with them in advance) for locating a person entitled to the grant until after the solicitor has been instructed and the grant extracted, and agreeing that if the estate proves to be *bona vacantia*, or if the solicitor does not ultimately take instructions for whatever reason, the genealogist will waive the fee.

An alternative approach is to apply for a grant of representation under s.116 of the Senior Courts Act 1981, which gives the court a discretionary power. The solicitor would again need to contact a firm of genealogists and ask if it is willing to carry out a no-cost initial assessment of the likelihood of tracing next of kin. If the results of the initial assessment are good, the solicitor can then apply for leave to be appointed as administrator while the next of kin are traced and then apply for the grant himself or herself.

The Treasury Solicitor must be informed of the application for a grant although it does not need to be informed of the s.116 application. The registrar will require to see the evidence relating to the likelihood of tracing the next of kin, showing that it is appropriate in the circumstances to make such a grant.

In the *Probate Section Journal*, May 2004, Richard Grosberg reported that a member of the Probate Section executive had obtained a grant of representation under s.116 on such a basis despite initial opposition from the Treasury Solicitor. The member then employed a firm of genealogists on a normal fee-paying basis to trace the next of kin. Before embarking on this course it is important to ensure that the assets are protected so as to prevent undue liability. It is also possible that no next of kin will be traced, in which case the estate will have to be passed to the Treasury Solicitor.

There may be cases where there is an immediate danger to the assets of the estate. If so, consider applying to the court for a limited grant *ad colligenda bona*. This is a limited grant issued where there is a pressing need for a grant and it is not possible to wait for the issue of a full grant. It can issue to anyone irrespective of whether or not that person has any right to take out a general grant to the estate. It is not necessary to say whether there is a will or an intestacy nor to do any of the usual clearing off. A caveat does not prevent the issue of an *ad colligenda* grant. However, it is normally limited to 'collecting and getting in and receiving the estate and doing such acts as may be necessary for the preservation of the estate' and ends when a full grant issues.

If applying for an *ad colligenda* grant, the grounds justifying the application must be set out (for example, land which needs to be made secure against vandals or squatters, debts which need to be paid to avoid interest or penalties, volatile assets such as shares which need to be dealt with). The difficulty with an application on this basis is that the Probate Registry may ask why the matter is not being referred to the Treasury Solicitor.

Ex gratia payments

It is possible to apply for *ex gratia* payments in exercise of the Royal Bounty to redress hardship or for some other good cause. The Treasury Solicitor's Department publishes guidelines as to the way in which this discretion will be exercised on behalf of the Crown as do the solicitors for the two Duchies.

Grounds include:

- services rendered;
- a testamentary document invalid as a will;
- an unmarried partner; or
- a factual relationship such as a step-child brought up by the deceased.

If the Treasury Solicitor succeeds in identifying a member of the deceased's family, the estate is no longer *bona vacantia*. The Treasury Solicitor will not adjudicate between claims nor become involved in subsequent disputes between kin.

16.3 UNCLAIMED CLIENT ACCOUNT MONEY

With one exception solicitors can only withdraw such money from the client account with the written authorisation of the SRA. The SRA may impose a condition that the solicitor pay the money to a charity which gives an indemnity against any legitimate claim subsequently made for the sum received. See Solicitors' Accounts Rules 1998 (SAR), rule 22(1)(h).

The exception is where the amount withdrawn does not exceed £50 and the solicitor pays the funds to a charity. The solicitor must comply with the requirements contained in SAR, rule 22(2A) as to attempts to establish the identity of the owner of the money.

Note that the solicitor will need to apply to the SRA, whatever the amount involved, if the money to be withdrawn is not to be paid to a charity. This situation might arise, for example, if a solicitor has been unable to deliver a bill of costs because the client has become untraceable.

16.4 CLIENTS AND BENEFICIARIES LACKING MENTAL CAPACITY

The guidance notes to rule 2 of the Solicitors' Code of Conduct 2007 make the point that under the Mental Capacity Act 2005 the question of capacity relates to the particular decision that needs to be made, and it is entirely possible for someone to lack capacity to make certain decisions but have the capacity to instruct a solicitor on other matters. However, the retainer is terminated when a client loses capacity. In such a case it is particularly important that the client, who is in a very vulnerable situation, is not left without legal representation. You could notify the Court of Protection or look for someone legally entitled to provide you with instructions, such as a deputy, or an attorney under an enduring or lasting power of attorney, or take steps for such a person to be appointed.

If a beneficiary is mentally incapacitated (and cannot therefore give a good receipt) it may be appropriate to consider the appointment of a receiver through the Court of Protection, or payment into court under s.63 of the Trustee Act 1925.

On very difficult points, guidance may be obtained from the Law Society's Practice Advice Service and the SRA's Professional Ethics Team (see **Appendix F**). *The Elderly Client Handbook*, 4th edn (Law Society, 2010) may also assist.

16.5 DISABILITY

Under the provisions of the Equality Act 2010, solicitors must ensure that they do not discriminate against disabled people by, for example, refusing to provide a service, providing one at a lower standard, making an increased charge or not making a reasonable adjustment to enable the disabled person to use the service effectively. All service providers, including solicitors, must ensure that their services are provided in a way that makes them accessible to disabled people. For example, you should consider the size of font on paper materials and websites.

The question of reasonable adjustment is difficult. Reasonable adjustments might include:

- changing the way a service is provided;
- providing an additional aid or service, such as an induction loop, if this will help or enable someone to access the service;

- removing or altering physical features, such as doors, lighting or glass screens, if these create barriers to accessing the service;
- providing the service in an alternative way.

One of the most difficult disabilities for wills and probate solicitors to deal with is visual impairment. The RNIB offers a visual awareness course which gives guidance on best practice for helping clients with impaired vision. A benefit of attending the course is that the RNIB's Wills and Legacies Advisory Service is then able to recommend your firm to the visually impaired. Its *See it Right* book and companion CD-Rom gives essential guidance on making information accessible to blind and partially sighted people.

For more information, see the Law Society's Equality Act 2010 Practice Note.

16.6 COPY DEATH CERTIFICATES AND BANKING PROTOCOLS

Probate practitioners were concerned when HMSO issued Guidance Notes (No.7, dated 27 October 1999, revised 4 January 2001) stating that because of the potential for photocopy documents to assist in the perpetration of fraud, their use was no longer acceptable. This obviously meant an increase in the cost of administering estates.

However, the Law Society agreed a protocol with the British Bankers Association, the Building Societies Association and the Association of British Insurers. The agreement means that, instead of having to send original certificates to asset holders, solicitors can send a death certificate verification form giving a guarantee that they have in their possession and inspected an original. The protocol letter and form are set out in **Appendix A2**. Solicitors can reproduce the letter and form electronically; the form must remain unaltered although the letter can be modified.

Not all banks and building societies will accept the protocol letters and some solicitors have experienced difficulty even with those that allegedly do so.

The Law Society has since agreed protocols with certain banks to bring clarity to probate-related dealings between advisers and the bank. The protocols set out the information the bank will require from the solicitor on first contact or shortly thereafter and the information that the solicitor is likely to require from the bank. The intention is to reduce delay in dealing with the account or investments. The Protocols are set out in the Law Society's Estate Administration: Banking Protocols Practice Note (20 August 2009).

The following protocols have been agreed:

- Nationwide protocol – 20 August 2009;
- Lloyds TSB protocol – 18 January 2008;
- HSBC protocol – 26 March 2008.

16.7 EXTRACTING A GRANT FOR NON-SOLICITOR PRACTITIONERS

Solicitors may be asked to make an application for a grant on behalf of a bank or will and administration company. Be cautious about accepting unsubstantiated figures. A company called Legacies (Will and Probate Services) Ltd was wound up in 2002 after an investigation by the Department of Trade and Industry into its financial affairs. The company had instructed solicitors to obtain grants on its behalf on the basis that the estates involved were excepted (they were frequently not excepted). The company had then siphoned off £4.8 million due to beneficiaries of the estates to cover its own losses.

Solicitors who prepare an oath swearing that an estate does not exceed a stated figure when they have not made sufficient enquiries may find that they have themselves committed an offence and/or that they are implicated in the offences committed by others.

16.8 PERSONAL REPRESENTATIVES AND PERSONAL LIABILITY

16.8.1 Personal representatives' liability for unpaid IHT on PETs and lifetime chargeable transfers

The primary liability for IHT on lifetime gifts is on the transferee. However, PRs have a secondary liability where tax on lifetime transfers and property included in the estate as a result of the reservation of benefit provisions is unpaid 12 months after the month of death.

The PRs' liability to tax is limited to the value of the estate but is not affected by a certificate of discharge.

There is no statutory right to recover from those who were primarily liable except in the case of a reservation of benefit (IHTA 1984, s.211(3)) although such a right may exist as a matter of general law (see *Private Client Business 1998* (Sweet & Maxwell), p.58).

To clarify the position, the following edited note was published in [1989] *Gazette*, 22 November:

> Personal representatives are liable for:
>
> - the inheritance tax payable on potentially exempt transfers (PETs) where the transferor dies within seven years of the transfer, if the tax has remained unpaid by the transferee for 12 months after the end of the month in which the death of the transferor occurs (Inheritance Tax Act 1984, s.199(2)); and
> - any additional tax on *inter vivos* chargeable transfers payable as a result of the death.
>
> A similar problem for personal representatives exists where property is treated as part of the death estate by virtue of the reservation of benefit rules. Such property will be treated as part of the donor's estate on death (Finance Act 1986, s.102(3)).
>
> The Solicitors Indemnity Fund Ltd (SIF) confirmed that where a solicitor incurred a civil liability in the course of his or her private practice then, subject to the provisions of

> the indemnity rules currently in force, that liability would be indemnified by the Indemnity Fund but only to the extent that otherwise funds are unavailable.
>
> Further enquiries should be referred to your insurers.

Subsequently, following representations from the Law Society, HMRC confirmed in a letter of 11 February 1991 that, without prejudice to the application in an appropriate case of IHTA 1984, s.199(2):

> The Capital Taxes Office will not usually pursue for inheritance tax personal representatives who:
>
> - after making the fullest inquiries that are reasonably practicable in the circumstances to discover lifetime transfers; and so
> - having done all in their power to make full disclosure of them to the Board of Inland Revenue,
>
> have obtained a certificate of discharge and distributed the estate before a chargeable lifetime transfer comes to light.

The problem for PRs is determining what HMRC will regard as 'the fullest inquiries that are reasonably practicable in the circumstances'. The IHT400 toolkit recently published by HMRC emphasises the importance of making enquiries about gifts and encouraging clients to keep records. HMRC is unlikely to be satisfied that a simple enquiry represents 'the fullest enquiries that are reasonably practicable'. Practitioners are advised to look at bank statements and follow up any inconsistencies relating to assets.

16.8.2 PRs and the pre-owned assets charge

Taxpayers who derive a benefit from property which they have disposed of or to the purchase price of which they have contributed are subject to an income tax charge on the value of the benefits received, as from 6 April 2005. It is possible for taxpayers who are liable to pay the pre-owned assets income tax charge to opt out of the regime and into the IHT reservation of benefit provisions within the relevant time limit. The election is made (using form IHT500) on or before the relevant filing date which is 31 January of the year of assessment that immediately follows the first year in which the taxpayer would otherwise be chargeable (or such later date as HMRC may, in a particular case, allow (Finance Act 2004, Sched.15, para. 23(3)(b)).

There will then be no charge to income tax. However, the property will be treated as part of the taxpayer's estate for IHT purposes under the reservation of benefit provisions. The donee who is the person primarily liable for the IHT on the gifted property has no say in the matter.

In the case of a couple who are married or in a civil partnership who jointly owned a property and who are both caught by the pre-owned assets rules, if they both wish to have it treated as property subject to a reservation, they must both make an election. An election by one cannot affect the other. Hence one of them may choose to pay the income tax charge in respect of their share, whilst the other may elect for the gift with reservation of benefit provisions.

Once made, the election can be withdrawn or amended by the taxpayer *but only before* the relevant filing date (Finance Act 2004, Sched.15, para.23(5)). It cannot be withdrawn by the taxpayer's PRs.

Points for PRs

The election is sent not to the local Inspector of Taxes but to the Pre-Owned Assets Section, HMRC Trusts and Estates Inheritance Tax, Nottingham (see **Appendix F**). They will inform the local tax office and record the election. There will be a check on death for any elections made by the taxpayer with a view to the collection of IHT.

Before applying for a grant, PRs should make enquiries to see whether or not the taxpayer made any elections. HMRC Inheritance Tax will want to see reservation of benefit reported on the IHT400 and, where an election exists but no mention is made on the IHT400, HMRC Inheritance Tax will ask why. (Professional advisers should clearly impress on clients the importance of keeping copies of elections safe and easy to locate.)

The PRs should, as soon as possible, make sure that the donee knows of the election. It is the donee who is primarily liable for the IHT. The election is likely to increase the IHT payable on the rest of the death estate as the property subject to the reservation will benefit from a proportion of any available nil rate band.

The PRs must remember their secondary liability for IHT on the reservation of benefit property.

16.8.3 Personal representatives' liability for unpaid tax on the death estate

PRs are liable for IHT on the deceased's death estate (excluding settled property). Liability is limited to the extent of assets which the PRs have received or should have received.

PRs remain liable to the extent of assets which they received and handed on to the beneficiaries. The case of *Howarth's Executors* v. *CIR* [1997] STI 640 (and discussed in [1997] *Trusts and Estates*, June, 71) illustrates the danger to PRs. An employee of a firm of solicitors acted as co-executor in an estate. One of the assets of the estate was land on which the instalment option was exercised. The land was transferred to one of the beneficiaries on the undertaking that he would be responsible for the payment of the instalments. Before the end of the 10-year period, the beneficiary became bankrupt, leaving tax unpaid. The land was sold and, as the Inland Revenue had not registered the charge over the land, the purchaser took free of the charge. The solicitors' employee was held personally liable.

The moral is clear: be very careful about distributing assets where there is an outstanding tax liability. Indemnities from beneficiaries will be worthless where a beneficiary has no assets. PRs may wish to consider charging assets before transferring them to beneficiaries, for IHT.

16.8.4 Personal representatives' liability to creditors

PRs are always in danger of a claim from unsatisfied creditors arising after assets have been distributed to beneficiaries. They can protect themselves from unknown claims by advertising for claimants under s.27 of the Trustee Act 1925. However, sometimes they may know that a possible liability exists but be uncertain as to the amount. Section 27 is then of no help, since it protects PRs only against unknown claims.

Unquantifiable liabilities may arise perhaps under leases where the deceased was a tenant or as a result of the deceased being a member of Lloyd's. Limited protection is available in respect of leases under s.26 of the Trustee Act 1925. For a discussion of possible liability for trustees arising from the ownership of leasehold property see [1997] *Trusts and Estates*, 94.

In many cases the only solution may be to apply to the courts for guidance. This is obviously an expensive option and PRs may wonder if the cost can be justified. In the case of *Re Yorke (Deceased), sub nom. Stone* v. *Chataway* [1997] 4 All ER 907, Lindsay J gave guidance on this subject in the context of possible liability in the estates of deceased Lloyd's Names. He stated that as only a court order can give complete protection, it cannot be wrong for executors to insist upon the protection of a court order where an estate has contingent liabilities.

In *Re K (Deceased)* [2007] EWHC 622 (Ch) the court held that the same approach was appropriate in relation to disputed claims against the deceased and 'stale' claims where it was unclear whether or not they were statute barred. The court will take a practical view and might in an appropriate case conclude that no protection beyond the personal liability of the beneficiaries is needed. Even if the court concludes that a greater degree of protection is required, it is not bound to protect the potential creditors in respect of the full value of their claims.

16.8.5 Personal representatives' liability for unpaid tax of the deceased

PRs may have the misfortune to face a demand from HMRC for arrears of lifetime tax due from the deceased. How far back can HMRC go and can it impose a penalty on the PRs?

The time limits changed on 1 April 2010 for assessments made after that date. There are, therefore, two sets of time limits which may apply.

Assessments made before 1 April 2010

Section 40(1) of the Taxes Management Act 1970 provides that no assessment in respect of the income or gains which arose to a deceased person during his or her lifetime can be made beyond the end of the period of three years beginning with the 31 January next following the year of assessment in which he or she died.

Section 40(2) of the Taxes Management Act 1970 provides that assessments on the PRs of a deceased person for the purpose of making good to the Crown a loss of tax or national insurance contributions due to fraudulent or negligent conduct may only be made within the time limit allowed, for any year ending not earlier than six years before his or her death.

Example

If a taxpayer died on 15 May 2003 all assessments would have to be made by 30 January 2008. The furthest back that an assessment can be made is for tax year 1997–98 under s.40(2).

Assessments made on or after 1 April 2010

Section 40(1) of the Taxes Management Act 1970 provides that no assessment in respect of the income or gains which arose to a deceased person during his or her lifetime can be made later than four years from the end of the year of assessment in which he or she died.

Section 40(2) of the Taxes Management Act 1970 provides that assessments on the PRs to recover any tax lost as a result of the careless or deliberate behaviour of the deceased (or another person acting on behalf of the deceased whilst they were alive), may only be made within the time period allowed for a year of assessment that ended not earlier than six years prior to the date of death.

Example

If a taxpayer died on 19 November 2010, all assessments must be made by 5 April 2015 (four years after the end of the year of assessment in which death occurred). The furthest back that an assessment can be made is for tax year 2004–05 under s.40(2).

Where a person who had incurred a penalty died, s.100A(1) of the Taxes Management Act 1970 allowed HMRC to charge the penalty on the PRs of the deceased. HMRC now accepts that s.100A(1) was incompatible with art.6 of the European Convention on Human Rights. Section 100A(1) was repealed by Sched. 24, para.29(b) to the Finance Act 2007.

HMRC gave an undertaking to PRs who offered to pay penalties because of the uncertainty surrounding penalties sought under s.100A(1). The letter stated the amount paid in respect of penalties would be repaid should the Department or the courts decide penalties arising from the default of a deceased taxpayer should not be imposed on the deceased's PR. HMRC has written to those PRs who were sent this letter advising them repayment will be made.

Note that different time limits exist in relation to EU taxes. The Recovery of Duties and Taxes etc. Due in Other Member States (Corresponding UK Claims,

Procedure and Supplementary) Regulations 2004, SI 2004/674 came into force on 1 April 2004. These regulations require the United Kingdom to provide effective enforcement and recovery of unpaid taxes in other EU Member States. A certificate signed by appropriate local fiscal officials stating that certain taxes (and interest) remain unpaid will provide sufficient evidence for UK purposes to enable recovery procedures to be taken in the United Kingdom. The relevant time limits applicable for the enforcement and collection of taxes due in other EU Member States will be the time limits applicable in that local jurisdiction. PRs may not therefore be able to rest comfortably on the UK time limits in relation to deceased persons. For a full discussion of this and the position in relation to non-EU foreign taxes, see an informative article by Stephen Arthur in the May 2005 issue of the *Probate Section Journal*.

Penalties

For the rules on penalties see **15.7**.

16.9 BANKRUPTCY

More and more firms are handling insolvent estates, which were once a rarity. An estate is only insolvent if the debts and liabilities cannot be paid, and is not insolvent if these can be settled, even if none of the legacies can be paid.

16.9.1 Sources of information

The legislation governing the administration of an estate which is insolvent is the Administration of Insolvent Estates of Deceased Persons Order 1986, SI 1986/1999 (AIEDPO 1986). There are many specialist publications such as:

- P. Totty, G. Moss, N. Segal, *Insolvency* (Sweet & Maxwell, looseleaf).
- S. Schaw-Miller and E. Bailey, *Personal Insolvency – Law and Practice*, 5th edn (LexisNexis, 2011).
- J.R. Martin and N. Caddick, *Williams, Mortimer and Sunnucks: Executors, Administrators and Probate*, 19th edn (Sweet & Maxwell, 2007).

There is also a useful article by Duncan Bailey ('Interaction between beneficiaries and creditors') in [2008] *Trusts and Estates Law & Tax Journal*, March.

16.9.2 A brief outline of procedure

When conducting the administration of an insolvent estate, there are three possibilities:

1. Administration by the PRs under the directions of the court pursuant to an administration order (CPR, Part 64). This means that the administration is

dealt with by the PRs under the direction of the court. The courts are not anxious to undertake such a role and professional advisers rarely consider this route.

2. Administration in bankruptcy following an insolvency administration order made by the bankruptcy court. Creditors or PRs can petition. In either case the order vests the estate in the Official Receiver. Subsequently, a trustee in bankruptcy will be appointed.
3. Administration by the PRs out of court. This is the most common method of administration. It is generally the most economic and straightforward method. Remember that creditors are entitled to take a grant. PRs do not need to be qualified insolvency practitioners (AIEDPO 1986, art.4(3)).

Whether the estate is administered by a trustee in bankruptcy or by the PRs out of court, AIEDPO 1986 provides that the same rules apply to the respective rights of creditors, to provable debts, to the valuation of future and contingent liabilities and to the priority of debts.

PRs must be careful to pay debts in the order of priority set out in the Insolvency Act 1986, s.328 and s.329. This is:

- bankruptcy expenses followed by funeral, testamentary and administration expenses;
- preferential debts (as defined in Insolvency Act 1986, Sched.6, e.g. remuneration of employees for the four months before death to a maximum of £800 as provided for in the Insolvency Proceedings (Monetary Limits) Order 1986, SI 1986/1996);
- ordinary debts;
- interest;
- deferred debts (e.g. a loan from a person who is the deceased's spouse at the date of death).

PRs will be personally liable if they pay an inferior debt before a superior one and there are insufficient funds for the superior one. They also incur personal liability if they pay one creditor in full when there are insufficient assets to pay all creditors in that class. However, in this case there is a defence if payment was made in good faith at a time when they had no reason to believe that the estate was insolvent.

Although PRs and trustees in bankruptcy follow the same rules when administering an insolvent estate, a trustee in bankruptcy does have certain additional powers. A trustee can:

- challenge transactions made at an undervalue and transactions made to prefer some creditors at the expense of others;
- disclaim onerous property;
- apply for an order for sale of an asset in which third parties have an interest (typically the matrimonial home). Where the application is first made by the trustee in bankruptcy more than 12 months after the deceased's property vested in him, the court will assume, unless there are exceptional circumstances, that

the interests of the creditors outweigh all other considerations (Insolvency Act 1986, s.335A(3)). PRs can also apply for such an order but there is no such assumption so they may have more difficulty.

PRs can petition for the appointment of a trustee in bankruptcy if they decide they do not wish to administer the estate themselves. PRs should follow this course if it becomes clear that there are assets which can be recovered only by a trustee in bankruptcy. Alternatively any creditor who could have petitioned for bankruptcy during the deceased's lifetime may petition for an administration order. The PRs will be required to deliver to the Official Receiver the deceased's books of account and records.

Once a trustee in bankruptcy is appointed, the appointment relates back to the date of death. Any disposition made by the PRs in the period between death and the vesting of the estate in the trustee in bankruptcy is void unless made with the consent of the court or subsequently ratified by the court (Insolvency Act 1986, s.284). This is to give effect to the policy that unsecured creditors should be paid rateably.

PRs may be in difficulties as a result of the relation back. They may have started the administration unaware of the existence of liabilities which mean the estate is insolvent. In *Dick* v. *Kendall Freeman* [2005] WTLR 1619 the executor asked the court to ratify payments covering a nine-year period from death to the appointment of a trustee in bankruptcy, many of which were to the executor's own firm. The court ratified payments made in the two years following death but refused to ratify subsequent payments on the basis that after that date it was clear that the estate was insolvent and it should, therefore, have been administered on that basis. The executor should have followed the insolvency order from that point and only made payments for the benefit of the estate as a whole, not for the benefit of individual creditors. He had not done so and, as a result, the court would not ratify the payments.

It is, therefore, important for PRs to be careful when administering estates to follow the insolvency order as soon as there is any possibility that an estate may be insolvent. Provided they do so, the court should be willing to ratify payments made by them even if a trustee in bankruptcy is appointed.

16.9.3 Will you be paid for acting in relation to an insolvent estate?

The rules on solicitor-executors charging for administering estates have changed as a result of the Trustee Act 2000. Solicitors' charges are no longer regarded as a legacy but instead s.35(3)(b) provides that charges are to be regarded as 'administration expenses'.

As such they are treated in the same way as the charges of a trustee in bankruptcy and have priority over the preferential debts listed in the Insolvency Act 1986.

There are, however, problems.

1. Bear in mind that, although administration expenses have priority, the estate may be too small to cover them. Therefore, if there is a chance that an estate

will be insolvent, try to assess the risk before committing a substantial amount of time to the estate. It may help if potential PRs complete a client questionnaire detailing assets and liabilities early in the administration process. The Questionnaire for Personal Representative Clients (available in packs of 25) is published by the Law Society. Solicitor-executors and, indeed, other executors, may want to renounce. It is important not to intermeddle in an estate which may be insolvent.

2. Terms of business letters (see **Chapter 3** on client care) for solicitors employed by PRs may incorporate a clause governing the position in relation to costs incurred if the estate turns out to be insolvent, say Professional Ethics at the SRA. Even though they are entitled to an indemnity from the estate, PRs are personally liable for the solicitor's costs.

16.9.4 Joint property

A Court of Appeal decision (*Re Palmer (Deceased)(A Debtor)* [1994] 3 WLR 420, CA) held that jointly held property passed to the co-owner on death as usual and was not available to the administrator of the estate.

The effect of this decision was reversed by s.421A inserted into the Insolvency Act 1986 by s.12 of the Insolvency Act 2000. The trustee of a deceased insolvent can apply to the court to recover the value of the deceased's former interest in joint property from the survivor for the benefit of the estate. The trustee can only make the application where the petition for the insolvency order is presented after 2 April 2001 and within five years from the date of death. When deciding whether or not to make the order the court must have regard to all the circumstances of the case including the interests of the creditors and the surviving joint tenant but, unless the circumstances are exceptional, the court must assume that the interests of the creditors outweigh all other considerations.

In practice, there are problems with this provision:

1. Given that the application can be made up to five years after the death, the asset may have increased or decreased in value since death. What will the court do if the asset has changed in value? In the case of increases in value, it is clear from the wording that the court can only order a payment equal to the value at the date of the death. If the asset has decreased in value, the court will presumably take that decrease into account when deciding on the terms of the order.
2. The surviving joint tenant may have died before the order is made. If the survivor's estate is above the IHT threshold, IHT will have been paid and will have been calculated on the whole value of the joint property. There is no obvious procedure for recovering that tax.

16.9.5 Deceased Lloyd's Names

The well-publicised problems at Lloyd's meant that many Names were faced with unquantifiable losses, and to solve the problems Equitas was created.

Names waived their claims against Lloyd's and in return received debt and litigation credits and reinsurance of outstanding open years into Equitas. All business for 1992 and prior years of account was reinsured to close with Equitas upon payment of the appropriate premium.

There was a possibility of claims being made against the Names (or their estates) if the resources of Equitas proved inadequate and it failed. This presented a problem for PRs who faced the possibility of personal liability if they distributed the estate without providing for this contingent liability. The Society of Trust and Estate Practitioners (STEP) brought the test case referred to at **16.8.4** above (*Re Yorke Deceased, Stone* v. *Chataway* [1997] 4 All ER 907) hoping that the judgment would remove the need for individual applications to be made for all estates in a similar position. Instead, while the court approved the use of Equitas, it said that PRs would face different levels of risk depending on the circumstances of the case and that they could only obtain full indemnity by applying to court for directions. In appropriate cases, judged to be low risk, PRs could take indemnities or rely on insurance.

There is a streamlined form of application available which will be heard by a Master rather than a judge. This is dealt with in *Practice Statement: Chancery Division: Estates of Deceased Lloyd's Names* [2001] 3 All ER 765.

The procedure applies to cases where the only, or only substantial, reason for delaying distribution of the estate is the possibility of personal liability to Lloyd's creditors and:

- all liabilities of the estate in respect of syndicates of which the Name was a member for the years of account 1992 and earlier have been reinsured into the Equitas Group; and
- all liabilities of the estate in respect of syndicates of which the Name was a member for the years of account 1993 and later:
  - are in respect of syndicates which have closed by reinsurance in the usual way;
  - are protected by an Estate Protection Plan issued by Centrewrite Ltd; or
  - are protected by EXEAT insurance cover provided by Centrewrite Ltd.

The Practice Statement contains a specimen witness statement to support the claim form and a specimen draft order, although both are likely to need adapting to suit the circumstances of the case.

The risk of liability falling on an estate has been much reduced. There was a substantial increase in reinsurance cover to Equitas as from 31 March 2006, significantly lowering the risk of default by Equitas.

Further, as from 30 June 2009 all 1992 and prior year non-life business underwritten at Lloyd's by open and closed year Names, together with the benefit of substantial reinsurance, was transferred to a company to be called Equitas Insurance Limited under the insurance business transfer provisions contained in Part VII of the Financial Services and Markets Act 2000. The transfer binds all policyholders as a matter of UK law meaning that names, and the PRs of deceased names, no longer have any liability for 1992 and earlier years of account within the European Economic Area. However, the extent to which the Part VII transfer will be recognised by courts of other overseas jurisdictions in the event that a claim is brought against a Name in that jurisdiction after the transfer takes effect is uncertain. Therefore, PRs may still wish to make an application to court.

16.9.6 Bankrupt beneficiaries

A PR who pays a legacy direct to a bankrupt beneficiary rather than to the trustee in bankruptcy may risk personal liability. There is a distinction between a beneficiary who becomes bankrupt after the date of death and one who is already bankrupt at that date.

Beneficiary becoming bankrupt after the date of death

When a trustee in bankruptcy is appointed, all the property belonging to or vested in the bankrupt at the commencement of the bankruptcy vests in the trustee (Insolvency Act 1986, ss.283–306).

A bankrupt who is entitled to undistributed property under a will or on intestacy at the date of the bankruptcy has an asset, a chose in action to compel due administration of the estate. The benefit of this asset vests in the trustee in bankruptcy, just like the other assets of the bankrupt.

This means that the person entitled to such assets on distribution is the trustee in bankruptcy not the beneficiary. The recent decision in *Raymond Saul & Co (A Firm)* v. *Holden* [2008] EWHC 2731 (Ch) confirms that the trustee is entitled to the assets even if the beneficiary has been discharged from bankruptcy before the date of the distribution.

There is no clear authority as to whether the trustee in bankruptcy is entitled to require PRs to make payment a second time. However, the beneficiary is not entitled to the property and so cannot give the PR a good receipt. There is clearly a danger that such a claim might be successful. In *Rooney* v. *Cardona* [1999] 1 FLR 1236 the Court of Appeal held that a bank who paid the proceeds of a Married Woman's Property Act policy to the bankrupt husband instead of to the trustee in bankruptcy had to pay again irrespective of whether or not the bank had notice of the bankruptcy.

Beneficiary who is already bankrupt at the date of death

Where the beneficiary is already an undischarged bankrupt when he becomes entitled to property passing by will or on intestacy, his chose in action is after-acquired property.

A bankrupt is required to inform his trustee in bankruptcy of the acquisition of any after-acquired property (Insolvency Act 1986, s.333(2)) and the trustee in bankruptcy may then claim it by serving a written notice on the bankrupt (Insolvency Act 1986, s.307(1)).

A trustee in bankruptcy has no right to after-acquired property until notice has been served so PRs must insist on seeing the notice before paying the trustee. Once the trustee has served notice, the PRs would pay the wrong person if they paid the bankrupt.

PRs may inadvertently pay a beneficiary who has been declared bankrupt after the date of the death and who has not disclosed his inheritance to his trustee in bankruptcy. The position is not entirely clear and PRs may well feel that it is worth taking steps to protect themselves and avoid possible disputes with a trustee in bankruptcy.

To protect themselves from allegations of improper behaviour where they have paid a beneficiary who was subject to the provision of the Insolvency Act either at the date of death or during the period of administration, it is sensible for PRs to carry out a bankruptcy search against the names of beneficiaries of the estate.

Some practical points on bankruptcy searches are given below.

1. **Where to search?** Bankruptcy petitions and bankruptcy orders are registered in the Bankruptcy section of the Land Charges Register in the register of pending actions and the register of writs and orders respectively. This is irrespective of whether the bankrupt is known to own land.

   The Insolvency Service has details of bankruptcies that are either current or have ended in the last three months.
2. **How long does registration last?** Registration of a petition or order continues for five years from the date on which it is made and then terminates unless it is renewed (Land Charges Act 1972, s.8). Registration is not cancelled when a bankrupt is discharged unless there is a specific court order directing cancellation.

   Personal representatives will be able to see from the search whether a beneficiary was bankrupt at the date of death or has become so since.
3. **Against what names should a search be made?** PRs should search against the following versions of a beneficiary's name:

   - The name as written in the will.
   - If different, only the first forename and the family name.
   - Any name the beneficiary gives as their true name.
   - If different, the first forename and the family name.
4. **When should a search be made?** A search at the date of death will not be

sufficient as beneficiaries may be declared bankrupt after the date of death (as in the *Raymond Saul* case referred to above). It will be wiser to search immediately before making a payment to a beneficiary.

If searching immediately before distribution, it is important to search the Land Charges Register which provides information for the last five years.

However, it is worth making an Insolvency Service search too as it is quick and free and gives the contact details for the trustee or Official Receiver whereas the Land Charges Register just gives the case number in the local county court. Also the Insolvency Service search shows Individual Voluntary Arrangements (IVAs) with details of the supervisor.

Example

Ted dies on 5 January 2009. He leaves half the residue of his estate to his nephew, Ned. Ned is declared bankrupt on 12 January and receives automatic discharge 12 months later. Ted's PRs are not ready to distribute the residue until May 2010. An Insolvency Service search in May will not reveal Ned's bankruptcy but a Land Charges search will.

---

5. **IVAs**. These normally contain a provision under which the individual 'covenants' to disclose any 'windfall'. Such an arrangement is a personal contract between the debtor, the creditors and any trustee of the IVA.

At the time of writing the Law Society is preparing a Practice Note on Bankruptcy Searches. Readers should look at the website to check for publication.

16.10 PERSONAL REPRESENTATIVES SEPARATELY REPRESENTED

The following opinion was originally published in [1986] *Gazette*, 3 September, 2561–2 and may be of assistance if one PR wishes to seek separate advice from the other(s). Despite its age it remains a good summary of the position. (Text in italic has been superseded by the Solicitors' (Non-Contentious Business) Remuneration Order 2009, see **Appendix B**.)

COSTS: PERSONAL REPRESENTATIVES SEPARATELY REPRESENTED

The following notes are issued by the Law Society's Non-Contentious Business Committee. Since the Joint Agreed Case was reported in [1985] *Gazette*, 24 October, 2987, the number of enquiries which the Society has received from practitioners indicates a need to publish more detailed guidelines. The following guidelines have been settled by counsel but practitioners should note that the Society has no power to determine matters of law, and that matters of dispute may ultimately fall to be determined by the court.

1. The basic principle is that a personal representative is entitled to an indemnity from the estate in respect of costs and expenses properly incurred in the course of his

office. Trustee Act 1925, s.23 expressly empowers personal representatives to employ and pay a solicitor to transact any business or to do any act required to be transacted or done in the administration of the estate.

2. The indemnity will not, however, be available (where there is more than one personal representative) to each personal representative who chooses to instruct his own separate solicitor, as the right to instruct a solicitor is limited by the overriding principle that personal representatives must act properly in exercising their rights and powers. In particular they must not make, or cause there to be made, any wasteful or unnecessary payments out of the estate.
3. Thus it is considered that in a normal case it is incumbent upon personal representatives to agree upon the joint instructions of solicitors.
4. In certain cases it may be proper for more than one firm to be instructed, where, for example, in the case of a large landed estate, different skills are required; in such a case it is unlikely that more costs would be incurred than if one firm dealt with all the work.
5. It is, of course, always open to a personal representative to seek independent legal advice separately from the advice given by the firm instructed on behalf of all the personal representatives, but in such circumstances he will normally not be entitled to an indemnity from the estate for the cost of doing so, and will have to pay such costs personally.
6. Mere personal animosity between personal representatives does not justify the appointment of a separate firm so as to increase the costs payable by the estate.
7. Exceptional circumstances justifying the instruction of a separate solicitor at the expense of the estate might include a case where a personal representative became aware of a *devastavit* or breach of trust by his fellow personal representative and required independent legal advice as to his position; or when the instructed solicitor refused or failed properly to carry out his instructions, thus necessitating the instruction of another firm (although here, strictly, no additional costs should be incurred, as the defaulting solicitor would not be entitled to recover his costs).
8. It is also open to personal representatives to agree that they should be separately represented provided that the estate does not thereby bear any additional costs. As the instruction of two firms in respect of the same work will inevitably involve extra work, it will avoid subsequent dispute if the personal representatives also agree in advance to bear personally the extra costs involved (and agree the proportions in which they will do so).
9. Any personal liability incurred by personal representatives may, of course, be charged to the estate with the concurrence of all the beneficiaries, provided that they are all *sui juris* and are properly advised.
10. Where a personal representative instructs a practitioner in circumstances where he knows that another firm is already acting for the estate he should be made aware of the likelihood that he will be personally responsible for his costs.
11. A distinction may need to be made between the fees charged to the personal representatives by the appointed firm of solicitors on the one hand and fees charged by a solicitor-executor on the other hand. Provided that the 'professional charging clause' expressly so provided a professional executor may properly charge for his time and trouble in acting as an executor, as distinct from his firm's charges for legal work transacted. More than one professional person may be appointed executor and may be entitled so to charge, but such charges will in both cases be of a different nature from the fees of the firm jointly instructed by the personal representatives to do legal work.
12. Beneficiaries who take legal advice in connection with the administration of an estate will rarely be entitled to recover from the estate their costs so incurred, but

they may be entitled to recover such costs from a defaulting personal representative who will not in such circumstances be entitled to recover them from the estate.

13. The Society is also asked from time to time to advise as to how the legal fees should be calculated in cases where more than one firm is involved in the administration of an estate. Opinions published in the Society's Digest in the past indicated a split of two-thirds/one-third; these were however published at a time when solicitors' fees were charged on a straight percentage of the value of the estate. *Since the Solicitors' Remuneration Order 1972 this element is only one of the factors to be taken into account in assessing what is fair and reasonable in each case; the two-thirds/one-third split is therefore no longer appropriate. The value element does still have to be taken into account, and will be recognised in the fair and reasonable charges of the respective firms, bearing in mind the amount of work carried out by each firm, the degree of responsibility involved and other factors set out in Article 2 of the Solicitors' Remuneration Order 1972.* This is subject to the overriding principle expressed in para. 8 above that the estate itself should not normally bear the additional expense occasioned by the employment of more than one firm.'

16.11 UNSUITABLE PERSONAL REPRESENTATIVES

PRs may be passed over under Senior Courts Act 1981, s.116: an application to the High Court may be made if it appears that the person apparently entitled to take the grant is unsuitable. The person next entitled to the grant will not necessarily be appointed.

An application for the removal of a PR may be made under Administration of Justice Act 1985, s.50. For a discussion of s.50, see **12.5.4**.

The Family Division has power to revoke grants under NCPR 1987, rule 41. Normally the consent of the grantee is required before revocation can take place. However, 'in exceptional circumstances' a district judge or registrar can revoke a grant without the grantee's consent. Where an executor or administrator refuses or neglects to participate properly in the administration of the estate, it may be possible to get the grant revoked. It is worth contacting the registry to see whether or not the circumstances of the case would justify such an application. Where they do, it represents a simpler and cheaper solution than a s.50 application.

16.12 PROBLEMS FROM CLIENTS

16.12.1 Distressed clients

Clients coming for help and advice on probate may be suffering grief and distress. Bereavement can generate many and conflicting emotions, which are not always expressed as one might expect. Sometimes clients' feelings spill over, so that the conduct of the administration is affected, for example by a family quarrel.

Helping bereaved clients, and coping with clients' feelings and emotions, can be difficult for practitioners. This is an added (and often unrecognised) source of stress for many practitioners, who may feel ambivalent about how to respond to clients and how to deal with their feelings.

Christopher Clulow, Director of the Tavistock Institute for Marital Studies in London, considered some of these issues in a number of short articles in the series 'Only Connect' in the journal *Family Law* during 1992 and 1993. Although directed mainly to solicitors working with divorce, the articles would be of great value and interest to all private client practitioners. There are helpful articles on the difficulties of working with emotional clients by Elizabeth McManus in the February 2006 issue of the *Probate Section Journal* and by Patricia Wass in the May 2007 issue.

It may be worthwhile ensuring that your office holds an up-to-date list of local voluntary and other sources of help and support for distressed and bereaved clients.

Solicitors may be approached by a client involved in a major tragedy. The Law Society's Practice Advice Service operates the Multi-Party Action Information Service (MPAIS) which exists to link the solicitors' firms instructed by those involved and their families and friends. Before applying for a Group Litigation Order (GLO), the solicitor should consult with the MPAIS and once a GLO has been made, firms are required (see CPR Practice Direction 19B, para.11) to supply a copy to the Law Society at:

Multi-Party Action Information Service
Practice Advice Service
The Law Society
113 Chancery Lane
London WC2A 1PL
Tel: 0870 606 2522

and to the Senior Master, Queen's Bench Division, Royal Courts of Justice, Strand, London WC2A 2LL.

16.12.2 Dealing with sudden deaths abroad

After the Tsunami in December 2004 there was a great deal of media confusion over the distinction between the presumption of death and leave to swear death and whether or not a seven-year period was required.

If there is evidence that a person is dead, it is possible to take a grant at any point by applying to the probate registry under NCPR 1987, rule 53 for leave to swear death.

The application must be supported by an affidavit setting out the facts. It should deal with the following:

- when the person was last heard of;
- whether there have been advertisements;
- whether there was any relevant communication before the disappearance;
- whether there is a will and, if not, who is entitled on intestacy;
- the value of the estate;

- a statement that the person is dead;
- anything else of relevance.

If there is an insurance policy which will pay out on death, the company must be told of the application and sent a copy of the affidavit. It can oppose the application.

In cases where there is no evidence, a person can be presumed dead after a continuous period of seven years or more. This requires an application to court. It is necessary to prove that:

(a) there are persons who would be likely to have heard of him over that period;
(b) those persons have not heard of him; and
(c) all due inquiries have been made appropriate to the circumstances, without result.

Then the presumption of law is that the person died within the period.

Richard Bark-Jones, Partner at Morecroft Urquart, Liverpool and former chairman of the Law Society's Wills and Equity Committee wrote the following guidance on dealing with sudden deaths abroad for the *Probate Section Journal* shortly after the tragic events in New York of 11 September 2001:

> The recent appalling events in the United States may mean that some of you have to help clients deal with the sudden death of a relative abroad. Here are some general pointers to help you handle the situation.
>
> **If the body is found**
>
> Follow the usual procedure, i.e. arrange the issuing of the death certificate in the country of death. The British Embassy/Consulate is invariably helpful and can give some advice on local procedures.
>
> The application for the grant will follow normal procedures.
>
> **If the body is not found, but its whereabouts are known**
>
> The first port of call will be the deceased's employers (if not self-employed or on holiday) who should be able to provide evidence as to the whereabouts of the deceased.
>
> The second port of call will be the British Embassy/Consulate, which with the benefit of the information supplied by the deceased's employers, will advise on local procedures.
>
> Assuming a death certificate is issued, the application for the grant should be straightforward as there is no difficulty in asserting death.
>
> **If no body is found and the whereabouts are not known**
>
> Steps 1 and 2 as above.
>
> If no death certificate can be obtained in order to obtain the grant, the applicant can apply for leave to swear to the death on an ex parte application supported by a sworn Statement of Facts. This should set out all the known circumstances relevant to the disappearance and should list the deceased's assets and particularly any life policies (for obvious reasons).
>
> On obtaining leave to swear to death, the application for a grant should be straightforward although the wording of the oath will be different.

16.12.3 Discussing funeral arrangements

Most people shy away from a discussion of the practical arrangements for their own funeral even when making a will. In an interesting article 'We need to talk' published in [2010] *Probate Section Journal*, July at p.22 Tony Collinson advocated encouraging clients to engage. He talked about the new Dying Matters Coalition (**www.deathmatters.org**). This is an association with a broad and diverse membership led by the National Council for Palliative Care, the umbrella charity for all those involved in end of life care. The collective aim is to encourage more openness and engagement around end of life issues among the public. Members come from organisations in the NHS, voluntary and independent health and care sectors, a wide range of faith and community organisations, schools and colleges, trade unions, the funeral sector and the legal sector. Tony Collinson describes the literature developed by Dying Matters which: 'can help reframe the conversations solicitors have with their clients ... For instance, instead of asking "what do you want to happen to you when you die?", the coalition advocates asking 'how would you like to be remembered?'.

16.12.4 Arranging funerals

Solicitors may be asked a variety of questions about funerals. Whose responsibility is it to arrange and pay for the funeral? Do PRs have to carry out the deceased's wishes? What if there is a dispute between surviving relatives? Unfortunately, such disputes are becoming increasingly common, perhaps as a result of more complex family relationships. See Rossdale, *Probate and the Administration of Estates*, 4th edn (CCH, 2010) for more information. The following may also be helpful.

Some general principles were set out in *Burrows* v. *HM Coroner for Preston & Joan McManus* [2008] EWHC 1387 (Admin):

1. There is no proprietary interest in a deceased person's body (*Williams* v. *Williams* (1881–82) LR 20 Ch D 659). However, various people have rights and duties in relation to it. The deceased's PRs have the right to determine how and where the body should be disposed, even where other family members object.
2. Where PRs have not been appointed, the person with the best right to the grant of administration takes precedence.
3. The order of priority for persons with the best right to the grant of administration, and hence to the deceased's body, is set out in NCPR 1987, rule 22. However, the court has the power, under Senior Courts Act 1981, s.166 to appoint as administrator some person other than the person who would have the right under NCPR 1987, rule 22, where there are special circumstances which might displace the order of priority set out in NCPR 1987, rule 22, and it is necessary or expedient by reason of those special circumstances to displace the normal order of priority.

4. Only rarely is it appropriate to displace the order of priority (*Buchanan* v. *Milton* [1999] 2 FLR 844).
5. The European Convention on Human Rights also has an impact. The main aspect of the Convention that has application is art.8(1): 'Everyone has a right to respect for his private and family life'. In as much as domestic law says that the views of a deceased person can be ignored, it is no longer good law (*X* v. *Germany* (8741/79), unreported, 10 March 1981 and *Dodsbo* v. *Sweden* (2007) 45 EHRR 22). The views of a deceased person as to funeral arrangements and the disposal of his body must be taken into account. In this type of case, a person's wishes can be regarded as a special circumstance in terms of Senior Courts Act 1981, s.116.
6. In some cases, there will be more than one claim which will engage the art.8 right. For instance, in *Burrows* the deceased (a 15-year-old boy who had committed suicide) had been brought up by his uncle and wife and had had little contact with his natural mother, a heroin addict. However, in the last year of his life, he had met her on several occasions and a bond had developed between them. Both the family life that the deceased had enjoyed with his uncle and his family on one hand, and the family life he enjoyed with his mother on the other were relevant in relation to art.8(1).
7. Where there is a conflict in terms of the engagement of art.8(1), the court is required to focus intensely on the comparative importance of the different rights being claimed, and to balance those rights so as to minimise the interference with each to the least possible extent. On the facts of *Burrows* while the natural mother had the best right under rule 22 to take a grant, there were sufficient special circumstances to justify passing over her rights and giving the uncle the right to take the body and arrange the funeral.

    (a) The mother was incapable of handling the funeral arrangements, owing to her addiction. Although her sister had offered to handle the arrangements, she had no independent claim to do so.
    (b) The deceased had expressed a very clear wish to be cremated. His mother had acknowledged that wish, but had initially been prepared to override it.
    (c) The uncle and his wife were, in reality, the deceased's psychological parents.
    (d) The deceased had a stronger connection with the area where his uncle lived and wished to conduct the funeral, than with the area where his mother lived.

The first of these factors was determinative. It was necessary for the natural mother's rights to be displaced. She was incapable of assuming the responsibility.

The following additional points may also be helpful.

Nobody owns a dead body (see (1) above and *R* v. *Sharpe* (1857) 26 LJMC 47). This is presumably on the grounds of public health and public policy. However, there is a common law duty on an executor to arrange for the proper disposal of the deceased's remains.

As an executor's authority derives from the will and not from the grant, they are entitled to obtain possession of the body for the purposes of burial prior to the grant (by injunction under Senior Courts Act 1981, s.37 if necessary).

While there is no property in a dead body to support a claim for damages, this is no obstacle to an injunction for the delivery of the body. Injunctions are awarded on different principles.

An administrator also has a common law duty to dispose of the body but, as their authority derives from the grant, they may not be able to obtain an injunction for delivery of the body until they have obtained the grant.

A householder has a common law duty to dispose of a body. When the deceased lived alone the duty passes to the local authority (Public Health (Control of Disease) Act 1984, s.46(1)). Local authorities will not pay if there are assets and may instruct solicitors (through their bereavement services department) to trace relatives to authorise the cost of the funeral. If the deceased died in hospital, the duty of disposal falls on the hospital authorities.

In *Lewisham NHS Hospital Trust* v. *Hamuth* [2006] All ER (D) 145 there was a dispute as to the validity of the will and, therefore, as to the validity of the executor appointed in it. The deceased had died in hospital. The executor wished to carry out the deceased's instructions and cremate the body. The family wanted to have the body buried in the family plot. The court held that an executor in general had the right to make arrangements for the disposal of the body but that there was also a common law duty for a householder under whose roof a person had died to make arrangements for a dignified and decent burial. The hospital, being in lawful possession of the body and there being no way of resolving the dispute as to whether the executor was validly appointed within an acceptable time period, had the authority to decide the appropriate means for the disposal of the body.

Are the deceased's wishes binding?

It was held in *Williams* v. *Williams* (1881–82) LR 20 Ch D 659 that a person has no property in their body after their death. Thus, a testator could not dispose of his body by will and any wishes expressed in the will were not binding on the executors. However, we now have the case of the *Burrows* v. *HM Coroner for Preston & Joan McManus* [2008] EWHC 1387 (Admin), which states that the views of a deceased person as to funeral arrangements and the disposal of his body must be taken into account.

Many religious groups have strong views about burial or cremation (Judaism and Islam require burial whereas Hinduism requires cremation) while some environmentalists regard cremation as an improper use of fuel. It is, therefore, important to appoint executors who will respect the deceased's wishes.

When are organs available?

The Human Tissue Act 2004 (HTA 2004) received Royal Assent on 15 November 2004 and the final provisions were brought into force on 1 September 2006. It repeals the Human Tissue Act 1961, the Anatomy Act 1984, the Corneal Tissue Act 1986 and the Human Organ Transplants Act 1989, and introduces a new legislative framework making consent the fundamental principle underpinning the lawful storage and use of human bodies and the removal, storage and use of 'relevant material' from the bodies of deceased persons.

The need for consent under HTA 2004 relates to the purpose for which the 'relevant material' is used or stored.

The purposes listed in HTA 2004, Sched.1 include, amongst others, anatomical examination, public display, research in connection with the functioning of the human body, transplantation and education or training relating to the human health.

Anatomical examination

The consent required for 'anatomical examination' differs from that required for transplantation.

The phrase 'anatomical examination' is defined in HTA 2004, s.54(1) as meaning 'macroscopic examination by dissection for anatomical purposes'; 'anatomical purposes' is defined in HTA 2004, s.54(1) as 'purposes of teaching or studying, or researching into, the gross structure of the human body'.

In the case of donation of a body or 'relevant material' for storage or use for the purpose of 'anatomical examination' or 'public display', appropriate consent can only be given by an individual who has chosen to donate; consent cannot be given by someone else (s.3).

This consent must be in writing and is only valid if:

(a) it is signed by the person concerned in the presence of at least one witness who attests the signature;
(b) it is signed at the direction of the person concerned, in his presence and in the presence of at least one witness who attests the signature; or
(c) it is contained in a valid will of the person concerned.

The Human Tissue Authority accepts that it may not always be possible to obtain written consent from the individual who has chosen to donate their body or part of their body for anatomical examination, for example when a person with sufficient mental capacity is physically unable to write. It has therefore produced a model form for a representative to sign on behalf of a donor (see **www.hta.gov.uk**).

The potential donor must have sufficient mental capacity to make the decision to donate their body for anatomical examination and be able to indicate their wish verbally or physically. The consent form cannot be signed by the third party after death has occurred.

Documented and valid consent for 'anatomical examination' given before 1 September 2006 is treated as 'appropriate consent' under HTA 2004 ('Anatomical Examination: Code 4' – August 2009, note 20).

Note 23 of Code 4 suggests that an individual who wishes to donate their body for 'anatomical examination' in their will should be encouraged to fill in a consent form from their nearest medical school and keep a copy with their will. Although the precise wording in the consent form does not have to be used in the donor's will, it should resemble the wording on the consent form provided by the establishment to which they wish to donate their body. The Human Tissue Authority has produced a model body donation consent form (see **www.hta.gov.uk**).

Purposes other than anatomical examination

Consent for other purposes, for example organ donation, does not have to be in writing. However, written consent is advisable for the avoidance of doubt.

Such consent can be included in the will but because most organs have to be removed while the donor's heart is still beating (except in the case of corneas which can be removed a few hours afterwards), it is important to have some other way of making doctors aware of the donor's wishes. Many people carry donor cards but the most effective method is registration on the NHS Organ Donor Register (see UK Transplant contact details in **Appendix F**).

As an alternative a person can appoint a 'nominated representative' under HTA 2004, s.4 to represent him after his death in relation to consent for any purposes other than anatomical examination. Such an appointment can be made orally in the presence of at least two witnesses (s.4(4)) or in writing, in which case it must comply with the requirements of HTA 2004, s.4(5). The nominated representative's consent cannot be overridden by other individuals including family members.

There is a helpful article ('Organ grinding') by Jonathan Smith, a family law solicitor and mediator based in Litchfield, in [2002] *Solicitors Journal*, 4 September, 781. UK Transplant (since October 2005 part of NHS Blood and Transplant) will send registration forms to solicitors which clients can complete and return.

Inquests and post-mortems

Fairly obviously, if there is reason to believe that there will be an inquest, no one can authorise the use of organs without the consent of a coroner. The same applies if a post-mortem is likely.

Alternative burials

Many people now consider burials in woods, fields or gardens. They can arrange for this but will have to obtain the consent of the relevant local authority. This is because a body is treated as clinical waste and can, therefore, only be disposed of by a licensed operator in accordance with the Control of Pollution Act 1974 and the

Environmental Protection Act 1990. If relatives want to bury the body in the garden, they will have to take advice from the Environment Agency which has a list of minimum distances from the site of a grave to water, cabling and wells or boreholes. The Department of the Environment confirmed in a letter to the Natural Death Centre in 1994 that it is not necessary to apply for planning permission to bury up to two people in a back garden. Permission would be required to bury any more. It is possible to apply for a certificate of lawfulness as regards planning law, and the result of the application is recorded on a public register. If the application is refused, there is a right of free appeal.

The following useful summary is taken from Salford City Council's website:

> The burial site should be on land with a deep water table and be sufficient distance from watercourses so as not to pose a pollution threat.
>
> The Department of the Environment must be informed of your intentions to bury privately, but generally have no objections as long as the following standards are adhered to:
>
> - No burial to be permitted within 100m of a borehole or well spring.
> - No burial within 10m of drain, ditch or watercourse.
> - No burial in waterlogged/poor draining ground.
> - Electrical and other services must be avoided. You may need to contact the gas and electricity board and request plans of the land to ensure your own safety.
> - Safe excavation of the grave is important and a minimum of 1 metre (3 ft) of soil must be left on top of the coffin lid/over the body after the burial has taken place. You may want to consider asking a local gravedigger who is used to working in graveyards if he could dig the excavation for you.
> - There is a requirement to record the burial on the deeds to the property, in accordance with the Registration of Burials Act 1864.
> - A location map must be attached to the deed to confirm the position of the grave and details of the name of the deceased, age, date and place of death should be recorded. This will reduce the potential complication of the police being called if human remains are discovered during future garden maintenance or building work. There are concerns over the issue of future problems, e.g. who would want to buy a property with a body in the garden, but the prospective buyer has the right to know that someone is buried within the grounds of the property.
> - A Certificate for Burial issued by the Coroner or Registrar of Birth and Deaths (called the green disposal) will have to be obtained and any other procedural matters of the Registrar satisfied. The detachable section of this certificate needs to be completed and returned to the Registrar by the person who is arranging the burial. The Registrar does not record the place/location of the burial and this is why it is necessary to write these details on the deeds to the property.
> - If there are any infectious disease concerns relating to the deceased person, then you must inform the local Environmental Health Department.

The Natural Death Centre is a social entrepreneurial, educational charity that gives advice on all aspects of dying, bereavement and consumer rights in this area. It gives support on family-organised and environmentally friendly funerals and runs the Association of Natural Burial Grounds.

Turning to the even more esoteric it is also possible to have a burial at sea. Readers wishing to know the details are referred to Mathew Knight's article in (2000) 20 *Trusts and Estates Law Journal*, 8.

Cremation of body parts after post-mortem and of still born children

Under the Cremation Regulations 1930, SR&O 1930/1016, there was a problem where body parts had been removed during post-mortem and not returned at the time of burial. When the body parts were returned, relatives were not allowed to cremate them if the body had been buried, and the parts had to be buried with the body. Separate cremation of body parts was only permitted when the body itself had been cremated. Initial amendment was made by the Cremation (Amendment) Regulations 2000, SI 2000/58.

The position is now dealt with by the Cremation (England and Wales) Regulations 2008, SI 2008/2841, reg.19. It is now irrelevant whether the body was buried or cremated. However, the new regulations do not require cremation, and it will still be possible to bury the parts with the body or to have them incinerated as clinical waste.

Regulation 20 allows cremation of stillborn children.

Disputes between parents over child's funeral arrangements

In *Fessi* v. *Whitmore* [1999] 1 FLR 767, divorced parents were unable to agree on the funeral arrangements for their 12-year-old son. The boy lived with his mother in the Midlands but had contact with his father who lived in Wales. The boy was killed in an accident while visiting his father in Wales. The father had the boy cremated and wanted to scatter his ashes in the sea off the Welsh coast. The mother wanted to have the ashes interred in the Midlands with a service arranged in conjunction with the boy's school. The parties were unable to agree and an application was made to court. The court concluded that parents with parental responsibility both have an equal right and duty to arrange the child's funeral. Judge Boggis QC said that he was considering an issue where the parties had equal entitlement but conflicting proposals. This was akin to a dispute between trustees and he was, therefore, entitled to consider the issue and come to a conclusion 'which does justice and fairness to both sides'. He ordered that the remains should be disposed of in accordance with the proposals of the mother, in the Midlands. This was because there was a connection there with both sides of the family and this would provide a focus for all the family. For a fuller discussion of the case see the article by David Hershman in (1999) 11 *Trusts and Estates Law Journal*, 18.

16.12.5 Difficult clients

Sometimes solicitors will encounter clients who are hard to please. It may just have to be accepted, but in a proportion of cases there may be some misunderstanding which could be discussed and perhaps removed. Asking such a client what the problem is, if appropriate, may be worthwhile, or a colleague may be able to assist. Prompt action may help to avert a complaint.

16.12.6 Are you being misled?

Not all clients are honest. If solicitors suspect a client is misleading them or others involved, these concerns must be discussed with the client, no matter how difficult this seems. There may, of course, be a completely reasonable explanation. The risks of involvement in another's dishonesty are analysed in **Chapter 13**.

The SRA's Professional Ethics Team may be able to help (see **Appendix F**).

Solicitors should be aware of the dangers of money laundering and read the Law Society's Anti-Money Laundering Practice Note. The Practice Note sets out warning signs to watch for, albeit with the caveat that money laundering techniques change over time. For more information, see **Chapter 4**.

16.13 CHARGING CLAUSES

16.13.1 No charging clause

If a will does not contain a charging clause, the Trustee Act 2000, s.29 allows a trustee who acts in a professional capacity in relation to the management or administration of the estate to charge reasonable remuneration for services provided, no matter when the trust was created, provided that the co-trustees consent in writing. The provision is of no assistance to sole executors or administrators who will have to arrange the appointment of co-trustees.

Professional executors can charge for their time if the beneficiaries are all adult and *sui juris* and give their approval. It is possible for a solicitor-appointed executor or executrix to employ and pay individual partners in the firm, provided there is an express agreement that the solicitor-PR shall not participate in the profits nor derive any benefit from the charges: *Re Gates* [1933] Ch 913. However, it is better practice in such a situation to inform clients that this problem has arisen and seek their consent to a charge being made. If legal advice is to be taken by lay PRs, they will incur costs in any event.

16.13.2 Inappropriate charging clause

It is important to look carefully at a charging clause to check exactly who is entitled to charge and for what. Lay executors can charge if there is an appropriate charging clause but not otherwise. Charities complain that there is an increasing tendency for lay executors to seek to charge in circumstances where they are not able to do so.

A common form of clause is: 'Any trustee engaged in a profession or business may charge for all work done and time spent.' This will allow any professional or business person to charge for any work done. The following clause is more limited: 'Any trustee who acts in a professional capacity may charge.' This will only allow a trustee to charge for professional services rendered. Thus, an accountant could charge for accountancy services rendered and an estate agent could charge for valuations provided.

Also be careful if a company director is to be appointed. The usual wording of a person 'engaged in a profession or business' does not clearly apply to an employee. The *Encyclopaedia of Forms and Precedents* (LexisNexis) suggests the following:

> Any trustee, whether he is engaged in a profession or business, or merely acts in a personal capacity shall be entitled to charge ...

Even if a trustee is authorised to charge, the clause will normally authorise 'reasonable' charges. A solicitor should check to see whether the charges made are reasonable.

16.14 SOLICITOR-EXECUTOR WITNESSES THE WILL

Section 28 of the Trustee Act 2000 provides that a charging clause is no longer regarded as a gift for the purposes of s.15 of the Wills Act 1837. Solicitors who witness a will which allows them to charge for their services will no longer forfeit the benefit of the charging clause.

16.15 CHARGING CLAUSE IN INVALID WILL

If a will proves to be invalid (for example, as a result of faulty execution) all legacies fail and naturally a solicitors' charging clause (being analogous to a legacy) also fails.

In *Gray* v. *Richards Butler* [2001] WTLR 625, solicitors who had paid themselves under a charging clause contained in a will which proved to be invalid for want of due execution had to repay the residuary beneficiary of an earlier will. The court did exercise its inherent jurisdiction to order reasonable remuneration for work done by the firm which could have been undertaken for the earlier valid will.

16.16 APPOINTMENTS FROM DISCRETIONARY TRUSTS AND THE THREE-MONTH TRAP

Section 144 of IHTA 1984 provides that where property comprised in a person's estate immediately before death is settled by will and within two years of his death an event occurs on which tax would otherwise be chargeable, no tax shall be charged and the Act shall apply as if the will had provided that on the testator's death the property should be held as it is after the event.

Example

T leaves his substantial estate on discretionary trusts for the benefit of his wife and family. Eight months after his death the trustees appoint everything to his wife.

The whole estate will be treated as left to his wife and so will attract the spouse exemption.

Most practitioners are aware that if appointments are made out of a discretionary trust within three months of the testator's or testatrix's death, there will be no reading back for IHT purposes. This was highlighted in the case of *Frankland* v. *Inland Revenue Commissioners* [1996] STC 735 where, as a result the spouse exemption was unavailable and £2 million of tax was irrecoverable. See articles in [1996] *Solicitors Journal*, 4 October by Julie Evans and 25 October by Catherine Sanders. The wording of IHTA 1984, s.144 means that an appointment made within the first three months after death is not read back. Appointments to a spouse or charity will not qualify for exemption.

There is no three-month trap if appointments are made to create an immediate post-death interest or a trust for bereaved minors under IHTA 1984, ss.71A or 71D.

16.17 OTHER POINTS TO WATCH IN RELATION TO APPOINTMENTS FROM DISCRETIONARY TRUSTS

16.17.1 Retain proof of the appointment

The most common reason for a s.144 appointment is to unravel an unwanted nil rate band discretionary trust by appointing property to a surviving spouse. The aim of such an appointment is to obtain the spouse exemption on the property appointed and to obtain the benefit of the unused nil rate band of the first spouse to die when the survivor dies.

It is, therefore, important to retain evidence of the appointment as when the transferred nil rate band is claimed on the survivor's death. HMRC will require documentary proof that the nil rate band of the first spouse was not used.

Section 144 does not impose any requirements as to the form of appointment and indeed talks in terms of 'events' so an informal advancement of capital will suffice to engage s.144. In this case a trustees' minute evidencing the advancement must be made.

However, the trust instrument itself will normally require the use of a deed to exercise a power of appointment.

16.17.2 Make sure the right people make the appointment

It is the trustees of the discretionary trust who make the appointment. Trustees of private trusts must act together unless the trust instrument provides otherwise.

Normally, the trustees are the same people as the executors but problems can arise where some of the executors renounce probate or have power reserved to apply at a later date. Those appointed remain trustees unless and until they disclaim their trusteeship. A renunciation of probate is not sufficient to disclaim trusteeship: *Re Gordon* (1877) LR 6 Ch D 531.

A disclaimer can be inferred from conduct: *Stacey* v. *Elph* (1853) 1 My & K, although it is preferable to have a written disclaimer for the avoidance of doubt.

16.18 DEALING WITH MISTAKES

How mistakes should be handled depends on the nature and significance of the error, and the applicability of the relevant rules of the Solicitors' Code of Conduct 2007, but the following comments may also be of interest.

According to the Legal Complaints Service (LCS), relatively minor errors are usually best dealt with promptly by being frank with the client. Most clients will appreciate openness at an early stage and an explanation. It seems that clients find a lack of frankness (or an impression of it, from an absence of explanation, or failure to answer questions or reply to letters, etc.) more irritating, and more likely to found a complaint, than a prompt apology and explanation of the problem.

More serious mistakes create different issues. First, these should be discussed with your insurers. Second, clients may have to be advised to obtain independent advice.

In either case, the SRA's Professional Ethics Team and the Law Society's Practice Advice Service may be able to assist (see **Appendix F**).

If solicitors acting for the other side have made an error which they refuse to deal with, or they do not reply to correspondence, it is open to solicitors and/or their client to make a complaint to the LCS. Only the client, however, can ask for the complaint to be conciliated.

Conciliation can be an effective means of resolving less serious disputes – more information is available from the LCS. The Office of Legal Complaints will open its doors in 2010.

For more information, see the Law Society's Complaints Management Practice Note (21 January 2010).

16.19 SOURCES OF HELP

16.19.1 The court

The court can assist in a number of ways:

- an application under CPR, Part 64 may be made for help on a particular point, or for the court's assistance in the administration generally;
- a PR may be removed by the court under the Administration of Justice Act 1985, s.50; and
- the Trustee Act 1925, s.63 provides for payment into court, in appropriate circumstances, if trustees are unable otherwise to obtain good discharge.

The court can also assist if it is impossible to trace missing beneficiaries (see **16.1** above) and s.49 of the Administration of Justice Act 1985 allows the court to pronounce on the validity of wills if the consent of the beneficiaries has been obtained. Clearly, the cost of such an application means that approaching the court is not one's first recourse, but there may be in the end no other alternative. Personal representatives' costs would usually be met from the estate (but see **16.10** above for counsel's opinion on the costs of PRs separately represented). An excellent series of articles by Dawn Goodman of Withers appeared in [1994] *Solicitors Journal*, August and September, on how to avoid problems and how the court can help.

In *Re Barton (Deceased)* [2002] EWHC 264 (Ch) (20 March 2002) an executor failed to recover his cost incurred in challenging a deed made between the residuary beneficiary and an annuitant commuting the annuity to a lump sum. The residuary beneficiary had made it clear before the commencement of proceedings that it and the annuitant accepted the validity of the deed and that there was, therefore, no need to refer the matter to court. The case is an illustration of how careful executors and trustees should be to avoid unnecessary cost. The courts are not prepared to order costs from the estate where the application was misconceived.

16.19.2 Official Solicitor

The Official Solicitor (see **Appendix F**) deals with personal injury work for children and adults without mental capacity, and also acts for children in other cases, as next friend or *guardian ad litem* where appropriate. The Official Solicitor also acts as trustee, obtains grants of representation for the use and benefit of those without mental capacity, and is asked to administer estates of certain intestates to allow IPFDA 1975 claims to be made. The website of the Official Solicitor (**www.officialsolicitor.gov.uk**) has several useful publications and includes various Practice Directions.

16.19.3 Court of Protection

The Court of Protection makes decisions in relation to the property and affairs and healthcare and personal welfare of adults (and children in a few cases) who lack capacity. The court also has the power to make declarations about whether someone has the capacity to make a particular decision.

The court has the same powers, rights, privileges and authority in relation to mental capacity matters as the High Court. It is a superior court of record and is able to set precedents (set examples to follow in future cases).

The Court of Protection has the powers to:

- decide whether a person has capacity to make a particular decision for themselves;
- make declarations, decisions or orders on financial or welfare matters affecting people who lack capacity to make such decisions;
- appoint deputies to make decisions for people lacking capacity to make those decisions;
- decide whether an LPA or enduring power of attorney (EPA) is valid;
- remove deputies or attorneys who fail to carry out their duties; and
- hear cases concerning objections to register an LPA or EPA.

A range of publications guidance and court decisions are available from the court's website.

The Public Guardian, supported by the Office of the Public Guardian (OPG), carries out a number of functions to help protect people who lack capacity. It:

- manages a register of LPAs;
- manages a register of EPAs;
- manages a register of court orders that appoint Deputies;
- supervises deputies and works with other relevant organisations (for example, social services, if the person who lacks capacity is receiving social care);
- instructs Court of Protection Visitors to visit people who may lack mental capacity to make particular decisions and those who have formal powers to act on their behalf such as deputies;
- receives reports from attorneys acting under LPAs and from deputies; and
- provides reports to the Court of Protection, as requested, and deals with cases where there are concerns raised about the way in which attorneys or deputies are carrying out their duties.

The Public Guardian is also personally responsible for the management and organisation of the OPG.

It produces many publications which are all available from its website (**www.publicguardian.gov.uk**).

16.19.4 Probate registries

The Principal Registry is encouraging registrars to make contact with practices in their catchment areas, for example by meeting local law societies, which were asked to appoint a liaison officer to further this link. The probate registry offers a very reasonably priced oath-settling service in cases of difficulty – although there have been complaints of some firms using this service for routine oaths which presented no difficulty.

16.19.5 Mediation

Seemingly intractable disputes can often be settled with the help of a trained mediator.

16.19.6 The Law Society

The Private Client Section caters for solicitors who have an interest in wills and trusts, tax planning, investment advice as part of financial planning, Court of Protection, care planning for elderly clients and estate administration.

The Practice Advice Service answers solicitors' questions on legal practice problems in all areas of law.

Lawyerline is a service run by the Law Society to assist solicitors with questions about client care and complaints (tel: 0870 606 2588 or e-mail lawyerline@lawsociety.org.uk).

16.19.7 Solicitors Regulation Authority

The SRA's Professional Ethics Team offers confidential advice on the application and interpretation of the rules and principles of professional conduct. This advice encompasses such issues as how the rules affect solicitors' plans to develop their practices, or their relationships with clients, the court and others with whom they have dealings. Professional Ethics can be contacted at:

Solicitors Regulation Authority
Professional Ethics Team
Ipsley Court
Berrington Close
Redditch B98 0TD
Tel: 0870 606 2577

16.19.8 Insurers

Problems which may involve claims against solicitors need to be referred to their insurers. Policies are likely to provide that the solicitor has a discretion whether to inform the insurers of circumstances which the solicitor believes may result in a claim, and a duty to notify them of claims which have been made against the solicitor or which the solicitor learns will be made.

16.19.9 Specialist solicitors and counsel

Counsel's opinion may be necessary on a variety of matters. If the question is one of construction, s.48 of the Administration of Justice Act 1985 allows a barrister of 10 years' standing to give an opinion to the PRs on which the court may, without hearing argument, allow them to act.

Rather than approaching counsel, some practitioners may like to consider consulting another firm of solicitors. This is a practice which is becoming established in certain specialist fields such as pensions and contentious probate.

It may be particularly useful to approach a professional colleague if a difficulty also raises conduct or practice issues, since another solicitor will be more aware than counsel of the impact of the Solicitors' Code of Conduct 2007 and issues relating to practice as a solicitor.

16.19.10 Institute of Legacy Management and legacy officers

Where charities are beneficiaries, solicitors should be aware that charities are in a sense 'professional beneficiaries'. The legacy officers of the larger charities have a wealth of specialist knowledge, and it is well worth discussing with them problems arising from the administration of estates in which they are interested, as they may well have had previous experience of that very problem. The website of the Institute of Legacy Management has a number of fact sheets for solicitors (see **www.ilmnet.org**).

16.19.11 Within the office

All solicitors, from time to time, have files which they feel have become bogged down or which are a constant headache. One option is to try to make a deal with a colleague to exchange 'headache' files once a month. A different solicitor may be able to skip through something which has stalled a colleague for days – and vice versa.

16.19.12 Personal

Stress is a major cause of illness. Many solicitors face huge pressures and a heavy burden of others' expectations and responsibility at work. There are now numerous books on stress available which help to identify the symptoms and suggest solutions. There are helpful articles in the *Probate Section Journal* (available on the website, **www.probatesection.org.uk**) entitled 'Stress and legal practice' September 1999; 'A new look at workplace counselling' December 1999; and 'Stress out!' June 2003.

16.19.13 The Solicitors' Assistance Scheme

The Solicitors' Assistance Scheme (SAS) aims to serve the solicitors' profession by providing solicitors and their staff with initial independent and confidential advice and assistance in respect of professional, business or personal problems. In doing so it seeks to enable individuals requiring help to resolve their problems, such as:

- stress;

- professional problems;
- bereavement;
- illness (including alcoholism and drugs);
- financial worries (including insolvency and intervention);
- employment problems; and
- disciplinary problems.

See **www.thesas.org.uk** for contact details.

16.19.14 LawCare

To assist lawyers, the Law Societies of England and Wales, Scotland, and Northern Ireland, the Bar Council and ILEX have funded LawCare, a confidential advisory service to help lawyers, their staff and their immediate families to deal with the health issues and related emotional difficulties that can result from a stressful career as a lawyer. There is a free helpline (see **Appendix F**) or visit **www.lawcare.org.uk**.

16.20 PARTING COMPANY

Sometimes, solicitors and clients have to part company. Clients may terminate retainers on any grounds they wish. Solicitors may terminate retainers in more limited circumstances, which are set out in the Solicitors' Code of Conduct 2007, rule 2.01 and supporting guidance notes. They include a client's supervening incapacity, the breakdown of confidence and an inability to obtain proper instructions. The solicitor must give reasonable notice.

Richard Buxton (Solicitors) v. *Mills-Owens (the Law Society intervening)* [2010] EWCA Civ 122 is an important case for solicitors on termination of a retainer.

A term of the firm's retainer was that the firm could decide to cease acting for the defendant 'only with good reason'. The firm terminated the retainer because the client insisted on pursuing the case on a basis which both the firm and counsel instructed believed to be unarguable. Following the termination of the retainer, the firm submitted its final fee account. At first instance the court held that the firm was not entitled to terminate its retainer and as the contract was an entire contract could not recover any costs.

The Court of Appeal allowed the appeal. A retainer is an entire contract. A solicitor might terminate his retainer before the end on reasonable notice and if he had a reasonable ground for refusing to act further for the client. It was wrong to restrict the circumstances in which a solicitor could lawfully terminate his retainer to those in which he was instructed to do something improper. Here the firm had been retained to institute and take a statutory appeal to the end. The parties had agreed that the firm could terminate 'only with good reason'. In the circumstances, the firm and counsel had been right to consider points advanced by the defendant hopeless and not properly arguable. On the evidence, therefore, the firm had had good reason to terminate the retainer.

It was settled law that where a solicitor terminated an entire contract before completion and did so for good cause or on reasonable grounds, subject to any provision contained in the agreement between the parties, he was entitled to be paid for the work that he had done.

Lay and professional executors, or two or more lay executors, may disagree about a number of issues. Where executors cannot agree, one may seek independent advice. An opinion given by counsel in 1986 on costs issues arising out of such a step is included at **16.10** above. It is clear from this opinion that PRs seeking independent advice may not in every case find that their costs would be paid from the estate.

Other problems arise where it is clear, or feared, that a client intends to act dishonestly, for example, by saying outstanding tax is to remain unpaid. In such cases, despite the duty of confidentiality, you may have an obligation to inform others. See guidance notes 9–19 to rule 4 of the Solicitors' Code of Conduct 2007. In difficult cases the assistance of the SRA's Professional Ethics Team (see **Appendix F**) is always available. Some of the issues are considered in **Chapter 13**. Solicitors should also be aware of the Warning Cards issued by the SRA in relation to mortgage fraud and money laundering.

16.21 NON-CONTENTIOUS PROBATE RULES REVIEW

At the time of writing Lord Justice Munby is chairing a working group reviewing the Non-Contentious Probate Rules 1987. The proposed changes are sweeping and were described by Patricia Wass, the chair of the Probate Section (now Private Client Section) in the July 2010 issue of *Probate Section Journal* at p.20 as 'revolutionary in their concept, representing the biggest change in many years to the way that probate applications are handled'. A summary of the main points encompassed by the review is given below.

1. **Substantive law.** The working group is proceeding on the basis that the substantive law will remain the same. The group may identify some areas of law that need to be reconsidered in which case it will make those suggestions but that will not delay the rewriting of the rules.
2. **Future-proof.** The rules and underlying practices will be reviewed to ensure the processes are appropriate for a modern Probate Service and will be 'future-proof', allowing for changes in practice, procedure and technology, without necessarily requiring further changes to the rules.
3. **Language.** The rules and supporting guidance will be written in clear, user-friendly language (not simply removing the Latin expressions, but removing or explaining terms that are not clear to ordinary users).
4. **Practice directions and additional guidance.** The rules will be supported by practice directions and additional staff guidance (to replace the current

compendium and registrars' practice points). These documents will be available to all users. The practice directions will not simply be an expanded version of the rules, but will add practical guidance.

5. **Application form.** There will be an application form asking focused, factual questions which will enable the Probate Service to issue the appropriate grant.
6. **Online application.** The rules will allow for both paper and online applications.
7. **Personal applicant interview.** It will not be necessary to require personal applicants to attend for interview as a matter of routine. Applicants will be able to communicate with the Probate Service by telephone or by electronic means. The Probate Service will retain the right to call a personal applicant to interview where appropriate, and the working group will consider how the applicant can exercise the option of attending for interview if s/he wishes.
8. **The oath.** The oath will be replaced by a statement of truth. The criminal law must impose appropriate sanctions on applicants who deliberately falsify an application.
9. **Advice for applicants.** The telephone advice service and other information available to users will be reviewed to ensure that individuals receive the appropriate level of assistance to complete the application process.
10. **Fraud.** The revised processes need to be robust and ensure best practice for preventing fraudulent applications.

16.22 MISSING WILLS

It can be difficult to discover whether there is a will and, if so, where it is located. PRs run the risk of distributing an estate on the basis of an intestacy when there is, in fact, a will.

It is possible to register the location of a will with the Certainty National Will Register (**www.certainty.co.uk**). A registered will can then be located by a search of the register.

Where a will has not been registered, it is possible to use a different form of Certainty search. This issues a missing will notification to solicitors in the areas where the testator was most likely to have made his or her will, i.e. where he or she worked or lived.

CHAPTER 17

Accounting and distributing

Lesley King

17.1 INTRODUCTION

Paragraphs **17.2–17.4**, the specimen accounts for Victoria Thomas (at **17.3.1** below) and the explanatory notes which follow (at **17.3.2** below) are based on materials prepared by the College of Law for trainee solicitors. We are most grateful to the College for its help in allowing us to reproduce these edited sections.

An increasing number of firms are turning to computerised packages to produce their accounts (see **Chapter 19** and **Appendix D**). Another option is to engage a specialist firm with the experience and expertise to do the work more quickly than you can.

Even so, we have set out the essential elements of the accounts in this chapter.

STEP published an excellent booklet written by Jonathan Cooke, *STEP Accounting Guidelines*, which gives fuller guidance (available from STEP, see **Appendix F**). The book gives detailed examples of accounting for a typical estate and the three main types of family trust.

17.2 ESTATE ACCOUNTS

17.2.1 The duty to account

Personal representatives are reminded of their obligation to keep accounts by the wording of all the oaths leading to grants of representation (giving effect to s.25 of the Administration of Estates Act 1925).

The accounts should give a clear and accurate statement of the estate property and income, and contain full details of all receipts and payments (for which the appropriate corresponding documentation should be available). Personal representatives (PRs) who are solicitors are subject to the Accounts Rules (see **Chapter 5**) as well as the general law.

17.2.2 Form of accounts

The form of estate accounts varies. Some firms use the traditional 'side-by-side' format showing income and outgoings. Others, as here, use a 'vertical' layout. The aim is always to give the PRs and residuary beneficiaries an explanation of the administration of the estate in an easily understandable form.

There is no prescribed layout or form for estate accounts, so whatever format best suits the estate in hand may be used, but the simpler and easier the accounts are, the better. They must, of course, give enough detail to allow a proper appreciation of all the transactions which have taken place.

The following elements are standard.

Introduction

This is a narrative setting out:

- the date of death, the date and place of issue of the grant of representation, and the PRs' names;
- if there was a will, a summary of the gifts made; otherwise, an outline of the effect in the estate of the intestacy rules;
- the value of the gross and net estates and the amount of any IHT paid;
- details of any joint property passing by survivorship, variations made, elections under IHTA 1984, s.142, funds held back in respect of future tax liability and other relevant information.

Balance sheet

This shows the amount due to residuary beneficiaries at the date of preparation and the remaining assets less any outstanding liabilities.

Estate capital account

This shows the value of the estate for probate and IHT purposes, any transactions and matters taking place during the administration period which affect those values and the balance remaining.

It can be drawn up in two parts: (1) the estate at death based on the IHT and any corrective accounts submitted; and (2) the transactions and events taking place during the administration period. The first part would show the gross and net estates at death, as agreed for probate and IHT purposes, exactly as they appear on the IHT accounts and probate papers. The second would record transactions which took place during the administration period affecting the probate value of the estate – for example, sales for more or less than book value and administration expenses.

Alternatively, if the estate is simple, it is possible to combine the two parts to focus on the amount available for beneficiaries. Assets are shown at their probate value with an immediate adjustment for gains/losses in value of assets sold and adjustments for administration expenses.

It is important to show the value of assets at the date of death both to allow the beneficiaries to understand what has happened during the administration and because the beneficiaries will use the value at death as their acquisition cost (for CGT purposes) in relation to future disposals of the assets.

Sometimes there will be differences between the IHT account(s) and the estate capital account, arising from the different tax treatment and legal nature of certain kinds of property (for example, reversionary interests, being 'excluded property', are left out of IHT accounts but appear, as assets, in the estate accounts; conversely, the deceased's share of jointly owned property passing by survivorship will be included in the IHT account but, as far as the estate accounts are concerned, will only be mentioned for information in the introductory narrative).

Apportionments cause problems. Show income accrued up to the date of death as an asset for IHT purposes and include it in the net estate. However, for income tax and for distribution purposes (if the Apportionment Act 1870 has been varied) such amounts must be treated as income receivable after death. As such, they are credited to the income account. To avoid double counting, they must, therefore, be deducted from the net estate on the capital account.

Estate income account

This shows all the income received during the administration period. When tax is deducted at source (for example, company dividends) only the net amounts of income received need to be shown; otherwise put in gross receipts, with an entry showing the basic rate tax which the PRs have paid.

If equitable apportionments have been made, or if any income is apportioned to capital under the Apportionment Act 1870, show the full amount of the income that the PRs receive, with the amount apportioned to capital being shown as an appropriation of part of the total.

This account should also show individually any interim payments of income to beneficiaries so that they can check these against the annual certificates of deduction of income tax the solicitor has given them (form R185E). It is helpful to divide the income account into tax years and to show the income received for each tax year and the payments made for each tax year.

Show any interest paid on general legacies, and any income produced by property which was given specifically in the will, as deductions from the total income received. Expenses attributable to income can be dealt with in a similar way.

This account can be made up to each 5 April.

Beneficiaries' or distribution accounts

Carry forward the balances on the capital and income accounts to beneficiaries' accounts. If the beneficiaries are absolutely entitled, add the two figures together to show the total due and then deduct any amounts that have already been paid. If the state is passing to a mixture of exempt and non-exempt beneficiaries, deduct any IHT attributable to the share of the non-exempt beneficiaries.

Schedules or annexes

More detailed information can conveniently be put here, to keep the main accounts uncluttered. Schedules may cover:

- debts at death;
- dividends received during the administration;
- investments owned at death – this will usually be in two parts: (1) showing investments retained and appropriated to, or divided between the beneficiaries; and (2) showing the investments which were sold, along with gains and losses.

Notes

These may be helpful to draw attention to any aspects of the accounts which might otherwise be overlooked or unclear.

17.2.3 Planning for the end of the administration period

Solicitors should consider early on in the administration the discharge that the PRs will eventually seek from the beneficiaries and whether any special arrangements need to be made, e.g. if any beneficiary lacks capacity. A discharge from residuary beneficiaries will only be valid if there has been full disclosure of the estate assets, the dealings with them and of the balances available for distribution. Solicitors should also anticipate the end of the administration period by, for example, settling all tax liabilities and arranging to withdraw funds from banks and building societies in good time.

PRs will want approval of the accounts from the residuary beneficiaries and may consider withholding some of the assets until this is forthcoming. Receipts for cheques or assets should be obtained and filed with the estate papers. (See **17.7** below for guidance on obtaining receipts.)

17.3 SPECIMEN ACCOUNTS

The following specimen accounts for Victoria Thomas deceased illustrate the points made above, and are followed by notes, beginning at **17.3.2** below, explaining how these accounts were made up.

17.3.1 Victoria Thomas, deceased

Miss Thomas died on 3 May 2010. Lowe Snow & Co of Hixley held her will which was dated 15 August 1994 and (in summary) provided:

- revocation clause;
- executors: (1) Miss Emily Thomas and (2) Miss Amy Thomas both of 'Hillview', Hixley, Cheshire;

- charitable legacies (all registered charities):

  (1) £1,000 to Cheshire Home of Rest for Horses;
  (2) £250 to Hixley Dogs Home;
  (3) £250 to Cheshire Donkey Sanctuary;

- receipts clause;
- residue, after debts, legacies, testamentary expenses – 'to such of them my said sisters Emily Thomas and Amy Thomas as shall survive me and if both equally between them' (gift over to RSPCA in event of both sisters predeceasing: both survived);
- clause dispensing with consents to appropriation.

It was duly executed and attested.

Victoria Thomas: estate for probate and IHT purposes

	£	£
Spring Cottage	340,000.00	
Investments	39,512.00	
Barclays Bank plc	4,100.00	
Cash in house	21.00	
Lloyds TSB Bank plc	5,828.00	
Arrears of retirement pension	442.00	
Contents:		
sold gross	500.00	
other: valued	2,500.00	
GROSS ESTATE		392,903.00
Less		
Electricity	31.00	
Gas	52.00	
Income tax	295.00	
Funeral	1,025.00	(1,403.00)
NET ESTATE FOR PROBATE		391,500.00
Less		
Charitable legacies (exempt)	1,500.00	
ESTATE FOR IHT PURPOSES		390,000.00
IHT PAYABLE		
on first £325,000	NIL	
on £65,000 at 40 per cent		(26,000.00)
on delivery of account, on net non-instalment property (£50,000)	3,333.33	
on Spring Cottage	22,666.67	

The solicitors sent a covering letter with the accounts to the two PRs:

Dear Miss Thomas,

YOUR LATE SISTER'S ESTATE

I enclose the estate accounts which include an outline of your sister's will, and the amount of the estate and of tax and other payments paid and so on. We have not deducted income tax from the £150 this firm has allowed you as interest. You should, therefore, include it in your tax return for the tax year 200–/–.

Yours sincerely [etc.]

These are the accounts which were sent.

Accounts: Estate of Miss Victoria Thomas deceased

Included in these accounts are the following:

1. Introduction
2. Capital account
3. Estate income account
4. Beneficiary's account – Miss Emily Thomas
5. Beneficiary's account – Miss Amy Thomas
6. Schedule of investments showing probate values

Introduction

Miss Victoria Thomas, late of Spring Cottage, Tottenhall Road, Hixley, Cheshire died on 3 May 2010, aged 82. Probate of her will dated 15 August 1994 was granted on ... to Miss Emily Thomas and Miss Amy Thomas, the executors named in the will.

In her will Miss Thomas left these charitable legacies:

(1) £1,000 to the Cheshire Home of Rest for Horses,
(2) £250 to the Hixley Dogs Home,
(3) £250 to the Cheshire Donkey Sanctuary.

The estate remaining after payment of these legacies, and after payment of Miss Thomas's debts and funeral and testamentary expenses, was given to Miss Emily Thomas and Miss Amy Thomas equally.

The net estate for probate purposes amounted to £391,500.00. For inheritance tax (IHT) purposes the taxable estate amounted to £390,000.00, the legacies to the charities being exempt. IHT amounted to £26,000.00. This has been paid and final IHT clearance obtained.

The residue has been divided between the beneficiaries (Miss Emily and Miss Amy Thomas) and this is shown in the accounts. Miss Thomas's investments have been divided equally between the beneficiaries. The values stated in the beneficiaries' accounts form the acquisition value for the purposes of capital gains tax.

Part of the contents of Spring Cottage was divided between the Misses Thomas as they agreed, and the remainder was sold. Spring Cottage was sold at the agreed probate value. The estate's liability to income tax was met by deduction of tax at source.

Lowe, Snow & Co

Balance sheet as at [date of accounts]	**£**	**£**
Balance due to residuary beneficiaries (see beneficiaries' accounts)		
Miss Emily Thomas	67,617.98	
Miss Amy Thomas	67,617.99	
		135,235.97
Represented by		
Cash balances		
Barclays Bank deposit account	43,478.00	
Lowe, Snow & Co client bank account	91,757.97	
		135,235.97

Capital account	**£**	**£**
Spring Cottage, Hixley		
Probate value	340,000.00	
Net proceeds of sale		330,000.00
Investments per schedule at probate value		39,512.00
Barclays Bank plc account	4,039.64	
– Interest to date of death	60.36	
		4,100.00
Cash – in house		21.00
Bank A/c – Lloyds TSB plc, Hixley		
Current a/c	721.50	
Deposit a/c	5,000.00	
– Interest to date of death	106.50	
		5,828.00
Arrears of retirement pension		442.00
Contents of house and personal effects		
Distribution *in specie* (estimated value)	2,500.00	
Proceeds of sale of rest	443.25	
		2,943.25
GROSS ESTATE		382,846.25
Less		

Capital account	£	£
Debts due at death		
Eastern Electricity Co – electricity a/c	31.00	
British Gas – gas a/c	52.00	
Income tax due at death	295.00	
Funeral expenses		
G. Smith & Co	1,025.00	
Administration expenses		
Commissioner's fees	9.00	
Probate court fees	60.00	
Stockbroker Co – valuation fees	517.50	
Lowe, Snow & Co – charges for administering the estate	1,650.00	
VAT	288.75	
Inheritance tax	26,000.00	
		(29,928.25)
NET ESTATE		352,918.00
Less		
LEGACIES		
Cheshire Home of Rest for Horses	1,000.00	
Hixley Dogs Home	250.00	
Cheshire Donkey Sanctuary	250.00	
		1,500.00
RESIDUE		351,418.00
Divisible		
Miss Emily Thomas – one half	175,709.00	
Miss Amy Thomas – one half	175,709.00	
		351,418.00

Estate income account	£	£
Income tax year 2010 to 2011		
Dividends received		
1.9.2010	255.00	
Interest received		
Barclays Bank		
Interest to close a/c on 26.08.2010	76.02	
Lloyds TSB Bank, Hixley		
Interest to close deposit a/c 30.8.2010	45.60	

Estate income account	**£**	**£**
Refund of income tax	15.55	
		392.17
Less loan interest		
Lloyds TSB Bank, Hixley		
Interest on loan to pay IHT		(62.20)
		329.97
Divisible		
Miss Emily Thomas – one half	164.98	
Miss Amy Thomas – one half	164.99	
		329.97

Beneficiary's account	**£**	**£**
MISS EMILY THOMAS		
Share of residue due to you per capital account		175,709.00
Share of residue due to you per income account		164.98
Total due to you		175,873.98
Represented by –		
Transferred to you		
Shares at probate value		
630 Marks & Spencer ord. shares	3,795.00	
500 Tesco Stores ord. shares	1,620.00	
489 Royal Dutch Shell ord. reg. shares	8,316.00	
115 Schroders ord. shares	1,175.00	
865 Tate & Lyle ord. shares	4,850.00	
		19,756.00
Retained by you		
Share of furniture at agreed value		1,250.00
Interim payments to you		
10.7.2010	12,250.00	
13.11.2010	75,000.00	
		87,250.00
Balance now due to you		67,617.98
		175,873.98
MISS AMY THOMAS		
Share of residue due to you per capital account		175,709.00
Share of residue due to you per income account		164.99
Total due to you		175,873.99

Beneficiary's account	**£**	**£**
Represented by –		
Transferred to you		
Shares at probate value		
630 Marks & Spencer ord. shares	3,795.00	
500 Tesco Stores ord. shares	1,620.00	
489 Royal Dutch Shell ord. reg. shares	8,316.00	
115 Schroders ord. shares	1,175.00	
865 Tate & Lyle ord. shares	4,850.00	
		19,756.00
Retained by you		
Share of furniture at agreed value		1,250.00
Interim payments to you		
10.7.2010	12,250.00	
13.11.2010	75,000.00	
		87,250.00
Balance now due to you		67,617.99
		175,873.99

Schedule of investments

PROBATE VALUES

Amount	**Stock**	**Probate**	**Miss Emily Thomas**		**Miss Amy Thomas**	
		Value £	**No.**	**Value £**	**No.**	**Value £**
1,260	Marks & Spencer ord. shares	7,590.00	1,650	3,795	1,650	3,795
1,000	Tesco Stores (Hld-ings) ord. shares	3,240.00	900	1,620	900	1,620
978	Royal Dutch Shell ord. shares	16,632.00	640	8,316	640	8,316
230	Schroders ord. shares	2,350.00	400	1,175	400	1,175
1,730	Tate & Lyle shares	9,700.00	600	4,850	600	4,850

17.3.2 Notes on the specimen estate accounts

The accounts start with the narrative Introduction, giving details of the grant and explaining the distribution of the estate.

In this estate, apart from three pecuniary legacies, the entire net estate was divided between two beneficiaries. Thus all that is required is a *capital account*, showing assets and liabilities and the net residue, an *income account* showing income received during the administration, and *beneficiaries' accounts* showing the division of their entitlements and how these were met between the beneficiaries, and a *schedule* showing details of the investments.

17.3.3 Capital account

In preparing the capital account there is a choice: the account can be produced in two parts or in one.

- If the account is in two parts, the first part will mirror exactly the estate as disclosed in the HMRC account (amended by any corrective account). The probate value of all assets, whether or not sold, will be listed together with deductions permitted for IHT purposes, e.g. debts due at death, funeral expenses. The figure produced will therefore be the same as that agreed with HMRC, but of course it will not be the amount available for distribution to the beneficiaries: for example, administration costs may have been incurred which cannot be deducted for IHT purposes (e.g. IHT itself, solicitors' costs, probate court fees, etc.). These costs will have to be deducted in the second part of a two-part capital account, to produce a sum which does represent the net estate available for the beneficiaries.
- If the account is in one part (as here) it shows the net estate available for the beneficiaries. This method produces a different sum from the one shown in the IHT400, and shows the amount the beneficiaries are actually receiving after tax and administration expenses.

A one-part account is used in this example. Accordingly, for any items sold, e.g. Spring Cottage, the net proceeds of sale are used.

Some or all of the investments may have been sold. If so, the probate value of all the holdings will be included, plus or minus the gain or loss on sale as appropriate. (Details of the transactions would be shown in the schedule of investments.)

In this estate, and others where the investments are divided equally between the beneficiaries, the value included in the accounts is the probate value, i.e. value at the deceased's death. This is unlikely to be the same as the market value at the point when the shares are vested in the beneficiaries. However, any increase or decrease in value will be shared equally between the beneficiaries, so this produces no unfairness. The probate value is also the beneficiaries' acquisition value for CGT purposes.

All the assets, then, are listed at the probate value or actual realised value.

In relation to bank and building society accounts, etc., the probate value includes interest accrued to the date of death. For IHT purposes, this interest forms part of the deceased's estate and so is shown in the capital account. (Interest earned after death and before the closing of the account will be shown in the estate income account.) For income tax purposes, however, the accrued interest before death, and any interest received between death and the closing of the account are regarded as income of the PRs and should be included by them in their income tax return. Accordingly, the income shown in the income account is not the amount of income on which PRs actually pay income tax.

The contents of the house have been valued at an estimated £2,500. Some items have been sold and turned into cash. The actual amount received, i.e. the net proceeds of sale, is shown.

Once the gross estate is established, all the debts and liabilities are then deducted from the gross estate figure, including debts not permitted as deductions for IHT purposes.

A sum representing the net estate results. In this estate, of course, there are legacies to be paid before the net estate is distributed between the residuary beneficiaries. So, non-residuary gifts are deducted from the net estate figure, and then the division of residue is shown. These figures are transferred to the individual beneficiaries' accounts.

17.3.4 Income account

This deals with income received during the administration of the estate. In this estate, all the income is received in one tax year. If the administration straddled more than one tax year, two or more separate sets of figures would be shown.

If income is received net of tax, show the net figure. If income is received gross, the PRs will have to pay income tax at basic rate. This payment will be shown as a deduction from income. Also deducted here will be any payments out of income, such as interest on loans, interest on IHT, any solicitors' or accountants' charges related to post-death tax returns.

In this estate, income and capital are received by the same beneficiaries, and no such distinction has been made in the solicitors' charges. If different beneficiaries were entitled to income and capital, e.g. in a life interest, a proportion of the solicitors' charges, referable to income, would be deducted here.

Again, the net entitlement to income is shown, and the balances are taken to the beneficiaries' accounts.

17.3.5 Beneficiaries' accounts

The entitlements have been brought forward and listed. In this estate the beneficiaries are due capital and income.

Once the total due to a beneficiary has been ascertained, the account shows how this has been satisfied. There may be, as with Miss Emily Thomas, three elements:

- assets transferred *in specie*. Here, the shares were divided equally. As these were entered in the capital account at probate value, again probate values are used. Some furniture was also transferred *in specie* at values agreed between the beneficiaries;
- assets which were retained by the beneficiaries. This is regarded as an 'advance' of part of their respective entitlements, and brought into account;
- payments of cash on account, or interim distributions.

Balancing the books

The balance after these calculations represents the amount due to the beneficiary and all together should add up to the amount left in the client ledger, after costs and disbursements.

If these figures do not agree, something has gone wrong. It can sometimes be a trying process to find the mistake, but it must be found.

It could happen that a balance appears to be due from a beneficiary to the estate. This will usually mean that interim distributions were too big – interim payments should only be made after considering all future liabilities, such as tax and costs. A situation like this often causes great difficulty, as the beneficiary will, at the very least, be disappointed.

17.3.6 Schedule of investments

Rather than include on the capital account details of the investments, these can be listed in a schedule or annex. As no items have been sold this schedule is simple, giving capital values and showing the division of the shares between the beneficiaries. If numerous dividends had been received these could also have been recorded in a schedule.

If items had been sold, the sale price and any gain or loss could be shown. This information would be included in the capital account.

17.3.7 Release for personal representatives

Unless the PRs and residuary beneficiaries are one and the same, the beneficiaries should provide written approval of the accounts and a release from liability. Even when they are the same, a note of the beneficiaries' approval of the accounts might be advisable as far as the solicitors are concerned. This could take the form of a simple statement on the accounts indicating their approval.

17.4 CAPITAL GAINS TAX

Death is not a disposal. PRs acquire assets at their market value at the date of death. If they transfer assets to beneficiaries there is no charge to CGT. The beneficiary simply takes the asset at its value at the same value as the PRs acquired it.

If the PRs sell assets there is a disposal. The rate of CGT payable by PRs depends on the tax year in which the disposal is made:

- For tax years 2004–05 to 2007–08 PRs paid at the uniform trusts rate of 40 per cent.
- For tax years 2008–09 and 2009–10 PRs, like individuals, paid at the uniform rate of 18 per cent.
- For tax year 2010–11 PRs pay at 18 per cent on gains arising before 23 June and 28 per cent on gains arising on or after 23 June.

There are two significant planning points for PRs in relation to capital gains tax:

1. In the tax year 2010–11 the rate of capital gains tax remains at 18 per cent for individuals whose total taxable gains *and income* are less than the upper limit of the income tax basic rate band (£37,400 for 2010–11). However, a 28 per cent rate applies to gains or parts of gains above that limit. PRs should therefore consider whether they should transfer assets pregnant with gain to beneficiaries rather than selling them as PRs. The beneficiaries may only have to pay at 18 per cent on some or all of the gain (or may have losses available to offset the gain).
2. The fact that some or all of the beneficiaries are charities and, as such, exempt from CGT does not mean that there is any exemption from CGT for gains made by the PRs during the administration. To obtain exemption the sale must be made on behalf of the beneficiary. See **17.9.7** below.

As with individuals an indexation allowance will be given for periods ending 5 April 1998 but not thereafter. So, for assets held at 17 March 1998 and disposed of after that date an indexation allowance will be calculated for the period from acquisition up to and including 5 April 1998. For assets acquired after that date no indexation allowance will be available.

Taper relief was available to PRs and trustees who held assets for an appropriate period (one year for business assets, three years for non-business assets) against gains arising in tax years 1998–99 up to and including 2007–08. For tax year 2008/09 and subsequent tax years taper relief is not available.

PRs continue to receive the same annual exemption as an individual for the tax year of death and the two subsequent tax years. Thereafter, there is no exemption. There is, therefore, an incentive to make disposals in the initial three years.

PRs will be able to treat as allowable acquisition costs a proportion of the costs of obtaining the grant: details are set out in Statement of Practice SP2/04. Costs of transferring the asset to the beneficiaries are also allowable (see Taxation of Chargeable Gains Act 1992, s.6(1)).

When PRs transfer assets to legatees there is no disposal and the legatees acquire the assets at the value at the date of death for CGT purposes. It is advisable for the solicitor to inform specific legatees (or pecuniary or residuary legatees to whom assets are appropriated) of the value at the date of death of assets transferred to them; the legatees can then calculate their liability for CGT without having to refer back to the solicitor, perhaps many years after a file has been closed.

There are particular problems in relation to CGT where charities are entitled to assets. See **17.8**.

17.5 INCOME TAX

PRs do not pay higher or additional rate tax. They pay basic or dividend ordinary rate tax on all the income of the estate. They will pay the net income to beneficiaries together with an appropriate tax credit.

Up until 6 April 1995, beneficiaries were assessed to income tax on income of the estate in the tax year in which it was paid to them but at the end of the administration the total of income paid out was apportioned evenly over the whole administration period on a daily basis. This led to recalculation of the beneficiary's tax liability for each tax year of the administration. In cases where a beneficiary was close to the limit of a tax band the apportioning of income could take the beneficiaries into or out of a particular band.

Since 6 April 1995 income paid to a beneficiary is treated as income of the tax year in which it is paid and there is no apportioning of income at the end of the administration. This can result in a beneficiary paying an unnecessarily high rate of tax. For example, if PRs make no interim income payments and pay out all the income at the end of the administration period to a beneficiary, that beneficiary may be pushed into higher rate tax for that year. Had the payments been made in two tax years the beneficiary might have remained a basic rate taxpayer. PRs must provide residuary beneficiaries with form R185E.

The provisions relating to the taxation of income are now to be found in Income Tax (Trading and Other Income) Act 2005.

HMRC has published a 'toolkit' to accompany the trusts and estates return which includes a checklist, potential errors and links to relevant guidance on income and gains of estates and trusts. It is available on the Tax Agent and Adviser page of the HMRC website (**www.hmrc.gov.uk**).

17.5.1 Administration of the deceased's estate

This can be a challenging experience as PRs struggle to get to grips with details of the deceased's income in time to meet HMRC's deadlines. HMRC has this to say on the subject of deadlines on its website at 'Paying the deceased's tax':

PAYMENT DEADLINES

Income Tax is paid in two instalments – on 31 January and 31 July after the end of the tax year. Capital Gains Tax must be paid by 31 January. So the payment on 31 January can be made up of three elements:

- the final balancing payment of tax due for the tax year which ended on the previous 5 April
- Capital Gains Tax due on gains made in the tax year that ended on 5 April
- a payment on account of half the tax due for the current tax year

The tax due on 31 July is the second payment on account of half the tax due for the tax year that ended on 5 April.

If a tax payment is due soon you can ask the Tax Office to reduce it to nil until you have worked out how much tax is due for the period up to the date the person died. Contact the Tax Office shown on the tax bill.

If you can't pay the tax by the date it's due you'll have to pay interest from then until the date you pay it.

But if the tax became due after the deceased died and the executors or administrators of the deceased's estate cannot pay before they obtain probate or letters of administration, you'll only have to pay interest on that unpaid tax from the later of the due date for payment or 30 days from the grant of probate or letters of administration until the date you pay it. If this applies to you, the executors or administrators will need to ask us to adjust any interest charged.

We have set out below extracts from a helpful article by Mary Hase, formerly partner in charge of executorship at chartered accountants, Hereward Phillips. This article first appeared in [1997] *Solicitors Journal*, 20 June and we are most grateful to Mary Hase and to the *Solicitors Journal* for allowing us to reproduce it. It remains good advice.

ADDITIONAL TAX RESPONSIBILITIES FOR SOLICITORS

The introduction of self-assessment puts increased responsibilities on solicitors acting as or advising executors. Tax matters can no longer be left until an estate is fully administered. Put simply, good management of an estate is essential. It saves time, money and – above all – professional reputation.

As a result of self-assessment, solicitors are responsible for ensuring that an estate is administered in a tax efficient manner, with tax returns completed on time and payments made in stages for the current year according to the dates laid down by the new tax regulations.

In the past, it has been common practice for solicitors to leave sorting out the tax on an estate until the estate has been substantially completed. Such practice would now lead to a series of mounting fines for the executor and beneficiaries.

Tax planning

This is the key to success. Consider at the outset when the estate's income is likely to be received and plan the distributions accordingly.

Also consider the financial position of the beneficiaries at the beginning. For wealthy beneficiaries looking to minimise their tax liability it may be best to delay distributions and thereby postpone the impact of higher rate tax until a more convenient time. For those in the middle range the payments might be spread to avoid hitting the higher rate tax threshold. Needy beneficiaries may desire a speedy settlement but again spreading their entitlement over a number of tax years may be more likely to help them utilise allowances and fall beneath tax thresholds.

Remember too that a large income distribution in one year may affect the beneficiaries' tax payments on account in the next.

If in doubt, call in the accountants/tax advisers early to assist with the planning.

The solicitor, acting as executor, must advise the Inland Revenue of the estate's untaxed income and capital gains. The normal deadlines apply – 30 September if the Revenue are to calculate the tax, 31 January if not. However, the Revenue will not work out the income and chargeable gains for you. Beneficiaries who have an absolute interest must also be advised of the income element included in their distributions to enable them to include these figures on their personal tax forms. It is the executor's responsibility to ensure that beneficiaries can meet their deadlines, which may be 30 September if the beneficiaries do not wish to calculate their own tax.

Payments on account

Payments on account underline the importance of good management. Plan the date of cessation and work out how the resulting accounting will be done, so that the beneficiaries are provided with the necessary information in good time to complete their own tax returns and assess their own payments on account.

The basic rule is that a payment on account should be half the previous year's tax liability, excluding capital gains. This is fine when income flow is regular, but distributions from an estate may involve payments over the short term only. It can be particularly difficult for executors and beneficiaries with unreliable income sources to deal with the tax payments. Once assets are realised, and the ensuing untaxed income sources cease, the executor may seek to reduce the payment on account.

Executors should also beware of placing any cash sums received from the estate in investments which pay income gross, such as the money markets, even if this is on a temporary basis. If the liability turns out to be greater than that anticipated when the payment on account was assessed, the executors will be liable for interest and possibly penalties.

For smaller estates it is advisable to avoid these complications by selecting investments which deduct tax at source, even if it means sacrificing one or two interest points and the cash flow advantage of gross income.

For beneficiaries the problem is worse. They may be looking at total income, taxed and untaxed, and can have no idea what their payment on account should be unless the executors give them guidance on how much and when the income distributions are likely to be. Remember that for absolute interest beneficiaries, their distributions will be part income, part capital so merely telling them how much in total to expect is not sufficient.

For life interest beneficiaries, their whole distribution is income so the amounts and dates will suffice for them during the period of administration. Any balance unpaid will be taxable at the date the administration ceases so the date(s) should be planned and made known to the beneficiaries.

Trustees' responsibilities for tax returns start on the death of the person in question, though there may be nothing to report until the estate's assets are vested in them. If a discretionary trust is set up, the payment of income to the trustees or direct to the trust beneficiaries will trigger a liability at the trust rate. So the responsibility for submission of trust returns may start before the closure of the administration.

Even if no formal trust is set up under the will, often it is convenient to leave the estate's assets in the hands of the executors after completion of the administration. This becomes a bare trust and under self-assessment bare trustees are not liable to make returns or to calculate and pay basic rate tax on behalf of the beneficiaries.

Tax liabilities of the deceased

When someone dies, their tax liabilities become the responsibility of the personal representatives, who must then try to keep to the dates above. This may be difficult if the deceased's tax affairs were in arrears, or if there is a delay in obtaining letters of administration.

Problems would occur simply by a death occurring, say, in December. This is because the tax return for the previous year, with up to three tax payments, must all be paid by the following 31 January. These tax payments would be for (a) any outstanding income tax for the previous financial year, (b) capital gains tax for the previous year, and (c) the first tax payment for the current year. As yet, there appears to be no legislation giving the executor more time to assess the tax situation, or to wait until probate is granted, or, indeed for the penalties to be mitigated in these circumstances.

If delay is unavoidable, it would be advisable to write to the Revenue at the earliest opportunity (and before the relevant deadline has passed) explaining the situation, giving an indication of when matters could be dealt with and requesting no penalties.

Delays may be considerable where a will is contested and it may not be clear which beneficiary gets which assets if applications are to be made under the Inheritance (Provision for Family and Dependants) Act 1975. The rigidity of the self-assessment regime cannot cope with such uncertainties.

17.6 TOP 10 TAX TIPS

In an article in [2000] *Solicitors Journal*, 21 January, Mary Hase gave her top 10 tips for making the preparation of key tax reports relatively straightforward whether solicitors are preparing them themselves or instructing accountants. We are grateful to *Solicitors Journal* for allowing us to provide an updated list of tips.

As a preliminary two general tax planning tips:

If the beneficiaries have unused CGT exemptions and/or will be paying CGT, PRs may consider transferring assets to them for sale especially if the administration has exceeded three tax years.

If the beneficiaries are non-UK residents or if they have capital losses against which they could offset any gains, transfer assets to them prior to sale in order to avoid a tax liability.

Date the accounts

Show the starting date (the date of death) and the end date (the date the administration ends or the date of interim accounts). This will clarify which tax year you are dealing with.

List all assets

It is important to itemise all assets (not just those which are encashed) and what happens to them. This is because assets transferred to a beneficiary count as a distribution to that beneficiary when calculating the amounts to be shown on their tax return.

Keep a note of sub-totals

Make sure that you keep a record of income received each tax year and within each year, work out a sub-total for each income source. Even if you don't show this information directly in the accounts, it will help you to fill in the Statement of Residuary Income Forms 922 and also the tax certificates R185 (Estate Income).

Highlight gross income and the date received

It is the date of receipt which determines the fiscal year for which you complete the tax return. Bear in mind that if you do not receive a return, the onus is on you to ask the Revenue for the relevant tax return under Self Assessment.

If you do not receive a tax return and there are capital gains or untaxed income to report:

- Advise the Revenue before the 5 October after the end of the tax year (e.g. before 5 October 2011 for the tax year 2010/2011).
- Submit the tax return by 31 January following the end of the tax year in order to avoid the automatic penalty (e.g. by 31 January 2012 for 2010/2011).

However:

- If you miss the 5 October deadline but subsequently ask for the tax return and submit it with the tax by 31 January, you will avoid any penalties or interest.
- If you don't know which tax office deals with the estate's affairs, contact the tax office which dealt with the deceased during his lifetime and explain the position.

Keep running totals of any capital gains

Calculate the capital gains as they arise and keep running totals for each fiscal year. If the gains exceed the losses at the end of year, a tax return should be submitted. (Also be aware that if the gains exceed the annual exemptions at the end of the first three fiscal years, a tax return should be completed.) The procedure is as above. But do remember to retain enough cash to pay the tax due on the following 31 January.

Record distributions to beneficiaries

Note the date of all distributions to the residuary beneficiaries as they occur. Remember that any transfer of assets counts as a distribution, so list these transfers as well as cash payments. The dates will tell you the tax years for which R185s are needed. Remember the R185s must be given to the beneficiaries in good time for them to meet the deadlines on their personal tax returns, i.e. 30 September or 31 January following the end of the tax year.

General tips

Interest on TESSA or ISA accounts is taxable after the date of death. PEPs lose their tax exemption on death. Thereafter income and gains are taxable. The sale of the deceased's main residence may not be exempt from CGT – check to see whether the concession applies.

Income accrued and not paid at the date of death, but which is shown on the IHT 400 should be included as part of the estate income when it is received. Relief from double taxation can be claimed on form 922 by noting the relevant amounts. (However, it is only worth doing this calculation if a beneficiary pays higher rate tax.)

Deduct administration costs for R185 (Estate Income) calculations

When you work out income less deductions for the R185 calculations, you can deduct part of the administration expenses relating to income. Unless bills are rendered separately, you will have to estimate the amount which can be deducted, but it is important to reduce the tax liability for beneficiaries who are higher rate taxpayers. Deductions can be made for the 'management of assets of the estate properly chargeable to income'. This includes the cost of completing the income tax part of the tax return and completion of the Statements of Residuary Income and preparing the relevant figures for forms 922 in addition to the R185s.

Interest on loans for IHT

Record the dates on which you pay interest on any loans taken out to pay IHT. The interest is tax deductible so include it on the tax return. However, if you would not otherwise submit a tax return because there is no untaxed income or capital gain, you can claim a tax repayment against the estate's income which is taxed at source.

Interest on tax

Although interest on a loan to pay IHT can be deducted against estate income, any interest on IHT or other tax is only deductible against the beneficiaries' higher rate tax – and then only if they have limited interests in residue. No relief is given if the beneficiaries have absolute interests. All other income management expenses will reduce the beneficiary's higher rate tax whether limited or absolute interest.

Keep specific legacy income separate

Keep a separate record of income from assets which are specific legacies and advise the relevant legatee so that he can put the appropriate amounts on his annual tax return.

17.7 RECEIPTS FOR LEGACIES

The following article first appeared in [1992] *Gazette*, 14 October. It is reproduced here, edited and with a revised draft of the recommended receipt and discharge wording approved by the Law Society's Land Law and Succession Committee. Mr Richard Oerton revised the original wording of the receipt and discharge for the journal *Clarity*. This version is identical to Mr Oerton's with one minor change:

Receipts for payment of legacies

Periodically the Law Society receives complaints from beneficiaries who have been asked by solicitors administering an estate to sign receipts for their legacies before payment is made. This has been considered by the Land Law and Succession Committee (now the Wills and Equity Committee).

It should now be standard practice for all solicitors to write to legatees and beneficiaries early in the administration of an estate to inform them of their legacies and entitlements and then, when funds are available, to pay legatees and beneficiaries direct by cheque, unless other arrangements have been made.

The Committee (except as stated below) considers that it is no longer reason-able or necessary for legatees and beneficiaries to be asked to sign receipts in advance of payment and that such a practice is bound to generate additional correspondence and thus to add unnecessarily to the cost of the administration of the estate.

Precedents for simple forms of receipt for the payment of pecuniary, specific and residuary legacies are available. However, solicitors may find it more convenient to ask the legatee or beneficiary to acknowledge receipt by signing and returning a duplicate copy of the letter accompanying the cheque. In any case, Cheques Act 1957, s.3 provides that: 'An unindorsed cheque which appears to have been paid by the banker on whom it is drawn is evidence of the receipt by the payee of the sum payable by the cheque.'

Solicitors are also reminded of the protection for cheques which is afforded by the 'account payee' crossing under the Cheques Act 1992.

With regard to residuary beneficiaries, the estate accounts will first have to be approved by the personal representatives. When that has been done, solicitors should then, in most cases, proceed with the final distribution by sending the residuary beneficiaries copies of the approved accounts, and cheques in payment, with a request that the beneficiaries acknowledge payment by signing a receipt either endorsed on the accounts or supplied separately; the receipt to include, if needed, a discharge to the personal representatives.

If difficulties have arisen during the administration, there may be occasions when solicitors, before making final distributions, wish to make sure that the residuary beneficiaries are not going to object to the amounts. In such cases the residuary beneficiaries should be sent, in advance, copies of the approved accounts and be asked to sign a form of receipt and discharge to the personal representatives on the basis that they will be sent a cheque immediately upon the solicitors receiving back the signed form.

It is recommended that the receipt and discharge should be in the following form:

'THE LATE …

The estate accounts show the final sum due to me as £ …

I approve the accounts and will accept that sum in full satisfaction of all my claims against the estate. Please pay it by a crossed cheque in my favour and send it to me by post.'

Finally, it must be remembered that a discharge will only be fully effective if the beneficiaries have been given full details of all the assets and liabilities of and all dealings with the estate.

17.7.1 Problems with legacies to minors

PRs need to consider who can give a good receipt on behalf of a minor. First, look at the will to see whether it authorises parents or guardians to give a good receipt on behalf of the minor or whether it authorises the minor to give a good receipt at a specified age (usually 16).

Even in the absence of such authority PRs do not need to hold the legacy until the minor is 18. If the legacy is contingent, there will usually be trustees appointed who can hold the legacy. If it is absolute, the PRs can appoint trustees under s.42 of the Administration of Estates Act 1925 to hold the legacy.

There is a further alternative. In an interesting article in (1997) 1 *Private Client Business*, 37, Michael Waterworth of 8 Gray's Inn suggests that there is not (and has not been for some time) any problem with receipts for legacies to minors. As a result of the Children Act 1989 all parents with parental responsibility have the same rights, powers and duties as guardians appointed under Children Act 1989, s.5. These rights are set out in s.3 and include (emphasis added):

> the right of the guardian to receive or recover in his own name, *for the benefit* of the child, property of whatever description and wherever situated which the child is entitled to receive or recover.

The words in italic indicate that the parent or guardian will hold the property in a fiduciary capacity.

17.8 CHARITABLE BENEFICIARIES

There are a number of special factors to bear in mind if a charity is left a substantial gift. The rest of this chapter highlights the important issues. We are grateful to the Charity Commissioners for their advice, and the help of the Institute of Legacy Management and Brian Walsh of Hempsons in revising those parts of the Handbook covering charities, has been invaluable.

An excellent 40-page booklet entitled *Charities as Beneficiaries*, written for solicitors by ILM and the Law Society Private Client Section is available from the Private Client Section free to members and additionally or to non-members at £25. The booklet covers a very wide range of issues affecting taking instructions for wills where a charity is included, the information charities need to have when an estate is under administration and a number of specific issues such as the Royal Sign Manual, *ex gratia* payments, charity taxation and the apportionment of inheritance tax.

The Institute of Legacy Management website (**www.ilmnet.org/information**) is a useful resource. There are fact sheets on:

- capital gains tax;
- empty dwelling management orders;
- *ex gratia payments*;

- guidance notes for lay executors;
- Scottish charity regulation;
- the role of the Official Solicitor and Public Trustee;
- the Royal Sign Manual direction;
- Wilsons press release re accountant disciplined;
- Charities Act 1993, s.36.

It also has a charities database which can be used to find contact details and previous contact details for various charities.

17.8.1 Charities and wills

Charities now work very hard to maximise their legacy income. Because of the importance of legacies for charitable funding, the larger charities in particular are very knowledgeable about their rights and entitlements and are very experienced beneficiaries. They can be expected to be well organised and efficient. Remember that charities have a responsibility to protect their trustees against any claim that the charity has not sought its full entitlement.

Where a charity is a residuary beneficiary, solicitors are not *obliged* to inform them that they have been named in the will. Harman J reviewed the relevant case law in *Cancer Research Campaign* v. *Ernest Brown & Co* [1997] STC 1425 and said:

> Until an executor is fully satisfied that there has been a complete payment of all debts, he cannot be under any obligation whatever to pay any legacy or, to my mind, to give notice to legatees of their prospective gain.

However, although there is no obligation to inform a charity (or any other legatee), it is good practice to do so. The charity may be in contact anyway, as many charities subscribe to a notification service, so it is better to take the initiative. The charity will appreciate being sent a copy of the will and if possible a schedule of assets and liabilities to give an idea of their possible entitlement. It will usually be helpful to agree with the charity the basis on which they will be kept informed of the progress of the administration. Charities do not wish to increase the cost of the administration unnecessarily, but legacy officers need to know the likely timescale. Charities comment that they often receive fuller information when banks are acting as executors than they do when solicitors are handling the administration.

17.8.2 Checklist: charitable beneficiaries

The following reminders should help avoid problems:

1. Changed circumstances

A charity may feel a moral obligation to renounce part of its entitlement under a will (or even make a payment from the estate) if there are grounds for believing that, in the events which have happened, the will does not in fact carry out its maker's intentions. The charity will need full details of the circumstances justifying the payment.

A charity normally needs authority from the Charity Commissioners to make an *ex gratia* payment. They have a discretion to refer individual cases to the Attorney-General for a decision. Applicants can have their cases considered afresh by the Attorney-General if the Commissioners refuse authority. The Charity Commission's leaflet CC7 explains the procedure. The relevant legislation is contained in Charities Act 1993, s.27. In [2001] *Probate Section Journal*, March, Michael Carpenter, Legal Commissioner at the Charity Commission made three points:

(a) The application to the Commissioners must come from the trustees of the charity who must regard themselves as under a moral obligation. The Commissioners will not entertain an application from executors, members of the family, disappointed beneficiaries or their advisers.

(b) Where there is a genuine dispute, for example an IPFDA 1975 claim, the *ex gratia* regime is irrelevant. The charity has a power to compromise claims.

(c) A disappointed beneficiary may allege that a solicitor prepared a will negligently. A negligence action against the solicitor would not involve the charity so the charity would have no power to compromise it. However, *Walker* v. *Medlicott & Son* [1999] 1 WLR 727 determined that in appropriate circumstances a disappointed beneficiary might be expected to bring a rectification action. The charity would be affected by a rectification action and, therefore, might use its power to compromise. It would only consider compromise 'where there is a genuine case which is likely to be successful'. There may be cases where a rectification claim might fail for technical reasons unconnected with the substantive merits. The Commissioners will consider an *ex gratia* application from the charity in such a case provided the charity considers that it would be morally unacceptable not to carry out the deceased's wishes.

Changes do not always work to a charity's advantage – a gift may be adeemed, for example, and clients should be warned about this possibility when making a will.

2. Wrong descriptions

Problems of a different kind are caused by wrongly describing the intended charity in a will. It is quite common for wills to refer to charities that have never existed and it is then necessary to determine what happens to the gift.

Responsibility for correctly reproducing the institution's current name rests with the draftsman. Brightman J said in *Re Recher's Will Trust* [1972] Ch 526 that it was the draftsman's 'elementary duty' not only to get the name right but to ensure that the institution was in existence at the date of the will. It is possible to check registered charities on the Charity Commission's website (**www.charity-commission.gov.uk**). The ILM website has a useful database. If a charity is not registered, check its details with its treasurer.

Where the name is wrong, solicitors would expect to have to apply to court for a direction on how to apply the legacy. However, in a very useful article in [2001]

Solicitors Journal, 22 June, 568 (and now available on the ILM website), Victoria Forwood of the Government Legal Service Charities Team explained the procedure for applying to the Attorney-General for a direction under the Royal Sign Manual. Such a direction identifies the charitable beneficiary whose identity was previously uncertain. The PRs then administer the gift in accordance with the direction. Examples of such gifts are to 'the Cancer Research Trust', 'the association for the preservation of tropical rain forests', 'the Ethiopa Fund'. The procedure is quick (a matter of weeks unless there is a dispute) and cheap – the Attorney-General does not charge.

3. Charity dissolved

A different problem arises when a charity did exist at the date of the will but has ceased to do so by the date of death.

It may have amalgamated with another charity, in which case there will be no problem provided the will includes a standard provision dealing with amalgamation. Well-drawn wills normally include a provision allowing the PRs to give effect to a charitable gift which fails by paying the money to the institution which most closely resembles it. If the will does not include such a clause, the gift fails but the *cy-pres* rule may allow effect to be given to the gift if the will shows a generable charitable intention.

4. Incorporated charities going into liquidation after the date of death

The case of *Re ARMS (Multiple Sclerosis Research) Ltd* [1997] 2 All ER 679 highlights a particular problem in relation to incorporated charities. In that case a charitable company overspent and went into liquidation. The court had to decide whether legacies to the charity taking effect after the date of the winding up order but before dissolution were payable to the liquidator – so as to be available to the company's creditors – or whether, as the Attorney-General argued, the legacies were given and should be applied for the charity's purposes. The court directed that the legacies were payable to the liquidator.

This case is significant for the probate practitioner when administering an estate and also when drafting wills including legacies to incorporated charities. The draftsman should consider adapting the standard amalgamation/dissolution clause to create a substitution or to give executors a discretion where a legatee is in liquidation at the date of death but not yet formally dissolved.

This decision also illustrates the clear distinction between incorporated charities, which take legacies beneficially in their own right, as opposed to unincorporated charities which take for their charitable purposes. Gifts to incorporated charities are much more likely to fail if the charity no longer exists at death than gifts to unincorporated charities which are more likely to take effect as gifts for the purposes of the defunct charity. It is, therefore, particularly important when drafting gifts to incorporated charities to include substitutional gifts or to give the executors a power to apply funds to similar charities. It made no difference that one of the legacies in the *ARMS* case was expressed to be 'for the general purposes' of the charity.

5. Conditional gifts

If your client wants to give a gift on condition, find out from the charity whether the terms of the gift will be acceptable or feasible; alternatively, provide in the will for what is to happen if the charity declines the gift.

It is also important to make clear what is to happen if it is impossible to carry out the condition at the time of the testator's death (e.g. a gift which is conditional on a charity caring for the testator's pets and at the time of the testator's death there are no pets). Failure to do so will result in uncertainty and possible litigation (see *Watson* v. *National Children's Home* [2001] WTLR 1375). There is a useful article in [2001] *New Law Journal*, Christmas Appeals Supplement, 3 December, 23 by Lucy Hickman summarising points to bear in mind when drafting gifts to charities.

6. Delayed distribution

If your client wants to enable the PRs and trustees to be able to distribute a gift over an extended period of time, you need to draft this carefully. The Commissioners' Annual Report for the year 1990 highlights the decision in *Re Muller's Estate* (unreported) which concerns a gift using a precedent in *Williams on Wills*, 6th edn (Butterworths, 1987) vol. 2, p.1185. It was held that the gift implied that distribution would be made within a reasonable time, and hence this formulation may not be suitable if the client wishes to provide otherwise.

7. Form R185E

Form R185E (annual certificate of tax deduction) is especially important to charities. They need these certificates for each tax year of the administration, as evidence that tax – which they can reclaim – has been deducted. The amounts may be small in each individual estate but the total is a significant addition to charities' income. There is a statutory obligation (Income and Corporation Taxes Act 1988, s.700(5)) to provide residuary beneficiaries with details of income and tax deducted if they make a written request. However, the joint Law Society and ILM booklet *Charities as Beneficiaries* advises that it is good practice to produce such documents as a matter of course. Provided full accounts have been prepared, it should be possible to lift all information required direct from the accounts without further work. It is suggested that the accounts be structured to include estate income (whether gross or net) in a separate income account, broken down into years. These figures can then be easily entered on the form 922 which will form the basis for the production of the tax certificates.

In some estates, the amount of tax that can be reclaimed by the charity is minimal and the cost of the production of the certificates may outweigh any benefits. Charities will be unlikely to pursue tax certificates where their reclaim value is less than £20 and will often take a view on those between £20–£40.

The Institute of Legacy Management reports that firms sometimes say that there is no need for form R185E because their client account pays gross. However, it is important to remember that charities can reclaim not only tax on income which has arisen during the administration period, but also tax which has accrued prior to the date of death and not been paid (e.g. building society interest) – but not without form R185E.

Solicitors' failure to issue these forms is a complaint frequently made to the Law Society and it is the responsibility of the firm undertaking the administration, and not the bank or building society, to prepare them and send them to beneficiaries. Having to produce these forms is a chore but as the charities will continue to ask for them, producing them early will allow the file to be closed more quickly.

Complete form R185E with the tax district reference number. Without this number, charities cannot reclaim the tax shown on the certificate.

If the deceased was a non-taxpayer, and the tax district reference number is not known, the problem can be solved by writing to the local tax office. Send a copy of the estate accounts and ask HM Revenue & Customs to waive the need for tax returns for the administration period. The local tax district reference number can then be quoted on form R185E.

8. CGT

Charities are exempt from CGT. Where they have been left assets, they will normally want the assets sold. It is important for PRs to follow the correct procedure to save the estate suffering an unnecessary CGT bill. (See **17.9.7** below.)

9. Land: Charities Act 1993, s.36

Section 36 provides that no land held by or in trust for a charity can be sold without an order of the court or of the Charity Commissioners unless certain conditions are satisfied. PRs may have to comply with the requirements of s.36 if they make a sale on behalf of a charity. (See **17.9.8** below.)

10. Interest

Interest will be due on legacies not paid at the end of the executors' year and may be due beforehand.

11. Form of gift

Discuss with the charity the best way for them to receive the gift: in some cases an appropriation *in specie* may allow the charity to sell an asset and thus save CGT. The charity may customarily use a particular auction house or estate agency, with which they may have a special arrangement relating to fees, which may also be able to assist. Appropriation of assets can be done on paper, that is, without any necessity physically to transfer securities. The sale is then made as bare trustee on behalf of the charity. It is, however, important to have a written record of the appropriation. See point 14 and **17.9.7** below.

12. Deeds of variation

Consider deeds of variation to make the gift in the most effective way (see the points set out at **17.10** below).

13. Exempt and non-exempt beneficiaries

If the residuary gift is to both exempt and non-exempt beneficiaries, the problem of how to distribute the estate in the light of *Re Benham* arises. See **17.9** below.

14. Early notice

Sending a copy of the will at an early stage alerts a charitable residuary beneficiary to its entitlement and enables it to put forward its own wishes for the PRs' consideration. Obtaining the PRs' consent to briefing the charity on progress can also be worthwhile. However, PRs remain, of course, obliged to act in the interests of the estate as a whole, not just those of one particular beneficiary.

15. Interim distributions

Consider whether one or more interim distributions can be made. The Institute of Legacy Management comments that some firms only write to charities when the administration is complete, sending their first letter, estate accounts and cheque all together. The justification is that it saves costs. Crispin Ellison, formerly of the Institute of Legacy Management, says that most charities would agree to a little more in costs in return for more information during the administration and some interim distributions. He also comments that while banks charge more in his experience, their level of service in providing regular information and in their accounting is superior.

16. VAT

Charities are no longer able to recover VAT on costs associated with sales made in relation to land or buildings.

17. Indemnities

Do not ask for indemnities which are too sweeping as a charity will not be able to give an indemnity which goes beyond its share of the estate; it will normally want its indemnity to be conditional on the PRs not accepting, compromising or otherwise admitting any claim without the previous written consent of the charity.

17.9 THE PROBLEM OF *RE BENHAM* AND *RE RATCLIFFE*

The case of *Re Benham's Will Trusts*, [1995] STC 210 caused great problems for PRs. To some extent they have been alleviated by the later case of *Re Ratcliffe (Deceased)* [1999] STC 262. (The notes at **17.9.1** *et seq* have been written specially for us by Chris Whitehouse, Barrister of 2 Stone Buildings and we are most grateful to him for doing so.)

As a general rule a testator or testatrix is free to decide where the burden of IHT is to fall. Specific gifts are, in the absence of any direction to the contrary, tax free with the tax being paid out of residue. To preserve the value of exempt transfers, however, and notably of gifts to spouses and charities, IHTA 1984, s.41 provides that:

Notwithstanding the terms of any disposition:

(a) none of the tax on the value transferred shall fall on any specific gift if or to the extent that the transfer is exempt with respect to the gift; and
(b) none of the tax attributable to the value of the property comprised in residue shall fall on any gift of a share of residue if or to the extent that the transfer is exempt with respect to the gift.

In a simple case where residue is split between chargeable and exempt beneficiaries (for instance, between a testator's son and his wife) any tax attributable to the son's share must be borne out of that share; no part of that tax can come out of the portion of residue passing to the surviving spouse.

17.9.1 When is it necessary to consider *Re Benham* and *Re Ratcliffe*?

In practice, difficulties only arise if residue is split between chargeable and exempt beneficiaries. Commonly this occurs when part of the residue is left to charity with the rest passing to the relatives of the testator. A will leaving a specific legacy to charity with residue to the testator's or testatrix's family does not, therefore, give rise to problems. A second point to bear in mind is that *Benham* is concerned with the calculation of IHT on the chargeable portion of an estate. Accordingly, if that portion falls within the testator's or testatrix's nil rate band, no computational difficulties can arise.

17.9.2 Grossing up a chargeable share of residue

Given that IHTA 1984, s.41 prevents tax on a chargeable share of residue from being borne by an exempt share, how can the wishes of a testator that the net residue after payment of all expenses and IHT is to be divided equally between (say) his wife and daughter be satisfied? Only, it is thought, if the will provides for the chargeable share (in this example the daughter's share) to be grossed up to include the tax which is charged on it.

Example

Assume net residue of £100,000 to be divided equally between surviving spouse and daughter, estate rate 40 per cent.

- Option 1: deduct tax on £50,000 and divide balance (£80,000) equally: prohibited by s.41.
- Option 2: divide equally so that spouse gets £50,000 and daughter gets £50,000 but then bears tax so that she ends up with £30,000.
- Option 3: gross up daughter's share (X) so that both end up with the same, i.e.:

  X + (100X/60 = £100,000; therefore X = £37,500

  Both receive £37,500; gross value of daughter's share is £62,500.

	Spouse (£)	Daughter(£)	Tax Man (£)
Option 1	40,000	40,000	20,000
Option 2	50,000	30,000	20,000
Option 3	37,500	37,500	25,000

The facts of Re Benham's Will Trust

In this case, under clause 3 of the will residue was left as follows:

- upon trust to pay debts, funeral and testamentary expenses;
- after such payment 'to pay the same to those beneficiaries as are living at my death and who are listed in List A and List B hereunder written in such proportions as will bring about the result that the aforesaid beneficiaries named in List A shall receive 3.2 times as much as the aforesaid beneficiaries named in List B and in each case for their own absolute and beneficial use and disposal'.

List A contained one charity and a number of non-charitable beneficiaries; and List B contained a number of charities and non-charitable beneficiaries. By an originating summons, the executor sought, *inter alia*, the opinion of the court on the following questions:

- whether the wording in clause 3(b) meant that each qualifying beneficiary in List A should receive 3.2 times the sum taken by each beneficiary in List B, or whether the List A beneficiaries should between them receive 3.2 times the total sum taken by the List B beneficiaries;
- whether, in view of IHTA 1984, s.41 and the terms of the will, the non-charitable beneficiaries should receive their shares subject to IHT, or whether their shares should be grossed up; and
- whether the shares of legatees who predeceased the testatrix accrued by survivorship to the other legatees or became applicable for the payment of funeral and testamentary expenses and debts.

The deputy judge agreed that the choice between the two interpretations of clause 3(b) was not so clear that it could be said that there was no real doubt or ambiguity and he admitted extrinsic evidence under Administration of Justice Act 1982, s.21(1)(b). He then concluded that clause 3(b) directed payment of the residue to two groups of beneficiaries and, whilst the persons named in Lists A and B, respectively, took as between themselves in equal shares provided that they survived the testatrix, the part of the residue available to List A beneficiaries to share equally between them was a fund 3.2 times as large as the fund available for the List B beneficiaries.

On the second question, there were three possibilities:

- the non-charitable beneficiaries received their respective shares subject to IHT, which would mean that they would receive less than the charities;
- the non-charitable beneficiaries should have their respective shares grossed up, so that they received the same net sum as the charities; or
- the IHT was paid as part of the testamentary expenses under clause 3(a), and the balance was distributed equally between the non-charitable beneficiaries and the charities.

The deputy judge agreed that the third possibility was precluded by IHTA 1984, s.41. However, he did not agree that the charities should receive more than the non-charitable beneficiaries. The plain intention of the testatrix was that each beneficiary, whether charitable or non-charitable, should receive the same as the other beneficiaries on the relevant list. That result, he concluded, was consistent with the express terms of the will and s.41. Thus, he considered that the non-charitable beneficiaries' shares should be grossed up.

Finally, clause 3(b) made it a condition that any named beneficiary should be living when the testatrix died. Thus, the deputy judge said, the two funds should be divided between the beneficiaries in the two lists, after deleting those who had died.

17.9.3 Difficulties arising from *Re Benham*

The main difficulty posed by *Re Benham* lies not in the actual facts of the case (which were obviously somewhat unusual!), but in the assertion of the judge that 'the plain intention of the testatrix is that at the end of the day each beneficiary, whether charitable or non-charitable, should receive the same as the other beneficiaries'.

This view, if correct, would appear to result in the implication (as a matter of construction) of a grossing up clause in all cases where:

(a) the residue is left to be divided between exempt and non-exempt beneficiaries;
(b) the will provides for them to take in equal shares and there is no evidence that the testator did not intend *Benham* to apply; and
(c) the value of the estate is such that IHT is payable on the chargeable portion of residue.

This approach goes against the existing practice which had been to apply s.41 in such cases.

17.9.4 Attitude of HMRC Inheritance Tax

The attitude of the Revenue to the *Benham* case and the consequent problems of construing and drafting wills can be gleaned from the following exchange of correspondence.

The British Heart Foundation wrote to the Revenue in the following terms:

Re: Benhams Will Trusts

The British Heart Foundation, like many other charities, is alarmed at the potential threat to its income if, as has been widely propounded in the legal press, the decision in the above case is applied in cases where the will is drawn not in the terms of the *Benham* will but in the very much more common terms usually applied.

The cases I refer to are of course those involving gifts of residue to exempt and non-exempt beneficiaries, where the will directs the executors to pay IHT and legacies and then divide the residue. Our concern is that if the *Re Benham* judgment is applied then non-exempt beneficiaries wrongly benefit from the exempt status of organisations such as ourselves, contrary to s.41(b) of the IHT Act 1984; that is that charities as a whole could lose a great deal of money, part of which will effectively go towards paying the IHT of non-exempt beneficiaries, contrary to our charitable objects.

We at the Foundation believe that *Re Benham* really turns on the rather unusual terms of the will and has no general application to bequests of shares of residue between exempt and non-exempt beneficiaries as expressed in the common cases outlined above. We and other charities are currently considering two cases to be put to the court, but clearly a decision may take some time. Whilst this information may hold off executors from distributing estates along the lines of *Benham*, we would be obliged however if you would confirm the following: that the CTO's view is also that the *Re Benham* decision is inapplicable for this more common type of provision and that in such cases no IHT will arise that will deplete charitable shares of residue as a result of the *Benham* decision.

The response of the Revenue indicates that they will abide by a proper construction of the will (so that the fact that extra tax is payable if grossing up applies is not a factor to be taken into account):

> We consider the decision to be primarily concerned with ascertaining the intention of the testatrix and hence as not directly involving the Inland Revenue. In an attempt to be helpful, however, we would comment as follows.
>
> Like you, our view is that the decision followed from the particular facts of the case with the court deciding that the plain intention of the testatrix was that at the end of the day and therefore after the payment of tax each beneficiary whether charitable or non-charitable on the respective lists should receive the same amount as the other beneficiaries in that list.
>
> Generally speaking the court is concerned in such cases to establish the intention of the testator or testatrix from the wording of the will and admissible extrinsic evidence. If the will is drafted in common form with a direction to ascertain residue after payment of funeral and testamentary expenses and debts followed by a bequest of that residue then it is focusing on the ascertainment and division of disposable residue rather than on what each residuary beneficiary is to receive. Accordingly wills so drafted would not appear to involve *Benham* style grossing up computations.
>
> P. Twiddy

17.9.5 Re Ratcliffe

The testatrix gave her residuary estate to her trustees (the claimants) on trust, after payment of her debts and funeral and testamentary expenses, to hold one half for the two sons of her cousin ('the cousins') in equal shares absolutely, and the other half for four charities ('the charities') in equal shares.

The charities contended that the two half shares of residue were to be calculated after providing for the debts and funeral and testamentary expenses (and three legacies) but before payment of the IHT due on the cousins' half share. The cousins would thus receive less because of the deduction of tax. The cousins contended that there were to be equal half shares of net residue after payment of the appropriate amount of IHT, which was to be treated as a testamentary expense. They argued that this equality was to be achieved, as in *Benham*, by grossing up their beneficial share of residue to produce an initial unequal division of residue which would leave equal amounts once the tax was paid.

Blackburne J held that it was a question of construing the will to decide what the testatrix had intended. The wording used was a common form trust for sale. Blackburne J found that while the testatrix could have left her residue to be divided unequally as the cousins contended, there was nothing in the wording used to indicate that this was her intention.

Of *Re Benham* he said this:

> The difficulty that I feel about that decision is that, with all due respect to the deputy judge who decided it, it is not at all clear why he came to the conclusion that the testatrix's plain

> intention was that 'at the end of the day each beneficiary, whether charitable or non-charitable, should receive the same as the other beneficiaries in the relevant list'.

He went on to say that had he thought that *Benham* laid down some principle, then, unless convinced that it was wrong, he would have followed it.

However, he did not consider that it did and, accordingly, was not bound to follow it.

17.9.6 Practical advice on the distribution of residue

1. Whenever an estate which exceeds the nil rate band is to be divided between exempt and non-exempt beneficiaries, it is necessary to consider the wording of the will to determine whether or not the basis of division is clear.

   If the will clearly provides for the beneficiaries to receive equal amounts (*Benham* division) or unequal amounts (*Ratcliffe* division), that is the end of the matter. For practitioners who find themselves in the unenviable position of having to perform a *Benham* calculation there is an interesting article on software available to do the job in [1997] *Private Client Business*, April, 197–202 ('Software makes *Benham* calculations simple').
2. If not, everything turns on a correct construction of the document. A relevant exercise is to calculate the IHT that would be payable on the alternative bases of:

   (a) applying IHTA 1984, s.41; and
   (b) grossing up.

   It will normally be the case that, if grossing up occurs, the tax take is increased; chargeable beneficiaries get a greater slice of the estate and the loser will be the exempt beneficiary (i.e. either spouse or charity).
3. When the only beneficiaries of the residue are family members (typically therefore the surviving spouse and children) it is often possible to agree an approach which will resolve the difficulties. Commonly, the children will be prepared to accept that *Benham* should not apply thereby ensuring that more is received by their mother than would otherwise would be the case (and, of course, that less is received by HMRC!).
4. If a 'deal' is not possible, then counsel's advice may be taken and the executors may then act in accordance with his opinion. Executors should always be warned that it does not prevent them from being sued by disappointed beneficiaries and in reality the absolutely safe course is to go to the court for directions. (Note, in this connection, that the court's general power to excuse executors and trustees under Trustee Act 1925, s.61 depends on the executors satisfactorily showing that a failure to obtain the court's directions before carrying out the relevant distribution was not culpable.)
5. If full agreement cannot be reached between the beneficiaries as to what is to be done then the executors may decide to apply s.41 if an indemnity is given

either by the charity or by the surviving spouse. Given the uncertain value of such indemnities and the difficulties of enforcement, this approach cannot be wholeheartedly recommended.

Note: When drafting a will where residue is to be divided between exempt and non-exempt beneficiaries, make it clear whether the division is to be equal before consideration of IHT (*Ratcliffe* division) or whether the beneficiaries are to receive equal amounts after consideration of IHT (*Benham* division). The following are examples of suitable precedents.

Example: Benham division

I declare that the shares of my estate of any beneficiaries who do not qualify for exemption from inheritance tax shall be deemed to be of amounts such that the amounts received, after payment of inheritance tax due, shall be the same for all the beneficiaries named in clause –.

Example: Ratcliffe division

I declare that if the share in my estate of any beneficiary named in clause – does not qualify for exemption from inheritance tax, that share shall bear its own tax so that the amount received by each beneficiary named in that clause is the same before the payment of inheritance tax.

17.9.7 Importance of assent or appropriation of assets to charity entitled to residue

Charities benefit from CGT exemption in respect of gains realised on the disposal of assets if the gains are applicable and applied for charitable purposes (see s.256 of the Taxation of Chargeable Gains Act 1992 (TCGA 1992)). However, the exemption will only apply if the relevant property is beneficially owned by the charity. If, during the administration of an estate, an asset, which has increased significantly in value since the date of death, is to be sold, it will be important either for the asset to be vested in the name of the charity prior to the sale, or for the executors to execute an assent declaring that they hold the asset for the charity absolutely. Failure to take these elementary steps will mean that the gain will be realised by the executors and not by the charity and HMRC may claim CGT on the gain realised, even if the benefit of the sale proceeds will ultimately pass to the charity. The need to consider appropriation before sale is a good reason for consulting charities early in the administration.

Many of the major charities have very helpful notes advising executors on the correct procedure. We print by way of example the note issued by the Guide Dogs for the Blind Association:

> May we please draw the attention of the executors and their advisers to the fact that as a national charity we are exempt, under the provisions of TCGA 1992, s.256(1), from payment of capital gains tax on the sale of any securities made on our behalf.
>
> The exemption relates to any sale made on our behalf in respect of the residue or shares of the residue of the estate to which we are entitled.
>
> The procedure to be followed to comply with HMRC requirements is that the securities should be appropriated to our account by a simple but clear designation in your books, or by a memorandum or resolution signed by the personal representatives in your files. Any sales subsequently made by you are made as bare trustee on our behalf under TCGA 1992, s.60.

Executors should be careful if they require an indemnity from the charity for the payment of administration expenses in return for the transfer of assets to the charity. HMRC may argue that such an indemnity is to be construed as a payment for the asset and accordingly a sale by the executors, or alternatively that the gain realised by the charity is not fully applicable and applied for charitable purposes.

A specimen memorandum of appropriation is available on the solicitors section of the ILM website (**www.ilmnet.org**) and is set out below for convenience.

Specimen Memorandum of Appropriation

Miss A N Other deceased

Miss Alicia Nora Other (The Testatrix) late of 1 Fairlawn Road, Leeds, LS12 9DW, died on 1 January 2000.

The will dated 1 January 1993 was proved by Robert Scott and Titus Oates at the Leeds Probate Registry on 1st April 2000.

Under the terms of the will, the ABC Charity of The Lodge, 25 High Street, Anytown is entitled to a one-third share of the residuary estate.

We, Robert Scott and Titus Oates, as Personal Representatives of Alicia Nora Other hereby give notice to ABC Charity that we have today together appropriated the stocks and shares set out in the Schedule hereto in part satisfaction of the said Charity's one-third share of the residuary estate of the Testatrix.

As from the date hereof, we the Executors declare that we shall hold the shares set out in the Schedule hereto as 'bare' Trustees for ABC Charity and not as Personal Representatives of Alicia Nora Other.

Suggested format for a schedule of investments appropriated to ABC Charity and referred to above

Name of Company	Number of shares appropriated (i.e. ABC Charity share)
XYZ plc	1234
ZZZ plc	4321
etc.	

Dated this ... day of ... 20....

Signed

Robert Scott
Titus Oates

We hereby acknowledge that we have received a Notice of which the above is a duplicate

Signed ... Date ...

For and on behalf of ABC Charity

For CGT purposes, the assets are deemed to have been appropriated at probate value. For the purposes of the estate accounts, investment values are usually taken to be the middle market price at the close of trading on the day of appropriation.

Where some of the investments need to be sold for administration costs or payment of legacies, the balance can still be appropriated to reduce the CGT burden. If the firm does not take these simple steps, then it may be in breach of its responsibilities to maximise the benefit to the estate. It might be worth noting that the major bank executorship departments now appropriate investments by default.

Some charities will choose to take investments *in specie*. Most of the larger charities are also companies limited by guarantee or are incorporated under Royal Charter, and have thc appropriate investment powers.

17.9.8 Charities Act 1993, s.36

Charities Act 1993, s.36 was enacted in order to ensure that charities are dealing properly with the disposition of real property in which they have an interest. Unfortunately, it has led to some confusion over the correct procedure where land is bequeathed to charities by will. The ILM instructed Christopher McCall QC to provide an opinion and settle a fact sheet, both of which are available on the ILM website (**www.ilmnet.org**). The following is a brief summary of the fact sheet.

Section 36 will have to be complied with when land in England and Wales held by or in trust for registered charities is sold, leased or otherwise disposed of.

The requirements of s.36

In order for a charity to effect a disposition of land, an order of the court or the Charity Commissioners is required, unless the following three requirements are complied with:

1. the disposition is not to a connected person;
2. the disposition is preceded by an agreement to effect the disposition;
3. before entering into such an agreement, the trustees comply with the procedure set out in s.36(3) or (5) which involves obtaining advice from a suitably qualified person on the merits of the proposed disposition.

The trustees must obtain and consider a written report on the proposed disposition from a qualified surveyor acting exclusively for the charity. Once the report has been obtained, the trustees should advertise the proposed disposition as advised by the surveyor. Once an offer has been made, they should consider whether the terms on which the disposition is to be made are the best which are reasonably obtainable by the charity. The requirements of the report are laid down by the Charities (Qualified Surveyors' Reports) Regulations 1992, SI 1992/2980.

When are personal representatives affected?

If land is disposed of by the PRs during the administration of an estate as part of the ordinary administration process the land is not charity land and s.36 will not need to be complied with. This applies even if a charity is acting as PR.

By contrast, where an appropriation has taken place, the PRs have no further power of sale other than at the instruction of the entitled beneficiary. Where a single charity is the beneficiary of the interest in land, and there has been an appropriation, trusteeship of the land for s.36 purposes automatically transfers from the PRs to the charity's trustees, who then have power of sale even though the legal title stays with the PRs; i.e. the PRs must do with the land what the charity tells them. Where there are two or more charities, the power of sale will remain with the PRs or nominated trustees if not the PRs themselves. They are therefore the 'charity trustees' for the purposes of s.36 and not the trustees of the individual charities. Section 36 will need to be complied with in the following circumstances.

- The land is, prior to entry into an agreement to effect a disposition of that land, appropriated by the PRs wholly to a charitable institution (the charity's trustees must comply) or wholly between two or more charitable institutions (the PRs must comply).
- The land is held in a trust of land, the life tenant of which has died, and the remainderman is a charitable institution (the charity's trustees must comply) or the remaindermen are all charitable institutions (the will trust trustees must comply).
- Land has been assented to the charity.

Section 36 will not need to be complied with wherever there is a mix of charities and non-charities. Thus s.36 will not apply where:

- Appropriation has the effect of creating a trust of land in which some of the beneficiaries are not charities.
- Land is held in a trust of land and is sold during the life of the life tenant even though the remainderman is a charitable institution.
- On the death of the life tenant, the remaindermen are not all charities.

Note that the requirements of the section must be complied with before entering into any *agreement* to effect a disposition of charity land. Failure to do so prior to exchange of contracts will mean that the contract is not enforceable, and can only be completed with the sanction of an order under s.36(1). See *Bayoumi* v. *Womens Total Abstinence Union Ltd* [2003] EWCA Civ 1548.

The government confirmed in September 2010 (Cabinet Office, Office for Civil Society: 'Making it easier for charities to sell and make other disposals of land: government response') that it supported proposals made in the earlier consultation paper to extend the definition of 'qualified surveyor' in the Charities Act 1993, s.36(4) to include suitably experienced fellows of the National Association of Valuers and Auctioneers.

It has decided to consider the regulation of sales and other disposals of charity land as part of the review of the operation of the Charities Act 2006, which will begin in 2011. The extension of the definition of qualified surveyor will be effected as part of any changes following the 2011 review.

17.10 ADMINISTRATION EXPENSES

The notes below are based on an article originally published in [1991] *Gazette*, 15 February by Alan Jarvis, a partner in Wilde Sapte & Co. We are most grateful to him for allowing us to adapt and update it.

17.10.1 Administration expenses and IHT

Most administration expenses are not deductible for IHT purposes. Careful planning at the time of the preparation of the will can, however, achieve an additional benefit whereby the administration expenses will, in effect, be deductible for IHT purposes.

For example, a testator leaves an estate of £725,000 with a gift to charity of £200,000 and the balance of the estate passing to a nephew absolutely.

The IHT position will be as follows:

Intended disposition		**£**
Value of estate		725,000
Legacy to charity		200,000
Residue to nephew		525,000
Less	inheritance tax on residue (£525,000 – £325,000) x 40%	(80,000)
	administration expenses	(6,000)
Net amount received by nephew		439,000

An alternative approach might be to give the nephew a specific legacy which after the payment of IHT, would leave him a net sum of £439,000. The residue of the estate would then pass to the charity. The revised IHT position will be:

Intended disposition	**£**
Gross legacy to nephew	515,000
Less inheritance tax on legacy (£515,000 – £325,000) x 40%	(76,000)
Net legacy sum due to nephew	439,000
Residue £725,000 – £515,000	210,000
Less administration expenses	(6,000)
Net residue payable to charity	204,000

Similarly, a benefit can be given to charity where none previously existed at no extra cost to a beneficiary:

Intended disposition	**£**
Gross estate due to beneficiary	725,000
Less inheritance tax	(160,000)
Net estate	565,000
Less administration expenses	(6,000)
Net amount received by beneficiary	559,000

Alternative disposition: legacy to beneficiary equal to £559,000 after payment of tax, residue to charity	
Legacy to beneficiary (£559,000 grossed up)	715,000
Less inheritance tax	(156,000)
Net amount received by beneficiary	559,000
Residue to charity (£725,000 – £715,000)	10,000
Less administration expenses	(6,000)
Net amount received by charity	4,000

17.10.2 Use of discretionary wills

Fine tuning to the degree mentioned in the above examples is not normally possible at the time of preparing the will since the estate is likely to alter in nature or value before death. Consideration might be given to two alternative approaches.

First, testators may wish to consider the establishment of a no-interest in possession will trust (see IHTA 1984, s.144). If a trust without a qualifying immediate post-death interest is established by will, any distributions or appointment from the trust within two years of death will be treated for IHT purposes as a disposition under the will occurring on death. The advantage, as demonstrated in either of the above examples, can be achieved with full knowledge of the value of the deceased's estate. The disadvantage of such a trust is that IHT will be charged in full on the application for the grant of representation, even if the intention is to make subsequent appointments from the trust that will attract the spouse or charitable exemptions. This problem may be avoided if the executors exercise their discretionary powers before making the application for the grant. They can do this since, unlike administrators, executors' powers commence upon death. (Do be careful not to make a distribution from the trust within three months of the death or the advantages of s.144 will be lost. This trap is pretty well known but *Frankland* v. *IRC* [1996] STC 735 shows the cost of getting caught out.)

Secondly, it is possible to effect a post-death variation of the will of the deceased under IHTA 1984, s.142.

17.10.3 Administration expenses and income tax

As most expenses of administration are not deductible for income tax, they will be paid out of the income of the administration which has borne tax at the basic rate. This will reduce the income which is distributed to the charity and, therefore, the scope for a repayment claim as the charity cannot reclaim the tax deducted from the income used to pay income expenses. The fewer expenses which are attributable to income, the greater will be the tax repayment to the charity. However, without specific power to pay income expenses out of capital, the level of expenses which are attributable to income will not be determined according to the executors' discretion but according to the law.

It may be appropriate to include in a will a direction that the executors shall have the power to pay administration expenses out of capital or income at their discretion, thereby enabling the executors to attribute all expenses to capital and allowing the charity to effect a full recovery of all basic rate tax paid.

In the absence of this power, it is important for the executors to ensure that no more than the correct amount of expenses is set against income. The matter should, however, be given careful thought and not merely determined by reference to the usual rough and ready estimate. Certain expenses may, upon a careful analysis, be properly attributable to capital rather than income.

17.10.4 Complaints about charities

The Charity Commissioners have a useful website (**www.charitycommission.gov.uk**). There are various helpful publications available there. See, in particular, CC47 *Complaints about Charities*.

CHAPTER 18

Probate practice checklists

Lesley King

Solicitors in private practice may adapt or adopt these checklists for the purpose set out on page iv of this Handbook, but not for any other purpose.

18.1 PERSONAL REPRESENTATIVES AND PLANNING CHECKLIST

Before you begin to deal with the assets and liabilities have you:

1. Obtained clear instructions from the personal representatives (PRs)?
2. Explained to the PRs:
   - their duties;
   - the nature and extent of the work to be done;
   - what is included in your retainer;
   - costs, charging, expenses;
   - Inheritance (Provision for Family and Dependants) Act 1975, statutory advertisements, deeds of variation, plus time limits – and noted relevant dates in your diary;
   - potential hold-ups: length of survivorship period, HMRC Capital Taxes, etc.;
   - any welfare benefits relevant and how to apply? (See **Chapter 10**.)

   Sent to the PRs:

   - information letter (see **Chapter 3**);
   - client care letter/leaflet (see **Chapter 3**);
   - copy will?
3. Obtained your clients' addresses and phone and e-mail address, fax numbers and their availability? Agreed reporting frequency and logged dates in your diary? Agreed billing frequency and logged dates in your diary?
4. Established an anticipated, realistic, timetable for completion of the administration? Confirmed this to PRs? Established target dates for completion of each stage? Logged these into your diary? Plus six-month and 12-month

anniversaries of death and other significant dates such as two-month anniversary of statutory advertisements? Established whether there is any need to obtain the grant urgently? If so, and if inheritance tax (IHT) is payable, checked with HMRC on possibility of submitting account with estimated valuations?

5. Checked will for validity? Contacted witnesses if affidavits are necessary?
6. Checked gifts for ademption, lapse, contingencies, etc.?
7. Checked form of ownership of assets (sole name, joint tenancy, co-ownership)? In case of assets which appear to have passed to the deceased by survivorship, checked whether there might have been severance by mutual agreement at an earlier stage?
8. Checked whether third parties allege rights in assets of the estate as a result of resulting or constructive trusts or proprietary estoppel?
9. Checked whether any lifetime gifts made by the deceased might be voidable on the basis of undue influence?
10. Obtained PRs' consent to contact residuary beneficiaries with copy will and estimated timescale? Obtained PRs' consent to contact legatees with estimated timescale?
11. Confirmed beneficiaries' and next of kin's addresses with PRs? Taken steps to trace any missing beneficiaries? Considered whether statutory advertisements are appropriate? The cost may not be justified where the executor is taking the entire estate. If appropriate, inserted statutory advertisements?
12. Informed:

    - deceased's bank or building society;
    - other professional advisers;
    - insurers;
    - others?

    Obtained figures for balances of funds held, accrued interest, etc.?

13. Arranged valuations? Instructed valuer to make valuation on basis of open market value and to state this on the valuation? Included balances and valuations on draft accounts? Obtained details of deceased's tax office and current position?
14. Established whether deceased was a member of Lloyd's? If so, decided whether:

    - it is safe to rely on indemnities or insurance; or
    - it is necessary to apply to court under *Practice Statement: Chancery Division: Estates of Deceased Lloyd's Names* [2001] 3 All ER 765 for leave to distribute without making provision for contingent liability in the event of Equitas being inadequate?

    Made application, if necessary?

15. Begun to prepare the accounts by:
    - listing all assets and estimated values;
    - deciding whether specialist advice is needed;
    - listing all liabilities?
16. Prepared list of asset holders needing to see the grant of representation?
17. Considered with PRs the method of payment of IHT? Made the necessary arrangements?
18. Established the nature of money coming into the office in terms of the Solicitors' Accounts Rules 1998 requirements? (See **Chapter 5**.)
19. Considered whether variation desirable?
20. In the case of a will trust without a qualifying interest in possession considered whether it is appropriate to make an appointment under IHTA 1984, s.144 to obtain reading back.

18.2 IMMEDIATE PRACTICAL ACTION CHECKLIST

1. Register death.
2. Check for directions re disposal of body in wills, personal assets log, and amongst papers.
3. Arrange funeral/cremation (as directed if appropriate).
4. Notify time, date and place to family.*
5. Deceased's house:
    - remove valuables (if to office, does your insurance cover value? Do any special conditions, e.g. regarding guns, apply?);**
    - arrange maintenance (e.g. drain water system) if appropriate;
    - cancel deliveries, e.g. milk, papers;
    - redirect mail;
    - lodge keys securely, not marked with address;
    - deal with insurers (special arrangements will have to be made if house is to be left empty), landlord and council tax as appropriate.
6. Deceased's car:
    - inform insurers;
    - transfer insurance, etc., if to be used by family;
    - arrange for security if not to be used.
7. Livestock and pets:
    - arrange for their immediate welfare;
    - check if prior long-term arrangements have already been made with friends or family (the Law Society personal assets log includes a point on pets);

- if not, pedigree pets may sometimes be returned to the breeder; otherwise animal welfare organisations could help (see **Appendix F**).

* Some firms counsel clients not to announce the death in the local or national paper, nor the funeral, because many families have – almost unbelievably – come back from a funeral to find that the house has been burgled.

** See the helpful article on firearms in this context by Peter Sarony in [1995] *New Law Journal*, Probate Supplement, 29 September.

18.3 TESTATE ESTATE CHECKLIST

1. Is the will valid and properly signed and dated, with an appropriate attestation clause, and correctly witnessed? If not, list remedial action needed and advise the client.
2. Is this definitely the last will? Are there any codicils?
3. Is there likely to be any dispute about the validity of dispositions included in the will? Did the testator or testatrix marry, form a civil partnership or divorce or dissolve partnership after the date of the will? Are any of the presumptions, e.g. capacity, validity, etc., likely to be rebutted? If so, is there any evidence of the circumstances surrounding the execution? Can the witnesses be traced if affidavits have to be obtained? List remedial action, and advise the client.
4. Does the will refer to unexecuted writings, chattels by memo, etc.? Is there a letter explaining why a person has not been provided for in the context of an IPFDA 1975 claim? Is a claim likely? (See **Chapter 11**.) Advise the client.
5. Is there any evidence of secret or half-secret trusts? If so, have the requirements for validity been met? If the will contains precatory words, can they be complied with?
6. Is there any evidence of an agreement that the will should be mutual? If so, where the death is of the first testator or testatrix make sure that the existence of the trust now binding on the property of the surviving testator is clearly recorded; if the death is of the surviving testator remember that the terms of any will left by the surviving testator cannot overrule the terms of the trust imposed on the death of the first testator.
7. If the will refers to contingencies, have they been satisfied?
8. Is all the property referred to in the will available for beneficiaries, or have any gifts adeemed?
9. Have all beneficiaries been traced? Do any gifts lapse?
10. Have any legacies been adeemed by subsequent lifetime gifts as a result of the doctrine of satisfaction?
11. Is the estate solvent?
12. Is there any evidence of PETs and other transfers?
13. Is a variation or appointment under IHTA 1984, s.144 appropriate?

18.4 INTESTATE AND PARTIALLY INTESTATE ESTATE CHECKLIST

1. The death: if the deceased and spouse or partner died together in an accident, remember 14-day survivorship period applies to spouses but not to others. Does this affect this estate? Advise client.
2. Has a search for a will been made? (If it is thought a will was made, the 'Wills and Whereabouts' page in the *Gazette*, Certainty, local solicitors, the deposit facility at the Principal Registry (see **Appendix F** for address) and enquiry of the deceased's bank, friends and relatives may all be of assistance.)
3. Will the estate be solvent? Does it exceed statutory legacy limits of £25,000/ £450,000? How will the existence of any undisposed-of property affect the payment of debts?
4. List the surviving relatives; in more complex cases drawing up a family tree is usually easier than describing relationship. Can they all be contacted? Will there be any problems establishing identity and relationship? Might there be an IPFDA 1975 claim? (See **Chapter 11**.)
5. Establish who will be entitled to the estate; note minor children's ages and the years in which they will attain majority.
6. Establish who will take the grant. Will two administrators be needed?
7. How will the statutory trusts apply, if at all?
8. Does the spouse wish to redeem the life interest and/or appropriate the matrimonial home? Log the 12 months' deadline from the issue of the grant into the diary. Does the value of the matrimonial home exceed the value of the statutory legacy? If so, what arrangements need to be made to cover the difference?
9. Is there any evidence of PETs and other transfers?
10. Is a variation appropriate?

18.5 THE OATH AND AFTER CHECKLIST

1. List assets and liabilities.
2. Is IHT account required? (See **15.3–15.4**.) Which pages?
3. Prepare oath and HMRC account.
4. Send tax cheque to HMRC. Lodge papers and receipted IHT421 at probate registry. Order plenty of office copies – it is false economy to order too few. Does timetable need adjusting? If so, inform PRs.
5. Prepare for payment of debts. Will assets need to be sold? If so, contact PRs and residuary beneficiaries: which ones? Arrange valuations if necessary. Consider tax implications – deed of variation, appointment from discretionary trust under IHTA 1984, s.144?
6. Update draft accounts. Update other lists. Review file generally, especially initial letters, and check expiry dates and deadlines – review schedule if necessary and advise client. Are charities interested in estate? If so, check

whether they wish assets to be appropriated to them to avoid unnecessary CGT. Check proceeds of sale of shares and land against probate valuations to see if assets qualify for IHT loss on sale relief (IHTA 1984, ss.178–189). If so, claim relief and file corrective account. Check proceeds of sale of assets generally against probate valuations to see if there are gains or losses for CGT purposes.

7. Log in diary due dates for IHT interest payments in relation to instalment option property, if appropriate.
8. Interim bill? (Did you agree this with the PRs in advance?)
9. Interim distribution? May be advisable to avoid a beneficiary receiving a large income receipt in one tax year pushing beneficiary into higher rate tax unnecessarily (see **Chapter 17**).

18.6 OBTAINING THE GRANT CHECKLIST

This checklist for the oath form, with reminders, has been specially revised and reformulated by Kevin Donnelly, Chief Clerk at the Probate Registry, Somerset House, and we are most grateful to him for doing so, and for permission to use it.

1. Extracting solicitors
   - Has your name, address (including post code), DX number and reference (if required) been included at the heading of the oath?
2. Name of deceased
   - Does the name correspond with the will (if any)?
   - If not, or if an alias is necessary for any other reason, has the true name been identified and the reason for the alias been set out in the oath by way of a footnote?
   - Was the deceased known by any other name or was the death registered in any other name? If so, these should be included on the oath (although these names may not appear on the grant).
3. Address of deceased
   - Has the last residential address been included? (A short stay in hospital can be ignored for these purposes.) Include post code.
4. Names of applicants
   - Are these the true names?
   - Do they correspond with the will (if any)?
   - Is an affidavit of identity required?
   - Has the applicant included any extra initials in his or her signature to the oath? (Any extra initials should be investigated and the oath resworn to show the true name if necessary.)

- Include address and post code.

5. Survival clause in will

- Does the will contain a clause providing that the executor or executrix must survive by a specified period before the appointment becomes effective?
- If yes, has the period expired?

6. Date of death

- Does the date of death given in the oath agree with that on the death certificate? (If the death certificate does not give a specific date of death, the oath should state when the deceased was last seen or known to be alive and when his or her body was found.)

7. Codicil

- Did the deceased leave any codicils to the will?
- If yes, has reference been made to them in the oath?
- If yes, have they been marked in accordance with rule 10 of the Non-Contentious Probate Rules (NCPR) 1987 by the applicant and swearing Commissioner?

8. Age of the deceased

- Has the age and date of birth of the deceased been included in the oath?

9. Domicile of the deceased

- Has the domicile of the deceased been included in the oath? (If the deceased died domiciled out of England and Wales and different systems of law operate within the country, the state of domicile must be shown, e.g. the State of Victoria, the State of New Jersey.)

10. Settled land

- Has the clause concerning settled land been included/completed? (This clause must be included in every oath.)

11. Life/minority interest

- Did the deceased leave a will?
- If yes, is the executor or executrix appointed in it applying for the grant?
- If no, or if the deceased left no will, does a life or minority interest arise out of the estate?
- Has the appropriate section in the oath been included/completed? (The oath must state, in terms, whether a life or minority interest arises unless an executor or executrix is applying for the grant.)

12. Title

- Have all the persons with a prior entitlement to the applicant been accounted for in the oath?
- Has the applicant's title been stated in full? (Unless all clearings have been included and the title stated in full the oath is certain to be queried and is likely to require reswearing.)

13. Value of the estate: Is the estate an 'excepted estate'? (See **15.3**.)

- If yes, have the band figures appropriate to the date of death been included in the oath?
- Has the net estate been stated to the nearest thousand?
- Have the words 'and this is not a case in which a HMRC account is required to be lodged' (or similar) been included in the correct clause? (Failure to include this clause will result in the oath having to be resworn.)
- If not, and the deceased died domiciled in England and Wales, has the total of all the estate passing under the grant been included?
- Does this total agree with that shown in the HMRC account?
- If not, has an explanation for the difference been included in the oath?
- If the deceased died domiciled out of England and Wales, has the relevant clause been amended to refer to estate only in England and Wales? (It is possible to have an 'excepted estate' for a deceased who died domiciled in Scotland.)

14. Jurat

- Has the oath and will/codicil(s) (if any) been signed by (all) the applicant(s) and swearing Commissioner(s)?
- Has the oath been dated and the place of swearing stated? (Please bear in mind that the oath and any supporting affidavits cannot be sworn before the solicitor extracting the grant or a member of his or her firm.)

Special types of application

1. Attorney grants

- Has the limitation to be recited in the grant been included in the oath? (The usual limitation is 'for the use and benefit of – [the donor] and until further representation be granted'.)

2. Grants for minors

- Are there two applicants?
- Is it necessary to lodge a nomination of the second applicant?
- If the application relies upon court orders, are court-certified copies available?
- Does the oath state that a minority interest arises?

- Does the oath have the correct limitation? (The usual limitation in such application is 'for the use and benefit of – [the minor(s)] until he/she/one of them shall attain the age of 18 years'.)

3. Domicile out of England and Wales

- Has the domicile of the deceased been described correctly?
- Have those facts upon which the deponent to the affidavit of law (if any) has relied when reaching his or her conclusions been included in the oath or another sworn document? (These facts are usually recited in the affidavit of law following the words 'I am informed and verily believe' or similar. If they are not sworn, the application will be delayed whilst the oath or affidavit is resworn.)
- Have the words 'in England and Wales' been added to the clause dealing with the estate?
- Are any foreign court documents to be used in support of the application copies certified by the court?
- Has the correct form of HMRC account (IHT201) been completed and controlled by the Capital Taxes Office?
- Has any necessary order under NCPR 1987 been obtained or approved? (It may not be necessary to have the order drawn before swearing the oath but prior approval of the district judge or district probate registrar must be obtained.)

4. Lost wills

- Has the original will been seen since the deceased's date of death?
- Was the will known to have been in the possession of the deceased up to the date of his or her death?
- If the answer to the first question is no and the second yes, does the evidence in support of the application rebut the presumption of revocation of the will by the deceased in his or her lifetime?
- Can the authenticity of the copy will be confirmed?
- Does the affidavit in support of the application exhibit the copy will to be proved?
- Does the oath in support of the application for the grant describe accurately the copy will being proved? (It is suggested that the affidavit(s) in support of the application be prepared in draft form in the first instance to enable any further evidence required by the district judge or registrar to be incorporated.)

Wills and codicils

1. Has the testator or testatrix signed the will?

- Has the will been witnessed by two witnesses?

- Does the will contain a properly worded attestation clause?
- Has the will been dated?

(Although these are obvious points, a large number of wills are rejected by the probate registries each year for these simple defects. The factors also apply to codicils. It may still be possible to prove a will/codicil with any of these defects if validity can be established under the Wills Act 1963.)

2. Does the will/codicil have any unattested alterations or additions?
3. Is there a valid appointment of executrix/executor(s)? (Care should be taken to ensure that the appointment is correctly worded; if there is any doubt, evidence of the testator's or testatrix's intention will be necessary.)
4. Did the deceased leave any codicils to his or her will?
   - If yes, are they all available?
   - Is the appointment of executors affected by the codicil?
   - Does the codicil confirm the will by the correct date? (If the date is not correct, evidence that the right will is being proved may be necessary.)
5. Have the will and codicils (if any) been marked by the applicant(s) and swearing Commissioner(s) in accordance with rule 10 of NCPR 1987?

IHT accounts

1. Has the correct account, appropriate to the date of death and type of application, been used?
2. Has the account been signed and dated by the applicant(s)?
   - Does the account need to be controlled by HMRC? (Although any account may be controlled, generally speaking this need be done only in the estates of persons who die domiciled out of England and Wales.)
   - Is the date of death of the deceased before 13 March 1975?
   - If the answer is yes, has the IHT account been sworn? (NB This is a requirement.)
   - Has the certificate regarding payment of IHT been signed?

Fees

1. Has the correct fee been paid?
2. Does the payment include the fee for any copies ordered?

Photocopies

Have you provided two A4 sized copies of the deceased's sworn will and, where applicable, codicil?

18.7 COLLECTING THE ASSETS, PAYING THE DEBTS CHECKLIST

1. Cancel/obtain refund/collect/return/pay/check:
   - council tax;
   - Department for Work and Pensions payments;
   - trade union or professional association subscription – and some death benefit may be payable;
   - club and other memberships such as charities, libraries, pressure groups, voluntary organisations, political parties and consumer and motoring organisations;
   - subscriptions: journals, magazines, book clubs;
   - borrowed items: library books, records, videos, hospital equipment such as a wheelchair;
   - payments made in advance by deceased, e.g. gas or electricity account may be in credit;
   - payments due to deceased which may be in arrears, e.g. pension;
   - laundry or dry cleaning, or items sent for valuation or repair;
   - items on hire: TV or washing machine, computer, possibly evening or formal dress;
   - relevant direct debits/standing orders, etc., at bank or building society;
   - milk, papers and other deliveries;
   - passport;
   - credit cards.
2. List all the assets and refunds and include a column for noting what happened to the asset, its value and relevant dates.
3. Is there any property abroad? How will this be dealt with? Do foreign law rules conflict with the will or the intestacy rules? Specialist advice may be needed.
4. Valuation: some items may be more valuable than one might expect. Certain charities, such as the PDSA, offer house clearance services (others may advertise in local papers and free sheets) but ensure that nothing possibly of value is overlooked. See specialist valuers address list (see **Appendix F**) for items needing an expert's opinion.
5. Send office copies of the grant to asset holders – use standard letters on a word processor to save time and get plenty of office copies, too few is a false economy. Include a request in letters to bank, building societies, etc., for all the necessary paperwork for closure of accounts to be sent.
6. Keep standard letters to creditors on a word processor to save time. Send these early so that relatives are not troubled by reminders about bills.
7. Make a list of all the deceased's liabilities, with columns for the dates and amounts of payments. Tick each off as it is dealt with.
8. Ensure that assets in your office are insured and listed, and any special regulations (e.g. re guns, antique or modern) are observed.

9. Pay bills promptly when funds becomes available – if this takes time, does the timetable need adjusting? If so, advise the client.
10. It may be helpful to keep all the paperwork related to paid debts (e.g. bills, receipts and correspondence, etc.) in a separate file once they are no longer current matters.

18.8 ACCOUNTING AND DISTRIBUTION CHECKLIST

1. Prepare any corrective account for IHT which has become necessary. For small amounts, correspondence may suffice.
2. If land or quoted shares have been sold for less than probate relief, consider whether it is appropriate to claim loss on sale relief under IHTA 1984.
3. Make interim distributions, but reserve enough money for outstanding tax, costs and other contingencies. Consider ensuring that PRs and residuary beneficiaries are satisfied with the draft accounts before making large distributions.
4. Ensure arrangements for payment of tax by beneficiaries have been made, where necessary.
5. Offer beneficiaries receiving substantial legacies your firm's investment advice if you are authorised or suggest that they seek independent advice. See also **Chapter 4** on undertaking investment business.
6. Do any beneficiaries need:
   - wills?
   - codicils?
   - tax advice?
   - lasting powers of attorney?
6. Have all beneficiaries received forms R185E where appropriate? This is particularly important for charities who will need to obtain refunds of income tax.
7. If problems in obtaining a discharge arise consider insurance, payment into court under Trustee Act 1925, s.63, etc.
8. Have the important dates for protecting PRs passed – two months for statutory advertisements, six months from date of grant for IPFDA 1975 claims? (See **Chapter 8** on probate time limits.)
9. Prepare accounts (or have them prepared for you).
10. Obtain receipts and discharges from beneficiaries.

18.9 CLOSING YOUR FILE CHECKLIST

1. Is your file closure letter satisfactory? It is an important document as it should stand proof that you have completed your work satisfactorily. To perform this function it should incorporate the following points:

   - It should explain why the file has been closed. This is usually because the matter has been completed. However, the client may have changed solicitors or decided to deal with the matter in person. This needs to be fully explained so that the client cannot allege later that you were still instructed. It is particularly important where you were retained to deal with only certain aspects of the administration.
   - It should explain exactly what work your firm has done and what the outcome was. There may be a misunderstanding between what you have done and what the client thinks you have done. It is better for the client to realise this at a time when further instructions can be given easily.
   - It should set out clearly any tasks which the client has to perform (for example, the payment of instalments of IHT) with, if necessary, exact timings and the consequences of failing to adhere to those timings.
   - Consider sending two copies of the letter to your client asking for one to be signed and returned.

2. Which documents belong to the client? See Solicitor's Code of Conduct 2007, rule 2, guidance note 11.
3. How long must the file be kept? See Law Society File Retention Practice Note (11 September 2007).
4. Which documents should be preserved? This list is not exhaustive:

   - documents belonging to the client;
   - documents of title;
   - significant correspondence with HMRC, returns, accounts, etc., particularly post-death variations and appointments under IHTA 1984, s.144;
   - court orders;
   - valuations (it may be advisable to supply probate valuations to non-residuary legatees – otherwise they will contact you in the future if CGT becomes an issue for them).

5. Consider asking the client if any old, but non-essential, documents could be of interest to a local history society or museum.
6. Could any of the letters or documents you prepared form the basis of stock letters for future use by you or within the office? If so, consider keeping these in a separate, indexed, precedent file.

18.10 EVALUATING CHECKLIST

Ten things I know now I wish I'd known then:

1.
2.
3.
4.
5.
6.
7.
8.
9.
10.

PART IV

Profitable probate practice

CHAPTER 19

Computing and technology issues

Charles Christian

19.1 INTRODUCTION

Shortly before writing this chapter, I attended a conference session given by a futurologist. Most of his presentation was outside the realms of legal practice but he did make one interesting throw-away remark. Commenting on the trend for a rapidly growing ageing population we now see in the United Kingdom (and the rest of Europe/the Western world) he said: 'if I were a lawyer, I'd want to focus on wills, trusts and probate work as that's an expanding market.'

This is an interesting comment as, if anything, the reverse is now true in England and Wales for, despite the old saw about 'nothing in life is certain except death and taxes', there are only about 7,500 solicitors in this jurisdiction who regularly handle probate work – and as few as 300 firms who handle probate in any real volume. This is not to say that there is no demand for probate practice – of the average of 560,000 deaths each year, about 180,000 result in applications for the grant of probate – but rather that the work is being gobbled up by banks and the likes of the Co-operative Funeral Service.

Such a state of affairs is something practitioners need to address by reading Kim Tasso's chapter on marketing, as simply buying a computer is not going to redress this issue – however, these figures do have one very important consequence for computerisation and information technology (IT) matters. Namely, if there are only a relatively small number of firms handling large (or even largish) volumes of probate work, there is insufficient demand to support a vibrant market for the supply of probate software and related systems. Indeed, in talking to some of the remaining players in this field (and since the previous edition of this book, we have seen a degree of consolidation, as well as the withdrawal from the market of some older 'legacy' vendors and products) they say their only real competition is Microsoft Word and the Excel spreadsheet.

This chapter, therefore, has something of a split personality.

- For those practitioners with only a limited volume of 'simple' probate work, where there are no trusts involved and deceased are not high net-worth individuals, with complex estates involving multiple properties and financial

investments, then you probably can still get by using some formulae programmed into Microsoft Excel to calculate inheritance tax (IHT), along with some standard document templates on your word processing software.
- For those practitioners with more complex, high value estates and/or seeking to handle higher volumes of probate work, read on ...

Thanks to the high profile coverage computer systems and IT-related matters now enjoy in the legal press, there is a growing belief among solicitors' practices that computerisation is the universal panacea for all problems. However, while it might be nice to think that if the firm is not making enough money out of probate practice, the easiest solution is to install a new 'probate case management software' application, not only is this a far too simplistic approach, but it could also prove to be commercially disastrous.

Leaving aside the cost and inevitable disruption (including the time taken up with administration matters that would otherwise be devoted to fee earning) associated with all computerisation projects, there is a risk of running foul of the old computer industry adage: GIGO – garbage in, garbage out. In other words, if the practice has problems, installing a computer will not fix those problems, it will merely computerise them.

That's the bad news. The good news is that a properly implemented law office computerisation project will yield positive benefits. And in the case of probate practitioners, at the very least this should include reducing the time and overheads associated with individual probate matters, so allowing them both to increase the volume of work they can handle and also to increase the profitability of that work. Or, to put it another way, technology is a tool that properly used will help you earn more money, get out of the office and away home earlier – and still keep the client satisfied.

19.2 TECHNOLOGY IN CONTEXT

The starting point for any discussion about legal technology must be with the premise that technology is not an end in itself but merely a tool to help implement a law firm's overall business and practice development plans. In other words, the emphasis is upon the creation of a joined-up, rather than a semi-detached, strategy.

Unfortunately, too many firms still approach computerisation projects from the wrong direction, putting the proverbial cart before the horse, and make the decision to invest in technology without fully thinking through its longer-term implications. Just because the firm down the road has bought a new probate system is not a good enough reason for your firm to buy one as well, it is important to look at the bigger picture. For example, where is your firm planning to go over the next five years? Will it still be doing private client work? Are there plans to expand or contract its probate practice? Are there any obvious problems with the way that probate work is currently processed that could benefit from technology? And what benefits is it envisaged that technology will deliver?

The answers to all these questions will help determine the firm's priorities; however, particular emphasis should be paid to the issue of the anticipated benefits of technology – or the 'return on investment' (ROI). Solicitors' practices are notorious for fudging the answer to this question and despite the fact a firm can currently expect to spend about 3 per cent of its annual turnover each year on IT (this figure assumes a firm has recovered from the cutback of the 2008–10 economic downturn and is now once more investing in practice development) the method of measuring the ROI is, to put it charitably, naive and unscientific. I have lost count of the number of times I have heard a firm justify some huge expenditure solely on the grounds that 'it will help us to provide a better service to our clients'.

Talk about stating the obvious – well, of course the firm hopes it is going to help provide a better service otherwise it would not be buying these systems. But warm, cosy, touchy-feely sentiments like that will not pay the bills – nor generate the fee income to keep the partnership happy. When assessing ROI the questions a firm should be asking are:

- 'How much money is this new system going to save us?' For example, will it be possible to cut down on the number of staff in the probate department?
- 'How much in extra fees is this system going to help us earn?' For instance, will the system enable the firm to handle more matters with the same staff resources?
- 'Will this system enable us to fix our costs?' – a key issue if you are tendering for volume instructions from a provider such as a bank, who will certainly be expecting you to operate on a fixed-fee basis.
- 'Will this system help us address other issues within our probate practice?' For example, do you need to speed up the process or else build-in quality control measures, whether for your own internal risk management purposes or else to ensure you meet with both professional and legal regulations and compliance, as well as any service level agreements/requirements of a volume provider of instructions.

Firms should also ensure that any ROI calculations focus upon profitability, as distinct from mere increases in turnover because more billable hours can be generated. If this increase in turnover has only been achieved by also increasing overheads, the slightest downturn in the economy – as we saw during the period 2008-10 – will put pressure on profit margins, which once again will not please the rest of the partnership. Lecture over, now let us start looking at the technology options available.

19.3 PROBATE SYSTEMS

Probate systems are a confusing area of law office automation in that the same term is often loosely applied by suppliers to a broad range of applications covering everything from will-writing software through to investment trust accounting and portfolio management systems. A listing and contact details of all the relevant systems suppliers are provided in **Appendix D**.

19.3.1 Will-writing software, electronic forms and precedents

Providing the products you use have been specifically designed for the professional market (rather than the home/DIY sector) there are some very good systems available which are suitable for probate solicitors in private practice. And, to repeat the old Law Society adage – 'if you want to stay in practice, you need to get a niche' – it may well be that the demographics of your local area means there is a commercially viable revenue stream to be had from offering will preparation services.

For example, in a rural area with limited public transport, sole practitioners may consider providing house calls, taking their laptop computers with them to provide will writing and other services to clients who would otherwise be unable to get to their offices. This also neatly highlights the true value of technology as a tool: in the right hands it can enhance the delivery of legal services to clients – in this instance, if the client cannot get into the office, the solicitor can take a 'virtual office' on a laptop to the client. Think outside the box.

Mention should also be made of the wide range of legal forms and precedents that now exist in an electronic format (typically on CD-Rom or via a download from the internet) so clauses can be selected and automatically incorporated within a document or deed without the need to retype any wording.

19.3.2 Wills and deeds registers

This is really just another name for a computerised index of all the wills that the firm holds copies of and where they are physically located. Back in the days of stand-alone technology, specific software packages were sold to handle this type of application. Today, with the emphasis in law firm IT on central databases, this type of information will usually be stored within an overall client/matter section of a practice management system or else it will be one of the elements of a probate case management system.

19.3.3 Trusts, portfolio management and other specialist systems

This area of legal work sees the practitioner moving beyond the conventional bounds of probate practice and into the broader private client/investment/financial services arena. Technically this is outside the scope of this book; however, with the rise in property prices and spread of personal financial investment, bringing many more estates up into values where IHT becomes an issue, we are seeing many more 'ordinary members of the public' (as distinct from high net-worth private clients) seeking advice on estate and tax planning matters where trusts may be relevant. A number of suppliers of probate systems also supply trust accounting and management applications. And, one supplier (but to my knowledge, only one) also markets a Court of Protection application.

19.3.4 Internet systems

Although there are still some firms offering online wills-related services, two factors have effectively killed this market. The first was the realisation of the complexity of the compliance issue – how do you ensure you don't breach five professional conduct rules before breakfast (never mind avoiding falling foul of the anti-money laundering regulations) when you are dealing with a virtual client? However, the real killer was that firms found there was simply not a commercially viable volume of demand for online wills services. Indeed, firms that did go this route discovered that the fees generated failed to even recoup the cost of the systems needed to deliver such services.

That however still leaves two valuable roles for the internet. The first is as a communications medium and searchable repository of information. This is going to become more important over the next few years as more 'e-government' initiatives are rolled out and it becomes quicker, more convenient and cheaper (particularly if government agencies extend the practice of offering financial incentives to complete forms online) to turn to the web rather than use traditional paper-based form filling methods. The Court Service continues to have a section of its website devoted to the Probate Service, which includes links to the HMRC capital taxes section. (**www.hmcourts-service.gov.uk/cms/wills.htm**).

The second role of the internet is in the delivery of legal services to clients and related third parties. This is particularly relevant in some areas of legal practice, such as residential conveyancing where typically the client, the estate agent and the mortgage lender (to whose panel the solicitor belongs) will be able to access matter progress reports online via a secure website known as an extranet. Increasingly 'client access extranets' are becoming a standard option within case management software although to date there has been very little demand for this facility by probate practitioners. To go back to my technology as a tool analogy – just because technology can do something, does not necessarily mean that your clients will want it or that you need to buy it.

19.3.5 Probate case (or workflow) management systems

These systems introduce an element of automation to probate work by building a workflow routine that effectively controls the way the work is processed. These can be very useful where work is being handled by a department and the partner in charge needs not only to be able to review and manage the progress of matters but also to ensure that tasks delegated to non-legally qualified staff take place within a sufficiently rigid framework, so there is no room for mistakes to be made.

For prospective purchasers there are a number of issues to consider here. The first is whether they have the volume of work or organisational structure to justify the workflow management approach? If lawyers are not prepared to delegate probate work to more junior staff the introduction of computerisation will merely turn fee earners in very expensive keyboard operators.

Another issue is whether the software is being sold on a stand-alone or an integrated basis. For example, some suppliers sell software on a stand-alone basis, so you can buy a probate workflow application and run it out of the box, with or without links to your firm's accounts or practice management software. (This is also sometimes called the 'best of breed' or 'point-solution' approach.) However, much of the software sold into the UK legal systems market consists of integrated products, so a firm cannot use one supplier's probate system unless that supplier's accounts system is also installed. If a firm is happy with its existing accounts/ practice management system then the cheapest and most hassle-free option will usually be to install either that supplier's own probate system or else that supplier's preferred probate software partner's product.

19.3.6 Probate accounts software

This is used to help practitioners compile estate accounts, print interim statements for beneficiaries and prepare completed IHT returns. Most of these systems also contain some form of workflow management-style diary reminders and checklists. Bearing in mind that the preparation of estate accounts can be one of the most time-consuming features of probate work, this is a system many practitioners would benefit from using. But when talking to software sales staff, be certain that they do not fudge this issue. Can it really handle all aspects probate accounts – for example can it produce IHT forms? And do not be fobbed off with promises that although the system currently only offers workflow facilities 'an accounts module is under development'. That is no good – you need to know what it can do for you now, not what it might be able to do at some dim and possibly very distant date in the future.

19.4 HOW PROBATE SYSTEMS CAN HELP PRACTITIONERS

This is a potentially contentious topic, for it does not matter how good a computer system may be in theory because unless a practice is prepared to invest adequately in training – so that its members really know how to operate the computers on their desks – the full benefits of the system will never be realised. Whatever else you do, do not skimp on training. Leaving aside this important qualification, there are six potential areas of benefit.

19.4.1 Achieving immediate objectives

There are a number of situations that can arise where computerisation is successfully undertaken to achieve immediate, relatively limited, short-term objectives. For example, suppose an experienced probate practitioner is heading for retirement and planning to work on a part-time consultancy basis. If the firm still has a healthy probate practice then investing in a probate accounts system that can act as an *aide-mémoire* for another less experienced lawyer and take over some of the donkey work on the estate accounts preparation work may be a cost-effective alternative to replacement of the consultant.

Similarly, if the firm were to win a major commercial client, such as a financial institution, and with it the prospect of a major increase in the volume of its probate work, then installing IT would be a cost-effective alternative to recruiting additional probate department staff. This also meets one of the measurements for ROI, namely how much will this system help us save?

19.4.2 Better information

In discussing computerisation most people tend to focus on the 'technology' aspect of information technology. However, the 'information' angle should also be remembered. Although computers have earned a poor reputation in the past for generating impenetrable reports of monumental length, modern systems are excellent tools for extracting valuable business information from large volumes of data – information that would be almost impossible to obtain (or at least take a long time and prevent staff from getting on with their normal work) using manual methods.

For example, access to detailed information about clients and work types allows firms to be more precise in their marketing and cross-selling efforts – which in the past probably involved little more than sending Christmas cards to every client name on the books, regardless of whether anyone in the firm had spoken to them in the last decade. (This aspect of legal software is increasingly referred to as client relationship management or CRM.)

For firms who anticipate that most of their probate work will be generated from the results of earlier wills campaigns (such as the annual Law Society 'Wills Week'), a good information system also allows the firm to become proactive rather than reactive, so clients can be periodically contacted to see if they need to review and update their wills. After all, this year's happily married shopkeeper could be next year's lottery winner with a younger spouse, new family and an increasingly complex network of commercial interests.

19.4.3 Greater efficiency and productivity

One of the more obvious benefits of computerisation is that IT is very good at doing relatively dull repetitive tasks very quickly and accurately, such as adding up long columns of figures. In the probate department this means error-free estate accounts can be prepared within hours whereas previously staff could have been tied up for days. This in turn means that the firm will now have the capacity to handle more work with the same or fewer resources, thus avoiding the need to recruit extra staff and/or allowing existing staff to be allocated to other tasks. Once again this meets the ROI criteria for saving money and/or helping the firm to make more money.

It is also worth noting that workflow and case management systems primarily come into their own in the context of helping manage the delegation of routine aspects of work to more junior staff – a particular boon for firms handling high volumes of work. However, even in those firms where probate work is handled by just one highly skilled solicitor, there can still be productivity gains. For example, there is always a degree of routine work associated with any matter, such as sending out client care letters, replying to correspondence and to enquiries about the progress of a matter, cheque requisitions for official fees, plus associated diary entries and updates to files and archives. The important point here is that the computer is not in anyway diminishing the role of the lawyer by automating some of these tasks, it is merely taking over some of the boring but necessary non-legal aspects of the business process. In other words, it frees lawyers from pushing around bits of paper and allows them to concentrate on the more interesting – and financially rewarding – legal work.

This has led to the suggestion that if a workflow system can automate just some of these tasks, perhaps only saving a fee earner five or 10 minutes a day, in the long term this can add up to a substantial saving in time. Ten minutes a day is the equivalent of 50 hours a year – which is quite a chunk considering the average English solicitor only bills a total of 1,250 hours a year. And, of course, if every fee earner in the firm enjoys the same benefits ... well, do the maths. In effect this is the 'little bang' approach to technology. The introduction of IT cannot be expected to dramatically change the firm's fortune in some kind of 'big bang' experience but the incremental benefits can become substantial over time. This also brings us back to my original comment that the role of technology in a solicitors' practice is to help you earn more money, get home earlier and still keep the client satisfied.

19.4.4 Better service

Having an IT system also opens up the possibility of offering services to clients which previously firms would have been reluctant to offer because of the additional workload involved. For example, producing interim accounts – or even interim distributions – for the beneficiaries of an estate becomes an automated click-of-a-button operation. Leaving aside the potential for generating extra fees (or taking less time to earn the same amount of fees) the ability to offer additional services is a plus point in terms of establishing a longer-term professional relationship with a client and helping to differentiate a firm from its competition. In broader practice development and marketing terms this is vital, because law firms cannot reduce their quality of service, competing on price is potentially ruinous, so the viable route is to offer a service that helps the firm to stand out from the rest of the crowd.

19.4.5 Increased profitability

If an IT system can help increase productivity among secretarial, clerical and fee earning staff, so that the same people can get through more work in the same or less time, then this will clearly have an impact upon the firm's profitability in that it frees them to get on with additional fee earning activities. However, computerisation can also bring about an increase in profitability by its potential for reducing overheads.

For example, it is not uncommon to find that smaller firms have an administrative 'tail' with a ratio of 1 to 2. In other words, for every fee earner in the firm, there are two back office staff (including secretaries). But, if IT is introduced, so fee earners can carry out jobs that would have previously involved dictating instructions to secretaries and waiting for these to be effected, it becomes possible to reduce the size of this tail.

A 1 to 1 ratio is the minimum to aim for, which typically will be achieved by sharing secretaries between fee earners, assigning some secretaries to quasi fee earning activities and reducing the reliance on 'temps'; however many firms have already achieved 2 to 1 or greater. Less reliance on support staff has, in turn, a number of other benefits. For example, it means it is possible to recruit more fee earners without also having to recruit a corresponding number of secretaries, which means that an expanding firm is likely to outgrow its existing office space less quickly than it would otherwise do.

Clearly employing proportionally fewer staff means that less is being spent on overheads, which in turn means increased profits. Equally, bearing in mind the competitive market in which solicitors operate, reducing overheads means that firms can also afford to compete on price (for example, against banks and other financial institutions) by cutting their margins yet still manage to make some profit on a matter.

19.4.6 Risk management, standards, compliance and quality control

Solicitors practise in an increasingly regulated and compliance-bound environment. And, while the vast majority of practitioners are honest and would never deliberately break or flout the rules, mistakes can and do happen. One attraction of all applications designed to perform specific tasks is that they create a framework the user has to follow so that, for example, when you first see a prospective client about the preparation of a will, you cannot start working for them unless they have acknowledged your client care letter/terms of business and provided evidence of their identity for compliance with the anti-money laundering regulations. As such, an IT system is also a quality control system, whether for your own internal risk management purposes or else to ensure you meet with both professional and legal regulations and compliance obligations. In addition, it can also ensure your service meets the standards set in any service level requirements of a volume provider of instructions.

19.5 THE PRINCIPLES OF IT PROCUREMENT

Along with salaries, accommodation and professional indemnity insurance, for many solicitors' practices their investment in a new computer system, or some related form of IT, will be one of the single largest financial commitments they ever take on. Current research suggests firms spend between 2 per cent and 7 per cent of their total fee income each year on IT, with smaller firms averaging 3.0 per cent and larger firms just over 4.5 per cent.

Furthermore, unlike buying conventional office equipment, such as a new photocopier, an investment in IT will potentially alter the way in which the whole firm operates. Bookkeepers, secretaries, receptionists, fee earners, partners and clients will all find that the new technology has some impact upon them and the legal services they either supply or receive. It is, therefore, essential that the IT procurement process is as efficient and problem free as possible, because if a firm gets it wrong, not only will a lot of time, money and effort have been wasted but the firm's commercial viability and professional reputation may have been irreparably compromised.

19.5.1 Strategy

Most solicitors probably know of 'computing disasters' that have occurred within other firms. However, what is not always appreciated is that the bulk of these disasters stem not from choosing inappropriate hardware or software but from attempts to implement fundamentally flawed IT strategies. The key element to bear in mind here (and I make no apology for repeating part of the message that appeared at the outset of this chapter because it is important) is that IT – even a stand-alone probate system – is not some self-contained entity but is instead merely an enabling technology or tool that should be regarded as an integral part of the practice's overall business development plan. If it wants to get its IT strategy right, a firm must first have (or devise) an appropriate general business strategy.

To give a simple example, there is no point spending time choosing a supplier of probate software, if the firm's only probate practitioner is considering retirement. In addition, any strategy should also take into account the firm's medium-term requirements and longer-term aspirations, for example opening new branch offices or diversifying into new areas of practice, such as trust and portfolio management. In other words, do not buy a system that meets only the immediate current needs, buy one that will also meet any future anticipated needs.

The first stage in devising an IT strategy therefore has nothing to do with computers but instead involves drawing up a business or practice development plan. Only once this is in place should partners begin considering how IT can be used to help implement that plan over the next few years.

Next comes the process of drawing up more detailed specifications and requirements – in effect a computerisation shopping list – that will help to realise the IT strategy. For example, is the proposed system intended to be used by one fee earner only as a productivity tool? In this case, a stand-alone software application that will run on a personal computer may be suitable. In contrast, is probate work to be handled by a department, with different tasks delegated between fee earning and secretarial staff? In this case, a networked case management product is going to be more appropriate. Whether or not a formal 'invitation to tender' (or ITT) document should be drawn up is a matter of policy, but the firm certainly must have a clear understanding of its requirements if prospective suppliers are to be properly briefed and their responses evaluated on a like-for-like basis.

19.5.2 Budgets

It is essential at this stage to consider budgets and the availability of finance to support the proposed investment in IT (whether from cash reserves, leasing, bank loans, etc.). An important factor to bear in mind is that calculating the overall IT spend is a lot more complicated than adding the cost of PC hardware and a single user software licence together and multiplying it by the total number of users.

Along with hardware and software, there is the cost of installing the supporting network cabling, which in older premises may mean major rewiring and redecorating exercises. There is also the cost of training, and it cannot be stressed strongly enough that it is essential to properly train everyone who is intended to use the computers. Then there are the ongoing running costs, including insurance, annual maintenance contracts, renewable software licences (where applicable), hardware and software upgrades, additional training for additional or replacement staff and computer 'consumables' such as replacement laser printer toner cartridges and pre-printed 'continuous' stationery.

As a rule of thumb today, in terms of capital costs, for a probate accounts software package, plus a PC to run it on and training, firms should budget on between £3,000 and £5,000 per user plus a further one-third of this capital cost for each subsequent year by way of ongoing running costs.

19.5.3 Finding a supplier

Having decided what it wants to buy and how much it is prepared to pay for it, the firm is now in a position to look for a suitable supplier. This may seem a daunting task, particularly when the total number of suppliers is considered. However, when broken down into logical stages, it becomes more manageable:

- First, thin down the number of contenders – if trust accounts, the case management approach or will-writing software are not required, drop them from the list.
- Contact the remaining suppliers for further information, such as brochures and promotional literature containing details of their track records and installations; visit their stands at exhibitions; attend any of the sales presentations you will inevitably be invited to, once they realise you are a prospect; talk to

contacts within the profession; reference websites given by the supplier and anyone else who has experience of dealing with them.

- Given the size of the probate systems market, this process will help whittle down the total number of prospects to a shortlist of two or three suppliers. In fact, your choice may be even more restricted if you are looking for software that is compatible with your firm's existing practice management system. Send these shortlisted companies copies of the tender document (if this has been drawn up) so that responses can be evaluated on a like-for-like basis.
- Visit their premises or user reference sites for detailed system demonstrations and discussions about how they would propose to handle the implementation of the project, including training. Incidentally, ensure that the key staff who will actually be using the proposed new system attend these demonstrations.
- Follow up any user references that are given and start exploring the contractual terms that are being offered, as this is frequently a protracted stage of the negotiations, not least because as lawyers you will inevitably find aspects of their contractual wording to disagree with!
- Take notice of your own business instincts. The relationship with the supplier does not end the day the new computer goes 'live' – the firm will be dealing with them for at least the next five to seven or even 10 years, so be certain these are people you feel you can trust and work with on a longer-term basis.
- Don't be blinded by science. Suppliers will often claim that their respective products are better than those of their competition because they have been developed using 'better' software development tools. This is all 'under the bonnet' stuff. What really matters is the functionality of the software – does it do the job you want it to do, in the way you want it done?
- Be clear what the firm is getting for its money. For example, how does the supplier of a probate accounts package deal with the fact that IHT rules change at least once a year, which may require both amendments to the way the software calculates returns and the incorporation of new forms to be submitted to HMRC? Is an automatic update included as part of the ongoing software maintenance contract or is this a chargeable extra?
- Finally, do take into account that price should not be the key factor (sadly, in many firms it still appears to be the only issue) in the selection process. Along with the ROI issues mentioned earlier, for those firms that lack their own in-house IT resources (and most firms with 30 or fewer members of staff fall into this category) the availability of what is sometimes called a 'trusted supplier' (someone who can be relied on to help out in a crisis) is essential. This kind of service is rarely provided by suppliers who have been selected purely on the basis of price. It is also arguable that 'implementation'(see **19.5.4**), including installation, training (especially of lawyers) and ongoing support, is even more important than selection.

19.5.4 Implementation

Now the firm is in a position to place an order. And is that it? Well actually no, for the firm is entering one of the most sensitive stages – implementation – where problems can frequently arise because insufficient management resources are devoted to this aspect of the project. By implementation we mean everything from the delivery of the system to the firm's premises, to the rolling out of the system and the completion of staff training. This is a management issue and at the very least a partner (i.e. someone who has sufficient 'clout' to make things happen if problems arise) should have responsibility for overseeing its progress.

Co-ordination will be essential to ensure that the installation of the network cabling, the delivery of the hardware, the loading of the software and the training of staff to use the new system is properly scheduled and takes place satisfactorily according to a mutually convenient and pre-agreed timetable. For example, it is probably wise to avoid the holiday season and the end of the firm's financial year – not least because the firm will normally be expected to pay for substantial chunks of the system on the completion of each of these stages.

Larger firms with experience of IT projects can probably manage implementation projects themselves but for smaller firms it makes more sense to leave the project management to its main systems supplier. This can be particularly important in multi-vendor situations, with hardware coming from one source, software from another, and yet another organisation installing the network cabling at your offices.

19.5.5 Training, training and more training

Although training should be part of the broader implementation process, I'm giving it an extra focus here because it is one area where law firms always try to make economies. At its most blatant this takes the form of 'sitting next to Nelly'. In other words the minimum possible number of people are sent on a formal training course and when they return to the office, they are expected to train up the other members of the staff, as well as trying to remember themselves how the new system works and continuing to do their day job. It may have worked in the past with some of the earlier (and simpler) legal systems but today it is a recipe for a dilution of knowledge in terms of the firm's overall understanding of how a system operates.

In effect, it is the training equivalent of Chinese whispers and can lead to serious problems when the original 'Nelly' has left the practice and those who sat next to her are now trying to train their own successors. There have been a number of occasions where firms have set out to purchase a replacement software system that can perform a specific function only to discover that their original system had that capability all along, but thanks to inadequate training no one in the firm realised it.

As mentioned before, computer systems are just tools whose value derives from how they are used. It therefore follows that if people are not trained in how to use them properly, the firm will not see a satisfactory return on its IT investments. Best advice is therefore that everyone who is going to use a particular system should receive full training in how to use that system. It should also be uninterrupted training, so the participants can concentrate on the course rather than being distracted by interruptions from clients and colleagues.

And it also means that the fee earners, who will be working with the software, must attend these sessions. This is one reason why it helps to have a senior member of the firm in overall charge of implementation, so they can compel the fee earners to attend. If not, left to their own devices, fee earners will often claim that they are 'far too busy' to attend training and then complain that the software is 'hopeless' when they later discover that they do not know how to use it.

Firms should also consider periodic 'top up' (or remedial) training, to ensure that everyone remains up to speed on how to use systems – not least because not everything taught during the initial intensive training sessions will be remembered. And, the firm needs to be able to cope with any upgrades that come along. A larger firm with its own HR department will be able to monitor the requirements for staff training. For smaller firms, the impetus may come from the systems suppliers, if the support calls coming through to their help desks have been monitored and analysed. And don't forget to invest in proper training for any newcomers who join your firm – modern systems are too complex to leave to 'Nelly'.

19.6 PROBATE SYSTEMS BUYERS' GUIDE

The Law Society's annual *Software Solutions Guide* is no longer being produced, which is a great shame, and it would appear that the Law Society's *PS Software Guide 2007* is now some three years out-of-date. However, the list in **Appendix D** gives the details of suppliers (in alphabetical order, with contact details) of probate systems and related software applications. Please note that software products are regularly upgraded in terms of their functionality. In addition, my own website (**www.legaltechnology.com**) contains a regularly updated probate systems buyers guide, which is intended to reflect any changes taking place between the publication of this book and any subsequent edition. For the record, I am not a computer consultant and hold no commercial interest in any of the vendors listed in **Appendix D**.

CHAPTER 20

Managing private client business for profit

Gill Steel

20.1 OVERVIEW

- Why plan at all?
- Obtaining commitment – stemming the decrease in profits.
- Reviewing existing services and the competition.
- Tactics, action plan and review.
- Structure of department and staffing issues.
- Knowledge management and IT.
- Risk assessment and quality management systems.
- Marketing.

20.2 WHY PLAN AT ALL?

Pressure on the management of law firms is increasing day by day. The legal profession is now close (6 October 2011) to a colossal change in the way legal services are delivered, managed and regulated. This is coupled, in the wider world, with the global recession; the development and introduction of sophisticated IT packages which streamline and improve performance; striving to contain operating costs and the increased sophistication of quality management procedures and risk management requirements.

In broad terms, the immediate impact of these (and other) radical developments, such as the growth in anti-money laundering regulation, have to a large extent affected firms as a whole rather than probate practitioners in particular. There is, however, a noticeable trend towards withdrawal from private client work by some more commercially minded firms and a dearth in quality practitioners available to lead and develop private client teams, as senior people retire and firms find it hard to recruit to replace them. There still is too little investment within probate departments in integrated case management systems and general improvements in the use of technology, even when within the same firm other parts of the practice have successfully introduced equivalent products. Overt promotional activity for private client work is often more directed at will making than at probate work.

As a result, most probate departments, in management terms, have only recently had to face significant change in the way services are offered and delivered, to meet increasing pressure from actual and potential competition. For many years, probate practitioners have been a steady, reliable but unchanging group producing constant, profitable fees in reasonable volume. In some firms this steady growth is criticised when other areas have significantly increased both turnover and profits; in others it has been the saviour as profits decline and some areas of work evaporate in the recession. Whilst it is not possible to increase the number of deaths in the geographic area served by a practice, it is possible to generate an increase in the number of people who choose to use the firm and the range of services offered to clients and potential clients at appropriate rates.

So the perceptions of the probate department and the firm within which it operates may be divergent. The danger is that those owners and managers of the firm who have little or no knowledge of private client work will demand a more transactional approach and as a result may insist on unrealistic financial targets which eventually leads to withdrawal from this area of work. There is another way. Probate practitioners could become more entrepreneurial and put across to their colleagues that the long-term relationship approach is what has kept a steady and to date profitable private client department. It should operate differently from the other departments, but nevertheless adopt appropriate improved management techniques.

The profession is at a crossroads and is faced with an unpalatable economic scenario in which traditional sources of core income are under threat (e.g. conveyancing) as other providers of legal services enter the market. More investment is needed in the use of technology and research to enhance innovation. Margins throughout the firm are becoming tighter as fixed costs are demanded from consumers yet government and regulators increase bureaucracy. As a result, partnerships must develop remunerative areas of practice and this means the attention of the managing partner inevitably turns towards what has been the ever-reliable probate department as a source of significant levels of fee income and profit. However, probate practice is itself facing increased competition from new entrants into the market such as Co-operative Legal Services which has an area on its website dedicated to probate services. Probate practitioners need to respond to this challenge by providing not only an efficient and friendly service for clients, but also an increasingly profitable income stream for the practice.

Such a situation demands a reconsideration of the way in which probate is delivered. Without in any sense compromising on the quality of work delivered or the relationship with the client, efficiency must be sought, revenue must be maximised and systems must be streamlined.

Probate practitioners need to look to their management systems to improve efficiency and enhance performance.

This chapter offers initial help and guidance. Readers may also find some of the publications of the Law Management Section of the Law Society helpful. These include the LMS Business Development Toolkit and the LMS HR Toolkit.

20.3 OBTAINING COMMITMENT: STEMMING DECREASING PROFITABILITY

Some firms do not have an overall business plan, but hopefully, these may be few in number. Even with an overarching firm plan some probate lawyers may not be familiar with the idea of a departmental plan. However, without a business plan it is impossible to stretch or challenge existing perceptions of what is reasonable, and it will be difficult to evaluate progress and performance. A departmental plan will identify the strategy, set the objectives to be achieved and provide that yardstick against which to measure successful performance.

Having a business plan for a department is not a foolish notion. It does not matter how small or large the department is, the need to know what it is aiming to achieve and whether it has done so is just plain common sense. How else will it be evaluated whether investments made were cost effective? How else will appropriate staff be chosen in the future?

Sometimes it helps to get started if practitioners pose for themselves and their colleagues a really wild question just to get the creative juices flowing. For example, if £500,000 could be invested in the next year (over and above the firm's current available funds) with the goal of achieving a thriving, more competitive and secure practice:

- What would you spend it on?
- Why would you choose those particular things/actions?
- How would you set about it?
- Who would be responsible for actioning it?
- When would you expect to achieve it?
- How would you know you had achieved it?

Once the group has done some freewheeling with those questions for a large sum, ask why were those priorities chosen and can any of those ideas actually become reality? If this is to happen, the partners must recognise that there is a balance to be had between the short-term issues of maintaining cash flow and profitability whilst at the same time investing resources in the future success of the practice by developing new ways of meeting the clients' needs. This includes finding enough time for managing the practice and the department. Time will be needed to reflect, plan and implement any changes effectively.

Concentrate on setting up a strategy for the firm's core business: if private client work is at the centre of the firm then it is important that you have a strategy for it to improve the overall profitability of the firm. Be creative about considering new ways of doing things! Is the firm's culture 'but this is the way we do things around here'? Why? Trying to improve competitiveness requires changing habits – your habits and those of your partners. Change can be a painful process, and managing change needs new skills, management skills, not just professional skills.

Sveiby and Lloyd in their book *Managing Know-How: Add Value … by Valuing Creativity* (Bloomsbury, 1987) identified 10 success factors for a professional organisation. How does your firm match up?

1. *Day-to-day leadership*. This is not just the technical ability to conduct the work but rather possessing the basic skills and attributes of the successful leader, which include: the ability to help others succeed, not just strive for personal success; the need to have a set of principles and to enthuse and motivate colleagues to achieve their roles; the ability to bring constructive new ideas on how to improve the practice and productivity of the team; and the ability to act as the team's coach, both collectively and individually nurturing and challenging everyone to achieve the identified goals.
2. *Quality control*. There has never been a greater need to identify the client's real requirements and at the same time acknowledge the standards of professionalism required to meet those requirements and those of the regulators. The more people in the team or conducting work of this type, the more important it is to have control over the outputs to minimise disappointment for clients, reduce negligent errors and to enhance the reputation of the firm. It is widely accepted that clients do not take into account technical competence when evaluating the 'quality' of the service they experienced – unless they are lawyers themselves how can they know whether they have been given the 'right' advice? Instead they rely on how the service was delivered. Was it:

   - reliable?
   - responsive to their needs?
   - accessible?
   - courteous?
   - a process of communication: information provision and active listening?
   - credible?
   - secure?
   - tailored to the specific client?
   - performed in satisfactory offices, by appropriately dressed staff using effective equipment?

3. *Respect for know-how*. Know-how is value-added information, the sort of information that arises out of complex problem solving. Law firms must therefore be know-how businesses since they are selling the ability to produce solutions to often complex problems. The probate team will often be dealing with technical details over taxation and sometimes difficult family problems, and the advice given will be based on solid experience gained from having tackled similar problems in the past. A firm needs to respect the building and sharing of know-how, as this is the main asset it is selling.
4. *Combination of professional and managerial know-how*. It is important to identify, develop and share know-how not only about technical matters but also about the management of the department and firm. The successful head of department will not just have basic knowledge and information about the probate system and law but needs the skills and attributes of the manager such as analytical, problem-solving, decision-making skills; social skills and

abilities; emotional resilience to cope with difficult situations; the ability to respond proactively to events; creativity; mental agility; balanced learning habits and skills (an independent learner with a 'helicopter mind' which can move between the theoretical and the practical) and plenty of self-knowledge so that he or she can identify when personal factors are influencing the decision-making process.

5. *A strong, well-defined culture*. So often it is the culture of a firm that is either enabling or inhibiting successful change. Every firm has a culture whether it has been explicitly identified or not. Effective managers need awareness of and understanding of the power dynamics within their firm. To get things changed will require the ability to identify where a particular source of power is in play and whether there is a particularly under-used source of power that can be brought into play.
6. *Focus on core know-how*. Firms that know what their clients actually want, as opposed to what the firm thinks they want, are on the right track to identifying what know-how is required to produce what the client wants. Firms that have focused on the main know-how to achieve what their client base wants have proved to be the most successful in terms of repeat business and recommendation.
7. *Know-how preservation*. Since know-how is hard to come by, as it is as much about experience and practice as it is about technical knowledge, capturing and preserving it when key staff leave is difficult to do but some firms are led by people who have identified that it is a key success factor for the future of their firm.
8. *Developing the people*. As we cannot do everything ourselves and remain sane it is vital that any professional service firm employs people who it recognises need to be continually developed to attain the changing skills relevant to the job in hand. More needs to be done by firms to help people find out what it is to serve a client, and about how to work with people, whether they are your juniors, your seniors or your colleagues.
9. *Changing key people*. The marketing adage that 'people buy people' is certainly true of private client practice in law firms. A successful firm will properly ensure succession planning so that when people change a client is kept informed and retained rather than left floundering.
10. *Stable structures*. If a successful firm is to be achieved or maintained, it will be necessary to create or preserve stability. Looking only at the short term does not help practitioners to develop policies for long-term stability.

The above ideas should have got your creative juices flowing. It will be apparent that if there is no commitment from all the equity partners (the owners of the business) to allow you, as head of department, to devote some time to planning, managing and implementing the plan (non-chargeable work), then if the firm focuses only on personal billing levels you will find yourself being criticised. Far better to explain what you propose to do, with a view to maintaining your sanity and your partners' equilibrium. Also, if all the partners decided independently to reorganise their area of work or department at the same time, then the firm's cash flow would take a nose-dive!

If the head of department is to spend time thinking, planning and coming up with ideas to develop his or her area of practice then some fee earning work must be *delegated* to other people: junior people. Why is this not being done already?

- Great emphasis is placed on personal billing; in a recession there is a danger that senior people hoard what work there is to maintain their personal level of billing.
- In general practices do not hold individual partners responsible for finding ways of reducing the costs of the way the firm delivers the particular legal service; partners are usually only responsible for finding and doing the work.
- There is a reluctance to 'invest' time in coaching and supervising staff, and yet people are the key resource in know-how businesses.
- Fear: if you delegate you will have to find other work of a more complex nature to do and may feel out of your depth.

If planning for change is to be successful, the head of department will need the support not only of the owners of the firm but also of the staff in the department, office or firm – the team. It is vital to ensure that a well-integrated, effective and supportive team is in place. This requires talking to all in the team, both individually and as a group, about their concerns, views and ideas. Use this as an opportunity not to criticise but rather to listen and learn. Research and practice shows that a well-balanced team will outperform any other team.

A group of people become a team if they have:

- a strong leader;
- respect for one another;
- a clear idea of what is expected of them and why;
- an incentive to share resources for the benefit of each other;
- an ability to resolve conflict between themselves; and
- an interest in their own future.

20.4 IDENTIFYING THE BEST OPPORTUNITIES: REVIEW EXISTING SERVICES AND THE COMPETITION

As a team, you should review everything:

- Consider what is going on in the world at large: the demographic changes resulting in an ageing population; government policy making the provision of care for the elderly a major area of concern; the social structure making it less likely for families to care for elderly relatives; the technological revolution making it easier to work from home and find suppliers via the internet, so making it more important for firms to harness its power to remain competitive;

the state of the economy which affects the 'feel good factor' of not just potential clients but also the partners and staff; the availability of appropriately trained staff.

- Gather as much background information as you can. Free annual statistical reports, fact sheets, and research publications are available to download from the Law Society at **www.lawsociety.org.uk/aboutlawsociety/whatwedo/researchandtrends/researchpubs.law**.
- Examine what services are currently offered by the firm in this area, e.g. wills, probate, lasting powers of attorney, living wills, tax advice, help with care in the community decisions.
- Identify current and future potential competition in the area from all sources for these services, e.g. other law firms now (name rivals and identify their strengths and weaknesses), but also will-writing companies and individuals making their own wills (as they represent substitutes for your service) and accountants or large investors such as companies with a consumer focus, e.g. supermarkets, looking to expand into probate services in the future (as these represent threats from new entrants into the field).
- Review which of the services currently offered are profitable and why, and which are not and why. What determines profitability?
  - How much does it cost to deliver the service, e.g. overheads, staff salaries?
  - How much are buyers prepared to pay for the service? If they can do it themselves and see no perceived value in what you can do, then will they really pay? The rewriting of the Non-Contentious Probate Rules 1987 which at the time of writing is under way, is likely to make personal applications easier.
  - Can you minimise the costs and maximise the price?
- Consider any agencies and bodies locally which might provide services and information to the elderly. To what extent are they also substitutes for the service offered by your department? To what extent could some clients, who could not afford to pay your fees but need appropriate help, be referred to them? What can be learnt from the way these bodies approach this potential client group? Can such referrals work both ways?
- Decide what resources the firm already has available or is prepared to commit to this project, e.g. money, time, people (with their particular strengths and weaknesses) and technology.
- Examine what services are often needed but which are not currently provided, e.g. independent financial advice, something solicitors are well placed to offer.

20.5 TACTICS, ACTION PLAN AND REVIEW

20.5.1 Defining aspirations

At the outset of the planning process, management needs to set acceptable standards of financial performance. Questions which need to be resolved include:

- What are acceptable billing figures?
- What are acceptable profit levels?
- What are the required levels of growth?

These targets will be affected by the factors which motivate the practice as a whole. Different firms are driven by different motivations and the business plan must reflect these differences. Motivation will generally be composed of a balance between:

- money;
- power;
- material gain;
- promotion;
- status;
- improving the environment;
- job satisfaction; and
- helping others.

20.5.2 Content of the business plan

Having defined departmental aspirations, an analysis of how to meet those aspirations must be undertaken. There are two simple but effective tools which assist with this task.

PESTE analysis

A PESTE analysis is a review of the external influences and factors operating on the department. It covers the following issues:

P: Political
E: Economic
S: Sociological
T: Technological
E: Environmental

A PESTE analysis within a probate department might consider the following:

1. Political:

    (a) Structural reforms, recent political decisions that have made an impact:

- (i) abolishing the professional prohibition on 'touting' for work;
- (ii) authorised probate practitioners;
- (iii) Legal Services Act 2007.

(b) Financial changes with political origins, e.g. introduction of the transferable nil rate band.
(c) Legislative changes, changes in the law you advise on, and changes in how you practise.

2. Economic: general economic forces impacting on:

(a) ownership of more than one property;
(b) reluctance to pay for optional services during a recession or time of distress;
(c) increasing wealth based largely on property values;
(d) declining estate values due to lifetime giving, care fees and equity release.

3. Sociological:

(a) Social attitudes influencing demand, e.g.:

- (i) towards home ownership;
- (ii) towards cohabitation, divorce and the second family;
- (iii) towards civil partnership.

(b) Consumer awareness affecting client expectations, e.g.:

- (i) price awareness;
- (ii) heightened consumer awareness of legal rights;
- (iii) greater service standard expectations.

(c) Demographic trends, e.g.:

- (i) population trends;
- (ii) age structures, nationally and regionally.

4. Technological: office equipment:

(a) computers have revolutionised business;
(b) methods of doing business, e.g. online banking facilities, telegraphic transfers, e-mail, video-links and others.

5. Environmental:

(a) office location, i.e. ease of access by public transport;
(b) use of 'green' products such as recycled paper.

SWOT analysis

A SWOT analysis is a review of the internal influences and factors operating on the department. It covers the following issues:

S: Strengths
W: Weaknesses
O: Opportunities
T: Threats

Consider the internal strengths and weaknesses of the department or team, and then plan to:

- maximise opportunities (capitalising upon strengths); and
- minimise threats (in order to eliminate weaknesses).

A SWOT analysis is often carried out by examining the department's:

- structure;
- administration;
- finance;
- services;
- partners;
- staff;
- clients;
- know-how and IT; and
- marketing.

A SWOT analysis carried out against these management disciplines within a probate department might consider the following:

1. Structure:

   (a) Does the department have a suitable shape? What are the partner/fee earner/support staff ratios?
   (b) Is the department's management structure appropriate?

2. Administration:

   (a) Who is responsible for administration?
   (b) Does the quality of that administration meet client and staff needs?
   (c) Do the department's systems have their intended effects? What are their intended effects? Could the systems be streamlined to make them more efficient?

   Be ruthless with office procedures. Question everything. Are there any gaps in what you perceive your clients want and what the individual client expects of your service because of that client's:

   (i) past experience of your firm?
   (ii) own needs?
   (iii) view of your competitors' services?
   (iv) knowledge through word of mouth recommendation?

(v) knowledge of any promotional information you have supplied?

Probate is a process that lends itself to standardisation. Where possible, aim to develop uniform procedures within the team. Retain only those steps in the process that are essential, and deliver a quality service in the way the type of clients that the firm serves will recognise as 'quality'.

3. Finance:

(a) Are you charging enough?
(b) What are your profit/billing expectations?
(c) Is your credit control effective?
(d) Are you effective at recovering all your chargeable time?

4. Partners:

(a) Do the partners have the necessary management skills to develop the department?
(b) What is the partnership's attitude towards delegation, teamwork and communication?

5. Staff:

(a) Do you have the right calibre of staff? Do they understand their jobs?
(b) Are your staff properly trained? Do they have skills which are different and more valuable than those of the competition, e.g. bereavement counselling skills, the ability to communicate well with the deaf and blind?
(c) Are they motivated?
(d) Are you over-/under-staffed?
(e) How do you monitor staff performance?

6. Clients:

(a) Who are your clients?
(b) Where are your clients?
(c) What do they want of you?
(d) Are your clients satisfied with your performance?
(e) Do you converse and write in plain English and in such a way as to get the best out of every interaction with your clients?
(f) Ask yourself why do clients ask a law firm to undertake probate work? Perhaps:

(i) they do not know how to do it themselves;
(ii) they do not have the time to do it;
(iii) it would not be an effective use of their time;
(iv) the particular case is too complicated;
(v) there is a dispute and someone independent is required to deal with it;

(vi) they have no choice, the testator or testatrix appointed partners in the firm as executors.

There are many more reasons but whichever reason applies in a particular case will have an effect on how that client perceives the quality of the service you are providing. If the case is complicated the client may be looking to you because your firm is regarded as having an acknowledged expert and the client may only want to deal with that expert. The 'client' may have no choice about dealing with your firm, as members of the firm are the executors. This may be resented, e.g. where the 'client' has acted in an estate personally before and the process holds no mystique. He or she may well focus on how quickly you finish the job and how cheaply you do so.

7. Know-how and IT:

(a) What will the future impact of technology be?
(b) Can you use IT more effectively?
(c) Can you make better use of existing equipment?
(d) Consider how technology can serve you and provide meaningful systems that manual methods could not. Do not just seek to computerise what you already do. Try to see if there is a better way of delivering the service that can be computerised. Often manual systems have grown up over the years in a piecemeal fashion and have become 'the way it has to be done'. Yet the only reason the existing way was developed was because with a manual system it was not possible to organise it in any other way; whereas now you are not limited to manual solutions – computers are there to help!
(e) The client expects you to do things in the most cost-effective way. Why should the client pay for your time to do something manually when the job could be done at a fraction of the price and more efficiently if a particular computer system was used?
(f) Can you make it easy to share skills and experience gained by one person with others in the team, and thus keep those skills and knowledge even if that person chooses to leave? It is no good investing in an IT system, and finding out that only one person knows how to use the system/package just as that person goes on maternity leave!

8. Marketing:

(a) Have you thought through an effective marketing strategy?
(b) Are you providing the right services? Can you keep in touch with the developments in this area to such an extent that you know before your competitors about any changes to rules, services (such as social service delivery in your area), law?
(c) Is your marketing spend sufficient to meet your strategic goals?

20.5.3 Strategic plan

Having carried out the PESTE and SWOT analyses in the light of the department's aspirations, the strategic goals of the department will become clear. Strategic goals will often be very simply expressed and, depending on the aspirations of the firm, will probably be about achieving improved profitability or sustaining profits. It is a good idea not to have too many strategic goals but rather to focus on the key goals which must be achieved under the main headings of:

- Information technology.
- Human resources.
- Finance.
- Quality and risk.
- Marketing.
- Management.

Examples might include:

- to increase the profitability of the private client department by 5 per cent by 31 December 20**; or
- to identify suitable members to join a private client alternative business structure before 6 October 2011.

In today's volatile trading conditions, an appropriate 'strategic window' for planning purposes is perhaps two to three years. Anything longer is unrealistic, as the PESTE and SWOT factors affecting the department are likely to change radically over such a length of time.

Developing a strategy and implementing it is about wanting to succeed. It is hard work! Features of a strategy that contributes to success are:

- it comprises goals that are simple, consistent and longer term;
- it displays a profound understanding of the competitive environment;
- it contains an objective review of resources available; and
- it is effectively implemented.

20.5.4 Operational plan

Once the strategic goals have been established, the next step is to consider the implementation issues and develop an operational plan. The operational plan defines the activities the department must undertake in order to achieve its strategic goals. For example, if the strategic goal was to increase the private client department's profitability by 5 per cent by 31 December 2011 this might translate into a number of operational goals including, for example, 'to increase the number of wills written per month by 20 from 120 to 140 by 31 December 2010'. This is often the main part of any business plan. It is generally short or medium term in character, covering only a one- to two-year period.

The team's commitment to any plans is essential. Without it the plans will never get off the drawing board. Developing a workable strategy needs the people at the 'bottom' to contribute – after all, it is the team who will have to carry it out.

Consult people; encourage ideas; develop suggestions; assess skills

This is where involving the team is essential. Play to their strengths and minimise their weaknesses. As head of department, do you know what are their personal career goals? Could the attainment of those goals be involved in the delivery of the firm's goals? Is an environment where people will freely express their areas of weakness without fear of criticism encouraged? Why not agree with your partners that the team has a combined fee target, whilst agreeing with the team a division that allows you development time, as team leader?

Is sufficient management information available to review fee income at least monthly against the team target? To check how and where the fees were generated? (Always thank introducers of business.) Can you review overheads and identify the cost of supplying the services offered in the way you do?

Structure actions; allocate jobs; delegate; set targets

A useful exercise is to take separate sheets of paper for each of the team's goals and draw up a table to be completed of:

- what needs to be done to achieve it;
- who is to take responsibility for each of these actions;
- how much time will be needed or is available to spend on each action;
- what is the deadline for completion of the action;
- how the team will know that the action has been achieved; and
- what budgets have been set for the activity.

Give people a few weeks to consider what actions they are prepared to commit to and then arrange a follow-up meeting. For example, the strategic goal of increasing the volume of wills written demands consideration of a wide range of issues – research into the marketplace, promotional activity, allocation of additional work, and so on. As the team leader, ensure that the end result is a workable and practical set of actions, which different members of the team have taken responsibility for implementing. Ensure that the team agree a fixed date in the future to conduct an evaluation.

Budgeting is vital but often poorly thought through. Unless there is a strategic reason which justifies it, there is little point in undertaking a promotional campaign if the expenditure involved will be greater than the level of profit that the promotion is anticipated to yield. The budget should therefore include profit and loss and cash flow projections for the period under consideration.

20.5.5 Goals

At all stages of the planning process goals need to be SMART:

- *Specific*: stated in such a way as to aid verification. What evidence would be required to establish success?
- *Measurable*: so that specific data can be collated to identify achievement (or otherwise).
- *Achievable*: to stretch but not over-challenge the individual and the team.
- *Realistic*: avoid arbitrary quantifications such as stipulating a 20 per cent reduction when there are no grounds for thinking this is any more or less attainable than a 50 per cent or 100 per cent reduction.
- *Timed*: how far ahead is it necessary or sensible to set certain objectives – one month/one year? Without imposed deadlines the plan will lose impetus as short-term priorities intervene.

20.5.6 Evaluation and review

If you have not documented what you are trying to achieve, by whom and by when, then the chances are you will not achieve your goals. If you have not considered what 'success' will look like, how will you know whether or not you have achieved it?

Periodically examine how you are doing, what worked and what did not. Were the actions identified successfully completed within budget and on time? If not, why not? What lessons were learnt as a result of trying to achieve the goals set? How can this experience inform the next stage of planning? Then continue with the next stage of action planning.

Ensure that your strategies keep up with the marketplace in which you operate by ongoing review and action. If you do, then you are certain to succeed.

Continually ask yourself the question: how can we get better at what we do?

20.6 STRUCTURE OF DEPARTMENT AND STAFFING ISSUES

The single largest overhead incurred in any probate department is likely to be the payroll and its associated costs. Given the very high ratio of payroll costs to income generated, it is vital to ensure that the best possible value is obtained from the firm's investment in staff.

As a simple example, a significant impact of poor personnel management is often high staff turnover. This not only subjects the department to the disruption encountered when a key member of staff moves on, there are also the significant costs incurred in replacing that member of staff and a learning curve to be overcome when a new member of staff begins work.

Good personnel management practices will ensure that staff are properly motivated, committed to the practice, properly trained and resourced and dedicated to meeting the needs of clients.

Within the department, however small, various roles will be performed:

- **Head of department** holds principal responsibility for the effective and profitable operation of the department. The role encompasses responsibility for:
  - development and implementation of departmental operating plans geared to meeting targets established by the firm;
  - establishment and achievement of departmental budgets and targets;
  - provision of coherent leadership and management support;
  - supervision, training and development of departmental staff; and
  - marketing of the department and development of the department's client base.
- **Fee earners** hold principal responsibility for the delivery of prompt, effective and accurate advice and services. The role encompasses:
  - provision of legal advice and assistance to the firm's clients;
  - development of excellent working relationships with clients and referring agencies alike;
  - familiarisation with and use of the department's IT systems;
  - familiarisation with and adherence to the department's prescribed operating systems and procedures;
  - maintenance and development of relevant technical legal knowledge and skills;
  - direction of support staff to maximise the performance of the department; and
  - resolution of client/referrer enquiries which cannot be dealt with by the support staff.
- **Support staff** hold principal responsibility for providing secretarial and administrative support to the collective fee earning staff. The role encompasses:
  - provision of word processing services and the completion of forms as directed by the fee earners;
  - attending to clients on the telephone and taking messages accurately;
  - establishment and maintenance of accurate filing facilities on behalf of the fee earners and head of department;
  - data input of time records;
  - maintenance of fee earners' diaries and appointments;
  - provision of photocopying services to the department;
  - preparation and sorting of incoming and outgoing mail;

- familiarisation with and adherence to the firm's prescribed operating systems and procedures; and
- answering routine enquiries relating to progress.

It may be that one person fulfils all the roles or that there are several people fulfilling the same roles. When reviewing the structure of the department and its ability to deliver the operational and strategic plans which have been devised, a review of the functions which have to be performed, the roles of the team members in conducting each of the functions and the relevant competencies of personnel to conduct them, is essential.

Some practitioners battle on with unrealistic caseloads believing the firm will not agree to any further staff assistance because overall fee income is low, without looking at why the income is low. If the same person is responsible for organising the way work is done, attracting the work, as well as doing it, it is inevitable that too much emphasis will be placed by that person on doing the work rather than on the significant question of how the work could be achieved in a more cost-effective way.

A cheaper member of staff can justify his or her salary and contribute to the profits much more quickly than a senior member of the firm. The workload of the senior manager could be made more realistic and real improvements to the bottom line achieved just by changing the staffing mix.

The larger the team the more essential it is that the department head is relieved of day-to-day fee earning and allowed to concentrate on the management of the team and its development in line with the strategic goals it has to achieve. This is always hard for professional people, who have undoubtedly been chosen to head up the department or team because of their seniority or technical legal know-how. Whilst their experience will still be called into use and their knowledge of particular clients will inevitably involve them in client contact the effective manager will try to delegate most of the routine matters to free up valuable planning and implementing time.

Gaining commitment from others in the team to take on some of these more routine matters and caseload will only be achieved if promises to deliver on matters that only a partner or manager can implement are kept. This means setting an exemplary example of being a person who can manage their time and their work to beneficial effect. There are only 24 hours in the day and seven days in the week for each and every one of us. The Prime Minister has no more time each day than the head of a department in a law firm. So it is not about having more time, it is about how we use the time available. Achievement is about being focused, organised and effective.

There are plenty of courses, books and programmes to help people to rethink how they manage themselves, but the biggest hurdle is to recognise that this may be a weakness; arrange to do something about it and keep an open mind as to what you may need to alter in your life to change what are essentially bad habits. Remember, it is easy to make New Year's resolutions but so much harder to achieve them.

When the services that the department is to offer clients and the ways in which those services will be delivered have been explored, it will be apparent what legal skills are needed in the team. However, it is also important to work through the processes that are necessary to have in place to deliver these services, and the non-legal skills required in order to operate the processes that are just as essential to the fulfilment of the plan. It then becomes easier to identify what competencies are needed to perform these functions and therefore what mix of staff skills, behaviours and attitudes will be required.

The more you can involve the team in identifying these competencies the easier it will be to develop a guide to job roles, comprising the critical success factors needed for each person to perform his or her role, and to identify any gaps in knowledge and skills which need to be filled by the recruitment of suitable additional staff, the utilisation of appropriate IT, or by the development of existing staff.

The more everyone in the team is involved in this exercise, the more likely it is that you will build a successful team where each member knows what is expected of them and the others in the team, how the individual skills fit together and who is responsible for what activities. It also helps when it comes to setting a pay structure where salaries can be set for the combination of factors within a person's job role for which that person is accountable. The critical success factors for which that person is accountable also provide the yardstick against which his or her own personal performance can be measured both on the job and when implementing regular appraisals to update training and development plans.

20.7 KNOWLEDGE MANAGEMENT AND IT

There are three kinds of knowledge:

- improvement of a process or service;
- exploitation of existing knowledge to develop new processes and services; and
- innovation by applying existing knowledge to produce new knowledge.

20.7.1 Developing knowledge

Managing information successfully means getting the right information, in the right form, to the right person at the right time to add value.

Hugh Garai in *Managing Information* (Gower Publishing, 1997) identified four principles of information management which he argued can turn worthless data into powerful intelligence, which, when applied, will generate effective change:

1. Data + Relevance + Purpose = Information.
2. Information + Insight = Understanding.
3. Understanding + Communication = Intelligence.
4. Intelligence + Action = Effectiveness.

So to work smarter, you need to be able to:

- distinguish between useful information and data;
- sort, order and display information in the most communicative way; and
- identify innovative ways of using the information to add value.

The huge increase in the use of specialist software applications in law firms and departments is changing staffing levels, so that departments are being asked to do more with fewer people who are rarely qualified solicitors. Clients want the ability to have 24 hours a day, seven days a week access to the progress of their matters. Without harnessing the use of IT how can this realistically be done? Case management systems accessed via a web-based product and secured by codes and encryption are already used by some firms, and those who have yet to address these issues and make the investment required are already behind the game.

Management must be allowed to invest development time in order to address these issues, and training time to ensure that equipment and software is being used properly. Otherwise, you will still have to perform to your clients' chosen standards – which may mean working until you drop – or you will eventually lose those clients to other organisations who are prepared to invest and learn.

The result of focusing on developing the knowledge that the client actually wants to access and making it available to them is an improvement in your service which adds value for which a client will pay.

20.7.2 Knowledge from resources such as books, lectures, cases, conferences, precedents

In the search for profit, one of the most popular ways of boosting the bottom line is to reduce the overhead costs, so advocating expenditure on sources of knowledge may not be well received. Actually, what would make both common sense and economic sense would be if the business made a better return on its expenditure on gaining knowledge. Instead of individuals being trained or seeing training as merely gathering continuing professional development points, the firm should want to see more focus in the choice of training and more use by all relevant practitioners in the firm of the information gained by the individual.

Basically, lawyers are selling knowledge based on their experience and skill. It therefore makes sense for a firm to take the explicit knowledge gained from these sources and to enable all who need to access this knowledge to do so freely at any time, e.g. by having access to the firm's precedents via laptop and portable printer when visiting a terminally ill client to prepare an emergency will.

For more information about knowledge management see Chapter 8 'Knowledge management' of Peter Scott (ed.), *Practice Management Handbook*, 2nd edn (Law Society, 2009).

20.7.3 Personal knowledge gained from experience and practical observation

A powerful selling point for any organisation is the experience and skill of its people. This is often the most difficult source of knowledge to capture but as any firm will know if a senior lawyer has died suddenly, or retired without some succession planning having been done, once a source of tacit knowledge about individual clients or tried and tested schemes or just plain human psychology which comes from a lifetime of dealing with people disappears, it can take years to recover, if it ever is.

Trying to identify this kind of experience as knowledge is the first step to being able to design systems to capture it.

If the firm adopts the 'eat what you kill' approach to profit sharing rather than the traditional 'lockstep approach', where rewards reflect a person's long-term contribution to the firm not just current personal profitability, then it is hard to change the culture to one where individual knowledge and experience need to be captured for the long-term good of the firm, whether or not that individual is there. There is no incentive on the individual partner to encourage 'his' clients to be 'firm' clients.

20.7.4 Sharing knowledge

Of systems

It is not just legal knowledge that needs to be shared but experience of the use of any systems in place in the firm, such as file management systems, accounting procedures, how the firm prefers to set out its estate accounts, etc.

Understanding why a particular procedure is undertaken helps newcomers contribute to how systems might be improved or streamlined. Systems that ossify are an impediment to progress but equally checks and safeguards, recognised as such, will more likely be honoured if the people obliged to follow them understand the reason for them.

Of access to information

We need to recognise the old adage 'knowledge is power'. If people are rewarded for keeping information to themselves, then the power is held by individuals and this stops people from being open and willing to share. Shared knowledge is greater power in the marketplace for your firm and that means encouraging understanding of the means of access to as much information as possible within your firm, e.g. enabling fee earners and administrative staff to obtain billing guides and client account balances, rather than this being done only in the accounts department.

Availability

Sharing personal knowledge and experience requires senior people to be available to the more junior. This can be expensive in the short term but over time the investment in developing the younger individuals will be securing the succession to your firm for the future. People may want increasing salaries but they also want opportunities to develop and the chance to see a career path. If senior partners take time to talk to younger lawyers and help them to understand why a problem is usually approached a particular way, this can smooth the transition for clients when the time comes and the senior partner is no longer available. However, if the culture of your firm generally is not positively disposed to this kind of approach, who will carry it forward and so keep these people in whom you have invested within the firm when you retire?

Rewarding the creation of 'firm's knowledge' not just personal knowledge

People often need incentives to change their behaviour. If people are to share what they know, it must become positively pointless to hoard knowledge and it must be made much more financially rewarding to share it. For example, promotion may depend on how well someone acts for the benefit of the team by entering course summaries into the department's knowledge bank for sharing internally.

20.7.5 Training

In developing systems

To what extent does the firm encourage people to learn how to solve a problem? Do solicitors ever attend courses on large changes, such as the tax treatment of trusts, and then never develop the systems needed in the firm to address the changes?

Training in technical matters tends to dominate the training budgets of many firms; however training on how to go about designing and implementing a system for use in the firm, or how to manage a project like the selection and installation of a new IT system, will often be much more useful to senior people. A large organisation may have specialist people to organise this sort of thing, but unless they also have input from you as the probate practitioner, the resulting system may have severe shortcomings that you and your team have to deal with on a daily basis.

In use of systems

It is a common complaint of staff that partners produce a new system, particularly IT systems, and simply say 'there you are, now get on with it'. This type of 'sink or swim' approach is far from cost effective. Work output plummets, stress levels soar and everyone is unhappy. If only the installation and training budget for new IT were at the top of the list of items when purchasing a new system, then some of the 'hidden' costs of change would be properly identified and dealt with in a positive way.

How can a member of staff show a new employee how to use something when they have only learnt by trial and error, which often means half of what the system has to offer is never used? It is human nature to learn enough to get your daily work done and not spend time on learning what else the system can do, even if this might mean missing out on useful shortcuts or safety procedures.

In technical aspects

Achieving strength and depth in the wider areas of law within the probate department helps once more to sell the services of the firm. There is the need to have the ability to undertake estate planning, living wills, financial services, community care planning, as well as the core services of will drafting, lasting powers of attorney preparation and administration, probate and intestate succession and trust drafting and administration.

20.7.6 Using software and the internet

For a further discussion of computing and technology issues see **Chapter 19**.

Estate accounts packages

There are a number of companies offering estate accounts packages for probate and trusts. The Legal Technology Insider website (**www.legaltechnology.com**) contains regularly updated information about what is available.

Some companies offer integrated systems which include probate as part of a suite of software but this is often not as good as the stand-alone systems, several of which have originally been the brainchild of probate practitioners who have developed the program to help themselves with their day-to-day work.

Case management software

This is where the system acts as a comprehensive supporter of the workflow in the probate field, supplying as it does templates, databases of contacts, probate registries, local authorities, standard letters and the forms used in the process. The idea is that you enter the details once about the deceased and the deceased's estate and those databases are interrogated by the system as required to complete the IHT400, the oath, letters to institutions, beneficiaries, executors, etc.

The main advantage is that this enables paralegals to help with the work and reminds the practitioner what to do next, often through the use of task lists or diary reminders.

Forms: data entry only, self-calculating, integrated

Whether or not case management systems are necessary (most firms will have a series of good manual systems which can deal with most of the probate process adequately), the use of technology to complete forms, particularly tax forms, is a must.

Simple forms are available on screen where the details are entered every time. Apart from saving the storage of hard copy stationery and ensuring, through a maintenance package with the supplier, that the most up-to-date form is always used, this data entry type of form does not provide the practitioner with very much more.

Some tax forms are integrated with the production of estate accounts. There are estate accounts packages which include, e.g. IHT400, as the information needed for the one activity is clearly needed for the other, and this might be set up to extract the data when input once and then utilise it for the other use.

Some types of tax form are self-calculating. HMRC itself has now put the integrated version of the IHT400 on its website, allowing the practitioner to download it from the website, enter the client's data offline, save it, and have the program calculate the tax due. Once all the information has been entered, it can be printed off and submitted in the usual way. This software is free, and all that is needed for saving and printing is an additional piece of low-priced software from Adobe (**www.adobe.com**).

As with all software, it takes time to become familiar with it, but once it has been mastered it can save so much time and therefore money. It can also mean that the quality of service to the client improves, as practitioners can produce a set of accounts at the push of a button rather than struggling with the file for half a day!

Library information

The excellent *Internet Newsletter for Lawyers* produced by Delia Venables and Nick Holmes (see **www.venables.co.uk**) has debated the pros and cons of developing an electronic library in comparison with a print library. Electronic libraries are useful research tools, and avoid the danger of 'losing' books and periodicals within an office just when they are needed. It is easier to keep the electronic files up to date (simply by loading the update CD), rather than having to file paper updates, an important but time-consuming job.

However, lawyers are often working not on current law but on the law that applied some time earlier when the cause of action arose, for example, and therefore still need access to paper versions that may contain the relevant information rather than the 'current' information provided electronically. Some legal databases do provide access to 'historic' legislation.

Another difficulty is that there is no industry standard as to how systems are updated. Whilst it is easy to update stand-alone PCs with update CDs, it can be impossible to do so over a network. This may require individual machines to be loaded with relevant CDs, a logistical nightmare and hard to police in order to ensure that your firm complies with user licence conditions.

Websites and e-mail alerts

We live in an age of information overload and certainly within the law there is a plethora of ways that we can access information over the internet – see, for example, **www.lawskills.co.uk** a site specifically designed for estate and trust practitioners.

As many commentators have noted, the law on the internet is not comprehensive nor is it easily accessible for research purposes. This is because the approach taken by each website is independent of the others. Government-supplied statutes are available but not all statutes which are still current. Some case reports are available free of charge on the internet: try **www.bailii.org**. Alongside the freely available information are the subscription-only sites and these are often set up so that users can indicate their chosen area of interest and have delivered to their computer each day an e-mail of developments and articles upon any of those selected subjects, for example LexisNexis and Lawtel.

The daily or periodic update via e-mail is, in theory, a wonderful tool – but how many people actually read them and then save what they need and delete the rest? Are you one of those people who print them all out and add the paper to the growing heaps of reading which are the lawyer's lot? New means of acquiring knowledge need new skills in harnessing it and making it work for you.

20.8 RISK ASSESSMENT AND QUALITY MANAGEMENT SYSTEMS

20.8.1 Risk assessment

To ensure that professional indemnity insurance premiums are kept at manageable levels, risk assessments need to be undertaken. If the firm is committed to the provision of quality services then file management will be at the heart of the office's systems and procedures. The two are linked, as those firms that have gained the Lexcel Quality Mark promoted by the Law Society have found that the premiums quoted for indemnity insurance are sometimes reduced or maintained. See for example the LMS Risk Management Toolkit published by the Law Management section of the Law Society.

It is acknowledged that implementing a file management system will inevitably incur administrative time, but at some stage it is likely that this will become a professional standard, so as always it is better to experiment with it whilst it is not compulsory rather than be faced with having to instigate systems under pressure. There are many firms and individuals who will testify to the advantage of having to implement similar approaches in the litigation areas of practice to continue to offer publicly funded work.

One way of checking whether systems and procedures are safe and reliable is to identify the possible risks that can arise in the probate process and check if robust safety systems are in place.

A few common risks are identified below with their obvious risk management actions alongside.

Risks	**Actions**
Delay – giving rise to complaints	File management system for keeping files under review and moving
Failure to attend to tax matters – giving rise to penalties	Software to help complete forms; training to understand compliance during the administration; checklist/diary to recognise due dates
Missed deadlines – leaving you exposed to negligence	Central diary system
Over-distribution to beneficiaries – giving rise to personal (if PRs) or firm liability to meet shortfall	Estate accounts package should minimise risk of paying out before IHT paid but still need file management system review before distribution
Sending money to wrong person/ address – breach of confidence and potential loss	Accurate database, properly trained staff, file management system to review
Overlooking usefulness of deeds of variation – leaving you exposed to negligence claims	Knowledge and skill as to whether relevant and how to implement them; diary system to record by when deed should be completed
Failure actively to manage investments – giving rise to personal liability for any loss	Training to obtain knowledge and skill over asset management and realisation to deal promptly to best effect

20.8.2 Quality management systems

There are a number of quality management standards which are appropriate for incorporation within law offices and probate departments but perhaps the Law Society's practice management standard Lexcel, which represents Law Society guidance on good management practice are the most appropriate. Specific to the legal profession, the Lexcel system covers:

- management structure;
- services and forward planning;
- financial management;
- managing people;
- office administration;
- case management;
- file management.

The Law Society arranges external accreditation and audit of the standard under the brand name of 'Lexcel'. Accredited practices are able to make use of the Lexcel logo and take part in Lexcel promotional initiatives. The audit process is simplified for those firms which are already accredited under other quality management standards. For an up-to-date statement of the practice management standard and Lexcel, see the 4th edition launched on 23 October 2007 which is accessible from the Law Society's website at **www.lawsociety.org.uk/productsandservices/lexcel.page**.

The standard:

- requires external assessment and audit of the firm seeking accreditation;
- measures the quality of the management systems in place within the practice, and not the quality of the legal advice and experience on offer;
- requires a measure of strategic planning to have been carried out;
- requires defined systems to be in place for the delivery of the product or service on offer; and
- requires effective mechanisms for personnel management, training and development to be in place.

The quality management standard provides a framework within which efficient management practices can be developed and implemented. In particular, systems for the efficient running of client files, incorporating safeguards to minimise the possibility of error or client dissatisfaction, are a key feature of quality management systems within the legal environment.

The need for such systems is clear. When the Solicitors Indemnity Fund (SIF) was the profession's main insurer 5 per cent of claims by number and 4 per cent by settlement amount were attributable to wills and probate matters. Penalty deductibles (effectively, an additional deductible of 50 per cent) arose from failure to:

- execute a deed of variation within two years (IHTA 1984, s.142(1));
- give written notice to HMRC within the six months permitted under IHTA 1984, s.142(2).

20.8.3 File management systems

The checks and balances inherent in an efficient file management system can be broken down into a series of key areas:

- response to enquiry and collection of marketing information;
- providing costs information and follow-up;
- allocation of work;
- opening a file;
- use of checklists;
- undertakings;
- arrangement of file contents;
- file supervision to include fee earner review, file review and the legal process;

- updating the client;
- file closure; and
- complaint handling systems.

20.8.4 Response to enquiries

The provision of telephone quotations is often seen as a mere irritant. Many probate practitioners, when asked to give a quotation over the phone, will do so briefly and without any attempt at 'selling' the service or the department. It is important to:

- give responsibility for responding to enquiries to the person who is best equipped to do it – not necessarily a partner but ideally someone with:
  - a good telephone manner;
  - sales experience; and
  - an outgoing personality;
- prepare a checklist of all the information that must be provided to the client;
- take a positive approach: not a defensive attitude to competitive pricing;
- cross-sell: ensure that the client is well aware of all the issues and services attached to his initial enquiry. You may, for example, encourage clients to consider a lasting power of attorney whilst discussing wills (see **Chapter 21** on marketing);
- capture information: it is vital to keep a record of the enquiry and to find out from the client what prompted the enquiry in the first place. Knowing the source of the enquiry will enable firms to monitor and plan their marketing strategy for the future.

20.8.5 Information on costs and follow-up

This is a major source of client dissatisfaction and complaint. It is compulsory under the Solicitor's Code of Conduct 2007 to address how costs will be calculated at the outset and in particular to provide terms of business setting out whether the 'value' element will be used in calculating the bill in a probate matter. For a further discussion see **Chapter 3**.

Even if it was not compulsory it is certainly true that the full and adequate provision of information about the likely costs of the matter, at the start and during its progress, will assist the client by providing a clear expectation. Failure to provide this information inevitably leads to shock at the size of the final bill. One of the most frequent complaints in probate matters is the unexpected nature of the bill.

It is important to agree the funding arrangements and payment terms. To help convert an enquiry into firm instructions, it is essential to follow up initial enquiries with a personalised letter. Ensure that the response is made on the day of receipt of the initial enquiry, unless this is patently unreasonable, and that it is accompanied by appropriate sales or promotional literature, particularly information concerning related services.

The details of the quotation, the client and the source of the enquiry should be recorded for future follow-up and in order to monitor sources of work and conversion rates.

20.8.6 Allocation of work

The successful probate department will be efficient in confirming instructions in writing to the client and obtaining the necessary data from the client to progress the matter.

Upon receipt of the confirmed instructions, allocate the work to the most appropriate fee earner. This means achieving a balance between:

- experience;
- workloads;
- nature of the instructions; and
- value of the work.

Failure to control the workload being handled by an individual fee earner spells potential disaster, particularly if file management/supervision procedures are absent.

At the same time, undertake a case planning exercise to try to identify problem areas as the matter progresses. In a probate matter, such a planning exercise might cover:

- difficult interpretations of law;
- beneficiaries lacking capacity;
- insolvent estate;
- all assets in possession of deceased;
- outstanding tax or other liabilities;
- whether deed of variation necessary/appropriate;
- IHT implications;
- whether statutory advertisement for creditors required; and
- whether charities have been properly identified.

The case planning exercise might also seek to establish targets and key dates relating to:

- assets collected;
- liabilities settled;
- time limits (variation, etc.);
- interim billing;
- grant of probate; and
- distribution, interim and final.

20.8.7 Opening a file

By now, the vast majority of the information required in order to carry out this function should be available. Client details are available and must be transferred on to the file and on to any electronic database or case management software, if in place.

20.8.8 Use of checklists or case management systems

Fee earners should complete checklists at key stages in the conduct of the matter and will be prompted to do so by case management systems. The purpose of a checklist is to act as an *aide-mémoire* to ensure that all relevant professional issues have been properly addressed prior to moving forward to the next stage in the matter.

If all is as it should be, the checklist will act as evidence on the file to confirm this: if the checklist throws up an omission, no matter how major or minor, the fee earner will be prompted to go back into the file to rectify the identified problem.

20.8.9 Undertakings

Strict control is required over the granting of undertakings, which bind the firm and its partners. Any undertakings, other than standard wording undertakings (e.g. those recommended by the Law Society in a conveyancing transaction), should receive a partner's prior authority.

A central register of undertakings granted should be established in addition to a clear record being placed on the file. Many firms now use a system of synopsis sheets on the front covers of files, which summarise key data relating to the file: it is sensible to include space on the synopsis sheet to show when an undertaking has been granted. Verbal undertakings should always be confirmed in writing.

20.8.10 Arrangement of file contents

Case files should be laid out neatly to ensure easy accessibility to all information by all fee earners and support staff and to enable supervisors regularly to review work. Working papers should be arranged so that:

- all correspondence is in sequence on a filing clip;
- all file notes/attendance notes are stored in sequence on the correspondence clip;
- a synopsis sheet is prominently attached to all files;
- deeds and other documents of title are stored in secure filing facilities, properly cross-referred to the file; and
- any other papers are neatly arranged on the file.

20.8.11 File supervision

Supervision of the management of the matter breaks down into two areas:

- fee earner supervision; and
- file review.

Fee earner supervision

Supervision equates to effective support of the fee earner. The objective of supervision is to ensure that:

- all fee earners know who is supervising them;
- arrangements to ensure supervision of the conduct of case work are in place and understood within the department;
- arrangements are in place for a regular independent review of case files in terms of procedural and legal content; and
- arrangements are in place to supervise the conduct of work carried out by non-fee earning staff.

The supervision process tends to be divided into three areas:

- checking of incoming post;
- checking (but not necessarily signing) of all outgoing post; and
- regular supervision meetings.

The level of supervision required will depend upon the experience of the fee earner concerned. Fee earners who are considered to be of sufficient experience should be granted the ability to supervise their own post, but they should still be subject to regular supervision meetings by their supervisor.

Base the frequency of supervision meetings on the fee earner's experience. Meetings should include coverage of issues such as:

- new cases taken on;
- existing workloads;
- progress on current cases;
- problem clients;
- the outcome of cases;
- training needs;
- undertakings granted or given;
- any other problems encountered.

The purpose of the meeting is for the supervisor to guide and assist the fee earner in the delivery of legal services.

File review

All files should be subject to independent periodic review. The review should cover both procedural matters and substantive legal issues. A supervisor who is independent from the day-to-day conduct of the matter should carry out the review.

The frequency of reviews is dependent upon the experience of the fee earner involved: five files per quarter will give an accurate, cross-sectional overview of the workload of most fee earners. The file review should be evidenced by means of a file review sheet which should be signed off and agreed by both parties to the review process. The review should check at least the following issues:

- substantive legal issues properly addressed;
- papers referenced;
- file notes used consistently;
- undertakings recorded;
- conflict of interest check conducted;
- requirements or instructions of the client recorded;
- advice given recorded;
- action to be taken recorded;
- costs arrangements recorded;
- terms of business despatched;
- key dates recorded and backed up;
- client properly updated;
- changes in costs notified.

Any poor levels of compliance should be drawn to the fee earner's attention and rectified within an agreed period of time.

20.8.12 Updating the client

Fee earners should ensure that clients are appropriately updated throughout the matter and this includes ensuring that:

- information about action taken in a case, or its handling, is given to the client promptly;
- information relating to delays is passed on to the client immediately.

Both of the above points should be evidenced on file, either by attendance notes or by means of a copy letter to the client.

20.8.13 At the end of the matter

Proper procedures need to be put in place to ensure that any outstanding points are properly dealt with before the file is closed formally within the firm. This is best achieved by means of a file closure checklist. Issues addressed on the checklist should include:

- that the client has been informed of the outcome of the matter;
- that the client (or beneficiary in a probate) has been accounted to for any outstanding money;
- that interest on the client account has been calculated (where applicable);
- that original documents have been returned to the client unless storage arrangements have been agreed;
- that, where appropriate, the client has been informed about arrangements for storage and retrieval of papers;
- that the client has been advised whether the matter should be reviewed in the future, and if so, when;
- that final bills have been received and settled and that account balances are zero;
- that a future review date (if applicable) has been diaried forward and that a file destruction date has been allocated.

20.8.14 Complaint systems

Complaint systems are not put in place simply to provide clients with the ability to whinge. Complaint systems are a part of the process of assessing client satisfaction. They are a means of identifying problems, resolving those problems and ensuring that the resulting benefit is passed on to the client base. Complaint systems should include a means not only of resolving the initial client complaint, but also of planning to ensure that the problem which gave rise to it never recurs. We should now treat queries over costs or fees as a complaint.

In probate matters it is possible that complaints are received from residuary beneficiaries, particularly in cases where members of the firm are the only executors, and our rules dictate that the residuary beneficiaries would have to approve the costs in any event.

20.9 MARKETING

For further discussion see **Chapter 21**.

20.9.1 New customers versus existing clients

Profitable organisations recognise that the best source of profit and sustainable revenue is gained by focusing on existing clients. It costs far more to convert a prospective client into an actual client than to sell more services to an existing client.

This assumes, however, that the client is a potential repeat buyer of the services offered and that the segment of the market being targeted will generate good and profitable business. If the type of client and the type of service are not in a profitable segment of the market, no amount of selling to them will generate good business.

The current emphasis stresses client relationship management (CRM), i.e. that a firm should develop close alignment with its clients, being able to customise its messages and activities to the different needs and values of its clients.

20.9.2 Client relationship management

The smaller firm has probably been practising CRM for years: it offers a service that is personal to each client. This works for as long as only one person deals with that client, but as the firm grows and as the personnel change it is inevitable that the 'closeness' of the service offered originally is weakened, and faced with this clients often choose to take the opportunity to move to another practice.

To learn enough to differentiate between clients the firm will need to have a system for capturing each individual's contact with the client (particularly if it wishes to cross-sell probate services to clients who have only used the litigation or conveyancing services) so that it can keep track of the dialogues and interactions which will help with your side of the work that the firm proposes to do for the client.

Clients find it much more difficult to start over with another firm, so you need to help them to create their own barrier to leaving your firm behind. You are trying to build and keep their trust. To keep them biased towards your firm, you need to find out what the client values from the way your firm delivers its services and then make sure that this is what you deliver to the client.

Clients are always going to value things that make their life easier – the challenge is to find out what this might be for the probate service. Can frequent visits to the office be avoided, thus saving them time, by giving clients regular reports, or allowing them access to basic information over the internet? The more your marketing can identify what the individual client is doing (behaviour) and thinking (feelings) the more emotional attachment there will be to your firm if you address these behaviours and feelings, and the more likely it is they will stick with you.

Everyone in the team needs to be able to adapt his or her delivery to suit the level of sophistication of the particular client. Do be clear about:

- what the service offered actually entails;
- how much this service is actually going to cost;
- how the level of cost is justified for the type of service provided; and
- how any problems will be dealt with.

Make contact with the bodies who are providing services to the elderly locally: provide free advice, join the local committee, discover what they are looking for from the lawyer. In this way, the profile of the firm to undertake work in this field in your area will be raised, encouraging referral of work.

Market the team's services by undertaking seminars to local groups, to clients, with the local care agencies, and write editorials for publications. However, you cannot market successfully until you are clear about what it is you are marketing.

When the firm has developed its own specific value chain to its satisfaction it can promote this value to its clients, e.g. by having better IT and systems than rival firms to collect all information necessary both accurately and efficiently (lower cost advantage), or by performing activities in a unique way, such as producing the will at the person's place of work or home to increase perceived value to the client (differentiation advantage).

In the will-drafting sector, solicitors are not the only people offering the service, so it is important to benchmark not just other solicitors' value chains (which is difficult outside groups such as LawNet or outside local areas) but other organisations or firms that might see this as a service to offer.

Several years ago the Law Society commissioned a benchmarking study of other professions and commercial companies in relation to client care. The result of this was that solicitors were advised to manage expectations and communications. The report recommended that:

- You are specific and clear in all communications:
  - use of plain English – have you ever appraised the competence of the practitioners in your firm in this respect?
  - use of guidance notes and leaflets – does your firm have clear terms and conditions of business or client care guide? Do you use explanatory leaflets that you have tried and tested for understanding by lay people?
- You know the concerns of your audience, i.e. the different needs of different types of client:
  - Scenario 1: you are invited to speak at an Age UK lunch club about what is involved in making a will; you are permitted to promote your own firm's will-making service. What would you say?
  - Scenario 2: the Excess Bank plc invites you to a seminar it is holding for some of its high net worth clients. The Bank does not have its own will-drafting service. It is recognised as being expert at putting its customers first. Do you offer to make a presentation? What would you say?
  - Scenario 3: the local branch of the Institute of Directors is holding a trade fair. Do you take part? How would you present the firm's will-writing service?
- You match content and style to your market, i.e. if you only act for scenario 1 clients, it is no good offering a scenario 3 service.
- You never commit without being able to deliver: it is a marketing adage that you should always under-promise and over-deliver, i.e. promise to produce a new will in two weeks' time and produce it in one week.
- You make rules and guidelines accessible to all:
  - internally, involve staff in designing and monitoring;
  - externally, ensure lay people can understand what is intended.

20.10 SUMMARY

1. Take your firm's business objectives.
2. Apply them to your department's strategic aspirations.
3. Review your firm's competition for similar services.
4. Conduct a PESTE and SWOT analysis of your department and its service provision.
5. Compare these with the competition and set your department some benchmarks.
6. Set down the department's agreed operational plan and allocate responsibilities for achievement between people in the team.
7. Be clear and precise about how you will know whether you have achieved your operational goals.
8. Implement your plan.
9. Review your performance against the plan.
10. Take forward what you have learnt to the next planning cycle.

CHAPTER 21

Marketing wills, probate and other private client services

Kim Tasso

21.1 INTRODUCTION

This chapter aims to:

- dispel the myths about marketing and business development and to explain the core concepts that are relevant to wills and probate practitioners;
- provide an analysis and planning framework to help probate practitioners understand their present position, articulate what they want to achieve and to develop effective action plans;
- offer practical guidance on selecting which of the many marketing approaches are appropriate for probate practitioners in their different markets – including the digital marketing revolution and topics such as social media, blogs and Twitter; and
- share insight through comments and marketing case studies from a variety of probate practitioners around the United Kingdom.

Marketing is not a concept that is comfortable for many wills, trust and probate practitioners. There is still a feeling that those in 'the death department' should resist the modern management approaches that their colleagues in the commercial departments have embraced and that by simply doing great work and keeping clients satisfied they will continue to prosper. Whilst I wholeheartedly agree that you must have strong technical expertise and provide excellent service as the foundation of a successful probate practice, I – and many probate practitioners – know that much more must be done to secure the future of a probate practice. I hope this chapter helps persuade you of the merits of this view and provides the tools you need to embrace marketing.

It should be noted that the markets for and marketing of wills can be significantly different from the markets for tax, trusts and probate. Also, the marketing approaches accessible and suitable for sole practitioners and high street firms are different from those used by their colleagues in the larger firms. This chapter will try to address these different perspectives and needs.

Market comment: Boodle Hatfield

Boodle Hatfield is based in Mayfair in London and Oxford. It has a total of 32 partners, with ten in the private client department.

There is a general feeling that the Legal Services Act 2007 will not have too much impact on the higher end of the market, because the service that firms like ours provide is part of an integrated package that high net worth individuals will probably continue to use for their overall planning much as they have done in the past. However, we believe that it will have an impact on the lower end of the market.

All the research indicates that the general public, and particularly younger people, are likely to start going to large organisations such as Tesco or their banks. The attraction of a known and trusted brand is very strong and the image of solicitors is often of being expensive and unapproachable. We are concerned that the changes to legalisation will impact on the quality of advice and the protection of the public. Clearly there is a danger that if people with no formal qualifications, no insurance and no regulation are allowed to write wills then mistakes will happen and the public will not be as protected.

On the more positive side, as house prices start to rise again, more people will need tax planning advice and this may encourage them to continue to seek advice from solicitors. HMRC is becoming more demanding in terms of having correct values before the grant of probate is obtained so we may see more people seeking legal advice as a result. There is also a growing need to interact with lawyers in other jurisdictions as people become more mobile and own more assets overseas. There is therefore a greater need for assistance on issues such as residence, domicile and international taxation and succession from solicitors.

Furthermore, the world is becoming more litigious and therefore the demand for contentious probate support will increase – there are more fragmented and complicated family structures now and increases in individual wealth will probably lead to further increases in disputes over wills/will trusts.

21.2 UNDERSTANDING THE BASIC PRINCIPLES OF MARKETING

21.2.1 What is marketing?

Some people think that marketing is the preserve of those in the marketing department – managing the production of brochures, seminars and websites. But this is only a small part of the picture, because real marketing involves all those who provide wills or probate advice, and extends to issues such as market research, the analysis of present clients and future opportunities, strategic decisions of what services will be provided to whom and how and at what price.

'Marketing is the management process responsible for anticipating and meeting client needs profitably' is the Chartered Institute of Marketing's official definition and one that few professionals would argue with – after all, isn't every lawyer there to meet the needs of their clients whilst making a modest profit?

Marketing is a philosophy that focuses – at every point in the firm – on the needs of the client. From a service delivery perspective, all members of the firm who have contact with clients and referrers (whether as a receptionist, switchboard operator, secretary, trainee, legal executive, etc.) create an impression of the firm and the probate team and either support or undermine the marketing effort. From a cross-selling perspective, everyone in the firm must be aware of what the probate team has to offer, including its particular strengths and how to introduce clients to the services available.

Marketing comprises a number of elements that are blended together into what is called 'the marketing mix':

- *Product* – The legal expertise and the way in which advice is delivered. Very often clients of the wills and probate team will be unable to determine whether the legal advice they receive is good or bad. However, they will make a judgment about the service depending on how that advice is delivered to them. Was the receptionist friendly? Were the meeting rooms pleasant? Did the solicitor make an effort to understand their particular concerns? Were things explained in a way that was easy to understand? Were letters and documents in a consistent style? Was it easy to contact the solicitor concerned? Were messages answered promptly? Were the right information and particular aspects of the service available online? Were the benefits and value received good enough? To what extent is the service from your firm different from or better than the service available from other providers – whether these are will writers, other solicitors or internet-based services?
- *People* – It follows then that the lawyers and their support staff are a critical part of the marketing process and must therefore be included in the marketing, planning and service delivery process. This is likely to involve training and internal communications programmes for them.
- *Place* – The various markets where the services are promoted and delivered or the channels involved, e.g. high street office, out of town offices, at a client's home and web-based services. There are many different markets for wills and probate practitioners, such as the general public, financial advisers and directors within commercial organisations. These markets will also have different needs; for example young married couples will have concerns relating to their own families and their relatives, different from the concerns of older people living on their own or in care homes. Similarly, those with little wealth and few assets will have needs that are different from the needs of those with significant assets that may be within trusts or overseas.
- *Price* – Some markets may choose their advisers on the basis of price alone whereas others will be more concerned with the reputation of the adviser, their past relationship, other services provided, or the particular service or value provided.
- *Promotion* – This concerns all those communications activities designed to alert clients, referrers and potential clients to your wills and probate services and to generate new clients and new work.

These different elements are explored further in the remainder of this chapter but it is important that all elements are considered together. A promotional campaign alone is unlikely to succeed.

There is often some confusion within the legal profession about the terms 'marketing', 'selling' and 'business development'. They are distinct activities aimed at different parts of an ongoing and integrated cycle (see **Figure 21.1**).

Figure 21.1 The business development cycle in law firms

21.2.2 What is selling?

Marketing is concerned with identifying needs in the market (therefore research and analysis are important), identifying or developing the services that meet those needs and communicating the appropriate messages to the market. Marketing is also concerned with developing the reputation or brand of the firm, service or individual. If marketing is successful then enquiries and opportunities to meet with potential referrers and clients will be generated.

When you move from communicating with a market to communicating with a particular individual or organisation, you have moved into the selling phase. Here the focus is on the specific needs of that one individual rather than the generalised needs of the whole market. Some argue that selling is more orientated to 'pushing' the product or service being sold, although in the legal market the most successful selling is driven by the needs of the buyer.

Typically in a law firm, selling is the preserve of the lawyers who talk to and meet with clients and who have the experience and knowledge to promote their own and the firm's services. Sometimes, there is a formal tendering process (or 'beauty parade') involved if there is a large volume of work or a legal panel at the client organisation – for example, with local authority social services teams.

When you convert a prospect through successful selling (this may be the way you field enquiries through the web or on the telephone, or as a result of meetings) it results in the firm gaining a client. However, one set of instructions does not a client make. Continued marketing and selling to that client (within the framework of a client relationship management (CRM) programme: see below) will be needed to ensure that further instructions are received for additional or new services. This is a vital activity in every law firm, as usually around 80 per cent of a firm's income is from existing clients and referrers. Typically, this area of client or relationship development is where the majority of lawyers focus their efforts.

Whilst some will argue that you only undertake one probate per client, the essence of this is true – but a wills client or someone receiving tax advice for a significant family estate who is looked after through many years will continue to instruct the firm. An accountant or independent financial adviser (IFA) who refers a number of clients and matters across will continue to do so as long as the relationship and service is good and contact is regular.

This view of marketing should dispel the myth that it is only about new business: a major component of law firm marketing is about developing the existing client and referrer base through relationship marketing.

21.2.3 Consumer (private client) versus business-to-business (commercial) marketing

Before we embark on a practical framework to get you marketing your probate and wills practice, you need to appreciate that marketing techniques vary depending on the nature of your target clients. The importance of segmenting the market into smaller, more manageable chunks with common characteristics or needs must be considered. Clever segmentation can result in a highly profitable niche practice, which makes achieving a premium fee for specialist work easier.

When promoting wills, you are typically targeting private individuals or families. There are over 60 million people in the United Kingdom and they can be grouped by socio-economic group, by age, by location, by household, by lifestyle and in various other ways. Even though the firm may have focused on a particular group, it would be difficult and not very cost effective to try to mail all members of that group or to spend hours in one-to-one meetings. So, more indirect methods of marketing might be adopted, such as advertising or media relations. The members of each group or segment will have common interests or needs that can be addressed within a specific marketing campaign. The smaller and more focused the segment, the easier it will be to reach the members with a suitable marketing tool and the easier it will be to tailor your message to address their specific needs.

Some elements of the private client market are keen to use the internet, and there are a number of examples of successful websites that provide an efficient online solution to simple wills and probate matters. Similarly, other elements of the private client market appreciate a much greater level of face-to-face interaction when dealing with legal matters, perhaps even in their own home environment. By segmenting the market, the service, the price and the promotional activity can be tailored more precisely to their needs.

Case study: Kaye Tesler technology

Michael Kaye, principal of high street practice Kaye Tesler & Co., uses an innovative website to target a specific segment.

People my age ask each other for recommendations. Those at university and the younger generation think nothing of getting online and seeking the information they need that way. It is a fundamental attitude and buying shift.

We are targeting those in the 35–50 year age group whose parents or elderly relatives have smaller estates – there is rarely any inheritance tax. They don't want advice – they know how to gather and distribute the estate – they want a finished product in applying for the relevant grant. The interactive website makes them read through some explanatory material and prompts them for the information we require. This information then goes direct into our computer system so the relevant forms and documentation are produced. We state the relevant warnings and disclaimers for those with more complicated needs. Our site has generated enquiries and probate work for several years and demand for this service has increased. More surprisingly, it has generated a lot of ex pat probate work and a number of probate claims especially matters under the Inheritance (Provision for Family and Dependants) Act 1975. Technology means we can provide an efficient, interactive service that meets the specific needs of our target clients while generating spin-off conveyancing and litigation work. The internet environment means that the small firms like mine are on an even playing field with the largest firms in the country.

For example, you might adopt a radically different approach and decide to target businesses in your area, offering a will-writing service to their employees. There are significantly fewer businesses than individuals and there is a greater wealth of information about them in various public directories and publications. Business people are less likely to be reached effectively through advertising so it might be appropriate to adopt a more direct approach to marketing to this group: by direct e-mail, through seminars or perhaps by arranging for a lawyer to make visits to employers' premises. Their needs will be different too: whereas individuals might need a will for peace of mind, to provide for their children, to minimise their tax liabilities on death, etc., a business will have different priorities. If a company offers a will-writing service to its employees it might be because it is genuinely concerned with staff welfare, it might be more concerned with minimising time away from the place of employment, or it might wish to minimise difficulties for the company's pension scheme in the event of death in service. Therefore, the way of reaching the business audience will be different and the message communicated needs to be different.

A further alternative might be to decide to reach referrer organisations to generate will or probate business, such as retirement homes, hospices, doctors, accountants, advice centres, charities or even banks. Here you are targeting organisations so the business-to-business techniques are more likely to be effective.

Case study: Russell-Cooke – referrer relationships

Russell-Cooke is a 150-lawyer firm with offices in Putney, Kingston and Central London. As well as a thriving private client practice, there is a specialist French property and estates administration team and a residential conveyancing team who work together. Michael Parkinson is a partner, formerly at a leading City firm, who now works alongside head of the private client team Richard Frimstone.

Most of our marketing activity is ad hoc and tends to focus on developing relationships with referrers – we have great relationships with accountants who are a rich vein of work and law firms where we target those without private client teams or who lack cross-border expertise. Interestingly, law firms who are dealing with probate disputes sometimes appoint us as neutral administrators.

We spend a lot of time being chased by investment managers but the work for them or from them is always limited – clients very rarely seek new investment advisers – they have their existing relationships which continue unless there is a disaster. On the other hand, we spend a lot of time with accountants where we can push out some work to them but they understand that it is more about working together for the same clients and providing a really good specialist and expert service than it is about reciprocal arrangements.

In marketing terms, this is the difference between consumer (private client) and business-to-business (commercial client or referrer) marketing. Often, lawyers do not make this distinction and use the wrong technique as a result. As a rule of thumb (there are always exceptions), if you are marketing to consumers you use indirect methods, while for businesses you use more direct approaches – although the digital revolution has blurred the distinctions. The following are the various techniques that could perform these tasks:

Indirect methods (for private individuals)	Direct methods (for organisations)
Advertising	Networking
Signs/posters	Selling (presentations and visits)
Media relations and publicity	Tenders and pitches
Sponsorship	Direct and digital marketing
Literature (left on display)	Literature (mailed)
Websites	Seminars/briefings
Word of mouth	Hospitality and entertaining
Outsourced (paying a third party organisation for leads)	Telemarketing

21.2.4 A marketing framework for probate practitioners

What follows is a framework to guide practitioners through the various steps to prepare them for effective marketing with a marketing plan to focus their marketing, selling and client development activities. It may seem that a lot of analysis, thinking and planning has to take place before taking any real 'action'. However, many solicitors' marketing fails because insufficient attention is paid to precisely these issues.

21.3 ANALYSING THE PRESENT SITUATION

21.3.1 Analysing current work, clients and sources

Let us start by looking at the sorts of sources of work and clients that a probate practitioner might have:

Those inside the firm	Those outside the firm
Private clients Matrimonial Personal Residential conveyancing Financial services	Private individuals Low income People with ageing parents High net worth/rich clients Company directors
Commercial clients	**Referring individuals**
Corporate/commercial: directors, senior employees, shareholders employment: senior employees	Existing/past clients those who know the solicitor personally
Other	**Referring organisations**
Staff, friends and family	Surveyors/agents Advice centres/bureaux Banks Carers Hospitals/homes Funeral directors Other law firms Accountants

Or it may be possible to produce a diagram of the particular dynamics in this market, like the example in **Figure 21.2**.

This illustrates the great variety of clients and prospective clients (both private and commercial), sources of referral, or work and needs with which wills and probate practitioners must get to grips. Prepare a similar diagram for your own firm. If the firm does not have the necessary information then an early priority is to ensure that systems (usually a client and contact database and a work referral or lead tracking system) are established to collect this information in the future. Marketing without sound information is rather like building on sand – it is without foundation and liable to crumble away.

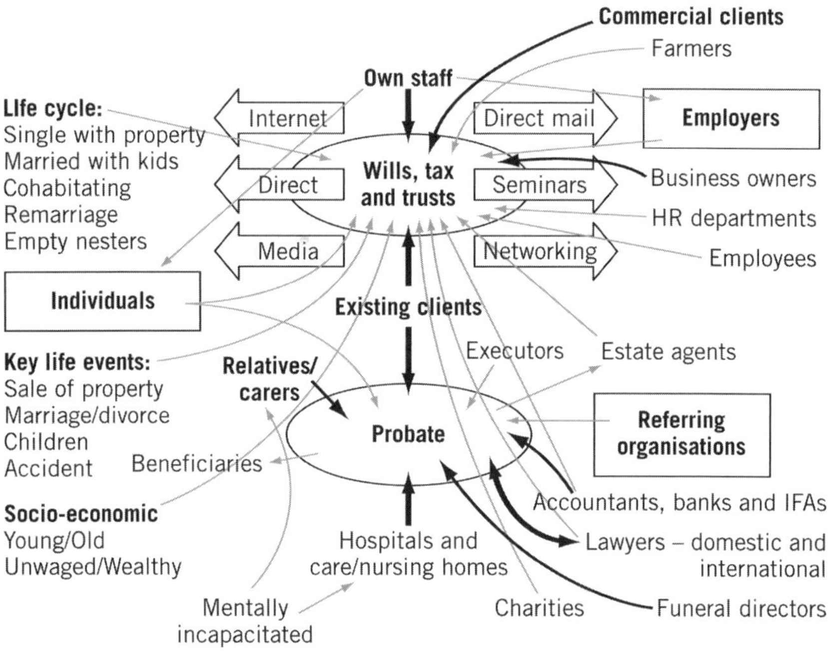

Figure 21.2 Market mapping example

This analysis should provide three or four areas on which you need to concentrate. Or it may show that the marketing challenge is to alter radically the nature of clients and work being generated.

Case study: Laytons – client mix/international/referrers

Ian Burman, partner, is head of the Laytons Private Client group (as well as its Charities Group) which comprises seven lawyers in the London office and a team of five lawyers, headed by Philip Laidlow, in Manchester. He established the Private Client team in 1989 and the Beachcroft Private Client group joined three years ago. He is Chairman of STEP in Central London.

We have a healthy mix of domiciled and non-domiciled clients – and the non-domicile work is increasing. We have some useful offshore connections with intermediaries which we developed more by happy accident than design. But it is a small world – once a non-domiciled comes to the United Kingdom, meets you and likes you then they are more than likely to mention you to their family, friends and colleagues back home and the momentum starts.

If the time is available, talking to existing clients and referrers will be an invaluable aid to future marketing. It will help you to identify why people come to your firm, what they like (and do not like) about the service, what additional help or advice they would like and what it is about your firm that is different from others. It will also provide insight into the clients' point of view and their existing and emerging needs. Time and effort spent investigating the perceptions and satisfaction of existing clients is always paid back.

21.3.2 Reviewing your skills, staff and services

The next thing is to review the skills and abilities of the staff who are promoting and servicing the wills and probate work. Do they have any specialist expertise, for example, in complicated tax issues, in contested wills, in situations with cohabiting couples, with overseas assets? If your firm has some expertise that is unlikely to be found in comparable firms then this may provide a key point of difference which will make targeting and marketing much easier. The need to differentiate your service in some way is important for effective marketing.

Are there any gaps in your expertise? You might identify areas where new or different skills need to be developed within the wills and probate team. Alternatively, your research may reveal that the service provided by some parts of your team is not generating sufficient client satisfaction or is the source of complaints. Training may be needed, or changes in systems and procedures. If there are weaknesses, it may be sensible to concentrate marketing efforts on only those areas where you know you are strong.

Are staff able and motivated to provide great service and to sell? Perhaps interpersonal skills training to develop their enthusiasm, confidence or 'bedside manner' should be considered. It may be useful to review the rewards system so that they are encouraged to invest time and energy in winning new business. Even if you decide to take on the major share of marketing yourself, it is still vital to ensure that all those who have contact with clients understand what you are trying to achieve, and that they deliver the services in the way you have promised and achieve a high level of client satisfaction.

Case study: Royds internal organisation

Royds is a long-established City firm near St Paul's with 17 partners and departments covering corporate, commercial litigation, employment, commercial property but over 20 per cent of its business is from private client, family and residential conveyancing services. Patrick Hart, family partner and head of the Family Wealth department, comments:

We have long seen the synergies between our private client and family teams and our residential conveyancers predominantly work on the properties of the clients of these departments. It therefore made sense to combine them into a super-department which we call the Family Wealth department to provide a truly seamless service – with one partner providing a single point of contact to all the expertise and services needed by a client. This fits in neatly with our 'Partners for Life' positioning which is a core value of the entire firm.

21.3.3 Analysing the market

Now that you understand where your work comes from, and the resources available to develop and deliver work in the future, it is time to look outside your firm to consider issues that may affect your future marketing success. A starting point may be some online research to get a feel for the overall size of the market. For example, if you are targeting the elderly market you need to understand the size of the market – there are 20 million people in the United Kingdom over 50 and they are responsible for 30 per cent of all consumer spending. Sixteen per cent of the population was over 65 in 2007 and this segment grew by 31 per cent. The over-85 segment grew by 65 per cent and is now at 1.2 million.

If you want to focus on the wealthier segments, you might use something like the ACORN tool from CACI to look at the profile of a particular area. Its classification of the 7.9 per cent 'affluent greys' of the population is in contrast to the 2.7 per cent of 'prudent pensioners'.

Case study: Royds – market segments

Whilst we have a long tradition of serving the needs of large family estates and international finance and business people, we have recognised that more recently we have significant numbers of sports people, celebrities, media personalities and entrepreneurial company directors. There is also a growing client base amongst those with specific religious needs (especially Jewish and Islamic faiths) and the LGBT (Lesbian Gay Bisexual and Transsexual) community.

We have had success with a service that promotes family, private client and residential conveyancing services to the employees of large City institutions through a specialist intranet service. We also generated significant interest approaching large City law firms, the global firms of accountants and financial institutions to provide tailor-made packages of legal services for their senior employees.

Furthermore, there were 502,000 deaths in England and Wales in 2006 – the lowest level since 1954 and 230,000 grants of representation, of which 70 per cent were managed by solicitors. If you are more focused on the Court of Protection work it may be useful to see how the national statistics – 2 million people lacking capacity to make decisions looked after by 6 million carers – and over 11,500 people with dementia from black/minority groups – compare this with your region. These ideas provide a starting point – but how do these figures apply to your particular geographic area and the particular segments that are of interest to your firm?

Standard Life research indicates that 57 per cent of UK adults have no will and a further 19 per cent have experienced significant changes that are not reflected in their wills. When the increasing wealth and rising property prices in the United Kingdom are considered, it becomes apparent that the importance of making a will and planning for IHT will become an issue for many more thousands of people than in the past. You can explore the figures on the number of estates being taxed on the Government's online statistics websites.

The long-term changes in the market that might affect future needs for wills and probate should also be taken into account. A review of political, sociological, technological and economic factors may alert you to imminent changes that will drive different client needs and different services. There are many changes that might impact on the future flow of your work: for example deregulation, the impact of civil partnerships, or the rising number of second and third marriages leading to increasingly complex potential claims on estates.

Market comment: Forshaws Davies Ridgway LLP

Forshaws Davies Ridgway LLP is a 17-partner firm in the North West with offices in Warrington, Stockton Heath and Frodsham. Emma Stride is a partner who qualified in 1990.

Over the past 20 years, there has been a significant change in the awareness and expectations of clients. Their demands have increased. They are entitled to more information in writing than ever used to be the case and thus, quite rightly, have greater knowledge about the standard of service they should receive. Beneficiaries expect to receive their entitlements without delay. Many clients from the older generation have embraced the IT revolution and now quite happily use e-mail. Being retired and having time on their hands often means that they are waiting at their computer for a swift response. To alleviate the pressure, practices and procedures need to be streamlined to become as efficient as possible. Where specialist advice is being offered, it is important to be able to demonstrate that this is the case and membership of professional bodies, such as STEP and ACTAPS, is always beneficial. We are living in an ageing population. Life expectancy is increasing. According to the Office for National Statistics, the number of people over pensionable age (taking account of the change in the woman's retirement age) is projected to have increased from nearly 11.4 million in 2006 to 12.2 million by 2011 and will rise to nearly 13.0 million by 2026, reaching over 15.2 million in 2031. It is still a fact that 60 per cent of people die without having made a will which, when set against the above figures, leaves an enormous proportion of the population who will potentially die intestate.

The next step is to think about local demands and needs. The demand in your area may be different from that in other parts of the country depending on, for example, the demographic socio-economic spread of the local population, the prevailing attitudes towards planning, the extent of nursing and private care homes and facilities and the nature of the competition in the area. This information can be found by researching at local reference libraries or contacting local government agencies who often have concise overviews of areas and the main economic and social trends. Networking at local events will also enable you to learn about the dynamics within your local marketplace and will provide vital marketing intelligence. It will have the added benefit of raising your firm's profile for all its services.

Case study: Local market analysis at Rix & Kay

Our three offices operate in very different markets. Uckfield has mature and established professional residents who are in well-paid jobs or running businesses. We have done talks for groups of professionals – GPs on the subject of IHT and we plan to extend this to groups of dentists, vets and even school teachers in due course. However, at Brighton it is a younger, more mobile market with distinct market segments including entrepreneurs and financial services. This means that we have to adapt the services we offer and the marketing approach for the different markets.

A key issue to consider will obviously be the strengths and weaknesses, strategies and activities of your competitors. These may not all be solicitors, and you will also need to consider banks, accountants (especially those with tax and trust departments), financial advisers and independent will writers. In any market you will face a variety of competitors – but just collecting information about your competitors is not sufficient. The information must then be used to modify your approach and activities in order to find a different market position offering different benefits.

21.3.4 Pulling your research together

An analysis of your internal strengths and weaknesses and how these translate into external opportunities and threats may help to identify the key issues on which you need to act. As you consider each opportunity and threat, think what needs to be done – as a specific action – to resolve or grasp the situation. The more time spent synthesising the key findings of your internal and external research, the easier it will be to develop a marketing strategy and action plan that works for you. Encourage all members of your probate team to participate in a discussion about the market and how it is changing – they are a good source of additional information and ideas, and if they are to participate in any changes in the way that the service is delivered or in any specific marketing activities, they will need to know what you are doing and why.

21.4 DECIDING WHAT WORKS FOR YOU

21.4.1 Setting objectives

By looking at the business plan for the firm, you will see the firm's overall objectives, both the financial targets and in terms of the perception and impression that the firm wishes to create in the market and the nature of the key clients it wishes to target. It is at this stage that many wills and probate practitioners find a difficulty, especially if the firm is focusing on developing commercial work rather than private client work. It may also be difficult if there are other practice groups targeting similar client and referrer groups to those targeted by the probate and wills team. All of these groups will need to work together carefully in this case to produce an integrated plan for marketing to private clients.

Once the firm-wide and short-term (usually one year) objectives have been identified, it will be possible to go on to develop short-term and longer-term objectives for the wills and probate team. Setting objectives that are measurable and realistic (see the discussion of SMART goals at **20.5.5** above) is hard, but without these it will be difficult to focus your marketing efforts appropriately and it will be impossible to measure the success of your marketing.

21.5 AGREEING STRATEGY

The external and internal analyses are complete and your objectives are set. The next challenge is to agree an overall strategy for the future – this involves making a number of hard decisions, which will enable efforts to be focused on those areas most likely to yield the results you seek. These decisions might include:

- the markets (and particular segments) which will be targeted;
- the particular services and benefits to be developed and offered;
- how the teams for service delivery and marketing are to be organised – and whether you need to do anything to increase automation or efficiency;
- the balance of effort between marketing to existing as opposed to new clients – this may relate to how much work you think you can generate from other areas of the firm;
- whether a largely indirect (to individuals) or direct (to referrers) approach will be adopted;
- whether there are any particular campaigns – addressing specific issues and/or territories; and
- the particular marketing techniques that will be deployed. This is important where you must consider the cash and time available to invest in business development – some techniques use more cash, whilst others use more time.

Case study: Marketing strategy at Forshaws Davies Ridgway LLP

Forshaws Davies Ridgway LLP is a long-established practice and we have a large bank of wills. In the past, we have always been able to rely on the work generated by those wills and the associated existing clients. The legal services market is changing and becoming increasingly competitive and it is no longer enough to sit back and wait for the work to come to us. The Legal Services Act means that competition is likely to continue to increase over the coming years. We also feel that greater emphasis needs to be given to pre-death work in our marketing strategy – wills, powers of attorney, planning for future care and the like. Our marketing focus is largely on education as we strive to show the public why planning for death is important. National media has also recently become more aware of these matters and we do see noticeable trends when key matters are covered by national television shows.

Case study: Laytons – working with intermediaries

In the early days I invested a lot of time into building a reputation. I wrote a chapter in Tolley's *Administration of Estates* and throughout the 1990s wrote many articles and presented papers and lectured at conferences – both on charity topics and on traditional private client matters. I presented a series of workshops for a leading firm of IFAs on IHT and tax planning at half a dozen centres around the United Kingdom to provide them with a working knowledge of tax and how it works. As a result, I was the first point of contact for them whenever they needed a lawyer after that. Laytons was supportive – they knew that once I had done as much as I could with the existing client base I would have to go out and generate new work. There were early good results – so they could see that it was working.

It has taken a consistent and high level of effort to make and maintain relationships with a variety of intermediaries – whether they are accountants, charity specialists, financial advisers or even other lawyers. But it pays off as the work is flooding in – during the recession last year our Private Client group had our second best year in terms of fee income. And that was in a year when the tax regime was really hammered by the Government.

21.5.1 Agreeing your target market and position

The market and client analyses should be used to identify which particular segments of the market you will focus on. Typical choices include high net worth individuals, as opposed to the lower value mass market. Other segments might include those, for example, with agricultural estates or international assets. Other approaches may focus on particular demographics such as age, gender or occupation. Lifestyle segmentation is another approach. There are many ways to segment the market and the choice will dictate the best methods of marketing – through intermediaries or directly, through advertising or seminars, and so on.

Case study: Boodle Hatfield international referral management

An increasingly significant part of our business is the contentious trust/probate market. These large cases are often international, always extremely complex and usually involve several firms of lawyers from different jurisdictions. The referral network is strong, and lawyers tend to recommend lawyers with whom they have worked well in the past. Marketing in this area is therefore primarily relationship building. During a case it is important to build a rapport and to introduce younger members of the team as much as possible to deepen the relationship. Once the matter is over, it is important to keep in touch through visits, e-mails and newsletters – and sometimes a gentle reminder that another firm 'owes' you a referral doesn't do any harm! The relationship activity should be backed up by PR activity so that the firm's brand in the international arena is strong, the right directory listings are obtained, and the lawyers attend (and speak at) the type of conferences where international intermediaries gather.

The next stage is to decide what position you want to achieve in the market. If all the other wills and probate service providers are pushing the low cost, prepackaged wills 'product', then look at whether there are opportunities for firms offering a higher priced, more tailored 'service'. If others are targeting the low income families, consider targeting the wealthy. If others are focusing on reaching the 'man in the street', why not consider reaching the executive in the boardroom or local employers?

A key element of your positioning will be trying to identify what it is that your firm offers that others do not. This may be expertise in a particular area, it may be your accessibility, it may be your client care philosophy, it may be innovative use of IT (for example providing internet delivery) or the degree of integration with other legal and financial services. Unless a 'cost leadership' strategy is being pursued, a suitable differentiation strategy must be identified.

If it is not possible to differentiate your firm across the whole market, then a particular niche in the market must be identified and selected. For example, a suitable 'segment' might be accounting firms over a certain size with no tax planning capabilities, or agricultural estates.

It is important that your strategy takes a slightly longer-term view as well. Use the positioning stage to identify where you want your wills and probate practice to be in, say, three or four years' time.

Case study: Royds – international seminars

The firm has significant international clients and connections. We sent a team of private client and commercial lawyers to the Middle East where we worked with a global bank and a local law firm to provide a series of seminars on a range of ex-patriot issues. As well as generating high value tax planning work we also received significant instructions from wealthy individuals conducting commercial and real estate transactions in the United Kingdom.

21.5.2 Balance of effort between targeting existing or new clients

Once your desired position in the market is agreed, you then need to decide to what extent you are focusing on developing existing clients and referrers compared to the development of new business. Long-established firms will probably devote more effort to developing and extending existing relationships, whereas newer or smaller firms are more likely to focus on winning new clients.

21.5.3 Direct or indirect approach

As discussed above, another key decision is the extent to which the firm will seek to market to individuals with wills, trusts and probate needs, compared to an approach through intermediaries. Most probate practices will concentrate on targeting accountants, charities, care organisations and such like for referral work. When marketing wills, however, it is more likely that the individuals themselves will be approached. It is likely, therefore, that different strategies and marketing campaigns will be appropriate, depending on the specific needs and services being promoted.

Case study: Forshaws Davies Ridgway LLP – referrers

We have found that many individuals understand that they require a will but do not see it as a priority and therefore the use of promotions can generate work as they focus on members of the public. We as a firm have strong connections with a number of local charities, including the local hospice, and through these charities we also run promotions which provide income or legacies to the charities.

21.5.4 Packaging the product and the people

An integral part of deciding strategy and positioning will be agreeing what it is the firm is selling in the market. Some firms have differentiated the services of their wills and probate team by packaging together a range of services such as wills, living wills, lasting powers of attorney and advice on financing long-term care either in an 'elderly citizens' package or as a 'families with ageing relatives' package. Some firms 'package in' tax, financial, trust and conveyancing services in different combinations to suit the particular needs of slightly different audiences.

Case study: An integrated approach at Boodle Hatfield

At Boodle Hatfield we take an integrated approach to marketing our private client services. Our clients are generally high net worth individuals to whom we provide long-term, complex tax, trusts and succession planning advice, often acting for one family over a number of generations. Probate services and will writing are therefore part of that integrated package of advice we provide, usually over a number of years (and often to generations of the same family).

The actual legal 'product' is similar in all such packages: what differs is the particular needs of the particular target audience being addressed and the emphasis. The packaging can shift the emphasis away from things people are reluctant to consider (the lack of a will when they die) to more positive issues, such as financing the education of grandchildren. Another approach might be to package the way the advice is offered or delivered. For example, there are some highly innovative websites which offer a fixed price procedure for straightforward grants of probate in low value estates or will drafting.

Case study: Specialist expertise and service development at Rix & Kay

Lisa Jones is a partner at Rix & Kay. The firm has 13 partners and around 100 staff in offices based in Brighton, Uckfield and Seaford in Sussex. There are two partners and 18 staff in the Private Client team.

We are fortunate in that we already have a specialist team dedicated to elderly client and Court of Protection work, where we have good links. We recognised there was a need to develop services for a growing elderly population and are getting work from local authorities in this area – having recently succeeded in winning a tender application for block local authority work along with two much larger City firms.

Members of our team have undertaken tax qualifications in order to support the increasingly complex needs of the directors of commercial clients. We have also invested in specialist software so that we can undertake the processing work for probate on a more cost-effective basis – freeing up lawyer time to concentrate on the relationship and advisory aspects.

Some firms have taken this a step further by extending the services provided beyond legal advice, for example, working with bereavement counsellors or with psychologists. The 'trusted adviser' status of many private client solicitors means that they could easily extend – particularly with the advent of multidisciplinary practices – to providing property management, contract management, therapy, house removals or even lifestyle management services as part of the service caring for older, infirm or overseas clients.

Case study: Royds – international services

Whilst we always had a fair amount of non-domicile work, the recent recruitment of a senior private client lawyer who has experience working in-house for trusts at a number of offshore territories such as the Cayman Islands, British Virgin Islands and the Bahamas means our offering in this respect is now much stronger.

Case study: Russell-Cooke – products and specialist services

As well as having a full service private client team serving the domestic market – which has a strong reputation in the area of cross-border matters – we are well known for our French team which deals with both the administration of French estates and French property matters.

In addition to packaging what the firm is actually offering, you need to consider the way in which the advice is delivered and this involves taking a long and hard look at everyone (lawyers, paralegals, secretaries and switchboard staff) involved in client communications for wills and probate services. Ensuring that everyone becomes a valued and integral part of the service promise will require training, communication and involvement in the marketing, planning and implementation process, so if you have not involved them in the process so far, do so now. This can be achieved through team meetings, where you explain what you are trying to achieve and ask those present to discuss the barriers they perceive to those goals and the help they will require in delivering the promise. An alternative approach would be to appoint people to specialist roles, such as handling telephone enquiries, explaining the service, or first meeting management.

21.5.5 Pricing

If they perceive no other differences in what is being offered by different suppliers, clients will choose on price alone. Therefore, if there is no perceived difference in the will-writing or probate service offered by your firm or any other provider, price will dominate the decision. A key element of marketing is to move clients away from thinking about the price to thinking about the benefits of the service and other factors, such as speed, accessibility, ease of use, friendliness, personal service, etc. This is called differentiation.

The price must equate to the value of the service as perceived by clients. They are not interested in the cost of providing that service (i.e. the time taken to produce a perfect document). Therefore, price must be considered in both strategic terms (what are my broad hourly or fixed fee rates and what level of profitability does the firm wish to achieve?) and in tactical terms (how much for this particular piece of work?). Some firms are becoming more creative in pricing, moving away from hourly rates to fixed price deals, value billing, retainer arrangements or shared risk and bonus arrangements. This gives clients the benefit of certainty.

For those operating at the lower end of the market, attention must be paid to the pricing strategies of the online providers as these will shape client expectations. At the time of writing, a quick search reveals the following: **www.tenminutewill.co.uk** offers a will for £29.95 and a lasting power of attorney for £27.95 (£39.95 for a pair); **www.lawpack.co.uk** appeals to business owners with a will for £14.99; **www.doityourselfwills.co.uk** offers a will at £9.95. Increasingly, banks and charities are offering wills free of charge, as a loss leader, in order to gain loyalty and custom in other areas.

Case study: Laytons – pricing

I'm not too worried about the changes in the market. If people want to use Tesco Law or do things cheaply on the internet then that's fine – I'm not going to compete with that. My charge out rate is £370 an hour and clients are happy to pay that because we believe we add value to what they want to achieve. Most of the larger law firms who retained a private client team have priced themselves out of the market – they are very expensive. We have a good reputation – we are ranked in the Legal 500 – and a lot less than those at the top of the market.

Market comment: Russell-Cooke – pricing

The larger law firms are more focused on the corporate drivers in their businesses and this makes their private client work more expensive. If they are looking to add value to their oligarch billionaire clients then their existing private clients are likely to be eased out.

21.5.6 Promotion and internal marketing

The objectives, analyses and strategies should reveal where the firm's marketing efforts are to be focused and should have indicated the types of marketing tool that will be most effective in achieving them. The following section identifies some of the key issues to consider when planning to use some of the most common marketing tools.

21.5.7 Advertising

Advertising is where a media owner (e.g. a directory, a newspaper, a magazine, a radio station, a poster site operator, a TV channel, a website) is paid to reproduce your message exactly as you require. There are two elements to the cost: the cost of designing and producing the advert, and the cost of the media space.

Advertising is a tool to get a simple message to a large audience that is perhaps difficult to reach by other means. It is generally more suited to winning legal aid or private client work. Common places where probate practitioners advertise for private client work include telephone directories, local newspapers and poster sites near advice centres. There are a growing number of magazines targeted at the older generation (for example, the Saga magazine has incredible reach amongst the wealthy over 55s) and some firms place adverts in magazines produced by charities or other advisers. There are over 1,400 trade and technical journals which are targeted at specific business, professional or trade audiences. For example, there are magazines aimed at accountants, independent financial advisers, funeral directors, nursing home staff and those who care for the elderly.

The advent of the internet means that some firms are experimenting with pay per click (PPC) advertising linked to search engines. You can see examples of this easily by typing a phrase such as 'Wills in Birmingham' into Google. As well as the organic search listings, you will see sponsored links at the top and right hand side of the screen – this is where people have paid to have their advertisement shown when the relevant key words are entered. They use tools such as Google Adwords to select and test the chosen key words and set a budget for how much they are prepared to pay for each click-through in a specific period. Most firms will have a dedicated landing page on their website for those who click on these online advertisements.

One-off adverts are rarely effective, so if advertising is the chosen tool, it will be important to make sure that adverts will appear on more than one occasion over a suitable period of time as part of a campaign. You must be clear on the following points before any advertising is attempted:

- Who is my target audience and what media will reach them efficiently?
- What key message am I trying to convey?
  - Is it simple and clear?
  - Does it focus on a specific need and mention benefits?
  - Is it sufficiently different from other solicitors' advertisements?
- What action does it prompt the reader/viewer to take?

With all marketing activities, be sure that the firm can respond to any enquiries that are generated (have switchboard and reception staff been briefed?) and that the response to the advert can be measured to assess its effectiveness. The increasing popularity with online PPC advertising is that you can see exactly how many people clicked on your advert, visited your website and subsequently subscribed to mailing list, RSS feeds (updates from your website or blog) and made enquiries online.

Most solicitors focus on display adverts. Other types to explore include: inserts in printed media; messages on appointment cards; posters; give-aways; leaflets in counter top dispensers; door-to-door leaflets; cable television (considerably cheaper than national or terrestrial television and much more focused on particular areas or audiences); local radio and the promotional materials of non-competing organisations targeting the same audience.

Case study: Russell-Cooke – location signage

We are fortunate with our location on the top of Putney Hill – within sight of the mainline train station and at the crossroads of the main South Circular road. Our sign is prominent so there is a strong level of awareness of the firm locally. At our Kingston office we have a similar advantage – everyone coming over Kingston bridge cannot fail to see our office signs. It's amazing how many people comment on the visibility and effectiveness of our signs. The geographical base is a good complement to our expert London reputation.

21.5.8 Direct mail and e-mails

Direct mail or e-mails are a cost-effective method of reaching commercial clients and referring organisations. The starting point is some form of database which contains, as well as the name of the individual, their position, the name of the organisation, its address, telephone number and e-mail address. Other useful information would be specific areas of interest (e.g. tax advice, overseas property), other relationships or services used within the firm, a list of past contacts and any other information that helps with analysis and segmentation. There are many mailing lists that can be purchased or hired from organisations which specialise in list development or from those, such as magazine owners, who make their lists of subscribers commercially available.

Short, simple letters or e-mails following the AIDA rule (attention, interest, desire and action) are effective, especially when the follow-up action is low commitment (e.g. sending in for an information pack, requesting a copy of a helpful checklist or visiting a website) rather than high commitment (e.g. calling a solicitor or attending a meeting). A covering letter will increase the chances of any brochure or newsletters being read. It may be helpful to facilitate an easy response by providing reply-paid envelopes or freephone telephone numbers. Most firms have websites with further information – and sections that are tailored to particular issues or campaigns – and some have invested in setting up modest call centres to manage enquiries.

Be creative in thinking what might be sent to people that will be of value – items should be focused on specific messages or issues. Copies of articles or of speeches delivered by partners in the firm, feedback or testimonials from clients facing similar situations, invitations to informal briefings or receptions and notification of books or speeches in preparation could all be used. Although there has been a tendency for law firms to produce high quality, glossy promotional materials, direct mail will work just as well (sometimes even better) if the materials are produced smartly and inexpensively in-house. Such items can often feel more immediate and personal than their glossy counterparts. They can also be tailored to specific needs, topical issues or special audiences with ease.

E-mail can be used to communicate on a regular basis with existing clients and referrers as well, helping to build relationships, provide added-value service and keep your firm's name 'front of mind'. This is particularly cost-effective and easy to do if a specialist e-mail alert system is employed.

Please be aware though that there are laws affecting the use of e-mail. You may e-mail clients and referrers but you cannot e-mail prospects unless they have given permission ('opted in') for you to do so.

Case study: Educational video at Sugdens

Kevin Ludgate, a partner at Sugdens solicitors in Huddersfield, produced a short video called 'Making a Will – Explained', which comes complete with a glossary which explains terms such as executor, intestate, residue, trust and witness in the video case cover. He also produced a short colour flier that he mailed out to promote the video. The video is rated 18 with an explanatory statement saying 'Essential viewing for all adults in England and Wales!'. The video explains very simply why you need a will and the likely contents through some realistic examples – a young couple, a middle-aged couple and an older single woman. The feedback he received was excellent and he provides the leaflets and video to intermediaries, building societies, accountants and the like. Kevin's rationale for this exercise was that he had found from research that although people were interested in learning more about wills, they were rather put off by the prospect of meeting a solicitor and the possible cost that might be incurred. A video that they could watch in their own homes at their leisure would overcome both potential problems. He also considers that if a potential client spends 30 minutes watching a video – rather than asking him questions for an hour on general background and common issues – it will make his life easier too: a win-win situation.

21.5.9 Public relations (including media relations)

'Public relations' is a broad term which covers a whole range of activities involving the firm in two-way communications with the various publics it serves. Relevant publics for probate practitioners might include existing wills/probate clients, other clients of the firm, potential clients, local referrers, the local media, existing staff, potential staff, the legal profession and government officials.

Media relations

This is one of the most useful tools for probate practitioners, i.e. communications with the printed and broadcast media. Timely press releases about topical issues, offering the expert views of the firm's tax, probate or private client experts, short articles providing practical advice, articles containing checklists to help readers assess their situation and 'legal problem pages' are all inexpensive (but time intensive) ways of getting your message across. If you regularly scan the main newspapers you can be ready to provide comments and advice when a high profile will or probate case hits the headlines. However, unlike in advertising, the editor will always have the final say on what items are used and the manner in which the material is used, so you have much less control. Unless you have some experience of dealing with the media it is often useful to employ the services of someone who does – freelance press officers can be used on an occasional basis and their rates are often very reasonable. It should be possible to find a public relations officer with good knowledge of and contacts within the media you have targeted. Sue Stapely's book *Media Relations for Lawyers*, 2nd edn (Law Society, 2003) is an excellent introduction.

Case study: Media relations at Seddons

Seddons is a Central London law firm specialising in property, disputes, people and enterprise. The firm has over 70 staff in the heart of the West End from where it serves the needs of many types of commercial organisations.

Marvin Simons, Head of Litigation said 'Arguments arising from care issues or people's involvement with terminally ill friends or relatives prior to their death are on the increase. The rise of so-called "vulture syndrome" – when beneficiaries fall out over the dead person's money, belongings or property – has been blamed for the increase. Last year Seddons commissioned a survey of 3,000 adults which disclosed that one in 10 have been – or are currently – in dispute following a death in the last six months.

It also emerged that three in 10 fear that they will be squeezed out by family members following a relative's death. A quarter admitted they were worried they would end up with nothing and one in five were concerned they would not be treated fairly. Around 17 per cent said they had been promised something by a relative but never received it and 37 per cent did not trust people in their close or extended family. The survey also found 15 per cent would remain in touch with an elderly relative just to be included in their inheritance. On average disputes take 12 months to resolve, yet the majority of people (45 per cent) receive no more than £250 in total. We issued a press release and spoke to national, regional and specialist media – as well as some radio stations – and generated significant publicity as a result. We also received ongoing press coverage (some even a year later) whenever the topic arose again in the general news.'

Case study: Boodle Hatfield and media relations

Public relations is an important part of our marketing. Our partners speak regularly on key conference platforms, we write articles in technical journals in the United Kingdom and those aimed at offshore intermediaries, and also write less technical articles in the type of 'lifestyle' magazines which are read by our clients.

Increasingly, firms are using blogs – a sort of informal, online diary area in an area of their website – to post regular updates and comments (see below). These fulfil a similar role to news releases and can be picked up by the mainstream media to generate further publicity.

Publications

Typical publications might include a firm brochure, a private client brochure or leaflets describing the services offered by the wills/probate team. Again, the key words here are 'focus' and 'benefits'. Too many solicitors' publications focus on 'we' the firm rather than 'you' the client and contain features rather than benefits. Truly client-facing publications will be written from the clients' point of view (e.g. problems, needs, questions, concerns, issues, etc.) rather than the firm's point of view (location, departments, services, etc.). Ideally, publications should contain guidance and advice so that they really add value to the reader.

Newsletters will serve a number of purposes. Whether they are general and aimed at of the firm's clients, or focused on the needs of particular groups (such as private clients, elderly clients, professional carers, etc.), they will:

- alert readers to changes in the law;
- educate them on possible needs they might have;
- provide simple advice so that they can help themselves;
- explain difficult legal issues in simple terms;
- demonstrate the expertise of your lawyers;
- remind them that the firm is proactive and able to assist;
- cross-sell services of the firm; and
- secure the loyalty and memory of existing or dormant clients.

Events

Events which target existing or potential clients or referrers would also fall under the public relations umbrella. Some firms take exhibition or stand space at local county or town shows – an opportunity to meet, face-to-face, local people who might be clients or potential clients and to re-establish contact with local referrers and intermediaries. Stands at trade exhibitions (e.g. for professional carers or home operators) can also be useful if targeted properly.

Case study: Laytons – networking and events

You have to be very selective when it comes to attending events. You can go along to some and it is full of lawyers all chasing the same clients. You need to think about who you are targeting carefully. You can spend a lot of time trying to reach specific individuals but it is always easier to develop a relationship with a key intermediary – through which you can potentially reach hundreds of their clients.

The firm organises an annual party – last year it was at the Tower of London – and the private client lawyers invited clients and key referrers. Most of our entertaining is on a one-to-one basis although we did take about eight people from a large trust company to a day of racing at Ascot. It's important to find something that your clients and intermediaries value and is personal to them.

Speakers

The firm might be able to provide 'expert' speakers to address the audiences of local business, trade or social groups. Organisations such as the Institute of Directors, the Chambers of Commerce and Business Links are often heavily targeted by other solicitors, so seek out more unusual organisations. Similarly, representatives of the firm could be sent to network at these events, the aim being both to develop contacts that might generate or refer business in the future and also to gather vital information or market intelligence about local needs and competitors and to ensure that the firm's name appears regularly at local events.

Seminars

Seminars are covered separately below.

21.5.10 Internal marketing

This area of public relations – communicating with those within the firm – is vitally important to wills and probate practitioners because other members of the firm will be an important source of referrals for your department and because sometimes you may be targeting similar audiences to others in the firm. In smaller firms it is easier to talk informally to the partners, assistants, trainees and secretaries within other departments without having to arrange special meetings or prepare lists of the services provided, the clients served and ways in which you can help each other develop business.

Internal marketing is important because limited resources will be available within the wills and probate team. However, the marketing and communication load can be significantly spread if all members of the firm understand what the team is offering, to whom, the relative benefits and how to 'pass across' clients or referrers who have the sorts of questions or problems with which the probate and wills team can help.

Case study: Internal marketing at Rix & Kay

Internal marketing is important too. All departments are aware of the need to cross-sell the firm's services and do, especially the family, private client and commercial teams. The directors of our commercial clients are keen to make wills and look at ways to save tax. We make sure we attend each others' departmental meetings to identify and pursue such opportunities.

Case study: Internal marketing and cross-selling at Forshaws Davies Ridgway LLP

As a full service legal practice we have a large client base to whom we market our wills and probate services. We actively encourage clients to amend their will whenever there is a major change in their life, whether that is moving house or a change in marital status. We therefore find that marketing to our conveyancing and matrimonial clients provides a significant level of wills work, as well as some interest in powers of attorney and trust matters. This cross-selling of services is key to our marketing strategy.

21.5.11 Organising events and networking

Organising events can take a huge amount of time and preparation. Support staff will need to assist with preparing invitation lists, monitoring the response and the myriad of logistical arrangements (e.g. room preparations, catering, cloakrooms, handouts, audio-visual materials, etc.). At the most informal level, a selection of clients, potential clients or referrers could be invited to your office for lunch or a glass of wine. This provides them with an opportunity to network with other people. However, people may be often invited to 'plain' cocktail parties and receptions, so it will help considerably if there is something that will make your event different, for example, an external guest of honour or by giving the event a theme. Better still, provide a business rationale for the event: so, for example, invite a group of staff involved in residential and nursing homes to an informal round table discussion where issues of common concern (with a legal flavour but not entirely legally focused) can be discussed.

The events taking most effort are those where your legal expertise is being presented or showcased – for example, a briefing for small firms of accountants on IHT planning, or a seminar for high net worth people on the impact of the Chancellor's annual budget. It is often better with high net worth clients to package any wills, tax and probate topics with other private client topics such as property transactions, overseas investment funds, and so on. Inviting external speakers to these events will both increase the attractiveness to your invitees and reduce the burden on your staff of preparing materials. Some firms invite guest speakers to talk on non-legal topics – such as their expeditions to remote parts of the world, their sporting achievements or careers in interesting places or even curators to talk about some aspect of art – to provide a hook as 'entertainment' to their private client events.

Case study: Boodle Hatfield seminars

We maintain regular contact with our clients through e-mail newsletters, newsflashes and client entertainment. This year we are organising a series of seminars for our clients and other professionals. Some of our clients are sharing their own practical experiences, for example on the pitfalls of running a family business or on issues for landed estates, or how to approach philanthropic giving within the family structure. Our delegates are finding it invaluable to hear practical tips from others in the same boat as them. We also regularly invite smaller groups of clients to cultural events such as Garsington, the London Handel Singing Competition or the theatre.

Networking can be used to achieve a number of purposes and can be done at your own and other people's events. For example, you can raise the profile of your firm in the local business community or amongst a particular audience (e.g. local social services people or local GPs). You can effect introductions and start to establish personal relationships with referrers or potential clients. Networking may also be used to help develop your understanding of the needs, interests and motivations of your target audience. It is important that you undertake a systematic analysis of the groups available for networking – too many firms focus only on the legally oriented events where they are only likely to meet other lawyers. There are thousands of other groups – use a reference such as the British Directory of Associations to expand your horizons or check out local media to discover groups specific to your region or town.

Case study: Russell-Cooke – entertaining

Richard has done a lot of article writing, lecturing and contributed to probate textbooks – as have I and others. The audience is mainly other professionals and raising our profile amongst the most highly regarded advisers.

We sponsor Esher Rugby Club which means that we get an allocation of free tickets which are good for client entertaining. We provide some support to the Rose Theatre in Kingston where again we put the tickets that we receive to good use.

Talking to people (and listening carefully to what they say) is one of the best ways to gather market intelligence. Regular attendance at a particular organisation's meetings or events will increase your chances of being recognised and establishing ongoing contacts. Offering to present on topical subjects or to explain complicated legal issues with a wide appeal in a simple way and being seen on speakers' platforms will help to raise your profile. People at the events will then feel a little easier about approaching you in future. Many older probate practitioners have built their successful practices by becoming totally embedded in the local community over decades through community groups, specialist interest or hobby groups or school and religious groups.

Case study: Theatre sponsorship

A small practice in the West Country places a range of inexpensively produced but attractive leaflets on all its services in dispensers at a local theatre. A wills leaflet states that it has members of the Society of Trust and Estate Practitioners and that it also offers an investment management service. This is an example of integrated marketing, where the firm's sponsorship of a popular local arts venue provides: (a) an excellent opportunity to entertain clients and intermediaries in a location where there is a clear link to the firm; (b) publicity and awareness raising from the strong branding in the signage supporting the sponsorship; (c) advertisements in event programmes; and (d) marketing materials on display in a location where they know members of their target audience – better off people of a slightly older generation – will see and read them.

21.5.12 Presentations

After establishing contact (or, indeed, having created an opportunity to establish contact), a short presentation about a topical issue alongside some information about the credentials and experience of your firm, your team and your services will ensure that the relevant information is conveyed efficiently and accurately. Yet not everyone is comfortable making presentations and some lawyers have little experience in public speaking. It is helpful to prepare audio-visual materials (whether these be pre-written sheets to talk against, PowerPoint slides or CD or web-based presentations) to guide the speaker and provide additional interest for the audience. Advance planning and rehearsals are vitally important if a poor quality presentation is not to undermine your professional skills. Summaries of talks should always be distributed, with your name, the firm's name and contact details marked discreetly but clearly on each separate sheet.

21.5.13 Webinars and podcasts

Instead of arranging actual events, some firms have started to use electronic alternatives. For example, a webinar is where the presenter speaks over a telephone line or through a PC while their slides are shown on screen at the remote location of the participants. The advantage of this is that you do not need to get everyone in the same location, although the disadvantage is that you miss out on the opportunity to network with people and make more informal contact. Some firms have found that they can record webinars on popular topics and make them available on an ongoing basis through their websites or popular sites such as YouTube.

Podcasts are similar except they are only providing the commentary rather than the visual elements of an event. These can be downloaded by people and listened to on their PCs or MP3 players.

Case study: Laytons – website

We don't rely on the website. Private client work is all about personal relationships and trust. When clients meet you they assume that you know what you are doing – their only decision is 'Do I like this person?' and you cannot do that on the internet. The internet simply allows them access to us and the services we provide.

Case study: Russell-Cooke – website

The website is a really important source of work on the cross-border and other specialist fronts. If you Google anything relating to cross-border or French or other complex issues then you are likely to find articles by the experts at Russell-Cooke will appear high in the search results.

21.5.14 Social media

There is growing interest in the use of media such as Facebook, LinkedIn and Twitter to promote legal services to both private individuals and organisations. Often, firms will have a blog (see above) where they make regular, informal posts regarding general and legal developments. These blogs can generate a following by readers subscribing to an RSS feed so that they automatically receive updates. Some firms use Twitter (a micro blogging site where posts are limited to just 140 characters) to promote material on their website and blog. There are a couple of examples of firms developing significant followings for their regular Tweets on subject as diverse as issues for ex-pats and those interested in probate.

LinkedIn is a network that is used by many professional and technical users (there are reportedly over a million lawyers worldwide on the system). As well as placing your profile and details of your expertise online, LinkedIn enables you to connect with colleagues, clients, referrers and other contacts who then automatically see any changes to your profile or groups that you might join. Some law firms have created groups focused on private client, probate or elderly client needs. And within these groups they often pose discussion questions or polls where others contribute. It is a good way in which to demonstrate your expertise by participating in debates and offering responses to questions or requests for help.

Case study: Seddons – blogs and social media

We run a series of blogs one of which is targeted at 'People' covering family, private client, wills, probate and residential property matters. Whenever something relevant arises in the mainstream media we try to add comments and advice that relates to ordinary people. We use Twitter to promote the links to blog entries and we also e-mail the links to selected clients, contacts and referrers. We also expand on some of the blog posts in our regular e-newsletters to clients. Together these activities raise awareness of Seddons, increase our visibility in the search engines and drive traffic to our website.

21.5.15 Professional selling

Where the majority of your business development is targeted at third party organisations, then you will need to be familiar with professional selling techniques. Whilst you are effectively selling whenever you convert an enquiry into a client, the sales cycle, processes and technique are quite different for winning business from a referrer or a charity or commercial organisation. You may need to develop relationships with numerous individuals and maintain contact over many months – perhaps years – before you can win the necessary trust and learn sufficient information to make a formal proposal of services. Training in professional selling techniques will improve the confidence and effectiveness of your efforts in this area and allow you to focus your time and attention on tackling each target.

21.5.16 Tenders and pitching

If you are trying to develop business from an organisation – such as a local authority, bank panel or large property business – you may need to undertake a structured selling campaign and go through the process of preparing and presenting a detailed tender. This is a specialist activity where you will need the support and advice from those experienced in this type of activity – for example, those in the commercial departments. The documents you prepare are fundamentally different from any brochures or marketing materials, they are sales documents that must be tailored to the specific issues and needs of the organisation and where you must pay particular attention to how your service is different from and better than competing firms.

21.5.17 Future developments

Technology and markets are changing fast and new marketing approaches are appearing all the time. At the time of writing we are witnessing the start of the smart phone era – with some of the larger law firms developing Apps (applications) for the iPhone. I suppose that it is possible that someone might develop an iPhone App for some aspect of the private client market – for example, with 'push' alerts for when tax regimes change causing a need for modifications to your financial or property assets.

21.5.18 Client relationship management (CRM)

As I mentioned at the start of the chapter, winning new clients is not the sole objective as probably 80 per cent of your work will come from existing clients and referrers. Therefore, you need to devote time and attention to develop programmes to ensure that you remain close to those existing clients and develop the relationships further. This can be achieved alongside some of your activities to attract new business by, for example, ensuring that existing clients receive all relevant newsletters and bulletins and invitations to events and hospitality. Or you may develop activities – such as key account management and client listening programmes – to ensure that you pay special attention to particularly important relationships. An essential tool here is a really good database system that enables you to capture all the relevant contact information, grade the quality of your relationships and indicate the particular areas of interest and nature of relationship management approaches that suit each individual.

Case study: Boodle Hatfield client relationship development

We work very hard at nurturing the relationship with the clients themselves to ensure that they stay loyal and hopefully recommend others. Enthusiastic clients are a great way of obtaining opportunities with others in their social group. Of course, the most important thing is to provide proactive and high quality legal advice, but it is also important to deliver this through a lawyer with whom the client builds empathy over a period of time. We try to match the personality of our lawyers as well as their legal skills to a family. We also introduce lawyers to the younger generations so that they start to build their own relationships. Some get very involved with family activities. This year one of our young lawyers is cycling four 'stages' of the Tour De France (two weeks ahead of the professionals) with some of our clients to raise money for their family charity. There's nothing like shared blisters and aching muscles on training weekends to help build a long-lasting relationship!

21.5.19 Referrer and intermediary management

If you are adopting the indirect approach that was mentioned above then the lion's share of your business development activity will be directed at individuals at referring organisations. Some of the techniques mentioned above will still be appropriate – you will need to raise your profile, send regular information to keep you 'front of mind' and invite them to events where you can catch up and possibly meet each other's contacts.

Some firms will have specific programmes aimed at particularly important referrers – such as a 'five-to-five' meeting where you get five of your staff together with five of their staff to get to know each other better or perhaps a 'young professionals' networking event where the junior people from each of your firms can start building relationships. Perhaps you might plan some form of collaborative activity – such as contributing to each other's newsletters or a joint seminar.

Case study: Probate disputes through referrers at Forshaws Davies Ridgway LLP

We have considerable experience of assisting clients with probate disputes. Due to our reputation and ability in this area we undertake work referred to us by other solicitors and probate professionals. The death of a loved one can be a traumatic time and if there is a dispute regarding the will then this can be even more upsetting and complicated. Many of our peers understand the requirement for specialist knowledge in these matters and therefore refer such matters to our experts so as to provide their clients with the quickest resolution and minimum upset.

Case study: Boodle Hatfield and referrer events

The most valuable source of referrals tends to be from intermediaries and we have developed a shortlist of key intermediaries with whom we work regularly. This has been carefully researched to identify firms who have the same approach to clients as we do and with whom we can build a good working relationship on mutual client activity. We try to refer work to them whenever we can and hope to receive referrals from them as well. We have get-togethers to share technical knowledge. We also regularly socialise with them, both at events organised by ourselves and at industry events. The next event is a World Cup 2010 Table Football competition.

21.5.20 Outsourcing your marketing

Some firms decide to take the ultimate indirect route to marketing and decide to outsource their marketing. This means that they effectively pay a third party to generate leads and work on their behalf. Whilst it can be effective, you must assess the quantity and quality of the leads generated and keep a close eye on the cost per case. Furthermore, you need to assess the risk associated with the source(s) abruptly ending or suddenly deciding to increase the price per lead once you have become dependent.

Case study: Seddons – outsourced marketing

We have experimented with paying for externally sourced leads – for example, by paying an annual subscription to various bodies which then generate interest through mainstream campaigns or online promotion and pass them through to the relevant firm. We found that they vary in effectiveness over time so they must be constantly reviewed for return on investment.

21.6 DEVELOPING AND IMPLEMENTING YOUR PLAN

21.6.1 Developing a marketing and action plan

A marketing plan will be needed in order to draw together the results of your analysis, objective setting, strategy development and consideration of the various marketing tools available. A typical marketing plan would address the following issues:

1. Introduction.
2. Where are we now? An analysis of the current situation.
    - External analysis – general trends, competition, local market.
    - Internal analysis – fees, clients, sources of work, services, skills, people.
    - Summary of critical issues to address.
3. Where do we want to be? Our goals.
    - The firm's goals – financial, clients, work, reputation.
    - The probate, trusts and wills teams goals – short, medium and long term.
    - How we will monitor and measure effectiveness.

4. How will we get there? Our overall strategy.

- How we will organise and resource our marketing and business development effort.
- Additional research and preparation required (e.g. development of a database).
- Product – legal expertise, service delivery, relationships and brand.
- People – recruitment, training, communications, work process, service standards.
- Place – market segmentation, target markets, referrers/clients.
- Price – charging methods and payment plans.
- Promotion – choice of public relations, direct marketing and other tools in appropriate campaigns.

Case study: Marketing planning at Rix & Kay

The major challenge for us is prioritisation. We have lots of ideas about what we could do to generate interest in different areas from the various markets. We are also very conscious of the need to match the different lawyers to the various markets and to their preferred style of marketing. There is a firm-wide marketing plan and it is adaptable to the different areas of work – some elements are highly relevant to the private client team and others less so. We recognise that we have only limited time for marketing so we need to spend time considering the different opportunities so that we focus our efforts accordingly. We have common themes across all specialisations – such as the need to provide a 'cradle to grave' service and we have workshops where every member of the team comes together to consider the marketing activities for the firm and team overall and the campaigns supporting specific market or specialist service promotion.

---

5. Budgets and action plan.

The next stage is to prepare a short, clear, task-orientated action plan, assigning the names of the responsible individuals and the target dates by which the tasks will be completed. The action plan will achieve a number of things:

- ensure that those activities which will help to achieve the objectives are selected;
- ensure priorities are assigned to those actions;
- ensure that you are realistic about what can be achieved with the human and financial resources available;
- communicate to everyone in the probate team (and in the wider firm) exactly what is planned and their role and responsibilities; and
- help you to monitor progress.

An example of a suitable action plan for a solicitor in a probate department is shown below:

Week	Month	Activity
1	January	Analyse past information about sources of work
1	January	Analyse past information about nature/types of client
2	January	Talk to 10 intermediaries to ask them for their views on the services provided by the team
3	January	Attend two meetings with other practice groups in the firm to identify ways in which joint marketing can be conducted
1	February	Research a list of 30 local financial advisers
2	February	Research a list of the 20 nearest small accounting firms
3	February	Attend a meeting of the corporate and commercial group to identify 10 high net worth directors who may be interested in tax and estate planning
4	February	Identify the main local business and consumer media and read some back copies to identify opportunities for placing articles
1	March	Prepare a checklist of the sorts of legal questions most likely to be asked by elderly clients/nursing home residents and their families
2	March	Prepare a short article for the local hospital about the issues surrounding relatives and lasting powers of attorney
3	March	Visit the three main referrers of past work
3	March	Identify two local organisations which should be targeted for networking
4	March	Initiate a series of regular blogs from a dedicated area of your website on a specific issue
1	April	Research and arrange for team members to start attending local groups regularly for profile raising, intelligence gathering and relationship development

21.6.2 Developing campaigns

If your private client department is large, it may be that you have to break down your marketing plan into a series of self-contained campaigns – where you group a range of activities around a particular theme or geographical area over a period of time. It can be of considerable assistance to the team if you set out the analysis and planning activities first, describe the profile raising and contact generating that must take place to generate a presence in the market, before indicating where time will be required for a period of concentrated meetings.

As an example, one campaign may have the following elements:

	May	Jun	Jul	Aug	Sep	Oct
Preparation	xxxx					
Analysis – internal	xxxx					
Analysis – external	xxxx					
Planning	xxxx					
Profile raising		xxxx				
Website and alerts		xxxx				
Media relations		xxxx				
E-newsletters			xxxx		xxxx	
Networking				xxxx		xxxx
Contact development			xxxx	xxxx		
Referrer visit programme			xxxx			
Networking external events	xxxx					
Seminar programme	xxxx	xxxx	xxxx	xxxx	xxxx	xxxx
Selling				xxxx		xxxx
Follow-up calls		xxxx	xxxx		xxxx	xxxx
Meetings			xxxx	xxxx	xxxx	xxxx
Presentations and pitches					xxxx	xxxx

Case study: Boodle Hatfield organising for marketing

Marketing private client services is hard work. The most effective activity is relationship building with carefully targeted people, and that has to be done by the lawyers themselves. Their marketing teams have an important role to play in identifying the right targets, organising the right events and ensuring everything is carefully recorded in a good CRM system.

21.6.3 Agreeing a budget

The main cost in marketing probate services will be the time of the solicitors involved in the marketing. Firms often budget out-of-pocket marketing expenditure very carefully but fail to think about how much time will be used and whether sufficient return on that time investment will be achieved. Many great marketing plans never deliver the desired results because the lawyers are simply too busy to devote sufficient time to implementing them.

Therefore, the budget should be prepared in two parts. The first is the out-of-pocket expenditure and should cover items such as advertising (especially directory entries), postage for mailings, catering for events, website design, membership and attendance of local events, entertaining people at lunches and dinners, the production of marketing materials such as leaflets and presentation aids (although many of these can be produced in-house at no cost by using advanced word processing or desktop publishing facilities) and sponsorship. As a rule of thumb, professional firms should spend around 2 per cent of their gross annual fee income on marketing and business development.

Consider the overall fee income of the probate team and think about what proportion of that should be spent on marketing. Remember that if little or no marketing has been done in the past, more cash might be needed in the first year than in subsequent years.

The second and more important part of your budget is agreeing how much time each solicitor and support person will spend on marketing each week or each month. The action list, having broken down the various marketing activities into their component tasks, might help with estimating. Alternatively, a specific amount of time each week or month can be allocated for each fee earner to spend on marketing and selling. It may be necessary to adjust the time recording system to capture and report on non-chargeable time spent on marketing. One of the main reasons why solicitors (particularly non-partners) do not invest time in marketing is because they feel that they only receive recognition and reward for chargeable time.

21.6.4 Monitoring results

After an initial burst of enthusiasm, the marketing initiatives of many law firms flounder and fade away. This is often because there are no mechanisms for:

- monitoring what is happening (and taking action to ensure that it does happen); and
- feeding back results and success stories to keep motivation high.

Two parts of your marketing need to be monitored: the process and the results. In the early days there may be few results, and it is likely to take a few months before any results materialise. The action plan can be used to tick off what actions have been completed. The amount of non-chargeable time being spent by various solicitors on marketing activities can be reviewed. A record should be kept of how many events are attended, how many mailings are issued, how many press releases, articles or blogs are produced, how many referrers met and so on.

Monitoring the results may require some changes to the firm's internal systems. It will be useful to be able to monitor additional work from existing clients or referrers and to pinpoint enquiries and work as a direct result of each marketing activity. Logging calls, enquiries, meetings, instructions, income or the amount of press coverage are all valid ways to measure the success of marketing. Websites now have the ability to monitor how many visitors there have been to the site, the number of enquiries generated and the number of subscribers to e-mail alert or newsletter lists.

However, at the end of the day the only true measure will be whether the marketing activity delivers the objectives which were set at the beginning of the planning process. That is why it is so important that time is spent ensuring that the objectives are clear and measurable at the outset.

APPENDIX A1

Anti-Money Laundering Practice Note (extracts)

[29 October 2009]

CHAPTER 11 – MONEY LAUNDERING WARNING SIGNS

11.3 PRIVATE CLIENT WORK

11.3.1 Administration of estates

The administration of estates is a regulated activity. A deceased person's estate is very unlikely to be actively utilised by criminals as a means for laundering their funds; however, there is still a low risk of money laundering for those working in this area.

Source of funds

When you are acting either as an executor, or for executors, there is no blanket requirement that you should be satisfied about the history of all of the funds which make up the estate under administration; however you should be aware of the factors which can increase money laundering risks.

Consider the following when administering an estate:

- where estate assets have been earned in a foreign jurisdiction, be aware of the wide definition of criminal conduct in POCA and the provisions relating to overseas criminal conduct
- where estate assets have been earned or are located in a suspect territory, you may need to make further checks about the source of those funds

The wide nature of the offences of 'acquisition, use and possession' in section 329 of POCA may lead to a money laundering offence being committed at an early point in the administration. The section 328 offence may also be relevant.

Be alert from the outset and monitor throughout so that any disclosure can be considered as soon as knowledge or suspicion is formed and problems of delayed consent are avoided. A key benefit of the *Bowman* v. *Fels* judgment is that a solicitor who makes a disclosure is now able to continue work on the matter, so long as they do not transfer funds or take any other irrevocable step.

How the estate may include criminal property

An extreme example would be where you know or suspect that the deceased person was accused or convicted of acquisitive criminal conduct during their lifetime.

If you know or suspect that the deceased person improperly claimed welfare benefits or had evaded the due payment of tax during their lifetime, criminal property will be included in the estate and so a money laundering disclosure may be required. Information on the financial thresholds for benefits can be obtained from **www.dwp.gov.uk** or **www.hmrc.gov.uk**.

While administering an estate, you may discover or suspect that beneficiaries are not intending to pay the correct amount of tax or are avoiding some other financial charge (for example, by failing to disclose gifts received from the deceased less than seven years before death). Although these matters may not actually constitute money laundering (because no criminal conduct has yet occurred so there is no 'criminal property'), you should carefully consider their position in conduct terms with respect to Rule 1.01 of the Solicitors' Code of Conduct.

Grant of probate

A UK grant of probate may be required before UK assets can be released, while for overseas assets the relevant local laws will apply. Remain alert to warning signs, for example if the deceased or their business interests are based in a suspect territory.

If the deceased person is from another jurisdiction and a lawyer is dealing with the matter in the home country, it may be helpful to ask that person for information about the deceased to gain some assurances that there are no suspicious circumstances surrounding the estate. The issue of the tax payable on the estate may depend on the jurisdiction concerned.

11.3.2 Trusts

Trust work is a regulated activity.

Trusts can be used as a money laundering vehicle. The key risk period for trusts is when the trust is set up, as if the funds going into the trust are clean, it is only by the trustees using them for criminal purposes that they may form the proceeds of crime.

When setting up a trust, be aware of general money laundering warning signs and consider whether the purpose of the trust could be to launder criminal property. Information about the purpose of the trust, including why any unusual structure or jurisdiction has been used, can help allay concerns. Similarly information about the provider of the funds and those who have control of the funds, as required by the Money Laundering Regulations 2007, will assist.

Whether you act as a trustee yourself, or for trustees, the nature of the work may already require information which will help in assessing money laundering risks, such as the location of assets and the identity of trustees. Again, any involvement of a suspect jurisdiction, especially those with strict bank secrecy and confidentiality rules, or without similar money laundering procedures, may increase the risk profile of the retainer.

If you think a money laundering offence has, or may have, been committed that relates to money or property which already forms part of the trust property, or is intended to do so, consider whether your instructions involve you in a section 328 arrangement offence. If they do, consider the options for making a disclosure.

11.3.3 Charities

In common with trusts, while the majority of charities are used for legitimate reasons, they can be used as money laundering/terrorist financing vehicles.

If you are acting for a charity, consider its purpose and the organisations it is aligned with. If you are receiving money on the charity's behalf from an individual or a company donor, or a bequest from an estate, be alert to unusual circumstances including large sums of money.

There is growing concern about the use of charities for terrorist funding. HM Treasury maintains a consolidated list of individuals and entities to whom you may not provide funds, economic resources, and in relation to terrorism, finacial services. See also 7.10 of this practice note.

11.3.4 Powers of attorney/deputyship

Whether acting as, or on behalf of, an attorney or deputy, you should remain alert to money laundering risks.

If you are acting as an attorney you may learn financial information about the donor relating, for example, to non-payment of tax or wrongful receipt of benefits. You will need to consider whether to make a disclosure to SOCA.

Where the public guardian has an interest – because of a deputyship or registered enduring power of attorney – consider whether the Office of the Public Guardian (OPG) needs to be informed. Informing the OPG is unlikely to be tipping off because it is unlikely to prejudice an investigation.

If you discover or suspect that a donee has already completed an improper financial transaction that may amount to a money laundering suspicion, a disclosure to SOCA may be required (depending on whether legal professional privilege applies). However, it may be difficult to decide whether you have a suspicion if the background to the information is a family dispute. You can get legal advice on this through the Law Society's AML directory.

APPENDIX A2

Death certificate verification form and protocol letter

DEATH CERTIFICATE VERIFICATION FORM [1] – For use by Solicitors

Registration District:	....
Place of death	....
Parish (if specified) & County	....
Entry number	....
Date of death	....
Cause of death [**2**]	....
	....
	....
	....
Name of doctor [**3**] certifying death	....
Name of informant [**4**]	....
Name of registrar [**5**]	....
Date of birth [**6**]	....
Sex [**7**]	....
Maiden name [**8**] (if applicable)	....
Previous married name (if applicable/known)	....
Occupation	....

I/We certify that I/we have examined the death certificate of

(client's name)	....
(client's address)	....
	....

and that the said certificate contains the information as recorded above. **A copy is kept on the client file for my/our information to which you may request access.**

Signed: (Partner)	....	Date:	....
Full name	....		
Firm Name:	....		
Firm Law Society number	....		

Firm's stamp

GUIDANCE NOTES

1. Only information contained in the certificate may be recorded on this form. Where information for a particular field is not recorded in the certificate, or not known, please state 'not recorded on certificate' or 'not known'. This form is not appropriate for use in lieu of an interim death certificate or a foreign death certificate.
2. This information is important in the event of an early claim on an underwritten policy. Each and every cause of death must be recorded as they appear in the certificate.
3. On occasion, usually in connection with an attempted fraud, the name of the doctor certifying the death may be important.
4. This information may be important in the context of an attempted fraud and in helping to identify if there is a spouse which may be relevant in the case of protected rights or guaranteed minimum pensions under pension plans where the provider has discretion over the beneficiary.
5. In some cases the signature may be illegible (and the name is not printed). If this is the case, please state 'signature illegible'. This does, at least, confirm that the Registrar has signed the certificate.
6. Identifies any possible mis-statements of age.
7. Allows comparisons with information provided at date of inception. (gender is not always obvious from the forenames).
8. Confirms identity of a woman who has married since policy inception but omitted to provide this information.

Dear

Re: [...] deceased Ref: [...] [*account/policy/pension number*]

We regret to inform you that [...] [*full name*] died on [...] at [...]. We act for [...], who are personal representatives of [...].

We are in possession of a certified copy of the entry of the death, the full details of which can be found in the attached schedule.* We confirm that we will forward the copy of the death certificate if the [...] [*bank/insurer/pension provider*] requires it.

We would be grateful if you would please note the fact of this death and take such action as is required.

We would be grateful if you could also provide precise details of all [...] [*accounts/insurance policy/assets*] held by you and their value as at [...] [*date of death*] for the purpose of administering the estate.

Yours faithfully

**Insurers/Pension providers will also require birth and marriage forms to be completed for certain purposes.*

APPENDIX A3

Disputed Wills Practice Note

[16 April 2009]

1. INTRODUCTION

1.1 Who should read this practice note?

Solicitors dealing with wills and probate.

1.2 What is the issue?

If a will you have prepared is disputed you may be asked to disclose information about the circumstances surrounding its preparation and execution.

Law Society advice on this issue was affirmed by the Court of Appeal in [*Larke* v. *Nugus* [2000] WTLR 1033].This practice note highlights that advice and provides supplementary information on disclosing such information, the consequences of failing to do so, and protecting the estate.

2. CIRCUMSTANCES IN WHICH YOU SHOULD DISCLOSE THE CONTENTS OF A WILL

Under the Solicitors' Code of Conduct 2007 your duty of confidentiality continues after the end of the retainer. When the client dies, the right to confidentiality passes to the personal representatives; an administrator's authority does not begin until the court grants letters of administration.

2.1 Legal background

The question of confidentiality in relation to a disputed will was considered in *Larke* v. *Nugus*. At that time the Law Society's advice on disputed wills was:

> If the testator is dead, the solicitor must not disclose any information before probate is granted, except to the executors, without the consent of the executors. But this will not necessarily apply where a solicitor is asked to disclose information about a Will which he has prepared and which is in dispute.
>
> Privilege cannot be claimed by one person claiming under a deceased testator's Will as against another person having a similar claim in respect of matters communicated by the deceased to the solicitor during the lifetime of the deceased. The testator's solicitor could be compelled by the court under subpoena to answer questions directed to liciting communications made to him by the testator in the course of preparing the Will if put to him by either party.
>
> Where a serious dispute arises as to the validity of a Will, beyond the mere entering of a caveat and the solicitor's knowledge makes him a material witness, then the

solicitor should make available a statement of his evidence regarding the execution of the Will and the circumstances surrounding it to anyone concerned in the proving or challenging of that Will, whether or not the solicitor acted for those who were propounding the Will.

This advice was confirmed and upheld in the case by the Court of Appeal (Civil Division) in *Larke* v. *Nugus*.

The Court of Appeal made it clear that the information required related to both:

- the circumstances in which the testator gave instructions for the will
- the circumstances in which the will was executed

2.2 [Senior Courts] Act 1981

If you have prepared a will you have knowledge that makes you a material witness if the will is disputed. The court has power under the [Senior Courts] Act 1981, s122, to order persons with knowledge of any document that is or purports to be a testamentary document to attend court and answer questions relating to the document.

You should therefore provide the information in advance to try to limit the costs of a full hearing.

2.3 Civil Procedure Rules

The court has power under Rule 31.16 of the Civil Procedure Rules to order pre-action disclosure of documents in order to either:

- dispose fairly of the anticipated proceedings; or
- assist the dispute to be resolved without proceedings; or
- save costs

You should make available any documents in your possession that are relevant to the proceedings to avoid the cost of unnecessary applications to court. Providing this information promptly when a Will is initially challenged may dispel suspicions and save costs in the long run.

You should make a full attendance note at the time the will is prepared. You should also preserve the file. See Law Society Practice Note on Retention of Files.

3. GOOD PRACTICE ON RECEIPT OF A REQUEST FOR INFORMATION

3.1 Where there is no suggestion of negligence

The following applies where a will you have prepared is in dispute, but there is no suggestion of professional negligence.

When requested, in what is known as a '*Larke* v. *Nugus* letter', you should provide the following information to anyone who has an interest in the dispute, whether or not you are acting for any of the parties:

- a full statement of evidence as to its preparation, and the circumstances in which it was executed, together with
- a copy of requested documents

The quickest and easiest way of complying with such requests will often be to copy the contents of the Will file.

As a potential witness in proceedings, you may not charge for time spent compiling the statement or documents however a reasonable charge may be made for photocopying.

3.2 Where there is a possibility of negligence

You should take the following steps where there is a possibility of negligence in the preparation of the Will:

1. inform any lay executors and beneficiaries of the Will that they may wish to take independent advice as to whether or not the Will was negligently drafted, and
2. immediately inform your practice's insurers of the existence of a potential claim

4. CONSEQUENCES OF FAILURE TO PROVIDE FULL INFORMATION

In *Larke* v. *Nugus*, the Court of Appeal refused to order those challenging the Will to pay the costs of the challenge even though the Will was found to be valid. This was because the solicitor who had prepared the Will refused to make information available at an early stage which, had it been given, could have prevented a full trial. The claimants' costs, therefore, were ordered to be paid from the estate and reduced the amount available for the beneficiaries of the valid Will.

The beneficiaries of an estate that has been reduced in this way would be justified in bringing an action against the solicitor who had failed to disclose the information at an early stage to recover the lost costs.

As the purpose of a *Larke* v. *Nugus* letter is to prevent money being spent on futile litigation by the provision of early pre-action disclosure, the onus is on you to provide a prompt reply and relevant evidence to facilitate early settlement.

Providing a response shortly before trial, when most of the costs have been incurred, is unlikely to protect you from an adverse costs order. You should therefore provide a full response to a request within a reasonable period, for example: two to three weeks, or as long as it is necessary to:

- retrieve the file
- consider the contents
- copy any necessary parts of the file
- provide the statement to the relevant parties.

5. RISKS OF ACTING IN DISPUTES

You may find yourself in a difficult position, if a Will you prepared is disputed, particularly if the Will appoints you as executor. You may feel strongly that the Will is valid and that those disputing it are misguided but you should consider your position carefully.

5.1 Risk of incurring costs

As an executor you are a fiduciary with duties to the beneficiaries of the estate, whoever they turn out to be. If you are partisan in the litigation, you risk a costs order being made against you personally. Provided you act neutrally in any litigation the costs of the executor should come out of the estate. So far as the warring parties are concerned, it is no longer the case that costs in probate litigation will necessarily be ordered from the estate. Costs are at the discretion of the court, and it is increasingly the case that the unsuccessful party will have to bear them.

To avoid being at risk of costs you should therefore remain neutral and allow the beneficiaries of the Will or next of kin to pursue the litigation. Your only obligation in the proceedings is to provide information and to preserve the estate.

5.2 Conducting litigation on behalf of the beneficiary

There may sometimes be circumstances in which it is difficult for the beneficiaries to conduct the litigation and you may wish to do so on their behalf. If so you should:

- be clear that you are making yourself a party to the litigation with all the risks of adverse costs orders being made against you
- protect yourself where possible by taking out an indemnity for costs from adult beneficiaries

The safest course of action is for you to suggest to the beneficiaries that they seek separate advice.

6. PROTECTING THE ESTATE PENDING RESOLUTION OF THE DISPUTE

6.1 Application for temporary grant

Irrespective of whether or not a particular Will is valid, steps should be taken in relation to the assets and liabilities of an estate. These can include the duty of the executors to ensure that assets must be secured and liabilities paid. However, the identity of the true executors may be uncertain if the Will is in dispute. In these circumstances, the parties to the dispute, and those advising them, should consider at an early stage how best to protect the estate.

Where it is possible, after the agreement of the parties to the dispute, you or another agreed party,usually a professional, should apply to the Probate Registry for a temporary grant, or grant *ad colligenda bona defuncti*, to deal with the assets and protect them until a full grant can be obtained.

6.2 Agreement regarding steps in the administration

Where an executor or administrator has already taken a grant, you should agree with the parties to the litigation what steps will be taken in the administration. It is easy for an executor who is involved in a dispute to overlook simple steps such as cashing in premium bonds after they cease to be eligible for prizes or investing cash in high interest accounts.

7. MORE INFORMATION

7.1 Professional Conduct

The following section of the Solicitors' Code of Conduct 2007 is relevant to this practice note:

- Rule 4.01 Duty of confidentiality

7.2 Legal and other requirements

- [Senior Courts] Act 1981, s 122
- Civil Procedure Rules, Rule 31.16

7.3 Status of this note

Practice notes are issued by the Law Society for the use and benefit of its members. They represent the Law Society's view of good practice in a particular area. They are not intended to be the only standard of good practice that solicitors can follow. You are not required to follow them, but doing so will make it easier to account to oversight bodies for your actions.

Practice notes are not legal advice, nor do they necessarily provide a defence to complaints of misconduct or of inadequate professional service. While care has been taken to ensure that they are accurate, up to date and useful, the Law Society will not accept any legal liability in relation to them.

For queries or comments on this practice note contact the Law Society's Practice Advice Service.

7.4 Terminology

Must – a specific requirement in the code or legislation. You must comply, unless there are specific exemptions or defences provided for in the code or relevant legislation.
Should – good practice for most situations in the Law Society's view. If you do not follow this, you must be able to justify to oversight bodies why this is appropriate, either for your practice, or in the particular retainer.
May – a non-exhaustive list of options for meeting your obligations. Which option you choose is determined by the risk profile of the individual practice, client or retainer. You must be able to justify why this was an appropriate option to oversight bodies.
Testator – The person who made the will
Executor – The person responsible for carrying out the terms of the will
Beneficiary – The person/s named in the will
Fiduciary – The person entrusted with property or power on behalf of the beneficiary
Subpoena – The summoning of a witness or the submission of evidence to the court
Grant ad colligenda bona defuncti – The application for a temporary grant from the Probate Registry to deal with the assets of a deceased estate.

7.5 Further products and support

7.5.1 Law Society Practice Advice Line

The Law Society provides support for solicitors on a wide range of areas of practice. Practice Advice can be contacted on 0870 606 2522 from 09.00 to 17.00 on weekdays.

7.5.2 Other practice notes and Law Society materials

- File retention practice note
- *Probate Practitioner's Handbook* available from the Law Society bookshop.

7.5.3 Solicitors Regulation Authority Contact Centre

Assists solicitors with enquiries relating to practising certificates, continuing professional development (CPD) and other general enquiries. Telephone 0870 606 2555 **www.sra.org.uk**

7.5.4 Association of Contentious Trust and Probate Practitioners

The Association provides resources for solicitors, barristers and legal executives working in this area, including a letter template for requesting information from solicitors about the preparation of wills. **www.actaps.com**

7.6 Acknowledgements

The Law Society thanks the Wills and Equity Committee for their assistance with this practice note.

APPENDIX A4

Estate Administration: Banking Protocols Practice Note

[20 August 2009]

PRACTICE NOTE

This practice note is relevant to any solicitor involved in the administration of estates.

Solicitors often experience difficulty and delay during the estate administration process in relation to assets held by banks and building societies.

This practice note contains protocols that set out procedures agreed with banks and building societies to clarify and speed up the estate administration process. This is a joint initiative with the Society of Trust and Estate Practitioners (STEP).

These are the first in a series of agreements with major banking organisations, aimed at helping the profession negotiate the different administrative procedures for releasing assets held, in order to wind-up an estate.

The following protocols have been agreed:

- Nationwide protocol – 20 August 2009
- Lloyds TSB protocol – 18 January 2008
- HSBC protocol – 26 March 2008

Note that these do not address professional conduct or legal requirements.

BANKING PRACTICES PROTOCOL BETWEEN NATIONWIDE BUILDING SOCIETY, THE LAW SOCIETY OF ENGLAND AND WALES AND THE SOCIETY OF TRUST AND ESTATE PRACTITIONERS

This protocol has been agreed between Nationwide Building Society, the Law Society of England and Wales and the Society of Trust and Estate Practitioners. The purpose is to bring clarity to probate-related dealings between advisers and Nationwide Building Society.

Set out below is the information Nationwide Building Society will require from the solicitor/STEP member on first contact or shortly afterwards. If this information is provided, delays in dealing with the account or investments will be reduced.

What information will Nationwide Building Society require from the solicitor/probate practitioner on a first approach?

1. Death certificate/death certificate verification form/Interim death certificate.
2. Date of death.
3. List of names, such as maiden names, in which accounts were held.

4. Verification of the status of the practitioner to include confirmation of authority to act on behalf of the executors/next of kin. In the case of solicitors a letter on headed paper with the Law Society roll number quoted; and in the case of STEP members a letter on headed paper with the STEP membership number quoted will be sufficient.
5. Correct address for correspondence in connection with the accounts of the deceased.
6. Approximate value of the estate.
7. Information regarding the will to confirm the existence of the will and the names of the executors.

Set out below is the information that the solicitor/STEP member is likely to require from Nationwide Building Society and also an outline of how Nationwide Building Society might respond to such requests.

1. Confirmation of the numbers of all accounts in the name of the deceased (including those held jointly).
2. Details of the balance on all accounts in the deceased's name (including joint accounts) at the date of death and, where appropriate, the amount of accrued interest to the date of death.
3. A certificate showing any interest paid and tax deducted during the period from 6 April last to the date of death [and for the previous tax year].
4. Details of all standing orders and direct debits in force at the date of death and confirmation that a stop has been placed on them (Only applicable for sole accounts).
5. Confirmation that the Nationwide Building Society will allow the balance on accounts to be used before production of the grant of probate for payment of inheritance tax, settlement of funeral expenses and payment of probate fees.
6. Correct address for correspondence in connection with the accounts of the deceased.

Account closure

1. Information sent no more than fifteen working days after receipt of the request.
2. Closing balance sent no more than ten working days after receipt of grant of probate.
3. Closing balance statement sent no more than ten working days from closure of the account.
4. When a deceased customer holds both credit and debit balances on accounts with the Nationwide Building Society, Nationwide will apply set-off rules, and clear any Nationwide debts, providing the solicitor/STEP member with settlement on the net figure. The solicitor will be advised of the net balance via the date of death figures.

BANKING PRACTICES PROTOCOL BETWEEN LLOYDS TSB, THE LAW SOCIETY OF ENGLAND AND WALES AND THE SOCIETY OF TRUST AND ESTATE PRACTITIONERS

This protocol has been agreed between Lloyds TSB, the Law Society of England and Wales and the Society of Trust and Estate Practitioners. The purpose is to bring clarity to probate-related dealings between advisers and Lloyds TSB.

Set out below is the information that Lloyds TSB will require from the solicitor/STEP member on first contact or shortly afterwards. If this information is provided, delays in dealing with the account or investments will be reduced.

1. Death certificate/death certificate verification form.
2. Date of death.

3. List of the deceased's names, such as maiden names, in which accounts were held or may have been held, and last address of the deceased prior to death or admission to hospital/nursing home etc.
4. Account numbers of relevant accounts if known.
5. Verification of the status of the solicitor/probate practitioner. The verification procedure for STEP members who are not solicitors must be agreed direct between STEP and Lloyds TSB. To verify non-solicitor STEP members please contact the Membership Department at STEP Worldwide on tel 020 7838 4890.
6. Correct address for correspondence in connection with the accounts of the deceased.

Set out below is the information that the solicitor/STEP member is likely to require from Lloyds TSB and also an outline of how Lloyds TSB might respond to such requests.

7. The numbers of all accounts, including internet accounts, in the name of the deceased, including those held jointly. This information will be provided automatically by Lloyds TSB subject to full name and address disclosure by the solicitor/STEP member, but note that where the deceased is the second named on the account, disclosure is not automatic and additional enquiries may be necessary.
8. Details of the balance on all accounts in the deceased's name (including joint accounts) at the date of death and, where appropriate, the amount of accrued interest to the date of death.
9. Confirmation that the current account balance will be placed on deposit, pending closure on production of the grant of probate. The solicitor/STEP member must specifically request this information. Lloyds TSB can 'place funds on deposit on request' only via specified 'executor accounts'. The solicitor/executor/STEP member will be asked to complete an application form and the process will be subject to Lloyds TSB's 'know your customer/anti-money laundering rules'.
10. Full details of any items the bank is holding in safe custody on behalf of the deceased. The solicitor/STEP member must specifically request this information. Note that Lloyds TSB staff may not know the nature of items being held, so the solicitor/STEP member or an agreed agent may need to visit to inspect and value the items.
11. A certificate showing any interest paid and tax deducted during the period from 6 April last to the date of death (and for the previous tax year). The solicitor/STEP member must specifically request this information.
12. Any dividend or interest counterfoils which the bank is holding. The solicitor/STEP member must specifically request this information. Note that Lloyds TSB operates a BACS system so is unlikely to hold many counterfoils.
13. Details of all standing orders and direct debits in force at the date of death and confirmation that a stop has been placed on them. Note that the solicitor/STEP member should consider the effect of a stop being put on certain payments if someone remains resident at the former address of the deceased.
14. Confirmation that the bank will allow the balance on accounts to be used before production of the grant of probate for payment of inheritance tax, settlement of funeral expenses and payment of probate fees.
15. Confirmation that the correct address for correspondence has been noted on all accounts in the name of the deceased.
16. Where available, details of any transfers over £3,000 which have taken place in the last seven years. The solicitor/STEP member must specifically request this information. Note that Lloyds TSB is unlikely to retain information beyond six years.
17. Correct address for correspondence in connection with the accounts of the deceased.

18. Where possible, details of the accounts held in the name of the deceased across the Lloyds TSB group. The solicitor/STEP member must specifically request this information.

Account closure

19. On closing an account Lloyds TSB is to confirm that the account has been closed; the closing balance will be sent within a reasonable time.
20. Bank statements for the period from the date of death to closure, and the closing balance, is to be sent to the solicitor/STEP member and not the lay executor.
21. When a deceased holds both credit and debit balances on accounts with Lloyds TSB, the bank will apply set-off rules and clear any Lloyds TSB debts, providing the solicitor/ STEP member with settlement on the net figure. The solicitor will be advised of the net balance via an assets and liabilities pro forma. The type of accounts included in calculating a net balance will include: savings accounts, current accounts, unsecured loan accounts and credit card accounts.
22. The time periods suggested in relation to account closures are:
    (a) information to be sent no more than fifteen working days after receipt of the request
    (b) closing balance to be sent no more than ten working days after receipt of grant of probate (although it may not be possible to supply this information in the case of shares and investments)
    (c) closing balance statement to be sent no more than ten working days from closure of the account

BANKING PRACTICES PROTOCOL BETWEEN HSBC, THE LAW SOCIETY OF ENGLAND AND WALES AND THE SOCIETY OF TRUST AND ESTATE PRACTITIONERS

This protocol has been agreed between HSBC, the Law Society of England and Wales and the Society of Trust & Estate Practitioners. The purpose is to bring clarity to probate-related dealings between advisers and HSBC.

Set out below is the information HSBC will require from the solicitor/STEP member on first contact or shortly afterwards. If this information is provided, delays in dealing with the account or investments will be reduced.

What information will the bank require from the solicitor/probate practitioner on a first approach? We suggest the following may be useful:

1. Death certificate/death certificate verification form.
2. Date of death.
3. List of names, such as maiden names, in which accounts were held.
4. Verification of the status of the solicitor/probate practitioner to include confirmation of authority to act on behalf of the executors/next of kin (and in the case of solicitors a letter on headed paper with the Law Society roll number quoted should ensure that delay is kept to a minimum).
5. Correct address for correspondence in connection with the accounts of the deceased.
6. Approximate value of the estate.
7. Information regarding the will to confirm the existence of the will and the names of the executors.

Set out below is the information that the solicitor/STEP member is likely to require from HSBC and also an outline of how HSBC might respond to such requests.

Please confirm that the bank will be able to supply the following once the solicitor/probate practitioner has supplied the information listed above.

8. Confirmation of the numbers of all accounts in the name of the deceased (including those held jointly).
9. Details of the balance on all accounts in the deceased's name (including joint accounts) at the date of death and, where appropriate, the amount of accrued interest to the date of death.
10. Confirmation that the current account balance will be placed on deposit pending closure on production of the grant of probate.
11. Full particulars of any items the bank is holding in safe custody on behalf of the deceased.
12. Full particulars of any items the bank is holding as security on behalf of the deceased.
13. A certificate showing any interest paid and tax deducted during the period from 6 April last to the date of death [and for the previous tax year].
14. Any dividend or interest counterfoils which the bank is holding.
15. Details of all standing orders and direct debits in force at the date of death and confirmation that a stop has been placed on them.
16. Confirmation that the bank will allow the balance on accounts to be used before production of the grant of probate for payment of inheritance tax, settlement of funeral expenses and payment of probate fees.
17. Confirmation that the correct address for correspondence has been noted on all accounts in the name of the deceased.
18. Correct address for correspondence in connection with the accounts of the deceased.

Account closure

On closing an account please confirm that information and the closing balance will be sent within a reasonable time. We suggest the following time periods:

19. Information sent no more than fifteen working days after receipt of the request.
20. Closing balance sent no more than ten working days after receipt of grant of probate.
21. Closing balance statement sent no more than ten working days from closure of the account.
22. Without a grant a signed indemnity may be required to release over £5,000, but with a grant there is no limit on the amount that can be released.

APPENDIX A5

File Retention Practice Note

[11 September 2007]

FILE RETENTION: RECORDS MANAGEMENT – RETENTION AND WILLS, DEEDS AND DOCUMENTS TOGETHER WITH SUPPORTING DATA

1.1. The information set out below has been developed by the Wills & Equity Committee of the Law Society in order to help practitioners identify issues that should be considered before relevant files are 'weeded' or destroyed.

Aims

1.2. The aims of this exercise are:

(a) to remind the profession of the possible circumstances in which a challenge to the practice of the firm is more likely to succeed if protective measures are not put in place.
(b) to encourage the profession to offer and maintain a high level of service to clients by adopting some of the practice management suggestions set out below.

The background to the project

1.3. The December 1986 guidance under Annex 12A of the Guide to the Professional Conduct of Solicitors has now been superseded by the new Solicitors' Code of Conduct, which does not contain guidance published in the same format. It should be noted that Rule 5 (business management) in the new Code of Conduct – which came into force on 1 July 2007 – requires principals in a firm to make arrangements for the effective management of their firm and these arrangements must include, amongst a list of other things, the safekeeping of documents as assets entrusted to the firm.

1.4. Following the splitting of regulation of the profession from representation in January 2006 and after the coming into force of the new code, on 1 July 2007, there is an information gap that could and should be filled by the representative part of the Society producing advice as necessary, although the Professional Ethics helpline (0870 606 2577) of the regulatory part of the Law Society will still be able to advise practitioners on matters in this area.

1.5. The Wills & Equity Committee takes the view that the former 12A guidance does not contain sufficient good practice information to allow it to be used as a ready reference source by solicitors on a day to day basis, since it operates more at the level of principle rather than practicality. The Wills & Equity Committee hopes that the attached good practice information can be used as a practical source on a day to day basis.

1.6. It is hoped that the good practice advice and information set out below will be of practical help to solicitors: it is not, nor is intended to be definitive guidance on the possible options available to the profession.

General position in relation to storage and destruction of wills and will files

1.7. *For how long should the original will be retained?* With will related material you need to bear in mind that an original will stored by you is the property of the client and after the client's death, it is the property of the estate. On this basis you should consider storage of the original until after the death of the client, or until you are able to return the original to the client.

Some firms store the will indefinitely, while others have a policy of holding the original will for fifty years from the date of its creation. There is no absolute rule, but it is suggested that solicitors should err on the side of caution, even if the firm believes or knows that a later will has been made.

At some point the firm may consider destroying the original will, after consultation with the client, if you know or have been told by the client that a new will has been made. You should consider and inform the client that occasionally the validity of the subsequent will might be challenged and then a prior will might be proved as the last will of the deceased. It is also possible that in cases where undue influence is alleged or where an Inheritance (Provision for Family & Dependants) Act 1975 claim is made an earlier revoked will may be produced as evidence of a settled or disturbed pattern of behaviour or thought by the testator. If a will is revoked you may wish to consider keeping a copy in your records.

With wills the limitation period does not start to run until the testator has died (see discussion of limitation periods in 1.26 below) and so the general six year limitation from the time the case is concluded is of little relevance.

1.8. How long should will files and supporting documentation be retained? When framing a policy on storage and disposal of will related documentation a firm should consider a number of matters.

The file belongs to the client, subject to a limited number of documents which can be removed and which belong to the firm. Documents which come into existence during the retainer fall into four broad categories: (i) documents prepared by you for the client and which have been paid for by the client belong to the client; (ii) documents prepared for the firm's own benefit or protection for which the client has not been charged belong to the firm; (iii) documents and letters written by the client to you where property passes to you on despatch belong to the firm; (iv) documents prepared by a third party during the course of the retainer and paid for by the client belong to the client. (see *Cordery on Solicitors* for more detail).

If the client cannot be contacted or is unable to respond or make a decision, the firm will have to make a risk assessment before destruction of any such material, including consideration of whether the firm's insurer's should be consulted.

For will files and related material you need to bear in mind that the limitation period does not start to run until the testator has died (see discussions of limitation periods in 1.26 below). The general limitation period applicable in will related cases is 6 years from the date of death of the testator.

Therefore consider:

(a) storing the file and any other supporting documentation for as long as the will is stored.
(b) editing the file and supporting documents so that the most important material is kept. You will have to decide whether to edit soon after the file is closed, or several years thereafter. An advantage of editing the file soon after the end of the transaction is that the relevant issues will be fresh in your mind. If the file is left to be edited at a later stage bear

in mind that your memory of issues may have dimmed and that you may no longer be working at the firm, leaving editing to be carried out by someone unfamiliar with the matter.

(c) keeping an abstract with the original will setting out significant matters.

Editing information

In order to help you decide how to handle a will file containing material such as instructions, retainer letters, general correspondence, drafts and attendance notes, you should assess if there are any unusual circumstances or disposals (see 1.9 below) that might be questioned by for example, a disappointed beneficiary.

You may decide that it is worth keeping the whole file, or selected material recording instructions or attendance notes of advice you gave to the client warning of matters such as a possible Inheritance (Provision for Family and Dependants) Act 1975 claims, or an abstract setting out how the matter was handled.

If you retain the original will while destroying the file, you may decide keep a note of the destruction with the will, so the absence of papers can be explained at a later stage (see reference to *Larke* v. *Nugus* immediately below) to show that the destruction was carried out in accordance with good business practice.

Even where you might know or suspect that a client has made a new will, it is still possible that the validity of a subsequent will could be challenged so you should consider making a risk assessment of whether originals should be destroyed or copies kept where the original has been sent to the client. You might also think of advising the client that all supporting papers will be destroyed unless claimed and then keep a record of this notice.

Prior to destruction of papers you should consider *Larke* v. *Nugus* [2000] WTLR 1033 and established guidance from Professional Ethics that where there is a dispute about the circumstances in which a will was made, and where requested, a solicitor should make available a statement of evidence regarding the execution of the will and the circumstances surrounding it, to anyone who asks the solicitor for such a statement, whether or not the solicitor acted for the person making the request.

Coding your files

It may be worth the firm building subject coding into the filing system for stored wills and files to enable staff to check which clients have particular provision in their wills related to, for example taxation of trusts, this should help identify all clients with circumstances that may be affected by a subsequent change in the law.

Your retainer should set out if you have any obligation to advise a client of a legal or taxation regime change, but even where there is no obligation to advise the client you may decide to inform clients of a change so that they have the option of coming back to you for a review of their affairs.

Money laundering rules – 'relevant business'

The Money Laundering Regulations 2003 require that for 'relevant business', evidence of identity is to be retained for at least five years after the business relationship ends and for details of a transaction to be kept for a five year period from the date on which all activities taking place in the course of the transaction were completed.

Note that will-writing is not treated as relevant business

Note that trust and probate work is relevant business for the purposes of money laundering rules.

Destruction of files where there have been lifetime disposals/transfers of property at an undervalue

1.9. *What sort of transactions related to the work I've done for my will client should I think of keeping with the will or recording on the will file?* Listed below is the sort of transactions where you need to consider retaining the file regardless of the standard conveyancing or other general firm policy on limitation periods.

(1) deeds of gift
(2) gifts of land
(3) transfers at an undervalue
(4) right to buy where funds came from someone other than the purchasing tenant/s
(5) lifetime gifts

Such transactions might be challenged in the future by someone alleging that there were, for example, capacity issues or that undue influence, fraud, negligence or, mistake was in play around the time a will was made or property disposed of. A disappointed beneficiary might ask why a hoped for share of an estate is non-existent or reduced and your files may be called for. Therefore you should consider keeping records (see reference to *Larke* v. *Nugus* at 1.8 above) with the will that could explain why, for example there was a conveyance at an undervalue, and recording that appropriate advice was offered to the client at the time. You should bear in mind that memories fade with time and that relevant staff may not be around at the time of a challenge who were around when the transaction happened or the will is challenged, so without adequate records you may not be able to defend the advice given by the firm.

If related transactions are undertaken by a separate department such as the Property department there is a risk that the relevant records will be kept in property files and that the Property department may have a policy of file destruction after a shorter period of time (i.e. 6–12 years). You should consider how you can best ensure that all relevant documents, advice and information about the affairs of a will client are preserved in an accessible form (also see 1.15–1.21 discussing storage of electronic data).

Remember that a standard 6 year limitation period may not protect you in will related cases where, for example, undue influence is alleged and note that in *Humphreys* v. *Humphreys* [2005] 1 FCR 712 (Ch D) there was a successful challenge thirteen years after the transaction.

1.10. *How should retention of general files and related property transactions be dealt with?* Your firm may have different policies on the appropriate time for storing property transactions and wills files. Where a transfer of land has been made which could have a bearing on the dispositions in a will you should try to ensure that the link is noted and that a record is kept on the will file (which may be retained for longer than the property file) particularly if advice about the effect and consequences of the transfer has been given by other colleagues in the firm (the information could concern the sale of shares in a family company or business or agricultural property).

You may also keep a general file recording contact with a particular client which is not related to any major transaction, but which contains pertinent information about, for example, family dynamics or the intentions of the client. You should not overlook such files when assessing what should be retained with the will (see also the discussion in 1.8 and 1.9 above).

Practical problems – on the terms of the retainer, storage, production of documents, charges and client consent to destruction

1.11. *How soon can I destroy information and documents on the file at the end of a will transaction?* Your retainer may have set out what will happen to papers, however bear in mind that the original will and certain other papers are not your property and should not be destroyed without written permission from the client.

If nothing has been agreed at the outset in your retainer, you should seek to contact your client and return any papers that you do not intend to retain.

If you cannot contact your client for some reason then you should document your efforts to trace the client and then carry out a review before deciding whether to retain or destroy material. You may wish to consider passing very old documents to a local authority archive as an alternative to destruction, but note the position regarding client confidentiality or legal privilege if the client may still be alive or recently dead (see 1.13–1.14). The National Archives recommends that where personal data needs to be stored for the life of the relevant individual and the date of death is not known it should be held until that individual would have reached 100 years.

You may also wish to take note of the appropriate limitation period (see question 1.26) before deciding when to destroy the file and what if anything from the file you should retain, whether as an original or a copy. Consider that certain papers such as attendance notes and copy e-mails may later help to explain why certain actions were taken. You may wish to refer to the facts of *Larke* v *Nugus* (1.8 above) and *Humphreys* v *Humphreys* [2005] 1 F.C.R. 712 (Ch D).

You may need your client's permission if you wish to put records of documents they own on microfilm, and so it may be worth dealing with such questions in your retainer letter as a matter of routine.

The requirement under schedule 11, paragraph 6(3) of the Value Added Tax Act 1994 should also be taken into account. This says that records and papers relevant to VAT liability have to be kept for six years.

Also note the anti-money laundering requirements set out in 1.8 above.

1.12. *Can I charge my client for storage, copying or production of old records and documents?* Your retainer should set out charges for storage, if any, and charges for copying the file or producing a document from storage. You might consider reminding the client that there is a cost to your business for storage and retrieval of documents from deep storage, particularly where the material is kept off site.

Confidentiality and legal professional privilege

1.13. *Are family members or beneficiaries entitled to disclosure of family papers?*

Confidentiality – After the client's death, the right to confidentiality will pass to the client's executors and it can only be waived by them. If the family members are personal representatives, it will be their decision whether to disclose information to beneficiaries.

There is an exception in cases where the validity of the will is in dispute. In such a case, the solicitor who prepared the will should make available a statement of his or her evidence regarding the execution of the will, and the circumstances surrounding it, regardless of whether or not the solicitor is acting for those named as executors in the will. The statement should be available to anyone who is a party to probate proceedings or whom the solicitor believes has a reasonable claim under the will (*Larke* v *Nugus* – 1.8 above).

Privilege – 'Legal advice privilege' protects a client's communications to and from his lawyer made for the purpose of seeking legal advice or assistance. Legal privilege belongs to the client, and only he/she can waive it. Privilege of the client passes to the personal representatives on death.

1.14. *Does confidentiality or legal privilege prevent me from providing information about the circumstances in which a trust was established, to beneficiaries under that trust?*

Confidentiality – Yes. The information will be confidential to the settlor during his lifetime. On his death the duty to keep matters confidential will pass to his/her personal representatives. An executor's powers derive from the will, where as an administrator's powers derive from the grant of representation. Accordingly, if the client died intestate, the administrator's authority to waive confidentiality will date from the issue of the grant.

Privilege – Privilege prevents any information being given to the beneficiaries during the settlor's lifetime unless the settlor waives privilege. On death of the settlor the right to assert privilege passes to the settlor's successors in title (the personal representatives – see 1.11 above).

Data protection and electronic storage

This information highlights some of the basic issues concerning data protection. More extensive information on all aspects of data protection is available from the Information Commissioner at: **http://www.ico.gov.uk/**

1.15. *Do I treat electronic data the same as paper based information?* The same issues of principle arise with electronic data as with other material, so you always need to consider limitation periods, ownership, confidentiality, privilege and make an adequate risk assessment etc, prior to destruction. However electronic data is subject to further regulatory safe guards as set out in the Data Protection Act 1998.

1.16. *Does the Data Protection Act 1998 require me to destroy personal data on beneficiaries and family members shortly after the will has been made?* The Data Protection Act 1998 allows you to retain personal data stored in an office the information on file without breaching the Act for as long as necessary for one or more specified lawful purposes (see further information).

1.17. *Are my paper files subject to the Data Protection Act 1998?* Personal data contained within files in paper format are subject to the Act only if they are held in a relevant filing system (*Durant* v *FSA* 2003).

1.18. *How does the Data Protection Act 1998 affect electronically stored information?* See 1.15–1.16 above. All personal data which are held in electronic format, including scanned documents which were formerly held in hard copy form, are subject to the Act.

1.19. *Is electronic storage of all file material safe, or could the material be corrupted?* It is much easier to corrupt electronic data, whether by accident or design, than paper. Systems need to be in place to safeguard the authenticity, reliability, accessibility and security of all electronic material.

1.20. *Is storing relevant e-mails containing relevant advice and discussion of cross-departmental issues on one matter safe?* E-mail is both unreliable and an insecure medium. If necessary, encryption should be used to safeguard the confidentiality of information transmitted via e-mail. E-mail should not be relied upon as a storage medium. Information should be stored in a system, whether paper or electronic, which manages it according to its function and content, not its format.

1.21. *The firm is upgrading its IT systems in a few weeks. What issues should I keep in mind when thinking of how to transfer electronically stored data?* It is a mistake to treat all data as though it were of equal value. Only business critical data or data of clear reference value should be migrated to new systems; the remainder should be destroyed according to an agreed retention and disposal policy prior to any migration occurring. This is particularly important where personal data is concerned, since migration is a form of processing and should therefore not be undertaken if there is no longer any need to retain the data.

Migration of large quantities of data is additionally a costly process and can also result in loss or corruption of data elements. Before data transfer to a new system, the firm should consider to whether or not data is likely to be corrupted by the migration process.

Storage issues in relation to file transfer within firms, use of external storage facilities, firm merger and office relocation

1.22. *Our firm has moved to new offices where there is no longer as much storage room for old files. My partners have asked me to rationalise the private clients departments' files and to dispose of a target of 50% to reduce the cost of paying for external storage. The other partners think that there are few issues involved in disposing of files beyond the usual 6 year limitation period. What should I tell my partners?* You should refer your partners to the sections of this good practice advice on limitation periods (1.26 and 1.8 which looks at ownership of papers), so that they are aware of the risks of disposing of will related files where a claim could well be brought far beyond the normal six year period.

1.23. *Our firm has just merged and some of our old will files have gone astray. What are the issues I should consider?* Loss of a file may amount to inadequate professional service or negligence where deeds are lost, so you may need to contact your insurer to record the loss and you should consider contacting your client to discuss what remedial action can be taken, if any, if original papers such as wills have been lost. If a claim arises in relation to lost papers the courts will weigh the available evidence to assess your part in the matter.

Family solicitors and advice where you feel you have a particular understanding of the needs of the client

1.24. *I have been advising the family for years and feel I understand what they all want. I do not think the lifetime transfers I have been involved with will be challenged. Do I need to make/keep records of why the transfer/will was made?* A solicitor should always keep a proper note of the advice that was given to the client together with details of the execution of the will/transfer if the solicitor was involved regardless of whether or not the solicitor believes that there may be a subsequent challenge.

In cases where you have a good relationship with a number of members of a family, you might think that you understand how they will react. However even in these circumstances you should consider that you may not have the complete picture of family dynamics and finances. Where there is an unusual disposal such as a gift at an undervalue, or where the will, leaves unequal shares to children, it would be prudent to keep detailed records of the instructions and your advice in case in definitely in case of a later challenge. Challenges could come after a breakdown in family relations long after you made the will or as a result of changing fortunes of family members. It is impossible to predict when such situations will arise so it is important to be prepared for such possibilities.

1.25. *Should storage of powers of attorney or living wills be linked to storage of will related material?*

Powers of attorney – The original power of attorney belongs to the client and so the power of attorney should not be destroyed without the client's prior consent or until you are satisfied that actual revocation has taken place or that the client is dead. Where a later power of attorney is made it cannot automatically be assumed that revocation of an earlier power of attorney has taken place. See *Re E* [2000] 1 FLR 882.

Alternatively the power could be given to the client and you will have to make a risk assessment if you then consider destroying the file and copies of the power.

Even where a new power has been created bear in mind that the validity of the later document could be challenged so the earlier power may be required. In addition you should note that the different types of power of attorney can run concurrently. An ordinary power of attorney is not automatically revoked by the creation (applicable until October 2007) or existence of an unregistered enduring power of attorney or from October 2007 the creation of a registered lasting power of attorney, where capacity of the donor has not yet been lost.

Bearing this in mind you must be cautious about destroying both original powers of attorney and related files. You must also consider if you wish to store documents, files or abstracts linked to the creation of a power of attorney with will related material so that your firm holds a complete picture of the client's affairs and wishes during life.

Living wills – If the client chooses to store a living will with your firm rather than with a doctor, you may wish to consider keeping the living will with the will, power of attorney and other such papers since the terms may have some bearing on the client's general wishes during life. However note that the living will must be readily accessible since production may be required at very short notice.

Limitation periods

1.26. *Which limitation periods need to be applied when destroying old files?* The limitation period may vary depending on the type of work.

Wills files – When considering whether a file should be destroyed you should note that in wills cases successful claims can be brought well after the usual contractual period of 6 years from the end of the retainer or time the work was completed/ applicable in many other matters. In wills cases the limitation period does not start to run until the client dies and the will comes into effect.

Trusts – For breach of trust the normal limitation period under the Limitation Act 1980, s.21 is six years from the date of the breach or the time the breach is discovered (subject to special provisions for fraud and for a trustee in possession of trust property).

Personal representatives – For claims against personal representatives the limitation period is twelve years from the date on which the right to receive the property accrues (Limitation Act 1980, s.22 (a)) or from the date the right to receive the share accrued which may be from the end of the executors' year rather than the date of death.

Discoverability – Under s32 of the Limitation Act 1980 the limitation period does not start to run until the claimant discovers the mistake, fraud or concealment or could have discovered it with reasonable diligence.

Disability/undue influence – Note that the limitation period, whichever applies, may not start to run until a claimant, deemed to have been under a disability (for example a minor child, a person with capacity problems, or someone suffering undue influence) has become free of that disability. So, for example, where a cause of action is apparent, a minor child will have 6 years from the date of attaining 18 years to take action.

APPENDIX A6

Making Gifts of Assets Practice Note

[16 July 2009]

1. INTRODUCTION

1.1 Who should read this practice note

This practice note is for solicitors who advise clients about transferring their assets to family and friends before they die.

1.2 What is the issue?

Clients may ask about transferring property or investments to their next of kin, family members, or friends in order to mitigate large tax bills after their death, or as a means of providing funding for their future care. Whether they wish to gift assets or offer them at significant undervalue, you must advise your client about the benefits and risks of doing so, and clarify your role and responsibilities in the process.

Some clients may have received advice from non-solicitor legal advice services that included unjustified claims about gifting of assets to avoid the assets being considered for inheritance tax or care fees liability.

2. TAKING ON A CLIENT

2.1 New clients

Before taking on a new client, you should check whether they retained another solicitor or adviser before you, and find out why they decided to change. If you are concerned, you should ask your client if you can contact their previous adviser so that you can establish all the facts of the case.

You should also satisfy yourself that your client is making the gift freely and has not been unduly influenced, especially where someone else purports to be giving instructions on behalf of the client. If indirect instructions are being given, you should confirm the instructions with the client, ideally in person without anyone else being present.

2.2 Conflict of interest

You should clarify who you will be acting for and who you will be receiving instructions from. You must consider any possible conflict of interest where you receive instructions from a donee, especially if you already act for the donor. Rule 3.01 of the Solicitors' Code of Conduct 2007 indicates when instructions must be refused.

If you are asked to act for both parties, you must make them both aware of the possible conflict of interest, and should advise one of them to take independent advice. You should explain you may be unable to disclose all that you know to each of them. You may also be unable to give advice to one of them which conflicts with the interests of the other. Both parties must give their consent to the arrangement in writing. If you remain in any doubt, you should not act for both parties.

2.3 Money laundering

There is a risk that clients seeking to transfer assets may be involved in money laundering or fraud. The Law Society's anti-money laundering practice note will help you to spot warning signs and gives information on what to do if, for example, your client attempts a transaction involving criminal property.

When you accept instructions from a client, you enter into a binding contract with them and you are obliged to follow their instructions. However, Rule 2.01 of the Solicitors' Code of Conduct creates an exception to this. Rule 2.01 requires that you do not act for a client if it would involve you in a breach of law or your professional obligations.

2.4 Professional negligence and file retention

To protect yourself in the event of a subsequent dispute or a professional negligence claim, you must retain evidence of the advice you give your client. Your file notes and correspondence will normally be covered by legal professional privilege or the duty of confidentiality. A court will not usually order discovery of a solicitor's file unless there is prima facie evidence of fraud, but has done so where there are public policy considerations – see *Barclays Bank plc* v. *Eustice* [1995] 1 WLR 1238. It is possible that a trustee in bankruptcy, or a local authority bringing proceedings under the Insolvency Act 1986, section 423-425, may persuade the court to override privilege.

3. ADVISING YOUR CLIENT

Your role is more than just drawing up and registering the necessary deeds and documents to effect the making of a gift. You must ensure that the client fully understands the nature, effect, benefits, risks and foreseeable consequences of making the gift, in order to enable them to form a view as to the wisdom of the proposed transaction.

Assessing your client's understanding of the implications of making the gift may help you to determine whether they have the capacity to make the decision, or whether they are subject to undue influence from family or other beneficiaries.

Since your advice will depend to a large extent on your client's motivations for disposing of their assets, you must first find out:

- what they are seeking to achieve
- who they wish to receive the gift
- what types of assets are involved

You should spend time with your client to enable you to:

- evaluate their instructions
- clarify their domestic and financial circumstances
- establish that they own the assets they wish to dispose of, and
- assess whether they have the mental capacity to make the gift.

The Mental Capacity Act 2005 (MCA) and MCA code of practice state that your client should be able to understand relevant information, use it to make a decision, and communicate that decision to you. The leading case of *Re Beaney (Deceased)* [1978] 1 WLR 770 sets out the test of capacity to make a gift, and states that capacity to make a gift will vary depending on the size, nature and circumstances of the gift.

Further, you should stress to your client that your advice is the best possible advice at the time it is given. You should point out that the unexpected can and often does occur and that the best laid plans can go wrong, so donors should always adopt a cautious approach.

In many cases, your client will be the person intending to make the gift, but you may be approached by a next of kin acting on their behalf. In this case, you should confirm your instructions with the client in person, preferably in private, so as to ensure that they are capable of making the decision and that they have not been unduly influenced by the donee or next of kin.

3.1 Establish your client's objectives and understanding

To enable you to provide relevant advice, you should do both of the following:

1. ensure that you receive full instructions
2. ensure that your client fully understands the implications of their proposed transaction.

3.1.1 Why the client is considering a gift

You should ask why your client has decided to make the gift, as you may be able to suggest more effective ways of achieving the same objective, for example: does your client wish to ensure that a particular person inherits an asset? This objective could be achieved simply by making a will.

Other points to consider could be:

- Is your client seeking peace of mind by making the gift? Do they think it provides certainty for the future or satisfies a moral obligation?
- Will the gift affect others who might have expected to eventually inherit a share of the asset?

If the intention in making the gift is to avoid tax, you should ensure that your client is aware of all tax implications, including Inheritance Tax, Capital Gains Tax and Pre-Owned Asset Tax. There are additional considerations if your client retains the benefit of an asset after giving it away. For instance, if the recipient of the gift dies before the donor, the asset may be subject to Inheritance Tax.

If your client is seeking relief from the worry and responsibility of owning an asset, granting a lasting power of attorney to a family member may be a better way of dealing with this issue.

If your client wants to avoid the value of their assets being taken into account for means testing, such as when they foresee the need to pay for long-term care, your advice must deal with the consequences of such an action, including tax implications and the risks in relation to deprivation of assets.

3.1.2 Issues involved in the clients decision

There may be other issues involved in your client's decision which you should be aware of, including where:

- Your client is infirm or disabled, and an adult child or other relative has given up a paid job or the chance of career advancement to provide full-time live-in care in the expectation of inheriting the home on their death.

- Your client is no longer able to pay for the upkeep or improvement of their home, and their child or children have been funding these in the expectation of inheriting the property.
- The home or other asset is a part of a family business which would no longer be viable if the asset were not included. For instance, a farm might not be able to function without the farmhouse.
- The asset was vested in the name of your client but was funded in whole or in part by their son or daughter.

3.1.3 Nature and extent of the assets

You should request details from your client regarding the nature and extent of the assets being disposed of, and whether your client expects to receive anything in return, including:

- whether the asset is the family home, or an interest in a property or business
- whether the gift will include art, antiques, jewellery or investments
- whether the gift is a one-off or one of a series
- the extent of the gift in relation to the rest of your client's assets, including assets held on their behalf or in trust by others, and the impact on their standard of living
- if they are making an outright gift, offering a loan, setting up a trust, or acquiring a share in a business or property owned by the donee
- whether your client expects to receive anything in return for their gift and, if so, what is the magnitude of their expectation? For instance, they may propose to give their house to a family member and in return remain there for the rest of their life. In this case, you would need to talk to your client about rent, insurance and maintenance of or alterations to the property
- the age, health and circumstances of the donee, including if they are reliant on means-tested benefits or local authority funded care, noting that a donee may die first or become involved in divorce, civil partnership dissolution or bankruptcy proceedings
- whether they expect the donee to provide care or financial assistance
- whether they intend the gift to take effect immediately or later, for example perhaps on your client's death or if they go into a care home
- whether your client has already made gifts to the donee or others.

A proper assessment of the implications of making a gift of the asset both for your client and the donee is best achieved by listing the benefits and risks, and thinking about other issues such as tax and future care. You should also tell your client that if the gift is made outright, they cannot assume that the asset would be returned to them upon request.

3.2 Benefits of transferring assets

If your client transfers assets to a family member or carer:

- There may be savings in relation to Inheritance Tax and administration costs upon the death of the client.
- The client may avoid the need to sell assets to pay for care fees.
- The asset may not be taken into account if your client has to undergo means testing for benefits or publicly funded services.
- Your client may be relieved of the burden of responsibility for the asset.
- It may reduce delays in processing their estate on their death.
- There may be savings in both time and expense in applying for a court order from the Court of Protection in the event your client loses mental capacity and there is no relevant power of attorney in force.

3.3 Risks in transferring assets

Among the risks involved are the following:

- The value of the home may still be taken into account for funding long-term care as there are anti-avoidance measures in relation to means-testing. This is set out further at 5.1.2 Means testing.
- If your client subsequently needs to move into a home but does not have the resources to pay for their care themselves because of the gift, the local authority may only pay for the basic level of care, leaving your client to rely upon the financial support of others to enable them to move into a home of their choice.
- The donee may not provide the support expected, resulting in suffering for your client – for example, by not topping up care fees, or by moving your client prematurely into residential care home in order to occupy or sell the family home.
- If the donee dies or runs into financial difficulties and the donor continues to live in the gifted home, your client may be made homeless.
- The relationship between the donor and donee, since parties can and often do fall into dispute and even become quite hostile to one another.
- The donee may later put pressure on your client to liquidate the gifted assets.
- If your client transfers their home, they may be deprived of opportunities to adapt to changing circumstances – for example by downsizing, or releasing equity to pay for adaptations or care at home, so the donor may be left with no option but to move into a care home.
- The person to whom the assets have been gifted may lose their entitlement to benefits and/or services based on personal means testing.
- If the arrangement is challenged, there could be additional legal fees.

3.4 Tax implications

There are many issues arising in relation to tax as a direct result of transferring assets. For example:

- There may be no Inheritance Tax saving as long as your client receives benefit from the asset – for example, if they continue to live in the home after transferring it to a child.
- There may be an Inheritance Tax liability if the donee dies before the donor, or if the donor dies within seven years of making the gift.
- The Capital Gains Tax main residence exemption will be lost unless the donee lives in the property.
- There may be no automatic uplift to the market value for Capital Gains Tax on the donor's death.
- Stamp Duty Land Tax and additional administrative burdens may be payable.
- Under the pre-owned assets rules, your client may be subject to an Income Tax charge after the transfer.

3.5 Other consequences

As well as the more practical issues, you should ask your client to think about their general approach to their future once they have transferred assets including:

- What effect making the gift could have on their future standard of living?
- If a main motivator in gifting assets was to avoid means testing for future care provision, how would your client feel if this situation didn't arise?
- Does the benefit outweigh the risk?

- What effect would transferring an asset have on others who might have expected to inherit a share of it?
- What might happen if relations between your client and the donee deteriorate?

4. SPECIAL CONSIDERATIONS

4.1 Joint donors

Where your clients are seeking to make a joint gift, you should consider the position of each donor separately. Where the donors may have children from previous relationships, you should consider their obligations to those children. You must also make your clients aware of any potential conflict of interest between the two of them in terms of your advice.

You must establish whether both donors have capacity to make the gift and whether either donor is exerting undue influence on the other.

Where the gift to a third party is the home in which the couple are living, there will be the same risks as with individuals providing the gift, however if the gift is of a share in the home by one of the donors to a third party, you should fully explore the implications for the potential survivor.

It is common for spouses, civil partners or cohabitees to contemplate a gift of their home to avoid its value being taken into account in relation to means testing for care home fees. You should tell the donors that if only one of them goes into care, there are circumstances in which the value of the share of that donor will not be taken into account, where the other donor remains in the home. However, the value of the resident's home is disregarded in the following circumstances:

- during a temporary stay if it is occupied by a spouse, civil partner, person living with the resident
- as a spouse or civil partner or relative who is aged sixty or over or is incapacitated
- if it is occupied by someone else and the local authority exercises its discretion
- for the first twelve weeks of a permanent stay in a care home.

4.1.1 Establish the nature of the donors' relationship

You should ascertain the relationship of the donors because different considerations apply for marriage, civil partnership, cohabitation or living together on a non-sexual basis.

For married couples and civil partners, you should make your clients aware that they benefit from the inheritance tax exemption on the transfer of assets between them both on death and during their lifetime. So a gift of an asset to a third party during their lifetime may not result in any tax saving on the first death of the couple. The survivor's expenses may increase due to living alone at the time as income is reduced because of lost pensions. To ensure that the survivor is left with sufficient assets following the first death, it may be preferable to retain assets, either absolutely or in an interest in possession trust until the death of the survivor. The survivor's estate will then benefit from the transferable nil rate band if it is still in force at that time.

For cohabitees, there is no inheritance tax exemption on gifts between them so a lifetime gift to a third party may appear to have a tax saving advantage. However, you should explore the implications for the survivor. As with a married couple, the survivor may well have increased living expenses or have a fall in income following the first death. It may still be better to choose a gift of the nil rate band to a discretionary trust of which the surviving cohabitant is a beneficiary.

It is not uncommon for joint donors to be living together on a non-sexual basis, for example children and parents, or siblings or for a parent to make a gift of the property to their children.

In these circumstances, you should remember that there is an automatic presumption of undue influence in the making of lifetime gifts where the donor is a child and donee a parent. This will necessitate separate advice for the donor(s) and the donee as a means of rebutting such a presumption.

You should also establish whether the donor(s) have taken into account the needs and expectations of each other and any other children. However unlikely it may appear to be, the consequences of the death of the donee before the donor(s) needs to be considered both from the point of view of inheritance tax and of succession to the property. The donor may be at risk of losing the property.

4.2 Multiple donees

Often, the gift will be to more than one donee, such as to multiple children, including where joint donors have children from different relationships.

These situations greatly increase the potential problems and risks. For example, the death of a donee before the donor is more likely, as is divorce, financial hardship, bankruptcy or incapacity of one or more of the donees. There is also the possibility that in the future the donees may disagree about issues concerning the donor(s) and the assets.

It is unlikely to be appropriate for one person to act for both the donor(s) and all the donees. Each party is likely to need separate legal representation to ensure their particular interests are considered.

5. GIFTING ASSETS TO FUND FUTURE CARE

Many clients will be motivated to transfer assets because they fear they will have to sell their home to pay for care and wish to protect their family's inheritance.

To advise your clients properly, you should familiarise yourself with:

- the eligibility criteria for NHS-funded continuing health care
- charging and funding arrangements by local authorities for residential and continuing health care
- when care must be provided free of charge
- any means testing criteria applied by local authorities which charges for care.

There is no foolproof way of avoiding the value of assets being taken into account for means testing. Anti-avoidance measures in the law allow some gifts to be ignored by the authorities, and even set aside by the court. The measures are subject to periodic change, might apply retrospectively, and are pursued more vigorously by some authorities than others.

5.1 Local authority care provision

Local authorities are not allowed to take responsibility for a person who is an NHS responsibility, but they must assess anyone who appears to it to be in need of community care services. These include residential accommodation for those who by reason of age, illness or disability are in need of care and attention which is not otherwise available to them, and domiciliary and community-based services enabling people to continue to live in the community. Relevant legislation:

- National Health Service and Community Care Act 1990, section 47
- National Assistance Act 1948, section 21
- National Assistance Act 1948, section 29, including functions under the Chronically Sick and Disabled Persons Act 1970, section 2

On the results of their assessment, they must decide whether there is a need to provide community care services. If that is the case, the person in need of care is likely to be subject to the financial means test.

5.1.1 Paying for care

If your client can afford to pay for a place in a care home, they can arrange this independently, though they should have a needs assessment to consider all their care options including whether and how much financial assistance would be available from their local authority. The assessment of need for care provision does not depend on the need for funding. Some care homes do not provide accommodation for local authority-funded residents.

Where the local authority pays or contributes to the cost of care:

- A standard weekly charge is fixed which represents the true economic cost of providing the accommodation, or a weekly charge is agreed for a place in an independent home which should represent the cost of the place to the authority.
- Residents must generally contribute in accordance with their resources up to the weekly charge, but no one should be required to pay more.
- The local authority will either pay the full weekly charge to the care home and collect the resident's contribution or, with the agreement of all parties, pay the home net of the person's assessed contribution, with the resident paying this to the care home direct.
- The contract should state what is included in the charge and what are extras.

If your client wishes to move to a care home which is more expensive than the local authority will pay on the basis of their assessed needs, and if the local authority can show that there are suitable homes with vacancies in the local area, you should note that the cost difference will need to be topped up by a third party such as a family member.

5.1.2 Means testing

For those who cannot afford the standard charge for their care, local authorities will make an assessment of their ability to pay. This is reviewed annually, though a reassessment can be requested at any time.

The assessment applies to both permanent and temporary care, and is based on the means only of the person in need of care: a partner's or spouse's resources are not taken into account, though jointly owned assets may be assessed. The National Assistance (Assessment of Resources) Regulations 1992 (as amended) and the Charging for Residential Accommodation Guide set out how fees are calculated. Half the occupational and private pensions of a resident can be disregarded if they are paid to a non-resident spouse or civil partner.

The basis of assessments for care provision is largely in line with that for income support, but there are some significant differences:

Some capital is disregarded, and everyone is allowed to keep a set level of capital. The level is set each year in the National Assistance (Assessment of Resources and Sums for Personal Requirements) (Amendments) (England) Regulations and the National Assistance (Assessment of Resources and Sums for Personal Requirements) (Amendments) (Wales) Regulations.

Notional capital and notional income rules may apply where the local authority believes there has been deliberate deprivation of asscts.

A small amount of income is disregarded if it would have been incorporated into the assessment for the Savings Credit element of Pension Credit. This is to ensure that pensioners who save still see some benefit of this when they are resident in a care home.

The local authority may agree to defer payment by means of a legal charge on the resident's property, so that the resident does not have to sell their home during their lifetime. The resident must contribute to their care fees from available resources, making up any shortfall through the legal charge. Interest starts to accrue 56 days after the resident's death. A deferred payment option will not be provided where the resident's income or capital is assessed as being above the upper capital limit outlined in the National Assistance (Assessment of Resources) Regulations.

All residents retain an allowance for personal expenditure on toiletries, stationery and treats, etc. This is set each year in:

- the National Assistance (Assessment of Resources and Sums for Personal Requirements) (Amendments) (England) Regulations, and
- the National Assistance (Assessment of Resources and Sums for Personal Requirements) (Amendments) (Wales) Regulations.

The local authority has discretion to increase the allowance, but it should not be used as top-up towards more expensive accommodation.

Local authorities should offer to carry out a benefits check on residents' behalf, since it is in their interests to ensure that people in care homes are receiving maximum state benefits.

5.1.3 Anti-avoidance measures and deprivation of assets

In most cases, the intention behind making gifts of assets is the most important factor. If a local authority believes that an asset has been given away with the intention of creating or increasing entitlement to means tested benefits, it may decide that the donor has notional capital of equivalent value to that of the asset given away.

Your client will be particularly vulnerable if they are deemed to have notional capital since, although the local authority is obliged to provide care, this does not have to be in a residential home. Moreover, your client may not be entitled to financial assistance towards the fees. The local authority may still be obliged to provide care, but the local authority could seek payment using debt recovery methods, as in the case of *Robertson* v. *Fife* [2002] UKHL 35.

A local authority financial assessment must follow the needs assessment. There is a question mark regarding whether *Robertson* v. *Fife* would stand up in England because of the slightly different wording of the legislation, such that the local authority would refuse to provide the care because the notional capital makes it otherwise unavailable (see 'Community Care and the Law' from paragraph 8.91), and as such are arguably under no obligation to provide residential accommodation under s.21 National Assistance Act 1948. However, the person might qualify as a vulnerable adult, regardless of notional capital, where they are in need of such accommodation because they cannot arrange their care or no longer has any resources to fund their care.

If the local authority believed that a significant part of the intention to transfer an asset was to increase entitlement to financial assistance, they could impose a charge on the asset after it had been gifted, or even recover the asset. For a local authority to pursue a claim they would have to show what the donor's intention was at the time of disposal. It may be difficult for the donor or donee to give evidence as to the donor's intentions and if another purpose of the gift cannot be established or indicated, the judge may conclude that it must have been to avoid means testing.

One way to establish the intention is the foreseeability or immediacy of the need for care. Any decision to reject or accept the evidence requires an overall assessment of that evidence by the local authority – see *Beeson* v. *Dorset County Council* [2002] HRLR 15. If, for example, your client was fit and healthy and could not have foreseen the need for residential care, it would be unreasonable for the local authority to treat the transfer of assets as deliberate deprivation. However, *Yule* v. *South Lanarkshire Council* [1999] 1 CCLR 546, states that there was no time limit on local authorities when deciding whether a person had deprived themselves of assets for the purposes of avoiding residential care fees.

If a local authority were to pursue a claim for care funding, your client could challenge that decision but would bear the burden of proof that the authority's decision was *Wednesbury* unreasonable – *Associated Provincial Picture Houses Ltd* v. *Wednesbury Corporation* [1948] 1 KB 233. This process could be protracted, involving local authority complaints and ombudsman procedures, and this could be very stressful for your client and expensive if it involves court proceedings.

5.1.4 Enforcement of fees for care

Local authorities can take steps to recover contributions towards care charges, and their assessment of ability to pay may take into account property that has been given away for the purpose of avoiding means testing. Their enforcement options include:

- taking proceedings in the Magistrates' Court to recover sums due as a civil debt (section 56, National Assistance Act 1948)
- imposing a charge on any property belonging to the resident, with interest chargeable from the day after death (sections 22 and 24 of the Health and Social Services and Social Security Adjudication's (HASSASSA) Act 1983)
- imposing a charge on property transferred by the resident, within six months of going to residential care or while in care, on property transferred by the resident with the intention of avoiding contributions (section 21, HASSASSA Act 1983)

If the debt for unpaid contributions reaches £750, the local authority could start insolvency proceedings to declare the resident bankrupt. Transactions at an undervalue may be set aside within two years, or within five years if the person made bankrupt was insolvent at the time of the transaction, which is unlikely. See sections 339–341 Insolvency Act 1986. A gift may be set aside without time limit and without bankruptcy if the court is satisfied that the transfer was made for the purpose of putting assets beyond the reach of a potential creditor or otherwise prejudicing the creditor's interests. See sections 423–425, Insolvency Act 1986.

This provision is exceptionally wide, and the court has extensive powers to restore the position to that which it would have been had the gift not been made. The Court of Appeal in *Derbyshire CC* v. *Akrill* [2005] EWCA Civ 308, considered the application of section 423, concluding that the section could apply where a person transferred his house by deed of gift to his children for the purposes of putting it beyond the reach of those who might have a claim in respect of the costs of his imminent residential care.

Although some local authorities have threatened to use insolvency proceedings, few have actually done so, perhaps because of lack of expertise, cost or the prospect of bad publicity. However, with increasing pressures on local authority resources to provide community care services, the incidence of this may rise in the future. There is evidence that families can be placed under considerable pressure to pay for care, even where the gift was entirely innocent.

5.2 National Health Service-funded care

You may be asked by clients who are already in receipt of care for advice on mitigating the cost of this. You may consider whether the National Health Service (NHS) should fund care, whether wholly or in part.

Section 1 of the National Health Service Act 2006 requires the Secretary of State to promote a comprehensive health service in England with the aim of improving people's physical and mental health, and effectively preventing, diagnosing and treating those who are ill. Section 3 sets out the duty to provide services for the care of those suffering from illness to the extent necessary to meet reasonable requirements. This includes accommodation for the purposes of health services provided under the act. Similar provision applies in Wales under the NHS (Wales) Act 2006.

Strategic health authorities and primary care trusts carry out this function on behalf of the Secretary of State in England, and local health boards have the responsibility in Wales.

NHS fully funded care is provided in this context, defined in the NHS Continuing Healthcare (Responsibilities) Directions 2007 as 'a package of care that can be arranged and funded by the NHS to meet both physical and mental health which have arisen because of illness'. Thus, the NHS would fund the full cost of care for eligible people in care homes, including accommodation and board, and those in their own homes would receive the cost of their both their health care and any social care funded by the NHS.

5.2.1 Extent of NHS-funded care provision

Where someone's care is primarily one of health, the full cost of care is the responsibility of the NHS. However, the distinction between care services that can and cannot be provided as part of a package of services is one of degree, and in borderline cases it depends on a careful appraisal of the facts of the individual case.

The Court of Appeal considered whether a local authority could lawfully provide nursing care for a chronically ill patient in the case of *R* v. *North & East Devon Health Authority ex p Coughlan* [2000] 3 All ER 850. In that case her care included nursing care but was not confined to it. A very general indication as to where the line is to be drawn between lawfully providing care or not is dependent on whether the nursing services were either:

1. Merely incidental or ancillary to the provision of the accommodation which a local authority is under a duty to provide.
2. Of a nature which it can be expected that a local authority could be expected to provide.

The judge confirmed that where the individual's care was primarily one of health, the full cost of care was the responsibility of the NHS. Until recently, in England it was the local NHS body's responsibility to determine what they meant by a primary health care need, whereas in Wales it remains up to the local health board. In any event, the NHS body must publish guidance on how eligibility for continuing NHS health care is determined, based on a full assessment of the relevant facts such as the quantity and/or quality of care need and how this is weighed to determine the person's eligibility. See *R (Grogan)* v. *Bexley NHS Care Trust* [2006] EWHC 44 (admin).

5.2.2 Eligibility for NHS-funded care in England

Eligibility is determined following a full multidisciplinary assessment of the individual's needs which indicate a primary health care need. Certain characteristics of need and their impact on the care required to manage them may help determine eligibility. These characteristics are:

- Nature – the types of need, and the overall effect of those needs on the individual, including the type (quality) of interventions required to manage them
- Intensity – both the extent (quantity) and severity (degree) of the needs, including the need for sustained care (continuity)
- Complexity – how the needs arise and interact to increase the skill needed to monitor and manage the care
- Unpredictability – the degree to which needs fluctuate, creating difficulty in managing needs, and the level of risk to the person's health if adequate and timely care is not provided

Eligibility and ineligibility should not be based on:

- the setting of care

- the ability of the care provider to manage care: only where the successful management of a health care need has permanently reduced or removed an ongoing need will this have a bearing on eligibility
- the use, or not, of NHS-employed staff to provide care
- the individual's financial position
- the need for/presence of specialist staff in care delivery
- the existence of other NHS-funded care
- any other input-related, rather than needs-related, rationale.

The National Framework for NHS Continuing Healthcare and NHS Funded Nursing Care in England came into operation in October 2007. The framework is accompanied by a decision support tool, screening tool and fast-track tool for those with apparent and immediate needs.

5.2.3 Eligibility for NHS-funded care in Wales

Eligibility in Wales is based on satisfying one of the following criteria:

- The nature or complexity or intensity or unpredictability of the individual's health care needs (and any combination of these needs) requires regular supervision by a member of the NHS multidisciplinary team, such as the consultant, palliative care, therapy or other NHS member of the team.
- The individual's needs require the routine use of specialist health care equipment under supervision of NHS staff.
- The individual has a rapidly deteriorating or unstable medical, physical or mental health condition and requires regular supervision by a member of the NHS multidisciplinary team such as a consultant, palliative care, therapy or other NHS member of the team.
- The individual is in the final stages of a terminal illness and is likely to die in the near future.

Guidance for Wales is contained in WHC (2004) 54: NAFWC 41/2004, which is supported by *All Wales Continuing NHS Health Care: Framework for Implementation in Wales*, published in 2004. Further advice to the NHS and local authorities on continuing NHS health care (NAFWC32/06) was given in 2006 following the *Grogan* judgement.

5.2.4 Registered nursing care funding

Your client may receive financial support, even if not eligible for continuing NHS health care, if they live in a care home registered for nursing care, and receive registered nursing care by a registered nurse. This includes any service provided by a registered nurse which involves the provision of care, or the planning, supervision or delegation of the provision of care, other than services which, having regard to their nature and the circumstances in which they are provided, do not need to be provided by a registered nurse. See section 49(2) of the Health and Social Care Act [2001]. Nursing home residents in both England and Wales are now eligible for a contribution of a flat rate towards their care fees.

5.2.5 Transitional arrangements for those in a nursing home before 1 October 2007

Before 1 October 2007, the level of need for residents was assessed as low, moderate or high, with a different financial contribution at each level. Those residents who were on the former high band (£139/week) continue to be funded at the higher level (uprated annually) as the change would otherwise put them in a worse financial position. They can continue to remain on the high band until either:

- their care needs decrease to what would be the middle of low band level and they become entitled to the single rate
- they move from the nursing home
- they no longer need nursing care but choose to continue to reside in a nursing home
- they qualify for continuing NHS health care
- they die.

5.2.6 Aftercare under section 117 of the Mental Health Act 1983

The Mental Health Act 1983 at s.117(2) creates a joint duty on the NHS body and social services to provide, in cooperation with relevant voluntary agencies, after-care services for certain mentally ill people, until such time as they are both satisfied that the aftercare service is no longer required.

Section 117 of the act applies to those who have been detained under:

- Section 3 (which provides for the compulsory admission of a patient suffering from any mental disorder to hospital for treatment)
- Section 37 (a hospital or guardianship order made by the Crown or Magistrate Court)
- Section 45A (a hospital direction made by the Crown Court), or those who have been subject to a transfer direction made by the Secretary of State under sections 47 or 48.

NHS bodies and social services should not charge for services provided under section 117.

See *R* v. *Redcar & Cleveland BC ex p Armstrong*; *R* v. *Manchester City Council ex p Stennett*; *R* v. *Harrow London BC ex p Cobham* [2002] 4 All ER 124.

The act does not define what is meant by aftercare services, but in *Clunis* v. *Camden and Islington Health Authority* [1998] QB 978, 992 Beldam LJ commented that these 'include social work support, support in helping the ex-patient with problems of employment, accommodation or family relationships, the provision of domiciliary services and the use of day centre and residential facilities'.

It is up to the appropriate authority to determine which aftercare services, within the framework of the care plan, should occur before discharge.

Aftercare services should continue until, after a joint assessment, the NHS body and local authority are satisfied that the person no longer needs them. It is for the authority providing the services to take the lead in deciding when aftercare is no longer required. Funding can end if the patient is no longer in need of mental health care, though in practice this point is unlikely to affect many people. See *R v Richmond Upon Thames LBC ex p Watson*, *The Times*, October 15, 1999/ LGO complaint into Bath and North East Somerset Council No 06/B/ 16774.

6. MORE INFORMATION

6.1 Solicitors' Code of Conduct

- Rule 2.01: Taking on clients
- Rule 3.01: Duty not to act

6.2 Law Society products and support

6.2.1 Practice Advice Service

The Law Society's Practice Advice Service provides support for solicitors on a wide range of areas of practice. The Practice Advice team can be contacted on 0870 606 2522 from 09:00 to 17:00 on weekdays.

6.2.2 Law Society publications

- Anti-money laundering practice note
- *Conveyancing Handbook*, 16th Edition
- The *Elderly Client Handbook*, 3rd Edition
- *Health and Social Care Handbook*
- *Mental Capacity Act 2005: A Guide to the New Law*, 2nd Edition
- *Solicitors' Code of Conduct 2007*, June 2009 Edition
- *Solicitors and Money Laundering*, 3rd Edition

6.3 Further reading and reference

6.3.1 Client capacity to give instructions

- Mental Capacity Act 2005
- Mental Capacity Act code of practice
- *Re: Beaney (Deceased)* [1978] 1 WLR 770: test of capacity to make a gift

6.3.2 Publicly funded care

- National Framework for NHS continuing healthcare and NHS-funded nursing care
- Age Concern advice about continuing care
- *Robertson* v. *Fife* [2002] UKHL 35: local authority recovery of care fees
- Department of Health continuing care website
- NHS Continuing Healthcare (Responsibilities) Directions 2007
- Delayed Discharges (Continuing Care) Directions 2007
- National Health Service (Nursing Care in Residential Accommodation) (England) Directions 2007
- Nursing Guide Handbook October 2007
- Health Service Ombudsman's (HSO) Second Report for sessions 2002-2003 – NHS funding for long term care
- HSO's NHS funding for Long term care follow up report 2004–2005
- HSO case no E.22/02/02–03 (The Pointon Case)
- Health Committee Report on NHS Continuing Care Sixth Report of Session 2004–2005 (April 2005)
- The Parliamentary and Health Service Ombudsman's report *Retrospective Continuing Care Funding and Redress* – 13 March 2007
- National Assistance (Assessment of Resources) Regulations 1992 as amended
- Circular LAC (99)9 *Charging for Residential Accommodation Guide* (CRAG) (copies available from the Department of Health, PO Box 777, London SE1 6XH. Fax: 01623 724 524. E-mail: doh@prologistics.co.uk).
- Department of Health website

6.4 Status of this practice note

Practice notes are issued by the Law Society for the use and benefit of its members. They represent the Law Society's view of good practice in a particular area. They are not intended to be the only standard of good practice that solicitors can follow. You are not required to follow them, but doing so will make it easier to account to oversight bodies for your actions.

Practice notes are not legal advice, nor do they necessarily provide a defence to complaints of misconduct or of inadequate professional service. While care has been taken to ensure that they are accurate, up to date and useful, the Law Society will not accept any legal liability in relation to them.

For queries or comments on this practice note, contact the Law Society's Practice Advice Service.

6.5 Terminology in this practice note

Must – a specific requirement in the Solicitor's Code of Conduct or legislation. You must comply, unless there are specific exemptions or defences provided for in the code of conduct or relevant legislation.

Should – good practice for most situations, in the Law Society's view. If you do not follow this, you must be able to justify to oversight bodies why this is appropriate, either for your practice or in the particular retainer.

May – a non-exhaustive list of options for meeting your obligations. Which option you choose is determined by the risk profile of the individual practice, client or retainer. You must be able to justify why this was an appropriate option to oversight bodies.

APPENDIX A7

Non-contentious costs

[Practice Advice Service, October 2010]

INTRODUCTION

This booklet, prepared by the Practice Advice Service, is not intended to be a fully comprehensive guide to non-contentious costs but attempts to cover those areas that generate the most frequent enquiries from solicitors. The booklet provides information on charging in non-contentious matters. It also discusses billing generally and the procedures available to clients who may wish to challenge solicitors' costs.

Solicitors should in particular familiarise themselves in more detail with:

- Solicitors' (Non-Contentious Business) Remuneration Order 2009
- Solicitors' Code of Conduct 2007, in particular Rule 2 which deals with Client Relations and Rule 10
- Sections 56, 57, 70, 71 and 72 of the Solicitors Act 1974
- Legal Services Act 2007 Schedule 16, s64(3)

Booklets on contentious costs (entitled 'Contentious Costs') and conditional fee agreements (entitled 'Payment by Results') are also available. For advice on solicitors' costs generally, please telephone the Practice Advice Service on 0870 606 2522 or e-mail **practiceadvice@lawsociety.org.uk**.

[...]

REVIEW OF CIVIL LITIGATION COSTS BY LORD JUSTICE JACKSON

In November 2008 Lord Justice Jackson was selected by the Master of the Rolls to conduct a fundamental review of the rules and principles governing the costs of civil litigation and to make recommendations which would promote access to justice at proportionate cost. A preliminary report was published in May 2009 and the final report on 14 January 2010. The full report can be viewed at **www.judiciary.gov.uk**.

If, in due course, the recommendations in the Jackson Report are to be implemented, it will require this booklet and the other Practice Advice Service booklets, Contentious Costs and Payment by Results, to be amended. Until then we have highlighted the Jackson proposals where appropriate in each booklet. Some of the key proposals are:

(1) Cease recoverability for after-the-event (ATE) insurance premiums and success fees in civil litigation
(2) Success fees to be capped at 25% of damages
(3) Increase of 10% in general damages for pain, suffering and loss of amenity
(4) Referral fees paid by lawyers in personal injury cases to no longer be permitted
(5) Qualified one way costs shifting – unsuccessful claimants will not be required to pay the defendants costs but, unsuccessful defendants will continue to pay the claimants costs.

Qualified one way costs shifting to apply for personal injury litigation and possibly clinical negligence, judicial review, defamation claims and others

(6) Fixed costs in all personal injury fast track litigation, for other types of cases a dual system eventually leading to fixed costs for all types of claims in the fast track
(7) Costs Council be established to annually review fixed costs and the guideline hourly rates
(8) Before-the-event (BTE) insurance should be actively promoted to encourage wider use
(9) Contingency fees to be permissible in contentious proceedings subject to regulations including a cap of a maximum percentage of damages that can be recovered in fees. An additional safeguard that the agreement will be invalid unless it is countersigned by an independent solicitor. The unsuccessful party will remain responsible for the successful parties costs on the conventional basis only
(10) Detailed assessment – to develop a new format for bills and to streamline the procedure through use of IT
(11) Abolition of the indemnity principle
(12) Alternative dispute resolution (ADR) – increasing lawyers, judges, small businesses and the publics' knowledge of ADR
(13) Contingency Legal Aid Fund (CLAF) and Supplementary Legal Aid Scheme (SLAS) – these are self funding and usually not-for-profit forms of litigation funding. The Government to review the viability of these schemes.

It remains to be seen whether and to what extent the recommendations in the Jackson Report will be implemented. Many of his proposals require primary legislation, whilst others would need changes to the Civil Procedure Rules which will still require Ministry of Justice approval.

WHAT IS NON-CONTENTIOUS BUSINESS?

Non-contentious business is defined in s.87(1) Solicitors Act 1974 as 'any business done as a solicitor which is not contentious business'.

Work done preliminary to proceedings is non-contentious provided proceedings are not subsequently begun. The keyword is 'begun'. So, for example, if a solicitor takes instructions on a personal injury matter and the parties reach settlement before proceedings are issued, the work is regarded as non-contentious.

Please note: When proceedings have been issued, it is a moot point as to whether all prior work leading to the action automatically becomes contentious. Please see obiter comment of Lord Justice Brooke in *Crosbie* v. *Munroe* [2003] EWCA Civ 350.

If solicitors in England and Wales are involved in work where proceedings are issued abroad, the work will be regarded as non-contentious. But please note Rule 2.04(2) of the Solicitors' Code of Conduct 2007 in regards to fee arrangements.

Examples of contentious and non-contentious business

	Contentious	*Non-contentious*
1.	Proceedings actually begun in the County Court, High Court, Magistrates Court, Crown Court and the Court of Protection.	Proceedings before all tribunals other than the Lands Tribunal and the Employment Appeal Tribunal. **The recent case of *Tel-ka Talk Limited* v. *HMRC* (in which The Law Society intervened) reconfirmed the position that proceedings before tribunals are non-contentious. (Please see below for further information)**
2.	Proceedings actually begun before the Land, Property and Housing Chamber First Tier Tribunal and the Employment Appeal Tribunal.	Planning and other public enquiries including Coroners Court work.
3.	Contentious probate proceedings actually begun.	Non-contentious or common form probate business.
4.	Proceedings on appeal to the Court of Appeal, Privy Council and House of Lords.	Conveyancing, company acquisitions and mergers, the administration of estates and trusts out of court, the preparation of wills, statements and contracts, and any other work not included in the 'contentious' column.
5.	Proceedings in arbitration.	Criminal Injuries Compensation Authority.
6.	Motor Insurers Bureau Uninsured drivers' claims (proceedings issued).	Motor Insurers Bureau Untraced drivers' claims. Motor Insurers Bureau Uninsured drivers' claims (proceedings not issued).
7.	Work done preliminary to proceedings covered by 1-5 above including advice, preparation and negotiations provided the proceedings are subsequently begun (although see note above*).	Work done preliminary to the proceedings included in the 'contentious' column if such proceedings are not subsequently begun.
8.	Licensing (appeals to Magistrates Court)	Licensing (administered by Local Authority)

VALIDITY OF CONTINGENCY FEE ARRANGEMENTS IN TRIBUNALS

Tel-Ka Talk Limited v. The Commissioners of Her Majesty's Revenue & Customs (HMRC) June (Case No: SCCO Ref: PTH0904822)

In the case of Tel-Ka Talk Limited (the company) had appealed against decisions of HM Revenue and Customs (HMRC) to refuse repayment of VAT input tax credit claimed by the company.

As a result of the withholding of VAT, the company suffered cash flow difficulties, and experienced difficulty in funding the legal costs of the tribunal hearings.

The solicitors agreed to continue to act on a contingency fee basis and entered into a non-contentious business agreement. The contingency fee arrangement enabled the company to continue to pursue its claim and recover the VAT repayment it was owed by HMRC. HMRC argued that a contingency fee was unenforceable as tribunal proceedings were contentious.

The Law Society intervened in this case to protect access to justice. It was essential for the Courts to allow contingency fee arrangements with solicitors to be valid in order to ensure that the right to a fair hearing in a tribunal was not denied.

Master Hurst, Senior Costs Judge in this case ruled that the use of contingency fees or a no win, no fee arrangement in tribunal cases was lawful.

The judge considered whether proceedings before the Tribunal fall within the definition of non-contentious business as defined in s.87(1) of the Solicitors Act 1974.

The Law Society was successful in maintaining their long held views that work in Tribunals is non-contentious. Therefore, a Non Contentious Business Agreement in the form of a contingency fee arrangement under s.57 of the Solicitors Act 1974 can be lawfully entered into.

Master Hurst also referred to Lord Justice Jackson's review of Civil Costs in which he also stated that:

> 'The Employment Tribunals jurisdiction is characterised as non-contentious and so the use of contingency fees is not prohibited by either law or professional conduct rules'

Master Hurst was not persuaded that a Tribunal is a 'court' or that proceedings before a Tribunal are contentious business. He therefore concluded that contingency fees before a Tribunal are lawful.

*Please note that Parliament has specifically sanctioned the use of contingency fee arrangements in Employment Tribunals by the Damages Based Agreements Regulations 2010 ...

BASIS OF CHARGING IN NON-CONTENTIOUS BUSINESS

When charging for non-contentious work, consideration must be given to the Solicitors' (Non-Contentious Business) Remuneration Order 2009 (SI 2009/1931) made on 16 July 2009, which came into force on 11 August 2009 (see Appendix 1) Article 3 states;

> 'A solicitor's costs must be fair and reasonable having regard to all the circumstances of the case and in particular to –
>
> (a) the complexity of the matter or the difficulty or novelty of the questions raised;
> (b) the skill, labour, specialised knowledge and responsibility involved;
> (c) the time spent on the business;
> (d) the number and importance of the documents prepared or considered, without regard to length;

(e) the place where and the circumstances in which the business or any part of the business is transacted;
(f) the amount or value of any money or property involved;
(g) whether any land involved is registered land within the meaning of the Land Registration Act 2002;
(h) the importance of the matter to the client; and
(i) the approval (express or implied) of the entitled person or the express approval of the testator to –

  (i) the solicitor undertaking all or any part of the work giving rise to the costs; or
  (ii) the amount of the costs'

VALUE ELEMENT

In certain areas of work, such as probate, mortgages, commercial leases and domestic conveyancing amongst others, it may be appropriate to include a value element in the method of charging. Information on these specific areas is discussed in the subject areas below.

However, the question of whether a value element is used is a matter for agreement between the solicitor and the client; it is not mandatory. Where a value element is used, practitioners may wish to use the guidance that follows, which has been distilled from the decisions made by assessors in dealing with applications for remuneration certificates.

Where no specific information is given in the individual subject areas, the table below may assist:

Value band	*Percentage*
Up to £400,000	0.5%
On next £600,000 (maximum value £1 million)	0.375%
On next £1,500,000 (maximum value £2.5 million)	0.25%
On next £2,500,000 (maximum value £5 million)	0.125%
On next £5,000,000 (maximum value £10 million)	0.1%

CHARGING IN PROBATE AND IN THE ADMINISTRATION OF ESTATES

Fair and reasonable

In all cases the overall consideration must be that the charges are fair and reasonable, having regard to all the circumstances of the matter. The figures below should not be regarded as scale charges in any way and must always be exercised with discretion. In *Jemma Trust* v. *Liptrott* [2003] EWCA Civ 1476, the Court of Appeal stated that it would be best practice to agree the charging regime in advance with not only the executors but also, where appropriate, with any residuary beneficiary who is an entitled third party under the Solicitors' (Non-Contentious Business) Remuneration Order 1994 (now replaced by the Solicitors' (Non-Contentious Business) Remuneration Order 2009). The Court of Appeal held that a value charge can either be made in addition to an hourly rate, or it can be included in the hourly rate, but the value element must not be reflected in both charges. The comments of the court are reproduced in Appendix 4 below but it is recommended that practitioners read the Jemma Trust judgment in its entirety.

Where appropriate, charges may consist of two elements:

(a) Hourly rate

This should be an inclusive figure incorporating the fee earner's expense rate and any appropriate care and conduct uplift.

(b) Value element

Account may be taken of the value of the assets in the estate. In calculating the value element of the charge, the following approach may be helpful:

- **Consider the value nature and number of assets** It is usual to divide the estate (i.e. total value of the assets left after death) into two parts:
  - (i) *The deceased's residence* The value of the deceased's home, or as much of it as he or she owned, if it was shared with another person. For example, where the property is jointly owned, the value is reduced by half.
  - (ii) *Value of rest of the estate*
- **Apply an appropriate percentage** An appropriate percentage should be considered in the light of the circumstances of the case but the following may be helpful.

Solicitor not acting as an executor

Value of gross estate less residence 1%
Value of residence 0.5%

WORKED EXAMPLE 1 – SOLICITOR NOT ACTING AS EXECUTOR

So for example if the residence was valued at £200,000 and was owned by the deceased alone this would be calculated as follows: £200,000 × 0.5% = £1,000.

Then consider the value of the rest of the estate, which is say, £50,000 ignoring the value of the residence then apply 1%. The remaining calculation therefore is:

Rest of estate is £50,000 then apply 1% = £500
Therefore total value element = £1,000 + £500 = £1,500.

Solicitor acting as sole executor or joint executor with another person

Value of gross estate less residence 1.5%
Value of residence 0.75%

WORKED EXAMPLE 2 – SOLICITOR ACTING AS EXECUTOR

So for example if the residence was valued at £200,000 and was owned by the deceased as a joint tenant this would be calculated as follows:

Value of residence (£200,000 divided by 2) = £100,000 × 0 .75% = £750. Note the value of the residence is reduced by half as the deceased owned it jointly with another person.

Then consider the value of rest of the estate which is say £50,000 ignoring the value of the residence then apply 1.5%.

The remaining calculation is therefore:

Rest of the estate is £50,000 then apply 1.5% = £750
Therefore total value element = £750 + £750 = £1,500

High value estates

When dealing with high value estates, consideration should be given to reducing the value element percentage charged in order to ensure that the overall level of charge is fair and reasonable. For general guidance on this point, see the case of *Jemma Trust* v. *Liptrott* [2003] EWCA Civ 1476. In that case the Court of Appeal held that an appropriate charging regime was as set out in Appendix 3 of this booklet.

In the case of *Jemma Trust*, the Court of Appeal also noted that in the appropriate circumstances a regressive scale may also need to be applied to the value element related to the principal residence.

It is for individual practitioners to exercise their own professional judgment as to whether or not to apply the value element when charging for the administration of an estate.

CHARGING IN PROPERTY WORK

The following methods of charging may be appropriate.

Domestic conveyancing

Two methods are suggested:

(i) *Calculate hourly expense rate.* Add value element outlined in the table on page 9 of this booklet or
(ii) *Take a broad look at the circumstances of the transaction.* Calculate a single charging figure incorporating the time spent and what is fair and reasonable in all the circumstances. This single charging figure may comprise a fixed fee or an estimate. If an estimate is provided consideration should be given to updating costs information regularly. See Rule 2.03 of the Solicitors' Code of Conduct 2007 at **www.sra.org.uk**.

In practice the second method is more commonplace.

Leasehold work

Hourly rate

This should be a single figure incorporating the time spent together with what is fair and reasonable in all the circumstances.

Value element

The suggested formula for calculating the value element of charges for leasehold work is as follows:

(i) Take half the yearly rent.
(ii) Multiply it by the unexpired term of the lease (limited to 20 years).
(iii) Add any premium payable by the lessee and deduct any payable by the lessor.
(iv) Apply the following regressive scale to the value as calculated:

Value band	*Percentage*
Up to £400,000	0.5%
On next £600,000 (maximum value £1 million)	0.375%
On next £1,500,000 (maximum value £2.5 million)	0.25%
On next £2,500,000 (maximum value £5 million)	0.125%
On next £5,000,000 (maximum value £10 million)	0.1%

Is the formula applicable to an assignment as well as a grant of a lease?

In 'An Approach to Non-Contentious Costs' the above formula is described as a formula for establishing a capital value. It does not discuss whether or not a value element is applicable. If on an assignment the circumstances suggest a value element is justifiable, the formula can be used to calculate it.

Fair and reasonable

Please note that these figures do not constitute a recommended scale. The final figure should still be reviewed to ensure that the charges are fair and reasonable having regard to all the circumstances.

Calculating a value element when acting on a mortgage or re-mortgage

Where the lender does not have its own scale of charges, the following percentages of value may be appropriate:

When acting for purchaser/mortgagor	0.25%
When acting for purchaser/mortgagor and the mortgagee	0.25%
When acting for the mortgagee alone	0.5 %
When acting for the mortgagor alone	0.5 %

These percentages should be reduced if dealing with high values.

NON-CONTENTIOUS BUSINESS AGREEMENTS

Section 57 of the Solicitors Act 1974 as amended by section 98 of the Courts and Legal Services Act 1990 allows a solicitor to enter into an agreement with the client for remuneration of non-contentious work.

Form of the agreement

The agreement MUST:

- be in writing – s57(3)
- be signed by the person to be bound by it or by his/her agent – s57(3)
- have all the terms contained within the document

see *Chamberlain* v. *Boodle and King* (1982) 3 All ER 188 CA – it must be precise and unambiguous.

The agreement MAY:

(i) be entered into before, after or in the course of the transaction – s57(1)
(ii) provide for remuneration by a gross sum, or by reference to an hourly rate, or by a commission, or percentage, or by a salary, or otherwise – s57(2). The reference to hourly rate was added by s98 of the Courts and Legal Services Act 1990 which came into force on 1 March 1991
(iii) include all or any disbursements made by the solicitor in respect of searches, plans, travelling, stamps, fees, or other matter s57(2).

Effect of a non-contentious business agreement

A s.57 agreement can be referred for assessment if the solicitor seeks to rely on the agreement and the client objects on the grounds that it is unfair and unreasonable. The court has the power to enquire into the facts and may set aside or vary the agreement if it is found to be unfair or unreasonable – s.57(5).

If a s.57 agreement as to hourly rates is referred to assessment and the client objects to the amount of costs and not that the agreement is unfair or unreasonable, the agreed hourly rate will not be open to challenge but the court may consider the number of hours worked and whether they were excessive – s.57(7).

Enforcing a non-contentious business agreement

Simple debt recovery proceedings can be commenced – s.57(4).

Section 69 of the Solicitors Act 1974 must still be complied with before an action for recovery is brought by a solicitor. See Appendix 4

CONTINGENCY FEES

Rule 2 of the Solicitors' Code of Conduct 2007 prohibits a solicitor from entering into a contingency fee agreement for contentious work except where permitted under statute or by the common law (see Rule 2.04 of the Code of Conduct 2007). Contingency fees are permissible in non-contentious cases. …

The term 'contingency fee' is generic in that it covers all agreements where the fee (whether fixed, or calculated either as a percentage of the proceeds or otherwise) is payable only in the event of success. However, 'contingency fee agreements' are traditionally regarded as arrangements whereby the fee is calculated as a percentage of the proceeds recovered.

Conditional fee agreements (CFAs) are a form of contingency fee permitted under statute. They can be used for all non-contentious work except for family matters. However, CFAs are not commonly used in non-contentious matters as they are best suited to cases where costs are recoverable from the other side. CFAs could be considered in matters where it is possible that proceedings could be issued.

At the outset of a matter in which it is likely that proceedings could be issued (e.g. a personal injury matter), a solicitor could either;

- use a contingency fee arrangement contained in a Non-Contentious Business Agreement until proceedings are issued. At that stage, the retainer could not continue on that basis (see Rule 2 above), and the arrangement would have to be changed to an alternative fee arrangement. Solicitors should be aware that it is a moot point as to whether all work done for the client automatically becomes contentious once proceedings are issued. If this view is taken there is doubt as to whether the solicitor would be able to recover his pre issue costs;

- use a CFA from the outset, or
- use some other type of fee arrangement (e.g., hourly rate, fixed cost, etc.) from the outset.

For guidance on conditional fee agreements see the Practice Advice Service booklet 'Payment by Results' which can be downloaded from the Law Society website at **www.lawsociety.org.uk**.

In the area of contingency fees Lord Justice (LJ) Jackson proposes the following:

(1) Cease recoverability for after-the-event (ATE) insurance premiums and success fees in civil litigation
(2) Success fees to be capped at 25% of damages
(3) Increase of 10% in general damages for pain, suffering and loss of amenity
(4) Before-the-event (BTE) insurance should be actively promoted to encourage wider use
(5) Contingency fees to be permissible in contentious proceedings subject to regulations including a cap of a maximum percentage of damages that can be recovered in fees. LJ Jackson has proposed an additional safeguard that the agreement will be invalid unless it is countersigned by an independent solicitor. The unsuccessful party will remain responsible for the successful party's costs on the conventional basis only.

The full report can be viewed at **www.judiciary.gov.uk**

DAMAGES BASED AGREEMENTS

As of 9 April 2010 contingency fee agreements used in Employment Tribunal work must comply with the Damage-Based Agreement Regulations 2010 ('DBA Regulations') in order to be valid. The DBA Regulations were made under s.154 Coroners and Justice Act 2009 which inserted s.58AA CLSA 1990. The DBA Regulations apply to any person providing advocacy services, litigation services or claims management services in Employment Tribunal work and to all damage-based agreements signed on or after 9 April 2010 whether proceedings are issued or not.

A CFA could still be used for an employment matter and as such would fall outside the DBA Regulations provided that the amount of costs and/or any success fee is not determined by reference to the damages. For further information, please see the Law Society's Practice Note on Damages-based Agreement Regulations 2010 at: **www.lawsociety.org.uk/practicenotes**

BILLING THE CLIENT

Interim bills

Interim bills on account

These are in fact merely requests for payments on account of a 'final bill' to be delivered at a later date. It is not possible to sue on this type of bill and a client cannot apply for assessment of it.

In non-contentious matters, a solicitor must make any requirement for a payment on account of costs a condition of accepting instructions. Without this condition (or the client's subsequent agreement), a solicitor cannot terminate the retainer if the client refuses to make such a payment. This is something that should be considered at the outset of the retainer when terms of business are being agreed.

Interim statute bills

These are termed statute bills because they comply with all the requirements of s65(2) the Solicitors Act 1974 and result in all the consequences that flow from such compliance. The solicitor can sue on them and the client can apply for assessment of them. They are final bills in respect of the work covered and cannot be adjusted in light of the outcome of the case.

Interim statute bills can arise in two ways:

(i) **Natural break**. The Law Society's advice is not to rely on this ground except in the clearest circumstances. For limited guidance on what constitutes a natural break, practitioners should see *Chamberlain* v. *Boodle and King* [1982] 3 All ER 188 CA.

(ii) **Agreement**. Practitioners should make it expressly clear in their terms of business letter that they propose to deliver interim statute bills in the event of protracted work..

See the Court of Appeal judgments in *Davidsons* v. *Jones-Fenleigh* [1997] Costs LR (Core Vol.) 70 and *Palomo* v. *Turner* [2000] 1 WLR 37 regarding the distinction between statute bills and requests for payment on account generally.

Final bills

These can be rendered in the following circumstances:

(i) where the client has agreed to, or asked for, delivery of a final bill
(ii) at the conclusion of the matter
(iii) on the termination of the retainer
(iv) on an application to the High Court under s68 of the Solicitors Act 1974 to order the solicitor to deliver a bill.

Where interim bills on account have been rendered pursuant to s.65(2) of the Solicitors Act 1974, these should be disregarded for the purposes of the final bill and treated as requests for payment of money on account. The final bill should therefore set out the total amount of the solicitor's charges and disbursements with any additional mark up on the interim bills and should give credit for all payments received as a result of bills on account.

Content of bill

Schedule 16, s.64(3) of the Legal Services Act 2007 which came into force in March 2008 amended s.69 of the Solicitors Act 1974. This amendment allows solicitors to deliver their bills electronically, please see Appendix 4 for further information. A solicitor's bill of costs should contain sufficient information to identify the matter and period of time to which it relates.

The bill must also comply with s.69(2) of the Solicitors Act 1974 which requires that the bill must be –

(a) signed in accordance with subsection (2A), and
(b) delivered in accordance with subsection (2C)

(2A) A bill is signed in accordance with this subsection if it is–

(a) signed by the solicitor or on his behalf by an employee of the solicitor authorised by him to sign, or
(b) enclosed in, or accompanied by, a letter which is signed as mentioned in paragraph (a) and refers to the bill.

(2B) For the purposes of subsection (2A) the signature may be an electronic signature.

(2C) A bill is delivered in accordance with this subsection if–

(a) it is delivered to the party to be charged with the bill personally,

(b) it is delivered to that party by being sent to him by post to, or left for him at, his place of business, dwelling-house or last known place of abode, or

(c) it is delivered to that party–

  (i) by means of an electronic communications network, or
  (ii) by other means but in a form that nevertheless requires the use of apparatus by the recipient to render it intelligible,

and that party has indicated to the person making the delivery his willingness to accept delivery of a bill sent in the form and manner used.

If the bill is not properly signed, it is still valid but will be unenforceable in the courts.

The bill should show disbursements separately from the solicitor's fees, see s.67 of the Solicitors Act 1974.

In order to comply with the VAT regulations, when a third party is paying the solicitor's costs, the bill must be made out to the client, but it should state that the bill is payable by a third party.

Gross sum and detailed itemised bills

It is for the solicitor to decide whether to deliver a gross sum bill or one containing detailed items.

In a contentious matter, a client who has received a gross sum bill has the right to require a solicitor to deliver a detailed itemised bill to replace the original bill, see s64(2) Solicitors' Act 1974.

This right does not apply in non-contentious work.

REMOVAL OF THE REMUNERATION CERTIFICATE PROCEDURE

Prior to 11 August 2009 the Solicitors' (Non-Contentious Business) Remuneration Order 1994 set out the procedure which applied when a solicitor delivered a bill for non-contentious business. This included the right of the client to request the solicitor to obtain a remuneration certificate from the Legal Complaints Service if the client disputed the amount of the bill. Article 6 of the Order required that the solicitor informed any entitled person, in writing, of:

- their right to a remuneration certificate;
- their right to assessment by the court; and
- the solicitor's right to charge interest on a bill.

The Solicitors' (Non-Contentious Business) Remuneration Order 2009 (SI 2009/1931) which came into effect on 11 August 2009 and abolished remuneration certificates from that date. (See Appendix 1). As a result of this Order, clients and entitled third parties* who dispute bills in a non-contentious matter issued on or after 11 August 2009 no longer have the right to request that their solicitor obtains a remuneration certificate. Solicitors must now comply with rule 2.05 of the Solicitors Code of Conduct 2007. (Please see below for further detail).

The Solicitors' (Non-Contentious Business) Remuneration (Amendment) Order 2010 (SI2 010/2262) makes further minor changes as a result of the specific provisions of the Legal Services Act 2007 which came into force on 6 October 2010. The net effect of this further amendment is that if the Legal Ombudsman has made a direction which restricts or limits a solicitors' fees under section 137(2) of the Legal Services Act 2007, then any applicable interest that is to be charged on the solicitors' unpaid costs is to be calculated by reference to the limited fee that has been directed by the Legal Ombudsman.

*Entitled third party is defined in s.2 of the Solicitors' (Non-Contentious Business) Remuneration Order 2009.

ASSESSMENT OF THIRD PARTY COSTS

Section 71(1) of the Solicitors' Act 1974 provides:

> (1) Where a person other than the party chargeable with the bill for the purposes of section 70 has paid, or is or was liable to pay, a bill either to the solicitor or to the party chargeable with the bill, that person, or his executors, administrators or assignees may apply to the High Court for an order for the assessment of the bill as if he were the party chargeable with it, and the court may make the same order (if any) as it might have made if the application had been made by the party chargeable with the bill.

The practical effect of this section is that if a client is required to pay a third party's solicitor's costs, he may be entitled to have the bill of costs assessed as if he were the party chargeable.

This provision may for example be useful in the following situations:

(i) Residuary beneficiaries may apply for assessment of the costs of the solicitor who is administering an estate whether or not the solicitor is an executor of the estate
(ii) A mortgagor who would like the costs of the mortgagee's solicitor assessed
(iii) A tenant required to pay a landlord's solicitor's charges

Information on precautions which a lessee's solicitors can take to prevent a dispute arising over a landlord's solicitor's bill is contained in a Law Society Council statement printed in the Law Society's *Gazette* on 19th December 1984 and reprinted in the Law Society publication 'An Approach to Non-Contentious Costs' (see details at the front of this booklet). See also rule 10.02 of the Solicitors Code of Conduct 2007.

In Rule 2 of the Solicitors' Code of Conduct 2007 (see **www.sra.org.uk**), the solicitor must advise the client of their potential liability for any other party's costs. Where appropriate, solicitors are advised to obtain a fixed figure or agree a cap on a third party's costs.

Where an undertaking is given as to costs, it is an undertaking to pay 'proper costs' unless otherwise stated. This enables the giver of the undertaking to apply for assessment of the bill and, provided that the recipient is notified of this promptly, the undertaking will take effect on the bill as assessed. See Guidance to Rule 10 paragraph 32 of the Solicitors' Code of Conduct 2007. The application for assessment is under section 71 of the Solicitors Act 1974.

The landlord's solicitor should inform his client that he may look to him for payment if the tenant does not pay his costs.

ASSESSMENT OF SOLICITOR AND CLIENT COSTS

There are two bases for the assessment of costs, the standard basis and the indemnity basis, and on neither basis will the court allow costs which have been unreasonably incurred or are unreasonable in amount (Rule 44.4 (1) of the Civil Procedure Rules (CPR)).

On an assessment on the indemnity basis, there is no reference to proportionality and any doubts as to whether costs were reasonably incurred or were reasonable in amount is resolved in favour of the receiving party. However, on an assessment on the standard basis, the court will only allow costs which are proportionate to the matters in issue and will resolve any doubt which it may have about whether costs were reasonably incurred or reasonable and proportionate in amount in favour of the paying party.

The client can apply for an assessment of his/her solicitor's costs under section 70 of the Solicitors Act 1974.

Time limits under section 70 of Solicitors Act

The client has a right to assessment within one month from the date of the delivery of the bill.

If the application is made after one month but before twelve months from the date of delivery of the bill, the court's permission is required for the bill to be assessed.

Except in special circumstances, no order for assessment will be made:

(i) after twelve months from the delivery of the bill or
(ii) after a judgment has been obtained for the recovery of the costs covered by the bill, or
(iii) after the bill has been paid, but before the expiration of 12 months from the payment of the bill.

In relation to the application of section 70, practitioners should also have regard to the Court of Appeal decisions in *Thomas Watts & Co (a firm)* v. *Smith (Malcolm Davies)* [1998] Costs LR 59 and *Turner* v. *Palomo* [2000] 1 WLR 37. Both of these decisions appear to allow the client a common law means to challenge a solicitor's bill outside the statutory limitations of s.70. The practical effect of this means that where a solicitor sues for non-payment of fees, any summary judgment will be for assessment of damages and not for a liquidated amount.

Also note the House of Lords' decision in *Harrison* v. *Tew* [1990] 2 AC 532 which stated that the Court had no power to order assessment under s.70 outside the statutory period.

Assessment procedure

Rule 48.10 of the Civil Procedure Rules sets out the procedure to be followed where the court has made an order under Part III of the Solicitors Act 1974 for the assessment of costs payable to a solicitor by his client and is as follows:

The solicitor must serve a breakdown of costs within 28 days of the order for costs to be assessed.

The client must serve points of dispute within 14 days after service on him of the breakdown in costs.

If the solicitor wishes to serve a reply, he must do so within 14 days of service on him of the points of dispute.

Either party may file a request for a hearing date:

(i) after points of dispute have been served; but
(ii) no later than 3 months after the date of the order for the costs to be assessed.

This procedure applies subject to any contrary order made by the court.

Precedent P showing the breakdown of costs is annexed to the Practice Direction accompanying Rule 48.10. This Practice Direction also deals generally with the practicalities of the assessment process.

Where to apply

Rule 47.4 deals with the appropriate venue for detailed assessment proceedings. This should be read in conjunction with s69(3) of the Solicitors Act 1974.

Who should apply?

It is usual for the client to apply for assessment although it is possible for a solicitor to apply to have his own costs assessed (see Rule 48.10(5)). The latter is inadvisable because the solicitor will generally be unable to recover his costs for attending the hearing if the client fails to attend.

Costs of assessment

The costs of assessment will follow the event. If a solicitor's bill is reduced by one fifth or more, then the solicitor will bear the costs of the assessment. If the bill is reduced by less than one fifth or is not reduced, the party chargeable will pay the costs. See Solicitors Act 1974 s.70(9).

The one fifth figure is calculated on the total of the bill *excluding* VAT.

On the subject of Detailed Assessment the Jackson Report proposes to develop a new format for bills and to streamline the procedure through use of IT. The full report can be viewed at **www.judiciary.gov.uk**

RECOVERING YOUR COSTS

Before you sue

Provided that a solicitor's bill complies with the requirements of s.69(2) of the Solicitors Act 1974 (see Appendix 4) recovery proceedings for costs may be commenced after one month has elapsed from the date of delivery of the final or interim statute bill. However, in circumstances where the client is about to quit England and Wales, to be declared bankrupt or to compound with his creditors or do any other act which tends to prevent or delay the solicitor obtaining payment, a solicitor may seek leave to issue proceedings within a month, see s.69(1) of the Solicitors Act 1974.

It should be noted that a solicitor will be prevented from issuing recovery proceedings for costs where the client has made an application to the court for detailed assessment of the costs within one month of delivery of the bill or where he has obtained an order for the bill to be assessed – see s.70(1) and (2) of the Solicitors Act 1974.

Before bringing proceedings to recover non-contentious costs, or if you deduct your costs (other than disbursements) from money held for or on behalf of a client or estate in satisfaction of a bill and an entitled person objects in writing to the amount of the bill within the prescribed time, you must do the following under the 'emergency' rule:

- Inform the client or other entitled person in writing of their rights in relation to having the bill assessed by the court under sections 70, 71 and 72 of the Solicitors Act 1974
- Inform the client or other entitled person in writing that you are entitled to charge interest on the outstanding amount of the bill in accordance with article 5 of the Solicitors' (Non-Contentious Business) Remuneration Order 2009

From 11 August 2009, you are no longer required to provide the client with information about their right to request a remuneration certificate as this procedure has been removed. You should amend any standard documentation accordingly.

Interest on costs

Article 5 of the Solicitors' (Non-Contentious Business) Remuneration Order 2009 deals with interest payable on unpaid costs in non-contentious matters and entitles the solicitor to charge interest from one month from the delivery of the bill of costs ,

Unless otherwise agreed with the client, the rate of interest will be 8 per cent per annum. This has been the interest rate on judgment debts since 1 April 1993 (see Judgment Debts (Rate of Interest) Order 1993 SI 93/564).

Service of a statutory demand

A solicitor can serve a statutory demand shortly after delivery of a bill and can, after the expiration of one month from the delivery of the bill, issue a bankruptcy petition provided 21 days have expired from service of the statutory demand.

A petition, but not a statutory demand, is an 'action' within the meaning of s69 of the Solicitors Act 1974.

In general solicitors should be wary of following this route as there is a power to set aside a statutory demand on the grounds of injustice. See *Re a Debtor (No 88 of 1991)* [1992] 4 All ER 301.

Note also the decision in *Turner* v. *Palomo* which may have the effect of outlawing statutory demands on the basis that the amount on a solicitor's bill is still subject to assessment by the court if there are proceedings. As it is not a liquidated demand there is no right to serve a statutory demand. An application for this case to be heard by the House of Lords was refused.

FURTHER READING

Law Society Practice Notes which are available at **www.lawsociety.org.uk**.
Guide to Good Practice published by the Law Society. Available from the Law Society bookshop at **www.lawsociety.org.uk**.
Solicitors' Code of Conduct 2007 is available online at **www.sra.org.uk**.
Cook on Costs 2010 by Michael J Cook, published by Butterworths.
The Expense of Time, 5th edition, a concise guide to calculating the annual expense and hourly expense of fee-earners in your firm. Photocopies are available from the Law Society library.
An Approach to Non-Contentious Costs, 1st edition (revised 1995), a guide to the key aspects of non-contentious costs. Photocopies are available from the Law Society library (telephone 0870 606 2511).
Fixed Costs, Kerry Underwood, 2nd edition.

Updates and guidance on cases and general developments are provided by the Law Society as appropriate. Solicitors should regularly refer to the Law Society's website at **www.lawsociety.org.uk**.

SPECIAL INTEREST GROUPS

International

For law firms, solicitors, and foreign lawyers seeking to develop their international business and build global relationships and profile, our innovative International Division provides the contacts, tools and information your firm needs and opportunities to progress your international career. [**www.lawsociety.org.uk/international**]

Junior lawyers

The Junior Lawyers Division provides a clear voice for student members of the Law Society enrolled through the SRA, trainees, and solicitors with up to five years' active PQE. [**www.lawsociety.org.uk/juniorlawyers**]

Law management

The Law Management Section focuses on the full range of practice management disciplines, including HR, finance, marketing, IT, business development, client care, quality and risk. [**www.lawsociety.org.uk/lawmanagement**]

Probate

The Probate Section [Private Client Section] focuses on wills, financial planning, trusts, tax planning, Court of Protection, care planning and estate administration. [**www.lawsociety.org.uk/probate**]

Property

The Property Section focuses on areas including e-conveyancing, housing, land registration, money laundering, planning and environment, as well as tax and revenue. [**www.lawsociety.org.uk/property**]

Civil Justice Section

The Civil Justice Section focuses on all areas of dispute resolution including arbitration, litigation and mediation. [**www.lawsociety.org.uk/civiljustice**]

Competition

The Competition Section focuses on UK and EU competition law policy, practice and procedure, providing practitioners with opportunities to engage in dialogue and debate and encouraging candid engagement between the profession and officials in the relevant institutions. [**www.lawsociety.org.uk/competition**]

Other groups

We also maintain a list of useful practitioner associations and groups at **www.lawsociety.org.uk/productsandservices/support/groupssections.law**.

[APPENDICES

- Appendix 1: The Solicitors' (Non-Contentious Business) Remuneration Order 2009 [see **Appendix B**]
- Appendix 2: High value probate cases
- Appendix 3: Extract from *Jemma Trust* v. *Liptrott*
- Appendix 4: Amendments to s.69 Solicitors Act 1974]

APPENDIX B

Solicitors' (Non-Contentious Business) Remuneration Order 2009, SI 2009/1931

Made 16th July 2009
Laid before Parliament 20th July 2009
Coming into force 11th August 2009

The Lord Chancellor, the Lord Chief Justice, the Master of the Rolls, the President of the Law Society, the president of Surrey law society and the Chief Land Registrar (in respect of business done under the Land Registration Act 2002, together constituting the committee authorised to make orders under section 56 of the Solicitors Act 1974, in exercise of the powers conferred on them by that section and having complied with the requirements of section 56, make the following Order:

Citation, commencement and revocation

1. (1) This Order may be cited as the Solicitors' (Non-Contentious Business) Remuneration Order 2009.

(2) This Order comes into force on 11th August 2009 and applies to all non-contentious business for which bills are delivered on or after that date.

(3) The Solicitors' (Non-Contentious Business) Remuneration Order 1994 is revoked except in its application to non-contentious business for which bills are delivered before this Order comes into force.

Interpretation

2. In this Order –

'client' means the client of a solicitor;

'costs' means the amount charged in a solicitor's bill, exclusive of disbursements and value added tax, in respect of non-contentious business;

'entitled person' means a client or an entitled third party;

'entitled third party' means a residuary beneficiary absolutely and immediately (and not contingently) entitled to an inheritance, where a solicitor has charged the estate for his professional costs for acting in the administration of the estate and the only personal representatives are –

(a) solicitors (whether or not acting in a professional capacity);
(b) solicitors acting jointly with partners, managers or employees in a professional capacity;
(c) employees of a solicitor sole practitioner acting in that capacity; or
(d) managers or employees of a recognised body acting in that capacity;

'manager' has the same meaning as in the Legal Services Act 2007 (see section 207 of that Act);
'paid disbursements' means disbursements already paid by the solicitor;
'recognised body' means a body recognised by the Law Society under section 9 of the Administration of Justice Act 1985;
'registered European lawyer' means a registered European lawyer within the meaning of the European Communities (Lawyer's Practice) Regulations 2000 who is registered with the Law Society;
'residuary beneficiary' includes a person entitled to all or part of the residue of an intestate estate; and
'solicitor' includes a registered European lawyer and a recognised body.

Solicitors' costs

3. A solicitor's costs must be fair and reasonable having regard to all the circumstances of the case and in particular to –

(a) the complexity of the matter or the difficulty or novelty of the questions raised;
(b) the skill, labour, specialised knowledge and responsibility involved;
(c) the time spent on the business;
(d) the number and importance of the documents prepared or considered, without regard to length;
(e) the place where and the circumstances in which the business or any part of the business is transacted;
(f) the amount or value of any money or property involved;
(g) whether any land involved is registered land within the meaning of the Land Registration Act 2002;
(h) the importance of the matter to the client; and
(i) the approval (express or implied) of the entitled person or the express approval of the testator to –

(i) the solicitor undertaking all or any part of the work giving rise to the costs; or
(ii) the amount of the costs.

Security for costs

4. A solicitor may take from his client security for the payment of any costs, including the amount of any interest to which the solicitor may become entitled under article 5.

Interest

5. (1) A solicitor may charge interest on the unpaid amount of his costs plus any paid disbursements and value added tax, subject to the remainder of this article.
(2) Where an entitlement to interest arises under paragraph (1), and subject to any agreement made between a solicitor and client, the period for which interest may be charged runs from one month after the date of delivery of a bill.
(3) Subject to any agreement made between a solicitor and client, therate of interest must not exceed the rate for the time being payable on judgment debts.
(4) Interest charged under this article must be calculated, where applicable, by reference to –

(a) the amount specified in a determination of costs by the Law Society under Schedule 1A to the Solicitors Act 1974;

(b) the amount ascertained on taxation if an application has been made for the bill to be taxed.

Judge, CJ
Sir Anthony Clarke, MR
Paul Marsh
John Perry
Peter Collis
Jack Straw
Lord Chancellor

16th July 2009

APPENDIX C

Non-Contentious Probate Fees Order 2004, SI 2004/3120

The Lord Chancellor, in exercise of the powers conferred upon him by sections 92 and 108(6) of the Courts Act 2003, and section 128 of the Finance Act 1990 with the consent of the Treasury under section 92(1) of the Courts Act 2003 and after consultation with the Lord Chief Justice, the Master of the Rolls, the President of the Family Division, the Vice-Chancellor, the Head of Civil Justice and the Deputy Head of Civil Justice and the Civil Justice Council under section 92(5) and (6) of the Courts Act 2003, hereby makes the following Order:

Citation, commencement and interpretation

1. (1) This Order may be cited as the Non-Contentious Probate Fees Order 2004 and shall come into force on the 4th January 2005.

(2) In this Order –

(a) a fee referred to by number means the fee so numbered in Schedule 1 to this Order;

(b) 'assessed value' means the value of the net real and personal estate (excluding settled land if any) passing under the grant as shown –

(i) in the Inland Revenue affidavit (for a death occurring before 13th March 1975), or

(ii) in the Inland Revenue account (for a death occurring on or after 13th March 1975), or

(iii) in the case in which, in accordance with arrangements made between the President of the Family Division and the Commissioners of the Inland Revenue, or regulations made under section 256(1)(a) of the Inheritance Tax Act 1984 and from time to time in force, no such affidavit or account is required to be delivered, in the oath which is sworn to lead to the grant,

and in the case of an application to reseal means the value, as shown, passing under the grant upon its being resealed;

(c) 'authorised place of deposit' means any place in which, by virtue of a direction given under section 124 of the Senior Courts Act 1981 original wills and other documents under the control of the High Court (either in the principal registry or in any district registry) are deposited and preserved;

(d) 'grant' means a grant of probate or letters of administration;

(e) 'district registry' includes the probate registry of Wales, any district probate registry and any sub-registry attached to it;

(f) 'the principal registry' means the Principal Registry of the Family Division and any sub-registry attached to it.

Fees to be taken

2. The fees set out in column 2 of Schedule 1 to this Order shall be taken in the principal registry and in each district registry in respect of the items described in column 1 in accordance with and subject to any directions specified in column 1.

Exclusion of certain death gratuities

3. In determining the value of any personal estate for the purposes of this Order there shall be excluded the value of a death gratuity payable under section 17(2) of the Judicial Pensions Act 1981 or section 4(3) of the Judicial Pensions and Retirement Act 1993, or payable to the personal representatives of a deceased civil servant by virtue of a scheme made under section 1 of the Superannuation Act 1972.

Remission of fees

4. Schedule 1A applies for the purpose of ascertaining whether a party is entitled to a remission or part remission of a fee prescribed by this Order.
5. The Lord Chancellor may, on the ground of financial hardship or for other reasonable cause, remit in whole or in part any fee prescribed by this Order.

6. (1) Where by any convention entered into by Her Majesty with any foreign power it is provided that no fee shall be required to be paid in respect of any proceedings, the fees specified in this Order shall not be taken in respect of those proceedings.
(2) Where any application for a grant is withdrawn before the issue of a grant, a registrar may reduce or remit a fee.
(3) Fee 7 shall not be taken where a search is made for research or similar purposes by permission of the President of the Family Division for a document over 100 years old filed in the principal registry or a district registry or another authorised place of deposit.

Special exemption – Armed Forces

7. Where a fee has been paid or fees have been paid for the application of a grant (other than fee 3.2) and at the time of payment of that fee or those fees –

(a) the application for the grant was in respect of an estate exempt from Inheritance Tax by virtue of section 154 of the Inheritance Tax Act 1984 (exemption for members of the armed forces etc); and
(b) was in respect of a death occurring before 20th March 2003;

the Lord Chancellor shall upon receiving a written application refund the difference between any fee or fees paid and fee 3.2.

Revocation

8. The Order specified in Schedule 2 in so far as it was made under section 128 of the Finance Act 1990 shall be revoked.

SCHEDULE 1 FEES TO BE TAKEN

Article 2

Column 1 *Number and description of fee*	*Column 2* *Amount of fee*
1. Application for a grant	£40
On an application for a grant (or for resealing a grant) other than on an application to which fee 3 applies, where the assessed value of the estate exceeds £5,000	
2. Personal application fee	£50
Where the application under fee 1 is made by a personal applicant (not being an application to which fee 3 applies) fee 2 is payable in addition to fee 1, where the assessed value of the estate exceeds £5,000	
3. Special applications	£15
3.1 For a duplicate or second or subsequent grant (including one following a revoked grant) in respect of the same deceased person, other than a grant preceded only by a grant limited to settled land, to trust property, or to part of the estate	
3.2 On an application for a grant relating to a death occurring on or after 20th March 2003 and in respect of an estate exempt from inheritance tax by virtue of section 154 of the Inheritance Tax Act 1984 (exemption for members of the armed forces etc)	£8
4. Caveats	£15
For the entry or the extension of a caveat	
5. Search	£5
On an application for a standing search to be carried out in an estate, for each period of six months including the issue of a copy grant and will, if any (irrespective of the number of pages)	
6. Deposit of wills	£15
On depositing a will for safe custody in the principal registry or a district registry	
7. Inspection	£15

Column 1 *Number and description of fee*		*Column 2* *Amount of fee*
On inspection of any will or other document retained by the registry (in the presence of an officer of the registry)		
8. Copy documents		
On a request for a copy of any document whether or not provided as a certified copy:		
(a)	for the first copy	£5
(b)	for every subsequent copy of the same document if supplied at the same time	£1
(c)	where copies of any document are made available on a computer disk or in other electronic form, for each such copy	£3
(d)	where a search of the index is required, in addition to fee 8(a), (b) or (c) as appropriate, for each period of 4 years searched after the first 4 years	£3
9. Oaths		
Except on a personal application for a grant, for administering an oath,		
9.1	for each deponent to each affidavit	£5
9.2	for marking each exhibit	£2
10. Determination of costs		
For determining costs		The same fees as are payable from time to time for determining costs under the Civil Proceedings Fees Order 2008, (the relevant fees are set out in fee 5 in Schedule 1 to that Order)
11. Settling documents		£10
For perusing and settling citations, advertisements, oaths, affidavits, or other documents, for each document settled		

SCHEDULE 1A Remissions and part-remissions

Interpretation

1. (1) In this Schedule –

'child' means a child or young person in respect of whom a party is entitled to receive child benefit in accordance with section 141, and regulations made under section 142, of the Social Security Contributions and Benefits Act 1992;

'child care costs' has the meaning given in the Criminal Defence Service (Financial Eligibility) Regulations 2006;

'couple' has the meaning given in section 3(5A) of the Tax Credits Act 2002;

'disposable monthly income' has the meaning given in paragraph 5;

'excluded benefits' means –

(a) any of the following benefits payable under the Social Security Contributions and Benefits Act 1992 –

  (i) attendance allowance paid under section 64;
  (ii) severe disablement allowance;
  (iii) carer's allowance;
  (iv) disability living allowance;
  (v) constant attendance allowance paid under section 104 or paragraph 4 or 7(2) of Schedule 8 as an increase to a disablement pension;
  (vi) council tax benefit;
  (vii) any payment made out of the social fund;
  (viii) housing benefit;

(b) any direct payment made under the Community Care, Services for Carers and Children's Services (Direct Payments) (England) Regulations 2003 or the Community Care, Services for Carers and Children's Services (Direct Payments) (Wales) Regulations 2004;
(c) a back to work bonus payable under section 26 of the Jobseekers Act 1995;
(d) any exceptionally severe disablement allowance paid under the Personal Injuries (Civilians) Scheme 1983;
(e) any pension paid under the Naval, Military and Air Forces etc (Disablement and Death) Service Pensions Order 2006;
(f) any payment made from the Independent Living Funds; and
(g) any financial support paid under an agreement for the care of a foster child;

'the Funding Code' means the code approved under section 9 of the Access to Justice Act 1999;

'gross annual income' means total annual income, for the 12 months preceding the application for remission or part remission, from all sources other than receipt of any of the excluded benefits;

'gross monthly income' means total monthly income, for the month in which the application for remission or part remission is made, from all sources other than receipt of any of the excluded benefits;

'the Independent Living Funds' has the meaning given in the Criminal Defence Service (Financial Eligibility) Regulations 2006;

'LSC' means the Legal Services Commission established under section 1 of the Access to Justice Act 1999;

'partner' means a person with whom the party lives as a couple and includes a person with whom the party is not currently living but from whom the party is not living separate and apart;

'party' means the individual who would, but for this Schedule, be liable to pay the fee required under this Order;

(2) Paragraphs 2, 3 and 4 do not apply to a party who is in receipt of funding provided by the LSC for the purposes of the proceedings for which a certificate has been issued under the Funding Code.

Full remission of fees – qualifying benefits

2. (1) No fee is payable under this Order if, at the time when a fee would otherwise be payable, the party is in receipt of a qualifying benefit.

(2) The following are qualifying benefits for the purpose of sub-paragraph (1) –

(a) income support under the Social Security Contributions and Benefits Act 1992;.

(b) working tax credit, provided that no child tax credit is being paid to the party;.

(c) income-based jobseeker's allowance under the Jobseekers Act 1995;

(d) guarantee credit under the State Pension Credit Act 2002; and

(e) income-related employment and support allowance under the Welfare Reform Act 2007.

Full remission of fees – gross annual income

3. (1) No fee is payable under this Order if, at the time when the fee would otherwise be payable, the party has the number of children specified in column 1 of the following table and –

(a) if the party is single, the gross annual income of the party does not exceed the amount set out in the appropriate row of column 2; or

(b) if the party is one of a couple, the gross annual income of the couple does not exceed the amount set out in the appropriate row of column 3.

Column 1 *Number of children of fee-paying party*	*Column 2* *Single*	*Column 3* *Couple*
no children	£13,000	£18,000
1 child	£15,930	£20,930
2 children	£18,860	£23,860
3 children	£21,790	£26,790
4 children	£24,720	£29,720

(2) If the party paying the fee has more than 4 children then the relevant amount of gross annual income is the amount specified in the table for 4 children plus the sum of £2,930 for each additional child.

Full and part remission of fees – disposable monthly income

4. (1) No fee is payable under this Order if, at the time when the fee would otherwise be payable, the disposable monthly income of the party is £50 or less.

(2) The maximum amount of fee payable is –

(a) if the disposable monthly income of the party is more than £50 but does not exceed £210, an amount equal to one-quarter of every £10 of the party's disposable monthly income up to a maximum of £50; and

(b) if the disposable monthly income is more than £210, an amount equal to £50 plus one-half of every £10 over £200 of the party's disposable monthly income.

(3) Where the fee that would otherwise be payable under this Order is greater than the maximum fee which a party is required to pay as calculated in sub-paragraph (2), the fee will be remitted to the amount payable under that sub-paragraph.

Disposable monthly income

5. (1) A party's disposable monthly income is the gross monthly income of the party for the month in which the fee becomes payable ('the period') less the deductions referred to in sub-paragraphs (2) and (3).

(2) There is to be deducted from the gross monthly income –

(a) income tax paid or payable in respect of the period;

(b) any contributions estimated to have been paid under Part 1 of the Social Security Contributions and Benefits Act 1992 in respect of the period;

(c) either –

(i) monthly rent or monthly payment in respect of a mortgage debt or hereditable security, payable in respect of the only or main dwelling of the party, less any housing benefit paid under the Social Security Contributions and Benefits Act 1992; or

(ii) the monthly cost of the living accommodation of the party;

(d) any child care costs paid or payable in respect of the period;

(e) if the party is making bona fide payments for the maintenance of a child who is not a member of the household of the party, the amount of such payments paid or payable in respect of the period; and

(f) any amount paid or payable by the party, in respect of the period, in pursuance of a court order.

(3) There will be deducted from the gross monthly income an amount representing the cost of living expenses in respect of the period being –

(a) £315; plus

(b) £244 for each child of the party; plus

(c) £159, if the party has a partner.

Resources of partners

6. (1) For the purpose of determining whether a party is entitled to the remission or part remission of a fee in accordance with this Schedule, the income of a partner, if any, is to be included as income of the party.

(2) The receipt by a partner of a qualifying benefit does not entitle a party to remission of a fee.

Application for remission or part remission of fees

7. (1) An application for remission or part remission of a fee must be made to the court officer at the time when the fee would otherwise be payable.

(2) Where a claim for full remission of fees is made, the party must provide documentary evidence of, as the case may be –

(a) entitlement to a qualifying benefit; or

(b) gross annual income and, if applicable, the children included for the purposes of paragraph 3.

(3) Where a claim for full or part remission of fees under paragraph 4 is made, the party must provide documentary evidence of –

(a) such of the party's gross monthly income as is derived from –

(i) employment;

(ii) rental or other income received from persons living with the party by reason of their residence in the party's home;

(iii) a pension; or

(iv) a state benefit, not being an excluded benefit; and

(b) any expenditure being deducted from the gross monthly income in accordance with paragraph 5(2).

Remission in exceptional circumstances

8. Where it appears to the Lord Chancellor that the payment of any fee prescribed by this Order would, owing to the exceptional circumstances of the particular case, involve undue financial hardship, the Lord Chancellor may reduce or remit the fee in that case.

Refunds

9. (1) Subject to sub-paragraph (3), where a party has not provided the documentary evidence required by paragraph 7 and a fee has been paid at a time when, under paragraphs 2, 3 or 4, it was not payable, the fee will be refunded if documentary evidence relating to the time when the fee became payable is provided at a later date.

(2) Subject to sub-paragraph (3), when a fee has been paid at a time where the Lord Chancellor, if all the circumstances had been known, would have reduced or remitted the fee under paragraph 8, the fee or the amount by which the fee would have been reduced, as the case may be, will be refunded.

(3) No refund will be made under this paragraph unless the party who paid the fee applies within 6 months of paying the fee.

(4) The Lord Chancellor may extend the period of 6 months mentioned in sub-paragraph (3) if the Lord Chancellor considers that there is a good reason for an application being made after the end of the period of 6 months.

SCHEDULE 2 ORDER REVOKED

Article 8

Title	*Reference*
The Non-Contentious Probate Fees (Amendment) Order 2000	S.I. 2000/642

APPENDIX D

Probate systems buyers' guide

[Compiled by Charles Christian, July 2010]

The listing here gives the details of suppliers (in alphabetical order, with contact details) of probate systems and related software and/or online applications. Please note that software products are regularly upgraded in terms of their functionality. In addition, my own website at **www.legaltechnology.com** contains a regularly updated probate systems buyers' guide, which is intended to reflect any changes taking place between the publication of this book and any subsequent edition. Readers will immediately notice that since the last edition of this guide, many familiar names have vanished from the list as a result of consolidation within the legal IT industry or rebranding.

Supplier	*Product*	*Type of system*
Cognito Software **www.cognitosoftware.co.uk** 0121 543 6996	Custodiens	Probate case management and estates and trusts accounts
Digita (Thomson Reuters Legal) **www.digita.com** 01395 280218	Trust Tax	Trust and estate tax computations
DPS Software **www.dpssoftware.co.uk** 020 8804 1022	DPS Probate	Probate case management and estate accounts – recently upgraded and wills drafting
Eclipse Legal Systems **www.eclipselegal.co.uk** 01274 704100	Proclaim Probate	Probate case management and estate accounts – recently upgraded
FloSuite **www.flosuite.com** 01592 760601	Probate/Executry	Probate case management inc IHT forms
IRIS Legal Solutions **www.iris.co.uk/lega**l 0844 815 5575	IRIS Law (Enterprise and Business)	Probate case management and estate accounts
IRIS Legal Solutions **www.iris.co.uk/legal** 0844 815 5575	IRIS Opsis + IRIS AlphaLaw	Probate case management and wills drafting
IRIS Legal Solutions **www.iris.co.uk/legal** 0844 815 5575	IRIS Laserform IHT 400Full	Electronic forms and IHT400

Supplier	*Product*	*Type of system*
Isokon Systems **www.isokon.com** 020 7482 6555	Isokon	Probate case management and estates and trusts accounts and Court of Protection module
Legal Workflow **www.legalworkflow.com** 07977 249438	Bespoke Development Services	Bespoke development and customisation of probate systems
Legis Systems **www.legis.co.uk** 01489 580290	LegisSQL Probate	Probate case management and wills and IHT forms
Linetime **www.linetime.co.uk** 0113 250 0020	Liberate Probate	Probate case management and estate accounts
Movewithus **www.movewithus.co.uk** 01480 409568	Probate Service	Property-related support services for probate matters
MYOB **www.myob.com** 020 8997 5500	Trust Accounts	Specialist trusts system
Ochresoft Technologies **www.ochresoft.com** 01793 836730	Intelliworks Probate	Probate case management and estate accounts
Peapod LegalOffice **www.peapod-legal.co.uk** 0845 683 25172	Probate Office + Probate Assist	Probate case management and estate accounts and Assist product for IHT forms
Pennik Ltd **www.pennik.co.uk** 0845 601 5418	Pro-File	Probate case management and estate accounts and wills drafting
Pilgrim Systems **www.pilgrimsystems.com** 0131 555 9700	Lawsoft Probate	Probate case management
Practical Law Company **www.practicallaw.com** 020 7891 2901	PLC FastDraft Master Will	Will-drafting system with access to probate know-how resources
Solicitors Own Software **www.soslegal.co.uk** 01225 787700	SOS Connect Probate Workflow	Probate case management and will-drafting module
Sweet & Maxwell **www.sweetandmaxwell.co.uk** 020 7449 1111	Probate Plus	Low-cost CD-Rom, handles IHT calculations and forms
Timeslice **www.timeslice.co.uk** 020 7231 0073	Lawman Probate and Trust Manager	Trust and estate accounts

Supplier	*Product*	*Type of system*
The Wealth Works **www.thewealthworks.com** 01444 401333	Troika	Trust and estate accounts and administration

APPENDIX E

Further reading

Books and looseleafs for practitioners

Barlow, R., Sherrin, C., Wallington, R., Meadway, S., Waterworth, M. (2008) *Williams on Wills*, 9th edn, LexisNexis.

Bedworth, G. and Waterworth, M. (2008) *Rossdale: Probate and the Administration of Estates*, 4th edn, CCH Editions.

BMA and Law Society (2009) *Assessment of Mental Capacity*, 3rd edn, Law Society.

Bridge, S., Martyn, J., Oldham, M. (2010) *Theobald on Wills*, 17th edn, Sweet & Maxwell.

Butcher, C. and King-Jones, A. (looseleaf) *Probate Practice Manual*, Sweet & Maxwell.

Caddick, N. and Martyn, J. (2007) *Williams, Mortimer & Sunnocks: Executors, Administrators and Probate*, Sweet & Maxwell.

D'Costa, R., Synak, T., Winegarton, J. (2011) *Tristram and Coote's Probate Practice*, 31st edn, LexisNexis.

Dew, R. and Russell, C. (2005) *Ranking Spicer and Pegler: Executorship Law, Trusts and Accounts*, 25th edn, LexisNexis.

Endicott, D. and Jones, A. (2007) *Brighouse's Precedents of Wills*, 14th edn, Sweet & Maxwell.

Frost, M., Reed, P., Sartin, L. (2009) *Risk and Negligence in Wills, Estates and Trusts*, OUP.

Greaney, N., Morris, F., Taylor, B. (2008) *Mental Capacity: A Guide to the New Law*, 2nd edn, Law Society.

Jones, R. (2010) *Mental Capacity Act Manual*, 4th edn, Sweet & Maxwell.

Kessler, J. (2010) *Drafting Trusts and Will Trusts: A Modern Approach*, 10th edn, Sweet & Maxwell.

King, L. and Whitehouse, C. (looseleaf) *Administration of Estates*, LexisNexis.

Lush, D. (2009) *Cretney and Lush on Lasting Powers of Attorney*, 6th edn, Jordan Publishing.

Riddett, R. (2004) *Will Draftsman's Handbook*, 8th edn, Law Society.

Thomas M. (ed) (2010) *A Practitioner's Guide to Wills*, 3rd edn, Wildy, Simmonds and Hill Publishing.

Thurston, J. (2009) *A Practitioner's Guide to Executorship and Administration*, 7th edn, Bloomsbury Professional.

Ward, C. (2011) *Lasting Powers of Attorney: A Practical Guide*, 2nd edn, Law Society.

Waterworth, M. (2009) *Parker's Modern Wills Precedents*, 6th edn, Bloomsbury Professional.

Withers LLP (looseleaf and CD) *Practical Will Precedents*, Sweet & Maxwell.

Wright, C. (looseleaf) *Butterworths Wills, Probate and Administration Service*, LexisNexis.

APPENDIX F

Useful addresses

PROBATE REGISTRIES

The London Probate Registry

Principal Registry
First Avenue House
42–49 High Holborn
London WC1V 6NP
Tel: 020 7947 7462
DX: 941 London/Chancery Lane

District probate registries

Birmingham
The Priory Courts
33 Bull Street
Birmingham B4 6DU
Tel: 0121 681 3400
DX: 701990 Birmingham 7

Brighton
William Street
Brighton
East Sussex BN2 2LG
Tel: 01273 573 510
DX: 98073 Brighton 3

Bristol
Ground Floor
The Crescent Centre
Temple Back
Bristol BS1 6EP
Tel: 0117 927 3915
DX: 94400 Bristol 5

Cardiff Probate Registry of Wales
3rd Floor, Cardiff Magistrates Court
Fitzalan Place
Cardiff
South Wales CF24 0RZ
Tel: 02920 474373
DX: 743940 Cardiff 38

Ipswich
Ground Floor
8 Arcade Street
Ipswich IP1 1EJ
Tel: 01473 284 260
DX: 97733 Ipswich 3

Leeds
3rd Floor, Coronet House
Queen Street
Leeds
West Yorkshire LS1 2BA
Tel: 0113 386 3540
DX: 26451 Leeds Park Sq

Liverpool
The Queen Elizabeth II Law Courts
Derby Square
Liverpool L2 1XA
Tel: 0151 236 8264
DX: 14246 Liverpool 1

Manchester
Ground Floor, Manchester Civil Justice Centre
1 Bridge Street West
Manchester M60 1WJ
Tel: 0161 240 5700
DX: 724784 Manchester 44

Newcastle
1 Waterloo Square
Newcastle upon Tyne NE1 4DR

Tel: 0191 211 2170
DX: 61081 Newcastle-upon-Tyne 14

Oxford
Combined Court Building
St Aldates
Oxford OX1 1LY
Tel: 01865 793 055
DX: 96454 Oxford 4

Winchester
4th Floor, Cromwell House
Andover Road
Winchester
Hants SO23 7EW
Tel: 01962 897 024
DX: 96900 Winchester 2

Probate sub-registries

Bodmin
Market Street
Bodmin
Cornwall PL31 2AL
Tel: 01208 261581
DX: 81858 Bodmin

Caernarfon
The Criminal Justice Centre
Llanberis Road
Caernarfon, Gwynedd
Wales LL55 2DF
Tel: 01286 669755
DX: 744381 Caernarfon 6

Carlisle
Courts of Justice
Earl Street
Carlisle CA1 1DJ
Tel: 01228 521 751
DX: 63034 Carlisle

Carmarthen
14 King Street
Carmarthen SA31 1BL
Tel: 01267 242 560
DX: 51420 Carmarthen

Chester
Chester Civil Justice Centre
Trident House
Little John Street
Chester
Cheshire CH1 1SN
Tel: 0151 236 8264
DX: 702470 Chester 18

Exeter
Exeter Crown and County Courts
Southernhay Gardens
Exeter
Devon EX1 1UH
Tel: 01392 415 370
DX: 98442 Exeter 2

Gloucester
3rd Floor, Combined Courts Building
Kimbrose Way
Gloucester GL1 2DG
Tel: 01452 834 966
DX: 98663 Gloucester 5

Lancaster
Room 111, Mitre House
Church Street
Lancaster LA1 1HE
Tel: 0151 236 8624
DX: 145883 Lancaster 2

Leicester
Crown Court Building
90 Wellington Street
Leicester LE1 6HG
Tel: 0116 285 3380
DX: 17403 Leicester 3

Lincoln
360 High Street
Lincoln LN5 7PS
Tel: 01522 523 648
DX: 703233 Lincoln 6

Maidstone
Law Courts
Barker Road
Maidstone
Kent ME16 8EQ
Tel: 01622 202 048
DX: 130066 Maidstone 7

Middlesbrough
Teesside Combined Court Centre
Russell Street
Middlesbrough
Cleveland TS1 2AE

Tel: 0191 211 2170
DX: 60536 Middlesbrough

Norwich
Combined Court Building
The Law Courts
Bishopgate
Norwich
Norfolk NR3 1UR
Tel: 01603 728 267
DX: 97390 Norwich 5

Nottingham
Butt Dyke House
33 Park Row
Nottingham NG1 6GR
Tel: 0115 941 4288
DX: 10055 Nottingham

Peterborough
1st Floor, Crown Building
Rivergate
Peterborough PE1 1EJ
Tel: 01733 562 802
DX: 702305 Peterborough 8

Sheffield
PO Box 832
The Law Courts
50 West Bar
Sheffield S3 8YR
Tel: 0114 281 2596
DX: 742916 Sheffield 6

Stoke on Trent
Combined Court Centre
Bethesda Street
Hanley
Stoke on Trent ST1 3BP
Tel: 01782 854 065
DX: 703363 Hanley 3

York
Castle Chambers
5 Clifford Street
York
North Yorkshire YO1 9RG
Tel: 01904 666 777
DX: 720629 York 21

COUNSELLING AND SUPPORT

Age UK

207–221 Pentonville Road
London N1 9UZ
Tel: 0800 107 8977
www.ageuk.org.uk

British Association for Counselling and Psychotherapy

BACP House
15 St John's Business Park
Lutterworth LE17 4HB
Tel: 01455 883 300
www.bacp.co.uk

Counsel and Care

Twyman House
16 Bonny Sreet
London NW1 9PG
Tel: 020 7241 8555
www.counselandcare.org.uk

CRUSE Bereavement Care

PO Box 8000
Richmond
Surrey TW9 1RG
Tel: 020 8939 9530
www.crusebereavementcare.org.uk

National Association of Widows

3rd Floor
48 Queens Road
Coventry CV1 3EH
Tel: 0845 838 2261
www.nawidows.org.uk

LEGAL

Association of Contentious Trust and Probate Specialists (ACTAPS)

Frydenson & Co Solicitors
Central Court
25 Southampton Buildings
London WC2A 1AL
Tel: 0203 178 8777
www.actaps.com

Court of Protection

Archway Tower
2 Junction Road
London N19 5SZ
Tel: 0300 456 4600
DX: 141150 Archway 2
www.hmcourts-service.gov.uk

LawCare

PO Box 147
Benfleet SS7 3WX
Tel: 0800 279 6888

The Law Society

113 Chancery Lane
London WC2A 1PL
Tel: 020 7242 1222
Fax: 020 7831 0344
DX: 56 London/Chancery Lane
www.lawsociety.org.uk

Law Society's Private Client Section
Tel: 020 7316 5678
Fax: 020 7316 5775
www.probatesection.org.uk

Law Society's Practice Advice Service
Tel: 0870 606 2522

Law Society's Lawyerline
Tel: 0870 606 2588

Office of the Public Guardian

PO Box 15118
Birmingham B16 6GX
Tel: 0300 456 0300
DX: 744240 Birmingham 79
www.publicguardian.gov.uk

Principal Registry of the Family Division

First Avenue House
42–49 High Holborn
London WC1V 6NP
Tel: 020 7947 6000
DX: 396 London/Chancery Lane

Royal Courts of Justice

The Strand
London WC2A 2LL
Tel: 020 7947 6000
DX: 44450 Strand WC2

Official Solicitor and Public Trustee

81 Chancery Lane
London WC2A 1DD
Tel: 020 7911 7127
DX: 0012 London/Chancery Lane
www.officialsolicitor.gov.uk

Society of Trust and Estate Practitioners (STEP)

Artillery House (South)
11–19 Artillery Row
London SW1P 1RT
Tel: 020 7340 0500
www.step.org

Treasury Solicitor's Department, Bona Vacantia Division

1 Kemble Street
London WC2B 4TS
Tel: 020 7210 3000
www.bonavacantia.gov.uk

BENEFITS

Carer's Allowance Unit

Palantine House
Lancaster Road
Preston
Lancashire PR1 1HB
Tel: 0845 608 4321

Disability benefits advice and information

Tel: 0800 88 22 00

Disability benefits claims

Tel: 08457 123 456

PENSIONS

Pension Service

www.pensions.direct.gov.uk

Pension Tracing Service

Tyneview Park
Whitely Road
Newcastle Upon Tyne NE98 1BA
Tel: 0845 600 2537

The Pensions Advisory Service

11 Belgrave Road
London SW1V 1RB
Tel: 08456 012 923
www.pensionsadvisoryservice.org.uk

HMRC

Capital Taxes
Ferrers House
PO Box 38
Castle Meadow Road
Nottingham NG2 1BB
Tel: 0115 974 2400
DX: 701201 Nottingham 4
www.hmrc.gov.uk/cto/

Inheritance Tax Enquiries
HM Revenue & Customs
Ferrers House, PO Box 38
Castle Meadow Road
Nottingham NG2 1BB

Inheritance Tax Payments
HMRC Banking
St Mungo's Road
Cumbernauld
Glasgow G70 5WY

Pre-owned Assets Section
HMRC Inheritance Tax
PO Box 38
Castle Meadow Road
Nottingham NG2 1BB.
Tel: 0845 30 20 900
DX: 701201 Nottingham 4

Deceased Estates Helpline
Tel: 0845 604 6455

Deceased's Tax Office
0845 300 0627

Probate and Inheritance Tax Helpline
Tel: 0845 302 0900

Shares and Assets Valuation Helpline
Tel: 0115 974 2222

Trusts Helpline
Tel: 0845 604 6455

REGULATORY BODIES

Adjudicator's Office

8th Floor
Euston Tower
286 Euston Road
London NW1 3US
Tel: 0300 057 1111
www.adjudicatorsoffice.gov.uk

The Charity Commission

PO Box 1227
Liverpool L69 3UG
Tel: 0845 300 0218
www.charity-commission.gov.uk

Companies House

Companies House
Crown Way
Maindy
Cardiff CF14 3UZ
DX: 33050
www.companieshouse.gov.uk

Financial Ombudsman Service

South Quay Plaza
183 Marsh Wall
London E14 9SR
Tel: 020 7964 1000
www.financial-ombudsman.org.uk

Financial Services Authority

25 The North Colonnade
Canary Wharf
London E14 5HS

Tel: 020 7066 1000
www.fsa.gov.uk

Legal Ombudsman (Office for Legal Complaints)

PO Box 15870
Birmingham B30 9EB
Tel: 0300 555 0333 (0121 245 3050)
www.legalombudsman.org.uk

Office of the Legal Services Ombudsman

3rd Floor
Sunlight House
Quay Street
Manchester M3 3JZ
Tel: 0161 839 7262
DX: 18569 Manchester 7
www.olso.org

Solicitors Regulation Authority

Ipsley Court
Berrington Close
Redditch B98 0TD
Tel: 0870 606 2555
DX: 19114 Redditch
www.sra.org.uk

SPECIALIST VALUERS

Central Association of Agricultural Valuers

Market Chambers
35 Market Place
Coleford
Gloucestershire GL16 8AA
Tel: 01594 832 979
www.caav.org.uk

Fleurets

Chartered Surveyors – Hotel and Licensed Property Valuers
4 Roger Street
London WC1N 2JX
Tel: 020 7280 4700
www.fleurets.com

Institute of Revenues, Rating and Valuation

41 Doughty Street
London WC1N 2LF
Tel: 020 7831 3505
www.irrv.net

LAPADA, The Association of Art and Antique Dealers

535 Kings Road
Chelsea
London SW10 0SZ
Tel: 020 7823 3511
www.lapada.org

National Association of Goldsmiths

78a Luke Street
London EC2A 4XG
Tel: 020 7613 4445
www.jewellers-online.org

Society of Fine Art Auctioneers and Valuers (SOFAA)

2 Kingfisher Court
Bridge Road
East Molesey
Surrey KT8 9HL
Tel: 020 8941 7861
www.sofaa.info/

Stanley Gibbons Ltd (postage stamps)

399 Strand
London WC2R 0LX
Tel: 020 7836 8444
www.stanleygibbons.com

Wildy & Sons Ltd (valuation of legal books)

Lincoln's Inn Archway
Carey Street
London WC2A 2JD
Tel: 020 7242 5778
www.wildy.com

OTHER

UK Transplant

NHS Blood and Transplant
Organ Donation and Transplantation Directorate
Fox Den Road
Stoke Gifford
Bristol BS34 8RR
Tel: 0117 975 7575
www.uktransplant.org.uk

The Natural Death Centre

In The Hill House
Watley Lane
Twyford
Winchester SO21 1QX
Tel: 01962 712 690
www.naturaldeath.org.uk

Index